COUNTRY MUSIC

COUNTRY MUSIC

DAYTON DUNCAN

Based on a documentary film
by Ken Burns,
written by Dayton Duncan

With a preface by Ken Burns

Picture research by Susanna Steisel, Susan Shumaker,
Pam Tubridy Baucom, and Emily Mosher • Design by Maggie Hinders

 ALFRED A. KNOPF • NEW YORK • 2019

THIS IS A BORZOI BOOK
PUBLISHED BY ALFRED A. KNOPF

Copyright © 2019 by The Country Music Film Project, LLC

Published in the United States by Alfred A. Knopf,
a division of Penguin Random House LLC, New York, and distributed in Canada
by Random House of Canada, a division of Penguin Random House Canada Limited, Toronto.

www.aaknopf.com

Knopf, Borzoi Books, and the colophon
are registered trademarks of Penguin Random House LLC.

Library of Congress Cataloging-in-Publication Data
Names: Duncan, Dayton, author. | Burns, Ken, [date]
Title: Country music / by Dayton Duncan ; based on a documentary film by Ken Burns, written by Dayton Duncan ; with a preface by Ken Burns.
Description: First edition. | New York : Alfred A. Knopf, 2019. | Includes bibliographical references and index.
Identifiers: LCCN 2018047629 (print) | LCCN 2018048609 (ebook) | ISBN 9780525520559 (e-book) | ISBN 9780525520542 (hardcover)
Subjects: LCSH: Country music—History and criticism.
Classification: LCC ML3524 (ebook) | LCC ML3524 .D85 2019 (print) | DDC 781.64209—dc23
LC record available at https://lccn.loc.gov/2018047629

Jacket artwork design © 2019 Public Broadcasting Service

Manufactured in the United States of America
First Edition

PREVIOUS SPREAD, LEFT PAGE *Fiddlin' Bill Hensley, Asheville, North Carolina, 1937*

FOLLOWING SPREAD LEFT PAGE *Dolly Parton, Sevierville, Tennessee, 1971*

In memory of Joe Blake,

who constantly brought his buddy Dayton "home" to country music;

and Robert K. Burns Sr.,

who sang his grandson Ken many of the old songs.

The circle will be unbroken.

CONTENTS

OLD GHOSTS AND ANCIENT TONES

There are things that are part of the landscape of human life that we all deal with—the joy of birth, the sorrow of death, a broken heart, jealousy, greed, envy, anger. All of these things are what is in music. Because it is the art of the invisible. There's a truth in the music. And it's too bad that we as a culture have not been able to address that truth. That's the shame of it. . . . The art tells more of the tale of us coming together.

—WYNTON MARSALIS

IT MAY BE APOCRYPHAL, but we've stumbled across the anecdote from enough sources and in enough different places to satisfy any journalist's or historian's prickly conscience and ethical obligation. The late music critic Nat Hentoff first told us the story more than two decades ago when we were making a television series for public broadcasting on the history of jazz. Then, years later, working on this project, a history of country music, Marty Stuart, the unofficial historian and keeper of all things sacred about the music he loves, related the same tale to us. It seems that Charlie Parker, one of the great creative forces in jazz (and, with Dizzy Gillespie, the "inventor" of the hugely complex, fast-paced, dazzlingly virtuosic variety of jazz called bebop), was between sets at one of the clubs he played at on Fifty-Second Street in New York City in the late 1940s. Much to his fellow musicians' shock, they found him feeding nickels into the jukebox, playing country music songs. "Bird," they asked, using his famous nickname, "how can you play *that* music?" Parker replied, "Listen to the stories."

For most of the last forty years, we have made films solely about American history. We stated plainly when we were beginning our first film that we were uninterested in merely excavating the dry dates, facts, and events of American history; instead, we were committed to pursuing an "emotional archeology," "listening to the ghosts and echoes of an almost indescribably wise past." Eschewing nostalgia and sentimentality, the enemies of any good history, we have nevertheless been unafraid of exploring real emotion—the glue that makes the most complex of past events stick in our minds but also in our hearts. We consciously chose not to retreat to the relative safety of the rational world, where one plus one always equals two. We are most interested in that improbable calculus where one plus one equals three. That, to us, is, in part, emotional archeology.

For at least twenty years, we have often quoted the late historian Arthur Schlesinger Jr., who liked to say that we suffer today from "too much *pluribus* and not enough *unum*." We have been all about "*unum*" for decades, extolling as much as possible a bottom-up version of our past as well as a top-down one, looking for ways to accentuate what we share in common, not what drives us apart, widening the scope of American history, not narrowing it. We wished to exclude no one's story at a time when our tribal instincts seem to promote so much disunion.

We also began to see that our work and interests have always existed in the figurative space between the two-letter, lower-case plural pronoun "us," and the much larger, upper-case abbreviation for our country—U.S. There is a lot of room—and feeling—in there, between "us" and U.S.—the warmth and familiarity of the word "us" (and also "we" and "our"), standing in contrast to the sheer majesty and breadth of the history of *our* United States. We have been mindful, too, of what the novelist Richard Powers wrote: "The best arguments in the world won't change a person's mind. The only thing that can do that is a good story." It is with all those references and contexts in mind—and in heart—that we have, over the last several years, devoted so much of our creative energies trying to understand country music, the art that tries to tell the stories of those who feel like their stories aren't being told. We could not have come to it a moment sooner, but we are also glad we did not start it a moment later.

It is conventional wisdom, accepted by too many, that country music is somehow a lesser art form, a simple country cousin (literally), lacking the elegance and complexity of jazz, a suspect musical form which too often is easily relegated to the "lower forty" of our cultural studies, bottomland, not befitting the scrutiny of sophisticates and—God forbid—

scholars. Much to our delight, we have, over the last eight years of working on an eight-part, sixteen-and-a-half-hour series for PBS on the history of country music, and now this companion volume, discovered just the opposite. Country music turns out to be a surprisingly broad and inclusive art form that belies the narrow definition into which many have imprisoned it. The music's narrative arc offers a new and at times achingly personal perspective on our last turbulent century, its clarity and honesty a refreshing corrective to the recent corruptions of popular culture. It is the story, at heart, about so-called ordinary people, who many times lifted themselves out of unbelievable poverty and hardship, and following an inner ambition or a dream (or with the help and kindness of others), shared their own stories—what Charlie Parker *heard*—in words so powerful and heartbreaking, and in music so plaintive and moving, that they have allowed the rest of us to dream our own dreams as well. And what they have left behind (and continue to create) is a legacy of emotion, authenticity, and simplicity unmatched in American music.

It is tempting to segregate the various forms of Ameri-can music into their own pigeonholes, erroneously presuming that these forms had or have little in common. But they all—whether jazz, the blues, rhythm and blues, folk, rock, or country—share a common ancestry in the American South. Within the frictions and tensions between blacks and whites trying to negotiate their stories with one another is the story of the birth of American music in general and country music in particular. Our political and social histories correctly chart the indignities and injustices these frictions and tensions often produce. Country music is not immune to those sufferings, but it does, like other forms of music, suggest happier and more transcendent possibilities, a civilized alternative that tries to get beyond those tribal impulses that continually seem to beset us. It is important to affirm that the musicians and artists themselves seek only to follow their own muse, unconcerned with categorization and labels, and so they cross and recross the restrictive fence lines, the musical boundaries we have created for our simplistic filing system. To understand these complex interrelationships, and the sublime art and emotion they promote, requires only that we heed Charlie Parker's words: Listen to the stories.

Those of us lucky enough to be engaged with trying to come to terms with this utterly American music felt we had been granted a privileged glimpse into a wildly diverse American family. It is a story that quickly became *our* story, too. The basic constituent building blocks of our series, and now this book, are the pantheon of several dozen great country artists our narrative considers and asks the viewer and reader to get to know. From Jimmie Rodgers and the original Carter Family to Dolly Parton and Garth Brooks; from Johnny Cash and his superbly talented daughter Rosanne to Hank Williams, his son Hank Jr., and his granddaughter Holly; from the Maddox Brothers and Rose to Merle Haggard and Buck Owens and Dwight Yoakam; from Loretta Lynn and Charley Pride and Faron Young to Kris Kristofferson, Felice and Boudleaux Bryant and Roy Acuff; from George Jones and Tammy Wynette to the Louvin Brothers and Naomi and Wynonna Judd; from Emmylou Harris and Bill Monroe to Marty Stuart and Connie Smith, from Ernest Tubb and Bob Wills and Gene Autry to Willie Nelson and Earl Scruggs and Roger Miller, we felt as if we were getting to know real people—almost as if they were members of our own family. There were the black sheep and the patriarchs, the sage mentors and the stage mothers, the addicts and the orphans, the sinners and the saved, the song catchers and the wordsmiths, the lovers and the loners, all the various branches and offshoots of this complicated family that was also—amazingly—asking us in, asking us to stay for supper.

Everywhere we explored this story, we found generosity and human kindness. Her grade school teacher let little Brenda Lee, a child star and singing sensation, put her head down in class to rest from the arduous travel schedule her fame demanded of her. When Mel Tillis's teachers recognized that he could sing without the stutter that affected him and his brother and father, they would take him from class to class, letting him sing—and starting, as he remembers, his career in show business. Lefty Frizzell brought a teenage Merle Haggard onstage with him and "gave me," Haggard said, "the courage to dream." Bill Monroe did the same for Ricky Skaggs . . . when he was only six. There were slights and

indifference, too: "The human being has a history of being awful cruel to something different," Haggard told us, as he and countless others had to escape the prejudice inflicted on them. Sometimes that pain was paradoxically the deciding factor in their success—their art came from seeing that cruelty and rising above it in songs of agony and grinding hardship.

In no other musical idiom had we ever come across this palpable sense of belonging to such a complex American family—the hundreds of people and their fans—who populate and animate our series. It is a hallmark of this far-reaching and sometimes dysfunctional family that once you're in, once you've been accepted, you're in for life, and that kind of loyalty and kindness, but also a good bit of inevitable tension, permeates the whole of the tale we try to tell.

In the beginning of our story, we noticed an unavoidable and in some ways welcome tension between the Old World (that is, the old Europe, which brought us the fiddle, and the old Africa, which brought us the banjo) and the New, which would "steal" and adapt and synthesize songs and instruments and attitudes, as a uniquely American sensibility was taking form, expressed so perfectly in the "hill country" music coming out of western Virginia and eastern Tennessee, the Carolinas and

OPPOSITE *A crowd in Backusburg, Kentucky, gathers to hear stars from* The Grand Ole Opry, *1934.*

ABOVE *Young Ricky Skaggs performs with his parents, Dorothy and Hobert, 1961.*

the hollows of Kentucky. But country music's much revered ancestry, the "old ghosts" and "ancient tones" that Mississippian Marty Stuart invokes in an interview for our film, has had its own tensions with this new, restless, almost omnivorous musical form. In any given era, country music has always wanted to push its own boundaries, always wanted to try something else, always wanted to swallow whole this new thing or that, always wanted to move away from its roots. And then, just as forcibly, it has always wanted to move back to an earlier era, to embrace all the old traditions, all the old ghosts and ancient tones, whether they be centuries or just decades old. It was exhilarating to see this all being worked out right before our eyes: a respect for the past and a willingness to toss it aside for whatever was feeding the artistic appetite of the moment. One is reminded of Abraham Lincoln's 1862 Message to Congress, where *his* country is undergoing its own almost bipolar breakup. The president's speech careens between a respect for tradition: "Fellow citizens, we cannot escape history. . . . The fiery trial through which we pass will light us down in honor or dishonor to the latest generation"; to a realization that everything has to be remade, completely reinvented: "The dogmas of the quiet past are inadequate to the stormy present. . . . As our case is new, so we must think anew, and act anew." As we traveled the five score years of the arc of our film series, we saw time and time again this ferocious need to be different, and yet, almost at the same time, this passionate, deeply felt and deeply American desire to remain the same. It lit *us* on fire.

Those tensions extended to black and white, of course; that *is* the age-old American issue (Lincoln knew it); it is a tension that country music was destined to inherit at its very beginning. The Mount Rushmore of its early stars—Jimmie Rodgers and A.P. Carter, Bill Monroe and Hank Williams—all had an African-American mentor who gave them an appreciation for the blues and enabled each to be better than he was before. Country music has not spent much time focusing on that, but we found the reality of it to be resonant and deeply revealing. It runs both ways, too. Many African-American artists, like Charlie Parker, but also DeFord Bailey, Ray Charles, and Charley Pride, found in country music their own inspiration—and their curiosity and contributions broadened the music's appeal and legitimacy.

The tension between Saturday Night and Sunday Morning, the sinner and the saved, the rascal and the responsible one, runs throughout all of American music, but no more so than in country music. Jimmie Rodgers, the music's first

superstar, Hank Williams, perhaps its greatest songwriter, and Johnny Cash, its towering, transcendent patriarch, were all familiar with the dark side, the Saturday night of dimly lit bars and too much alcohol, infidelity and other temptations of the road, and they all celebrated an outlaw streak, an exultation of the rogue, that extends from them through Willie Nelson, Kris Kristofferson, Waylon Jennings, right up to the present. On the other hand, the Carter Family seemed to embody a centuries-old ideal of Family, Mother, and the Church that runs genuinely (and sometimes sanctimoniously) through the music and the country it tries to represent. Their example would be mirrored in generations of future stars more interested in promoting virtue in their music than vice. But as is often the case, those disparate polarities coexisted *within* the same artist, and the profoundly human music they made as a result reflected their never-ending search for some kind of redemption.

ABOVE *Fans at the Blackboard honky tonk have fun listening to Buck Owens and His Buckaroos, 1956.*

Rosanne Cash told us that her father "could hold two opposing thoughts at the same time and believe in both of them with the same degree of passion and power." His art was the mitigating, the reconciling force. He "worked out all of his problems onstage," Rosanne continued. "That's where he took his best self, that's where he took all of his anguish and fears and griefs, and he worked them out with an audience. That's just who he was. And [he] got purified by the end of the night." On the other side of the coin, the reality of A.P. and Sara Carter's strained marriage and her passionate love affair with her husband's young cousin is the stuff of almost unbelievable melodrama.

There is in country music, as in all things, an inherent tension between men and women, but we've never worked on any film before now that has had such strong and assertive women, whose artistic expression of their own struggles predates any feminist or Me Too movement. From Sara Carter chafing at a distant and distracted husband, to Kitty Wells defiantly proclaiming in a number one hit, "It Wasn't God Who Made Honky Tonk Angels"; from Loretta Lynn's subversively proto-feminist songs "Don't Come Home a-Drinkin' with Lovin' on Your Mind" and "The Pill," to Reba McEntire's willingness to confront enduring women's issues in songs like "Is There Life Out There?"; not to mention the incredibly successful career of Dolly Parton; women, and their stories and art, make up a huge part of our sprawling, multigenerational, almost Russian novel–like series and this book.

More tensions central to country music continued to surface and continued to multiply as we pursued our story. Ever present was the conflict between art and commerce—that is to say, whether to be a copycat of some earlier success, or, as Garth Brooks explained to us, "go down being true to yourself." (Spoiler: Brooks chose to be true to himself, but did not go down.) The influential singer-songwriter Guy Clark told his up-and-coming fellow Texan Rodney Crowell, "You're a talented guy. You can be a star. You probably have the talent to do it. Or you can be an artist. Pick one. They're both worthwhile pursuits." Fortunately, many of the artists we meet and follow in our series end up having it both ways. But a record's triumph always bred in the businessmen who sold them a desire to clone whatever had just worked—the death, it would seem, of creativity in any endeavor. Still, in the late 1950s and early '60s, some record producers, hoping for crossover success in the lucrative pop market, created the Nashville Sound, smoothing out country's rougher edges, adding sweet strings and backup vocals, and ended up having hit after hit. Chet Atkins, the genius session guitarist turned genius producer, was once asked what the Nashville Sound was. He jingled the change in his pocket.

There were also geographical tensions in a music that was never one thing, never something easily categorized or labeled. From the "ancient tones" of the hill country music springing out of the farmhouses and hamlets of Appalachia to the rough, wide-open songs of California's Central Valley, country music has absorbed—and, for the most part, tamed—all its many and varied constituent parts. The Deep South gave us the mournful blues and aching heartbreak of Jimmie Rodgers and Hank Williams (along with a huge dollop of hell-raising fun), and Texas and Oklahoma supplied dozens of defiant, fiercely independent singer-songwriters, all willing to buck traditions imposed from on high by country music's masters back in Nashville. Along our southern border, Mexican music filtered up and influenced an untold number of country music singers and songwriters, including one of the very best, Kris Kristofferson. And the West gave us cowboy songs and honky-tonk ballads that tumbled out of rowdy saloons, songs filled with longing and resentment—and having a good time.

ABOVE *A Mexican-American farm worker plays his guitar and sings in a California migrant labor camp, 1935.*

Country music comes from the country, of course, but cities—Atlanta, Chicago, Dallas, Bakersfield, and especially Nashville—are central to its growth. Where you're from, and what you still remember about home, and still wish for, is key in country music. Where you're going, and how you're planning to get there, figures prominently as well. Roy Clark, the owner (he lets us know) of two custom-made tuxedos, wasn't afraid to brag about or wear on the TV show *Hee Haw* the bib overalls he wore as a boy in Meherrin, Virginia. Everyone (it seemed) *heard* songs in a particular place. And that place and those tunes became at times one and the same thing. When Hazel Smith first listens to George Jones singing "He Stopped Loving Her Today" on the car radio, she has to pull off I-64 near Nashville, she explains, and cry. Garth Brooks, from Oklahoma, has a similar experience, rooted in *his* place: "I was going to the store with my dad and I remember coming out of Turtle Creek, up there where I was going to take a left by the blue church, heading north to Snyder's IGA, and my dad had his radio on . . . and this lady says, 'Here's a new kid from Texas and I think you're going to like him.' And it was George Strait. . . . And it was that day, I looked and said, 'That's what I want to be.'" Marty Stuart told us, "When I was growing up on Route 8, Kosciusko Road, in Philadelphia, Mississippi, the Gulf, Mobile & Ohio ran right behind our house. . . . And I used to dream about getting on that train and riding. . . . I didn't want to go to New York. I didn't want to go to Hollywood. I wanted to go to Nashville and play the kind of music that touched my heart."

The biggest tension was the most obvious and the most difficult to reconcile: the tension between the words and the music. As filmmakers, we understand a bit about that dynamic as we seek to find the right balance between our words and the images that accompany them. Or vice versa. It's a fundamental challenge, and each successful film has to find its own organic equilibrium. It is the same in country music, where the words and the music often add up to so much more than what the notes on the page indicate. That was where the art was made. That was when the whole became much greater than the sum of its parts. We looked for that moment everywhere, but it refused to yield

to any formula of discovery and *always* defied description. Everything, every song that tumbled out, success or failure, was unpredictable in the extreme. Gradually, we began to see the film we were making as a complex overlay of *all* these tensions. From the first episode to the last, songs and their lyrics became akin to our human characters. Some were like Marty Stuart's "ancient tones," around as long as the hills have been, their truths, however, as fresh as today. Some were brand new, shockingly new, but they often sounded as if they were hundreds of years old. Some were like "heirlooms," as Dolly Parton told us, songs passed on from generation to generation to generation. In our series, these songs appear and reappear, "old ghosts" (Marty would say again), as powerful in their rebirth and influence as, say, the music and memory of Hank Williams. In this way, we follow an old hymn that is rearranged by an African-American minister, only to be reworded by the Carter Family, finally ending up as Woody Guthrie's "This Land Is Your Land." "Mule Skinner Blues," one of Jimmie Rodgers's greatest tunes, undergoes no less than three more "rebirths" in our film—with Bill Monroe, the Maddox Brothers and Rose, and Dolly Parton each reimagining it for a new generation. "Will the Circle Be Unbroken," about burying one's mother, becomes one of the most joyous and most sung songs in all of American music, its sad lyrics left essentially unchanged.

RIGHT *Mother Maybelle Carter performs at the Opry, with Chet Atkins (left) on the guitar, 1955.*

Along with this often exhilarating appreciation of the tension between the virtuous and the rascal, between black and white, and men and women, between regions, between the conformist and the contrarian, between the authority of tradition and the thrill of the experimental, country music is also hugely about rising up from the bottom, about striving, and the overweening ambition to better oneself and one's family. A disproportionate number of country music's greatest stars were born into a stultifying poverty reminiscent of the Great Depression. (For many of our characters it *was* the Depression.) Dolly Parton's parents paid the doctor who delivered her with a sack of cornmeal. Roger Miller came from a town in Oklahoma so small and so poor "that we didn't have a town drunk, so we had to take turns." Rose Maddox from Boaz, Alabama, and her brothers and parents, had to live in a warren of unused drainage culverts, along with many other families and transients, all labeled "Okies" by their unforgivingly hostile California neighbors. Country music became their way up and out. So impressive is this manifest ambition and obvious drive—the need to escape the specific gravity of that poverty (or other childhood traumas)—that we all came to see this poverty as an essential ingredient of each artist's greatness. Negotiating and reconciling grief and loss, privation and suffering, made them better equipped to pass on the essential truths country music has always been able to convey.

The key for many of us was understanding what the musicians and singers and songwriters themselves understood country music to be. In interview after interview, they all came back to us with words like "simplicity" or "authenticity" or "truth." Loretta Lynn told us, "If you write the truth . . . and you're writing about your life, it's going to be country. It'll be country 'cause you're writing what's happening. And that's all a good song is." Speaking of Sara Carter's remarkable voice, Rosanne Cash said, "[It's] like wailing at the grave, that kind of keening . . . so plainspoken and so without any kind of embellishment or frill, just telling the truth, one note at a time." For Hank Williams, it could be summed up in just one word: "sincerity." Referring to Williams and his stunningly direct and exceedingly emotional lyrics, Rodney Crowell said, "When an artist gets it right for themselves, it's right for everyone." Emmylou Harris, the angel who more than once has "rescued" country music and reminded its listeners of its core values, echoed Hank Williams, saying, "The simplicity of country music is one of the most important things about it. It's about story and the melody and the sound and the voice and the sincerity of it."

Eventually, for many of us struggling to understand this deceptively simple music, all those old tensions would at times evaporate, the binary combat subsumed by larger, more important *human* themes only art (especially music, not exposition) seems capable of comprehending. And so our film gradually became, as well, about life and death, collaboration and reconciliation, loneliness and despair, falling in and out of love, missing someone, sinning, forgiveness and redemption. We found ourselves searching each other's eyes for help as we listened and watched, finding that we were all unexpectedly in tears as the lights came back on in our editing room after a screening. At first, we didn't quite understand the music's great gift. Finally, we realized it was right in front of us, in the elemental directness of the songs nearly everyone we interviewed spoke about and the startling complexity of the artists we ended up highlighting in our series. In the end, it came down to *recognition*—of ourselves, of the other, of the immense power at the heart of those words and music. "At the end of the day," Vince Gill, who wrote one of the most poignant hymns in all of country music, told us, "all I've ever wanted out of music was to be moved. I love the emotion of music. . . . There's something that it does to my DNA that I can't explain." Neither can we. But it's there. Help yourself.

KEN BURNS
Walpole, New Hampshire

ABOVE *A young Hank Williams, who became the "Hillbilly Shakespeare," c. 1940*

THE MUSIC of the Southern mountaineer is not only peculiar, but like himself, peculiarly American. Nearly all mountaineers are singers. Their untrained voices are of good timbre, the women's being sweet and high and tremulous, and their sense of pitch and tone and rhythm remarkably true.

The mountain people do sing many ballads of old England and Scotland. . . . [S]ome have been recast, words, names of localities and obsolete or unfamiliar phrases having been changed to fit their comprehension.

The mountaineer is fond of turning the joke on himself. He makes fun of his own poverty . . . his hard luck and his crimes. Once touched by religious emotion, however . . . the deeps of his nature are reached at last.

There are simple dance tunes, with a rollicking accompaniment . . . peculiar fingerings of the strings, close harmonies, curious snaps and slides and twangs, and the accurate observations of an ear attuned to all the sounds of nature. The fiddler and the banjo player are well treated and beloved among them, like the minstrels of feudal days.

[T]hese tunes are bound with the life of the singer, knit with his earliest sense-impressions, and therefore dearer than any other music could ever be—impossible to forget as the sound of his mother's voice.

Surely this is folk-song of the highest order. May it not one day give birth to a music that shall take a high place among the world's schools of expression?

EMMA BELL MILES,
The Spirit of the Mountains (1905)

1

THE RUB

The Sources of Country Music, *by Thomas Hart Benton,
1975. Commissioned by the Country Music Foundation
and now displayed at the Country Music Hall of Fame
and Museum, Benton's six-by-ten-foot mural depicts the
music's diverse roots: mountain ballads and square dance
tunes, hymns and spirituals, cowboy songs and African-
American blues. When Benton was already in his eighties,
he threw himself into the project at the encouragement of
country star Tex Ritter. In the early evening of January
19, 1975, Benton told his wife he was going back to his
studio in their Kansas City carriage house to decide if he
was finally finished with the painting, in which case he
would sign it. She found him there later, collapsed on the
floor and dead from a heart attack, with the mural still
unsigned.*

COUNTRY MUSIC was not invented; it emerged. It rose from the bottom, up: from the songs Americans sang to themselves in farm fields and railroad yards to ease them through their labors; and songs they sang to each other on the porches and in the parlors of their homes when the day's chores were done. It came from the fiddle tunes they danced to on Saturday nights to let off steam, as they celebrated the end of another hard week of work; and from the hymns they chanted on Sunday mornings, when they sought forgiveness for their earthly transgressions and found comfort in the promise of eternal salvation when their life on earth had ended. It filtered out of secluded hollows deep in the mountains and from smoky saloons on the edge of town; from the barrios along the southern border and from the wide-open spaces of the western range.

Most of all, its roots sprang from the need of everyday Americans—especially those who felt left out and looked down upon—to tell *their* stories. Country music, the songwriter Harlan Howard said, is "three chords and the truth."

In the early 1920s, after centuries of being handed down, person to person, country music would become more than a haphazard collection of songs cherished by people on the lower rungs of the nation's social and economic ladder. It would become a business. And over the course of the twentieth century, as it sometimes struggled to shed its homespun image and become accepted by mainstream society, country music would continue evolving, adapting to changing times, constantly mingling with other forms of American music to create something new.

But even as it broadened and changed, it would also find itself constantly returning to its roots, circling back to its origins. "All of American music comes from the same place," said Ketch Secor, a multi-instrumentalist and member of the string band Old Crow Medicine Show. "It's just where it ends up—and country music is one of the destinations. It's what American folk music has come to be called when it followed the path of the fiddle and the banjo."

● ● ●

Nothing goes but old-fashioned fiddling. Just pure elbow grease and awkwardness and a tune that gets

into your feet. I figure that any tune that will let a man keep his feet still ain't worth the playing.

FIDDLIN' JOHN CARSON

By June 1923, John Carson had been playing the fiddle for nearly forty years—ever since his grandfather first gave him one at the age of ten—and although music was his passion, he had relied on other work to get by: toting pails of water to African-American railroad gangs as a boy, then, as a young man with a growing family to support, making $10 a week for sixty hours of labor in the burgeoning textile mills of Atlanta.

But on Saturday nights, in the crowded factory neighborhoods, Carson started to make a name for himself—and a little extra money—playing at square dances for families who had migrated from their farms to find work in one of the South's biggest cities.

ABOVE *Fiddlin' John Carson*

OPPOSITE *Four early musicians. Country music, Ketch Secor said, "followed the path of the fiddle and the banjo."*

FIDDLING
JOHN CARSON
COMING!
To Appear in Person at Fiddlers Convention
In Pelham, Ga.
FRIDAY and SATURDAY Nov. 22nd and 23rd.

He's A Radio Star!

He's on the Okey Record Producing Company's payroll and his records are in demand all over the nation. Carson is an Old Timer and as Original as the Violin he plays.

He is as much at home before a New York audience as he is in Pelham.

TOP *Fiddlin' John Carson, far right, at the 1925 fiddlers' convention in Mountain City, Tennessee. Carson happily played for any crowd he could find, from farm auctions and store openings to communist rallies and Ku Klux Klan gatherings, like the one advertised on the bank window.*

ABOVE *Carson's exposure on Atlanta's WSB radio station, where he played for free, landed him paid engagements throughout the region. "Radio," he said, "made me."*

Known as "Fiddlin' John," Carson soon began appearing wherever a crowd could be found: store openings and farm auctions, Confederate veterans' reunions and political events ranging from Ku Klux Klan gatherings to a rally in support of a communist organizer. He even showed up outside the Fulton County courthouse during a celebrated murder trial, performing some ballads he had composed about the case, while his children hawked the sheet music for ten cents apiece. He showed up again for the throng that came to see the corpse of the accused man, after a mob had taken him from his cell and lynched him.

Carson's biggest audiences were at the Georgia Old-Time Fiddlers' Convention, held in Atlanta's Municipal Auditorium. Each year several thousand people came to hear fifty or more fiddlers—and a music that reminded them of simpler times and the rural homes of their past. "Going to a dance was like going back home to Mama's or to Grandma's for Thanksgiving," said music historian Bill C. Malone. "Country music is full of songs about little old log cabins that people have never lived in, the old country church that people have never attended. But it spoke for a lot of people who were being forgotten, or felt they were being forgotten. Country music's staple, above all, is nostalgia—just a harkening back to the older way of life, either real or imagined."

With his easy sense of humor and natural showmanship, as much as his skill on the fiddle, Carson became a crowd favorite, often winning the convention's top prize of $50.

Even though he—and many of the other contestants—had been factory-working city dwellers for decades, Carson gladly cooperated with newspaper reporters and convention publicists who preferred to portray the musicians as rustic hayseeds. On the stage and in newspaper interviews, he often claimed to have just arrived from the remote hamlet of Blue Ridge in the north Georgia mountains. "The only things I [do] really well is moonshining and fiddling," he told one reporter, "and since the 'revenooers' caught me . . . the old lady 'lows I better quit for good. That leaves me only the old fiddle."

In 1922, his audience expanded again, thanks to a new technology. *The Atlanta Journal* began operating the South's first radio station, whose call letters, WSB, stood for "Welcome South, Brother." For a while, the new station struggled to find enough talented live performers to fill the broadcast schedule. "Anyone who could sing, whistle, recite, play any kind of instrument, or merely breathe heavily was pushed in front of the WSB microphone," one of the station managers remembered. "In a short time, almost everybody in Atlanta who could ride, walk, or crawl to WSB had participated in a program." He added, "None of the talent was paid, but that made no difference. They trouped to WSB to perform, and Aunt Minnie stayed home to listen."

Carson saw an opportunity, even if he had to play for free. Backed by a three-piece string band, he became the first of the region's skilled old-time musicians to perform on the air. So many telegrams and telephone calls poured into WSB that the station asked him back for weekly appearances. The radio exposure, in turn, brought him invitations to play at paid performances in country schoolhouses and small-town theaters throughout the region.

As he neared the age of fifty, Fiddlin' John Carson could finally quit his day job as a mill worker to become a full-time musician. "Until I began to play over WSB," he admitted, "just a few people in and around Atlanta knew me, but now my wife thinks she's a widow most of the time because I stay away from home so much, playing around over this part of the country.

"Radio," he said simply, "made me." But an older form of technology would now bring Carson and his kind of music to even more people.

Ever since Thomas Edison's invention of the phonograph in 1877, Americans had been buying the machines for their homes, and sales of records to play on them had risen steadily—by the early 1920s, surpassing $100 million a year. Most of the music was confined to "highbrow" stylists like

opera tenor Enrico Caruso, Broadway stars like Eddie Cantor, or Paul Whiteman's popular dance band.

Then, in the summer of 1923, a young man named Ralph Peer, from Independence, Missouri, would change all that. "You couldn't possibly be a success—at least, it would be unusual to be a success—if you knew too much about music," Peer later recalled. "You have to be a businessman and a prophet, and you also have to be somewhat of a gambler. The real secret is continuous activity. You can't rest."

By the age of thirty-one, Peer had risen through the ranks of the new General Phonograph Corporation, which had carved out a niche in the booming industry with records aimed at America's significant immigrant populations. Italian, German, Russian, Scandinavian, Polish, Greek, Turkish, Yiddish, Slovakian, Lithuanian, and Chinese households all could buy music recorded in their own languages.

In 1920, Peer had discovered another untapped niche in the market. With the company's Okeh label, he recorded

TOP *By continually finding new niche markets for record sales, Ralph Peer would change the course of American music history. He was a gambler, he admitted, and his success was based on a willingness to try something new.*

ABOVE *Mamie Smith's recording of "Crazy Blues" proved so popular among African Americans that Peer began signing up more black musicians for Okeh's "race" records.*

Peer's records in his grandfather's downtown furniture store and had helped arrange the Atlanta sessions. Brockman suggested bringing in a musician who had become something of a local radio celebrity on WSB playing old-time music. It was Fiddlin' John Carson.

Peer was reluctant at first. A year earlier, Texas fiddler Eck Robertson had recorded two songs—"Sallie Gooden" and "Arkansas Traveler"—for the powerful Victor Talking Machine Company, but they had not sold well. Peer was uncertain much of a market existed for that kind of music. Brockman convinced him to give Carson a try by guaranteeing to buy at least five hundred copies for sales in Atlanta alone. With nothing to lose, Peer brought Fiddlin' John in to record him playing an old minstrel song, "The Little Old Log Cabin in the Lane."

Peer was unhappy with the quality of the recordings, but took the wax masters back north and, true to his word, sent finished copies to Brockman in Atlanta a few weeks later. As soon as they arrived, Brockman put Carson in front of a large crowd gathered for the opening of the Georgia fiddlers' convention and placed the largest phonograph player he could find on the stage next to his artist. After Carson performed "The Little Old Log Cabin in the Lane" for the audience,

vaudeville singer Mamie Smith's "Crazy Blues," which sold 75,000 copies in its first month. Peer learned that African-American Pullman railroad porters were buying them by the dozens and taking them south for resale to their friends. He quickly arranged to record other black musicians for what the label called its "race" records: stride piano player James P. Johnson, slide guitarist Sylvester Weaver, the Virginia Female Jubilee Singers, and others.

Seeking more black musicians to record, in June 1923 Peer brought Okeh's engineers to Atlanta with brand-new transportable equipment and set them up in a vacant warehouse on Nassau Street. But after recording two female blues singers and a quartet from Morehouse College, he was disappointed that he hadn't gathered more material.

He found his solution from Polk Brockman, who promoted

TOP *In 1922, Texas fiddler Eck Robertson had recorded two songs for the Victor label, but they had not sold well.*

RIGHT *Fiddlin' John Carson's recordings for Okeh in 1923 were an immediate success in Atlanta, persuading Ralph Peer that he had discovered yet another untapped market. Carson, seen here touring with his daughter "Moonshine Kate," now billed himself as a "record artist" as well as a radio star.*

Brockman played the record with the same song and offered his supply for sale. "They sold," he said, "like hot cakes." Then he called Peer and ordered thousands more.

Peer now realized that there was another segment of America eager to buy recordings of music they were familiar with—essentially one more niche waiting to be filled: predominantly white working-class Southerners. He contacted Fiddlin' John to arrange for more sessions in Okeh's New York studio—and started looking for other artists like him.

Peer soon proclaimed in an advertisement that Okeh had "uncovered a brand-new field for record sales" and now offered "Old Time Pieces" that were setting off, he said, a "craze for this 'Hill Country Music.'"

"I'll have to quit makin' moonshine," Carson joked to a reporter, "and start makin' records."

THE MUSICAL MELTING POT

The phonograph companies [have] opened a new market, one that they had not dreamed existed: a wide market among the folk of the mountains, of the mining districts and the timberlands. Plain folk to whom the story is the important part of any song; who like the accompaniment simple and the words understandable.

COLLIER'S MAGAZINE

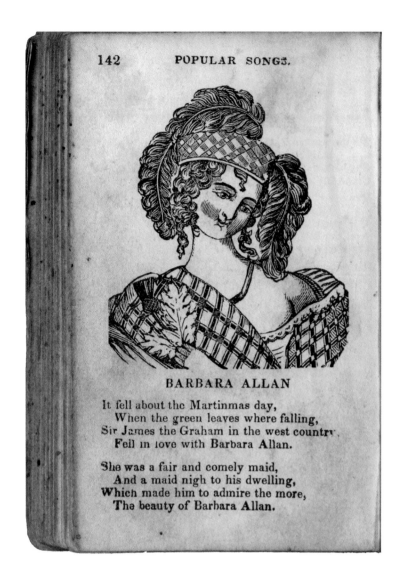

Ralph Peer may have discovered a new field for record *sales* in the 1920s, but the music was anything but new. It sprang from many roots, some of them older than the nation itself.

The first colonists brought with them ballads from the British Isles that were already centuries old—songs that told stories, often of lost loves, murders, or tragic events. Some were passed along in the New World relatively unchanged from generation to generation.

"Barbara Allan," the plaintive story of an unrequited love, a broken heart, and two deaths, dated all the way back to the 1600s. It was nearly three hundred years old when Bradley Kincaid, who had learned it from his uncle in Kentucky, first sang it on the radio. The song received such an overwhelming response that he sang it on the radio every week for a solid year.

Bascom Lamar Lunsford, a lawyer and amateur folklorist from Mars Hill, North Carolina, had collected more than three hundred old songs in his travels through southern Appalachia. Peer recorded him performing some of them in 1924, including "I Wish I Was a Mole in the Ground," the last song, Lunsford said, that his dying mother had requested to hear. Known as "the Minstrel of the Appalachians," Lunsford would soon organize the Mountain Dance and Folk Festival in Asheville to keep the old-time music alive—and he would write the lyrics of what became a standard in its own right: "Mountain Dew."

For generations, Americans had also been adapting melodies from the Old World by attaching new lyrics to match their experiences in the New World. "Bury Me Not on the Lone Prairie" came from an old sailor's song, "The Ocean Burial." "The Streets of Laredo," about a dying Texas cowboy, took its tune from an Irish ballad, "The Bard of Armagh,"

ABOVE *When this version of "Barbara Allan" was published in a songbook in New York in 1840, the song was probably two hundred years old. It was already popular in 1666, when Samuel Pepys noted in his diary that he had enjoyed hearing the "little Scotch song" at a New Year's party in England.*

TOP *Just as in the distant past, news-making tragedies often became the subject of popular songs. In 1903, a train disaster in Virginia was turned into "The Wreck of the Old 97," which borrowed its melody from "The Ship That Never Returned," written in 1865.*

RIGHT *The plight of Floyd Collins, trapped for weeks in Kentucky's Mammoth Cave, created national headlines—and then became the topic of Columbia Records' biggest hit of 1925, "The Death of Floyd Collins."*

written around 1700. "The Wreck of the Old 97," a ballad recounting the story of a notorious train accident in 1903, borrowed its melody from a tune out of the 1800s, "The Ship That Never Returned." Ralph Peer first recorded it in 1923 with Henry Whitter, and although it didn't sell well, it caught the attention of Vernon Dalhart, who talked the Victor label into releasing a version of his own. It became old-time music's first million-seller and vaulted Dalhart into instant stardom.

Born in Jefferson City, Texas, Dalhart's original name was Marion Try Slaughter. He had been trained at the Dallas Conservatory as a classical singer before moving to New York, where he appeared in Puccini operas and Gilbert and Sullivan shows. (He adopted his new stage name from the two Texas towns where he had once worked as a cowhand.) When his career on the stage foundered, Dalhart decided to try a different type of music. He sang "The

Wreck of the Old 97" and for its flip side, the equally popular "The Prisoner's Song," with an affected twang, but kept some of the precise diction of his formal training, which may have helped his sales. One loyal fan said he bought Dalhart's records "because you can hear the words to what he's singing real good and clear through all that hiss."

Another tragedy brought Dalhart another big hit. In 1925, trying to discover a new entrance to what became Mammoth Cave National Park in central Kentucky, Floyd Collins found himself stuck in a narrow passageway. Rescuers tried in vain for more than two weeks to reach him, and as his plight became a national sensation, Polk Brockman commissioned a blind musician named Andy Jenkins—who performed regularly on Atlanta's WSB and specialized in writing ballads after someone read him newspaper stories—to quickly churn out a song about the incident. Dalhart's version of "The Death of Floyd Collins" became Columbia Records' biggest success of 1925.

That same year, Carson Robison, who played guitar on many of Dalhart's singles, provided him with another song taken from the headlines. It was based on the sensational trial in Dayton, Tennessee, in which John Scopes was convicted of violating a state law against the teaching of Darwin's theory of evolution. Its recurring line at the end of each

chorus was, "the old religion's better after all." Dalhart would go on to record it—and many of his other hits—multiple times for other labels, ultimately using seventy-nine different pseudonyms, in order to make more money from the same song.

Nowhere was music more essential than in church. The hymns people sang on Sunday mornings warned them of God's eternal judgment, but also offered the promise of salvation—even to the sinners who had been out carousing on Saturday night. "The best Christian in the world is the one who realizes that he needs to be," said Don Reid of the Statler Brothers, a gospel quartet. "You know, you've got to experience Saturday night sometimes to know what Sunday morning's all about."

Jazz musician and composer Wynton Marsalis agreed: "Human beings, what do we think about? We've got very basic things. We think about our sexual relationship that we need to propagate our species and makes our life sweet and also bitter; and our relationship to whatever our Lord is. So we put those two things right together: the Saturday-night

ABOVE *A frontier baptism in a Kansas river offers the promise of a new life.*

function and the Sunday-morning purification. And you've got to get purified on Sunday so you can do the same thing again next Saturday."

Many churchgoers, especially in the rural South, couldn't read music, so singing schools were organized to teach people a basic system called shape notes. Songbook publishers dispatched traveling quartets to demonstrate how to add harmony to the songs—and then sell their products.

At singing conventions and gospel tent revivals, people congregated to sing old spirituals, originating from black churches, or popular hymns like "Will the Circle Be Unbroken," written in 1907, and a cheery gospel tune from 1899, "Keep on the Sunny Side," inspired by the writer's invalid cousin who asked that his wheelchair always be pushed "on the sunny side" of the street. Sometimes, revival organizers simply set religious lyrics to popular melodies everyone already knew. "Why," the saying went, "should the Devil have all the good tunes?"

The instruments people played came from every corner

TOP AND ABOVE *A church-sponsored singing school in West Virginia and a songbook page with a variant of shape-note music*

OPPOSITE *The choir in an African-American church in Kentucky sings for the congregation.*

of the globe. Fiddles were the most common, having been brought to America by successive waves of immigrants. The first known fiddle contest in North America was advertised in Virginia in 1736—forty years before the Declaration of Independence, and nearly two centuries before Eck Robertson was defeating the competition in Texas and Fiddlin' John Carson was winning state championships in Georgia.

Over time, each section of the new nation developed its own homegrown style of playing, but they all served the same primary purpose: providing music for people to dance to.

Like many of the tunes, "Soldier's Joy" came from Celtic roots. It was already old when Scottish bard Robert Burns attached sarcastic lyrics to it about a veteran recounting how much he "liked" being in the army. By the time of the American Civil War, the words had changed to mention morphine

ABOVE AND OPPOSITE, TOP *The fiddle came from Europe, and the banjo arrived with slaves from Africa. On plantations in the South, black musicians mastered both instruments and played them for their masters' entertainment—and their own.*

and alcohol as a soldier's most trusted friends. In the 1920s, Gid Tanner and His Skillet Lickers, with Clayton McMichen and Lowe Stokes on fiddle and Riley Puckett doing the singing, made it one of their signature hits. Country star Charlie Daniels would reference it—and another old favorite, "Fire on the Mountain"—in 1979 within his song about a different fiddle contest, "The Devil Went Down to Georgia."

The banjo, second only to the fiddle early on, came to America as a gourd with a fretless neck, brought by slaves from Africa. By the early 1800s, it had evolved into the instrument of choice for many musicians.

"The banjo, for the first hundred years, is a black instrument," said Rhiannon Giddens, a banjo and fiddle player and founding member of the Grammy-winning Carolina Chocolate Drops, an African-American string band. "It's known as a plantation instrument. That is where it is played. Dance is a main form of entertainment. Who's playing for the dances? You had a lot of African servants, also known as slaves; they are the players for these dances. They learn these European [fiddle] tunes and so the fiddle and the banjo start getting combined on the plantation. It's an African-

American innovation, this idea of those two instruments together. You don't have country music without fiddle and banjo. And you don't have fiddle and banjo music without black people."

By the 1920s, Charlie Poole, a textile worker from Eden, North Carolina, had become the best-known banjo player in the nation. He had broken several fingers playing baseball, on a drunken bet that he could catch a hard-thrown ball without a glove. The bones weren't set properly, resulting in permanently curled fingers on his right hand, but they allowed him to develop a unique three-fingered style that differed from the prevailing "clawhammer" or "frailing" method.

With his North Carolina Ramblers, Poole often performed for tips from his fellow mill workers—"lintheads," as they were known—on Saturday afternoons after their half-day shift. Then he landed a recording contract with Columbia in 1925, and when the Ramblers became one of the most popular string bands in the nation, he was finally able to quit work in the mills and appeared in the Gibson company's catalog promoting their instruments. A prodigious drinker—he once clubbed a policeman over the head with his banjo during a

ABOVE *North Carolina's Charlie Poole was the nation's best-known banjo player in the 1920s. A baseball injury to his right hand permanently curled some of his fingers, which prompted him to innovate on his technique.*

Once the guitar arrived in America, musicians of all races and ethnicities put it to use for a wide range of styles, and it began to rival the fiddle and banjo in popularity.

brawl—Poole died at age thirty-nine, at the end of a bender that had lasted thirteen weeks.

The guitar came to America from other lands, too. After trying to open his own guitar factory in Germany—only to face opposition from established violin makers—Christian Frederick Martin immigrated to New York and in 1833 started producing small gut-string guitars whose light sound made them appropriate for the guitar's main market at the time: polite parlor music. Then black, Hawaiian, and Latino musicians adapted it to more diverse styles, and when Martin's grandson designed a new model in the early twentieth century—with a larger body and stronger neck to permit steel strings—the guitar began to rival the fiddle and banjo in its use. Orville Gibson of Kalamazoo, Michigan, made guitars, too, and innovated with the design of another instrument from Europe: the mandolin.

Riley Puckett, of Alpharetta, Georgia, had been blinded as an infant by a lead acetate solution used to treat a minor eye irritation, but he developed a distinctive guitar style that, combined with his smooth voice, made him an early favorite on Atlanta's WSB radio station. Besides becoming an important member of Gid Tanner's Skillet Lickers, Puckett had success of his own as a soloist. In 1924, he recorded "Rock All Our Babies to Sleep," a mournful song about a husband with a roaming wife, to which he added extended yodels, mimicking a vocal style that had swept the nation in the mid-nineteenth century after some Tyrolean singing troupes from Switzerland toured the United States.

Not all of the music people considered "old-time" was actually rooted in the deep past; nor did it spring exclusively from the rural South.

Long before phonographs and radio, traveling shows had crisscrossed the countryside, bringing theatrical performances that featured music between acts, written by professional songsmiths from the cities. Beginning in the 1840s, Stephen Foster created a string of heartfelt songs that ended up in the parlors of homes across the nation: "Jeanie with the Light Brown Hair," "Oh! Susanna," "Beautiful Dreamer," and "Hard Times."

Though he was a Northerner who traveled only once below the Mason-Dixon Line, Foster also contributed many more tunes that were spread by itinerant minstrel shows—white professional musicians, dressed in blackface, who danced and performed songs that the audiences believed imitated African-American music and simultaneously sentimentalized life in the antebellum South: "Camptown Races," "My Old Kentucky Home," "Old Folks at Home."

The only source of income for a professional songwriter like Foster was the royalties from sales of sheet music. His songs were immensely popular, but because of lax copyright laws, when he died, in New York City's Bellevue Hospital in 1864 at the age of thirty-seven, he was virtually penniless.

Many other songs that became considered quintessentially southern and rural came, in fact, from northern, urban sources. "Carry Me Back to Old Virginny" was written by James A. Bland, a college-educated African American born in Flushing, New York. "Dixie," played at the inauguration of Jefferson Davis when he became president of the Confederacy, was credited to Daniel Decatur Emmett of Ohio, who

ABOVE *Stephen Foster wrote both popular sentimental songs like "Beautiful Dreamer," which people sang in their home parlors, and tunes like "My Old Kentucky Home," romanticizing pre–Civil War plantation life, which traveling minstrels performed.*

TOP *A traveling minstrel group, some in blackface, arrives in a small village.*

ABOVE, LEFT *A poster for Christy's Minstrels, one of the nation's most popular minstrel groups. They specialized in performing Stephen Foster songs.*

ABOVE, RIGHT *Sheet music for some of James Bland's songs. Bland, a college-educated African American from New York State, wrote "Carry Me Back to Old Virginny," among other minstrel tunes.*

may have learned it from the Snowdens, a neighboring black family.

Minstrelsy continued after the Civil War—the principal conduit of pop music to Americans, North and South—but as the nation became more urbanized when the twentieth century dawned, vaudeville shows, which played in theaters, began to overtake it. And the music that vaudeville made popular increasingly came from the publishing houses concentrated in New York's Tin Pan Alley.

Minstrel shows were fading, but their songs would live on. In 1924, Emmett Miller, a vaudevillian and former minstrel star who still performed in blackface, released "Anytime (You're Feeling Lonely)"; a year later, Peer recorded him singing "Lovesick Blues," a Tin Pan Alley tune to which Miller, too, added a novel yodeling break in his voice. Eddy Arnold would make "Anytime" a hit a generation later, and Miller is said to still have been performing in the late 1940s in a club in Nashville's Printer's Alley when Hank Williams was becoming a country sensation in nearby Ryman Auditorium singing "Lovesick Blues."

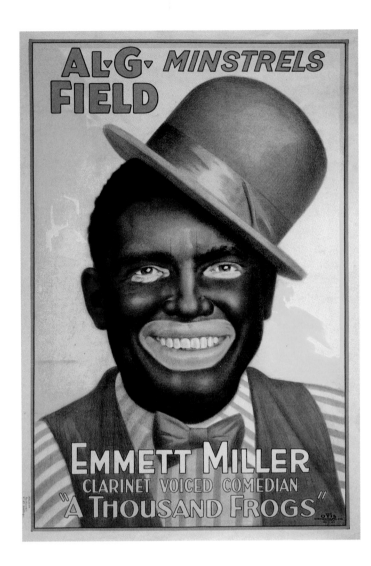

In its own way, Miller's "Lovesick Blues" also demonstrated something essential about the multiple sources that had come together to create the music Ralph Peer was now recording. It drew deeply from race music—even if that music was increasingly performed almost exclusively by whites, most of them Southerners.

"In the South, you have the most intense injustice, but you also have people living together," said Wynton Marsalis. "You had the intensity of slavery, you have the cultures coming together. You have a depth of human tragedy in the South; you have this type of bondage in the context of freedom; you have a lot of opposites that create richness. That's where a lot of our Southern music comes from."

"I think that friction is a good way to look at the music, because of this rub between white and black," added Ketch Secor. "Country music comes from the South because this is where slavery happened. It's that simple."

"The rub," Rhiannon Giddens said, "is people mixing. It starts going back and forth and it becomes this beautiful mix of cultures. And what happens is, always, the people who are

TOP, LEFT *Emmett Miller's 1925 Okeh hit "Lovesick Blues," which included his own unique yodeling, would become the breakthrough song for Hank Williams a generation later.*

TOP, RIGHT AND ABOVE *Much of country music evolved from the mix of races and cultures in the South—a complicated "rub between white and black" that continued long after slavery was abolished.*

living together and who are working together are combining and making this music. The heart spoke musically to each other. And then somebody from the . . . up, up here, says, 'Oh, we can't have that. You guys can't be doing stuff together.' It's like they don't want us to know how mixed we are. That's what the rub is."

By the 1920s, slavery had been abolished for more than half a century, but segregation was still rigidly enforced in every aspect of life—except in the music that kept crossing the racial divide. "African-American style was embedded in country music from the very beginning of its commercial history," said Bill C. Malone. "You can't conceive of this music existing without this African-American infusion. But then, as the music developed professionally, too often, African Americans were forgotten."

• • •

Country music wasn't called that yet, but it was music of the country. It was a combination of the Irish; the recently freed slaves, bringing the banjo into the world; the Spanish effects of the *vaqueros* down in Texas; the Germans bringing over the "oom-pah" of polka music, all converging.

I think it's definitely American. It's a combination of all the influences that came together in America, especially in the 1800s. The melting pot was a musical melting pot.

JOHN MCEUEN, THE NITTY GRITTY DIRT BAND

Sprouting from so many intertwining roots—old ballads and hymns, Tin Pan Alley compositions, minstrel shows, and African-American blues—the music Ralph Peer and his competitors began recording in the 1920s was hard to categorize or precisely define. But for marketing reasons—for their catalogs and for display purposes in retail stores—the companies needed a name for it.

The record labels tried a variety of names: "Old Familiar Tunes," "Old Southern Tunes," "Old-Time Melodies of the Sunny South," "Songs from Dixie," even "Native American Melodies." Peer's Okeh label at first referred to its new category as "Hill Country Music" or "Old Time Tunes."

In 1925, Peer recorded a spirited string band fronted by Al Hopkins in New York City. As they were leaving, Peer asked what name he should use for the band in his advertising. Hopkins answered, "Call us anything. We're nothing but a bunch of hillbillies from North Carolina and Virginia."

Peer had the name he needed: he called them "The Hill Bil-

THE HILL BILLIES

40336 { CRIPPLE CREEK, Orchestra, Vocal Chorus by Al. Hopkins — The Hill Billies
10 in. .75 { SALLY ANN, Orchestra, Vocal Chorus by Al. Hopkins — The Hill Billies

lies." Soon, magazines and newspapers were referring to the entire genre as "hillbilly music," and the name stuck.

Not every artist appreciated the term, or the way they were often portrayed as quaint and quirky backwoods hayseeds. College-educated Bradley Kincaid found it insulting; Charlie Poole steadfastly refused to dress like a rustic farmer, demanding that his band wear formal suits for all publicity photos and performances. Even one of Al Hopkins's band members objected to the word. " 'Hillbilly' was not a funny word," he said. "It was a fighting word."

"If you're an outsider and you're saying it's 'hillbilly music' because you don't know any better, it's almost like a racist remark," said singer-songwriter Dolly Parton. "But if we're hillbillies, we're proud of that. It's our music."

ABOVE *When Ralph Peer named Al Hopkins's band "The Hill Billies," Okeh was promoting the music as "Old Time Tunes." But magazines soon began calling the whole genre "hillbilly music," a term some musicians resented but others gladly adopted.*

OPPOSITE, TOP *At traveling medicine shows, musical performances attracted the crowds for the "doctor," who then pitched his "snake oil." Kapoo Indian Medicines promised a salve that could kill worms and cure coughs.*

OPPOSITE, BOTTOM *In Kansas, Dr. John R. Brinkley started his own radio station, which featured live music and crop reports mixed in with pitches for his medical clinic, where he claimed he could restore men's sexual potency by transplanting goat glands into them. He became fabulously wealthy.*

As long as it helped sell records, many performers were fine with it—including Fiddlin' John Carson, who had already adopted the persona of a country bumpkin from north Georgia, rather than the former mill worker from Atlanta he really was. His daughter, Rosa Lee, now performed with him as a sassy hillbilly girl everyone called "Moonshine Kate," even though she was a city girl, born and raised in Atlanta.

TUNING IN

In a medicine show, you come into town, you set up in the town square, and you hawk an elixir. You've got this remedy, and you pass out handbills and you take personal testimonials from paid dudes out there in the audience. And they tell you about how wonderful they feel, how their dropsy went away and how their sores and festering wounds have healed because of this corn whiskey, this snake oil.

So, you've got your product. And music is only there to push your product. Music is just like the soapbox you stand on; it's all about the message. The radio changed everything.

KETCH SECOR

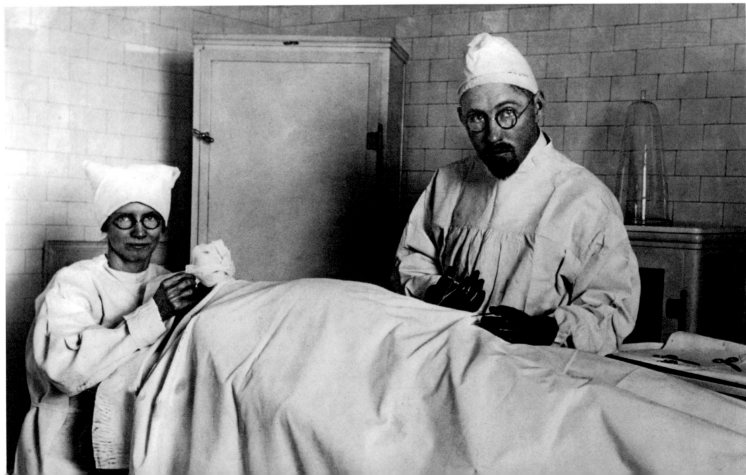

From the time KDKA in Pittsburgh became the nation's first licensed radio station in 1920, Americans quickly embraced the new technology that brought them news and entertainment from far away. Within four years, the number of broadcasters mushroomed from 1 to 556. And to attract listeners, they all borrowed from one of the oldest traditions of mixing music and commerce: the traveling medicine show.

In tiny Milford, Kansas, Dr. John R. Brinkley, who had once peddled cure-alls in traveling medicine shows (and who had purchased his medical certificate for $100 from the Eclectic Medical University in Kansas City), set up a clinic that promised to restore aging men's sexual potency by a special technique he had developed: implanting billy goat testicles into them. One patient attested that Brinkley's so-called "rejuvenation" procedure had allowed him to father a son, whom he proudly named "Billy."

To promote his business, in 1923 Brinkley started radio station KFKB—for "Kansas First, Kansas Best"— and filled most of the broadcast day personally dispensing medical advice, inviting listeners to his clinic, and assuring them that "a man is as old as his glands." He filled the rest of the schedule with crop reports, weather forecasts, and live music by "Uncle Bob" Larkan, the Arkansas state champion fiddler.

In Shenandoah, Iowa, in 1924, the owner of a mail-order seed store opened station KFNF—"Keep Friendly, Never Frown"—by stringing a long horizontal wire between two tall towers. Over the air, he staged fiddle contests and live music from groups named the Cornfield Canaries and the Seedhouse Girls, in between pitches for his products. When sales skyrocketed, his chief competitor in town started KMA, "The Corn Belt Station in the Heart of the Nation," and before long Shenandoah, population five thousand, was flooded with visitors from all over the Midwest who wanted to watch the broadcasts in person—prompting both companies to build ornate auditoriums, arcade shops, a miniature golf course, and tourist cabins to accommodate the crowds.

They were soon eclipsed by the giant Sears, Roebuck and Company in Chicago, which launched station WLS (the "World's Largest Store"). It featured a wide variety of programming—dance bands, classical music, radio plays, sports, and religious services on Sundays. But on Saturday night, April 19, 1924, it experimented with *National Barn Dance*, modeled after a program of square dance music already popular on Fort Worth's WBAP.

The experiment almost failed. A Sears executive had turned on the radio to entertain his guests at a fancy dinner

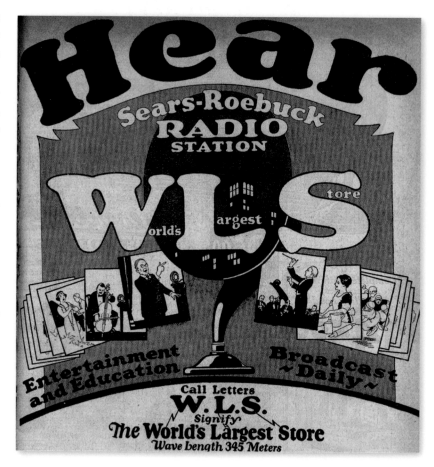

party in Chicago and was appalled at the hillbilly fiddle music coming out of it. He ordered the station to cancel the show, but when thousands of letters poured in from twenty states, *National Barn Dance* was reinstated—and quickly became the premier show of its kind in the nation.

Station managers at WLS eventually realized that most of the listeners weren't actually staging square dances in their homes to the program's music—they were more interested in the songs—and the format changed to highlight solo artists and smaller acts. One of the earliest stars was Bradley Kincaid, who had received his first guitar when his father traded a prized foxhound for it. His performances of traditional songs generated more than 100,000 letters a year to WLS, and Sears began marketing a Bradley Kincaid Houn' Dog Guitar in its catalog, while sales of his first songbook went to six printings to keep up with the demand. Booked for his first public concert in Peoria, Kincaid was startled to find a line of people several blocks long. When he asked what

---

ABOVE *Sears, Roebuck and Company, the catalog retailing powerhouse in Chicago, broadcast a variety of programming from station WLS (for "World's Largest Store"), but its* National Barn Dance *proved to be its most popular show.*

was happening, a man in the crowd answered, "Why, that radio singer from WLS is going to be here."

Meanwhile, in Nashville, Tennessee, the success of stations like Chicago's WLS and Atlanta's WSB caught the attention of Edwin Craig, the son of the founder of the National Life and Accident Insurance Company. A radio station, Craig believed, might provide an effective way to help the company's 2,500 salesmen, who sold low-cost sickness and burial policies door to door to working-class families in more than twenty states.

Craig's father was against it at first, believing that a radio station would be a waste of money and a distraction from National Life's business. But Edwin Craig persisted, arguing that it would increase the company's name recognition and sales. With his father's reluctant permission, Craig set up a studio on the fifth floor of the company's downtown office building, with thick carpets and pleated drapes hung from the ceiling to improve the acoustics, and began broadcasting on October 5, 1925, with the call letters WSM, which stood for the insurance company's motto: "We Shield Millions."

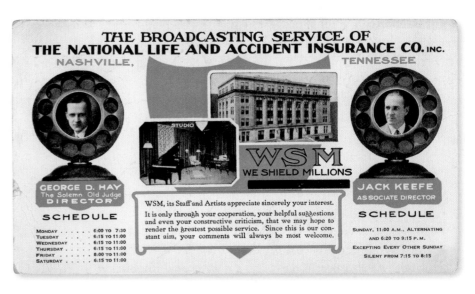

TOP *Bradley Kincaid (with guitar, seen here broadcasting from the Sherman House Hotel kitchen) was an early WLS star. Sears offered copies of his Houn' Dog Guitar, and fans eagerly bought Kincaid's songbooks.*

ABOVE *In Nashville, Tennessee, the National Life and Accident Insurance Company launched a radio station to help promote its policies. The call letters, WSM, came from the company's slogan, "We Shield Millions."*

All of the programming was performed live: Vito Pellettieri and his Radio Five playing Vivaldi and popular songs; Miss Daisy Hoffman, the piano teacher of Craig's daughter, doing solos; bedtime stories for children read every night at seven o'clock by Bonnie Barnhardt; and an orchestra led by Craig's cousin, offering music suitable for polite social dancing.

As WSM's program director, Craig recruited the personable George D. Hay, who had just been proclaimed America's favorite announcer on Chicago's WLS the year before. Though only thirty years old, Hay called himself "the Solemn Old Judge" and often punctuated his broadcasts by blowing on a wooden riverboat whistle.

On November 28, 1925, Hay invited an elderly musician named "Uncle Jimmy" Thompson, a fiddler since before the Civil War, to perform on the air. He called his instrument "Old Betsy," which he said had been passed down from his ancestors in Scotland, and that night he played for a solid hour. When Hay suggested he had done enough, Thompson answered, "A man don't get warmed up in an hour. Tell the neighbors to send in their requests, and I'll play them if it takes me all night."

The response persuaded Hay to schedule a regular

ABOVE *Despite his youth, WSM's program director, George D. Hay, called himself "the Solemn Old Judge." On November 28, 1925, he asked the aging "Uncle Jimmy" Thompson to play on the air, and the overwhelming response persuaded the station to start its own weekly Barn Dance.*

LEFT *Among the groups that appeared for free on WSM's Barn Dance was a string band led by Dr. Humphrey Bate, a prominent Nashville physician (center, with dog). Hay promoted them as the Possum Hunters, dressed as hillbillies.*

ness, he joined the minstrel and vaudeville circuit. Known as "Uncle Dave" Macon, he entertained audiences with his versatile banjo picking, his mixture of old-time and Tin Pan Alley songs, and his boisterous antics, like twirling his banjo between his legs or shouting and hollering as he played.

Macon was proud to be called a hillbilly—in 1924 he had been the first to use the term in a recording. He billed himself as "the struttinest strutter that ever strutted a strut." When he joined WSM, Judge Hay dubbed him "the Dixie Dewdrop."

Saturday-night *Barn Dance* on WSM, using local talent willing to work for free. Dr. Humphrey Bate, a Vanderbilt-trained physician from a prominent Tennessee family with a passion for old-time music, brought his string band to the show. Hay liked their music, but insisted that they needed a new name and a different image. Dr. Bate and His Augmented Orchestra soon became the Possum Hunters.

Hay would do the same makeover with other bands. The Binkley Brothers Barn Dance Orchestra was renamed the Dixie Clodhoppers. Ed Poplin's band became the Poplin-Woods Tennessee String Band. "The Solemn Old Judge" didn't stop there. He also named the Dixieliners, the Gully Jumpers, and the Fruit Jar Drinkers, insisting they take on hillbilly personas, even if they were urban sophisticates.

The biggest star of WSM's new *Barn Dance* didn't need any help from Judge Hay with his image. David Macon had once made his living driving mule wagons near Murfreesboro, playing his banjo as he traveled, and singing, it was said, "in a voice you could hear a mile up the road on a clear night." When gas-powered trucks put him out of the freighting busi-

I didn't play while I was working, but whenever we stopped to eat or take a break, I'd pull out my harp and start blowing on it.

One time I was working for a white feller in a cornfield and he told me that if I worked for him, I'd have to leave my harp at home. "Well," I told him, "if I do, I'll have to stay at home with it." I meant it, too.

DEFORD BAILEY

Another regular on WSM's *Barn Dance* was the man Judge Hay nicknamed "the Harmonica Wizard." DeFord Bailey was born in 1899, about forty miles east of Nashville, the grandson of a former slave who had been freed early in the Civil War and joined the Union army for the duration of the con-

---

Two of WSM's biggest stars were "Uncle Dave" Macon (top, left), who played banjo, sang, and told jokes; the other was DeFord Bailey (above, right), "the Harmonica Wizard."

flict. Instead of a baby rattle, Bailey told people, his parents gave him a harmonica.

At age three he was stricken with polio and confined to his bed for nearly a year. It left him with a slightly deformed back and stunted his growth. Bailey was barely four feet ten inches tall, weighing less than a hundred pounds, and by 1925 he was living in Nashville, where he had held a series of jobs: a houseboy for several wealthy families, working in the kitchen at the Maxwell House Hotel, operating the elevator in the Hitchcock Building, shining shoes at a local barbershop— all the time developing his own style on the harmonica. "If I don't blow my harp, I hurt," he said. "God put that on me to make me play. He wanted me to use my talent."

One of his favorite tunes was "The Fox Chase," a song that dated back to Irish bagpipe music and that Bailey had heard his grandfather play on the fiddle. Bailey's version added the shouts of the fox hunter urging his hound dog on, without skipping a beat on the harmonica.

His playing caught the attention of Humphrey Bate, a harmonica player himself, who recognized Bailey's skill and insisted that Judge Hay let him perform on WSM's show. Hay

was so impressed, he threw his wooden whistle into the air at the end of the performance and told the audience, "I'm letting you know, DeFord Bailey is the best harp player that was ever knowed out of four hundred years."

Along with Dr. Bate's Possum Hunters and Uncle Dave Macon, Bailey quickly became one of the *Barn Dance*'s most popular performers, appearing on it more than any other act. Between the broadcasts—like some of the show's other stars—he spent the week touring to other towns. Crisscrossing the segregated South with Uncle Dave Macon, whose father had been a captain in the Confederate army, Bailey was only allowed to stay in some hotels when Macon claimed DeFord was his valet.

Meanwhile, the hillbilly image Hay promoted for the show had begun to grate on Nashville's business leaders and social elite. Edwin Craig's country club friends complained that the *Barn Dance*, even though it was broadcast only once a week, was damaging the city's image and self-proclaimed reputation as "the Athens of the South."

But Craig enjoyed the music and ignored letters from Nashville's upper crust urging him to drop the show, preferring instead to focus on messages from out-of-town listeners expressing their enthusiasm for it.

ABOVE, LEFT AND RIGHT *WSM transmitted its programs from two 165-feet-tall towers, with a flat-top antenna strung between them. Some of Nashville's elite complained that the* Barn Dance *was ruining the city's image as "the Athens of the South," but Edwin Craig knew it was reaching the insurance company's core clientele: working-class families.*

Needless to say, we thoroughly enjoy your Saturday night program. I have one request to make, and that is when your harmonica artist puts on the "Fox Hunt," that we are given some advance notice as to what to expect.

Last night my old Irish Setter bird dog was laying in front of the fireplace when your artist reached the point in his playing where he repeated the words, "Get him, sic him." Before anyone could interfere, my old dog had turned over two floor lamps and a smoking stand.
MRS. HOLLOWAY SMITH, JEFFERSON CITY, MISSOURI

To mollify his critics, Craig compromised in 1927 by broadcasting a more refined show from NBC just before the *Barn Dance*. It featured the New York Symphony conducted by the eminent composer Dr. Walter Damrosch. "The members of our radio audience who loved Dr. Damrosch and his symphony orchestra," Judge Hay recalled, "thought we [on the *Barn Dance*] should be shot at sunrise and did not hesitate to tell us so."

One night, Damrosch closed his show with the orchestra imitating the sound of a train coming into a station. When Hay came on the air immediately afterward, he ad-libbed. "Friends," he intoned, "the program which just came to a close was devoted to the classics. However, from here on out, for the next three hours we will present nothing but realism. It will be down to earth for the earthy."

With that, Hay called on DeFord Bailey to perform "Pan American Blues," a harmonica piece Bailey had developed that, with a single instrument, duplicated the sound of a steam locomotive as it starts off slowly, picks up speed, and then fades away into the distance. He had worked on the song for more than a decade and named it for the Pan-American Express, the luxury passenger train that passed through Nashville every day on its run from Cincinnati to New Orleans. "Some people can play the train," he said, "but they can't make it move like I do."

When Bailey was finished, Hay told his listeners, "For the past hour, we have been listening to music taken largely from grand opera. From now on, we will present the Grand Ole Opry." With that, he blew his trademark wooden whistle and told his entertainers, "Let's keep it close to the ground, boys," meaning "nothing too fancy."

Within a few weeks, the program had a new name. It was no longer the WSM *Barn Dance*. It was *The Grand Ole Opry*.

Edwin Craig had no way of knowing that it would eventually become the longest-running show on American radio, but he was satisfied with what he'd started two years earlier. His new program was perhaps not yet as well known as WLS's *National Barn Dance*, but with 1,000 watts—the only station with that much transmitting power in the South, other than Atlanta's WSB—it was doing exactly what he had intended: reaching a far-flung audience to help National Life's sales force.

"Would you please send one of your agents down here to insure my carpets, floors, shoes, and everything in connection with the household?" one listener from New York State wrote. "Your Saturday night 'shindig' has got my floors down to the second plank, and I am afraid someone will drop

OPPOSITE AND ABOVE *Improvising one night in 1927, after WSM had broadcast the New York Symphony, Judge Hay opened the* Barn Dance *program by saying that instead of "grand opera," people would now be hearing "the Grand Ole Opry." With that, the Saturday-night show had its new name. It would eventually become the longest-running show on American radio.*

[through] on my barrel of preserves." A family from Oklahoma sent in a similar testimonial: "We had a house full Saturday night past," it said. "All enjoyed the program very heartily and said for us to look for them back again. I have two babies insured with your company."

THE ROAD TO BRISTOL

The advent or revival or whatever you choose to call it of what are described as the "hill-billy" songs signifies more than a mere vogue of such publications. "The Death of Floyd Collins" . . . and other such songs which have had fairly widespread popularity may mark the initial move in the passing of jazz. . . . All of this undoubtedly shows the earmarks of a new phase of the popular music and record business.

THE TALKING MACHINE WORLD

Melodically, we're keeping it pretty simple here. We're working with the major chords, you know? This is not jazz. This is country. And we keep it simple.

The music is simple, in a way. But the truth is very complex. So you have this balance of a simple melodic section, maybe, but this really complex thing of life.

DIERKS BENTLEY

By 1927, the decade known as the Roaring Twenties had reached a full head of steam. The nation's wealth had more than doubled, and for the first time, more than half of all Americans now lived in towns and cities, not farms. Although Prohibition had made the manufacture and sale of liquor illegal, people still found plenty of ways to drink.

It was called the Jazz Age, when young women called flappers, with bobbed hair and short skirts, danced to the hot, syncopated music that originated in New Orleans and was sweeping the country.

For some, like the automobile tycoon Henry Ford, the new music represented everything they considered wrong with the country's moral direction. Ford considered jazz a

"Jewish conspiracy to Africanize American taste," according to historian Bill C. Malone. To counteract it, Ford encouraged his car dealers to sponsor traditional fiddle contests, leading up to a highly publicized national championship; and he published a book describing old-time dance steps—all in the belief that it could somehow turn people away from jazz and restore American culture to a simpler and seemingly more virtuous past.

But others considered the rising popularity of hill-billy music with equal disdain, along with the people who seemed to enjoy it the most. "The hillbilly," the editor of *Variety* magazine scoffed, "is of the 'poor white trash' genera. The great majority, probably 95 percent, can neither read nor write English. Theirs is a community all unto themselves. Illiterate and ignorant, with the intelligence of morons, the sing-song, nasal-twanging vocalizing of a Vernon Dalhart or a Carson Robison reciting banal lyrics of 'The Prisoner's Song' or 'The Death of Floyd Collins' intrigues their interest." But, the editor added, "it's a vast market."

Ralph Peer didn't agree with either Henry Ford or *Variety*. No one had done more to bring both kinds of music to the public. Since recording Fiddlin' John Carson and other hill-billy acts, he had also brought more black musicians into the studio for his race records: W. C. Handy; Jelly Roll Morton; Gus Cannon's Jug Stompers; and King Oliver and his Creole Jazz Band, with a young Louis Armstrong on cornet. "People

---

OPPOSITE, TOP, AND THIS PAGE *In the midst of the Jazz Age, automobile tycoon Henry Ford (seen here visiting Atlanta's WSB) did everything he could to steer people back toward traditional fiddle music and square dances, while* Variety *disparaged "Hill-Billy" music and the "poor white trash" who listened to it. Ralph Peer continued recording both styles of music, including Gus Cannon's Jug Stompers (Cannon on left with banjo) and others like Jelly Roll Morton and W. C. Handy for Okeh's race records. Peer, his son said, "saw music through glasses that had no color."*

didn't consider these styles of music—Southern rural music, black music—to be music of importance," his son, Ralph Peer II, said. "To him it was important because it was different. He really saw music through glasses that had no color. What separated him was his willingness to try something new and to find artistry in types of music that other people had sidelined."

To Peer, hillbilly music and the blues shared some common roots and often borrowed from each other as they evolved. But as a businessman, he was less interested in music theory than in profits—and by July 1927, he was enjoying plenty of them.

He had left his job with the Okeh label and joined the biggest recording company in the nation, the Victor Talking Machine Company, after making them an unprecedented offer: he would work for no salary, if he could control the copyrights of the songs and collect the publishing royalties, which at the time amounted to two cents per record sold.

Then he offered his artists something equally unprecedented: he would pay them $50 plus expenses for recording a song, but rather than buying the copyrights outright for a nominal fee and keeping the royalties, as most publishers did, he would share a portion of future publishing royalties with them, if they had written the song. He called it a "square deal," one that had been denied artists in the past, and many

In 1927, Peer came to Bristol, on the Tennessee-Virginia state line, to record more songs by his top star of the moment, Ernest "Pop" Stoneman (center, with guitar) with his Dixie Mountaineers and other groups from the area. The sessions would ultimately attract two other acts—the Carter Family from Virginia and Jimmie Rodgers from Mississippi—that would change the course of country music.

of his musicians were lured by the incentive to follow him to the Victor label.

Among them was Ernest "Pop" Stoneman, a carpenter from the Blue Ridge section of southwest Virginia, near the town of Galax. When Stoneman had heard some of the early hillbilly recordings in 1924, he told his wife he could sing better than that—and went to New York to prove it. His recording for Peer of "The Sinking of the Titanic" became one of the biggest hits of the day. Soon, he was Victor's top hillbilly artist and making enough money to buy some land and build a new home for his wife and growing family, which would eventually number twenty-three children.

Peer wanted to make more recordings of Stoneman and his Dixie Mountaineers. Stoneman suggested that Peer come to nearby Bristol, a city that sits astride the Virginia-Tennessee border, promising that the region was home to plenty of other acts that would make the trip worthwhile.

Peer and two engineers arrived in Bristol in late July and set up their temporary studio on the second floor of a vacant building, a former hat company on the Tennessee side of Bristol's principal street. They were using new equipment now, which Victor had developed to greatly improve the fidelity of the sound. It used an electric carbon microphone, instead of a horn, that permitted performers to sing with greater intimacy, rather than shouting to be heard. They put a carpet on the floor and raised it up like a tent for better acoustics, with all the equipment except the microphone hidden from the view of the artists.

On July 25, Stoneman and his group laid down ten tracks for Peer. The next day Ernest Phipps and His Holiness Quartet performed six rousing gospel songs. By the third day, when Stoneman returned to record again, Peer became worried that not enough artists were turning up. He invited the editor of the *Bristol News Bulletin* to attend the morning session, hoping for some free publicity. He got it:

Intensely interesting is a visit to the Victor Talking Machine recording station, located on the second floor of the building formerly occupied by the Taylor-Christian Hat company in Bristol. This morning Ernest Stoneman and company were the performers and they played and sang into the microphone a favorite in Grayson County, Virginia, namely "I Love My Lulu Belle."

The quartette costs the Victor company close to $200 per day—Stoneman receiving $100 and each of the assistants $25. . . . He received from the company over $3,600 last year as his share of the proceeds on his records.

Bristol News Bulletin, July 27, 1927

The $3,600 Stoneman had reportedly made from his recordings the year before was nearly four times the average yearly income in America. "This worked like dynamite," Peer recalled. "After you read this, if you knew how to play 'C' on the piano you were going to become a millionaire. The next day I was deluged with long-distance calls from the surrounding mountain region. Groups of singers who had not visited Bristol during their entire lifetime arrived by bus, horse and buggy, train, or on foot."

A half dozen new acts, eager to become stars, were quickly added to the recording session, including a gospel group called the Alcoa Quartet; the Bull Mountain Moonshiners; Red Snodgrass's Alabamians; the West Virginia Coon Hunters; and a twenty-member church choir, the Tennessee Mountaineers.

But much more important to Peer—and to the future of country music—would be two other acts who showed up in Bristol the next week: a family trio from nearby Maces Spring, Virginia, named the Carters; and a former railroad brakeman from Meridian, Mississippi, Jimmie Rodgers.

Success, Peer once said, is "the art of being where lightning is going to strike." It was about to strike for him—twice—in the same location. "The only thing missing in the newspaper ad," said country star Marty Stuart, "was, 'Bring your songs. Bring your talent to the microphone to audition,' and, it should have said, 'We're going to start an industry now.' Because that's what happened."

Among the artists Peer recorded in Bristol were Blind Alfred Reed (top, center, below a poster that misspells his name) and the West Virginia Coon Hunters (above).

KEEP ON THE SUNNY SIDE

ABOVE *Marriage photo of A. P. Carter and Sara Dougherty, June 18, 1915. After the wedding, Carter moved Sara from Rich Valley to Poor Valley, on his side of Clinch Mountain, near Maces Spring, Virginia.*

The Carter Family were elemental. It's like the atom. It was the beginning of the building blocks for the rest of us. Those songs, they were captured rather than written. They were in the hills like rock formations.

So, in 1927, those first Bristol recordings, these songs that were part of the collective unconscious were gathered together, documented forever, with these plaintive voices and these elemental guitars. The bedrock was formed for the rest of us.

ROSANNE CASH

Alvin Pleasant (A.P.) Carter was thirty-five years old that summer of 1927, trying to make ends meet in the southwest corner of Virginia, in one of the state's most impoverished counties—in an area called Poor Valley. He had been born with a palsy, a slight shaking in his hands and sometimes in his voice, that his mother blamed on a lightning bolt that had struck the ground next to her when she was picking up apples on the mountainside just before his birth.

But A. P. Carter possessed a talent for music, and though his schooling ended when he was ten, he had learned to play the fiddle and read the shape-note songbooks used in the local Methodist church, impressing people with his rich bass voice as he grew into a lanky six-foot-two-inch man.

He took a job selling fruit tree saplings, rambling for miles on foot from farm to farm, and in 1914, after crossing Clinch Mountain to find customers on the more prosperous side called Rich Valley, he heard a young woman's clear and deep voice singing nearby. It caught his interest. So did the singer herself.

Sara Dougherty was barely sixteen at the time, already skilled on the autoharp she had purchased from Sears, Roebuck at the age of ten and steeped in old mountain ballads and gospel hymns. A year later, A.P. and Sara married, and A.P. brought her by wagon to a two-room cabin in Poor Valley, later building a more proper home in the foothills of Clinch Mountain, not far from Maces Spring.

As restless as he was ambitious, A.P. would be gone for weeks at a time over the next ten years, selling his trees while leaving Sara to care for their three children, tend the crops, chop firewood, and handle all the responsibilities of a mountain home without his help.

When he was home, they sang at church gatherings. After one man gave Sara $10 because, he said, she had "the prettiest voice I ever heard," A.P. got the notion that they might make a little money with their music. Another time, when their car broke down, he arranged for an impromptu concert in a schoolhouse, bringing in enough cash to fix the vehicle.

In 1926, a scout for the Brunswick label appeared in the region. They went to an audition and sang "Anchored in Love." But Brunswick was looking for a singing fiddler, and suggested that A.P. bill himself as "Fiddlin' Doc Carter," putting Sara in the background because, he said, a woman in the lead could never be popular.

A.P. wouldn't agree. Instead, he added another woman to the group—a younger cousin of Sara's named Maybelle Addington, a shy teenager who had learned to play the banjo from her mother, as well as the autoharp. Then she took up the guitar—and mastered it. When Maybelle married A.P.'s brother, Eck, a mail clerk on the railroad, the couple moved to a two-story house he built for them less than a mile from A.P. and Sara's home. There were now three Carters in the group.

In late July 1927, A.P. announced that they were going to Bristol to audition for Ralph Peer. A few weeks earlier, the local Victrola dealer had told him about the upcoming recording sessions, but the newspaper account of Pop Stoneman's financial success may have galvanized his decision. The women were reluctant at first. Sara was still nursing her third child, and Maybelle, now eighteen, was eight months pregnant. Eck was against it, too, since his wife was so far along. But A.P. was insistent, persuading his brother to lend him his car by promising to weed Eck's cornfield in exchange.

On July 31, they set out over hilly roads so rough and rutted it took all day to make the twenty-six miles to Bristol. They forded a river, and then blew a tire that A.P. had to patch in the hot sun—and repatch two more times before they finally pulled into the city to stay with one of his sisters.

The next morning, August 1, they auditioned for Peer. His response was the opposite of the Brunswick scout's. "As soon as I heard Sara's voice," he recalled, "that was it. I knew it was going to be wonderful. I began to build around it."

That evening, the Carters returned to record four songs,

beginning with "Bury Me Under the Weeping Willow," an old tune Sara and Maybelle had known all their lives. Although A.P. hadn't written the original, Peer considered his arrangement of it—and the others they played—different enough for Carter to claim a composer's credit, and to permit Peer to be the publisher, an important point Peer now stressed with all of his artists. Holding the copyright was essential for their future mutual profits.

ABOVE *Carter spent much of his time away from home, selling fruit tree saplings, leaving Sara to tend to all the chores at home and raise their three children. But sometimes the two performed at church gatherings and schoolhouse concerts.*

The trio performed two takes of each song that night: Sara singing lead and playing autoharp; Maybelle on the guitar and adding harmony; A.P. joining in occasionally. When the session ended, Peer mentioned to A.P. that he hadn't seemed to sing much in them. "No," Carter answered, "I just bass in every once in a while."

But Peer was impressed. These were old songs that would strike a familiar chord with the audience he was trying to reach, but with something of a new sound to them. He invited the Carters to come back the next morning for another session. When the time came, only Sara and Maybelle showed up—A.P. may have been getting Eck's car tire replaced—and Sara seemed a little irritated by his absence.

It didn't bother Peer. He had Sara sing two solos with Maybelle on the guitar: "The Wandering Boy," a mother's lament about a son who wouldn't stay at home, and a tune Sara said

she didn't like but agreed to perform at Peer's urging, "Single Girl, Married Girl," which compares the carefree life of an unmarried woman to the burdens of a wife left at home to care for her babies. Perhaps it cut too close to her own situation.

With the sessions concluded, and $300 in their pockets as payment for recording six songs, the group now called the Carter Family headed back to Maces Spring. This time the tires held up, but the car got stuck fording Holston River, forcing them to get out and push it across. "We made it home," Sara remembered, and "never thought no more about it. We never dreamed about the record business turning out the way it did." A.P. started hoeing Eck's cornfield, just as he'd promised.

Meanwhile, back in Bristol, Peer was about to record someone else who would also change hillbilly music forever.

RECORDING BOOK
Copy for

Page 6156

Serial No.	Mark	Date		Artist	Title, Composer, etc.	Publisher	Copyright by	Date of Copyright	Listed	Catalog No.
				BRISTOL TENN.(Rec)	TUESDAY AUGUST 2, 1927					
BVE 39758-1	H¹	9/9		WHITTER (Mr. Henry)	Henry Whitter's Fox Chase	R. S. Peer	Same	1927		
2	M	"		(Harmonica Solo)	(Whitter)					20878-9
3	D	"		(Hillbilly)	"	"	"	"		
BVE 39759-1	H¹	"		"	Rain Crow Bill		"	"		
2	M	"		"	(Whitter)					20878-13
				ALCOA QUARTETTE	(Mr. W.B. Hitch(Bass) Mr. L.J. Wells(Baritone) Mr. J.H. Thomas(2nd Tenor)					
				(Hillbilly)	Mr. J.E. Thomas (1st Tenor) Inst: Unaccompanied)					
BVE 39756-1	D	8/23		"	Remember Me O Mighty One	R.S. Peer	Non			
2	M	"		"	(Joanna Kirkel)					20879-9
BVE 39757-1	D	"		"	I'm Redeemed		"			
2	M	"		"	(James Rowe-S. A. Camus)					20879-13
				CARTER FAMILY	Inst: Guitar-Auto Harp					
BVE 39754-1	H¹	9/9		(Mabel-Sarah-Mr. A.P.)	Single Girl, Married Girl	R.S. Peer	Same	1927		
2	M	5/25		(Own Accom)	(Carter)					20937-9
				(Hillbilly)	NOTE:-Mr. Carter not in This Selection					
BVE 39755-1	M	9/9		"	The Wandering Boy	"	"			20877-13
2	H¹	"		"	(Carter)					
					NOTE: Mr. Carter not in This Selection					

JTB/BB

OPPOSITE *Maybelle Addington (left) was Sara's (right) younger cousin; when she married A.P.'s brother, Eck, she, Sara, and A.P. became a trio.*

TOP *Recording sheet for the Carter Family session in Bristol, August 2, 1927. On this second day, as noted, only Sara and Maybelle performed. A.P. may have been getting a tire replaced before the drive home. Though some of the songs were old ones, Peer decided that A.P.'s arrangements were original enough to give him a composer's credit—and Peer the publishing rights.*

RIGHT *The Carter Family: Maybelle played guitar and sang harmony, A.P. occasionally added bass harmony, and Sara played autoharp and sang lead. When Ralph Peer heard Sara's voice, he said, "I knew it was going to be wonderful."*

THE SINGING BRAKEMAN

Somebody told me a story one time about Red Foley and Bob Wills and Ernest Tubb. They got together one time, and they were all big Jimmie Rodgers fans and they said, "Could we agree on our favorite ten, top ten, Jimmie Rodgers songs?"

Wills said, after a lot of debate and talk, they couldn't get it down to less than fifty.

MERLE HAGGARD

James Charles Rodgers was still a month shy of his thirtieth birthday in August 1927, but he had already packed several lifetimes into those years, most of them spent in constant motion. He was seeking, in his own carefree way, the chance to prove to people in his hometown of Meridian, Mississippi, that he wasn't the no-account drifter most of them considered him to be.

ABOVE *Jimmie Rodgers as a young boy. Raised principally by his spinster aunt in Meridian, Mississippi, he spent as much time listening to traveling salesmen swapping stories and shooting dice at barbershops as he did attending school.*

RIGHT *Rodgers and his second wife, Carrie Williamson Rodgers, and their daughter Anita. "His pockets all had holes in them," Carrie said. "Any money that went into them went right on out again."*

His mother had died by the time he was six. His father, who quickly remarried, was often absent, working as a foreman for the New Orleans & Northeastern Railroad. Little Jimmie ended up in the care of a spinster aunt, who was charmed by his irrepressible good humor and indulged his adventurous spirit. He started skipping Sunday school, then school itself, preferring instead to shoot dice with the shoeshine boys at a local barbershop, listen to traveling salesmen swap stories, or haunt Meridian's theaters, which offered silent movies between vaudeville acts on their stages.

He picked up the mandolin, then the banjo, then the guitar; won an amateur contest singing "Bill Bailey, Won't You Please Come Home"; and at age thirteen ran away for a while with a traveling medicine show, before his father retrieved him in Alabama and put him to work as a water boy for the railroad's mostly black crews who laid and maintained the tracks. Still in his teens, Rodgers learned their songs and entertained them with his own rendition of "Casey Jones." Off and on for the next decade, he held a series of railroad jobs—flagman, baggage man, and then a brakeman on the run between Mississippi and New Orleans—but it was never steady work.

He married at the age of nineteen, was separated in less than a year, hoboed around the country, and then came back to Meridian. In 1920, after his divorce came through, he married Carrie Williamson, the seventeen-year-old daughter of a Methodist preacher, relying often on her family for financial support and a place to live as he jumped from one job to

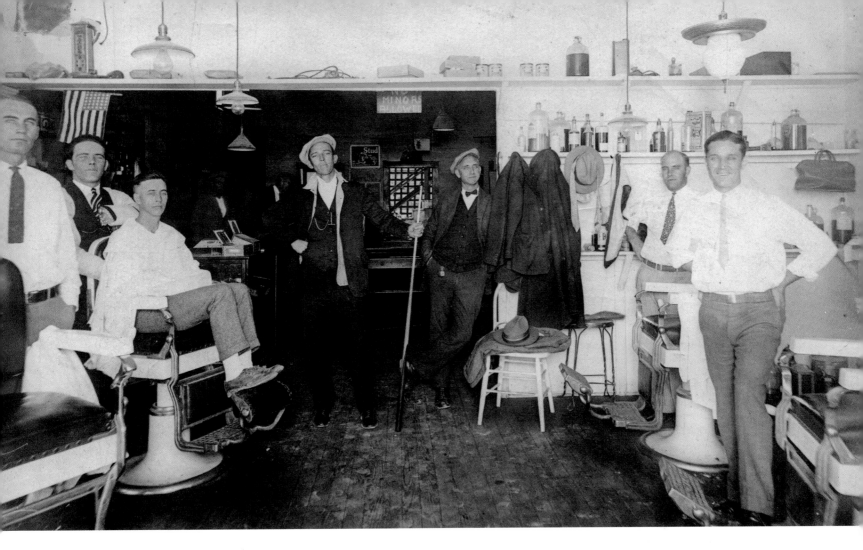

another. Nine months after the wedding, Carrie gave birth to a daughter, Anita.

When he wasn't working, he loafed around poolrooms and rail yards. When he was working, his paychecks quickly disappeared—on tickets to shows, on every phonograph record he could buy, and on a men's perfume he had discovered in New Orleans: Black Narcissus, whose scent, he thought, masked the harsh smell of railroad fumes. "It was chicken one day, feathers the next—but it seemed that our chickens were mostly all feathers," Carrie recalled:

> He always declared that money was no good until after you'd spent it; then it was good, for it had furnished you and those around you with the good things of life. His spendthriftiness worried me, especially when he tossed his money away—receiving for it nothing but a good time or perhaps some useless gewgaws.
>
> His pockets all had holes in them. Any money that went into them went right on out again.

Rodgers joined a traveling show in 1923, performing some blues numbers he had picked up, but the gig was cut short when he got called home after his and Carrie's six-month-old second daughter died. Without any money, he rode a boxcar to Meridian and borrowed cash from friends for her burial plot. "That black hour," Carrie said, "came near crushing [his] dauntless spirit forever."

A year later came more bad news. Working once more for the railroad, Rodgers developed a hacking cough. Carrie noticed flecks of blood in his handkerchief. A doctor diagnosed the problem: it was tuberculosis, at the time the leading cause of death in the United States. There was no known cure.

He spent three months in a charity hospital, and when he was released, it was clear that his railroading days were over. Rodgers turned to music as his last chance to support his wife and remaining daughter. "He refused to be downed," Carrie said. "He had to be doing something, for the sake of his eager soul as well as for the sake of his loved ones."

He played for dances around Meridian and briefly joined a

ABOVE *Pool halls and barbershops were among Rodgers's favorite hangouts. This one was a combination of both. (Rodgers is holding the pool cue.)*

medicine show, strumming a banjo in blackface on village street corners while the so-called doctor peddled snake oil to passersby. He would visit stores and talk the owners into selling him a guitar on credit, then go to the nearest pawn shop to hock it for cash.

He drove the family to Arizona, but his illness didn't improve, so he sold their car and got railroad passes for them to try Texas, where they ran out of money. Back once more in Meridian, "about all he had," a friend remembered, "was the clothes on his back, a warped-neck guitar, and that cough in his lungs."

In early 1927, Rodgers moved his family to Asheville, North Carolina, hoping the mountain air would improve his health. He arranged for a free apartment in exchange for being the building's janitor and earned a little cash as a part-time cab driver, but focused most of his energy on the city's music scene. He met a string band trio called the Tenneva Ramblers and formed a quartet, renamed the Jimmie Rodgers Entertainers, which debuted that summer on Asheville's brand-new radio station WWNC (for "Wonderful Western North Carolina").

The group was barely scraping by, and in dire need of a better car for touring, when one of the members decided to ask his father, a barber in Bristol, Tennessee, for help. Rodgers went along with him. They arrived on August 1—the same day the Carters were doing their first recordings—and, after making arrangements for a slightly newer car, went to a boardinghouse run by the band member's mother, just across the street from the building Ralph Peer was renting. Here they learned that the town was full of musicians trying to make records with the Victor label. The next morning, they managed to talk with Ralph Peer, who agreed to audition them, without any promises.

They hurried back to North Carolina for the other band members, as well as Carrie and her daughter, and returned to Bristol on August 3. Carrie was skeptical; Jimmie was as optimistic as ever. "A victor is a winner, isn't he?" he told her. "And a peer is the top of the heap."

But that evening, as they rehearsed in the boardinghouse, the group fell apart. The other members, who considered Rodgers an inferior musician, wanted to record as the Tenneva Ramblers, not the Jimmie Rodgers Entertainers. An argument broke out—and ended when Rodgers said they could do what they wanted; he would record by himself with just his guitar.

On the afternoon of August 4, Rodgers entered the makeshift studio first, alone; he said the Tenneva Ramblers would come in later. Peer had no problem with the new arrange-

ment. "I liked him the first time I saw him," Peer recalled. "He was an individualist. He had his own style [and] it wouldn't fit with a bunch of fiddles."

Rodgers sang only two songs that day, "The Soldier's Sweetheart" and "Sleep, Baby, Sleep," assuring Peer that with a little more time, he could come up with a lot more that could be copyrighted. That evening, while the Tenneva Ramblers were recording, he left Bristol with Carrie and their daughter, heading north in the car the band member's father had bought a few days earlier.

During his two weeks in town, Peer recorded more than

OPPOSITE *Diagnosed with tuberculosis, Rodgers could no longer hold a railroad job and turned to music as a way to support his wife and daughter. He traveled with a medicine show, appearing in blackface to attract a crowd.*

ABOVE *Jimmie Rodgers (left) and the Tenneva Ramblers, Asheville, North Carolina. The night before their recording session with Ralph Peer in Bristol, they argued and broke up.*

Letter	Pitch	Serial No.	Matrix No.	Selection, Composer, Publisher, Copyright, Etc.	Wax	Rec.	F. Cur.	Level	Amp Set	Eqlzr.	Fil.
				Bristol Tenn.August 4th.1927.#408 State St.2nd. & 3rd.Floors.							
				Inst-- Guitar. (Own Accomp.)							
BVE	100	39767	1	* The Soldiers Sweetheart.	55-322	138	9	5-5	46	No	No
BVE	100m	39767	2	Comp.J.Rodgers.	55-333	"	"	4-4	44	"	"
BVE	100	39767	3	Pub. & Copyr.R.S.Peer.1927.	55-333	"	"	5-5	46	"	"
BVE	100	39767	4	036 C298	55-333	"	"	5-5	46	"	"
BVE	100	39768	1	Sleep Baby Sleep. (Jimmie Rodgers) Peer Intl., BMI	55-333	"	"	5-5	46	"	"
BVE	100	39768	2	Copyr.No Information.	55-329	"	"	4-4	44	"	"
BVE	100	39768	3	Non Copyr. R.S.Peer. Time 2.00 to 4.20	55-335	"	"	5-5	46	"	"
				Camden-Studio #1. November,30th 1927. (With Guitar--playing own Acc)					CS-EE		
BVE	96	40751	1	Ben Dewberry's last Run.	55-383	59	9				
BVE	96	40751	2	Comp-Andy Jenkins. Pub.& Copy- R.S.Peer.1928.	56 SP	"					
				Inf.Verbal by Mr.Peer.							
BVE	100	40752	1	If Brother Jack were here.	55-383	"	"				
BVE	100	40752	2	Comp-J.Rodgers. Pub.& Copyr-R.S.Peer--1928	55-365	"	"				
				Inf.Verbal by Mr.Peer.							
BVE	100	40753	1	Blue Yodel.	55-354	"	"				
BVE	100	40753	2	Comp-J.Rodgers. Pub.& Copyr-R.S.Peer--1928	55-364	"	"				
				Inf.Verbal by Mr.Peer.							
BVE	96	40754	1	* Away out on the Mountain.	55-278	"					
BVE	100	40754	2	Comp-K.Harrell. Pub.& Copyr-R.S.Peer--1928	55-399	"					
				Inf.Verbal by Mr.Peer.							
				(Time 1.30 to 4.25)							

#LPM-2531

* LPM/LSP 3315 - THE BEST OF THE LEGENDERY JIMMIE RODGERS
January 1965 Release
Shipped12/21/64

* LPM/LSP 3315 - THE BEST OF THE LEGENDERY JIMMIE RODGERS
January 1965 Release
Shipped 12/21/64

ANLI-1209   + CPL-2504

Blue Yodel
FOX TROT

Lyrics and Music by
JIMMIE RODGERS

two dozen performing acts. A few of them—like Pop Stoneman and his family—would go on to have long careers in the music business; most would soon be forgotten. But by discovering the Carter Family and Jimmie Rodgers, Ralph Peer had set the future of country music in motion.

"I think Jimmie Rodgers represented the rambling side of country music—the desire to hit the road, leave responsibilities behind, to go out and experience the world," historian Bill C. Malone said. "The Carter Family, on the other hand, embodied the sanctity of the home and of the family, particularly 'Mother,' who kept the home together. And those have been two important impulses in country music ever since, sort of the reverse sides of the same coin."

The recording sheet (top, left) for Rodgers's Bristol session, August 4, 1927, and for the later session in Camden, New Jersey, on November 30, which included his song about Thelma, "that gal that made a wreck out of me." Peer released it as "Blue Yodel" (top, right), highlighting the vocal touch that became Jimmie's trademark.

THE BLUE YODELER

Jimmie Rodgers was conflating the blues with the rural white experience and sound. I think this went on a lot—we just don't see it until he showed up. And, of course, he had that little yodel.

DOUGLAS B. GREEN, RIDERS IN THE SKY

He had songs that spoke in the language people understood about subject matter they understood. He had this wonderful ear and this wonderful voice, and his delivery was totally unheard of. I think it came out of the black blues and mixed in with his yodeling—and they called him "the Blue Yodeler."

MERLE HAGGARD

That November, shortly after his first recording had been released, Rodgers showed up unannounced in New York City with only $10 in his pocket. He checked in to an expensive hotel, showed the desk clerk a copy of his new record, and brashly told him to charge everything to the Victor company. Then he called Ralph Peer to say he was ready for another session.

Among the four sides Rodgers recorded a few days later was one he had strung together from a mixture of songs he had heard over the years: a standard twelve-bar blues melody with snatches of borrowed lyrics that introduced Thelma, "that gal that made a wreck out of me," but bragged, "I can get more women than a passenger train can haul." Then it warned, "I'm gonna buy me a pistol just as long as I'm tall" and "I'm gonna shoot poor Thelma just to see her jump and fall."

To it he added what he called a "blue yodel," something he had been developing that also drew from deep roots: the Alpine yodels that came to America in the 1840s, then were adopted by black and blackface minstrel singers at the turn of the century, and more recently by recording artists like Riley Puckett and Emmett Miller. He was "tacking yodels onto just about everything," Carrie remembered. "Even his share of conversation around the house was largely yodels."

Regardless of where Rodgers came across the individual elements of the song, his combination of them was uniquely his own: lyrics that were a little saucy and audacious, but delivered in an easy conversational style with the slight trace of his Mississippi accent, and with the repeated vocal gymnastics that worked like instrumental breaks. Peer released the song under the title "Blue Yodel" in the spring of 1928. It was an immediate hit.

Rodgers had even greater success with a song recorded in a third session, also derived from African-American blues and jug band musicians: "In the Jailhouse Now." It quickly became Victor's third-biggest-selling record—ahead of their leading pop artists Paul Whiteman, Fred Waring, and their preeminent star of the time, the crooner Gene Austin.

Jimmie and Carrie had settled temporarily in Washington, D.C., and when her brother paid a visit, Rodgers drove him around town, slowly, with the windows open on the car, so he could hear what was coming out of the music houses. "The whole city," he said, "was listening to Jimmie Rodgers." Back in Mississippi a few weeks later, the brother-in-law heard the same thing from farmhouses he passed. "It was his voice, and his yodeling," he remembered. "It came from almost every house. I knew then he was destined to be great."

By midsummer of 1928, with the release of more songs, "Brakeman's Blues" and a number Peer titled "Blue Yodel Number 2," royalties started pouring in—$1,000 a month—which Rodgers spent as quickly as they arrived. He paid $1,500 for the "Jimmie Rodgers Special," a personalized Martin guitar with gold inlay, his name spelled out in mother of pearl on the neck, and the word "Thanks" emblazoned on the back. Other artists, with other labels, were now rushing to produce cover versions of his hits, trying to imitate his style.

To capitalize on his success, Rodgers began a tour of major theaters and auditoriums in the South, making $500 a week, sometimes appearing in

TOP *Rodgers paid for this publicity shot shortly after his solo recording session in Bristol. "I liked him the first time I saw him," Peer said. "He had his own style."*

RIGHT *As sales took off and royalties started to pour in, Rodgers paid $1,500 for a personalized Martin guitar. His name was spelled out on the neck, and at the end of a performance he could flip the guitar over to say "Thanks" to his audience.*

CLOCKWISE FROM TOP LEFT *The Carolina Theater welcomes Rodgers to its stage; an advertisement in Quitman, Mississippi, promotes an upcoming appearance by the "Blue Yodeler"; an autographed photo that Jimmie signed, "When better cars are built I will buy one. Yours yodeling, Jimmie Rodgers"; and Rodgers, in his brakeman outfit, posing with a fan.*

his brakeman's outfit—a blue jumper and striped cap with a railroad watch hanging from a big gold chain—and billing himself as "the Singing Brakeman." Other times, in dapper clothes, he called himself "America's Blue Yodeler."

Thousands of people turned out in Norfolk, Atlanta, Memphis, New Orleans. In Chattanooga, where 1,400 people filled the Soldiers and Sailors Memorial Auditorium for two straight nights, the local paper's theater critic, who panned Rodgers's music, nevertheless admitted, "More people were entertained by the yodeler . . . than witnessed any performance of grand opera presented in the auditorium last week." Asheville welcomed him back with the headline "Jimmie Rodgers Left City Broke: Returns as King of 'Blue Yodel.'"

Appearing before a huge International Men's Bible Class in Miami, he admitted he didn't know any church songs, so he sang "In the Jailhouse Now" and the racy "Frankie and Johnny" instead. They gave him a standing ovation. "If they like you when you're nice," he told Carrie, "they'll forgive you when you're naughty."

Then he made a triumphant return to Meridian, the town that only recently had considered him a worthless drifter who didn't pay his bills. He arrived in a shiny new car, wearing expensive clothes and diamond rings, and made a public point of settling his old debts. Booked for an extended stay with a tent show, Rodgers added a string of personal appearances and autograph sessions at local music stores. He caroused with old friends, despite his increasing exhaustion from the tour.

Each performance left him weaker, dripping in sweat and gasping for breath. His temperature rose to 103 degrees. One night, he blacked out backstage. Chest X-rays revealed that his tuberculosis was now active in both lungs, and a doctor told him that without proper rest, he wouldn't live more than another year or two.

Instead, Rodgers booked himself on another tour, this time at $1,000 a week, and went to New York for another recording session with Ralph Peer. Rodgers appealed to wide audiences, Peer said, "because he had what was a *popular* version of hillbilly; he used hillbilly, but he also used Negro. . . . [And] many of the songs he recorded were popular. They had a verse and a chorus. He got them from many sources. He could record anything."

By now, Peer was making even more money than Jimmie Rodgers—nearly a quarter of a million dollars in three months' time—thanks to his publishing royalties from all the artists he had signed across a variety of musical genres. With Rodgers, he would continue issuing a long list of "Blue Yodels"—eventually reaching "Blue Yodel Number 12"—but beginning in the New York session, Peer began experiment-

ing with new orchestrations and styles that included much more than simply Rodgers on guitar: jazz ensembles, small orchestras, African-American jug bands, ukuleles, champion whistlers, or simply musicians Rodgers happened to have met the day before a recording session. Regardless of the arrangement, Jimmie would insist on throwing in a yodel so his fans wouldn't be disappointed.

To help him come up with more songs that could be copyrighted, Rodgers had enlisted Carrie's sister, Elsie McWilliams, a Meridian housewife and Sunday-school music teacher with a gift for turning an overheard phrase or random incident into a melody with lyrics. Her brother-in-law couldn't read musical notations—"crazy little fly specks with funny tails," he called them—so she often came to teach her new compositions to him in person. In all, she would write or contribute to more than a third of Rodgers's recorded songs.

At one session in Dallas, which included the Hawaiian steel guitar player Joe Kaipo, Elsie heard Jimmie say, "I'd like to have me one of them hula-hula girls," and that night she came up with a new song, which they recorded the

ABOVE *Elsie McWilliams, Jimmie's sister-in-law, provided more than a third of Rodgers's recorded songs. He couldn't read musical notation, so she had to join him at sessions to teach him what she had written.*

next morning: "Everybody Does It in Hawaii." With its suggestive double entendres, the song earned a warning from *Variety* that record dealers should "not sell this into polite families," because, the review said, "it's never made clear what everybody *does* in Hawaii."

At another session, out in Hollywood, to accompany Rodgers, Peer brought in a twenty-eight-year-old trumpet player who was headlining at the New Cotton Club in Los Angeles. It was Louis Armstrong. Equally charismatic in person and always pushing the boundaries of his music, just as Rodgers did with his, Armstrong would go on to become the most influential jazz artist of all time. "My father wanted to get them together to see what would happen, to have that chemistry experiment," Ralph Peer II said. "He knew their artistic talent. So bringing them together was an idea that seemed to serve both their purposes. The music that resulted was this wonderful fusion that we all benefit from today of music from genuine black community roots and genuine rural Southern roots coming together."

Disc Reviews

Jimmy Rodgers

(Victor 22143) More "Frankie and Johnny," and backed by "Everybody Does It in Hawaii." Dealers should use discrimination and not sell this into polite families or for juvenile consumption.

It's never made clear what everybody does in Hawaii. That leaves the sensitive listeners in a state of unrelieved embarrassment.

TOP AND MIDDLE *With Joe Kaipo (second from right), a Hawaiian steel guitar player, and the Burkes Brothers, Rodgers recorded Elsie McWilliams's new song, "Everybody Does It in Hawaii." Its suggestive lyrics earned a warning from* Variety *that the song was not for "polite families or for juvenile consumption."*

RIGHT *Ralph Peer brought jazz artist Louis Armstrong to a session with Jimmie Rodgers in Hollywood to record "Blue Yodel Number 9" ("Standin' on the Corner"). Both men would be remembered for expanding the boundaries—and popularity—of their respective genres. Bringing them together, Peer's son said, was a musical "chemistry experiment."*

Together, with Armstrong's wife Lil on the piano, they recorded "Standin' on the Corner," renamed by Peer as "Blue Yodel Number 9," telling the story of a Tennessee hustler arrested on Beale Street in Memphis. (Years later, Jerry Garcia of the Grateful Dead would record his own acoustic version, and it would ultimately be selected by the Rock and Roll Hall of Fame as one of the five hundred songs that shaped rock and roll.)

Meanwhile, Rodgers had decided to relocate to Kerrville, in the Texas Hill Country, whose dry climate had attracted several sanitariums for treating tuberculosis. He announced plans to build an expensive mansion, the Blue Yodeler's Paradise, and had publicity pictures taken of him wearing a big Stetson, cowboy chaps and boots, and a gun and holster.

He added some new songs to his repertoire—"Prairie Lullaby," "The Cow Hand's Last Ride," "Moonlight and Skies," and a song Elsie McWilliams wrote to fit yet another image he now presented to the public: "the Yodeling Cowboy," in which his yodeling was decidedly less "blue." The Texas legislature was impressed enough by his makeover to name him an honorary Texas Ranger. And a generation of his followers would be inspired to believe that all cowboys not only sang, but also yodeled.

In the fall of 1929, Peer brought Rodgers to a studio in Cam-

TOP *Hoping the dry climate would help his worsening tuberculosis, Rodgers moved his family to Kerrville, Texas, where he built a mansion he called the Blue Yodeler's Paradise.*

ABOVE, LEFT AND RIGHT *Having moved to Texas, Rodgers happily added a new persona for his publicity. Not just "the Singing Brakeman" or "America's Blue Yodeler," he was also now "the Yodeling Cowboy." For generations to come, singing cowboys would be expected to yodel like Jimmie.*

den to make a short film, *The Sing-ing Brakeman*. Since the advent of talking movies with Al Jolson's *The Jazz Singer* two years earlier, many executives in the music industry had seen the "talkies" as a threat to live performances. Vaudeville was dying because of it, they contended. Peer, on the other hand, saw the new medium as another opportunity for his stars to become better known; Mamie Smith would soon appear in her own short film, singing about jailhouses. In Rodgers's nine-minute film, he approaches what is meant to be a depot, dressed in his railroading outfit as if checking to see if there's a train coming that might need his services. Then, at the request of some women there, he agrees to sing a few songs.

Just as Peer had predicted, the short film of his performance made Rodgers even more popular. Despite his fragile health, he was now a full-fledged celebrity—and not just in America. Peer had already arranged for his music to be released in England, Australia, India, Japan, and, ultimately, Africa.

When they were first introduced to phonographs and records, the Kipsigi tribe of Kenya would construct a minor deity based solely on the sound of Rodgers's music and his voice, a spirit they sang to in special ceremonies. They called the spirit *Chemirocha*.

TOP *In 1929, in the early years of the "talkies," Peer had Rodgers star in a nine-minute film,* The Singing Brakeman, *in which Jimmie sang three songs. It made Rodgers even more of a celebrity.*

ABOVE *Rodgers's music spread across the world, from Europe and Africa to India, Australia, and, as this disc of "Dear Old Sunny South by the Sea" demonstrates, Japan.*

WILDWOOD FLOWER

If Taylor Swift or Carrie Underwood, or whoever the hottest girl of the moment is, wants to know where they come from, they need to go all the way back to the voice of Sara Carter, because she was the first one. It's Sara, then there's been everybody else. It's that simple.

As far as guitar playing goes, there's Maybelle, then there's everybody else. That's the genesis of it all.

MARTY STUART

Back in November 1927, A. P. Carter got word from the owner of Bristol's music store to drop by. When he arrived, he was handed a shiny disc with the first release of the Carter Family by Victor records, with "The Poor Orphan Child" on one side, and "The Wandering Boy" on the other. With it was a letter from Ralph Peer. Initial sales were good, it said; more than two thousand copies had been sold in Atlanta in one week. Carter asked the store owner if he could listen to the record, since he didn't personally have a Victrola in Poor Valley. Then he hurried home to show it to Sara and Maybelle.

A few weeks later, Victor released a second record that included "Single Girl, Married Girl," the song Sara had not wanted to sing. It sold even better—and Peer now invited them on an all-expenses-paid trip to his studio in Camden, New Jersey, for another session, where they recorded twelve more songs.

Among them was "Keep on the Sunny Side," which A.P. would adopt as the Carter Family's signature tune, and another song that had been handed down in Maybelle's family for generations. "My mother sang it," she said, "and *her* mother sang it." It dated back to 1860, a vaudeville song called "I'll Twine 'Mid the Ringlets," originally composed by J. P. Webster of Manchester, New Hampshire, with lyrics by Maud Irving, and over the years it had spread in various forms into the folk vernacular under different names.

The Carters' version was titled "Wildwood Flower," featuring Sara singing alone, with Maybelle demonstrating a guitar technique she was perfecting, in which she picked the melody with her thumb on the bass strings while simultaneously providing the rhythm and chords with her other fingers. "I didn't even think about it," she said. "I just played the way I wanted to and that's it." It would come to be called the "Carter scratch."

Maybelle's technique would become one of the most copied guitar styles in country music history. "To me, Mother Maybelle as a guitarist was maybe the most iconic instru-

mentalist that we've ever had," said Vince Gill. "There's rhythm and there's the melody—and at its simplest place, it still carries maybe the most poetry." John McEuen remembered hearing from the daughter of famed rock guitarist Duane Allman how her father taught her mother to play "Wildwood Flower" on the guitar. "That's how powerful the Carter Family music was," McEuen said. "There's not a guitar player that's picked up a six-string, I don't think, that hasn't touched on some Carter Family music."

Peer paid the Carters $600 for their second session—as much money as a farmer in their part of Virginia might make

ABOVE *If Jimmie Rodgers represented the "Saturday night" side of country music, the Carter Family represented the "Sunday morning" side, but both acts had a profound impact on the music's development. Sara Carter was its foundational female singer. Maybelle Carter developed a unique guitar style, the "Carter scratch," that influenced generations of guitarists.*

in a year at the time—and when "Wildwood Flower," with "Keep on the Sunny Side" as its companion, sold more than 100,000 records, and royalties started arriving in Maces Spring, A.P. was able to buy his first automobile.

More sessions were scheduled, requiring more copyrightable songs. A.P. scoured the immediate area, searching for them among his neighbors, returning with his pockets filled with scraps of paper containing bits and pieces of lyrics. But he had trouble remembering melodies, so Sara and Maybelle would set the words to old ones they had known for years. At home, the trio would practice the new arrangements.

A.P.'s song-gathering journeys began taking him farther afield. In the summer of 1928, he was in Kingsport, Tennessee, in the black section of town, when he met a blues singer and slide guitar player named Lesley Riddle, who had lost one leg in an accident and now supported himself playing on street corners and railroad depots. A.P. invited him to help in the hunt for new songs, and Riddle accepted—ultimately making fifteen trips with Carter through Virginia, East Tennessee, North Carolina, and parts of Georgia.

"He'd go ninety miles if he heard someone say that someone had an old song that hadn't ever been recorded or didn't have a copyright," Riddle recounted. "He'd just go in [people's homes] and tell them, 'Hello, I was told by someone that you got a song, kind of an old song. Would you mind letting me hear it?' So they'd go and get it and sing it for him." While Carter wrote down the words, Riddle focused on memorizing the melodies. "I was his tape recorder," Riddle later recalled. "Then I'd learn it to Sara and Maybelle."

Riddle also shared some blues guitar stylings with Maybelle and introduced the Carters to hymns sung in African-American Pentecostal and Baptist churches, which they added to their own gospel and sacred selections. One melody he taught them, with Maybelle playing bottleneck guitar, was "When the World's on Fire." The Carter Family would later reuse the basic tune for another song, "Little Darling, Pal of Mine." A few years after that, Woody Guthrie—an admirer of the Carters—would incorporate it into his classic, "This Land Is Your Land."

Unlike Jimmie Rodgers, who toured constantly, the Car-

ABOVE *In his need to collect more and more songs to record, A. P. Carter hired Lesley Riddle (right, with Brownie McGhee), an African-American blues singer and slide guitarist. On their trips together, Carter would concentrate on the lyrics, and Riddle was responsible for remembering the melodies.*

ters stayed close to home. Maybelle was now a mother, too—her daughter Helen had been born shortly after the Bristol sessions; a second daughter, June, came along in the summer of 1929. Sara had her own three children to care for, and she hated public performances in front of total strangers.

But A.P. organized short trips in which they were fed and housed overnight by rural fans. He tacked up posters on barns and trees, announcing an appearance by the trio in churches, schools, or small-town theaters. Admission was from fifteen to twenty-five cents. "The program," the posters promised, "is morally good." During perfor-

TOP *The Carter Family outside Maybelle and Eck's home in Poor Valley. Sometimes, neighbors gathered to listen to them practice for upcoming recording sessions.*

RIGHT *Unlike Jimmie Rodgers, the Carter Family did not tour extensively, but on short trips they made appearances in nearby schools and churches and were housed by their fans. A.P. would put up posters advertising programs that were "morally good."*

LOOK!
Victor Artist
A. P. CARTER
and the
Carter Family
Will give a
MUSICAL PROGRAM
AT *Roseland Theater*
ON *Thursday August 1*

The Program is Morally Good

Admission 15 and 25 Cents

A. P. CARTER. Mace Spring. Va.

mances, A.P.'s attention sometimes seemed to wander. "If he felt like singing, he would sing," Maybelle said. "If he didn't, he'd look out the window. So we never depended on him."

Most of the time, the Carters stayed in Poor Valley, where neighbors often gathered outside their house just to hear them practice for the increasing number of recording sessions Peer was scheduling: in Camden, Atlanta, Memphis, and Charlotte. The session fees of $50 per song and the royalties from record sales—700,000 copies in two years—provided a steady income and some measure of prosperity. A.P. bought larger pieces of land and a sawmill to convert some of his woodlands into lumber. Sara got herself some perfume and a mink stole. Maybelle purchased a bigger guitar, a Gibson, for $275. Both women briefly indulged themselves by buying motorcycles they drove around the fields.

TOP, LEFT AND RIGHT *As record sales collapsed with the start of the Great Depression, in June 1931, Ralph Peer decided to have his two biggest acts record some songs together in Louisville, Kentucky. In addition to the music, he had them read corny scripts in which they pretended to be visiting each other's homes and promoted the record as "a great event."*

OPPOSITE *After a joint recording session in Louisville, Rodgers and the Carters went their separate ways. He would become known as "the Father of Country Music." They would become "the First Family of Country Music."*

Then, in October 1929, the financial bubble that had fueled the Roaring Twenties burst. The stock market crashed, and the nation descended into what would ultimately be called the Great Depression. Banks and businesses failed by the thousands. Millions of workers lost their jobs. In major cities, destitute residents relied on breadlines and soup kitchens merely to survive.

The recording industry was hard hit. Between 1929 and 1930, record sales in the United States dropped from $74 million to $46 million, then to $17 million in 1931. No artist was immune, although for a while sales of Carter Family records held up—partly thanks to their song "Worried Man Blues," their best seller of 1930, which seemed to both capture the nation's mood and express the hope that "I won't be worried long."

By this time, worries were becoming evident in A.P. and Sara's relationship, too. He could be remote, with flashes of temper, and obsessed with the demands on his time for song-

mie Rodgers, whose music was rooted in minstrelsy and the blues, and who happily cultivated the public image of a fast-living scamp—Saturday night.

But for two hot days in Louisville, Peer did his best to bridge the gap. Rodgers and Sara Carter sang two duets. They were the only duets he ever recorded: a sentimental song, "Why There's a Tear in My Eye," and "The Wonderful City," a pious gospel number to which they nonetheless added Rodgers's trademark yodels. Later, all four tried their hand at a tune hardly out of the Carter Family songbook: "Hot Time in the Old Town Tonight."

Peer's main idea consisted of recording two skits he had written for them. In the first, though in fact they were in downtown Louisville, they pretended that Rodgers had dropped in unexpectedly on the Carters in Virginia—"the first cowboy we've seen in a long time," A.P. says, telling Rodgers about his coon dogs treeing two possums, then fetching Jimmie a drink while Sara and Maybelle sing for him.

In the other skit, the tables were turned: the Carters supposedly had shown up in Texas and knocked on Jimmie's door. After a little banter, he asks his wife to go get some chickens for dinner, while he and Sara sing a few lines of "T for Texas" to Maybelle's accompaniment.

When the session ended, they posed for a publicity photograph and went their separate ways, never to see each other again.

writing. Sara became disenchanted even with going for the necessary recording sessions—"all the folderol," she called it.

But in June 1931, the Carter Family headed for Louisville, where Peer wanted to bring his two biggest acts together for some joint recordings he hoped would boost sales in the midst of hard times.

Jimmie Rodgers—"the Singing Brakeman" and "the Blue Yodeler," now also promoting himself as a singing Texas cowboy—would meet them there.

Only a music entrepreneur like Ralph Peer would think of joining the Carter Family, the epitome of rural wholesomeness—Sunday morning—with their repertoire of gospel songs and mountain ballads, together with Jim-

THE TB BLUES

To this day, I cannot put my finger on why the appeal of Jimmie Rodgers was so broad. He sang in a funny voice. He yodeled all the time. But there was something, that unexplainable something, that made him special, made him a star.

He talked about us. He was our representative. As country people, he was our ambassador. He was a rogue, just like the rest of us. He had hard times, just like the rest of us. But we appreciated him dressing up in his cool clothes and driving in his fancy car and talking about us country people. He represented us well. That's why he's the Father of Country Music.

MARTY STUART

ABOVE *Rodgers sent this photograph to the Carters, inscribed "To my good friends" and expressing the "hope we have many more recordings together." But they would never meet again.*

We get to go to the other side of the tracks when we buy Jimmie Rodgers records. We're able to go to those juke joints that we're not invited to. Whether we know it or not, that's where the appeal is.

KETCH SECOR

By 1932, Jimmie Rodgers was more popular than ever. Hard-up farmers, the story went, would come to town and tell storekeepers, "Give me a sack of flour, a slab of bacon, and the latest Jimmie Rodgers record."

Fans wrote him letters as if all his songs were true stories from his life. They asked why he had wanted to shoot poor Thelma, and about his time in the jailhouse or out on the open range; they even castigated Carrie on the belief that she had loved another man while Jimmie served as a brakeman riding the rails. "They proved the sincerity that was in his voice as he sang," she recalled. "He'd had troubles. He'd suffered. Those truths were in his songs."

With the famous humorist Will Rogers, he made a tour of the Southwest on behalf of the Red Cross for victims of the Depression and the Dust Bowl. Playing off the fact that their last names sounded the same, though were spelled differently, Will Rogers called his companion "my distant son." Their appearances raised $300,000 in much needed funds.

But the deepening economic crisis affected Jimmie, too. His records, which recently had sold half a million copies with each release and made him $100,000 a year, now were lucky to sell fifteen thousand. For the recording industry as a whole, things were even worse, down to a mere $5.5 million in total sales, less than 10 percent of what they had been a few years earlier.

"You're still at the top of the heap," Peer assured Rodgers, "but the heap isn't so big." Victor cut down on its list of artists: Pop Stoneman's royalties had dried up; Vernon Dalhart,

BELOW *Ralph and Anita Peer visiting the Rodgers family at Blue Yodeler's Paradise in Kerrville*

once a giant of hillbilly music, hadn't recorded in two years. To keep at least some money coming in to his favored acts, Peer began paying Rodgers advances of $250 for recording a song—$100 per song to the Carter Family—so they wouldn't be reliant on copyright royalties that were shrinking and slow to arrive.

He loaned Rodgers more than $5,000 toward his mortgage on the lavish Blue Yodeler's Paradise in Kerrville, but even that wasn't enough. Rodgers ended up selling it at a loss and moved into a much more modest bungalow duplex in San Antonio.

TOP, LEFT AND RIGHT *Rodgers and humorist Will Rogers toured the Southwest, raising money for the Red Cross to help victims of the Dust Bowl and Depression; Jimmie kept track of the receipts in a datebook.*

Despite his worsening health, Jimmie kept touring—in part to help pay his mounting debts, but also, it seemed, because he drew strength from the adoring crowds, even if they were now often in smaller towns, in venues like high school auditoriums.

He traveled in his favorite car, which he called "Thirsty, the Christmas Tree," in honor of its many gadgets, including a special pocket where he kept a fifth of bootleg whiskey handy. He would stop in the center of a town and play for free, gaining the publicity he wanted for that night's paid performance, then move on the next day.

Everywhere Rodgers went, legends grew up. A blind newsboy in McAlester was said to have been given a new guitar; a widow in another town was said to have her mortgage paid off. Sometimes he liked to invite pretty women to ride around town with him in his shiny car. After a stop in O'Donnell, Texas, people said he left two divorces and three separations in his wake.

And everywhere he went, his music resonated, especially "Mule Skinner Blues," a bouncy tune sung by a young man looking for work. The outlaw Bonnie Parker, in the middle of a crime spree with her lover, Clyde Barrow, spent some of their stolen money to buy every one of Rodgers's records.

In Brownwood, Texas, a young Ernest Tubb, who went hungry to save money for Rodgers's latest record, remembered people lining up for blocks to see him in person, paying a dollar and filling a local theater that had trouble getting half that crowd for a movie costing a dime.

But it all came at a cost. He traveled now with bags full of medicine, whose smell he masked with his Black Narcissus perfume. He took increasing doses of morphine with shots of whiskey to combat the pain that racked his chest with prolonged fits of coughing that brought up bloody spittle. His breath was often labored. He collapsed from exhaustion more frequently; had night sweats that kept him from sleeping.

He made no secret of the disease that was killing him—or how he intended to respond to it. "I'm not going to lay in one of these hospital rooms and count the fly specks on the wall," he told people. "I want to die with my shoes on." Carrie was

TOP *With his health worsening, the Depression deepening, and his debts mounting, Rodgers stepped up his touring, often in "Thirsty, the Christmas tree," a car loaded with special gadgets, including a secret pocket where Jimmie could hide a flask of bootleg whiskey.*

ABOVE *Rodgers waves from his car on a road across the desert.*

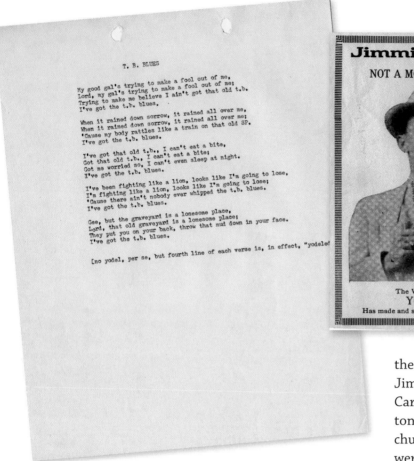

```
                    T. B. BLUES

My good gal's trying to make a fool out of me,
Lord, my gal's trying to make a fool out of me;
Trying to make me believe I ain't got that old t.b.
I've got the t.b. blues.

When it rained down sorrow, it rained all over me,
When it rained down sorrow, it rained all over me;
'Cause my body rattles like a train on that old SP.
I've got the t.b. blues.

I've got that old t.b., I can't eat a bite,
Got that old t.b., I can't eat a bite;
Got me worried so, I can't even sleep at night.
I've got the t.b. blues.

I've been fighting like a lion, looks like I'm going to lose,
I'm fighting like a lion, looks like I'm going to lose;
'Cause there ain't nobody ever whipped the t.b. blues.
I've got the t.b. blues.

Gee, but the graveyard is a lonesome place,
Lord, that old graveyard is a lonesome place;
They put you on your back, throw that mud down in your face.
I've got the t.b. blues.

[no yodel, per se, but fourth line of each verse is, in effect, "yodeled
```

especially worried. "I now came to realize the awful import of those two simple words: wasting away," she wrote, "and I asked myself frantically: How long? A month? Two? A year?"

He asked Elsie McWilliams to write him a song about his tuberculosis, but she refused, because it seemed too painful a topic. So he got a prisoner in a Texas penitentiary, who had submitted other tunes to him by mail, to compose "TB Blues," to which Rodgers added a final stanza: "Gee, but the graveyard is a lonesome place. They put you on your back, throw that mud down in your face."

Fans loved him all the more for it. Hundreds of thousands of other Americans had tuberculosis, too—"lungers" they were called—and many families had been touched by it in one way or another. At one performance, a person in

---

TOP, LEFT *When Elsie McWilliams refused to write Jimmie a song about his tuberculosis, he enlisted Raymond E. Hall, a convict in a Texas prison, to help him compose "TB Blues." Rodgers added the final verse (seen on this hand-typed copy) that begins, "Gee, but the graveyard is a lonesome place."*

TOP, RIGHT *In Crockett, Texas, fans were assured that Rodgers would appear at the local theater in person, not on the screen, and they had four chances to hear "The World's Greatest Yodeler."*

the audience shouted out some encouragement. "Spit 'er up, Jimmie," he said, "and sing some more." For the "lungers," Carrie recalled, his music and his persona were "a greater tonic than any physician had been able to prescribe. They chuckled: 'Old boy, Jimmie! He knows!' And their chuckles were good medicine."

On May 14, 1933, Rodgers arrived in New York City and checked into the same hotel near Times Square where he had stayed back in 1927, when he was a complete unknown and had brazenly pretended to be a recording star so the desk clerk would give him a room. Now he was the real thing.

With him was a private nurse who was needed to be near him constantly. His touring days were over—although he had rallied enough to make a quick trip to Paducah, Kentucky, with his bulldog, Mickey, to stage a performance on behalf of an old friend facing bankruptcy. He had lost weight; his face was pale and wan; but, his friend said, "Jimmie sang and pulled me out of a bad place."

Seeing him in New York, Peer was shocked at his appearance and insisted that he rest a few days before starting his recording session, which Rodgers had proposed in order to make a quick $3,000 for singing twelve new songs. He was worried about money for Carrie and their daughter Anita.

On May 17, in the Victor studio at 153 East 24th Street, he began the way he had started his recording career—just himself and his guitar. In two long, difficult days, he laid down six songs: a few more blue yodels, a cowboy ballad, and some sentimental songs about home. The tuberculosis was shredding his lungs and he was heavily sedated for the pain, sipping whiskey to clear his throat between takes. His voice

On May 24, Rodgers decided to come back, though Peer was in Camden for other recordings. He felt strong enough to stand at the microphone this time and performed four songs, resting on a cot in the rehearsal room between each take. He ended with "Years Ago," a song about a prisoner. Jimmie managed to play with his old vigor, characteristically infusing its plaintive lyrics with a bright pace and almost joyful voice. "I was happy, oh so happy, down in Mississippi way," he sang. "I was livin' with my pappy, fifteen years ago today."

was thinner, sometimes with a slight rasp, and he stumbled occasionally on his guitar riffs.

The engineers had to carry him to his cab after the second afternoon, and he rested for two days before returning to record two more songs, propped by pillows in an easy chair in front of the microphone. Rodgers was exhausted afterward, and they postponed the next session indefinitely for him to recuperate.

TOP *Jimmie and Carrie share a happy moment at Monmouth Beach, New Jersey, in 1932. Everyone, including his fans, knew his TB would kill him, but Rodgers kept performing—drawing strength from his audiences' reactions and providing them with what Carrie called "good medicine" in return.*

ABOVE, LEFT *On May 16, 1933, Jimmie wired Carrie from New York, complaining about cold weather and asking her to send him his blue serge suit; on May 21, he would send a postcard to friends in Texas promising to see them as soon as his recording sessions were completed.*

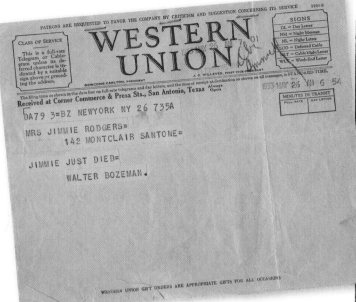

With his twelve songs done and the session completed, Rodgers felt reinvigorated. He took in Coney Island the next day, had hot dogs for lunch, drank a glass of newly legalized 3.2 beer, and napped in the sun.

But that night, back at his hotel, fits of coughing swept through him and he began hemorrhaging bright red spots onto his pillows. Shortly after midnight, he slipped into a coma. Then, in the early hours of May 26, 1933, Jimmie Rodgers died, drowning in his own blood. He was only thirty-five years old.

. . .

The Southern Railway added a special baggage car to its New Orleans run to carry the Singing Brakeman home. His pearl-gray casket, covered with lilies, rested on a platform in its center, with a photograph of Rodgers dressed in his railroad uniform, two thumbs up in the brakeman's signal that everything was ready to move on. Many members of the crew were old friends of his, including the engineer, who periodically set off the train's whistle as it made its way to Mississippi.

Big-city newspapers in the East made only passing reference to Rodgers's death, but in small towns throughout the South and Southwest it dominated the front pages. Solemn crowds gathered along the tracks to pay their respects as the train rumbled through on its way toward Meridian.

After lying in state at the Scottish Rites Cathedral, where mourners filed past his casket, and a funeral at the Central Methodist Church, he was buried in the Oak Grove Cemetery, beside the daughter who had died in infancy.

His career had lasted less than six years, but in that time

Jimmie Rodgers had recorded more than a hundred songs, many of which would be re-recorded for generations by other artists, as proof that they were staying true to the music's roots.

"His songs never go away," said Marty Stuart. "Generation after generation, genre after genre, the songs keep coming at you. Everybody that is anybody has recorded a Jimmie Rodgers song, or sung one along the way somewhere. Had it not been for Jimmie Rodgers, there would be a vast hole in the musical universe."

"He set the pace for people like Ernest Tubb, people like Hank Williams, people like me," Merle Haggard said. "A whole big section of country music wouldn't be here if it hadn't been for Jimmie Rodgers."

In the immediate aftermath of Rodgers's death, nearly twenty memorial songs were written and recorded about him and his life—including "We Miss Him When the Evening Shadows Fall," written by his sister-in-law collaborator, Elsie McWilliams, and sung by his widow. Record labels began searching among his many imitators for someone to replace him. Several already seemed eager to try to fill his shoes.

TOP, LEFT *On May 26, Carrie received a terse telegram informing her that her husband had died.*

TOP, RIGHT *Carrie and Anita Rodgers place flowers on Jimmie's grave on the day after his funeral in Meridian.*

OPPOSITE *In the baggage car that carried Rodgers's casket from New York to Meridian, friends from his railroad days placed this photograph. It shows a smiling Jimmie Rodgers in his brakeman's suit, holding his personalized guitar and giving the thumbs-up signal that the coast was clear to move on.*

2

HARD TIMES

I think hard times and country music were born for each other. There's a strange faith and hope that exists in country music, even in songs that have nothing to do with faith and hope.

MARTY STUART

I think people have always, from the beginning of time, had a need for stories. If you go back to these old ballads, they seem to be telling your story. They seem to resonate with something in your experience. And, to me, the best songs are universal in the message that they have.

"Hard Times" is something that still resonates, I think, for people. Poverty is very real and hard times are just around the corner for a lot of people. So a song like that has a message.

For me, the sad songs are the best because they make you feel better because, somehow, they connect you to the world: the fact that we're maybe all in the same boat.

EMMYLOU HARRIS

As she watches her family's belongings being loaded up, a woman's final companion in her empty house is a guitar. The combination of the Depression and the Second World War would produce the largest internal migrations in America's history.

B Y 1933, the worst economic crisis in United States history, the Great Depression, had entered its fourth devastating year. Nearly thirteen million workers had lost their jobs, and one out of every four farm families had lost their land, their home, and their livestock. A quarter of a million Americans under the age of twenty-one were homeless. According to a song by the Carter Family, the only place the Depression hadn't reached was in Heaven.

Between 1933 and 1945, nearly every aspect of American life would be strained and uprooted as never before. The economic cataclysm of the Depression would be followed by the United States' entry into the Second World War—and together, the twin crises would produce the largest internal migrations in the nation's history.

But in the midst of those dark and turbulent years, country music would manage to grow in popularity. Based as it was on the real-life experiences of America's working people, the music seemed to express perfectly what everyone was going through. Coping with hard times had always been one of its pervasive themes.

Meanwhile—as a new president, Franklin Delano Roosevelt, proved with his reassuring fireside chats—the still-young medium of radio would become increasingly central in American life, binding people together as they struggled to weather hard times.

* * *

My family were sharecroppers. The landlord, he got half of the cotton, which was about ten bales of cotton a year. That left us with five bales of cotton. So, it was about five hundred dollars a year, was my family's income.

DON MADDOX

In 1933, in the cotton fields near Boaz, Alabama, Lula and Charlie Maddox had finally given up trying to support themselves and their seven children as sharecroppers. Lula, who had always enjoyed dime novels about the Gold Rush of 1849, decided the family should uproot itself and move to California. "We sold everything we had, and they got thirty-five dollars for all their worldly possessions," remembered Don Maddox, one of the sons, "and we started walking to California the next day."

With their five youngest children, including their only daughter, Rose, the Maddoxes set out on foot, occasionally catching a ride from a sympathetic motorist. It took them five long days to travel just two hundred miles and reach Meridian, Mississippi. They spent the night at a Salvation Army shelter, where people explained how impossible it would be for a family to walk all the way to the West Coast. "So they took us down to the railroad yards the next day and showed us how to catch the trains," Don said. "We rode the rest of the way to California on freight trains."

That year, officials of just one of the nation's railroads, the Southern Pacific, reported that 683,000 transients had been discovered moving from town to town in the company's boxcars. The Maddox family was now among them.

ABOVE *During their departure from Oklahoma, a man comforts his family with a song.*

OPPOSITE *In Louisiana, a young migrant strawberry picker seeks solace with his guitar.*

FAMILY ROAMS U.S. FOR WORK

A hitch-hiking family of seven found shelter at Oakland's "Pipe City" after a cross-country trip from Alabama seeking work. The family comprises (left to right), **Calvin Maddux**, his father; Charles; Rose, Fred (standing), **Mrs. Lulu Maddux**, Henry and Kenneth. They have "ridden the rails" in their westward trek, and hope to make their home in California.—*Tribune Photo.*

Alabama Family Has 'Luck' In Arriving at 'Pipe City'

By ANNE CLARK.

From Gadsden, Alabama, to an unexpected haven in the "City Hall" of the unemployed was a long trail for the Maddox family, who have been "riding the rods" and hitchhiking the highways with their five children, penniless, in search of quest of employment.

"I worked for 10 years as a tenant on the same farm in Alabama," Maddox explained the family exodus. "Last year the flood ruined the whole crop. Then the owner lost his farm and we had to leave.

"When we rode the freight trains,

MRS. HUTTON OF BERKELEY DIES

BERKELEY, April 11.—Stricken last Thursday while pursuing her duties as assistant in the women's physical education department at the University of California, Mrs. Mary English Hutton, 65, widow of

In Oakland, California, they found temporary shelter living in a jumble of drainage culverts called "Pipe City." A reporter for the *Oakland Tribune* took their picture and wrote a story about them as an example of just how hard the Depression had become.

They moved to the foothills of the Sierra Nevada and tried panning for gold, with no luck. Things became so dire, Lula considered putting some of her children up for adoption so they might have a better life. Instead, they moved again, this time to the San Joaquin Valley, where they picked peaches and cotton alongside the thousands of other desperate families who were arriving every day from the South and from parts of the Great Plains ravaged by the Dust Bowl. Regardless of where the migrants came from, as they followed the crop seasons up and down the valley, they all were looked down upon by most Californians—and, Don Maddox

recalled, they all were called by the same derogatory name: Okies.

For the Maddoxes, life returned to the way it had been in Alabama: every member of the family still spent long days in the sun, stooped over, picking cotton for someone else. One hot day, eighteen-year-old Fred Maddox decided he'd had enough. "When I got out in that field," he said later, "all I could do was think, 'Boy, if I wasn't here, what I could be doin'.'" He stopped in the middle of a row, stood up, and stared at the sky. "What are you doin'?" his mother asked. "I'm a-thinkin'," he answered. "Everybody stop," she told the family. "Look at Fred, he's a-thinkin'." Fred had recently seen a hillbilly band playing at a local rodeo and heard they were paid $100 for the performance. "I'm a-thinkin'," he said, "we should go into the music business!"

Older brothers Cliff and Cal could play guitar; Rose, age

TOP AND ABOVE, RIGHT *The Maddox family's exodus from Alabama, by foot and by hopping freight trains, brought them to Oakland, California, where the only place they could live was with other dispossessed migrants in "Pipe City." The* Oakland Tribune *featured their story on April 11, 1933.*

eleven, liked to sing around the house. Fred didn't play any instrument, but he was a funny and persuasive talker. He charmed the owner of a Modesto furniture store into sponsoring them on a radio show by boasting that they had "the best girl singer there ever was" and even got the man to put up the money for a bass fiddle that Fred struggled to master. "He didn't know anything about playing bass and somebody said, 'Let me tune that thing for you,'" said Merle Haggard, who later became a friend of the family. "And he said, 'It ain't no use, I don't know where I'm at anyway.' And he just tuned it down and made sort of a percussion instrument out of it."

They weren't paid by the furniture store or the radio station, but they broadcast a show of music and lighthearted banter every weekday morning from 6:30 to 7:00 on Modesto's KTRB and used that exposure to land personal appearances that brought in some money. Billed as the Maddox Brothers and Rose, they were soon playing at rodeos and clubs from Susanville to Bakersfield. Lula made sure they always made it back to Modesto for their early-morning show, even if it meant driving all night.

In their travels, they met a young Dust Bowl refugee who was playing for tips in a nearby bar. His name was Woody Guthrie. Like the Maddoxes, Guthrie was a big fan of the Carter Family—his song "This Land Is Your Land" borrowed

its melody from a popular Carter tune, "Little Darling, Pal of Mine." Rose Maddox, in turn, grew fond of Guthrie's song "Reno Blues," about a lawyer who gets shot after promising a woman from Hollywood to get her a quick divorce from her cowboy husband. Rose soon incorporated it into their act, as "Philadelphia Lawyer." Rose employed a dramatic vibrato in her rendition, and at the song's climactic moment, the Maddoxes added the sound of a gunshot and a scream to signal the lawyer's demise.

When Guthrie heard the Maddox Brothers and Rose's version, he said, "my ears wiggled with pure joy." Don Maddox, who joined the band as the fiddle player, remembered another compliment Guthrie gave them: "He said we was the best thing that had come along in country music since the Carter Family. But the Carter Family, they were 'it' in my book; they're still 'it.'"

TOP, LEFT *Cliff, Rose, Fred, and Cal Maddox at a bar in Susanville, California*

TOP, RIGHT *Oklahoma's Woody Guthrie, a Dust Bowl refugee, also ended up in California and became a friend of the Maddox Brothers and Rose. Here, he performs at a migrant camp in the Central Valley for a small crowd.*

NATIONAL BARN DANCE

Radio was the most inexpensive form of entertainment available in the 1930s—and people sure needed some sort of entertainment during those years. Tune in to radio each night with no cost at all and you could hear the radio hillbillies. You could hear them early in the morning, at noon time, when people came home from work, or you could hear them on Saturday night at the barn dances. And the music just provided encouragement to people.

It enabled them to cope with hard times. You could lose yourself in the life of the cowboy, or the life of the hobo, or listen to a gospel song and gain assurance for a brighter day beyond this world.

BILL C. MALONE

Among the many businesses brought to their knees by the Great Depression, few were harder hit than the recording industry, whose sales had plummeted to a mere 5 percent of their peak in the 1920s. For Americans struggling simply to survive, buying a record was now a luxury they could no

longer afford, even when new cut-rate labels began offering them at thirty-five cents, less than half the price of a few years earlier.

But listening to the radio was free, and throughout the 1930s more and more stations realized they could attract large audiences by offering programs that featured old-time music. KMBC in Kansas City hosted the *Brush Creek Follies*; WOWO in Fort Wayne, Indiana, had the *Hoosier Hop*. There was Cincinnati's *Midwestern Hayride*, St. Louis's *Old-*

Fashioned Barn Dance, Des Moines's *Barn Dance Frolic*, and Virginia's *Old Dominion Barn Dance*.

In Virginia's Shenandoah Valley, singer Mac Wiseman remembered that his father had the first radio in the area. The family's house had no electricity, but his father made a tiny windmill that could generate just enough power to charge a battery that then ran the radio. "The radio had three dials on it," he said, "and you had to learn all the different numbers, like a bank vault combination, to get the stations. And people would gather in at our place to listen to the radio, and by that time Jacksonville, Florida, had a barn dance and Hopkinsville, Kentucky, and you could just go from one to another and listen all night. As one signed off, we'd hunt up another one. And my mom would cook 'em breakfast and they'd go home. We had one neighbor that was close enough, it was a good quarter of a mile away, but he would come out on his porch and listen as we played it with the windows open in the summertime."

Radio station WBT in Charlotte, North Carolina, had the *Crazy Barn Dance*, named for its sponsor, the Crazy Water Company, which promised that a teaspoon of its Crazy Crystals, dissolved in a glass of water, acted as a powerful laxative that could cure a wide range of ailments. The show was carried by fourteen stations in the Southeast, part of the company's aggressive promotional campaign that also included underwriting hillbilly bands, as long as they added "Crazy" to their names: the Crazy Mountaineers, the Crazy Hickory Nuts, the Crazy Blue Ridge Hillbillies.

Wheeling, West Virginia's WWVA beamed its Saturday night *Jamboree* toward the north and east, covering Pennsylvania, New York, New England, and parts of eastern Canada. One of its stars was the singer and comedian Louis Marshall Jones, who had already made a name for himself as "the Young Singer of Old Songs" on stations in Akron, Cleveland, and Boston.

Though only in his early twenties, Jones had a voice that seemed much older, so they nicknamed him "Grandpa Jones" and encouraged him to dress the part in old boots and a brush-handle moustache and to take up the banjo. He

OPPOSITE *Across the nation, like this woman tuning in her radio in Spencer, Iowa, Americans found a welcome reprieve from the hard times listening to barn dances like Indiana's* Hoosier Hop *and North Carolina's* Crazy Barn Dance.

ABOVE *In his twenties, Louis Marshall Jones performed as "Grandpa Jones" on WWVA in Wheeling, West Virginia. He was still in character—but no longer needing makeup—when he made his last appearance on the* Grand Ole Opry *in January 1998, shortly before his death at age eighty-four.*

would play the role for the next sixty years—long enough that special makeup to help him look like a grandpa was no longer necessary.

> While the intellectuals of wireless entertainment were racking their brains to build a Packard, WLS came along with a Ford among the amusements . . . the Alpha and the Omega of all the bucolic revues.
>
> [T]heirs is the last roundup for hillbilly talent, and artists of this type who have not faced its microphones are still on the fringe of the best yokel society.
>
> RADIO GUIDE, NOVEMBER 1934

But in the early 1930s, the show with the biggest audience was still the *National Barn Dance*, already a decade old, on Chicago's WLS, one of only twenty stations that had been granted a federal license for a powerful 50,000-watt signal.

The station was owned now by *Prairie Farmer* magazine, which promoted the *National Barn Dance* in its pages, as well as through a weekly fan newsletter and its annual *WLS Family Album*. In one six-month period, more than a million letters poured in from admiring listeners—a record for any station in the country, and proof, the owners boasted, that they were "the broadcaster with the greatest audience of the common, everyday folks on farms and in towns and cities."

So many people wanted to see the *Barn Dance* in person that WLS moved it to the 1,200-seat Eighth Street Theatre in downtown Chicago, charged a whopping ninety cents a ticket, staged two two-hour shows every Saturday night—

and, in the midst of the Depression, had to turn fans away at the door. During the 1933 Chicago World's Fair, the station arranged for part of the program to be broadcast remotely from an airplane circling over the city. Down on the ground, 35,000 people showed up for the performance at the fairgrounds during "Farmers' Week."

Musicians were paid only $20 per show, but they were eager to join the *Barn Dance*'s large cast, because the publicity often led to paying gigs during the rest of the week and the chance to launch a bigger career.

At age fourteen, George Gobel was just starting at Chicago's Theodore Roosevelt High School, but he was already the youngest member of the crew, nicknamed "Little Georgie, our little cowboy." Twenty years later, he would have his own national television show as a comedian.

TOP *WLS's* National Barn Dance *in Chicago was the nation's premier hillbilly radio show. John Lair (arm raised in the rear) led its energetic cast.*

LEFT *The show's youngest member was "Little Georgie" Gobel, who was signing autographs at age fourteen as "Goebel" before he changed the spelling of his last name. He would later become a famous television comedian.*

onstage, at first acting as a boy-crazy country girl—and then as a feisty wife, when she married her singing partner, *Scotty Wiseman*. In 1936, she was voted the most popular woman radio entertainer—of any genre—in America.

John Lair, the show's music director, recruited other Kentucky-born performers to join him as the Cumberland Ridge Runners string band, including the smooth-voiced Clyde Julian "Red" Foley of Blue Lick. Foley would go on to become one of country music's most durable stars, with hits ranging from the swinging "Chattanoogie Shoe Shine Boy" to the sentimental "Peace in the Valley," one of the first gospel songs to sell a million records.

Mac and Bob—Lester McFarland and Robert Gardner—had met at the Kentucky School for the Blind. Their close-harmony duets—and Mac's use of the mandolin—would influence country musicians for generations.

Arkie the Arkansas Woodchopper, one of the show's favorites, was actually Luther Ossenbrink from Missouri.

Myrtle Eleanor Cooper, known as Lulu Belle, always wore her trademark gingham dress, pantaloons, and lace-up boots

Lair would leave WLS to start his own show, the *Renfro Valley Barn Dance*, in his home state, featuring another act he brought with him: Lily May Ledford and the Coon Creek Girls, the first all-female string band. They became so popular they were chosen to perform at the White House along with the opera singer Marian Anderson and pop star Kate Smith for England's King George VI and President Roosevelt. Lily May said she was nervous—until she saw King George tapping his feet to the Coon Creek Girls' music.

But of all the stars created by the *National Barn Dance*, none would become more famous and wealthy—or contribute more to changing the image of hillbilly music—than a slim, sandy-haired singer from the southern Plains who had started his career as a slavish imitator of Jimmie Rodgers.

TOP *Lulu Belle (seen flirting with fellow* Barn Dance *star Red Foley, and in a WLS advertisement) was voted the most popular woman entertainer on American radio in 1936.*

LEFT *Led by Lily May Ledford (with the banjo), the Coon Creek Girls were the first all-female string band on radio—and were so popular, President Roosevelt invited them to perform at the White House.*

NUMBER ONE COWBOY

Here he comes; he's fence riding . . . he's repairing a fence right there. Now he's got that done, and he's very fast on his horse, and just as fresh as a daisy early in the morning.

He's our Gene Autry and he's going to sing for us, I'm sure.

WLS ANNOUNCER, *NATIONAL BARN DANCE*

Orvon Grover Autry had never intended to become a cowboy. Born in Tioga, Texas, in 1907, before moving to Oklahoma as a young boy, he grew up on a farm, not a ranch, and after buying a guitar from a Sears, Roebuck catalog at age twelve, he had no interest in guns or riding horses, a cousin remembered. "He just wanted to sit around," she said, "and play the guitar and sing."

After quitting high school, he took a job as a telegraph operator for the St. Louis–San Francisco Railroad, bringing his guitar along to pass the time during slow hours at the depot. In 1927, he traveled to New York City hoping to land a recording contract by singing an Al Jolson song. Two labels turned him away with the advice that he should instead learn how to yodel, a technique Jimmie Rodgers was beginning to make popular.

Back at his telegraph job in Oklahoma, Autry started practicing. Now calling himself "Gene," he landed some appearances on Tulsa station KVOO, and in 1929 returned to New York, where he was soon turning out covers of Rodgers's popular songs on an assortment of discount labels just as quickly as the Blue Yodeler released them on RCA Victor. He even recorded "TB Blues," Rodgers's deeply personal song about his losing fight with tuberculosis.

"Gene Autry was a slavish disciple" of Rodgers, according to country music historian Douglas B. Green, who also performs as "Ranger Doug" with Riders in the Sky. "In fact, you almost can't tell their voices apart on Gene Autry's 1928, 1929 records. And part of that was quite deliberate: if you could spend seventy-five cents to hear Jimmie Rodgers sing 'Blue Yodel Number Four' on RCA, you might be tempted to spend thirty-five cents to hear Gene Autry sing it on Conqueror."

Autry also dabbled in occasional risqué songs—"High Steppin' Mama," "She's a Hum Hum Dinger," and "She Wouldn't Do It," about parking in his car late at night with different women—but Art Satherley, a producer for the

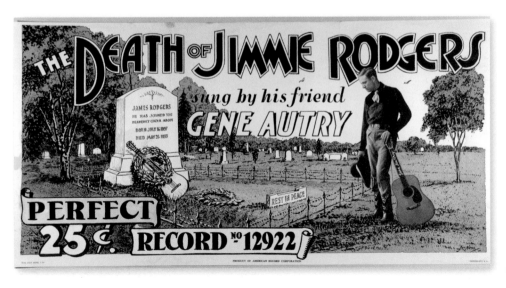

ABOVE *Young Orvon Grover Autry stands on his family porch while his sisters pose for a photograph, circa 1915.*

OPPOSITE AND LEFT *At first, Autry was one of many imitators of Jimmie Rodgers, but by the time the Blue Yodeler died in 1933 and Autry released four different tribute songs, he had changed his public persona. He was a singing cowboy. Like his hero, Autry (now calling himself Gene) had his name inscribed on the neck of his guitar.*

American Record Corporation, encouraged him to develop his own style and identity, especially after Autry's sentimental song, "Silver Haired Daddy of Mine," became a big hit in 1931.

Emphasize your Texas and Oklahoma roots, Satherley advised; be more of a westerner. But "that sort of stuff didn't sound very glamorous to me," Autry remembered. "My recollections of [farm] life included aching muscles and endless days in the sun and dust. I wanted to be a dreamy-eyed singer of love songs like Rudy Vallee."

He dropped his reticence when Satherley secured him a regular spot as "the Oklahoma Yodeling Cowboy" on a WLS morning show in

Chicago, where he abandoned his Jimmie Rodgers imitations in favor of songs like "The Last Roundup" and "Home on the Range," said to be President Roosevelt's favorite song. Autry began making personal appearances attired in fancy western clothes: ornate, handmade cowboy boots with his pants tucked in to show them off; a big belt buckle and a custom-made cowboy shirt with a scarf at the neck; all topped off by a wide-brimmed Stetson hat.

By 1933, when Alka-Seltzer began the first national broadcasts of the *Barn Dance* over the NBC network, Autry was a featured performer. The Sears catalog offered Gene Autry records at a special price of nineteen cents; a folio of sheet music called *Gene Autry's Cowboy Songs and Mountain Ballads*; and the Gene Autry Roundup Guitar for $9.65—with Gene getting a dime for each guitar. Over the air, he encouraged listeners to send in fifty cents for a Gene Autry songbook, and every week he'd fill a wastebasket with coins as he opened his mail.

TOP AND ABOVE *Autry (far left with the cast of WLS's* National Barn Dance*) became the show's featured star on national broadcasts—and the Sears catalog offered his Roundup Guitar to all the little cowboys who idolized him.*

He spent some of the cash on a new Martin guitar, just like the one his hero Jimmie Rodgers had, with his name inscribed on the fingerboard. But, except for their mutual burning ambition to be famous and rich, in many ways Autry was the opposite of Rodgers: humble, wholesome, and shy—"one of the cleanest young men you'd ever want to meet," an acquaintance said. He didn't drink or smoke and was always careful with his money. Though he hadn't graduated from high school, he had taken a correspondence course in accounting. "Even as a boy," he said, "I planned ahead."

When Rodgers died from tuberculosis in 1933, Autry quickly recorded four different tribute songs, all of them big sellers, but no longer as a pale shadow of the Blue Yodeler. He was a bona fide star in his own right—a singing cowboy— and now others were following *his* example.

Suddenly, singing cowboys—and cowgirls—were everywhere. And, regardless of whether real cowboys had ever yodeled to their cattle herds during the trail drives of the 1800s, they all were yodeling now. "Every group of men who are isolated develop a song tradition," said Douglas B. Green. "There are lumberjack songs; there are sailor shanties;

and the cowboys did, doubtless, sing, probably not nearly as much as it's shown in the Westerns, or we're led to believe. Once Gene Autry made it really popular, and building off the huge success of Jimmie Rodgers, then every cowboy had to yodel."

There was Tex Owens on KMBC in Kansas City; Texas Jim Lewis and his Lone Star Rangers on Detroit's WJR; and in New York City, on WHN, Tex Ritter, a deep-voiced Broadway star who actually was from Texas and a

TOP, LEFT *Tex Ritter, a serious student of the history of the West, performed on Broadway before heading to Hollywood, where he carved out a long career as a singing cowboy. His rendition of the theme song for* High Noon *won an Academy Award.*

TOP, RIGHT *Dolly and Millie Good billed themselves as the Girls of the Golden West, though they were from East St. Louis, not Muleshoe, Texas, as they claimed.*

ABOVE, CENTER *Like Gene Autry, Patsy Montana (originally Rubye Blevins from Hope, Arkansas) had started out imitating Jimmie Rodgers and his yodels. Her song "I Want to Be a Cowboy's Sweetheart" became the biggest hit for a female hillbilly singer of the time.*

serious student of the Old West. Ritter had appeared in the play *Green Grow the Lilacs*, which would later be turned into the musical *Oklahoma!*

Dolly and Millie Good, sisters from East St. Louis, performed as the Girls of the Golden West, and claimed they were from Muleshoe, Texas, and had learned to yodel by listening to coyotes howl.

Rubye Blevins of Hope, Arkansas, had tried making it as a female imitator of Jimmie Rodgers's songs, before adopting

---

TOP AND LEFT *In the film serial* The Phantom Empire, *Gene Autry had to battle the Muranians thousands of feet below the earth's surface and get back home in time to perform on his radio show.*

OPPOSITE, TOP *Movie poster for Gene Autry, "the screen's new singing cowboy star," in* Tumbling Tumbleweeds

OPPOSITE *Autry was soon the nation's most famous singing cowboy, and particularly the hero of boys who flocked to movie theaters every Saturday. One of them, Willie Nelson, remembered Autry as a cowboy who never lied and always won the girl.*

the name Patsy Montana. In 1933, she came to WLS's *Barn Dance*, where she was backed by the Kentucky Ramblers, who changed their name to the Prairie Ramblers. Her song "I Want to Be a Cowboy's Sweetheart"—which she wrote about an independent-minded woman who wants to ride beside her cowboy lover as his equal—became a runaway best seller.

In 1934, Gene Autry got the break that would take him and the singing cowboy to even greater heights of popularity. Hollywood wanted him.

Cowboy films had been popular from the time of William S. Hart and Tom Mix in the silent movie days. By the early 1930s, "talkies" had taken over, and the studios began making so-called B movies: cheaper productions that big-city theaters played before the main attractions, and small-town movie houses offered at twenty-five cents' admission for their Depression-strapped clientele.

Ken Maynard was their biggest star and incorporated some songs into his role. But Maynard was not much of a singer, and in 1934, for the making of *In Old Santa Fe*, his studio decided that Autry, WLS's new phenomenon, should be brought out to perform in a few scenes. Moviegoers ate it up.

The next year, Maynard—an alcoholic, prone to violent outbursts that created costly production delays—was fired. After taking riding lessons, Gene Autry replaced him. In a serial called *The Phantom Empire*, a mixture of science fiction and a Western, he played himself: a singing cowboy with a radio show, who also does battle with a race of people thousands of feet below the earth's surface, the Muranians, who are developing a powerful death ray. At the end of an episode, Autry would somehow escape from Murania and

HARD TIMES · 75

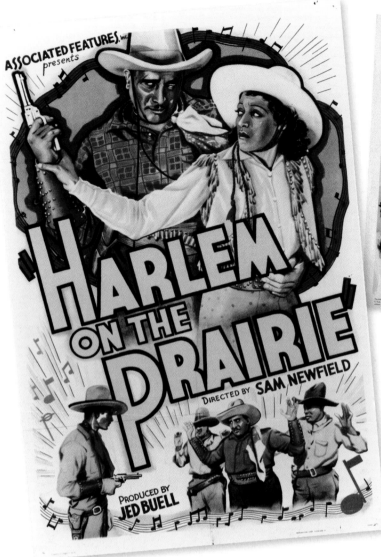

With the Depression deepening, Americans wanted an escape, and watching Gene Autry defeat the bad guys with his fists, court a pretty girl, and sing some happy songs was one of the best ways to do it. In Abbott, Texas, young Willie Nelson grew up going to Autry movies every Saturday. "Gene was my hero," Nelson said. "He was a good guy. You know, he never lied. And he always got the girl in the end."

Virtually every movie studio developed a singing cowboy. There was a Mexican singing cowboy, Tito Guízar, and a singing cowgirl, Dorothy Page. Herb Jeffries was born in Detroit and had recorded with Earl Hines's jazz band before coming to Los Angeles, where he sang at the Club Alabam and was recruited to star in a series of all-black Westerns, begin-

ride back to his ranch, just in time to sing another song on the radio.

With the success of *The Phantom Empire*, Autry moved permanently to California while Republic Pictures quickly cranked out a string of B movies with him as their star, appearing with his horse Champion and with his sidekick Smiley Burnette. He now took on more contemporary issues, often battling against corrupt politicians or ruthless businessmen—ten feature films in less than two years: including *Tumbling Tumbleweeds*, *Melody Trail*, *The Sagebrush Troubadour*, *The Singing Vagabond*, and *The Singing Cowboy*. Many of them cost less than $20,000 to produce—and each made nearly a million dollars.

In the 1930s, with Americans looking for diversions from the economic crisis gripping the nation, Hollywood provided a steady parade of B movies with new stars who wore cowboy hats and sang songs.

ning with *Harlem on the Prairie*, aimed at African-American audiences in big cities and segregated theaters of the South.

Tex Ritter followed Gene Autry to Hollywood, where his skills on a horse and on the stage—as well as his resonant singing voice—made him the star of more than eighty Westerns and boosted the sales of his records. Two decades later, though he didn't appear in it, Ritter's version of "Do Not Forsake Me, Oh My Darling" became the Oscar-winning theme song of *High Noon*. In the early years of the craze, even the rising film star John Wayne tried to be a singing cowboy, but he decided he looked silly pretending to play a guitar and lip-synching the words to a voice dubbed by another actor.

• • •

With so many singing cowboy films being made, the demand for new songs increased. No one was better at supplying them than the Sons of the Pioneers, who helped redefine

the sound of cowboy songs with their precise harmonies and their lyrics about the beauty of the West.

The group had been put together by Leonard Slye of Cincinnati, Ohio, who, like so many other Americans down on their luck in the early 1930s, had migrated to California, seeking a new chance. He drove dump trucks and picked fruit for a while, then placed an ad in the *Los Angeles Examiner* looking for musicians to join him in a cowboy band.

Among those who answered it was Bob Nolan, who was working as a lifeguard at the time, and showed up barefoot for his tryout with Slye. Originally from Canada, Nolan had

TOP *The Sons of the Pioneers created some of the most enduring cowboy songs of the era, like "Cool Water" and "Tumbling Tumbleweeds." The group was founded by Leonard Slye (standing, right) from Cincinnati, Ohio; its principal songwriter was Bob Nolan (standing, with bass fiddle), an admirer of Keats and Shelley.*

moved to Arizona as a teenager and fell in love with the desert landscape. A lover of poetry—Keats and Shelley were favorites—Nolan wrote the classic "Cool Water" when he was just sixteen.

He and the Sons of the Pioneers began supplying more songs and appearing in Hollywood Westerns with all the big stars: Gene Autry, Dick Foran, Charles Starrett—even pop crooner Bing Crosby, who came out with his own singing cowboy movie, *Rhythm on the Range*, in 1936. A song Nolan wrote provided the title for Autry's film *Tumbling Tumbleweeds*, which gave Autry his second million-selling record and provided countless other western singers with a surefire hit.

By 1937, the singing cowboy boom had spawned 530 Westerns in four years, most of them B movies often scoffed at by the critics, but adored by the fans, particularly youngsters from rural and working-class families. And when Gene

Autry released his new film *Public Cowboy No. 1*, its title was no exaggeration.

In addition to his films, he kept up a furious pace in the recording studio and touring the country, pulling his horse Champion in a trailer to towns where his movies had played. His wife, Ina, set up a filing system with the names and addresses of fans who had written to him; when he came to their town, Autry would check the local phone book and call them up.

Then, in early 1938, he told Republic Pictures he wouldn't make more movies for them until they paid him more than his current $5,000 per film. Lesser stars were receiving from

---

ABOVE AND OPPOSITE, TOP *When Gene Autry went on tour, he always took his trusted horse Champion with him—even for a publicity shot in a local barber shop.*

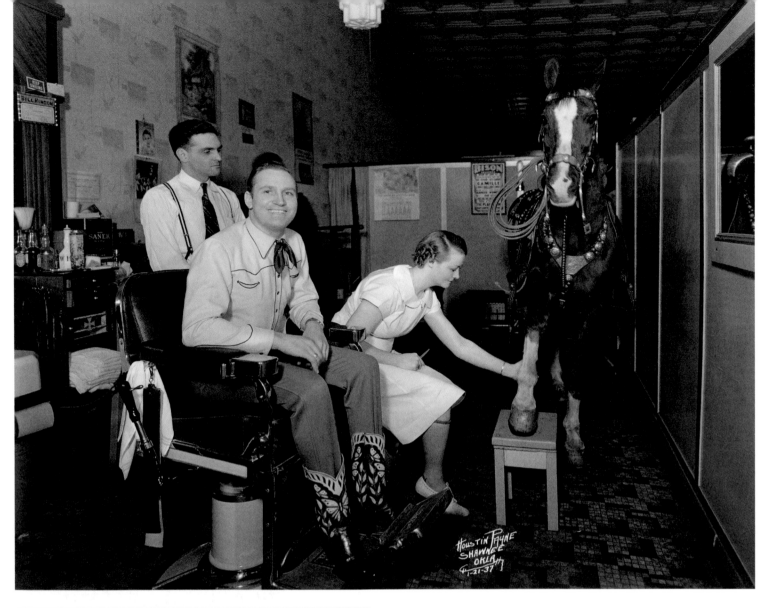

$12,000 to $21,000, he said, and "I think I am entitled to more money." He also demanded that Republic drop a provision in his contract that entitled the company to half of any money he received from endorsements and personal appearances.

Republic wouldn't give in. As a tactic to force him back to work, the studio auditioned for his replacement. Eventually they settled on an actor who had appeared in Autry's movie *The Old Corral*, under the stage name of Dick Weston. In reality, it was Leonard Slye of the Sons of the Pioneers, someone with a proven ability to sing as well as Autry himself.

The only problem was his name. The studio executives didn't think Leonard Slye sounded like the name of a movie hero. So they changed it. From now on, he would be known as Roy Rogers.

LEFT *Gene Autry's contract dispute with Republic Pictures prompted the studio to seek a replacement. They settled on Leonard Slye of the Sons of the Pioneers, but changed his name to Roy Rogers.*

THE FIRST FAMILY OF COUNTRY MUSIC

Time Life reviewed a box set once upon a time that had been released on the Carter Family, and they said, "In the light of perfect beauty, tears are the only answer." That says it so well.

There's our first lead guitar player in country music, Mother Maybelle. The foundational songs of country music were gathered, or written, by A.P. Carter. Sara Carter was the original great female vocalist in country music. She was so powerful. The Carter Family is the first family of country music.

MARTY STUART

Maybelle, as a guitar player, I don't know that you can overstate the influence of her guitar playing and that "Carter scratch," and everything that grew out of that. And Sara's voice, like wailing at the grave, that kind of keening, just pierces you, so plainspoken and without any kind of embellishment or frill, just telling the truth, one note at a time.

ROSANNE CASH

By 1938, the lingering Depression had taken a heavy toll on the Carter Family in Maces Spring, Virginia. Sales of their records had dropped to a few thousand per release, decimating their royalties. Sara Carter often refused to take part in what few live performances her husband, A.P., and sister-in-law, Maybelle, could arrange in the immediate area. A.P.'s sister Sylvia would substitute for her to keep a little cash coming in.

More troubling was the rift that had been growing over the years between A.P. and Sara. She considered him cold and constantly distracted, and his trips to collect more songs kept him away from home for weeks at a time. To help out with chores around the farm while he was on the road, A.P. hired his younger cousin Coy Bays—handsome, hardworking, affectionate, with unforgettable blue eyes. When it became clear that Sara and Coy were starting to fall in love, the extended family intervened. In the end, Coy's parents decided the best course was to leave for California and take him with them. Sara moved out of her and A.P.'s house to live with her parents across Clinch Mountain.

All of this posed a problem for Ralph Peer, who had been managing the trio and publishing their songs since he first recorded them in 1927. He had promoted them as the Carter *Family*, and when Sara refused to come to an upcoming recording session, Peer asked his wife, Anita, to reach out to her with a letter:

ABOVE *Sara Carter with her daughters, Gladys (right) and Janette*

Dear Sara, I realize that it would be distinctly awkward for both you and A.P. to work together again, but on the other hand the "Carter Family" has become well known and there is a chance to make some more money, even in these days of depression. Let me know if there is anything I can do. I have been divorced once myself, as I think I told you, so I can sympathize with you perfectly.

Even if you never live together again you could get together for professional purposes like the movie stars do.

Sara reluctantly gave in. She moved back to Maces Spring—spending the nights with Maybelle and her husband, Eck, and joining A.P. only during the day to practice for a series of recording sessions. In them, the Carter Family recorded some songs that A.P. had written about romance and abandonment, seemingly reflecting both his anger toward Sara and the love he still felt for her: "Are You Tired of Me, My Darling?" "You've Been Fooling Me, Baby," and "Tell Me That You Love Me."

But the Carter Family also recorded what would become one of the most enduring songs in country music history: an old hymn, "Will the Circle Be Unbroken," first written and published a generation earlier, in 1907, by Ada R. Haber-

shon and Charles H. Gabriel. In 1928, an African-American minister, J. C. Burnett, had rewritten and recorded it. A.P. reworked it some more, turning it into a vivid story about the death and funeral of a mother, reflecting both profound grief for the loss and religious faith in a family's ultimate reunion in heaven. (The Carter Family version was titled "Can the Circle Be Unbroken," but over subsequent years, the name reverted to the original.)

Told from the point of view of one of the deceased's children, it begins, "I was standing by the window, on a cold and cloudy day, when I saw

LEFT AND ABOVE *The songs and the image Ralph Peer promoted for the Carter Family put an emphasis on family, but by the late 1930s the rift between Sara and A.P. had widened. She and Coy Bays, a cousin of A.P.'s, had fallen in love, and Sara was no longer living with her husband.*

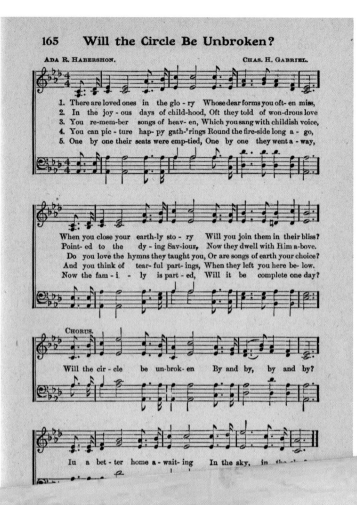

CAN THE CIRCLE BE UNBROKEN

I was standing by my window, on one cold and cloudy day
I saw the hearse come rolling, for to carry my mother away

Chorus:

Can the circle be unbroken, by and by Lord by and by
There's a better home awaiting, In the sky, Lord, in the sky

Lord I told the undertaker, undertaker please drive slow
For this body you are hauling, Lord I hate to see her go

I followed close behind her, tried to hold up and be brave
But I could not hide my sorrow when they laid her in the grave

I went back home Lord, my home was lonesome
For my mother she was gone
All my borthers and sisters crying, what a home so sad and lone

Chorus:

Okeh Record No. 03027
Carter Family

that hearse come rolling, for to carry my mother away"; but its chorus ends with the promise, "There's a better home awaiting in the sky, Lord, in the sky." The circle of family will be unbroken.

"You put that kind of suffering in music and art, and you're liberated," said singer-songwriter Rosanne Cash. "It's liberating because you're feeling it anyway. Do you want to take it in and let it destroy you, or do you want to put it out there and make it something beautiful?" Marty Stuart added, "The song tells us there's a better home awaiting. No more suffering. No more trials. No more heartache. No more struggle in this world down here below." Betty Johnson, who performed with the Carter Family on the radio in North Carolina as part of the Johnson Family Singers, said her grandmother particularly loved the song: "There will always be hard times. But you have to have faith that there's going to be a better time. Faith is what gets us going every morning. It just gives you this tremendous hope. That's what that song gives you." Alice Randall, a songwriter, said it was her grandmother's favorite, too: "My black grandmother, from Selma, Alabama, used to sing that song to me. It meant so much to my grandmother, whose grandmother was born enslaved. When families are broken apart, there is a place we will come together, that all that family that has been lost will be reunited. My grandmother rested on that song."

. . .

In 1936, Sara filed for divorce—A.P. was granted custody of the three children, with visitation rights for Sara—though they kept it as quiet as possible and continued making more records, earning $75 for each new song. "From a business standpoint," Peer told Sara, "it is important that the Carter Family should not be too badly broken up."

He presented them with an offer from the Consolidated Royal Chemical Corporation: they could have their own twice-a-day radio show that the company sponsored, be paid $4,000 each—nearly three times the average yearly wage at the time—and work only six months a year. The company even threw in a new car for A.P. The

accused him of "blatant quackery" and the Kansas medical board revoked his license in 1930, he had used his radio celebrity to run for governor as a last-minute write-in candidate, promising to graze his goats on the statehouse lawn and abolish all licensing boards. He narrowly lost. Then the Federal Radio Commission stripped KFKB of its license, saying it did not fulfill a "public purpose."

Undaunted, Brinkley had moved to Del Rio, got a license to practice medicine in Texas, and spent half a million dollars to build a new radio station, XERA, just across the river in Mexico, beyond the reach of American regulations—a so-called border blaster sta-

only catch: during the six months they worked, they would need to be in Texas.

Given the hard times, it was too good a deal to pass up. Strained but still presenting a public face of unity, in October 1938 they arrived in Del Rio to meet the owner of the station at the elaborate mansion he had built on the banks of the Rio Grande. It was Dr. John R. Brinkley, one of the earliest pioneers in understanding the power of radio for selling products and services—in his case, operations promising to restore aging men's sexual potency by transplanting goat testicles into them.

Brinkley had already made a fortune in tiny Milford, Kansas, broadcasting from his local station, KFKB. When the American Medical Association

OPPOSITE *The original "Will the Circle Be Unbroken?" was written in 1907 and appeared in this hymnal in 1921, years before the Carter Family ever started making records. It was rewritten and recorded in 1928 by J. C. Burnett, an African-American minister. Seven years later, A.P. Carter changed it some more as "Can the Circle Be Unbroken," telling a vivid story of a mother's death and a family's grief, as shown in this lyric sheet.*

TOP *Sara and Maybelle Carter outside XERA, the "border blaster" station across the Rio Grande from Del Rio, Texas, owned by the medical huckster John R. Brinkley, who had been run out of Kansas.*

RIGHT *Though now divorced, Sara and A.P. still performed together (with Maybelle, center) on XERA.*

tion, 500,000 watts in strength, ten times the power of WLS in Chicago or any other station in the United States.

Brinkley opened a new hospital to resume his special operations, and another one in San Juan, Texas, that treated hemorrhoids. "Remember," he told his listeners, "Del Rio for the prostate, San Juan for the rectum." It all made Brinkley richer than ever. Between 1933 and 1938, he and his staff operated on sixteen thousand patients and collected $12 million.

The Carter Family—including Sara and Maybelle's daughters—was now a long way from Poor Valley, Virginia, but they settled into their new routine. Once in the morning and once in the evening, they broadcast for thirty minutes on *The Good Neighbor Get-Together*, opening always with their theme song, "Keep on the Sunny Side," and promoting Consolidated Royal's two main products: a cold medicine called

Peruna, which was 25 percent alcohol, and Kolorbak, a hair dye that contained lead. "And while you heard the music, you also had to put up with the incessant merchandising," said historian Bill C. Malone. "The interesting thing about the border stations is, here you have some of the seediest, some of the most low-life merchandising and advertising imaginable, making it possible for these songs about 'Mama' and 'home,' and the 'old country church,' and the 'old-fashioned ways,' to be popularized, that they went hand in hand."

XERA, "The Sunshine Station Between the Nations," had a signal that was so overpowering, local ranchers heard the music on their barbed wire fences; Del Rio residents talking on the telephone sometimes had conversations interrupted by the broadcasts; and their children, it was said, got good reception on their braces. More important to the Carters' exposure, at night their program could be heard as far away

as New York, California, and Alberta, Canada. Their songs were now reaching people who might not otherwise have known about them.

In the dust-ravaged town of Littlefield, Texas, little Waylon Jennings's first childhood memory was of his father connecting the family radio to the pickup truck's battery so they could listen to the Carter Family. In Columbus, Georgia, fourteen-year-old Chester Atkins heard Maybelle's guitar picking on a radio set he had built from mail-order parts. And in tiny Dyess, Arkansas, a New Deal resettlement community for impoverished farmers, a boy named J. R. Cash was tuning in. "My father, as a young boy, would have listened to country music and known what it was because of the Carter Family," his son, John Carter Cash, said. "So many different artists in the 1930s were sitting around the radios in their living rooms and listening to the Carter Family. If it hadn't been for Dr. Brinkley and his radio station, and the fact that he had to move to Mexico to be able to do this, if it hadn't been for that, we wouldn't know country music as we know it today. So, thank you, Dr. Brinkley."

To gauge the group's drawing power, their sponsor promised that anyone who sent in a box top of the company's products, care of the Carter Family, would be sent their picture and a free Bible. Twenty-five thousand box tops arrived in a single week.

In February 1939, Sara Carter put the station's reach to a different use. She had not seen Coy Bays for years—and for most of that time had not received any response to the many letters she had sent him. During the evening show, she stepped to the microphone and said, "I'm gonna dedicate this [next song] to Coy Bays in California."

With that, Maybelle started strumming her guitar, and

OPPOSITE *On XERA, the Carter Family now also included A.P. and Sara's daughter Janette (back row between A.P. and the station announcer Bill Rinehart) and Maybelle's daughters (seated from left, Helen, Anita, and June). Their broadcasts reached listeners as far away as New York, Canada, and the West Coast.*

ABOVE *After hearing Sara Carter dedicate "I'm Thinking Tonight of My Blue Eyes" to him one night on the radio, Coy Bays drove the sixteen hundred miles from Greenville, California, to Del Rio. Reunited, the two were soon married.*

Sara began singing one of their earliest songs, "I'm Thinking Tonight of My Blue Eyes." "Oh you told me once dear that you loved me," she sang. "You said that we never would part; but a link in the chain has been broken; leaves me with a sad and aching heart." "Oh I'm thinking tonight of my blue eyes," the chorus ended, "and I wonder if he ever thinks of me."

More than sixteen hundred miles away, on the far side of the Sierra Nevada, in Greenville, California, the Bays family had gathered around their radio and tuned in to *The Good Neighbor Get-Together*. Up until that moment, Coy thought Sara had forgotten *him*; he had stopped writing her because he hadn't received her letters. His mother now admitted she had hidden them all.

"Mom," he said. "I'm gonna go get Sara." Then he set off for Texas. Reunited, they got married there on February 20. No one outside the immediate family was told of the new development.

A.P. was despondent. "He had no zeal after that," his son remembered. "He was lost." He was so ill at ease during subsequent broadcasts that the sponsors eventually sent him home a month before the contract ended—because, they believed, "he was transmitting his mood unwittingly over the air."

Sara and Maybelle continued broadcasting without him. Then Maybelle headed back to Maces Spring. Sara went with Coy to California.

TAKE ME BACK TO TULSA

To me, Bob Wills was one of the seminal figures of American music. When he was asked about it, it was just, "We were just playing music to get people to dance." And dancing is rhythm, so he'd fit his music to the rhythm that the dancers needed.

The instrumentation was what was different because it was fiddle based, guitar based, and that was what Western swing was and is.

RAY BENSON

If somebody don't like Wills, he's immediately under suspicion with me. I would say, "Let's go on to something else."

MERLE HAGGARD

By the late 1930s, a new sound was sweeping the nation—what *Variety* magazine called an "indelible notation on the evolution of jazz." Known as "swing," it had incubated in the dance halls of Harlem, but now an entire generation of Americans—white as well as black—danced to its beat, filling ballrooms and theaters all across the country: from the Paramount in Manhattan and the Aragon in Chicago to the Palomar in Los Angeles, where Benny Goodman thrilled audiences with his version of music

ABOVE AND LEFT *Bob Wills (seen with his father in 1915 and as a teenager in the Texas Panhandle) came from a long line of frontier fiddlers. By the time he was a young man, he was competing against his father and the legendary Eck Robertson in regional contests.*

first played by Louis Armstrong, Chick Webb, and Duke Ellington.

People were swinging in Tulsa, Oklahoma, too, crowding twice a week into a former automobile dealer's garage called Cain's Dancing Academy on North Main Street. But the music they moved to was different, representing its own unique cross-fertilization of genres.

Drums, bass, and a syncopated piano drove its pulse, just as they did in swing bands; and musicians were expected to improvise on their instrumental breaks, just as they did in jazz. But instead of saxophones, clarinets, and horns, this music featured the mainstays of a hillbilly band: fiddles and guitar.

It was Bob Wills and His Texas Playboys, making their own "indelible notation" on the evolution of country music. Jimmie Rodgers had connected hillbilly music with the blues. Gene Autry had given it a flavor of the Old West. Bob Wills gave it a beat—a raucous, dance hall beat from Texas, influenced by German, Czech, and Bohemian traditions, totally unlike anything from Appalachia or the Bible Belt of the Deep South.

With an ancestry that included English, Irish, Cajun, and Cherokee stock, James Robert Wills had been born on March 6, 1905, near Kosse, Texas, southeast of Waco, with fiddle playing in his blood. Both of his grandfathers were fiddlers; his father was a fiddler; and uncles on both sides of

his family were frontier fiddlers, too, some of the best in the Brazos River area.

As a boy, Wills absorbed all the music around him—including the blues he heard from the nearby shanties of African-American cotton pickers, whose children were his playmates. His musical horizons broadened again in 1913, when his family moved farther west by covered wagon to the Texas Panhandle, and he began accompanying his father to play at all-night ranch dances, including a birthday party for the legendary cattleman Charles Goodnight.

By the time he was a young man, Wills knew he wanted to be a performer. In regional fiddling contests, the championship often came down to Wills, his father, and Eck Robertson, who a few years earlier had made one of the first recordings of hillbilly music. One time, Wills played so long that his chin got infected, leaving lifelong scars after doctors had to scrape the bone clean.

He moved briefly to Roy, New Mexico, where he formed a band with some Hispanic-American musicians, developing a

ABOVE *The Light Crust Doughboys on the road, after Milton Brown had left the band. From left, W. Lee "Pappy" O'Daniel, Bob Wills, Herman Arnspiger, new singer Tommy Duncan, Sleepy Johnson, and the bus driver. O'Daniel parlayed the public exposure he received as the band's announcer into becoming governor, then U.S. senator from Texas.*

They were called the Light Crust Dough-boys. At first, the company required them to work in the flour mill when they weren't broadcasting, until the company manager, W. Lee ("Pappy") O'Daniel, realized how popular they were with listeners and paid them instead to show up for work and practice their music eight hours a day. Then he took them on the road in a special car, emblazoned with the company's name and equipped with its own public address system. O'Daniel himself insisted on accompanying them as the announcer; he would later capitalize on the publicity by becoming governor of Texas and then narrowly defeat a young Lyndon Johnson to win a U.S. Senate seat.

The Light Crust Doughboys' radio show soon began appearing on more powerful stations—WBAP in Fort Worth and others throughout the Southwest—and their music kept evolving. "All of a sudden, the Jazz Age is upon us and he's a young man, in Fort Worth, playing music—and jazz is the music of the day," according to Ray Benson. "The 1930s in Texas had brutal segregation and there were lynchings. It was 'American apartheid,' I'd call it. And here was Bob Wills imitating Louis Armstrong, Bessie Smith, Emmett Miller, and 'black' music. That, in itself, in Texas, was revolutionary."

When Milton Brown quit to start his own band, Wills auditioned sixty-seven vocalists before he found his replacement in Tommy Duncan, who had been singing at root beer stands

style of playing that incorporated their sound, along with the African-American blues he always loved. "So you've got fiddle tunes, the blues, and then you have the Mexican-American experience," said Ray Benson, a founder of the band Asleep at the Wheel. "He has a tune called 'Spanish Two Step.' It encompasses the feeling of the Hispanic music of the day. So Bob took all of those things and made it into what we call 'Western swing.'"

Restless for better opportunities, Wills moved to Fort Worth just before the Crash of 1929, and for a time had to support himself and his family wearing black-face, telling jokes, and dancing in a medicine show, before he and singer Milton Brown formed a band that was sponsored by the Burrus Mill and Elevator Company on radio station KFJZ.

ABOVE *Cain's Dancing Academy in Tulsa, where Bob Wills and His Texas Playboys played two nights a week.*

RIGHT *Capitalizing on Wills's celebrity, General Mills named a brand of flour for his band and gave him a royalty for every sack it sold.*

for tips. At the audition, Wills asked Duncan to sing one of his favorites, "I Ain't Got Nobody," a blues song recorded by Bessie Smith and Emmett Miller. It was one of Duncan's favorites, too, and when he copied Miller's yodel, note for note, he was instantly hired.

After a dispute with O'Daniel, Wills formed a band called the Playboys—appearing in pullover sweaters, like college students—and in 1934 moved them all to Oklahoma, where they ended up at Tulsa's KVOO, billed as Bob Wills and His Texas Playboys.

There he expanded the band—adding saxophones, horns, piano—as he expanded the sound he wanted. In every song, Wills interjected a falsetto "ah-haa" that became his trademark, the same way Jimmie Rodgers had made the "blue yodel" his.

By the late 1930s, Wills was a celebrity throughout the Southwest. He persuaded a subsidiary of General Mills to produce Playboy Flour, giving him a royalty for every sack it sold, and kept the band on the road four nights a week, with six radio broadcasts each morning, and two nights at Cain's ballroom, where fifteen hundred fans regularly came to dance to his music. To keep the crowd on their feet, he never called for an intermission—just let some musicians rest while the others continued playing. To keep his musicians on their toes, without warning he would nod to one—or dip his fiddle bow at them—to take the next instrumental break while he strutted around the stage.

"He was a showman," Merle Haggard remembered. "He was there to do his best to make you enjoy yourself and he was really comical, at the same time. It was a piece of work to watch him perform." "He was a colorful figure, à la Mick Jagger," Ray Benson added. "He pranced around onstage like a peacock. I got to know a lot of the old Texas Playboys who worked for Bob Wills. And one thing they said to me, all of them, was that when they got onstage with Bob Wills, he motivated them to play above what they could. They said he had these burning black eyes and this look that, when he looked at you, you went, 'Oh, my God, I better do something.'"

But Wills was a binge drinker, and sometimes missed engagements if he went on a bender; the band would say he had the flu and perform without him. His affairs with women brought him five divorces in six years, including with the widow of Milton Brown, whom he married and divorced *twice*. And he struggled with occasional depressions. "The only time we ever played sad songs," one band member said, "was when Bob was between marriages."

Nothing, however, seemed to dampen his growing popu-

ABOVE *Wills demanded the highest musicianship from his Playboys. They knew he could turn in their direction and motion for one of them to break into a solo. "He was there to do his best to make you enjoy yourself," said Merle Haggard, one of his many admirers.*

larity or his continuing musical innovations. Besides introducing drums to hillbilly music, he encouraged his steel guitar player, Leon McAuliffe, to adopt a technique first developed by Bob Dunn of Milton Brown's group. By raising and magnetizing the strings and attaching an electric pickup, hooked to an amplifier, it created a new sound, which McAuliffe popularized with Wills's recording "Steel Guitar Rag." More and more players copied it, and for many people the electric steel guitar would ultimately become as closely associated with country music as the fiddle.

In 1938, Wills recorded a new song he had written, adapted from his earlier "Spanish Two Step." He called this one "San Antonio Rose." It was a fiddle tune, with no lyrics at first, and it became the most popular hillbilly record of 1939. His publisher at the time, the Irving Berlin Music Company in New York, thought it could be even bigger if it had words, and they had one of their in-house writers provide them.

LEFT AND ABOVE *Even as he expanded his band, Wills kept them constantly on tour throughout the Southwest. His biggest hit came in 1940, when a band member wrote words to a tune Wills had written, "San Antonio Rose."*

Wills couldn't stand the new lyrics or the new arrangement Irving Berlin's people had provided. When his band played it, he complained, it sounded like a pop song and the audience didn't think it sounded authentic. He wanted something better. He gave one of his horn players a jug of whiskey and five dollars to come up with something new. The result was a song Wills called "*New* San Antonio Rose," and in 1940 he and his band, now with eighteen members, one of the biggest swing bands in America, recorded it.

The song was an instant hit. A year later, Bing Crosby would record his own version, which sold one and a half million records. With the success of "New San Antonio Rose," Wills and his musicians were not only the most popular dance band in five southwestern states, he also had a growing national audience. Fans would drive two hundred miles just to hear him and the Playboys in person. Hollywood invited him to California to appear in a singing cowboy movie, *Take Me Back to Oklahoma*, with Tex Ritter.

Because of "New San Antonio Rose," Wills said, "I went from hamburgers to steaks." In 1969, astronaut Pete Conrad would bring a tape cassette of the song along with him on the Apollo 12 mission to the moon. As his fellow astronaut Alan Bean described the view of Earth from outer space to a worldwide audience listening far below, "New San Antonio Rose" was beamed to everyone on the planet.

A GOOD-NATURED RIOT

For Edwin Craig and the National Life and Accident Insurance Company in Nashville, owners of radio station WSM, the 1930s proved to be a time of opportunity, despite the Depression.

When WSM was granted a federal license to become one of only three 50,000-watt "clear channel" stations in the South, Craig authorized spending a quarter of a million dollars to erect a new transmitting tower, said to be the tallest of its kind in the nation. It could beam WSM programs—and the insurance company's name—from coast to coast. In January 1934, 174,574 letters came in from listeners as far away as Washington State and Pennsylvania, where coal miners said they used WSM's daily broadcast of the whistle of the Pan American Express train passing by the tower as their signal to go home to supper.

Within Nashville, which considered itself "the Athens of the South," the station's more highbrow programming remained the most popular: like *Magnolia Blossoms*, featur-

ing opera stars and the Fisk Jubilee Singers; or the *WSM Hollywood Show*, with a full orchestra and twenty-voice chorus performing songs from popular movies; or special appearances by a Vanderbilt student named Frances Rose Shore, now calling herself Dinah Shore, singing with a big band.

But Craig particularly enjoyed WSM's Saturday-night show, the *Grand Ole Opry*, still hosted by the amiable George Hay, "the Solemn Old Judge," presiding over what he called "a shindig, barn dance and breakdown [with] old-time folk tunes [from] the Tennessee Hills." The colorful Uncle Dave Macon and his banjo anchored the cast of musicians, most of them dressed like caricatures of hillbillies. They created, Hay bragged, "a good-natured riot."

The show did not have the national prominence of WLS's *Barn Dance*, and Nashville's upper crust still considered it an embarrassment to the city's image. When his wealthy friends in the fashionable Belle Meade neighborhood complained that WSM preempted the broadcasts of Arturo Toscanini and the NBC symphony with the *Grand Ole Opry* on Saturday nights, Craig mollified them by arranging for the symphony to be carried on a smaller 1,000-watt signal that became the first commercial FM station in America.

ABOVE *In the depths of the Depression, WSM invested a quarter of a million dollars to erect a new 50,000-watt radio tower, the tallest of its kind in the nation. It extended the station's reach from coast to coast.*

And he grew even more convinced of his hillbilly show's appeal to rural and working-class listeners when his far-flung sales force reported a 30 percent increase in policies. *Someone* was listening—and liking the music they heard, whether it was on the *Grand Ole Opry* or *Rise and Shine*, an early-morning show that Hay also hosted, with many of the *Opry*'s hillbilly artists, timed around the schedules of working people.

TOP AND RIGHT *WSM offered an array of programs. Dinah Shore, a young Vanderbilt student, sang with Francis Craig's big band orchestra. But George Hay and his "good-natured riot" every week on the* Opry *presented a hillbilly image that Nashville's elite did not appreciate.*

During a golf outing to North Carolina, Craig hit a shot into a ravine, and when he went to retrieve the ball, a local string band was standing there, hoping he would put them on the air. Growing up in Olive Hill, Kentucky, country star Tom T. Hall remembered, he had his mother awaken him while it was still dark so he could listen to WSM's morning show with his father over an early breakfast: "They'd play country music until Belle Meade woke up, and then they'd go back to 'civilized' music."

ABOVE *WSM's Studio C, on the fifth floor of National Life's office building, hosted acts that ranged from orchestras, hillbillies (with George Hay, back right), religious singers (back left), and Jamup and Honey, a blackface comedy routine.*

OPPOSITE AND RIGHT *The search for a bigger venue led the Opry to the spacious Dixie Tabernacle in East Nashville, until neighbors complained about the crowds and traffic and then it moved again to the War Memorial Auditorium downtown. Even people in states far away from Tennessee were clamoring for tickets to the show.*

Crowds were now showing up at the weekly *Opry* broadcasts. In 1934, the company built a new studio on the fifth floor of the insurance building to hold the performers and several hundred people, and split the broadcast into two shows, at eight and ten o'clock. The result was mayhem—people jamming the stairs and elevators to get in, some hiding in closets and offices during the break to stay for the second show. The *Opry* had to move.

A theater on Belcourt Avenue, with seats for an audience of 750, became the *Opry*'s new home, but that soon turned out to be too small. In 1936, it moved to the Dixie Tabernacle in East Nashville, a barn-like structure with sawdust on the floor and wooden benches to accommodate three thousand people. About a quarter of them came from states other than Tennessee, and the overflow crowds, with their trucks and cars parked everywhere, quickly became a nuisance to the residents of the neighborhood. "It was no great surprise," the station manager said, "when a group of East Nashville citizens called on me one day and asked in

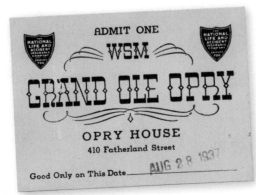

ADMIT ONE
WSM
GRAND OLE OPRY

OPRY HOUSE
410 Fatherland Street

Good Only on This Date ___ AUG 28 1937

grew in popularity, more highly trained artists joined the cast, expanding the quality—and the sound—of the music.

The Delmore Brothers—Alton and Rabon—combined precise guitar picking with tight, haunting vocal harmonies they had learned singing gospel music in northern Alabama. Technical improvements in microphones permitted their soft and sweet voices to hold their audiences spellbound.

Opry performers were paid only five dollars per broadcast, and they were required to be onstage every Saturday night. To keep the bigger stars, an artist bureau was instituted that booked them throughout the rest of the week within driving distance of Nashville. The Delmores were sent on the road with one of the show's original headliners and its only African American, DeFord Bailey, "the Harmonica Wizard." Traveling the segregated South, Bailey and the Delmores developed a close friendship. "They'd stick by me through thick and thin," Bailey said, including at restaurants that refused to serve a black man. "If you can't feed DeFord," the Delmores responded, "we can't eat here, either." "If the place wouldn't let me come in at all," Bailey added, "they'd drive down the road fifty miles or more to find another place that would."

In 1937, another professional act auditioned for the *Opry*. If Judge Hay hadn't been on an extended medical sabbatical, they probably would not have been hired. It was Pee Wee King and the Golden West Cowboys—totally unlike the hillbilly image and sound Hay had been developing for a decade.

Julius Frank Anthony Kuczynski had been born to a Polish-German family in Milwaukee and grew up playing polka music on his accordion in the Great Lakes region. He performed in a backup band on WLS for Gene Autry, changed his name to Pee Wee King and formed the Golden West Cowboys, then established himself at WNOX in Knoxville, developing his own brand of Western swing. Art Satherley had turned him down for a recording contract by telling him, "I believe what you have is salable, but I already have Bob Wills."

When he joined the *Grand Ole Opry*, King insisted that the local musicians' union, which previously had shunned *Opry* artists because most of them couldn't read music, accept his band as members. Soon, the entire show was unionized.

Upon his return from

a very nice way if we would take that bunch of musicians and get lost."

In 1939, the show moved again—back downtown, to the War Memorial Auditorium, where, for the first time, tickets were no longer free. Even with an admission price of twenty-five cents, the 2,200 seats were sold out every Saturday night.

In the early years, many of the *Opry*'s stars had been semiprofessionals, supporting themselves with regular jobs during the week. Even Uncle Dave Macon spent much of his time on his farm, plowing behind a mule. But as the show

---

ABOVE *When DeFord Bailey (seen here with Bill Westbrook of Bill Monroe's band) was denied a meal touring the Jim Crow South in between* Opry *broadcasts, his fellow musicians would keep driving until they found a restaurant that would serve him.*

RIGHT *Julius Frank Anthony Kuczynski, an accordion player from Milwaukee, was better known as Pee Wee King, who led the Golden West Cowboys to the stage of the* Opry.

his medical leave, Judge Hay was initially appalled at King's music and his band's cowboy clothes. Hay didn't like the accordion, and he objected when King introduced drums and an electric steel guitar to the *Opry* stage. But the band became one of the audience's favorite acts, and Hay ultimately admitted that King helped the show adjust to changing times. (King himself made a concession: conscious that he spoke in an unmistakable Northern accent, he had a band member from the South emcee his programs.)

Pee Wee King and the Golden West Cowboys may have broadened the music of the *Opry* far beyond the "old-time folk tunes of the Tennessee Hills," but in 1938 they were responsible for recruiting an artist who embodied it—and who would go on to personify the show for generations.

Roy Claxton Acuff was born on September 15, 1903, in Maynardville, Tennessee, about twenty-five miles north of Knoxville. His father, a part-time lawyer and Baptist minister, was a good country fiddler; his mother played piano

and guitar. Though he sang in church choirs and at his school's morning chapel services, Acuff seemed more interested in sports than music as a boy. He played football at Knoxville's Central High School and seemed destined to achieve his dream of playing professional baseball when the New York Yankees invited him to a summer training camp, until a near-fatal case of sunstroke ruined his chances. Recuperating at home, he listened to his father's record collection of Fiddlin' John Carson and Gid Tanner and the Skillet Lickers and took up the fiddle.

At age twenty-nine he spent a summer touring East Tennessee with a medicine show, providing music and comedy skits—sometimes in blackface—to draw crowds before the "doctor" sold them Mocoton Tonic, a cure-all that was 10 percent alcohol, and a remedy for corns so powerful, people allegedly could pour it on their boots and it numbed their

ABOVE RIGHT AND TOP *Young Roy Acuff had hoped for a career in sports, but found it instead in music. In 1938, Acuff's emotional and full-throated singing style (center) earned him a place on the* Grand Ole Opry *that he would keep for the rest of his life.*

feet. "I got a pretty good background in show business," Acuff said of the experience. "You sang to several thousand people in the open, and you couldn't get to them if you didn't put your lungs to the fullest test." He also learned to entertain audiences by imitating train whistles and doing tricks with a yo-yo.

By 1938, he and his own string band, the Crazy Tennesseans, were appearing on Knoxville radio shows, where Acuff learned to tone down his outdoor singing voice just enough, he said, so he didn't "blow the station off the air." It was there that Pee Wee King's manager encountered him and arranged for an on-air audition at the *Grand Ole Opry* on February 5.

TOP AND LEFT *Acuff soon became the Opry's headliner star—on the road and on the half-hour portion of the show carried nationally on the NBC radio network.*

Acuff was nervous at the start of the performance. His knees shook. A year earlier he had auditioned for the show, only to be told that he should find a better way to make a living. But this night, after a lilting dobro introduction, he launched into "The Great Speckled Bird," a religious song with lyrics based on a passage from the Book of Jeremiah and a melody taken from the Carter Family song "I'm Thinking Tonight of My Blue Eyes."

At the microphone that night, Acuff remembered his minstrel show days and *sold* the song to the audience, letting his voice resonate with emotion. This was not a typical string band with a singer; it was a singer with a string band. WSM officials were unsure about his performance—until a few days later, when their mail clerk asked, "What are we going to do about all these letters . . . about something to do with a bird?"

They swiftly signed Acuff for a regular spot on the *Opry*, as well as regular morning shows. With his band's name changed from the Crazy Tennesseans to the Smoky Mountain Boys, Acuff became the show's biggest star, beloved for his willingness to put everything into his songs. "I've cried onstage," he said, "not just for that audience, but . . . because I wanted to cry. Because it was hurting." Listening to him one night in Alabama, a young Hank Williams was struck by Acuff's palpable sincerity. "For drawing power in the South," Williams remembered, "it was Roy Acuff, then God."

"He's in a hillbilly string band, and in a hillbilly string band, there's no hierarchy," said Ketch Secor. "The fiddle plays all the time. The harmonica might play all the time. The jug might blow all the time. There's not even solos in hillbilly string band music. Nobody steps out. But the *Opry* was ready for a new era in which the star not only stood out, but he sold his own songbooks. He had his face on the record. Things were changing."

"While everybody else was donning cowboy hats and cowboy boots, and adopting cowboy monikers," Bill C. Malone said, "Acuff stuck to the old style and sang old-time songs that had been around, or at least sounded like they had been around, for generations."

In 1939, when the R. J. Reynolds Tobacco Company offered to sponsor a half-hour portion of the *Grand Ole Opry*, to be carried nationally over the NBC radio network, there was no question who would be the main attraction. It was Roy Acuff and the Smoky Mountain Boys.

THE BLUE GRASS BOYS

Bill Monroe is one of the most important musical figures that has ever walked through the gates of this town. When he arrived in Nashville, his sound was not yet fully formed. It was a vision in progress.

MARTY STUART

The 1930s witnessed an explosion of brother acts in hillbilly music. Besides the Delmore Brothers from northern Alabama, there was South Carolina's hard-charging Dixon Brothers, who worked by day in the textile mills of Darlington; and North Carolina's Callahan Brothers, who mixed blues with gospel. The Carlisle Brothers helped introduce the dobro steel guitar as a popular instrument; brothers Earl and Bill Bolick, performing as the Blue Sky Boys, preferred old-time ballads of death and sorrow like "Banks of the Ohio."

From Rosine, Kentucky, the Monroe Brothers had their own distinctive sound: Charlie on guitar and singing lead, with Bill providing high harmony while driving the beat with furious runs on his mandolin. In the mid-1930s, few other duos built a larger audience as they moved from radio stations in Indiana, Iowa, South Carolina, and North Carolina, making a string of hit records and playing at small venues in whatever region they happened to land.

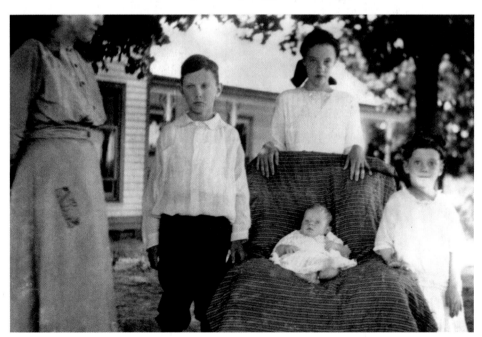

ABOVE *Young Bill Monroe (second from left) with family members in Rosine, Kentucky, shortly before his mother's death. His bad eye made him shy and lonely.*

Monroe's "Uncle Pen" Vandiver (top, left) encouraged his interest in music, and Arnold Shultz (above, with fiddle) furthered Monroe's musical training by introducing the blues. Bill and his brother Charlie (above, right, with guitar) had a successful duo career before their personal disputes drove them apart.

Of the two, Bill Monroe was the more unlikely to become a public performer. The youngest of eight children, he had been born on September 13, 1911, with a crooked eye, which made him the butt of constant teasing and turned him into such a shy boy that he would hide in the barn when he heard hoofbeats and the creaking of a wagon approaching the family farm.

His life became even lonelier at age ten when his mother died. Bill sought solace walking in the woods and, where no one else could hear him, singing the songs she had taught him. Her brother, Pendleton Vandiver—"Uncle Pen"—an accomplished fiddler, took the boy under his wing, bringing him along to local square dances and eventually letting him play backup on the guitar. Monroe also made friends with Arnold Shultz, a gifted African-American guitarist and fiddler, who inculcated the boy with an appreciation for the blues.

After the fifth grade, Monroe quit school to help support the family, something that became even more important when his father died in 1928. "You've got to realize that Bill Monroe came up during the Depression," said musician Ricky Skaggs, who later became an acolyte and friend of Monroe's. "He knew what it was like to work hard all day long. He used to tell me about cutting timber, himself, falling these trees, himself, rolling them down the hill, himself, onto a wagon, and taking them into town. And he said, 'You know when I'd get in close to town, Rosine, I'd stand up where everybody could see me, 'cause I'd really worked hard.' And that was his identity."

By the early 1930s, he had grown into a strapping young man, his bad eye had been corrected, and like so many other rural Southerners seeking employment in the Depression, he had moved to the industrial centers of the North, joining Charlie and an older brother working for the Sinclair Oil Company near Chicago.

They earned some extra money as square dancers for *National Barn Dance* shows at the 1933 Chicago World's Fair and performed occasionally as a trio on stations in Hammond and Gary, Indiana, before Charlie and Bill set out on a successful career as a duo. They were doing well in 1938, based at Raleigh's WPTF. Their song "What Would You Give in Exchange for Your Soul," one of sixty sides they had recorded on the Bluebird label, was their top hit.

But both Monroe brothers were stubborn and competitive—Bill was especially prickly—and they argued constantly about the direction of their music. One day, Charlie abruptly pulled out of town, formed his own band, the Kentucky Pardners, and landed a spot on WWVA's popular *Wheeling Jamboree* in West Virginia.

Bill responded by gathering three other artists into Bill Monroe and His Blue Grass Boys, named in honor of his home state of Kentucky. With them he began experimenting with a new sound: songs played in higher keys, for what he called a

BELOW *Bill Monroe (second from left, with his mandolin) and his Blue Grass Boys onstage at the* Opry

"high, lonesome sound," tinged with some blues influences. He was based at WFBC in Greenville, South Carolina.

In 1939, both brothers set their sights on Nashville and the *Grand Ole Opry*, which was now rivaling WLS's *National Barn Dance* as the premier showcase for hillbilly music. They each wanted to be part of it. Bill got to Nashville first and was given a guest slot on the October 28 broadcast.

When they walked onstage that night, the Blue Grass Boys didn't look like any of the other *Opry* acts. Bill detested the way Judge Hay had performers costumed like country rubes and instead dressed himself and his band members in high-top boots and riding pants, crisp shirts and Stetson hats. As they broke into their own propulsive reinterpretation of Jimmie Rodgers's famous song "Mule Skinner Blues," adding an infectious laugh to Rodgers's trademark yodel, it became immediately clear that they didn't sound like any of the other acts, either.

"Our music was pitched up at least two or three changes higher than anyone had ever sung it at the *Opry*," Monroe recalled later. "Those people couldn't even think as fast as we played," said his guitarist Cleo Davis. "There was nobody living who had ever played with the speed that we had."

Marty Stuart said one reviewer was "indignant that they would do such a thing to a sacred Jimmie Rodgers song,

singing it in the voice of a woman, playing blistering, hot rhythms." But the audience brought the Blue Grass Boys back for three encores. "If you ever leave," Judge Hay told Monroe, "you'll have to fire yourself."

In his dressing room at WWVA, Charlie Monroe had tuned in to the broadcast when he heard his brother singing. "He won't last on the *Opry*," Charlie scoffed. "Wait 'til people find out how difficult he is to get along with."

GRINDER'S SWITCH

As the music heard on hillbilly shows broadened and evolved during the 1930s, one thing that didn't change was the presence of comedy routines, a feature that stretched back to the days of vaudeville and traveling minstrel shows. It was an expected part of every performance, as common as including gospel hymns sung by the entire cast, with the audience invited to join in.

Uncle Dave Macon, as much a flamboyant comedian as banjo picker, made fun of his own weakness for drink, saying how his brakes gave out at the top of a steep mountain hill and he vowed if he survived the descent he would give up liquor forever. When he reached the bottom, he said, he pulled out his flask for a quick shot just to steady his nerves.

In the middle of songs, Roy Acuff often hammed it up by balancing his fiddle bow—and sometimes the fiddle itself—on his nose while the other band members performed instrumental breaks.

David Akeman was a skilled banjo player, part of Bill Monroe's Blue Grass Boys, before going on to a long career as a star in his own right—as Stringbean, dressed in a loud shirt and pants pulled down to his knees to make him look like an extremely tall hayseed.

On WLS, Pat Buttram did comedy routines for the *National Barn Dance*, then moved to Hollywood to become Gene Autry's laughable sidekick in singing cowboy movies. And the zany novelty group, the Hoosier Hot Shots, combined vaudeville and hillbilly music with songs like "When There's Tears in the Eyes of a Potato" and "From the Indies to the Andes in His Undies."

Blackface comedy, caricaturing African-American stereo-

LEFT *Roy Acuff liked to entertain audiences by balancing his fiddle on his nose. He also did tricks with a yo-yo.*

types, persisted long after minstrelsy, and not just on hillbilly shows. *Amos 'n' Andy,* created by two white actors, was one of the most popular nightly radio shows in the nation. At WSM, Judge Hay launched his own weekly minstrel show, with the blackface stars Lasses and Honey, which later became Jamup and Honey.

But the most improbable—and enduring—comedy star of the *Grand Ole Opry* was a college-educated aspiring actress from a prosperous Tennessee family who joined the cast in 1940. Her real name was Sarah Ophelia Colley. Her fans would know her as Minnie Pearl.

She was born on October 25, 1912, in Centerville, sixty miles southwest of Nashville, and nothing in Sarah Colley's upbringing seemed destined to produce the character she became on the *Opry* stage. Her father owned a lumberyard and a sawmill, and the home he provided for his family had one of the town's best libraries, its finest carriage, and one of its first automobiles.

As a young girl, she became sensitive that she wasn't as pretty as her friends—a "plain little thing," she remembered being called by her mother's social acquaintances—but she excelled in elocution and became determined to be a great actress. She enrolled at the exclusive Ward-Belmont School, the most fashionable finishing school for young women in

the state, located in a former plantation mansion in Nashville, where she studied Shakespeare and earned the leading role in *Taming of the Shrew,* as Petruchio.

After graduating in 1932, Colley landed a job with the Wayne P. Sewell Production Company in Atlanta, which helped rural towns in the South stage plays and variety shows with homegrown talent. For six years, making $10 a week, she traveled from one tiny hamlet to another, where she boarded with local families, recruited advertising from the businesses, distributed the company's costumes and stage sets, and directed the amateur casts before moving on to the next town ten days later for yet another production.

One cold winter night in January 1936, she arrived in a little village near Sand Mountain in northern Alabama, fifteen

TOP, LEFT *David "Stringbean" Akeman was as much a comedian as a banjo player.*

TOP, RIGHT *With clothes purchased at a secondhand store and stories that poked fun at herself, Sarah Colley became Minnie Pearl.*

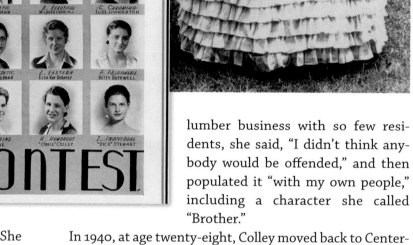

miles from the nearest railroad in Cullman. She boarded with a poor family in a log cabin, presided over by a woman in her seventies whose youngest of sixteen children, the same age as Colley, was simply called "Brother."

"When I left," Colley later remembered, "the old lady paid me the highest possible compliment. She said, 'Lord 'a' mercy, child, I hate to see you go. You're just like one of us.'"

She had been collecting stories and anecdotes as she traveled, slowly developing an alter ego she sometimes portrayed for friends. Colley named the character Minnie Pearl and outfitted her with clothes she purchased for less than $10 at a secondhand store: a pair of simple black shoes with low heels and one strap; white stockings; a plain, round-collared dress; and a cheap straw hat, topped with some dime-store flowers.

While many hillbilly comics painted on freckles and blackened some of their teeth, Colley didn't see her Minnie Pearl that way. "I never intended her to be a caricature," she said. "I dressed her as I thought a young country girl would dress to go to meetin' on Sunday or to come to town on Saturday afternoon to do a little [shopping] and a little flirting."

She created a hometown for her character: tiny Grinder's Switch, named after a railroad juncture used by her father's

lumber business with so few residents, she said, "I didn't think anybody would be offended," and then populated it "with my own people," including a character she called "Brother."

In 1940, at age twenty-eight, Colley moved back to Centerville, making $50 a month giving private drama lessons and overseeing an afternoon recreation program for schoolchildren funded by the Works Progress Administration, one of President Roosevelt's New Deal programs. After performing a Minnie Pearl sketch for the town's Rotary Club, she got a call from WSM's general manager, inviting her to audition for the *Grand Ole Opry*. She wasn't sure about it. She preferred pop music at the time and had never attended one of the shows. Knowing her genteel background, a few station offi-

---

Sarah Ophelia Colley (top, left, with her mother) came from a prosperous, sophisticated Tennessee family and attended the fashionable Ward-Belmont School in Nashville (top, right). Her mother's friends had called her a "plain little thing," but as her school yearbook shows (above, center) her friends loved her for her sense of humor.

one feller told me I was the homeliest girl he'd ever seen." She said another "feller just now told me I looked like a breath of spring. Well, he didn't use them words, exactly. He said I looked like the end of a hard winter."

cials were reluctant, too—"afraid," she said, that "the *Opry* audiences would find that out and suspect I was a phony [and] would think I was putting down country people."

But in November 1940, just before she went on the air for the first time, Judge Hay thought she looked scared and gave her what she later called "the very best advice any performer can get." "Just love them, honey," he said, "and they'll love you right back."

She greeted the audience with a big "Howwww-deeee!" and they gave her one back. Then she reported some news from Grinder's Switch and talked about Brother. And, as she would for the rest of her career, she poked most of her fun at herself. "I felt so at home when I got here," she said. "In fact,

The audience ate it up. That first performance generated hundreds of pieces of fan mail from people, she said, who "really felt they knew me, and they considered me a friend." Sarah Ophelia Colley answered them all as Minnie Pearl.

As Minnie Pearl (top, left), Colley was nervous before going onstage at the Opry *in 1940. "Just love them, honey," Judge Hay advised her, "and they'll love you right back." She was soon a popular fixture on the show, telling made-up stories from the fictional town of Grinder's Switch (above, left) and publishing her own newspaper (above, right), which fans bought for 25 cents.*

Much of what country music became in the 1940s was sort of developed by Gene Autry back in the 1930s. It didn't matter what kind of song they were singing, whether it was a folk song, a pop song, a country song, a yodel, they all had fringe and hats. Whether you were singing mountain songs in Pennsylvania, or Virginia, or you were playing Western swing in Texas, everybody wanted to dress up and look like glamorous cowboys.

DOUGLAS B. GREEN

By 1940, Gene Autry had long since settled his dispute with Republic Pictures and triumphantly returned to the silver screen, making $10,000 for every movie they cranked out and quickly eclipsing all the other singing cowboys who had followed his lead, including Roy Rogers.

Autry hosted his own radio show, *Melody Ranch*, sponsored by Doublemint Gum on the CBS network. He was receiving twenty thousand fan letters a week. Merchandisers paid him handsomely to put his name on cap pistols, cowboy boots,

lunch boxes, and bicycles. That year, with the Great Depression stubbornly hanging on, he earned $205,000.

In Washington, D.C., Autry was invited to attend a birthday party for President Roosevelt and presented him with a white Stetson cowboy hat. "They're good throwing hats too, Mr. President, in case you choose to throw one into the ring," he told FDR, who had not yet announced whether he would seek an unprecedented third term.

For an appearance at the Madison Square Garden rodeo in New York City, Autry paid the airline TWA $3,400 to fly his horse Champion across the country; they ripped out passen-

After returning to Republic Pictures, Gene Autry was a bigger star than ever, getting fan mail directed to his CBS radio show, Melody Ranch (above, left), taking Champion with him on airplane rides to the East Coast (left), and appearing in Washington, D.C. (above, right), to help President Roosevelt celebrate a birthday.

ger seats and put in a horse stall. Impressed by the response to his New York appearance, other rodeo producers signed him to appear in eight other rodeos for $100,000. During a tour of the British Isles, enthusiastic crowds greeted him in London, where he rode Champion into the swank Savoy Hotel. In Dublin, 300,000 people turned out to greet him.

But one of his biggest thrills occurred back home in Oklahoma, in the tiny town of Berwyn, population 227, after the release of his fiftieth movie. Autry had decided he could make even more money by producing his own rodeos, rather than appearing in someone else's, and had purchased a big ranch nearby, which he named the Flying A. Construction had started on the barns and fences, and the range was being stocked with horses and cattle.

On November 16, 1941, with the state's governor acting as emcee, and some 35,000 people overwhelming the small town, *Melody Ranch* was broadcast live from Berwyn, as it officially changed its name to Gene Autry, Oklahoma.

• • •

In the fall of 1940, the American Society of Composers, Authors, and Publishers (ASCAP), the organization responsible for collecting royalties for music played on radio shows and in movies, had suddenly announced that it was doubling the rate it charged radio stations across the country. Eighty-three percent of the tunes played on network radio were ASCAP songs.

Edwin Craig of WSM and his fellow board members at the National Association of Broadcasters saw the demand as a dire threat to their profits. They created their own competing group, Broadcast Music Incorporated—BMI.

Ralph Peer, the man who had helped popularize race and

ABOVE *In 1941, 35,000 people turned out as the tiny town of Berwyn, population 227, officially changed its name to Gene Autry, Oklahoma.*

hillbilly music, sensed an opportunity to provide that music with even greater exposure. Dominated as it was by New York publishers and Tin Pan Alley songwriters, ASCAP had shunned most old-time and black music in favor of pop and more mainstream songs. Peer now gave BMI a big boost by assigning to it much of his existing catalog of blues, Latin, and hillbilly songs, including the music of Jimmie Rodgers and the Carter Family. Other small publishers and other songwriters that ASCAP had ignored did the same thing.

On January 1, 1941, the broadcasters declared a ban on all ASCAP songs being played over the air and switched to BMI. Suddenly, even more Americans began hearing hillbilly music on their radios. "New composers," Peer told reporters, "are being given their first chance."

BMI's biggest hit was by a singer from Louisiana named Jimmie Davis, who had started out as one of the many imitators of Jimmie Rodgers and moved on to record a string of risqué, double entendre numbers like "Tom Cat and Pussy Blues" and "Do-Do-Daddling Thing" in the 1930s, before adopting the persona of a singing cowboy.

Though he may not have actually cowritten it, he copyrighted the bouncy "You Are My Sunshine" through BMI, and his version was quickly covered by Gene Autry, Bing Crosby, and Lawrence Welk, crossing over into pop music to become that year's recording sensation. Three years later, Davis would ride the song's popularity to win the governorship of Louisiana.

The New York Times reported that the sale of sheet music of BMI tunes was now "far ahead" of ASCAP music in the nation, and, it concluded, "Radio has demonstrated for five weeks that there still can be music without ASCAP." Within ten months, ASCAP reached a truce with the broadcasters. But by then, BMI had firmly established itself with more than 36,000 copyrights from fifty-two publishers. Tin Pan Alley's near monopoly on songwriting had been broken.

A year later, Roy Acuff launched a music publishing busi-

TOP *With the skilled songwriter Fred Rose, left, Roy Acuff opened a publishing business in Nashville, which would help the city develop as a business center for country music.*

ABOVE *In 1941, Jimmie Davis's "You Are My Sunshine" was the biggest hit for BMI, the upstart organization representing songwriters and publishers. Davis would ride the song's success into the Louisiana governor's office.*

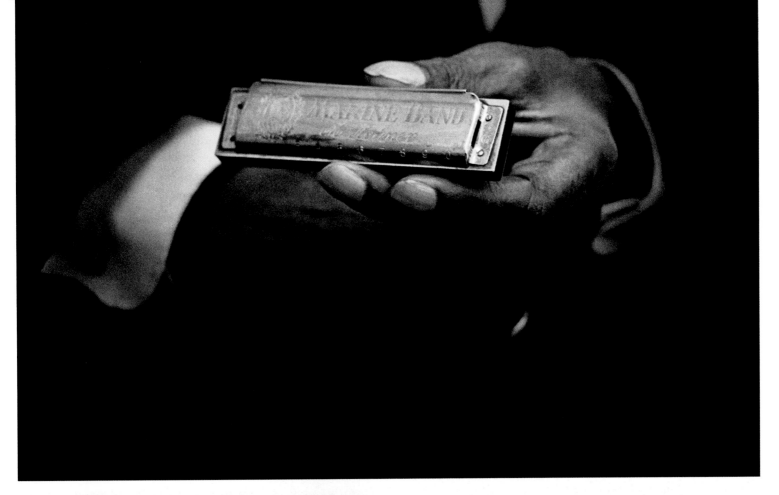

ness in Nashville with Fred Rose, a skilled songsmith who had composed many of Gene Autry's hits. Rose himself had switched from ASCAP to BMI, and the new Nashville company, Acuff-Rose, was soon delivering more hits—performed by Acuff, Bob Wills, and many others. Nashville's importance in the business of American music was growing.

But one casualty of the broadcasting war with ASCAP was DeFord Bailey, who had been a regular on the *Grand Ole Opry* from the beginning.

During the 1941 boycott, WSM's managers fired Bailey without any public explanation. Judge Hay would later say it was because Bailey wouldn't learn any non-ASCAP songs. "Like some members of his race and other races," Hay wrote, "DeFord was lazy."

Bailey disputed that. Over the years, he had sometimes complained to the show's management about his pay, saying he had been treated like a "civilized slave." He was forty-two years old, with a wife and three young children, when the *Opry* unceremoniously dropped him.

TOP AND LEFT *Though he had been an Opry star from its earliest days, in 1941 DeFord Bailey, the Harmonica Wizard, was unceremoniously dropped from the show. Twenty-four years later, on the show's fortieth anniversary, he would be invited back to perform.*

"DeFord could play," Wynton Marsalis said about the Harmonica Wizard, but while "the gene pool cries out for diversity, tribal tradition cries out for sameness. America, we're caught in between those two things. So our music has ended up being segregated—and that's not what the origins of the music would lead you to believe would be its trajectory."

"They turned me loose," Bailey said, "to root hog or die. They didn't give a hoot which way I went." He set up a successful shoeshine parlor in the back room of his home, and then expanded it to a thriving storefront in downtown Nashville. In 1965, on the fortieth anniversary of the *Grand Ole Opry*, he would finally be invited back to its stage.

SMOKE ON THE WATER

By the spring of 1941, the Carter Family's *Good Neighbor Get-Together*, now in its third season, was more popular than ever—not only being broadcast over Dr. John Brinkley's high-powered XERA, across the Rio Grande from Del Rio, Texas, but recorded on transcription discs and provided to a string of other "border blaster" stations along the Mexican border.

A. P. and Sara Carter had been divorced for two years, but the public was unaware of the split—and the family image was actually burnished by the inclusion of their teenage daughter, Janette, as well as Maybelle's three young girls, Helen, June, and Anita, who performed regularly on the show.

Then, a new treaty between the United States and Mexico closed XERA. Beset by lawsuits for fraud over his medical operations and hounded for unpaid federal taxes, Brinkley declared bankruptcy and would die, penniless, a year later. But the massive radio exposure provided by the "border blasters" had revived sales of Carter Family records. In October, RCA Victor called them to New York City for another studio session to generate more material to meet the rising demand.

Among the thirteen sides they recorded were some hymns Sara had learned at revival meetings in California, where she now lived with her new husband, and four written by Maybelle, including "Why Do You Cry, Little Darling," a plaintive song about a girl pining for her sweetheart who has been called away into the Army. With war already engulfing Europe and Asia, the nation's first peacetime draft had been instituted in the United States. Maybelle's song captured the worries and prayers of millions of Americans that they, too, would be drawn into the conflict.

In November, the Carter Family seemed poised for even greater national recognition. *Life* magazine was preparing a cover story about the increasing popularity of hillbilly music and planned to focus on the Carters as the prime example of how a genre once denigrated—or, at best, ignored—by the mainstream press had nonetheless prospered among everyday people during the Great Depression.

A photographer arrived in Maces Spring, and the whole family gathered for an extensive shoot. June Carter, age twelve, was so excited she saved all the burned flashbulbs as souvenirs of the event that was sure to make them all famous.

But the story never ran. *Life* magazine pulled it at the last moment, to make room for bigger news. On December 7, 1941, Japanese planes bombed Pearl Harbor, and the United States found itself at war with the Axis powers: Japan, Italy, and Germany.

As the nation mobilized its young men to enter World War Two, Maybelle's song now held even greater meaning to the women she sang for: "Every night I'll kneel by my bedside, and ask God to guide you each day, back to your sweetheart that's waiting and loves you more than I can say."

The day after Pearl Harbor, Tommy Duncan walked into radio station KVOO to tell Bob Wills and the other Texas Playboys, "I don't know about you guys, but I'm going to join 'this man's army' and fight those sons of bitches." Wills, age thirty-six, decided he would enlist, too, as did his steel guitar player Leon McAuliffe.

In Chicago, nearly fifty members of the *National Barn Dance* joined the service, including young George Gobel, who served as a flight instructor at a base in Oklahoma. It was stateside duty, he said later, but "there was not one Japanese aircraft that got past Tulsa." In California, members of the Sons of the Pioneers and the Maddox Brothers signed up, too.

Hawkshaw Hawkins, a young hillbilly singer from Huntington, West Virginia, interrupted his fledgling career to become a staff sergeant, ultimately stationed in France, where he fought in the Battle of the Bulge and earned four battle stars during fifteen months of combat.

The Delmore Brothers had formed a new quartet, the Brown's Ferry Four, which had to split up because three of

RIGHT *The entire Carter Family gathered for a* Life *magazine photo shoot at Maces Spring in November 1941. They expected it to make them even more famous, but world events intervened.*

Virtually every star now added songs reflecting the experiences and emotions of the war. "Smoke on the Water," released by Bob Wills and other artists, promised revenge against Japan and Adolf Hitler. Tex Ritter recorded "There's a Gold Star in Her Window," about a mother who had lost her son. Patsy Montana did "I'll Wait for You," offering a young woman's promise to her boyfriend, while Autry had a hit with "At Mail Call Today," a song he cowrote with Fred Rose about a serviceman overseas receiving a "Dear John" letter from the girl he loved back home.

Elton Britt had one of the biggest hits with his patriotic ballad "There's a Star-Spangled Banner Waving Somewhere," telling the story of a backwoods boy, disabled by a twisted leg, who nevertheless yearns to fight for his country. In 1942, it sold more than a million records and 750,000 copies of sheet music—and brought Britt an invitation to sing it for President Roosevelt in the White House.

• • •

them went off to war. Alton Delmore joined the Navy, Merle Travis became a Marine, and Grandpa Jones went into the Army.

Gene Autry told reporters, "I think the He-men in the movies [and] every movie cowboy ought to devote time . . . helping to win, until the war is over— the same as any other American citizen." To prove it, he was sworn into the Army Air Corps during a live broadcast of *Melody Ranch*. His income had risen to $600,000 in 1941; he traded that in for a sergeant's salary.

For a while, he continued his regular radio show, renamed *The Sergeant Gene Autry Show*, until he completed his flight training, earned his wings, and ended up copiloting a C-109 cargo plane on the dangerous flights over the Himalayas from India to China.

TOP AND RIGHT *Maybelle, A.P., and Sara pose for the* Life *photographer, as do Maybelle's daughters (from left) Anita, June, and Helen. June saved the spent flashbulbs as souvenirs of the event.*

ABOVE, LEFT *Henry and Don Maddox traded in their extravagant performance clothes after enlisting in the Army, but did not lose their sense of humor.*

ABOVE, RIGHT *Hawkshaw Hawkins of West Virginia was beginning his career as a hillbilly singer when the U.S. entered the world war. He would earn four battle stars in combat in Europe.*

LEFT *Gene Autry joined the Army Air Corps and became a copilot for cargo planes flying over the Himalayas from India to China.*

With men from every region of the country now thrown together on military bases across the States and overseas, the war introduced hillbilly music to millions of them who had never heard it before. "Servicemen from the North and from the West heard their buddies from the South singing the music in the barracks and on the troop ships," according to music historian Bill C. Malone. "People were leaving the farm, leaving rural life, moving into town, getting new jobs. A lot of people were moving into defense work. And so, the music moved as the people moved. World War Two nationalized country music."

Just like many better-known pop and jazz bands, Pee Wee King and the Golden West Cowboys toured Army camps, airfields, and hospitals with the Camel Caravan, sponsored by the R. J. Reynolds Tobacco Company, doing three shows a day for nineteen months and covering more than 75,000 miles across thirty-two states. Minnie Pearl went along to provide some humor to the homesick soldiers—and to chaperone the young "Camelette" girls who danced in frilled uniforms and handed out free cigarettes. Mentioning all the military police who guarded the gates, Minnie told the troops how personally touched she was that they all wore her initials—"M.P."—on their sleeves.

Polly Jenkins and Her Pals, a novelty act that incorporated cowbells and a xylophone that resembled a wheelbarrow into their music, performed at more than nine hundred USO shows in all forty-eight states. In 1944 she took out an ad in *Billboard* magazine saying she was "now booking dates to follow Hitler's funeral."

At a special outdoor event, Bob Wills and Bing Crosby got

ABOVE *During the war, Roy Acuff (second from left, top) and Bill Monroe (second from right) autographed bombs during a bond drive.*

ABOVE LEFT *WLS remembered the soldiers overseas in its 1944* Family Album.

together to record a duet version of "New San Antonio Rose," the song they had both made into hits, offering one single copy as a collector's item to whomever bought the most war bonds. The record went for $250,000.

In their barracks and field camps, soldiers got to know the latest hillbilly stars when the Armed Forces Radio Service added the *Grand Ole Opry* and *National Barn Dance* to its regular rotation of broadcasts. One poll it conducted in Germany found Roy Acuff to be more popular than Frank Sinatra. In the South Pacific, war correspondent Ernie Pyle reported that during the battle of Okinawa, Japanese soldiers charging the American position shouted, "To hell with Roosevelt! To hell with Babe Ruth! To hell with Roy Acuff!"

Hillbilly music was advancing on the home front, too, where the war effort had ended the Depression. Six hundred radio stations now featured it coast to coast. Under the headline "Bull Market in Corn," *Time* magazine proclaimed, "The dominant popular music of the U.S. today is hillbilly."

While some national publications didn't quite know what to make of the phenomenon, others were equally unsure about how to define—or what to call—the music itself. In 1941, *Billboard* launched its first regular column covering the genre under the title "Hillbilly & Foreign Record Hits of the Month." A year later, the column appeared under the name "Western and Race," which was changed in less than a month to "Western, Race and Polkas"—and then quickly changed again, to "American Folk Records: Cowboy Songs, Hillbilly Tunes, Spirituals, Etc."

On January 8, 1944, still under the broad category of "Folk Records," the music was popular enough that *Billboard* made its first attempt to rank individual record sales, based on reports of how many times they were played on jukeboxes throughout the nation. Al Dexter's hit song "Pistol Packin' Mama" was at the top, bolstered by a cover version sung by Bing Crosby and the Andrews Sisters.

ABOVE *As part of the Camel Caravan, Minnie Pearl toured military bases and hospitals in thirty-two states and entertained soldiers with her jokes.*

If the name of the music was in flux, *Billboard* had no question about its trajectory. "When the war is over," the trade magazine predicted, "it will be the field to watch."

After the Japanese formally surrendered on September 2, 1945, ending World War Two, Gene Autry happily returned to civilian life and started making movies again. But things had changed during his absence. Roy Rogers, who had received a deferment, had risen to the title of "King of the Cowboys," a role he would continue to play in the new medium of television. John Wayne, who had also received a deferment, was now Republic Pictures' biggest star, making Westerns without any music.

"The singing cowboy era, like all eras, like all fads, like all trends, has an arc and comes to an end, and I think World War Two sort of accelerated that," said Douglas B. Green. "I think World War Two changed the way we looked at movies.

ABOVE *Bing Crosby and Bob Wills recorded a duet of "New San Antonio Rose" at a war bonds rally and offered the single copy to the person who bought the most bonds. The winner paid $250,000.*

Gradually, 'Adult Westerns' came in. They were just much more serious; they weren't sunny and optimistic like the singing cowboy movies were."

The war had taught Autry a financial lesson. "I'll never again let myself get into a position where I'm depending on a salary alone which might be cut off by something like this," he said.

Autry remained a major celebrity, and the public still eagerly bought his records, but they shifted more toward pop music than cowboy tunes, and he began steadily building a business empire that would include radio and television stations, real estate, and a publishing company that increased his profits from new songs—like "Here Comes Santa Claus."

"Working with numbers was what I did best," he said later. "What I did less well was sing, act, and play guitar."

Ultimately, he would own a major-league baseball team, and by the time he died in 1998, he would be one of the four hundred richest people in America—and the only entertainer on the list.

Bob Wills's time in the service had been brief. The Army discharged him in 1943; he was older than most soldiers, out of shape, and his drinking led to discipline problems. He headed for California, where his shows outsold those of Tommy Dorsey and Benny Goodman. During the last years of the war, he was bigger than ever. The Venice Pier Ballroom became the Los Angeles County Barn Dance, where bands played all night to crowds of five thousand. It was double that when big stars like Bob Wills showed up—such a throng that the show's producers worried the pier might collapse. Soon, a circuit of dance halls stretched from Southern California through the Central Valley to the Bay Area.

One of Wills's youngest Central Valley fans was a ten-year-old in Bakersfield named Merle Haggard:

I heard on the radio that he was going to be at a place called the Beardsley Ballroom. I waited till Mama got in bed and give her time to go to sleep. And I got on my bicycle and rode over, it must be about five miles, and I went around to the back of the old dance hall and I stood on my bicycle seat and I could see in there.

And I could see Bob. I seen them all onstage. Tommy (Duncan) was singing. Bob had his fiddle and they all had on white shirts, cowboy hats, and dressed fit to kill.

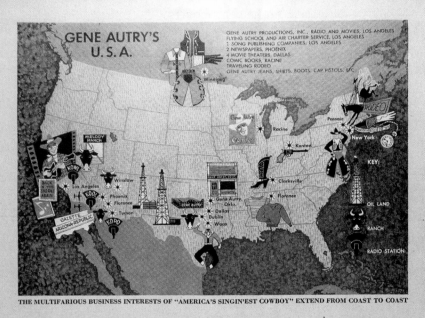

THE MULTIFARIOUS BUSINESS INTERESTS OF "AMERICA'S SINGIN'EST COWBOY" EXTEND FROM COAST TO COAST

GENE AUTRY, INC.

The business-minded star of singing Westerns has parlayed a horse, a guitar and an agreeable voice into a multimillion-dollar empire

And they had these GI haircuts and they were sharp on the stage.

And it was an intriguing moment for me. It didn't last very long. I got down off my bike and went home and went to bed before Mama knew I was gone.

Following the war, as Wills embarked on cross-country tours, his increased drunkenness sometimes impeded the perfection of a performance; he became ashamed and would cut the price his contract required. Some unscrupulous promoters began getting him drunk *after* the show, so he would return a portion of the gate receipts.

The "big band" era was fading, too—from 75 percent of record sales during the mid-1930s through the war, to just 25 percent in 1948—although Western swing, the sound Wills had helped invent, remained popular in the Southwest. Willie Nelson was now a teenager and was trying his hand as a young promoter who hired Bob Wills to play in Whitney, Texas: "I hauled a piano on the back of a pickup, so that his band could have a piano. I managed to take in enough money and pay him. And I got up to sing with Bob Wills, so it was as good as it gets."

After the war, with the singing cowboy craze beginning to fade, Gene Autry (above, with his wife, Ina, at their home) began building a diverse and hugely profitable business empire that included real estate, radio and television stations (top, left), and a music publishing company that released huge hits like "Here Comes Santa Claus" (top, right).

The war years brought other changes for the future of the genre most people still called "hillbilly music."

With the closing of the Mexican "border buster" stations, the Carter Family had tried to reestablish themselves at WBT in Charlotte, North Carolina, where they performed with the Johnson Family Singers. But after one season, Sara decided she had had enough. She yearned for a stable, domestic life with her new husband, Coy Bays, who had a steady job in California's Stockton shipyards.

In March 1943, the original Carter Family permanently disbanded. They did it without any formal announcement or special concert or radio broadcast. Sara went to California

Bob Wills (top, performing on his ABC radio show in California) became more popular than ever in the mid-1940s, until the "big band" era also started to wane. His Western swing music remained popular back in the region where it was born, though he now played in smaller venues in places like Coffeyville, Kansas (left).

and settled with Coy on a ten-acre cherry orchard they had purchased. A.P. moved back to the home-place in Poor Valley.

But Maybelle and her three girls—Helen, June, and Anita—still wanted a career in music. Maybelle's husband, Eck, served as their manager.

Billed as "the Carter Sisters and Mother Maybelle," they landed a job singing at a small Richmond, Virginia, station, and performed during the week at county courthouses, school gymnasiums, even on the top of concession stands at drive-in theaters.

Helen struggled with the accordion—until Pee Wee King informed her that she was holding it upside down. Anita was given a bass fiddle that was bigger than she was; sometimes she stood on a stool to play it. June, self-conscious that her singing voice was not as good as her sisters', became the act's comedienne, and at first slavishly patterned herself after Minnie Pearl—until Minnie saw her in action and told Maybelle, "This child is too good to go into a career doing imitations of someone else. She ought to be encouraged to get up her own act."

By 1946 they had moved to Richmond's biggest station, WRVA, performing every Saturday night on the *Old Dominion Barn Dance*, but dreaming,

as every hillbilly act now did, of someday making it to Nashville and WSM's *Grand Ole Opry*, something the original Carter Family had never done. Thanks to its infusion of stars—Roy Acuff, Pee Wee King, Bill Monroe, and Minnie Pearl—the *Opry* had now eclipsed WLS's *National Barn Dance* to become the undisputed premiere show of its kind in the nation.

And now, the *Opry* had a new home. In 1943, it had moved to a location just off Broadway, on Fifth Avenue: an imposing brick tabernacle built in 1892 by Thomas Ryman, a wayward riverboat magnate who had undergone a religious conversion and wanted a place he called "purely an outpost to catch sinners."

When the original Carter Family disbanded, Maybelle and her daughters formed their own act and performed on radio stations in Richmond, Virginia, like WRNL (above), before moving to the bigger WRVA. (From left, Anita with the bass fiddle, June on autoharp, Maybelle with guitar, and Helen on accordion.) June worried that her singing voice wasn't as good as her sisters', so she adopted a comic persona, "Aunt Polly Carter" (left), modeled after Sarah Colley's Minnie Pearl.

It seated more than three thousand people with long pews on the floor, and a spacious balcony, the Confederate Gallery, built to accommodate a reunion of Southern soldiers. For years, it had hosted more than church services: symphonies, ballets, theater, and the Fisk Jubilee Singers, an African-American gospel choir, were all featured. Enrico Caruso and Marian Anderson had performed there. President Theodore Roosevelt and Booker T. Washington had spoken from its podium.

Its acoustics were unmatched—"like being inside an old violin, surrounded by good seasoned wood," Pee Wee King said when the *Opry* moved in. With the war over, new stars were already rising on the Ryman Auditorium's stage, and in the late 1940s and '50s they would cement the *Opry*'s place as the preeminent venue in country music, where its artists would continue to push the music in every direction.

In 1943, the Grand Ole Opry moved to a new home on Fifth Avenue in Nashville. The Ryman Auditorium had been built as a tabernacle in 1892, with wooden pews on the ground floor and the Confederate Gallery above them. Performers and audiences appreciated the building's excellent acoustics.

3

THE HILLBILLY SHAKESPEARE

After the war, everybody came home supercharged. One of the things that went with that was an electricity and a bit of an energy that called for something besides fiddle tunes.

All of a sudden, it was about stomping and dancing, and that called for drums and that called for twanging guitars and a steel guitar that would cut through and get above the noise of the crowd and the fights. It always gets louder at a honky tonk and more rambunctious as you move toward midnight.

The edge moves closer to you, so you need an edgy sound that cuts through that. And electricity was your friend.

MARTY STUART

Hank Williams, "the Hillbilly Shakespeare," broadcasts on WSM.

WITH THE END OF WORLD WAR TWO, the cultural landscape of America began changing faster than ever. The soldiers returning home had not only experienced battle, but they had also come to know the societies of Europe and the Pacific; they came back to seek jobs more likely to be found in cities than on farms. More American women had now experienced life outside the domestic confines of home, working in wartime factories.

Change was taking place everywhere: in science, in the economy, in race relations, in art, in literature. Some older customs now seemed outdated, no longer suited to the modern world. The rapid changes brought new tensions, as well. In 1946, 600,000 marriages ended in divorce, a record number.

Country music, as it always had, adapted to the times. Songs that dealt openly with cheating and drinking—topics once considered beyond the pale of respectability—became as popular as songs with more traditional themes like Mother or a sentimental longing for home. The new songs had a new sound: a piercing electric guitar, a driving drum beat, insistent bass, and a voice that delivered lyrics about both good times and heartbreak with an emotional urgency.

The music had sprung up in darkened taverns and barrooms around the oil fields of Texas and Oklahoma, had spread to California with the migration of so many southwesterners, and then reached the industrial cities of the North. The beer joints were too noisy for musicians playing acoustic instruments and too small for the big bands that played Western swing for dancing. If a small live band wasn't available, the tavern owners kept the patrons happy with a jukebox in the corner that could boom out recorded music for a nickel per song. By 1946, there were nearly 300,000 jukeboxes in the nation. Four billion nickels were dropped into them.

For half a century, the term "honka tonk" had referred to a bar African Americans frequented to hear jazz or ragtime music. Now it described a place where predominantly white working-class people gathered to drink, smoke, and mingle—and gave its name to the new music they wanted to hear: "honky tonk."

The rise of honky tonk would be just one way country music changed in the late 1940s and early '50s. A Tennessee farmboy would go in the opposite direction, becoming a crooner of love songs that appealed to people who normally considered hillbilly music beneath them, giving the music a new respectability—and selling more country records than anyone ever had. The leader of a string band from Kentucky now assembled a new group of musicians and pushed the boundaries of one of the oldest forms of country music into its own category, with *its* own name.

But honky tonk would define the postwar era and create one of country music's biggest stars, a skinny singer-songwriter from Alabama, who could get any crowd rocking to his good-time beat and then bring them to tears with his songs of almost inexpressible heartache, written from his own personal torments. He would rocket to fame and be gone before he reached the age of thirty, but in six short years he would leave an imperishable mark on American music.

•   •   •

OPPOSITE *Couples dancing in Oklahoma*

ABOVE *The Texas Top Hands take a beer break at a honky tonk in Bandera, Texas.*

THE HILLBILLY SHAKESPEARE • 125

I loved Ernest Tubb. "Three chords and the truth," that's pretty much Ernest. His songs weren't complicated; anybody who could play a little guitar could sing them. And that's why I think he was so popular.

WILLIE NELSON

By 1946, the field of honky tonk singers on the radio and jukeboxes was already crowded—Ted Daffan, Al Dexter, Floyd Tillman, and many more—but no one was bigger than the six-foot Texan with a toothy smile and deep voice named Ernest Tubb.

Every Saturday afternoon, Tubb would broadcast a national half-hour radio show, the *Checkerboard Jamboree*, then perform on the live broadcast of Nashville's *Grand Ole Opry* from Ryman Auditorium. After the show, he would load his band, the Texas Troubadours, into his tour bus and set off for as many personal appearances as possible before he had to be back in Nashville for the next Saturday's broadcasts.

The mail he received was so heavy, three people had to collect it: requests for his fifty-cent songbook, or fawning letters from his 1,500-member fan club, nearly all of them women, who also received a regular newsletter that kept them informed of Tubb's upcoming schedule and allowed them to submit testimonials of their own. "Ernest Tubb is my Frank Sinatra," one woman wrote from Minnesota. "I cry when he sings 'Soldier's Last Letter' and swoon when he sings 'You Nearly Lose Your Mind.' That deep drop he takes on the word 'trifle' just sends me out of this world."

Personally, Tubb believed that part of his popularity was because his voice really wasn't all that good. Some people liked to play his records on the jukebox, he said, simply so they could brag to their friends, "I can sing as well as he can." Les Leverett, a longtime photographer at the *Opry*, remembered, "I've heard people say, 'Well, he never could sing.' And I said, 'No, and he goes to the bank every month and puts a lot of money in there because he can't sing.'"

After hearing his first Jimmie Rodgers record at the age of fifteen in Brownwood, Texas, and committing "In the Jailhouse Now" to memory, Ernest Tubb's sole ambition had been to follow in the footsteps of his idol, the Blue Yodeler,

whose death in 1933 Tubb called "one of the saddest days of my life."

In 1936, in San Antonio, he met Rodgers's widow, who befriended him by persuading RCA Victor to let him record some tribute songs about his hero. Soon enough, Mrs. Rodgers took him with her on a tour of small-town movie theaters in south Texas: Carrie Rodgers appearing as the living connection to her late husband; Tubb singing and playing the famous $1,500 Martin guitar—with the word "Thanks" emblazoned on its back—that Rodgers himself had once used. "With his memory as my inspiration," Tubb sang to each audience, "I'll pick up the torch that he laid down . . . to yodel your blues away."

But his days as a Jimmie Rodgers imitator ended suddenly in 1939, when a tonsillectomy left Tubb's throat so badly damaged he had to give up yodeling. He started writing his own songs, developed a warmer vocal style, and got work as a traveling musical ambassador for the Western Mattress Company in San Angelo. In 1941, a businessman who owned 150 jukeboxes in Fort Worth

Ernest Tubb's big break was touring small Texas towns with the widow of his hero, Jimmie Rodgers (top). She let Tubb perform with Jimmie's famous guitar emblazoned with "THANKS" on the back (above) and his name on the fret board (opposite).

gave him important advice: Tubb's records, he said, were popular in honky tonks during the afternoon, but when the crowds enlarged in the evening and wanted to dance amid all the noise, they switched to other artists' tunes. "They can't hear your records," the man insisted. "They're not playing your records; you need to make them louder."

At his next recording session, Tubb brought in a musician to play an electrified lead guitar for a song he had written, "Walking the Floor Over You." The new song became such a hit—as did the ones that followed—that the *Grand Ole Opry* brought him to Nashville and offered him a place in their cast in 1943. Once he started appearing regularly, he quickly became one of the show's most recognizable stars, and his record sales doubled from the exposure. By 1946, one trade magazine reported, Tubb was "the most imitated singer in radio today."

In 1947, Tubb and the comedienne Minnie Pearl headlined an *Opry* cast that played for two nights at New York City's Carnegie Hall, the palatial and prestigious venue for classical and popular music. "Boy," Tubb said at the start of the concert, "this place sure could hold a lot of hay."

Staid Carnegie Hall has been be-bopped by Lionel Hampton and jived by Woody Herman, but Thursday and Friday . . . it was conquered by hillbilly music and the place will never be the same again.

TOP *Tubb (far left, with guitar) toured the San Angelo area on behalf of a mattress company in 1939.*

LEFT *By 1947, he was headlining a* Grand Ole Opry *show with Minnie Pearl at New York's Carnegie Hall.*

These weren't just curious onlookers out for a night of novelty. These were serious devoted fans, almost rabid in their wild enthusiasm. Such screaming and wild applause after each number hasn't been heard in town since Frank Sinatra brought out the bobbysoxers at the Paramount.

New York is sold on hillbilly music.

Billboard magazine

That same year, Tubb opened a business in downtown Nashville, not far from the Ryman. The Ernest Tubb Record Shop was originally meant to be a mail-order operation, a way to offer country music fans an easier way to find the latest records of the artists they liked, although in the early years Tubb steadily lost money on it when 50 to 60 percent of the records came back broken and had to be replaced for free.

To publicize the store, Tubb started *Midnite Jamboree*, broadcast by WSM on location every Saturday night, immediately after the *Grand Ole Opry* signed off. Tubb served as the genial host, but preferred highlighting other artists and their songs rather than his own. He did it remembering Carrie Rodgers's generosity in helping launch him into the music business. "What can I do to repay you?" he had asked her. "Just do the same for others," she answered.

TOP *A crowd gathers outside Tubb's record shop on Commerce Street in Nashville; he would later move it to Broadway, not far from the Ryman Auditorium.*

ABOVE *Tubb performs on his* Midnite Jamboree, *broadcast live from his record store every Saturday night by WSM, immediately following the* Opry.

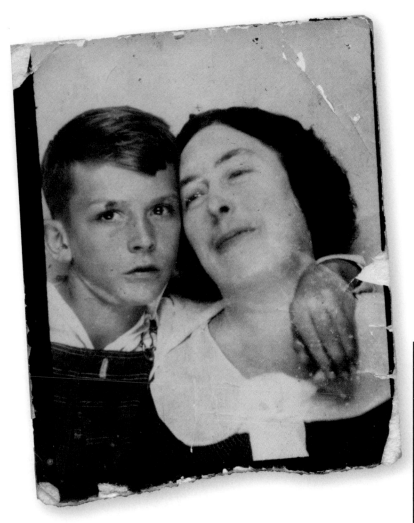

christened Hiram, after one of the kings in the Old Testament (though it was misspelled on his birth certificate as "Hiriam"). There was a raised spot on his spine, probably an early sign of spina bifida, though his parents didn't understand its significance.

His father, Lon, who had returned from World War One suffering from shell shock, worked a variety of jobs—farming a strawberry patch until a bad freeze ruined the crop, then in logging camps, until his condition required him to enter a veterans' hospital in Louisiana, in effect departing from his son's life.

But Lillie Williams, Hiram's mother, was a strong and ambitious woman. She moved her daughter and son to a succession of towns in southern Alabama: Garland, then Greenville, and finally Montgomery, where she opened up a boardinghouse in 1937, which some people in town

MOVE IT ON OVER

My mother used to sing me songs at night to make me go to sleep. And she was a pretty darn good singer. And later on in life I learned that those songs that I loved that she was singing me were songs by Hank Williams. So I was a huge Hank Williams fan before I even knew who Hank was.

BRENDA LEE

Hank Williams had the guts to put into words what we were all thinking and feeling but were too embarrassed to say. He cut right to the bone.

FRED FOSTER

In the late summer of 1946, Hank Williams was just a few days short of his twenty-third birthday. They had been a hard twenty-three years.

He was born on September 17, 1923, in a dirt-floor log house his parents rented in Mount Olive, Alabama, and was

believed doubled as a place for call girls to conduct their business.

Her son was frail and spindly, but a fun-loving teenager who preferred that people call him Hank, not Hiram. Lillie, who played the organ in church, encouraged his interest in music, sending him to a gospel, shape-note singing school and getting him his first guitar when he was eight. In Greenville he met a black street musician, Rufus Payne, known to everyone as "Tee Tot," who had spent his childhood in New Orleans, learning to play blues and early jazz. Payne took Hank under his wing, teaching him chords on the guitar and letting the boy follow along as he and his street band roamed through town, playing for handouts. "All the music training I ever had," Williams said later, "was from him."

In Montgomery, Williams shined shoes and sang on street corners while he hawked peanuts his mother had roasted. He had developed a taste for alcohol at the age of eleven, and when he won a local talent contest, singing a song he had written, "WPA Blues," he immediately spent his $15 prize partying with his friends. "He never stopped doing that," his mother would recall. "When Hank was in his chips, so were his friends, as long as the money held out. Always." At sixteen, Hank quit school.

His music caught the attention of radio station WSFA, which soon featured him on broadcasts as "the Singing Kid." He formed a band called the Drifting Cowboys, which played small-time gigs at theaters and schoolhouses in Alabama, Georgia, and the Florida Panhandle. Lillie was the driving force behind it: putting up handbills, collecting the money at the door—and constantly scolding (and sometimes hitting) her son whenever he strayed, which was often. But she also sometimes came to his defense, when drunks in the audience picked a fight with him. "There ain't nobody in this here world that I'd rather have standin' next to me in a beer joint brawl," Hank said, "than my maw with a broken bottle in her hand."

His repertoire was filled with songs of his musical heroes at the time, Roy Acuff and Ernest Tubb, mixed in with a few tunes of his own. One night, after listening to the *Grand Ole Opry* with a band member, he said, "Someday, I'm gonna be doing that." To which his friend replied, "If you keep drinkin', ain't nobody in the business gonna pay us no attention." In 1942, WSFA fired him for habitual drunkenness.

A year later, while working in a medicine show in Brundidge, Alabama, he met a pretty drugstore clerk who turned out to possess the same steely determination as his mother. Audrey Mae Sheppard had run off and gotten married at age seventeen, but was abandoned when she became pregnant. Though still technically married, and now with a young

daughter, she was irresistibly drawn to Williams, and they forged an immediate bond. "I knew what I wanted and I went after it," she recalled. "He was lucky with a God-given talent, and I was lucky with a few brains."

OPPOSITE, TOP *Young Hank Williams with his mother, Lillie. She bought him a guitar when he was eight and sent him to a gospel singing school.*

OPPOSITE, BOTTOM *When Hank began playing on radio station WSFA in Montgomery, Alabama, they called him "the Singing Kid." His mom was his manager; she scolded and cuffed him when he misbehaved, but also helped defend him in bar fights.*

ABOVE *Sometimes, Williams performed on street corners, selling peanuts Lillie had roasted.*

With the outbreak of World War Two, Williams was classified as 4-F because of his back problems, which had been aggravated by a fall from a horse. For a while, he and Audrey worked at the Alabama Dry Dock and Shipbuilding Company in Mobile, until she pushed him to go back to Montgomery and his music. In her own way, she was as influential as Tee Tot Payne, according to Hank Williams Jr.: "Rufus Payne, that's where those licks came from, but you don't want to forget Audrey Williams. She said, 'Look, you're good. Your music is good. Your songs are good.' You take out Rufus Payne and you take out Mama, and then maybe the guy sits down there and welds ships."

By the war's end, they were married and he was back on WSFA, the most popular hillbilly act in the area, though he always referred to his music as "folk songs [that] express the dreams and prayers and hopes of the working people." The station managers were concerned about his periodic drinking binges and couldn't understand his popularity, but local stores selling radio sets reported that the first question customers often asked was, "Will it pick up Hank Williams?" So they kept him on the air.

Opening for a local performance by Ernest Tubb, he told his idol that he had tried imitating Tubb's style and he had tried imitating Roy Acuff's more emotional delivery, but had finally found his own voice somewhere in between. Impressed, Tubb tried to interest his booking agent in taking the young man on. The agent already knew of Williams's unreliable reputation and declined.

In 1946, Hank and Audrey set off for Nashville anyway—"I just literally made him go," she said. Hoping to make a name for himself, he met with Fred Rose, the noted songsmith in charge of Acuff-Rose Publishing, one of the first music publishers in town. Rose took a quick liking to Williams and signed him to write a few songs for one of the company's stars, then helped him get a recording deal of his own, before Hank and Audrey returned home to Montgomery.

TOP *Audrey Mae Sheppard and Hank Williams, around the time of their marriage. He had a "God-given talent," she said, "and I was lucky with a few brains."*

LEFT *Hank (in white hat) and the Drifting Cowboys, at WSFA's studio, 1938, before he met Audrey*

Among the songs Williams recorded was one that showed the influence that Tee Tot Payne had wielded. It was called "Move It on Over," and after its release in June 1947 it became Williams's first hit. "They say 'Rock Around the Clock' is the first rock song," Hank Williams Jr. said. "I don't agree with that. 'Rock Around the Clock' is a direct steal of 'Move It on Over.' Listen to them, compare them sometime."

Royalties from the song permitted Williams to buy his first house and a fur coat for Audrey. But they were back in Montgomery, which now seemed even farther than 280 miles from Nashville and the big time.

ABOVE *Ernest Tubb, right, sitting next to Carrie Rodgers, shares a table with Hank Williams. Williams told his hero that he had developed a singing style somewhere between Tubb's and Roy Acuff's.*

RIGHT *A poster promoting Williams and his Drifting Cowboys, shortly after the release of "Move It on Over," shows that Audrey is already working her way into the act.*

Here's Another Kind of Program That's Important to You

The Grand Ole Opry and the other radio programs which come to you on our radio station, WSM, are intended for your entertainment, and every effort is devoted to making them just as fine as they can be.

We offer you another kind of program, too.

It is a program of security for you and your family, designed especially to fit your needs, and to guarantee for you and for them all the things you want them to have. Such a program, through Life Insurance, takes the uncertainties from life and helps you build for the future with security.

The Shield Man who represents the National Life and Accident Insurance Company in your community will be glad to give you the details of this plan.

Form 8113

The NATIONAL LIFE *and* ACCIDENT INSURANCE CO.
OF NASHVILLE, TENNESSEE

FIDDLES AND LIFE INSURANCE

WE SHIELD MILLIONS

The reason Nashville never goes away as a musical entity is it has its business act together. It is a very business-minded town. Guitar in this hand, briefcase in this hand. There's a lot of other towns that may have more soulful music. But the reason that Nashville never, ever falters is it has a business model and its business act together.

MARTY STUART

By the end of World War Two, hundreds of radio stations across the nation were broad-

Life Insurance for Every Member of the Family

WSM—650 ON YOUR DIAL
HOME OF THE GRAND OLE OPRY

casting weekly barn dance programs—from the *Ozark Jubilee* in Springfield, Missouri, to Philadelphia's *Hayloft Hoedown*, from the *Carolina Hayride* in Charlotte to Dallas's *Big D Jamboree* and California's *Hollywood Barn Dance*. But the lineup of stars at Nashville's *Grand Ole Opry* was unequaled, and WSM's powerful 50,000-watt signal beamed the show to both coasts from the Ryman Auditorium, "the Mother Church of Country Music."

The owners of the station, the National Life and Accident Insurance Company, couldn't have been happier. The show was doing exactly what Edwin Craig had hoped: selling insurance. The station's call letters, WSM, stood for the company's slogan, "We

Shield Millions," and the *Opry* had become its best calling card.

Bud Wendell was one of the company's salesmen in Akron, Ohio, going door to door, offering policies for as little as ten cents a week. "I'd introduce myself," he remembered. "I'd say, 'I'm Bud Wendell and I'm with the National Life and Accident Insurance Company of Nashville. We own WSM, and the *Grand Ole Opry*. Perhaps you've heard of the *Grand Ole Opry*? And I have a little gift here I'd like to give you. May I step in?'" Once inside he would give the gift he promised—a sewing needle packet, or a calendar, ruler, flower seeds, emery board, or fly swatter, all emblazoned with National Life's emblem and slogan. He also had a folder with a picture of Roy Acuff or Ernest Tubb or Minnie Pearl on it.

Now he had their attention: "A lot of their questions had to do with the artists. You know, 'Do you know Roy Acuff?' or 'Do you know Minnie Pearl?' Or 'We listened to the *Opry* last Saturday night and we sure loved the song that Acuff did.' But I'd try to get them onto the subject of life insurance. That's why I'm there; I'm not there to tell him the life story of any of the *Opry* stars. But the connection with the *Opry* was a tremendous door opener."

WSM was also accepting other sponsors for its shows, including the R.J. Reynolds Tobacco Company, which underwrote a segment of the *Opry* over the national NBC radio network. By the end of the decade, the *Opry* was generating $600,000 a year in advertising revenue, plus another $600,000 from its Artist Service Bureau, which booked tours for its stars in exchange for 15 percent of the gate receipts.

For the stars themselves, performing every Saturday night on the radio show for $30 a performance and then giving the Service Bureau a cut from their more lucrative personal appearances during the week represented a financial sacrifice. But being on the nation's top country music show provided them with the best exposure they could get to promote their records, as did being billed as official *Opry* artists on their upcoming tours. "For a country musician to be asked to join the *Opry*, that's kind of like saying do you want to go to heaven when you die," said country star Bill Anderson. "It's the top of the ladder; it's the ultimate. Do you want to play first base for the New York Yankees? Do you want to pitch for the Boston Red Sox? Do you want to be a member of the *Grand Ole Opry*? That's just about as good a question as anybody could ever ask. And there's only one answer: 'Yeah!'"

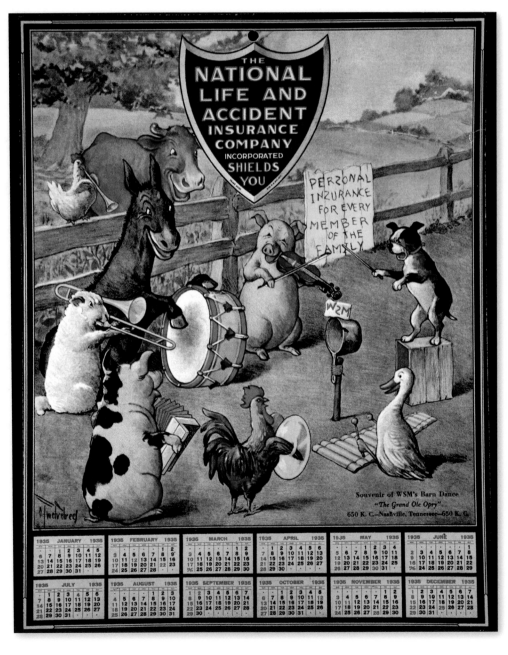

OPPOSITE *Door-to-door salesmen for the National Life and Accident Insurance Company gave prospective customers an array of gifts—like this brochure and pack of sewing needles—that connected the* Opry *to the company's products.*

RIGHT *Another promotional gift was this calendar with a barnyard band.*

I'LL HOLD YOU IN MY HEART

He spread the word. He was our first pop crossover. People bought Eddy Arnold records who wouldn't buy country records because, as Eddy said, he was "smooth." People who liked pop music also entertained the idea of an Eddy Arnold record.

RALPH EMERY

My grandfather was a romantic, so he really always focused in on love songs. They weren't about drinking or cheating, or anything like that, necessarily. They were about love.

SHANNON POLLARD

In October 1947, not long after Ernest Tubb had performed at Carnegie Hall, another star of the *Grand Ole Opry* appeared in another unlikely venue for a hillbilly singer. Eddy Arnold filled Washington, D.C.'s Constitution Hall for two straight nights. His music, prominently featuring a steel guitar, was unmistakably country. But he was just as unmistakably *not* another Ernest Tubb or Hank Williams.

Richard Edward Arnold was born on a farm near Henderson, Tennessee, on May 15, 1918, the youngest of six-

teen children. He spent his life never forgetting his humble beginnings—and being just as determined never to return to those circumstances.

On his eleventh birthday, his father died, so deeply in debt the family farm and implements had to be auctioned off, and the Arnolds found themselves as tenants working on what had been their own land. "A boy that works on a farm and does labor," Arnold remembered, "he does a lot of day-dreaming." Arnold's dream was doing anything other than chopping corn and wearing shirts his mother made from feed bags. He had been playing guitar since he was seven, and people seemed to enjoy listening to him sing. He decided music might be his way out.

Arnold left school after ninth grade and got a job in nearby Jackson, Tennessee, driving the hearse for a funeral home that allowed him to sleep there at night. He learned to read music and began performing on local radio stations. In 1938, he and a friend, Speedy McNatt, took the bus to St. Louis

and landed a job performing on the early-morning show at KWK as the Tennessee Harmony Lads. At night they played in taverns, returning to the station to nap in the lobby before their 6 a.m. sign-on. Arnold took a second job to pay for voice lessons, practiced incessantly, and dreamed of bigger things. "I knew where I wanted to go because I couldn't go back," he said. "There wasn't anything to go back to."

His big break came in 1940, after Pee Wee King invited him to join the Golden West Cowboys for a guarantee of $15 a week. Billed as "Smilin' Eddy Arnold," he would sing ballads, sell Pee Wee's songbooks at intermission, and for extra money sweep out the auditorium after each performance. In 1943, after touring Army bases with King and Minnie Pearl on the Camel Caravan, he went out on his own, singing on the *Opry* as "the Tennessee Plowboy" and doing a morning show on WSM right after Ernest Tubb's.

OPPOSITE, TOP *Young Eddy Arnold with his mother and father, Georgia and William. William's death threw the family into poverty.*

OPPOSITE, BOTTOM *Arnold and his friend Speedy McNatt—the Tennessee Harmony Lads—on the* Early Bird *show on station KWK in St. Louis*

ABOVE *On the* Opry *(top), Arnold was nicknamed "the Tennessee Plowboy." Young Harold Bradley, accompanying him on the guitar, would go on to become the most-recorded guitar player in history. A* Billboard *advertisement touts Arnold's record sales, his various radio broadcasts, and his live performances.*

People responded to his clean-cut image: neatly pressed slacks, a crisp white shirt, a handsome, square-jawed face, sometimes with a dapper rancher's hat on his head. They loved his music even more: a mellow voice that could not only croon love ballads, but also break into a smooth yodel on a favorite upbeat song, "Cattle Call."

On tour, unlike most musicians, he usually declined to carouse and drink the night away. One night in Fort Worth, Bob Wills invited him out to cruise the beer joints. Arnold turned him down. "I had a show to do the next day," he recalled, "and I wanted to get plenty of rest for it and be in good condition." In the morning, he preferred prune juice with his breakfast.

912

Associated Radio Co.

Here in Person!

Eddy Arnold

NOW!

hear

WALLY FOWLER

ASSOCIATED

GRAND OLE OPRY STARS TUE. MAY 28
MUNICIPAL AUDITORIUM WED. MAY 29

He was managed now by Thomas A. Parker, a former carnival promoter with a flair for publicity who insisted on being called *Colonel* Parker. On the road with Arnold, to attract attention to his star, Parker often demanded a police escort into town—or even when they went out for a hamburger. By 1947, with a long string of hit recordings to his name, two segments on the *Opry*, and a five-day-a-week national show of his own on the Mutual network sponsored by Ralston Purina, Arnold was a big enough star to tour without using the *Opry*'s name, saving himself the 15 percent they took from concert receipts.

At the end of the year, his song "I'll Hold You in My Heart" reached number one on *Billboard*'s ranking of hillbilly music. It would stay there for an unprecedented twenty-one weeks,

and be followed by four others. Of the six number-one country songs in 1948, Eddy Arnold had five of them. The entire music industry sold 177 million records that year; Arnold sold 6.5 million, nearly 4 percent of the national total.

By September 1948, Colonel Parker had convinced Arnold he could make more money on Saturday nights doing personal appearances than being in Nashville for the *Grand Ole Opry*. Roy Acuff had tried the same thing in 1946, but without the weekly exposure on the *Opry*, fewer people came to his shows, and he finally begged to resume his place at the Ryman. Most people thought the same thing would happen to Arnold.

On his final night, Arnold and his old friend Minnie Pearl hugged each other backstage one last time. Fans listening on the radio cried to think he was leaving the show. On his way out of the Ryman, someone scolded him about his departure, saying "The *Opry* made you." "If *it* made me," he answered, "why hasn't it made the Fruit Jar Drinkers?"

ABOVE *"Colonel" Tom Parker, far left, became Arnold's manager and persuaded him that he could make more money playing paid appearances on Saturday nights rather than staying with the* Opry.

BLUEGRASS BREAKDOWN

In music history, Bill Monroe, to me, is as important as Duke Ellington; he's as important as Charlie Parker, any of those guys. I mean you think about it, how many people have a genre of music that they started, that they can say, "This man right here started a whole new genre of music." Bill Monroe did that: bluegrass.

RICKY SKAGGS

I think there are archangels and I think there are cosmic forces by way of human beings that hit the planet. Bill Monroe was one. There's just one Bill Monroe. There's just one Mark Twain. There's just one Einstein, one Hemingway.

TOM T. HALL

Since his first appearance on the *Grand Ole Opry* in 1939, Bill Monroe had been one of the show's biggest attractions, the leader of the best-known acoustic string band in the nation, the Blue Grass Boys, named in honor of his home state of Kentucky. But Monroe was a perfectionist, never entirely satisfied with the music he and his band were playing. "When Bill put his band together and came to Nashville, in 1939, and got to be a member of the *Grand Ole Opry*, his music started changing," said Ricky Skaggs. "And he started looking for different sounds. I think in his brain he was hearing something that was unique, but he didn't know exactly what it was."

In late 1945, Monroe began reconfiguring the band's cast, bringing in Chubby Wise, who had popularized "Orange Blossom Special" on the fiddle; Cedric Rainwater on bass; Lester Flatt, from Duncan's Chapel, Tennessee, recently a member of Charlie Monroe's band, singing lead and playing guitar.

BELOW *Bill Monroe, center, and his reconfigured Blue Grass Boys onstage at the* Opry: *Chubby Wise on fiddle, Lester Flatt on guitar, and Earl Scruggs on banjo; bass player Cedric Rainwater is not in the shot.*

And to replace Dave "Stringbean" Akeman on banjo, during a series of auditions in Nashville's Tulane Hotel, Monroe discovered a quiet twenty-one-year-old from Flint Hill, North Carolina, named Earl Scruggs, and hired him on the spot.

Scruggs had been playing banjo since the age of four, and as a boy started experimenting with a three-fingered technique popular in western North Carolina's Piedmont. After working in a textile mill to support his widowed mother during the war, he had joined a band in Knoxville and further refined his propulsive, rolling style, so different from the "frailing" or "clawhammer" technique used by Stringbean and the *Opry*'s Uncle Dave Macon, both of them as much comedians as banjo players. Scruggs was definitely not a comedian. Almost painfully shy, he overcame his stage

fright by concentrating on making his lightning-like finger work appear effortless.

"Prior to Earl Scruggs, a lot of the banjo playing wasn't clearly defined," said John McEuen, the banjo player for the Nitty Gritty Dirt Band. "There was a lot of the frailing style and it wasn't a definite lead style. When Earl walked up anywhere near that mic, he was picking so hard and definite that his excitement would penetrate the audience. It would just make them nuts. He brought to it the same thing that Eddie Van Halen brought to rock and roll [with his] shredding guitar. It was so fast. It was what excited people." Eddie Stubbs, a WSM announcer, agreed: "He wasn't the first person to play with a three-finger roll. But he was the first person who came to Nashville with it." He added, "Earl Scruggs is one of the single most important musicians, not just in the history of country music, but he's one of the single most important instrumentalists in the history of the music of the world."

When Monroe heard Scruggs's fiery three-fingered roll, it was the "last cog that he needed for the machine to make the engine go," said Ricky Skaggs. "Earl is pretty good on the banjo," Uncle Dave Macon admitted after Scruggs debuted with Monroe on the *Opry*, "but he ain't a damn bit funny." The crowds, on the other hand, loved what he did with his instrument. Judge Hay, the *Opry* host, started introducing the group as Bill Monroe and His Blue Grass Boys, with Earl Scruggs, "the boy that makes the banjo talk."

Monroe liked the Blue Grass Boys' new sound, which now featured individual solo breaks in each song—Wise's furious fiddle, Monroe's extraordinary mandolin, and Scruggs's syncopated banjo, with Flatt keeping pace on his guitar and providing a strong lead voice while Monroe added his own high tenor harmony. "It was improvisational, the same as jazz music, but the fire was there," said Marty Stuart. "It gave country music a whole new sound. It was as powerful as when Louis Armstrong and the Hot Five finally found the magic. America had a new music then."

Thanks to their *Grand Ole Opry* broadcasts every Saturday night, and Monroe's relentless schedule of touring throughout the South, the band's style began influencing other string bands. In the mountainous southwestern corner of

OPPOSITE *Bill Monroe, standing, kept his Blue Grass Boys constantly on the road between* Opry *broadcasts. To reach the event advertised for Hummelstown, Pennsylvania, they would have driven nearly 750 pre-interstate miles from Nashville.*

LEFT *Earl Scruggs's exciting three-fingered rolling technique on the banjo was central to Monroe's new sound.*

ABOVE *Ralph Stanley (with banjo) and his brother Carter quickly adapted their music to reflect what they heard on the radio when Monroe's band played. Monroe was incensed when they recorded one of his songs, setting off a feud that lasted for decades.*

Virginia, the Stanley brothers—Carter and Ralph—were paying particular attention.

They had been raised in the Primitive Baptist Church, where entire congregations sang hymns a capella, led by a church elder like their father. But their mother loved playing the banjo, using the clawhammer style, and when young Ralph expressed an interest in it, she told him that for an upcoming present from her, he had a choice to make: he could have a pig to raise or he could have a banjo. Both were worth five dollars. "I was interested in hogs at the time," Ralph remembered, "but I picked the banjo." His brother Carter took up the guitar, and the Stanley Brothers soon began performing locally. "Ralph's voice sounded like it had coal dust in it, in a really cool way," according to Vince Gill. "And I love that brother harmony; I've always been a nut for that brother harmony that Ralph and Carter had together."

After serving in the war, they came home and formed the Clinch Mountain Boys, became regulars on WCYB in Bristol, and went to see the musician they admired the most, Bill Monroe, at a nearby performance. Ralph watched Earl Scruggs intently. "Well," Ralph recalled thinking, "I will have to try to get that style myself. So I started working on it."

Stanley soon became as proficient with Scruggs's three-fingered style as with the more traditional clawhammer technique his mother had taught him. For new material, the Clinch Mountain Boys sometimes memorized what they heard the Blue Grass Boys playing on the *Opry* and performed it on their own show in Bristol a few days later.

Monroe was temperamental, proud, and sometimes prickly. To him, being copied was an insult rather than a tribute. When the Stanleys released a song of his, "Molly and Tenbrook," on a regional label in 1948, Monroe was even more angry. He had recorded it a year earlier, but his label, Columbia, had not yet released it. Then Columbia signed the Stanley Brothers; Monroe retaliated by switching to Decca Records.

There were more aggravations. In 1948, two of Monroe's stars, Lester Flatt and Earl Scruggs, tired of making $60 a week as sidemen in a band that seemed always to be on the road, decided to strike out on their own. They eventually formed their own band, the Foggy Mountain Boys, named for a Carter Family song they often performed.

Once again, Monroe was incensed. He demanded that the

Opry not allow Flatt and Scruggs to perform there for a few years—and refused to even speak to them for much longer than that. He got some additional measure of revenge by stealing guitarist and singer Mac Wiseman away from the Foggy Mountain Boys, which infuriated Lester Flatt.

A little later, Flatt and Scruggs came out with an instrumental song Earl had written, "Foggy Mountain Breakdown," named for the new band. Except for a few changes, it closely resembled a tune Scruggs had worked on with Monroe, called "Bluegrass Breakdown." That only added fuel to the fire. "They'd work around each other and exist in the same industry, but nobody spoke for like twenty-five years," Marty Stuart explained. "Nobody can hold a grudge like hillbillies; I can attest to that."

This newest style of country music that Bill Monroe, Lester Flatt, and Earl Scruggs had created still had no name. In the midst of all the feuding, audience members at Flatt and Scruggs concerts would want to request a Bill Monroe tune dating from the time they were still a part of Monroe's Blue Grass Boys. But, as Everett Lilly, a member of the Foggy Mountain Boys, recalled, the fans were afraid even to mention Bill Monroe: "The public began to say, 'Boys, would you please do one of them old Blue Grass tunes like you used to do?' They knew me and Lester could sing them duets like him and Bill. They'd say, 'Would you please do an old bluegrass tune?' The public named Blue Grass music . . . through the fear to speak Bill's name to 'em."

STEP IT UP AND GO

Sometimes, you go someplace and you wonder if you're at the right place or not. But when you went to see the Maddox Brothers and Rose, you knew you'd come to the right show. You could not be at one of their shows and not be happy.

MERLE HAGGARD

In 1948, an old Jimmie Rodgers song got a new lease on life. Rodgers, country music's first superstar, originally recorded his "Blue Yodel Number 8"—"Mule Skinner Blues"—in the 1920s with just his guitar. In 1939, Bill Monroe had made his *Grand Ole Opry* debut with a stunningly energetic reinterpretation of it. Now an electrified band out in California's Central Valley gave it a honky tonk bounce. It was the Maddox Brothers and Rose.

OPPOSITE *When Earl Scruggs and Lester Flatt left Monroe's band to form their own, the Foggy Mountain Boys, Monroe was even more furious and stole guitarist and singer Mac Wiseman away from them, resulting in another bitter feud.*

They had arrived in California in the depth of the Great Depression, riding freight trains from Alabama and barely surviving as migrant farmworkers before taking up instruments and putting their young sister, Rose, in front of a microphone. They worked the bars and dance halls playing hillbilly music for others like them, economic refugees denigrated as "Okies."

When her brothers went off to war, Rose had approached the king of Western swing, Bob Wills, for a job. "And he said they already had a girl singer, so he wasn't interested in using Rose in his band," according to her brother Don Maddox. "And the way I heard it, Rose said, 'Well, if you don't use me, you're going to be sorry because when my brothers get home, we're going to put you out of business.' Later on, I heard that Bob Wills was telling that story to somebody and he said, 'You know, they almost did put us out of business.'"

Lula Maddox, the family matriarch and driving force behind the band, outfitted her children in flamboyant western clothes made by Nathan Turk, a Polish-born tailor in Hollywood, who had designed costumes for movie cowboys. As they made more money on the West Coast honky-tonk circuit, their mother decided they should travel in equally flashy automobiles; she went to a dealership and astonished the salesman when she pulled enough cash out of a cigar box to buy them a fleet of Cadillacs.

No one had ever seen—or heard—anything quite like it before: shows that included slapstick humor, shouts and hollers, songs that mixed honky tonk and boogie-woogie and blues, an electrified hillbilly sound in overdrive. Don came up with a nickname, "the Most Colorful Hillbilly Band in the Val-

OPPOSITE *From left to right, Cal, Henry, Rose, Don, and Fred Maddox, decked out in one of their special outfits made by Nathan Turk in Hollywood*

ABOVE *Three photographs of "the Most Colorful Hillbilly Band in the World"*

RIGHT *"You could not be at one of their shows and not be happy," said Merle Haggard. When he went to see them at age twelve, Haggard was most interested in hearing the band's teenage guitarist, Roy Nichols, center, between Don and Henry Maddox. Years later, Haggard would hire Nichols to play in his band.*

ley," then "the Most Colorful Hillbilly Band in the State," then "the Most Colorful Hillbilly Band in the United States"—and finally "the Most Colorful Hillbilly Band in the World."

One of their biggest songs, "Step It Up and Go," was a "prelude to rock and roll," according to Marty Stuart. "They put the boogie in country music, which went on to be 'Baby, Let's Play House,' 'That's All Right, Mama,' 'Rock Around the Clock.' You could see the embers starting, the seed had been planted."

By the late 1940s, the Maddox Brothers and Rose were the hottest country band in California. Fifteen years earlier, as destitute arrivals, they had lived in a concrete culvert in Oakland. Now they moved into a lavish house in Hollywood.

In 1949, twelve-year-old Merle Haggard went to see them in Bakersfield, intrigued not only by the Maddoxes' showmanship but also by their guitar player, Roy Nichols, who at age sixteen was already on his way to becoming a renowned musician. "And I paid some attention to the Maddox Brothers and Rose, but mostly to Roy," Haggard said. "And I remember my brother made the remark, he said, 'He don't have to pick cotton or go to school, either one.' I said, 'I want his job.'"

COUNTRY BOY

Jimmy Dickens didn't go out onstage to go over; he came out onstage to take over. And he did every time. He would say, "You know, they may not know who I am now, but when I get done with them, they will." He was fearless.

EDDIE STUBBS

In 1948, the *Grand Ole Opry* welcomed a new singer to the stage at Ryman Auditorium. From the coal-mining region of southern West Virginia, the oldest of thirteen children, James Cecil Dickens was twenty-eight years old and had been moving from one local radio station to another, learning how to entertain audiences and keep a show's sponsors happy by persuading listeners to buy whatever was being advertised. They were called "per inquiry" deals: for every order that came in, the artist would get a small percentage of the sale.

No one was better at it than Dickens. Only four feet ten inches tall, he turned his short stature into part of his act. His first hit, "Take an Old Cold Tater (and Wait)," told the story of a boy who was always last to be served at the dinner table. "That's why I look so bad and have these puny ways," he sang, "because I always had to take an old cold tater and wait." Working at radio stations in Dayton, Ohio, and Indianapolis—and promoting everything from fruit trees to kitchen utensils to patent medicine—he would stand on a chair to share the microphone with T. Texas Tyler, a six-foot-three-inch singer, and gladly adopted the nickname Tyler gave him: "Little Jimmy Dickens."

Impressed by his stage presence, Roy Acuff invited Dickens to Nashville, where he quickly won over the *Opry* audiences and honed the comic antics that would become his trademark by listening to advice from Minnie Pearl, who, he said, patiently taught him how to tell a joke better and not step on the crowd's laughter.

To further distinguish himself onstage, Dickens went to

RIGHT *Little Jimmy Dickens stands on a chair to share a microphone with T. Texas Tyler on Indianapolis station WIBC.*

Hollywood for flashier clothes. He found them at the main competitor of Nathan Turk, who was outfitting the Maddox Brothers and Rose. Nuta Kotlyrenko had been born in Kiev, in the Ukraine, but changed his last name to Cohn when he came to America. Childhood friends in Brooklyn, having trouble with his first name, called him Nudie. Now he ran Nudie's Rodeo Tailors in Hollywood, steadily attracting Western movie stars like Gene Autry and Roy Rogers and Rex Allen. To expand his business, Cohn also started seeking clients in country music, sometimes designing new, ostentatious outfits for them for free, simply for the exposure.

Little Jimmy Dickens was the first star from the *Grand Ole Opry* to appear in what became known as "Nudie suits." "I tried it both ways," Dickens said. "I tried it in a neat little businessman suit. Didn't work. But when I put one of these on and come on the stage it's, 'Wow.' I just seen the difference that it made in my appearance. I've been wearin' 'em ever since. And everybody started wearing Nudie suits. That's the main thing in country music, is to sell yourself to the audience, other than just singin' to them. 'Cause if I had to depend on my singin' I'd be up the creek."

Always looking for new material, Dickens soon found another hit song, "Country Boy," a bouncy tune with lyrics that celebrated a simple rural life in which he proclaimed, "I raise Cain on Saturday but I go to church on Sunday . . . [and] I'll be lookin' over that old gray mule when the sun comes up on Monday." It proved so popular when Dickens performed it on the *Opry*, fourteen extra verses were added for him to sing during all the encores the audience demanded.

The song came from an unlikely source. Boudleaux and Felice Bryant were hardly country bumpkins. He was the son of a small-town Georgia lawyer and had been trained as a classical violinist. She was a Sicilian American from Milwaukee who loved writing romantic poetry.

Named for the French soldier who had saved his father's life in World War One, Boudleaux Bryant had played in the Atlanta Philharmonic Orchestra symphony at age eighteen, but, hoping to make more money, he became an itinerant musician, playing Western swing and jazz, as well as hillbilly tunes, across the South and Midwest, making a name for himself as a hot fiddle player. He was part of a quartet working in the cocktail lounge of Milwaukee's Schroeder Hotel when he met his future wife and writing partner.

Matilda Genevieve Scaduto was the hotel elevator operator. She saw Bryant walking across the lobby and got his attention by splashing him with water from the fountain next to the elevator. They struck up a conversation. "And she took him downstairs, bought him a drink, and then immediately told him that she had dreamt of him all of her life and that they should be married," according to their son Del Bryant. "And they were hitched very quickly, or at least were doing what hitched people usually do very quickly." Boudleaux decided to call his new wife Felice.

With the birth of two sons, the couple struggled to survive financially, moving from town to town in a trailer they pulled behind their car. Meanwhile, Boudleaux began setting some of Felice's poems to music. When Fred Rose heard their song "Country Boy," he passed it on to Jimmy Dickens and urged the Bryants to relocate to Nashville. They moved into a trailer court some people called "Hillbilly Heaven" and ignored advice that while Nashville had some stars who wrote their own songs, no one really made a living there solely as a professional songwriter. That happened, they were told, only in New York.

To peddle their songs, Boudleaux began hanging out backstage at the *Grand Ole Opry*. He was known well enough as a fiddle player by many of the artists, who let him jam with them in the dressing room; they indulged him when he pitched them some of his and Felice's new tunes.

Little Jimmy Dickens would record a number of their songs: lighthearted, up-tempo tunes like "Out Behind the Barn," "Bessie the Heifer," and "I'm Little but I'm Loud," but also soulful ballads like "Take Me as I Am" or a song Felice had written for Boudleaux as a birthday present, "We Could."

Other artists soon followed suit—enough that a publisher from New York flew to Nashville to try to persuade the Bryants to move to the Big Apple, the nation's songwriting capital, and write show tunes for him. They turned him down. Nashville, they decided, might just be able to support people who wrote songs for a living.

ABOVE *Boudleaux Bryant was a classically trained violinist who learned he could make more money playing in swing and hillbilly bands. Matilda Genevieve Scaduto was an elevator operator in Milwaukee who loved and wrote romantic poetry. She and Bryant were soon married, and he called her Felice.*

LEFT *When the Bryants moved to Nashville, they lived in a trailer park with their sons, Dane and baby Del. Little Jimmy Dickens's success with some of their songs persuaded them that they could make it as songwriters.*

LOVESICK BLUES

If Hank would drink a little beer, he was alright. But you didn't want to be around if he was really snookered.

When Hank got on the hard stuff, drinking, you didn't want to be around him. He was belligerent when he was on the booze.

E. JIMMY KEY

Despite the success of "Move It on Over," Hank Williams seemed stuck in Montgomery, Alabama. He was popular there, but yearned to move to Nashville and the *Grand Ole Opry*, where his music could find a wider audience.

His marriage to Audrey had been turbulent from the start. There were constant tensions about her insistence on

ABOVE *Audrey and Hank Williams performing in Union Springs, Alabama. Her demands to be part of his act were one of many points of contention in their marriage.*

RIGHT *E. Jimmy Key was a member of the Strawberry Pickers band in Montgomery and a good friend of Hank Williams, who often stayed at Key's apartment whenever Hank and Audrey were fighting.*

being part of his act, troubles over money, angry fights during his recurrent bouts of heavy drinking. His Montgomery friend E. Jimmy Key saw it firsthand: "He and Audrey were constantly battling. I had an apartment. So when Hank and Audrey would have a fight, Hank would come move in with me. I came home for lunch from work, and he's sitting in the hallway, with his feet against the wall, in just his hat, boots, and shorts. And he was wailing away on 'Lovesick Blues.' He was just completely snookered. And it ticked me off. It just hit me wrong, 'cause he was, in the middle of the day, in the juice too much. And he said, 'What do you think about this song?' And I said, 'It ain't worth a damn. It won't sell ten records.'"

Williams's publisher, Fred Rose, continued to have high hopes for him and took a fatherly interest in his welfare. A recovering alcoholic himself (he had brought himself out of drunken ruin by adopting the tenets of Christian Science), Rose wrote a series of letters hoping to guide his young protégé back from the brink, as relations between Hank and Audrey unraveled:

February 18, 1948. Dear Hank: Sometimes we humans

act in a funny way when things are not going our way. We make plans, and when anyone interferes with our plans we have nervous breakdowns because we think that drowning our sorrows will make us forget our troubles, but this has never worked and never will work because when we wake up the next morning we still have our troubles plus a hangover that prevents us from thinking clear enough to think our way out of the problem we thought our way into. . . .

I'm opening my heart to you because I love you like my own son and you can call on me anytime when you are in a problem and I'll do anything within my power to help you help yourself.

March 18, 1948. Dear Hank, . . . I feel kinda let down today after receiving your call 'cause I knew you were drinking again and Hank that is something I refuse to go for because it only proves a man's weakness.

I know YOU LOVE AUDREY more than you are willing to admit and you are taking the wrong way out, slopping up a lot of poison that makes you feel sorry for yourself and makes your friends disgusted with you. If you really want Audrey back, get a haircut and buy a new suit, wash your face and throw that damn whiskey bottle out the window and become a man that she would be proud of.

I am trying to be your friend 'cause I know you need a friend. . . .

I know what I am talking about because I have gone through the same thing that you are going through now.

I am . . . Your friend.

April 3, 1948. Dear Hank, . . . You are destined for big things in the recording and songwriting field, and you are the only one who can ruin this opportunity. In the future, forget the firewater and let me take care of your business and you'll be a big name in this business.

Kind personal regards, I am . . . Your friend, Fred Rose

But Williams was unable to stop. He showed up drunk when a touring group from the *Opry* played in town and was so disheveled for a performance a few nights later the bar owner told the band he would hire the rest of them to play again, but not Hank Williams. His dream of going back to

February 18, 1948

Dear Hank:

Sometimes we humans act in a funny way when things are not going our way. We make plans and when anyone interferes with our plans we have nervous breakdowns because we think that drowning our sorrows will make us forget our troubles, but this has never worked and never will work because when we wake up next morning we still have our troubles plus a hangover that prevents us from thinking clear enough to think our way out of the problem that we thought our way into.

Hank, we live by rules and regulations (Principle) the same as your automobile. The Automobile Companies keeps your car running by, what they call, "factory specifications" and when your car gets away from these specifications it ceases to run and you take it to a mechanic who gets it back to "factory specifications" and "MAN" is the same way. You cannot hope to be successful while neglecting the Principle of health. The principle of success and all other secondary principles depend on the principle of LIFE because without life there is no such thing as success.

Don't let Audry pull the wool over your eyes by making you jealous. That is the first weapon a woman uses on a man she loves. Woman think they way to hold a man is to make the man think they are cheating and if the man is sucker enough to go for it, he is supposed to start drinking and become a tramp, these women want to be scalp collectors and see how many mens lives they can wreck, but they can always be crossed up by a man who uses common sense. All the man has to do, is know that, if his woman loves him, she will not be satisfied with any other man and , if she doesn't love him, he is a chump to want her. I think Audry loves you and that she is being very foolish try to hurt you but as the old saying goes "WE ALWAYS HURT THE ONE WE LOVE". The trouble with you kids is that, both of you want to be boss, Both of you have pride. Pride, is one of the most destructive lies on earth, it make people liars, it makes them pretend to be something they aren't, it ruins businesses, it breaks up homes, it is something we all should get rid of, as quick as possible, so we can enjoy the happiness of humility. The three hardest words in the English language to say are "I WAS WRONG" but when we do muster enough courage to say it, we feel a sense of victory, we find out we
(Cont.)

SONGS FOR HOME FOLKS
(SOLE SELLING AGENTS FOR MILENE MUSIC)

"ONL...   ...ay about three weeks
...   ...times, if you need me.

I am ...ng a little "Peace Prayer" that I wish you would learn by heart. It has helped me lots when I felt disturbed.

Your friend,
Fred Rose

March 27, 1948

...illian Williams
...McDonald
...mery, Alabama

...rs. Williams:

...have Hank sign the enclosed receipt for the money
...d return for our files.

...ent to Hank some-
...arrived

March 19, 1948

Hank Williams
...CARLOS HOTEL
...216
...cola, Florida

...Hank:

...tells me you called this morning for
...ey after me wiring you four hundred
...Just day before yesterday and this
...make very good sense. We have gone as
...can go at this time and cannot send
...e.

...have tried to be a friend of yours
...you refuse to let me be one, I feel that
...you are just using me for a good thing and
...This is where I quit. You have been very unfair,
...Calling my house, in the middle of the night
...and I hope you will not let it happen again
...as it isn't fair to Lorene.

...When you get ready to straighten out let me
...now and maybe we can pick up where we left
...ff but for the present I am all fed up with
...our foolishness.

...oping you come to your senses soon, I am

Your friend,
Fred Rose
Fred Rose

OPPOSITE *Williams's publisher, Fred Rose, was a skilled songwriter himself. He was also a recovering alcoholic who tried to get Hank to stop his destructive heavy drinking.*

ABOVE *Excerpts from some of the letters Rose sent to Williams (and sometimes Hank's mother), hoping to steer his protégé in the right direction.*

dark. And I think part of him struggled with that. He believed in the real redemptive nature of Christ. You know, "I have struggles like everyone else does, and I'm a sinner. And I do this wrong, but I have faith in my salvation."

HOLLY WILLIAMS

A year earlier, on the way back from a performance, Williams had been in the back seat of the band's touring car, sleeping off another bender, when his mother, who was driving, saw the beacon light of Montgomery's airport in the distance and tried to rouse him from his stupor. "Hank, wake up," she shouted. "We're nearly home. I just saw the light."

By the time they arrived, he had turned it into a song, closely based on a gospel tune written by Albert E. Brumley called "He Set Me Free." Hank's version was "I Saw the Light."

"'I Saw the Light,' whether you love Jesus or not, whether you're religious or not, it's a song that just sticks in your head like glue, and you can't stop singing it," said his granddaughter Holly Williams. "It's happy. It's up-tempo. At the same time, it's a song of redemption and this broken man who has seen the light."

"He addressed Saturday-night sinning and Sunday-

Nashville and playing on the *Grand Ole Opry* seemed more and more out of reach.

In late April, Audrey filed for divorce. "He has a violent and ungovernable temper," she stated in her complaint, "and during the last month has been drunk most of the time." She added: "I am afraid to live with him any longer."

• • •

He constantly, I think, was dealing with the battle of, I don't want to say good and bad, but more light and

---

TOP, LEFT *Hank Williams backstage on the road. He embodied country music's tension between Saturday night and Sunday morning.*

ABOVE *The handwritten lyrics of the first two verses and chorus of "I Saw the Light," a song of redemption for someone who had sinned*

ABOVE, RIGHT *The sheet music for "I Saw the Light" featured a photo of Williams in a church setting.*

morning redemption as well as anybody did," said singer-songwriter Rodney Crowell:

> You go howling at the moon on Saturday night. You wreck your car. You chase women. You come in drunk. But then, Sunday morning, you face the music 'cause somebody's mama and somebody's favorite aunt is going to grab you by the ear and drag you out of the bed and take you to church. And you're going to have to sit there and pay for the fun you had all over again.
>
> Hank Williams, to me, personifies it better than anyone. Everybody out there who's had Saturday night and Sunday morning can say, "He's telling us about our lives." And when you get it right, when an artist gets it right for themselves, it's right for everybody. "I Saw the Light," well, I venture to say, you don't see the light until you know the darkness.

By the time the Williams' divorce was finalized in May 1948, they had already reconciled. Hank had sobered up, and Fred Rose soon found a new radio station for him, which had just started its own barn dance program.

Broadcast from Shreveport's Municipal Auditorium on station KWKH's powerful 50,000-watt signal, *Louisiana Hayride* had ambitions to rival WSM's *Grand Ole Opry* and was searching for new talent to do it. Hank Williams quickly became the show's top star. And his most popular song on its stage was the one he had tried out on Jimmy Key back in Montgomery, the old vaudeville song Emmett Miller had recorded in 1925, "Lovesick Blues." In December 1948, he insisted on recording it, over the vehement objec-

tions of Rose, who called it "the worst damn thing I ever heard."

"You might not like the song," Hank had told Rose, "but when . . . I walk off the stage and throw my hat back on the stage and the *hat* encores, that's pretty hot." If "Lovesick Blues" didn't make it, he told a friend, "I'm thinkin' seriously of getting out of the business."

Within a few months of its release in early 1949, it was the nation's number one hillbilly song and would stay on the charts for nearly a year. "There's just something about it," said country star Dwight Yoakam. "There's a sentimental heartache to that song, but yet, there's still a raw-edged kind of raucous, mud-in-your-eye, flipping the finger at the world, because you feel this bad side of it. It's an interesting combination."

Royalty checks from "Lovesick Blues" and another hit, "Wedding Bells," amounted to $10,000. Williams's erratic career had turned around—and Audrey had given birth to a son, Hank Williams Jr., whose proud father lovingly nicknamed "Bocephus" (after the name of a puppet of *Opry* comedian Rod Brasfield). Hank and Audrey arranged to have their divorce annulled.

With his newfound success, Williams set his sights again on the *Grand Ole Opry*. They couldn't ignore his new star power, but the management there still resisted because of his reputation for drinking and missing shows. Fred Rose interceded again, offering the *Opry*'s manager and program

director the songwriting credit (and therefore the royalties) for a tune Rose had written, "Chattanoogie Shoe Shine Boy," that Red Foley recorded and took to number one.

On June 11, 1949, during Ernest Tubb's segment, Williams made his *Opry* debut, singing "Lovesick Blues" to such thunderous applause he was quickly asked to become a member.

With their baby son and Audrey's daughter, Lycrecia, the Williams family moved into a new house in Nashville. They filled it with furniture so expensive, Hank joked, he was afraid to sit on it. They added a bedroom, a den, and a two-car garage for their new automobiles, and bought horses to ride on the property's three acres. On tour in California, Hank added a new outfit, designed and made by Nudie Cohn.

In November, though still a relative newcomer to the *Opry*, he was asked to join other headliners on a two-week tour of American military bases in Europe. The cast included Red Foley, Roy Acuff, Minnie Pearl, and Little Jimmy Dickens. They performed in Wiesbaden, Frankfurt, Munich, Vienna, and Berlin, where Hank was issued a document written in Russian, in case he wandered by mistake into the Soviet-controlled zone. "They ain't gonna win the next war," he said when he saw it, "they can't even spell."

Back home, as 1949 ended, Hank Williams was the second-best-selling country singer of the year, with eight songs on the charts. Only Eddy Arnold, with thirteen, was ahead of him. And when Hank came to Montgomery as part of an *Opry* tour that packed the auditorium, Jimmy Key went to the dressing room to see his old friend. "I walked in and Hank didn't say hello or anything," Key recalled. "He just said, 'What do you think of "Lovesick Blues" now?'"

COUNTRY AND WESTERN

The Western field, which has shot to such popularity since the war, is a strange mixture of simple singers, pseudo cowboys who never rode a horse, and Arkansas fiddlers from Arizona. It's rife with jealousy; most of the stars being quite touchy about whether they are "folk singers" or "Western singers" and they themselves refer to other artists whom they dislike as "hillbillies."

SAN FRANCISCO CHRONICLE

From the very first recordings of Fiddlin' John Carson back in 1923, record labels had trouble naming the music that sprang from so many different roots. The growth of additional subgenres—cowboy songs, Western swing, honky tonk, bluegrass—made it that much more difficult to categorize it all and market it under a single word or phrase.

Most people referred to it as "hillbilly music," and *Billboard* magazine used that term for a while. In 1944, *Billboard*'s first

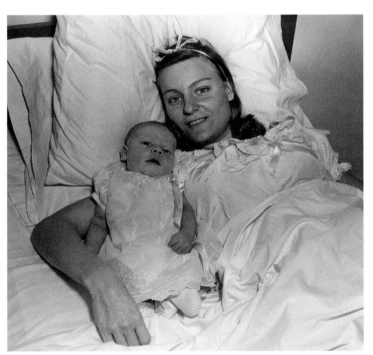

LEFT *Audrey Williams and baby Hank Williams Jr., born May 26, 1949. His proud father nicknamed him "Bocephus."*

OPPOSITE *Hank's success with "Lovesick Blues" finally landed him a spot on the* Opry *on WSM.*

ABOVE *The Williams family in their new home in Nashville. Audrey's daughter Lycrecia sits on the piano bench, while little Hank Junior is held tight on the piano's top by his father.*

mostly old standards, it also included songs of social protest that bothered some more conservative listeners, especially since the United States was locked in a Cold War against the Soviet Union and Americans were fighting a real war against communist China in Korea.

The Weavers—a folk quartet that included Ronnie Gilbert, Lee Hays, Fred Hellerman, and Pete Seeger—had a smash hit in 1950 with "Goodnight, Irene," and were touring the country when a newspaper named Seeger as a former member of the Communist Party. The group soon found itself blacklisted, and many of its records were removed from stores.

Caught up in the anti-communist backlash of the time was Woody Guthrie. "I ain't a communist necessarily," Guthrie had said, "but I've been in the red all my life." His musical background—growing up in Oklahoma and being driven to California by the Dust Bowl—sprang from the same country tradition that had inspired the Maddox Brothers and Rose. The melody of Guthrie's most famous tune, "This Land Is Your Land," came directly from a Carter Family song. "I think, in every sense of the word, Woody was a country singer," said music historian Bill C. Malone. "When you look at his style, his guitar playing, it was borrowed directly from Maybelle Carter. He admitted that. His songs were based on country melodies. He borrowed from the Carter Family and Gene Autry and Jimmie Rodgers and other people like that. But then he went to New York. He had begun associating with a different crowd, with these New York, urban people. He began to lose that country identification and began to be identified as a quote 'folk singer' unquote, and became the godfather of the whole urban folk music movement."

Moving forward, though they both shared common roots and often drew on the same songs—and though the definitions were arbitrary, driven as much by marketing as anything else—folk music and what was now "country and western" music became separate categories. "Somebody had to claim Woody, and the folk music community absolutely claimed Woody," said Marty Stuart, who believes Guthrie should be in the Country Music Hall of Fame:

> Country music missed by not claiming him as one of their own, because, in my mind, when I listen to Woody Guthrie, he's one of the purest country artists that God ever made. Woody Guthrie *is* American music. He *is* country music.
>
> Take it to the music. Put it on the music. Shine the light on the music and what the man wrote. Mighty powerful. "Deportee," "This Land Is Your Land," just start there and keep going to the end of the line. There you have country music: Woody.

popularity charts lumped it under the broader title of "folk records." Few artists seemed to mind. Hank Williams called his songs "folk music," though he was equally comfortable referring to himself as a hillbilly, a term many other performers considered degrading. Ernest Tubb and Red Foley, in particular, pushed for something different.

On June 25, 1949, *Billboard* added the phrase "country and western" (and substituted the term "rhythm and blues" for "race music"). "My feeling is that people who bought records called 'race' records and people who bought 'hillbilly' records were offended by those terms," said Douglas B. Green. "And the record companies finally got a clue and decided to change to more genial or politically correct, for the 1940s, terms: 'rhythm and blues,' and 'country and western.'"

Slowly the term "folk music" began to describe a music performed by groups more likely to be based in New York City than in Nashville. Though the category contained

ABOVE *When* Billboard *was persuaded to rename the music coming out of Nashville "country and western," the term "folk music" became more narrowly associated with artists like Woody Guthrie, who were more politically outspoken.*

・・・

By 1950, Nashville's position at the heart of the country and western music business was solidifying. Radio station WSM and its *Grand Ole Opry* hosted most of the music's biggest stars. The Acuff-Rose company had spawned other song publishers who saw money to be made in holding the copyrights to the tunes people loved to hear, and songwriters like Boudleaux and Felice Bryant were happy to provide them.

Some enterprising WSM engineers had formed the Castle Recording Company to take advantage of the local pool of artists and produced their records for a variety of labels, moving to the former dining room on the second floor of Nashville's Tulane Hotel for their studio. And early in 1950, as a WSM announcer introduced a popular morning show, which was carried nationally on NBC, he improvised a little—"for no good reason," he admitted later. "From Music City USA, Nashville, Tennessee," he proclaimed, "the National Broadcasting Company brings you *The Red Foley Show*."

It was more an offhand comment than a statement of fact—most music was still written and recorded in other places, and Nashville's leading citizens still preferred to call their city "the Athens of the South"—but for more and more country artists Nashville had become the Promised Land they all wanted to reach.

No one's pilgrimage covered more miles than Hank Snow's. Born Clarence Eugene Snow in Liverpool, Nova Scotia, in Canada's Maritimes, he suffered an abusive childhood and ran away at age twelve to serve as a cabin boy on fishing boats before being inspired by Jimmie Rodgers to try his hand at music.

He became an accomplished guitar player, changed his first name to Hank because it sounded more Western, and started appearing on Halifax radio as "the Yodelling Ranger." When his voice deepened and he could no longer yodel, he became "Hank the Singing Ranger."

RIGHT *Hank Snow's first songbook. He idolized Jimmie Rodgers and called himself "Canada's Blue Yodeler."*

ABOVE *Snow toured Canada with his trick horse Shawnee and changed his moniker to "the Singing Ranger." He was popular in his native country, but had trouble breaking through in the United States.*

A star in Canada, Snow had less luck breaking through in the United States when he moved south in 1944. He appeared on radio stations in Philadelphia, West Virginia, California, and then on Dallas's *Big D Jamboree*, where Ernest Tubb met him in 1949. Their shared obsession with Jimmie Rodgers formed an instant bond, and Tubb invited Snow to Nashville, highlighting him with slots on the *Midnite Jamboree* and eventually persuading the *Grand Ole Opry* to let him perform.

ABOVE *Snow finally made it to the* Grand Ole Opry, *where he became a star performer like Minnie Pearl.*

Snow's first appearance was underwhelming, and he was considering giving it all up and returning to Canada when a train song he had written and recorded, "I'm Moving On," suddenly hit the charts.

"It was like magic," Snow remembered. The audiences "were completely indifferent one week, and the next week they were wildly enthusiastic." The song would be the number one country song for twenty-one weeks, equaling Eddy Arnold's record for duration at the top of the charts. Hank Snow's place on the *Opry* was assured, and the former cabin boy from a Canadian province in the North Atlantic had become a certified American country and western star.

MOTHER MAYBELLE

I was asking Maybelle one night in Knoxville, she was doing a sound check, and she had the autoharp and she's trying to get it louder and it's starting to feedback, and I said, "Maybelle, what do you do when you have trouble with that mic?"

"Oh, I just do what I tell the girls to do when they have trouble with the mic: just smile real loud." Good advice.

JOHN MCEUEN

That same year, another group of country artists found their way to Nashville, although their journey was much shorter—and much less unlikely—than Hank Snow's. The Carter Sisters and Mother Maybelle, from Maces Spring, Virginia, now represented "the First Family of Country Music," since A.P. and Sara had gone their separate ways and left the original trio. Maybelle and her three daughters carried on the family business, at the urging of her husband, Eck.

Wearing dresses Maybelle had sewn from a wartime surplus silk parachute, the group performed on radio stations in Richmond, and throughout the week made personal appearances Eck would book for them. Anita, the youngest sister, had the best voice of the three. Helen, the oldest, was the most accomplished instrumentalist. June, the middle child, was high-spirited and outgoing, and though not as musically accomplished as the two other girls, often became the center of attention because of her natural sense of humor, which she deployed to create a comic character.

RIGHT *The Carter Sisters (with Mother Maybelle, second from left) were growing up, and like other country acts they dreamed of coming to Nashville and joining the* Opry.

"My mom was born an entertainer," said Carlene Carter, June's eldest daughter. "Mom made herself out to be not as good a singer as she was, because her sisters teased her all the time that she couldn't sing as good as them. So Mama kind of turned it into an act." She would sometimes get the audience laughing by pretending to have difficulty finding her note to start a song, her daughter remembered, "but she knew exactly where it was."

In 1948, they landed a job on the *Midday Merry-Go-Round* on Knoxville's WNOX, where Eck asked a gifted young guitarist to join the ensemble, even if his playing style, much different from Maybelle's distinctive "Carter scratch," leaned more toward jazz than old-time country music.

Chester Atkins came from the remote hollows in the East Tennessee foothills of the Clinch Mountains, where he had made his own crystal set to hear music on local radio stations. Shy and sickly as a boy, he had taken up the fiddle and then the guitar, drawn to the stylings of the Belgian-French jazz guitarist Django Reinhardt and the influential finger picking of Kentucky's Merle Travis, who had established himself as a top session musician on the West Coast.

Despite his virtuosity, Atkins had been having trouble making a living, bouncing from one station to another, many of which thought his music wasn't hillbilly enough for their audiences. "I got fired all over the country," he remembered. "I never really blamed anybody for firing me," he added. "I

CLOCKWISE FROM ABOVE, LEFT *Chester Atkins, left, with his sister Niona and brother Lowell in Luttrell, Tennessee, 1935; despite his talents, Chester was fired by one radio station after another because his guitar style was too sophisticated; in Springfield, Missouri, the Ozark Jubilee featured him and the Carters as a top act; when they finally arrived at the Opry, the crowds adored them.*

always felt they knew what they wanted and I wasn't giving it to them."

He was feeling defeated when the Carter Sisters and Mother Maybelle offered him an equal share of their receipts if he would become part of their act. The combination of his bluesy guitar playing, the Carters' firm grounding in traditional Appalachian ballads, and June's effervescent personality was an immediate success.

It caught the attention of a powerful station in Springfield, Missouri, whose call letters, KWTO, stood for "Keep Watching the Ozarks." In 1949, they became the featured attraction on a show syndicated across the nation, sponsored by Red Star Flour. When the company's sales increased, its main competitor, the Martha White Flour Company, which sponsored a segment on the *Grand Ole Opry*, pressured WSM to bring them to Nashville. This was an offer every country musician dreamed of. But there was a problem: they were told they couldn't bring Chet Atkins with them.

"The reasoning behind this, according to my mother," said June's son, John Carter Cash, "was that the *Grand Ole Opry* was concerned that Chet would come to Nashville and basically take over." "The *Opry* guys didn't want Chet around because he was going to take some work away from them," Carlene Carter said. "But Grandma had taken Chet kind of under her wing. And the girls, they adored Chet. Grandma stood up for him, and said, 'No, Chester's coming.'"

The *Opry* wouldn't budge about Atkins, but sweetened its offer if the Carters would come without him. Still, Maybelle and the girls held out.

After six months, WSM finally gave in. The Carter Sisters and Mother Maybelle, with Chet Atkins "and His Fancy Guitar," debuted on the *Opry* in September 1950. "The roof," June recalled, "came off that building."

They were hired to play four shows a week: a Sunday-morning gospel program, a daytime show called *Noontime Neighbors*, a show at the local veterans' hospital, and every Saturday night at the *Opry*, where June and Little Jimmy Dickens developed comic routines to entertain audiences between the singing acts.

Nashville would become the Carters' home—and Chet Atkins's home, too. He was soon sought after in the city's young recording industry as a session player, just as the other musicians had predicted. He would live in Nashville the rest of his life, and always tell people, "I owe everything to the Carters."

I'M SO LONESOME I COULD CRY

Songwriting is the most mysterious of all the trades. It cannot be explained. There's a craft that goes along with it, but at the same time, it's the divine gift; it's that thing you can't explain.

I guess he said it best, when somebody asked him, "Hank, how do you write them old sad songs?" He says, "Hoss, I don't write 'em. I just hang on to the pen and God sends them through."

The way I see it, if you're collaborating with God, the Creator, who made the mountains and the stars, and the moon and the sky, a three-minute country song is not that big of a stretch. But those kind of songs, like "I'm So Lonesome I Could Cry," "Your Cheatin' Heart"—unexplainable.

MARTY STUART

ABOVE *Hank Williams had a one-word explanation for the power of the songs he wrote and performed: "sincerity."*

Like Jimmie Rodgers, Hank Williams could neither read nor write musical notations. But he was now cranking out hit after hit. Most of his compositions were honky tonk songs with upbeat tempos that his audiences and jukebox operators seemed to prefer. But he was also skilled at writing and performing slower "heart" songs, like "I'm So Lonesome I Could Cry," which Williams himself considered his personal favorite. Many other songwriters—from all genres—point to it as a masterpiece, and cite it as one reason people called him "the Hillbilly Shakespeare."

"I think Hank Williams is a bit like Shakespeare," said Elvis Costello, the British rock and pop musician. "He could animate these simple words to sound like, as if they were everything in the world. That's an incredible talent." "Very simple, straight-ahead lyrics; no sentimentality in it," singer-songwriter Paul Simon said of the song. "It's so direct and true, and a singable three-chord song. A great balance of melody and story. It doesn't seem at all like he's working at it. And it's a gift. Hank Williams is just a freak-of-nature kind of thing—it wasn't before; it didn't come around again. Those songs, they last for lifetimes, if not forever."

"He used to say, 'I don't know what you mean by country music; I just write songs the way I know how,'" added Holly Williams, Hank's granddaughter and a singer-songwriter in her own right. "He was saying, 'Hear that lonesome whippoorwill. He sounds too blue to fly. The midnight train is winding low, I'm so lonesome I could cry.' It's

Williams would not have been able to understand the musical notations of the published version of his classic song "I'm So Lonesome I Could Cry" (above, left). He wrote his lyrics on anything handy, like the start of "The Driftwood Blues" (above, right).

this stunning, beautiful, heartbreaking loneliness. It's simple enough English, but it's just put together in these perfect little mazes of words that cut right at your heart. That's where the Shakespeare stuff comes in."

Hank Williams had his own explanation. His secret, he said, "can be explained in just one word: sincerity." "He made you think he was singing strictly to you," said Bill C. Malone. "This guy understands me. He knows the pain I feel. He knows what I've done and what I've experienced. He knows it just as well as I do, and this song he's singing, he's singing directly to me."

Headlining his own tours, Williams now drew adoring crowds wherever he went, holding them in the palm of his hand, one of the Drifting Cowboys remembered. "Once Hank walked out there . . . and curled up around that [microphone]," he said, "a naked lady coulda rode an African elephant behind him and wouldn't nobody have seen her."

During intermission, band members sometimes sold as many as a thousand Hank Williams songbooks a night. At the end of each tour, he would return with a suitcase bulging with cash that he emptied onto the cashier's counter at his Nashville bank for deposit. In 1950, Williams earned $92,000 in personal appearances and another $40,000 in recording and songwriting royalties.

Then he and Audrey spent the money as fast as he made it. She bought jewelry and new furniture and got them "his and hers" Cadillacs. He left extravagant tips at restaurants; sent money to people who wrote him with hard-luck stories; bought five hundred acres of land south of town and stocked it with cattle. Together, they opened Hank and Audrey's Corral, a clothing store in downtown Nashville, near Ernest Tubb's record store.

As a songwriter, Williams was constantly working, writing new lyrics while he traveled—on scraps of paper he stuffed

into his wallet, on hotel stationery, even on the cardboard that came with his pressed shirts.

To other stars, the Hillbilly Shakespeare seemed to have the golden touch. Touring with Bill Monroe, he co-wrote a tune, "I'm Blue, I'm Lonesome," that became a bluegrass classic. Backstage at the *Opry*, where he was now the show's big-

---

Like all country stars, Williams developed a close connection with his fans. He signs an autograph for a young admirer (top, left); mugs for a snapshot with some female fans at a restaurant's cash register (top, right); and poses backstage with a thrilled young man (above).

nine thousand people showed up at the city's Agricultural Coliseum to hear a show that included Hank Snow and the Carter Sisters and Mother Maybelle with Chet Atkins. Backstage, a teenager showed up with a guitar and asked his idol if he could sing "Hey Good Lookin'" as part of the show. But "that's my current song," Williams answered. "Aw, Hank, let *me* sing it," the boy pleaded. "Go ahead," Williams finally said. "I'll sing something else." He had plenty of other crowd-pleasing hits to choose from.

That same year, Williams was recruited to headline the largest traveling medicine show ever, sponsored by Hadacol, a foul-tasting elixir its makers promised could cure everything from cancer and epilepsy to heart ailments and tuberculosis. It contained vitamins, minerals, honey, and 12 percent alcohol—"enough alcohol to make people feel good," its promoter admitted privately, "and enough laxative for a good movement."

The caravan was a lavish extravaganza, with parades in each city, dancing girls in fancy costumes, and free admission to the shows for anyone with Hadacol box tops. Hank and his Drifting Cowboys, along with Minnie Pearl, were the only country acts, joined at different locales by movie stars like Cesar Romero and Jack Benny, and the prizefighter Jack Dempsey. Bob Hope appeared in Cincinnati but had to wait to walk onstage because the raucous crowd demanded five encores from Williams. When it finally quieted down enough, the comedian sauntered out wearing a cowboy hat. "Just call me Hank Hope," he said. After he was done, he told the show's manager he would never follow Hank Williams again.

The makers of Mother's Best Flour also saw Williams as a draw for their products, and he pre-recorded seventy fifteen-minute radio shows for them to distribute. Besides his hits—and always a hymn or gospel song—the broadcasts sometimes included recitations of poems he had written as his alter ego, Luke the Drifter, who dispensed moral advice Hank Williams himself never followed. And sometimes, over the objections of the band, the shows included vocals by Audrey, who, despite the limits of her vocal talents,

gest star, he would sometimes try out a new song for other artists and ask if they wanted it. If they *really* liked it, he would usually decide to record it himself.

Jimmy Dickens got the treatment when he was on tour with Williams and Minnie Pearl:

He said, "You need a hit." I said, "Well, who doesn't?" He said, "Let's just write you one right now. You got any paper?" And Minnie Pearl reached in her glove compartment and gave him a little pad of paper and he gave me a pen and he said, "Now write this down."

And he wrote me one line at a time, one line at a time. And in fifteen minutes he had written "Hey Good Lookin'." And he said, "Now you record this and it'll make you a hit." I said, "As soon as I can get in the studio it'll be put down."

About a week later, we were up at [the Ryman] and he said, "I recorded your song today." I said, "When it hits, you'll know that it's mine." He said it with a smile.

"Hey Good Lookin'" would be another number-one hit—for Hank Williams. In 1951, when Montgomery, Alabama, staged a huge homecoming for their hometown celebrity,

---

ABOVE *Little Jimmy Dickens thought he was going to be first to record Hank Williams's song "Hey Good Lookin'." Hank beat him to the studio.*

LEFT *Hank promotes Mother's Best Flour.*

seemed to crave the limelight that increasingly focused only on Hank.

Though the couple presented a public image of a happy marriage, their relationship was as explosive as ever, filled with fights and broken furniture. She suspected him of cheating on her; and when he was on the road, he suspected her of the same thing. "They loved each other. I think they truly did love each other," his friend Jimmy Key remembered, "but for some reason, they fought a battle, I think, every day."

After a few months of sobriety following their move to Nashville, Hank had resumed his bouts of heavy drinking, which escalated the tensions. Returning from a tour, a band member called Audrey to let her know Hank was in his cups again. She said she wouldn't let him in the house, so he should be taken to a nearby hospital to dry out. Another time, when she had locked him from their home, Williams checked into the Tulane Hotel and fell asleep in his room with a lit cigarette, which started a fire that resulted in him being arrested.

Occasionally, he turned to Mother Maybelle Carter. "Maybelle brought Hank within her fold," said John Carter Cash. "She reached out and took him into her heart and really was

like a mother to him in many different ways. My mother would tell me that he would come to the house sometimes late at night and would just sit in the kitchen area and have coffee and talk to Maybelle." "They worried about him a lot, and they'd try to steal his liquor, and pour it out," Carlene Carter said. "It was always done with a lot of love. There was never any judgment there. There was some cornbread and some stew, and some pinto beans with a ham hock in it, no matter what. She'd feed you and lift you back up, and talk to you, and counsel you. She'd just love on you until you felt better."

Williams continued to pour his troubles into his songs. When Audrey was hospitalized—she later claimed it was for a "little minor something," other accounts say it was for

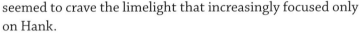

TOP, LEFT *Audrey Williams wanted publicity shots taken of the two of them, not just Hank.*

TOP, RIGHT *Hank relaxes backstage with a woman. Audrey suspected him of cheating on her when he was gone; he suspected the same of her.*

ABOVE *Hank and Audrey's marriage began unraveling again in the early 1950s. "They fought a battle every day," said Jimmy Key.*

reluctant to sing what he considered a "cowboy song," but Miller persuaded him by saying, "Listen to the words." Miller persisted because, he said, Williams "had a way of reaching your guts and your head at the same time. Nobody I know could use basic English so effectively." Bennett's version would soon jump to the top of the pop charts, prompting other popular artists—Perry Como, Dinah Washington, and Louis Armstrong among them—to record it as well.

"It was said one time that his songs could go to places that he couldn't because he was so pure as a country boy and as a country singer. His hillbilly fence might have stopped him," said Marty Stuart, "but the songs could go beyond the fence and go everywhere." Williams reportedly told people he didn't like Tony Bennett's version of his song; it was too "uptown." But band members remembered that whenever they stopped for a meal, Williams would go to the jukebox, put in some money, and make sure everyone there heard Tony Bennett sing his song.

More troubles plagued him. He fell off a stage in Canada, further aggravating his chronic back problem and sending him to the hospital to be fitted for a stainless steel and leather brace that made life on the road excruciating. Near the end of the year, after reinjuring his back in a hunting accident, he entered another hospital for an operation, then ignored his doctors' orders and left before it was fully healed to be home on Christmas Eve.

There, he and Audrey argued and fought for a week—he told a friend he had learned of her latest affair and it "busted my heart." She later accused him of physically attacking her, even firing his gun four times. By New Year's Eve of 1951, she had moved out with the children and called Hank to say she would never live with him again. Ten days later, she filed for divorce once more.

As the year ended, *Billboard* announced that Hank Williams's "Cold, Cold Heart" had been the top country song of 1951, and Tony Bennett's version had been number thirteen on the pop charts.

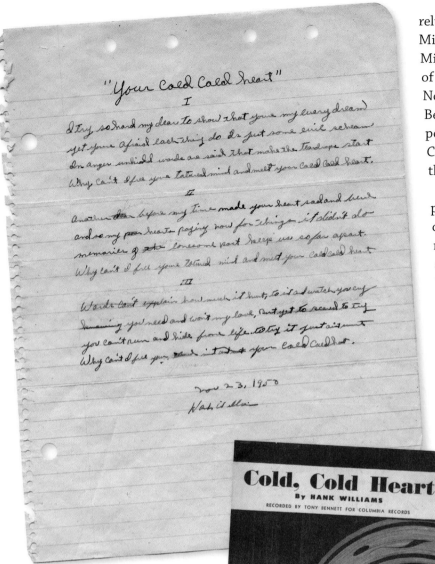

an infection after an abortion he didn't know about—she refused to let him kiss her. Back at home, he told the children's babysitter that his wife had "a cold, cold heart." Then he sat down, and in an hour wrote another classic: "Cold, Cold Heart."

"I think there's such beauty in the storytelling and in the lyrics," said singer-songwriter Vince Gill. "If you hear the words, 'Why can't I free your doubtful mind and melt your cold, cold heart,' if that doesn't stir something up in you, then we'll pass; we'll just let you go on by. But to me, that's as poetic as anything you could ever hear. And it's real."

As "Cold, Cold Heart" rose in the country charts, Mitch Miller, a big-label record producer in New York, urged pop star Tony Bennett to do his own cover version. Bennett was

TOP AND ABOVE *The handwritten lyrics to "Cold, Cold Heart" and the song's sheet music, after Tony Bennett's version topped the pop charts. Hank claimed he didn't like Bennett's version, but he always played it on the jukebox in bars and diners.*

Tony Bennett had been only one of many pop artists who found success covering country songs. Bing Crosby had charted hits with "You Are My Sunshine" and "Pistol Packin' Mama." "Chattanoogie Shoe Shine Boy," the song Fred Rose had given to two WSM executives in exchange for letting Hank Williams onto the *Grand Ole Opry*, was recorded by Frank Sinatra after Red Foley's version climbed the country charts.

In 1948, Stanley Davis Jones, a park ranger at Death Valley National Park, had written and recorded "Ghost Riders in the Sky," a song based on a story he said he had heard as a twelve-year-old about a band of doomed cowboys chasing "the Devil's herd" across an endless sky. Burl Ives covered it in February 1949, then Vaughn Monroe, a famous big band leader, in early March, followed quickly by Bing Crosby, the Sons of the Pioneers, and Peggy Lee. Before the year was out, Spike Jones's comedy orchestra had released a parody of the song, and Gene Autry had appeared in a movie using it as the title. *Billboard* reported that Vaughn Monroe's version was the biggest-selling pop song of 1949.

Three years later, country star Tex Ritter sang the theme song for the movie *High Noon*, which won the Oscar that year for Best Song in a Motion Picture. But it was crooner Frankie Laine's version that sold the most records.

None of those covers, however, equaled what happened to Pee Wee King's "Tennessee Waltz," which he and his vocalist Redd Stewart had written after hearing Bill Monroe's "Kentucky Waltz" on their car radio and deciding that Tennessee should have a waltz of its own. They scribbled lyrics onto a matchbox and recorded it in 1948, complete with fiddles, a steel guitar, and King's accordion.

Then pop star Patti Page decided to add it as the B side of her 1950 Christmas song, "Boogie Woogie Santa Claus." Within six months, 4.8 million copies of the record had been sold, along with 1.1 million copies of sheet music—earning the writers and the Acuff-Rose publishing company $330,000, before other artists in the United States and overseas increased its reach and royalties with even more versions. Everyone from Guy Lombardo to Petula Clark, Otis Redding, Manfred Mann, and Leonard Cohen would eventually record it, and for a while it was the best-selling song in Japan. Tennessee would make it an official state song.

"Tennessee Waltz" became a huge crossover success when Patti Page (top) recorded it; then it became a number-one song in Japan, sung by Chiemi Eri (bottom).

HONKY TONK ANGELS

By 1952, 1,200 radio stations, in every corner of the nation, were devoting at least two hours to country and western music every day. The Decca label reported that country records represented 50 percent of its sales; the giant Columbia label said its country and western catalog had nearly doubled in size and now represented 40 percent of its sales. And because of the lower costs to produce a country record, the company profits were that much higher.

"A jukebox loaded with hillbillies or westerns is as good as money in the bank," *Billboard* proclaimed. Under the headline "Country Music Is Big Business and Nashville Is Its Detroit," *Newsweek* reported, "Country music has become more than a regional manifestation, it has become a national desire." *The American Magazine* put it differently: "This noteworthy nation," it declared, "has been taken down bad with an epidemic called hillbillyitis." With his smoother version of country music, Eddy Arnold had now sold eighteen million records for RCA Victor, nine million of them in the last three years alone.

Hank Williams was the brightest star in the honky tonk firmament, but he was not alone.

Webb Pierce, from West Monroe, Louisiana, had two number-one hits to his name when he heard Hank Williams on the radio, singing "Back Street Affair," about an illicit love between a young woman and an older married man that ruins her reputation and makes them both the subject of small-town gossip. When he told Williams how much he liked it, he learned that Fred Rose had kept Williams from recording it, thinking it was too risqué. But, Hank said, "I think

anyone who's got guts enough to record it has got themselves a number one hit." Pierce rushed to release it, and just as Williams had predicted, got his third top song in a row—bringing him an invitation to leave the *Louisiana Hayride* for the *Opry*. Faron Young, known as "the Hillbilly Heartthrob," joined the *Hayride* as a protégé of Pierce, whom he hoped to follow to Nashville.

Carl Smith was already there. "My daddy had the 'it' quality," said his daughter, Carlene Carter. "He had that clear voice and he was good looking and the women swooned over him." Smith had arrived at WSM around the same time as the Carter Sisters. He and June soon became involved. "They called them 'the Sweethearts of the Opry' because they met on the *Opry* stage," Carlene said. "And my mom would always make these jokes about, 'Where's that nice Carl Smith?' Just with a little wink. So she had a crush. And he got a crush back. And so they got married, and I think they were happy for a good amount of time. But they had that career struggle,

TOP *Like Hank Williams, honky tonk singers Faron Young (left) and Webb Pierce (right) moved from the* Louisiana Hayride *to the* Opry.

LEFT *Carl Smith and June Carter, "the Sweethearts of the Opry." They married and had a daughter, Carlene.*

Lefty Frizzell (performing, top, and stopping for a fan photo, above) was Hank Williams's chief rival for dominance in the honky tonk world. "It was a toss-up to who was the hottest," said Merle Haggard, who idolized Frizzell.

where Mama had that ambition eating her up, and it caused a problem."

But of all the rising honky tonk stars, none was challenging Hank Williams for supremacy more than William Orville "Lefty" Frizzell from Corsicana, Texas, who had given up working oil rigs to sing and write songs. "A lot of people refer to that period as the period of Hank and Lefty," Merle Haggard said. "The jukebox was just full of Lefty Frizzell and Hank Williams, and it was a toss-up to who was the hottest."

Like Williams, who was five years older, Frizzell struggled with alcoholism and derived inspiration for his songs from his personal life. "I Love You a Thousand Ways" came from a number of poems written during a six-month jail term in New Mexico as an apology to his wife. "And the back side of it was called 'If You've Got the Money I've Got the Time,'" Haggard said. "Both of them went on to be country music standards. And that was his first record. And the next five records were treated the same way; they were all number-one records. So he was really hot around 1950, '51, '52."

Frizzell and Williams toured briefly together as "the Kings of Honky Tonk," though Hank privately complained to friends that he thought Lefty's voice was whiny. After their shows, the two would play their guitars in a hotel room and sing Jimmie Rodgers songs.

TOP *Kitty Wells performs at the* Opry.

ABOVE *The* Billboard *chart for August 23, 1952, shows that her song "It Wasn't God Who Made Honky Tonk Angels" has both answered— and bested—Hank Thompson's "Wild Side of Life."*

In early 1952, a song rocketed to the top of the country charts, sung by another honky tonk singer from Texas, Hank Thompson, who had made his name in Western swing with his Brazos River Boys. "The Wild Side of Life" was written by William Warren after his wife had asked him for a divorce, and then he saw her in a bar with another man and thought, "She quit me to go back to the wild side of life." Its melody came from the Carter Family's "I'm Thinking Tonight of My Blue Eyes," which Roy Acuff had also used in his famous song "The Great Speckled Bird." Its lyrics lamented, "I didn't know God made honky tonk angels."

"The Wild Side of Life" was still rising in the charts when a new song, with the same melody, "It Wasn't God Who Made Honky Tonk Angels," came out as a direct answer to it, sung by Kitty Wells. "It's a shame that all the blame is on us women," she sang. "Too many times married men think they're still single, that has caused many a good girl to go wrong."

Kitty Wells was no honky tonk angel. The happily married wife of Johnnie Wright, part of the popular duo Johnnie and Jack, and the mother of three, she preferred appearing in public in demure old-style gingham dresses. After several unsuccessful attempts at gospel recordings, she had agreed to do the new song simply to earn the session fee and had no expectations for it.

But her song struck a chord in women everywhere. "She

didn't even know the record was released," according to Eddie Stubbs. "Audrey Williams had been to Alabama and was driving back into Nashville and she was scanning the radio dial and she heard 'It Wasn't God Who Made Honky Tonk Angels' repeatedly. And she got on the phone when she got back to Nashville and she called Kitty and she said, 'Gal, you've got a hit on your hands.'"

It soon eclipsed "The Wild Side of Life" to become the first song by a woman to reach the top of *Billboard*'s country and western chart—and prompted Johnnie and Jack to rename their act. "Instead of being Johnny and Jack and the Tennessee Mountain Boys, and Kitty Wells, Kitty got top billing," Stubbs said. "Roy Acuff told them, at the time, 'You're making a huge mistake. There's always room for a girl singer on a show, but there's no girl singer headliners.'"

For a while, Wells was kept from broadcasts of the *Opry*—where Acuff was hailed as "the King of Country Music"—because her song was considered too outspoken. But the show's managers eventually relented, and Kitty Wells would go on to become one of the *Opry*'s most durable stars, an inspiration to future women artists known as "the Queen of Country Music."

I'LL NEVER GET OUT OF THIS WORLD ALIVE

I think when Hank split with Audrey, I think that was the beginning of the end. He wasn't good with her, and he wasn't good without her. He had to have her, he had to have somebody strong like that to keep him focused.

E. JIMMY KEY

As Hank and Audrey Williams's second divorce was finalized in 1952, he once more turned his personal sorrows into a song: "You Win Again." "Yeah, that was an Audrey song, 'You Win Again,'" Jimmy Key said. "It's a sad song, but it really tells a lot about his life at that point."

Williams moved in briefly with Ray Price, a rising country star, who remembered Hank calling Audrey

TOP *Hank Williams wrote "You Win Again" when Audrey divorced him for the second time in 1952.*

RIGHT *Williams has his arm around nineteen-year-old Billie Jean Jones after winning her away from Faron Young.*

every day, only to have her hang up. Then Williams tried to move on. He found a new girlfriend, Bobbie Jett, who soon became pregnant with his child. And when he appeared on national television, on *The Kate Smith Evening Hour*, it seemed clear that he was also infatuated with young Anita Carter, as they sang one of his new songs, "I Can't Help It If I'm Still in Love With You." "There's a huge crush going on there, big time," Carlene Carter said. "I don't know details, but you can see it. She certainly was in awe of him. You can see it in her eyes, a lot of love going on there in a shy girl. She was pretty young."

In June, Williams met another woman, nineteen-year-old Billie Jean Jones, who had accompanied Faron Young for a guest appearance at the *Opry*, and he was so taken by her beauty that he told Young, "If you ain't going to marry her, ol' Hank's gonna marry her." Soon enough, Williams had wooed her away and the two were engaged.

In a recording session in Nashville, where Chet Atkins sat in on guitar, Williams was so weak, he would fall into a chair to rest between each take. As they finished the last song, "I'll Never Get Out of This World Alive," Atkins remembered thinking, "Hoss, you're not just jivin'."

Despite it all, he was still writing and recording hit after hit. His song "Jambalaya" topped the country charts, and like so many others, became a pop hit as well when Jo Stafford covered it. Acuff-Rose, his publisher, reported that eighty-nine of his copyrights were recorded in the first half of 1952.

On tour, Williams continued drawing huge crowds, though he often was drunk or surly onstage—or simply failed to appear, sometimes even for his spot on the *Grand Ole Opry*. In Richmond, Virginia, with Ray Price as the opening act, he had trouble remembering the lyrics and staying on key, and walked off after three songs, leaving Price and the Drifting Cowboys to try to appease the angry crowd. After another ragged performance, a disgusted Roy Acuff told him, "You've got a million-dollar voice and a ten-cent brain."

At a concert in El Paso, he was in such bad shape that Minnie Pearl was asked to stay with him between performances to make sure he didn't miss the second show. She tried to brighten his mood by singing "I Saw the Light." He responded, "Minnie, there ain't no light."

On August 9, he missed another *Opry* appearance, despite being warned by Jim Denny, the show's manager, that it was his last chance to redeem himself. Two days later, after hearing reports that Williams was drunk during a show at a Pennsylvania music park, Denny called him up and fired him—"the toughest thing I ever had to do in my life," he said. Ernest Tubb, who was in the office at the time, said Denny had tears in his eyes. Informed of the decision, Edwin Craig, the president of National Life and Accident Insurance, the owner of WSM, told Tubb that it might force Williams to rehabilitate himself. "But it may work the other way," Craig added. "It may kill him."

But his physical condition was deteriorating. The operation on his spine had not eased his constant back pain, and now he added a steady mix of drugs to combat it: amphetamines to get himself going, sedatives to help him sleep, sometimes morphine to numb the pain. One bystander in California noticed that he seemed to have pills for breakfast. In Texas, a man hired to keep tabs on him for the *Opry* said, "He had pills in his hat band, his guitar, pills everyplace." His friend Jimmy Key remembered the time vividly: "The drinking was bad enough, but he progressed to other things. I went on out to the house and he came out, still in his underwear, and he looked like Death eating a cracker. I mean he was really, really sad to see."

ABOVE *Williams with his friend and sometime roommate Ray Price. Price often opened for Hank and the Drifting Cowboys and saw Williams's increasingly erratic performances firsthand.*

CENTER *By the time Williams appeared at the Skyline Club in Austin, Texas, on September 18, 1952, he had been fired by the* Opry *for his drunkenness.*

Fred Rose set out to keep his protégé's career intact. In Montgomery, he worked with Williams to polish two new songs Hank had written. One was "Kaw-Liga," about a wooden Indian in an antique store who falls in love with the statue of an Indian maiden, but loses her because he was never able to express his feelings. The other song was pure emotion. When she heard her son and Fred Rose working on it, Lillie Williams called it "the prettiest song I ever heard . . . so pretty it made my hair stand on end." It was titled "Your Cheatin' Heart."

As he made preparations to have the songs recorded, Rose also arranged for Williams to return to the *Louisiana Hayride*, which was

happy to have such a national star back on its stage, regardless of reports about his unreliability. Jerry Kennedy, who would go on to be a renowned session guitarist and record producer in Nashville, was just a kid in Shreveport at the time, and went to the *Hayride* to see his idol:

I remember going down around five o'clock for an eight o'clock show. I got on the first row. Unfortunately, Hank had been overserved, or something. It was probably close to ten o'clock before they brought him out; we had all been waiting. And he did the chorus to "Jambalaya" three times and walked off. That was my seeing Hank Williams.

I was definitely a big fan. So when I saw him do three choruses of "Jambalaya," it did not bother me in the least that that's all I had seen. I had seen Hank Williams.

On October 19, Williams and Billie Jean got married in New Orleans in as public a manner as possible. For tickets ranging from $1 to $2.80, people could attend the afternoon rehearsal or the evening ceremony, complete with a musical performance. Fourteen thousand fans attended.

Then Williams went back on tour for the remainder of 1952. "Those last days must have been a physical challenge," Marty Stuart said, "because the disease of alcoholism and drug addiction, on top of whatever physical ailments, and riding up and down the road in a back seat of a car to sing country music, was not a glamorous life. So it must have been just a physical nightmare—and a soul nightmare."

LEFT *A total of fourteen thousand paying fans attended the rehearsal and then the wedding of Hank Williams and Billie Jean Jones, staged at the Municipal Auditorium in New Orleans.*

ABOVE *Hank performed for both audiences.*

ney to the concert. "My father's dream in life, or the way he viewed himself and his place in the world, is that *he* should have been Hank Williams," Rodney said:

And we went and he put me on his shoulders. I remember the odor of the Brylcreem [on his hair] and I really think it is my second memory in life.

But the memory was made more vivid and more real because my father would constantly remind me, "I took you to see Hank Williams. Don't forget, I took you to see the Hillbilly Shakespeare." It was his legacy for me: "I took you to see Hank Williams."

For a retainer of $300 a week, Williams had brought on Horace "Toby" Marshall, who claimed to be a doctor, but in reality had a bogus degree he had purchased from a traveling salesman at a filling station. Before a performance, Marshall would let Williams have a few beers, inject him with something that made him vomit, then give him black coffee and Dexedrine and send him onstage. After the show, Williams was provided with some more beers, a few sedatives, and put to bed. More and more often the sedative was a new drug Marshall added to Hank's bag of pills: chloral hydrate, powerful and particularly dangerous when combined with alcohol.

On December 30, Williams prepared to leave Montgomery for two shows in West Virginia and Ohio. A winter storm canceled his plans to fly, so he hired seventeen-year-old Charles Carr to drive him in Williams's Cadillac, with his guitars, songbooks, and records packed in the trunk, along with a fresh supply of Marshall's chloral hydrate. They started late and made several stops—for Williams to buy beer and find a doctor who would provide him with a shot of morphine—before stopping for the night in Birmingham.

On the 31st, New Year's Eve, they set out early. Hank was in good spirits. After breakfast, he bought a bottle of bourbon and sang along with the radio at times. When they stopped in Chattanooga for lunch, he played Tony Bennett's version of "Cold, Cold Heart" on the jukebox and left a $50 tip.

It was snowing when they reached Knoxville and learned that the first show, scheduled for that night in Charleston,

His health worsened: chest pains that made it hard to catch his breath at times; a puffy appearance from his drinking and drug abuse; periodic incontinence often associated with spina bifida; his back pain now so acute that he sometimes lay on the floorboard of his touring car, crying because it hurt so much. "Every time I close my eyes," he said, "I see Jesus comin' down the road. He's comin' after ol' Hank."

"He had the taste of success and he had such a fear of losing it that I think that just kept pulling him and pulling him," said Jimmy Key. "Everybody was grabbing at him. Everybody wanted money; everybody wanted this, they wanted that."

He kept touring. In mid-December, he was in Houston, where James Walter Crowell took his two-year-old son Rod-

---

ABOVE *Despite his deteriorating health, Hank kept up his busy touring schedule in late 1952; sometimes his back pain was so severe, he would lie on the floorboard in the back of his new Cadillac and cry.*

CENTER *Williams's prescription for chloral hydrate, signed by his "doctor" Toby Marshall*

West Virginia, had been canceled and they were to proceed directly to Canton, Ohio, where four thousand people had paid $2.50 each for the New Year's Day show. Hank persuaded a doctor to give him two more shots of morphine before they departed at 10:45 p.m., with Williams lying down in the back seat, covered by his overcoat and a blanket, as they headed for Canton.

He never made it. Somewhere on the mountain roads between Bristol, Tennessee, and Oak Hill, West Virginia, in the early hours of January 1, 1953, Hank Williams, the Hillbilly Shakespeare, died in the back seat of his car. He was twenty-nine years old.

Fred Foster, a young clerk at the Irving Music store in Washington, D.C., went to his favorite café the morning of January 1, 1953, just as news of Hank Williams's death was starting to spread across the nation. A radio was on, playing one of Hank's songs: "And the DJ comes on and said, 'Well, there he is, folks, the late and great Hank Williams.' And so I said to the waitress, 'What? Is Hank Williams dead?' And she said, 'Oh, yeah. Haven't you heard? He's dead.' And I wept. I couldn't help it 'cause there was a loss, man, for all mankind, I thought."

Though it was a holiday, and Foster was only a lowly clerk at his record store, he managed to contact the regional distributor of MGM records on the phone and asked him, "How many Hank Williams records do you have?" The distributor guessed he had maybe fifty thousand. "Fine, I want them all by tomorrow," Foster said:

And the next morning, when I opened up the shop, there was a semi loaded with Hank Williams 78s; every piece of literature that had ever been printed about him that they had; posters and everything. We stacked the storage room completely full to the ceiling. Then we started stacking them down the aisles. And there was barely room to walk in the store.

The store's owner, George Friedman, was appalled and thought Foster had just bankrupted him, but reluctantly agreed to let the young man create a radio spot saying that the record shop was the only one in the region with Hank Williams's complete catalog. Foster was nervous as he headed to work the next morning:

I'm five blocks from the record shop and I see this great multitude of people, four and five abreast, covering the whole sidewalk. And when I get back to where they're coming in to order, the first guy up said, "I want five sets, complete, of everything."

I said, "Well, we also have Luke the Drifter." He said, "I said 'everything.'" I said, "Yes, sir."

I mean it was unreal. It was unbelievable—and for three or four days. I called back to the distributor and I said, "You've got another shipment of Hank Williams coming in?" And he said, "Yeah, we had to. We had none left." I said, "We want 'em all."

So, I don't know, we must have sold a hundred, a hundred and fifty thousand; I don't know. But George would slip a five in my pocket occasionally, "Wonderful job, Fred." I said, "I didn't do it for the money, George. I just knew that people who loved Hank like I do would want 'em."

TOP Poster for Hank's New Year's Day concert in Canton, Ohio. When news arrived that Hank had died, the cast was asked to perform anyway, beginning with "I Saw the Light."

LEFT Released posthumously, "Kaw-Liga" would be 1953's top-selling country song, and "Your Cheatin' Heart" would become a classic.

OPPOSITE *The crowd for Williams's funeral on January 4, 1953, was Montgomery's biggest since the day Jefferson Davis was inaugurated as president of the Confederacy. There was room inside the church for 2,750.*

TOP *From left, Little Jimmy Dickens (partially hidden), Bill Monroe, Roy Acuff, Red Foley, Carl Smith, and Webb Pierce perform "I Saw the Light."*

CENTER *Ernest Tubb sings "Beyond the Sunset," accompanied by the Drifting Cowboys.*

RIGHT *The Southwind Singers do a gospel song, "My Record Will Be There."*

Then Williams was laid to rest in Oakwood Cemetery. He was already becoming a legend. Released after his death, "Kaw-Liga" would become the top-selling country song of 1953. "Your Cheatin' Heart" would become one of his best-known songs—and for many people would define country music.

"'Your Cheatin' Heart' is probably my favorite," said Darius Rucker, who has been both a rock and country singer. "I think everybody that wants to sing country music should have to sit in a room and listen to 'Your Cheatin' Heart,' over and over, for an afternoon. The way his voice cries out for her. As a singer, it just makes you go, 'Man, that's what I want to do.'"

"The same way that Jimmie Rodgers spawned many musical children, I think the same could be said for Hank," said Marty Stuart. "And the most incredible part of the whole story to me was the short span of time in which he wrote and how long those songs have lasted, and will keep on lasting."

"I loved Hank Williams," said Kris Kristofferson. "He had his heart and his soul into every word. Every song he sang, to me, would sound like he believed everything in it. I wish

On Sunday, January 4, twenty thousand mourners gathered outside Montgomery's Municipal Auditorium for the funeral of Hank Williams—the largest crowd in the city's history since the day Jefferson Davis was inaugurated as president of the Confederacy in 1861.

Only 2,750 could fit inside, including two hundred African Americans who filled the segregated balcony, as Williams's open casket was placed at the foot of the stage, flanked by floral arrangements in the shape of a guitar.

Though the *Grand Ole Opry* had fired him just four months earlier, many of its stars attended the service. Ernest Tubb comforted Lillie Williams in the audience, then sang a hymn with the Drifting Cowboys. Red Foley performed "Peace in the Valley," and Roy Acuff joined him, Carl Smith, Webb Pierce, Jimmy Dickens, and Bill Monroe to sing "I Saw the Light," while June Carter sat with the crowd. The Southwind Singers, an all-black gospel quartet, also performed.

ABOVE *Ernest Tubb consoles Hank's mother, Lillie, as mourners file past his open casket before the funeral service begins.*

RIGHT *Billie Jean, second from left, is comforted by her parents; Audrey, far right, sits next to Hank's sister Irene.*

that he'd lived to be as old as I am, 'cause I know there was a lot of great songs in there that he wasn't around long enough to write."

"Everybody, nowadays, is, in a way, swimming in the wake of Hank Williams," said rock musician Jack White. "All roads sort of lead back to him. Hank Williams feels like America to me. When you hear that, you really are hearing America."

"What I loved about Hank Williams were those songs and the way he made you feel how much he must have hurt," added Vince Gill. "I was always drawn to the melancholy ones, more than the fun ones. 'Cold, Cold Heart,' 'Your Cheatin' Heart,' and 'I'm So Lonesome I Could Cry.' You can't say it any more plain, or any more poetic, than 'I'm So Lonesome I Could Cry.'"

ABOVE *Lillie Williams, surrounded by some of the letters of condolence from Hank's many fans*

"Just the sheer amount of music that he put out in a six-year period is unbelievable to all of us," said his granddaughter, Holly Williams:

In six years, he had eleven number-one singles; thirty-five Top Ten singles. He recorded nearly two hundred songs, recorded and wrote. The body of work is what keeps people coming back, not only the amount of songs, but the fact that they were all truly amazing. I've never heard a song of my grandfather's that I would consider as a throwaway.

If it's a fun, kitschy song that doesn't mean anything, it's still a great melody that you keep singing over and over; or it's a total heartbreak song. But this simple boy, born on a dirt floor, who can just rip your heart out— for generations to come we'll always refer back to him.

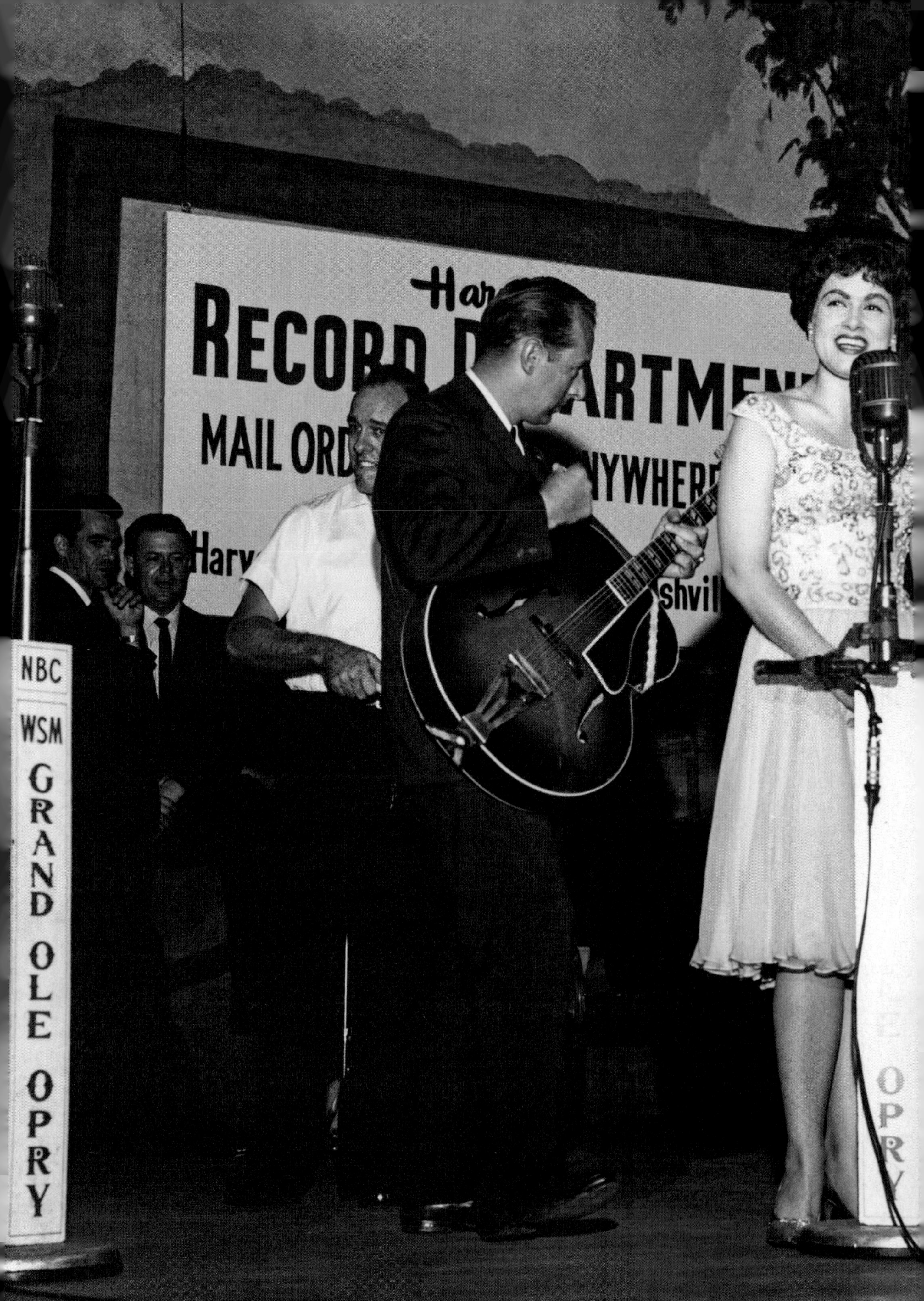
NBC
WSM
GRAND OLE OPRY

4

I CAN'T STOP LOVING YOU

Country music has always been a family. I think
one of the things that drew us together in the early
days, we were not the "toast of the town." We sought
comfort and strength and solace in being close with
one another. It was kind of an "us against them"
mentality, really.

BILL ANDERSON

Patsy Cline singing at the Grand Ole Opry

was represented by Tommy Duncan and Hank Thompson.

Honky tonk heroes Lefty Frizzell and Webb Pierce were there, as was Hank Williams's mother. *Grand Ole Opry* regulars Roy Acuff and Little Jimmy Dickens showed up. So did Ralph Peer, who had done more than anyone to record both hillbilly and race music in its early days.

Hank Snow's devotion to Rodgers's memory was as fervent as Ernest Tubb's: he had just released an album of Rodgers's songs and had named his son Jimmie Rodgers Snow in honor of his hero. With Rodgers's widow at his side, Snow presided at a ceremony unveiling a new monument to the man Meridian had once considered a worthless drifter but now claimed as its most honored native.

Rodgers, Snow proclaimed, "led the way for all of us, including Hank Williams, who's been called home." Only five months earlier, the industry had been shocked by the passing of Williams, who like Rodgers had mixed hillbilly tunes with the blues, endeared himself to his audiences with his rakish persona, and died young—but not before leaving behind hundreds of songs that would influence American music forever.

"Jimmie Rodgers handed it over to Hank," Snow added, "who bridged the gap between hillbilly and popular music." But the handing down—and the bridging of musical gaps—was far from over.

O N MAY 26, 1953, the twentieth anniversary of the death of Jimmie Rodgers, more than thirty thousand people flooded into his hometown of Meridian, Mississippi, to celebrate the man known as "the Singing Brakeman" and "America's Blue Yodeler." Ernest Tubb, a Rodgers acolyte and one of the organizers of the celebration, referred to him as "the Daddy of Country Music."

The array of stars that turned out demonstrated the broad embrace of the music Rodgers had helped popularize in the 1920s. The original Carter Family—A.P., Sara, and Maybelle—appeared together for the first time in ten years. Bluegrass innovator Bill Monroe and his brother Charlie put aside their long-standing feud for the day. Western swing

ABOVE *Hank Snow (right) and Justin Tubb unveil a statue to "the Father of Country Music" at the Jimmie Rodgers Memorial in Meridian, Mississippi, May 26, 1953.*

RIGHT *A photo of Rodgers looks down on a teenager who has just made a purchase at the Ernest Tubb Record Shop in Nashville. A new generation was looking for something different.*

In the 1950s and early '60s, radio formats were segregated, like the rest of American society. Rhythm and blues played on stations presumably for black audiences. Country and western was heard on stations presumably listened to by whites. But in truth, on each side of the racial divide, young people were tuning in to—and buying—both. The children of the postwar baby boom were now becoming teenagers and hungry for music different from what their parents had listened and danced to.

"A lot of times, in this community, or that community," said Darius Rucker, "you're told, 'You can't listen to this; you can't listen to that.' You know, 'We don't listen to that; we don't listen to this.' But people that are buying music and listening to music are a lot more open than you think they are."

With its diverse and tangled roots—from Appalachian ballads and cowboy songs to gospel and the blues—country music had always been a dynamic mixture of genres, perpetually striving to reach broader audiences and greater sales. Now, it would adapt again.

The sonic explosion that would both spring from country music and rock it to its core would include a poor boy from Mississippi and a restless, dark-eyed young man from rural Arkansas, with an unmistakable deep voice and a voracious passion for every type of American music. Their new sound would originate not in Nashville but farther west in Tennessee, along the Mississippi River in Memphis, where a pioneer record producer believed that this music could be a way to bring the races together.

TOP *Bill Anderson (left) at the WGAU radio station in Athens, Georgia; Walt Harper at WHOD in Pittsburgh. In a time of racial segregation, young people's taste in music knew no color barriers.*

· · ·

Only 240 miles apart, but universes apart when it comes to music. Memphis has always had a little more soul. It was more horn driven, more blues driven. It's not a country town, it's a river town.

There's a feeling in Memphis that you'll not find anywhere else. There's just a magic that comes up from the Delta and that surrounding country that's in the gumbo down there.

MARTY STUART

In 1954, a newly wed couple arrived in Memphis to begin their married life together. Johnny Cash, from Dyess, Arkansas, about fifty miles north and across the Mississippi River, was twenty-two years old and just out of the U.S. Air Force. His young bride, the former Vivian Liberto, was from San Antonio.

Cash had chosen Memphis because his older brother Roy already lived there, where he had a job at a car dealership. "Roy took my dad down to where he worked and there were two mechanics in the bay, Marshall Grant and Luther Perkins," said Rosanne Cash. "And Marshall told me that he looked up from the car he was working on, and he saw my dad standing in the doorway, this kind of skinny, black-haired restless guy; and Marshall said a chill started at the top of his head and went right down his spine. It was like he knew, that he knew something. And Dad came over to him and said, 'Roy says you boys play a little guitar.' And Marshall said, 'Very little.' And Dad said, 'Well, we ought to get together and play sometime.'"

But Cash's first priority was finding a job, and he soon

Music had always provided both solace and an escape from the harsh realities of life for Johnny Cash. He was born February 26, 1932, the son of an Arkansas sharecropper too poor to pay the state's poll tax to vote, and a pious mother who played piano three times a week at worship services in the Baptist church. His parents said that they had been unable to agree on a name for their third son, so they settled on the initials "J.R."

In 1935, during the depths of the Great Depression, they moved from south-central Arkansas, along with five hundred other destitute families, to the Dyess Colony, a resettlement community created by President Roosevelt's New Deal. It offered families a fresh start by providing homes, twenty acres of land, and small stipends for food and clothing, all of which the colonists repaid once they had cleared the trees for their fields and began raising crops. Young J.R. was picking cotton by the age of eight.

Their home had no electricity, and their only luxury was a battery-powered Sears, Roebuck Silvertone radio. They

started work as a door-to-door salesman for the Home Equipment Company. According to Rosanne, "He was the single worst appliance salesman who ever lived. At one point, he went up to a door, knocked on a door, and a housewife answered, and he goes, 'You don't want to buy anything, do you?'"

On his rounds one day, he came across an elderly black man playing music on his front porch and stopped to listen. Gus Cannon had once played in traveling medicine shows, and he had been leading a jug band on Memphis's Beale Street when Ralph Peer had recorded him back in the 1920s. Cash struck up a friendship and sometimes brought along his own guitar to play with Cannon and learn songs from him. "That's the narrative," Rosanne Cash said. "The slave songs and blues meet; the Delta, gospel, somehow Appalachian gets filtered in there. They meet and marry, and there's a story. That's country music."

> My father was a man of the American soil. He worked hard. He saw poverty. They worked that soil—the rich, black gumbo soil is what they called it, gumbo.
>
> JOHN CARTER CASH

ABOVE *Johnny Cash and his new bride, the former Vivian Liberto, August 7, 1954*

RIGHT *In Memphis, Cash met Gus Cannon, a former jug band performer whom Ralph Peer had recorded back in the 1920s. The two became friends and played together on Cannon's porch.*

would gather around it at night, after a hard day's work, and listen to the Carter Family show beaming up from the "border blaster" station in Mexico, or to Sister Rosetta Tharpe singing a mix of gospel and blues. "That was the light in his life," Rosanne Cash said. "The radio was his lifeline to the rest of the world, to the rest of his life."

J.R. had always looked up to his brother Jack, who intended to be a minister. But in 1944, Jack was fatally injured cutting fence posts when the saw blade ripped into his stomach. "I'm going to the light," he told the family as he died. "Can you hear the angels singing? Listen, Mama, can you hear them?" The family had to return to the cotton fields the day after Jack's funeral, Cash would always remember, and his mother would sometimes drop to her knees and say, "I can't go on." Then they would sing a spiritual and go back to work.

J.R.'s relationship with his father, who could be cruel and distant, was already strained. Now it worsened. Once, after drinking heavily, Ray Cash told his teenage son, "Too bad it wasn't you instead of Jack."

J.R. retreated into books about American history and the poems of Edgar Allan Poe. He went on solitary walks at night down the colony's dirt roads, and returned from one to tell his mother he would honor Jack's memory by becoming a gospel singer. She took in other people's laundry to buy him singing lessons, telling him, "God has His hand on you, son. You have a special calling, a gift."

After graduating from high school in 1950, Cash enlisted in the Air Force and listed his name as "John." Trained as a radio intercept operator, he was stationed in Landsberg, Germany, where he monitored the high-speed Morse code transmissions of Soviet Union bombers for three years.

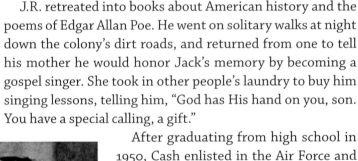

TOP, LEFT *Young Jack (left) and J. R. Cash in the cotton fields of Dyess, Arkansas*

TOP, RIGHT *Ray and Carrie Cash stand over the grave of their son Jack, 1948. He had wanted to become a minister. After Jack's tragic death, his little brother promised their mother he would honor Jack's memory by becoming a gospel singer.*

LEFT *J. R. Cash in high school*

ABOVE *Vivian Liberto at her family home in San Antonio, and the envelope to one of the many love letters Johnny Cash sent her from Germany.*

In his off hours, he learned to play some basic guitar chords, filled sheets of paper with song lyrics, dreamed of starting his own band, and wrote daily letters to Vivian, the pretty and petite Italian-American girl he had met during his training at an Air Force base near San Antonio. He returned to the States in the summer of 1954, and he and Vivian married. It was then that they decided to move to Memphis.

Cash had no intention to remain an appliance salesman. He wanted to be a singer. Soon, he and Marshall Grant and Luther Perkins were gathering each night at Grant's home to play music—some Hank Williams songs, but mostly gospel—while their wives played cards in the kitchen.

Their skills were limited—the only instrument any of them played was the guitar, and no one was particularly adept at it. But Memphis in 1954 would prove the best possible time and the best possible place for them to start.

ABOVE *Cash, during his time in Germany with the Air Force. He already was learning to play the guitar and was writing song lyrics.*

THAT'S ALL RIGHT, MAMA

Memphis, in the '50s, was just this hot stew. Tommy Dorsey was playing down the street in a hotel. And, at the same time, what they called "race music" was played on WDIA, which was really soul music, and B. B. King was a disc jockey, and Rufus Thomas was a disc jockey.

Elvis, Jerry Lee Lewis, Charlie Rich, Roy Orbison, my dad, they were all coming up there. All the guys listened to WDIA and were so profoundly influenced by it that you can say that that station and that music changed the course of modern country music through these guys, through these guys who came up through Sun Records.

ROSANNE CASH

There was a saying: "The blues had a baby and they called it rock and roll." And I always said, "Yeah, and I think the daddy was a hillbilly." So, I think rock and roll was a marriage of black and country music.

BOBBY BRADDOCK

The most popular tune on Memphis radio that summer was "That's All Right," a song written by Arthur "Big Boy" Crudup, an African-American Delta blues musician, whose original release had enjoyed only limited success on rhythm and blues stations. But this new version was something different. It was sung by a white teenager with long sideburns, slicked-back hair, and an almost angelic tenor voice. His name was Elvis Aron Presley.

He had been born in Tupelo, Mississippi, and like J. R. Cash grew up listening to every kind of music on the radio: from hillbilly tunes on the *Grand Ole Opry* to pop standards by Bing Crosby and Perry Como and then the blues by Muddy Waters. His personal favorite was gospel music, especially the kind performed by quartets like the Blackwood Brothers and the Statesmen, who combined tight harmonies with flashy showmanship. When Presley's family moved to Memphis in 1948, he regularly attended the monthly All-Night Gospel Singings at Ellis Auditorium to see them excite the crowds with their energetic, joyful shows.

By 1954, Presley had graduated from high school and was driving a truck for an electrical contractor when he stopped at 706 Union Avenue, the home of tiny Sun Records. Its owner, Sam Phillips, had previously recorded B. B. King, Howlin' Wolf, and other black artists who sang rhythm and blues—the music Phillips called "where the soul of man never dies." He wished he could find a white singer who could do the same thing.

"Sam Phillips has got to be one of the seminal geniuses of popular music," said singer-songwriter Paul Simon. "That he understood exactly what could be achieved by blending the

ABOVE *From left, Marshall Grant, Luther Perkins, and Johnny Cash play music while Vivian Cash and friends listen.*

OPPOSITE, TOP *Sam Phillips in his studio at Sun Records. His business card promises "All Types of Recording" and a handwritten note of his lists "Talent just waiting to be discovered."*

OPPOSITE, LEFT *B. B. King was a guitarist and deejay at Memphis station WDIA.*

OPPOSITE, RIGHT *Arthur "Big Boy" Crudup. His rhythm-and-blues song "That's All Right" would be transformed by Elvis Presley.*

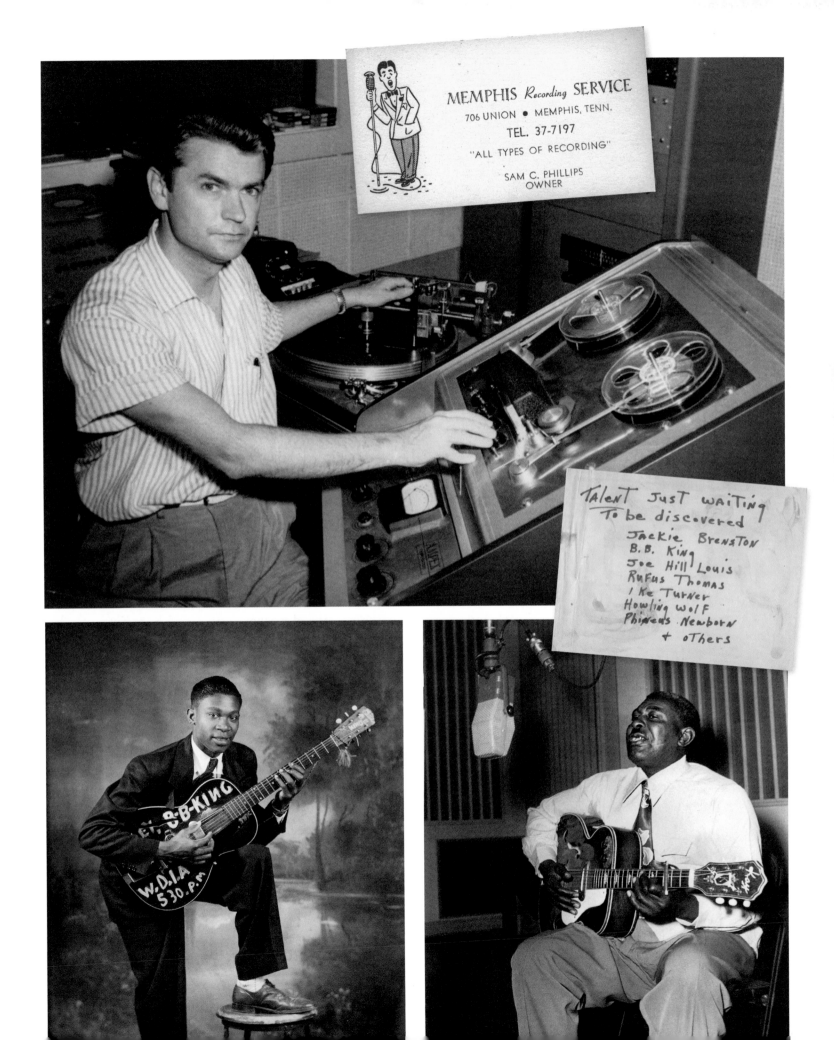

white and black cultures and that he looked for the vehicle to do that and found it in Elvis Presley and recognized it, and saw that as a way of bringing the races closer together—and that was his purpose—that's an extraordinary vision."

Phillips paired Elvis with two musicians from a hillbilly band called the Starlite Wranglers, guitarist Scotty Moore and bassist Bill Black, but initially was unimpressed when they cut "Harbor Lights," a Bing Crosby hit, and "I Love You Because," a country ballad Ernest Tubb had charted a few years earlier.

Then, during a break, Presley started goofing around on his own with Crudup's "That's All Right"—"jumping around

and acting the fool," one of them remembered. Black joined in on the fun with his slap-beat bass, and Moore started in on guitar.

"What are you doing?" Phillips asked from the control booth. "We don't know," they answered. "Well, back up," Phillips ordered. "Try to find a place to start and do it again." Then he started recording them.

"It's not black, it's not white, it's not pop, it's not country," he said when he shared the recording with a local deejay, who immediately put it on the air, playing it over and over as calls and telegrams flooded the station for more.

Phillips quickly scheduled another session to record something for the B side of the record he now wanted to release. Once again Presley and his musicians struggled to come up with something distinctive. All three of them knew Bill Monroe's hit song from 1946, "Blue Moon of Kentucky," a lilting waltz that had become a standard for every bluegrass string band. They started clowning around with it, just as they had with "That's All Right," and Phillips began recording again, using a homemade device to add a distinctive echo to the sound. "Hell," he said when they finished, "that's different."

The single that Sun Records rushed out became a regional phenomenon: rhythm and blues stations played "That's All Right," while country stations focused on "Blue Moon of Kentucky."

It was enough to earn Presley an invitation to play at the *Opry*. The audience responded politely, at best, while some *Opry* regulars grumbled that he had desecrated Monroe's classic song. "The first time I heard Elvis Presley, I hated him, because I was into bluegrass music," country star Charlie Daniels remembered. "I was bluegrass to the bone back then, and he sang

'Blue Moon of Kentucky,' one of my favorite Bill Monroe songs, and I thought, 'What's he doing to my song?'"

Fifteen years earlier, Monroe had caused a similar stir at his own debut on the *Opry* with his energetic reinterpretation of Jimmie Rodgers's "Mule Skinner Blues." History was repeating itself, said Marty Stuart: "Bill Monroe took Jimmie Rodgers's song and built another cornerstone, another pillar for country music to rest on. I think when Elvis took 'Blue Moon of Kentucky,' he took everything from his childhood that he had heard and loved, and he drove a new stake in the ground. Monroe didn't like it much when he first heard it. He thought they were kind of not doing the right thing by way of his music until the first royalty check came. And then I believe Monroe's tune went to, 'I told him if there's anything in this world I could do to help you out, you just let me know.'" (Monroe was impressed enough to release a hybrid version of his own that started with the original 3/4 waltz and then jumped into Elvis's supercharged 4/4 beat.)

But Presley and his music seemed too radical for the *Opry*, and they did not ask him back. Phillips sent him to Shreveport and the *Louisiana Hayride*, which had provided Hank Williams a platform when no one else would. The *Hayride*'s audiences loved him—and called him "the Hillbilly Cat."

Jerry Kennedy, who later became a renowned guitar player and record producer, recalled one of Presley's first appearances:

When Elvis came to the *Hayride*, I was really excited to get to go see his guitar player. I didn't even know Elvis's

ABOVE *An advertisement for Presley's single with "That's All Right" on one side and "Blue Moon of Kentucky" on the other. It was pop, hillbilly, and rhythm and blues—and an immediate hit in the Memphis region.*

LEFT *After the* Opry *didn't invite Presley back, he found a home at KWKH's* Louisiana Hayride, *where they called him "the Hillbilly Cat."*

In [his song] "Get Rhythm," Johnny says, "Get rhythm, when you get the blues, come on get rhythm." Isn't he sort of telling you how to make rock and roll, in a way? He's singing a country song and he's saying, "Get rhythm when you get the blues." Well, those are the ingredients for rock and roll, really.

JACK WHITE

Elvis Presley's success with Sun Records was not lost on Johnny Cash. In late 1954, Phillips showed up at his studio to find Cash sitting on the front stoop asking for an audition. Phillips invited him in and listened to him sing.

"There was something in his voice, and I guess Sam heard it," said former WSM announcer Ralph Emery. "But John wanted to be a gospel singer and Sam said, 'I can't sell gospel records. Write something that's not gospel and I'll cut it.' He thought maybe he could make lightning strike twice."

Cash told Marshall Grant and Luther Perkins they all needed to get more serious about their music. Perkins borrowed an electric guitar and Grant got a stand-up bass and began learning to play it. They started performing a few low-paying local gigs, and Cash persuaded his employer at the Home Equipment Company to sponsor a weekly fifteen-minute radio show on station KWEM.

Still, he wanted some original songs for Phillips to record.

name. And I had called a friend of mine, a disc jockey in Shreveport, and I said, "Who is the guitar player that's playing on that guy you just played whose name was kind of weird." And he told me, he said, "It's a guy named Scotty Moore. He's Elvis's guitar player." And he said, "They're doing the *Hayride* Saturday night."

A friend of mine and I went down, paid our money to get in to hear Scotty Moore. We are sitting there and Elvis comes out, with Scotty and Bill Black, and we are sitting there waiting for this instrumental that he would play. And Elvis steps back at that point, starts dancing. The girls start screaming. We never heard Scotty. So it was kind of a waste of our money, but it was worth it. And then, later on, I did find out who Elvis was.

Back in Memphis, the local newspaper declared, "A white man's voice singing negro rhythms has changed life overnight for Elvis Presley." Sam Phillips put it differently. "I went out into this no-man's land," he said, "and I knocked the shit out of the color line."

ABOVE *Elvis with his bandmates Scotty Moore and Bill Black, in 1954*

RIGHT *Johnny Cash and the Tennessee Two: guitarist Luther Perkins and bass player Marshall Grant*

On his way home from the Air Force, Cash had written a poem on the train, called "Hey, Porter." They put a simple melody to it, and began practicing. "They knew very few chords," said Rosanne Cash. "And there was no real riffing on Luther's part, but he could figure out these very simple and hypnotic lead lines on the guitar. But out of those limitations came a great style, undeniable. The simplicity of the accompaniment just created a frame for Dad's voice and the lyrics. There was just something about it; it was a completely unique sound."

"His voice is singular," added Elvis Costello. "The bass is a

ABOVE *Cash's song "Hey Porter" came from a poem he had written on the train home after his stint in the Air Force. To it, he and his band added a melody with what became their "boom chicka boom" sound.*

percussive and Luther Perkins just playing like the four notes that he seemed to only know. Everything is so angular. I literally think they sound like punk rock records, and I mean that as the highest compliment. I mean, they're just so vivid."

"There's something squirrely about you guys," Phillips said when he first heard their stripped-down style in the spring of 1955. But, he admitted, "it's different." For the flip side of "Hey, Porter," they played another Cash composition, "Cry, Cry, Cry," which took them thirty-five takes because Perkins kept muffing his guitar solos.

But listeners liked the "boom chicka boom" sound of Johnny Cash and the Tennessee Two. They were soon booked on tours with Sun Records' other star, Elvis Presley, usually with a better-known country and western artist, who got top billing. At concerts headlined by honky-tonker Webb Pierce, Cash got a good response as the opening act, but the crowds

went absolutely crazy for Elvis—and many left before Pierce walked onstage to finish the show.

Out on the road, the two young singers became friends. Elvis called Cash "old man," because Cash was three years older. Cash called Presley "the shaky kid" because of his electrifying stage presence, which now overwhelmed every show in which Presley appeared. Music historian Bill C. Malone was a student at the University of Texas in 1955: "I went down to the old Coliseum to see Hank Snow, who was my favorite at the time. And Hank had to cut his program short in order to let Elvis have a second show, or to let the people outside come in. As I watched Elvis, I thought I saw the beginning of the end of the music I loved. At certain points during his show, the young women would attack the stage, and I thought that was something young women shouldn't be doing. It took me a long time to recognize just what he meant to American music and just how strongly a part of country music he really was."

"The Hillbilly Cat, I think he was so different, he was so unique, they were trying to figure out what to do with him, where to put him, where does this guy go?" said Marty Stuart. "He didn't neatly fit into anybody's box. He wasn't exactly country, he wasn't exactly rock and roll, although he was all of those things. He wasn't exactly gospel, although he was all of that. So it took the world a moment to sort out what to do with him."

Also in 1955, the Hollywood movie *Blackboard Jungle* was released, featuring a song by Bill Haley and the Comets called "Rock Around the Clock," which became a national smash hit. Haley himself had once been a yodeling Western swing artist, back when the Comets

were called the Saddlemen, but an earlier song of his, "Rock the Joint," had caught the attention of Alan Freed, a deejay at a rhythm and blues station in Cleveland, who was credited with calling the music "rock and roll."

That same year, a blues guitarist named Chuck Berry went into Chess Records in Chicago, hoping to cut his first single, only to find the producer uninterested in most of his material—until he played a song he had adapted from an old Bob Wills fiddle tune called "Ida Red." It was always the crowd's favorite dance number, Berry said, at the integrated "salt and pepper" clubs in St. Louis where he performed. Intrigued by the notion of a hillbilly song sung by a black man, Chess Records released it, after reworking the lyrics to make it about a young man chasing his unfaithful girlfriend in her Coupe de Ville—and renaming it "Maybellene." Like "Rock Around the Clock," it would sell a million records, mostly to teenagers.

At the time, Elvis Presley and Johnny Cash were known

OPPOSITE *Cash and Presley backstage in Memphis. Elvis called Cash "old man"; Johnny called Presley "the shaky kid."*

ABOVE *A poster for a Hank Snow concert in Ocala, Florida. Elvis Presley is far from being the headliner, billed under Snow and other country stars Faron Young, the Wilburn Brothers, Mother Maybelle and the Carter Sisters, and Slim Whitman.*

RIGHT *Chuck Berry's first big hit, "Maybellene," was also a mixture of music genres; it transformed Bob Wills's fiddle tune "Ida Red."*

mostly in the South and Southwest, where country stations played their songs. Tours operated by the *Grand Ole Opry* and *Louisiana Hayride* booked them to attract younger people to their shows.

The term used to describe their music was "rockabilly."

"I think that most young people who heard rockabilly music in the mid-1950s just thought of it as music," according to Bill Malone. "It was just something that sounded good to them. And, in the beginning, the music they heard would have been on country stations and they thought of the music as being just another form of country. But as time went on and as it began to attract another audience, then they began gradually to divorce themselves from the music of their parents."

At a concert in west Texas featuring Elvis, Cash, and Porter Wagoner, a young singer from Lubbock named Buddy Holly opened the show. And at Sun Records in Memphis, Sam Phillips suddenly found himself inundated with aspiring rockabilly artists.

Jerry Lee Lewis, a flamboyant piano player from Ferriday, Louisiana, showed up after being turned down in Nashville. Roy Orbison came from

TOP *Roy Orbison and the Teen Kings in Tulsa, Oklahoma*

LEFT *Harold Lloyd Jenkins became a rockabilly star named Conway Twitty.*

OPPOSITE *"The Million Dollar Quartet": from left, Jerry Lee Lewis, Carl Perkins, Elvis Presley, and Johnny Cash during an impromptu jam session at Sun Studios, December 4, 1956*

the oil fields of Wink, Texas, at the suggestion of Johnny Cash, who had met him on tour. Orbison had a minor hit with "Rock House," a tune written by another newcomer to Sun Records, Harold Lloyd Jenkins, who had turned down a contract to play baseball for the Philadelphia Phillies after being inspired by Elvis's example. Jenkins was soon touring himself under a new name: Conway Twitty.

After signing with Phillips in 1955, Carl Perkins, the son of the only white sharecropper on an old plantation in west Tennessee, became a close friend of Johnny Cash after both men discovered they had scars on their fingers from picking cotton as young boys. Cash told him a story about a man he had met in the Air Force who prided himself on his spiffy clothes and always said, "Don't step on my blue suede shoes." Perkins turned that into his first major hit.

Wanda Jackson, a young country singer fresh out of high school in Oklahoma City, who wore cowgirl clothes and sang country ballads, joined one of the package shows for her first tour. She had never heard of Elvis Presley, who performed after her, and was in the dressing room with her father when they started hearing lots of screaming:

And Daddy said, "My gosh, I wonder if there's a fire, or something." So he runs out and he said, "Get your stuff together." And he came back and he's just shaking his head and he said, "Wanda, you've got to come see this for yourself. You'll never believe it."

He took me to the wings of the stage and I looked out and there was Elvis, doing all of his gyrations and singing, and all these girls down in front, screaming. And some were crying and reaching up for him. We had never seen anything like that.

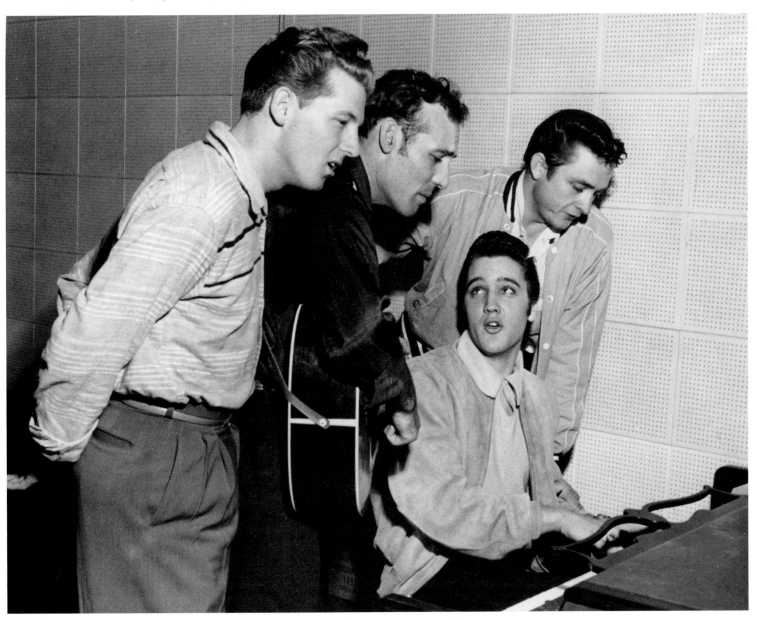

Jackson and Elvis became friends, and he advised her to switch styles from country and western to rockabilly: "We were just talking and he said, 'Wanda, you should get in on this new kind of music,' because, he said, 'things are changing.' He said, 'You know, I draw young people and they're the ones that are buying records now.' He already had this figured out."

Jackson put away her cowgirl clothes in favor of tight-fitting skirts and low-cut blouses her mother tailored for her. (At her debut guest appearance on the *Grand Ole Opry*, Jackson was told she couldn't appear with bare shoulders and was ordered to put on a jacket if she wanted to perform.) She would come to be called "the Queen of Rockabilly."

But the undisputed king of them all was the Hillbilly Cat, Elvis Presley. *Cashbox* and *Billboard* magazines reported that country deejays had voted him as the most promising new artist, and *Country & Western Jamboree* said that 250,000 readers named him "New Star of the Year."

Hank Snow had witnessed Presley's magnetic star power firsthand on his package shows. So had Snow's manager and business partner, Colonel Tom Parker, who had once guided Eddy Arnold's career. They encouraged RCA Victor to buy out Presley's contract with Sun Records for $40,000—at the

time, the most ever paid for a recording artist. After the contract was signed, Snow learned that Parker had squeezed him out of the deal and was now the exclusive agent for Elvis Presley.

In Nashville, Presley began his RCA career by recording "Heartbreak Hotel," which rose to the top five of the pop, country, and rhythm and blues charts simultaneously. His cover of "Blue Suede Shoes" soon began the same rise. By late 1956, Presley had been signed for Hollywood movies, and sales of his singles represented two-thirds of RCA's business. "It's hard to explain a phenomenon like Elvis," said Ralph Emery. "He just took off. I think people, in the beginning, didn't know what to do with him. Do you play him country? Do you play him pop? And then by the time he got down to 'Don't Be Cruel,' he was gone." Elvis Presley had outgrown the family of country music. He left for a career in the movies and the more lucrative pop market.

Meanwhile, Johnny Cash stayed put (although he incorporated a short segment into his performances in which he impersonated his friend, twitching his legs and curling his lips just like Presley). Cash was doing well enough to buy a house in northeast Memphis for his growing family: Vivian had given birth to two daughters, Rosanne in 1955 and Kathy in 1956. The *Louisiana Hayride* had made him a regular, and Marshall Grant and Luther Perkins quit their jobs as auto mechanics.

In July 1956, Cash made his first guest appearance at the *Grand Ole Opry*, where someone backstage told a reporter, "He'll be better than [Elvis] because Johnny's a true country singer, and Presley isn't and never has been."

OPPOSITE *Wanda Jackson and Elvis Presley (top) on the road. As the Queen of Rockabilly, Wanda performs at the Golden Nugget in Las Vegas (bottom), while an aging Bob Wills urges her on.*

ABOVE *Elvis in action, which drove his young crowds crazy*

MIDDLE *Johnny Cash added a comic impersonation of his friend Elvis to his own act, but he stayed with country music as Presley moved to pop and rock and the movies.*

RIGHT *An Elvis fan with a photo of her teen idol*

A new single of Cash's had just become his first number-one country hit. It was for Vivian, who had become worried that on his tours he would succumb to one of the well-known temptations of the road—one that Elvis was already famous for giving in to: the adoring female fans.

Talking about Vivian's concerns with Carl Perkins one night as they watched a group of girls follow Elvis to his dressing room, Cash said that as a married man, "I walk the line." Perkins replied, "That's your title."

"It's a simple song, a very simple song, except they change key every verse," said Paul Simon, an admirer of "I Walk the Line." "And that forces Johnny Cash to change the register of his voice. If it had a weakness, it would be that it was kind of episodic. It was

the writer and the singer. And the melody cannot be separated from the words, that none of it would work by itself, but there's this beautiful perfection in all of the parts. And that's 'I Walk the Line.'"

The song came from her mother's fear about her father's life on the road, Rosanne added. "And he wrote, 'I Walk the Line.' 'I'm going to stay true to you.' Of course, that wasn't true, but . . ."

Backstage at the *Opry* the night of his debut, after singing "I Walk the Line," Cash met for the first time someone whose voice he had once heard on his family's radio back in Dyess, Arkansas. It was June Carter.

like verse after verse, which is just kind of the same thing. 'This happens, that's why I walk the line; that happens, that's why I walk the line.' But he moves it in his register and so you feel some kind of three-dimensional depth that's happening. I think it allows the listeners to project their lives into the spaces. And that is what makes for people's favorite songs, is because they hear songs and their lives fit with those songs."

"The style came from his limitations, as both a guitar player and a singer at that time in his life," Rosanne Cash said. "He had no contrivance yet, only his raw influences and his woundedness that it came from, the purity of it and the stark lines of it—how perfect it is. Bob Dylan said that when he first heard that song on the radio, it was like a voice came from the center of the earth to deliver that song. That's part of the greatness of the song, is that that song cannot be separated from his voice. And I think that is one of the definitions of timelessness, is when the song cannot be separated from

OPPOSITE, TOP *Johnny Cash holds daughter Rosanne; Vivian holds Kathy.*

OPPOSITE, BOTTOM *Cash performs at the* Opry.

ABOVE *Cash signs autographs for Opry fans at Ryman Auditorium.*

RIGHT *Johnny Cash and June Carter backstage at the* Opry. *He had heard her voice on his family's radio in Dyess, Arkansas; now they were both rising stars.*

WSM
GRAND
OLE
OPRY

I think country music, blues music, folk music, rock music, you name it, I think it's all intertwined. They categorized me as rockabilly. Well, I didn't know it was rockabilly. I'm just singing songs, singing them like I sang. And then, all of a sudden, I was rock. And then, all of a sudden, I was pop. Then, all of a sudden, I became country.

I think, when a singer is absolutely passionate about what they do, I don't think you should pigeonhole them. I think they should just be everything they want to be. Because if you ask us artists when it's all said and done, it's music. That's all it is. Doesn't have a title.

BRENDA LEE

In 1956, Fred Foster left his job as a clerk in a record store in Washington, D.C., to take over promotion for the Mercury label's country music division. His bosses dispatched him on a long trip to the South, telling him, "Get on the road and don't come back until you find out why we're not selling." He was gone eight weeks, visiting retail outlets and radio stations.

At a record store in San Antonio, Texas, Foster was impressed with a new inventory system that showed the date they had ordered any release, how many had sold over any period of time, how many they had on hand, and how many were on order. "Why Baby Why" by Webb Pierce and Red Sovine was the top country and western song at the time. The store had sold fifty-two copies, had three in stock, and had none on order. Carl Perkins's "Blue Suede Shoes" had sold 1,300 copies and they had twenty thousand on order. "So I said to

the lady that was in charge of the inventory, I said, 'How do you account for the discrepancy here?'" Foster remembered. "She said, 'You ain't going to *give* country music away with them fiddles and banjos anymore. It's changed.'"

As rock and roll began taking over the airwaves and record sales, the postwar boom in country music seemed to go bust overnight. Speaking to a gathering of deejays in Nashville, Steve Sholes, the RCA producer now handling Elvis Presley, told them, "Your older listeners who want old country music sounds are wonderful people [and] loyal radio listeners . . . but they don't buy records, not enough to keep us in business; not enough to keep the old-fashioned country artist in guitar strings. It's the kids who want and buy the newer sounds."

More and more radio stations switched to a new "Top Forty" format that emphasized pop and rock music. The number of stations devoted to country shrank from six hundred to about eighty-five. Live "barn dance" programs began disappearing. "Country music just died on the vine," said Wanda Jackson. "You could dial your radio back and forth all the time, you couldn't find a country song. The general sense in the country and western community about rock and roll was, 'Maybe it will go away. If we just hang in there long enough, it will go away.'"

On some nights, the *Grand Ole Opry*—which had given Elvis the cold shoulder—found itself playing to a half-empty

OPPOSITE *While other radio barn dances were going off the air in the face of rock and roll's ascendance, the* Opry *still hung on. Here the cast gathers backstage in 1957 with Judge Hay front and center.*

RIGHT *But on many nights, they played to a half-empty theater. Minnie Pearl stands alone, on an uncommonly vacant Ryman stage; the postwar boom in country music seemed to have gone bust.*

Ryman Auditorium. NBC dropped its national network portion of the show in 1957. But the station's powerful 50,000-watt signal still reached many of the adult listeners the National Life and Accident Insurance Company wanted, so the show continued. And a new disc jockey, Ralph Emery, was hired for an all-night country music show.

"It was the longest air shift I ever had in my life; ten at night till five in the morning is a long time to be on the radio," Emery said. "When you're sitting there, just talking to a microphone, you're not really aware of the distance. But we reached into Canada and down into Florida. I used to play records for a Texas Ranger on a fishing boat in the Gulf of Mexico, right off the Yucatan Peninsula."

"[Emery] became a very powerful, powerful figure," said Eddie Stubbs, a WSM announcer. "And artists needed Ralph Emery. They needed radio. Their opportunities on television, at that time, were fairly minimal. But Ralph Emery was the person they went to see because they knew they could get in at any time and they knew that he had listeners." "There weren't many stations playing country music," Emery added. "I always thought that if the *Opry* had died and they had taken that show off, it would have killed country music. But because of WSM, and the *Grand Ole Opry*, and that all-night show, we hung on by our fingertips, because rock and roll was taking over everything."

Opry icons like Hank Snow and Ernest Tubb saw their record sales plummet—as well as the fees they could command for personal appearances. Tubb considered leaving music entirely to join his brother's insurance agency in Texas. "He was like a man grieving," a friend said, "like he'd had a couple of kids die."

Hoping to connect somehow with younger listeners, Tubb came out with a cover of Chuck Berry's "Thirty Days (To Come Back Home)." Hank Snow released "Hula Rock," whose chorus simply repeated the line "Rockin' and a rollin' in Waikiki" four times. Pee Wee King and His Golden West Cowboys tried their best with "Blue Suede Shoes," although it sounded more like a big band than Carl Perkins.

Webb Pierce's four-year string of number one singles had ended in 1956, and on tour he had been upstaged by Elvis Presley's wild gyrations and hard-driving beat. Now, desperate to appear relevant, he came out with a tune called "Teenage Boogie." Worried that his country fans might be offended by the more sexually suggestive lyrics of another song—called "The New Raunchy"—he released that single under the pseudonym of Shady Wall.

"The same way that honky tonk music kind of put old-timey string band music or the quaint songs of the Carter Family out of style a little bit," Marty Stuart said, "I think when rock and roll came through, some of the crooners and some of the more authentic, old-line country, Hank Williams kind of singing, it kind of got left behind by this new force and this new energy called 'rock and roll.'"

Ray Price was one country star who didn't get left behind. His response to the crisis in country music was to double down, ignoring rock and roll completely and sticking even closer to his country roots.

Price had been a struggling singer in Texas before Hank Williams befriended him, helping him get a recording contract and a place on the *Opry* and taking him on tour for a while. In the wake of Williams's death, Price had adopted the Drifting Cowboys as his band. "They were working a dance one night in Grand Junction, Colorado," according to Eddie Stubbs, "and this guy came up to the stage and said, 'You sound just like old Hank.' And a light went off that night.

ABOVE *While other radio stations dropped country music in favor of a Top Forty format, Ralph Emery's all-night radio show on WSM, beamed across the nation, helped keep country music on life support.*

OPPOSITE *Ray Price and the Cherokee Cowboys kept the fiddle and steel guitar alive with Price's popular "Texas shuffle."*

And he got to thinking, 'If I'm going to make it, I'm going to have to do things in my own way.'"

He found it with a song called "Crazy Arms," which featured a prominent walking bass line in 4/4 time—a beat that became known as the "Ray Price shuffle" or "Texas shuffle." It was perfect for dancing the Texas two-step. "It is one of the happiest kinds of music there is," said Darius Rucker. "Even when the song's not happy, a Texas shuffle makes you happy. You hear the beat and you just want to dance along." Price's friend Mel Tillis remembered, "Somebody asked old Ray one time, he said, 'Ray, can you define a shuffle?' And he said, 'Yes, it's a beat that makes a slow song feel fast.'"

Price also kept the fiddle and the steel guitar front and center. "If it hadn't have been for Ray Price," Eddie Stubbs said, "the fiddle may have gone away completely in country music. He kept the fiddle and the steel guitar going."

Other country singers went in a different direction—toward pop music. Ferlin Husky, in California's Central Valley, abandoned a steel guitar and fiddle accompaniment for a weeping ballad called "Gone." In early 1957 it topped the country charts, and went to number four on the pop charts—exceeded only by "Young Love," a song of teenage romance by Sonny James, a former barn dance performer from rural Alabama. "The happiest day in a country boy's life in those days was going pop, his crossing over, because country records didn't sell," according to Ralph Emery. "Jukebox operators, I think, were the only people that bought them."

Marty Robbins would prove to be the most adaptable musician in the fast-changing environment. Born Martin David Robinson in 1925, in a shack in the southern Arizona desert eight miles from Glendale, he had been constantly uprooted as his father, an alcoholic and petty thief, moved the family from place to place, including living for a while in a tent. When his parents divorced in 1938, his mother moved the children to the barrio on the wrong side of the tracks in Glendale, where Hispanics and poor whites lived—and where he learned to love Mexican music.

As a boy, he herded goats and worked on ranches in the summer, and used some of his money to spend his Saturdays watching Gene Autry movies. "I would sit so close to the

screen," he remembered, "that I got powder burns when the guns went off."

He dropped out of school in 1943 to join the Navy and served as a ramp operator of landing craft bringing Marines to shore in the battle of Bougainville Island, where he remained for fifteen months helping the Seabees bulldoze an airfield; made a name for himself as an amateur boxer; and learned to play guitar.

Back in Phoenix after the war, performing as Marty Robbins on a local country music show, his impressive vocal versatility caught the attention of Little Jimmy Dickens, who helped arrange a recording contract and a regular spot on the *Opry*. In 1953, Robbins's song "I'll Go on Alone" reached number one on the country charts, and he became known as "the boy with a teardrop in his voice."

When Elvis Presley began to emerge, Robbins covered "That's All Right, Mama," which did better on country radio than Presley's original. He charted again with a cover of Chuck Berry's "Maybellene."

The direction of Robbins's music took a new turn in 1956 with "Singing the Blues," a song brought to him backstage at the *Opry* by a young man in a wheelchair. "Singing the Blues" topped the country charts for more than three months, even beating out Presley's "Hound Dog." But Robbins was chagrined when the New York producer Mitch Miller recorded a version by Guy Mitchell, which reached number one on the pop charts and sold four times as many records.

After Guy Mitchell did the same thing to his next song, Robbins decided to go to New York himself and have Mitch Miller record him singing a tune he had written. "A White Sport Coat and a Pink Carnation" became Robbins's third number one country hit—and, more important to his bottom line, reached number two on the pop charts. Despite its success, he would never consider it a country song. But, he said, "I wasn't doing any good writing the songs I wanted to write, and I wasn't doing any good singing the songs I liked."

TOP *Twins Martin and Mamie Robinson near the shack where they were born in the Arizona desert. Martin would later adopt the stage name of Marty Robbins and cross over with songs like "A White Sport Coat and a Pink Carnation"; people referred to him as "Mr. Teardrop" because of the emotion in his voice.*

LEFT *In Philadelphia, Mississippi, Hilda Stuart was such a Marty Robbins fan that she named her son Marty in his honor.*

about his sons while cutting the hair of Boudleaux Bryant. Bryant and his wife, Felice, were among the first professional songwriters to establish themselves in the city. "Ike used to tell my dad about his boys and said, 'You know, I've got two boys and they really sing well. I really wish you would listen to them,'" said Del Bryant. "My father would say, 'Yeah, yeah, I'd like to listen to them; a little shorter here, please.' And, 'Can you take a little off here?'"

As it turned out, the Bryants had written a song meant for two-part harmony, but it had been turned down by dozens of artists. The Everly brothers decided to record it. Its title was "Bye Bye Love." They were on a month-long tour with Bill Monroe, making $90 a week doing tent

In Philadelphia, Mississippi, Hilda Stuart was so enamored by Robbins's singing, she named her son Marty in his honor. (His full name is John Marty Stuart, for his father and for the country star.) "'A White Sport Coat and a Pink Carnation' was the first Marty Robbins song I remember hearing," Stuart said. "And I thought he was a rock singer. And then I found out he was a country singer. Then I found out he was all of that."

shows in Mississippi and Louisiana, when the song exploded on the radio. In Queens, New York, young Paul Simon heard it on a local station:

I went to buy "Bye Bye Love" right after I heard it. There wasn't a record store in my immediate neighborhood so I had to take a bus and take a transfer and then another

Ira and Charlie Louvin, who came from the hill country of northeastern Alabama, where they grew up steeped in gospel and bluegrass music, now mixed their own "high lonesome" vocals with a more contemporary accompaniment that included an electric guitar and drum—and showed that traditional brother harmonies could survive in the age of rock and roll.

In 1957, two other brothers, Don and Phil Everly, ages twenty and eighteen, from Kentucky, had already been trying for two years without success to make it as a country duo in Nashville and were thinking of calling it quits. One day, their father, a barber (and skilled guitar player), was talking

---

ABOVE *Ira and Charlie Louvin carried on the traditional brother harmonies––and would go on to influence another generation of artists.*

RIGHT *The Everly Brothers, Phil and Don, exploded onto the scene with songs by Boudleaux and Felice Bryant, starting with "Bye Bye Love."*

to Artie [Garfunkel], and we tried to figure out how they were singing.

For their next song, the Everly Brothers turned again to Boudleaux and Felice Bryant. It was "Wake Up, Little Susie," about two teenagers falling asleep at a movie and fearing their reputation was now ruined. Helped by the publicity of being banned in Boston, where parents thought the song was too suggestive, "Wake Up, Little Susie" rose to number one on all three charts: country, pop, and rhythm and blues. With more songs written by the Bryants—"All I Have to Do Is Dream," "Bird Dog," and others—the Everly Brothers would sell more than thirty million records worldwide in three years.

And, although Memphis had given birth to the new hybrid of country and rhythm and blues, Nashville had now established itself as the place to write and record it.

bus, two buses, to get to a record store. I bought it and came home, put it on my player, loved it, flipped it over, played the other side. Loved it. Went to play it again, scratched the record. Just mortified.

Got back on the bus, took the second bus, went and bought another record. I couldn't even wait for the next day. I had to have it, again. I mean it was like an hour ride and then an hour ride back. And then I showed it

---

TOP *The Everly Brothers practice backstage while publisher Wesley Rose (center left) and songwriter Boudleaux Bryant listen. Bryant and his wife, Felice, wrote many of the brothers' hits, including (from left, in their original handwritten lyrics and music) "All I Have to Do Is Dream," "Wake Up, Little Susie," and "Bye Bye Love."*

MUSIC ROW

Country music wasn't always recorded in Nashville. The major label companies had studios in New York, Chicago, the West Coast. In some cases, they would go to Dallas, Texas, and record as well. But when Owen and Harold Bradley opened their studio, everything changed here.

EDDIE STUBBS

My brother, Owen, is the big daddy. He saw the big picture. He's the architect. He had a vision. He saw how the picture fit together, all the different pieces. I give him all the credit. I was just glad to be there and glad to plug in the guitar and play it.

HAROLD BRADLEY

Owen and Harold Bradley grew up in Nashville, where Owen had carved out a musical career: playing piano in dance bands as a young man; leading WSM's twenty-six-piece orchestra and becoming the station's music director; and moonlighting at Castle Recording, a small recording studio run by some WSM engineers in the downtown Tulane Hotel. Harold, ten years younger, had learned the guitar and, at Owen's urging, briefly joined Ernest Tubb's band as a teenager.

In the mid-1950s, WSM told its employees they could no longer have outside jobs, and the Castle studio was closing. Paul Cohen, a Decca executive who had used it and a small studio the Bradleys had opened in Hillsboro Village, informed Owen that he would be taking his business to a bigger, newer studio in Dallas, which had better equipment. He asked Bradley to come along. "He didn't want to leave," Harold recalled. "So, he said, 'I'll tell you what. Let Harold and I build you a studio. You put up $15,000; I'll put up $15,000. Harold will continue working for nothing.'" Cohen also promised that Decca would book one hundred recording sessions a year.

Bradley found a bungalow in a decaying residential neighborhood on 16th Avenue, southwest of downtown Nashville, paid $8,500 for it, and in 1955 opened a studio in what had

TOP *Owen Bradley, at piano, led dance bands and orchestras in Nashville before becoming a leading record producer. His younger brother Harold (third from right, back row) had played in Ernest Tubb's band as a teenager.*

ABOVE *The Bradleys converted a house on 16th Avenue into a sound studio to keep Decca's recording business in Nashville. As things picked up, they added a second, larger studio behind the house by attaching a military-surplus Quonset hut.*

been its basement. Decca chose to stay, and soon other labels began using the Bradleys' new studio. Business was so good, they erected a military-surplus Quonset hut in the backyard and equipped it as a second studio—and for filming performances, too, to send to television stations.

"We had a lot of other things going for us here," Harold Bradley said. "We had the *Grand Ole Opry*, so we had the musicians; we had the singers, who happened to also be songwriters, or there were songwriters who weren't musicians. It was all sittin' here waiting."

Then, RCA Victor built a brand-new studio a block away on 17th Avenue, which would be run by producer Chet Atkins, who had become one of the most sought-after session musicians in town.

Before long, Atkins and the Bradleys were busy making records—and other houses in the neighborhood were being converted into offices of booking agents and music publishers, offering songs to meet the growing demand. Eventually, the area would become known as Music Row.

RCA built a brand-new studio (top) a block away from the Bradleys', on 17th Avenue, where Chet Atkins (left), a top guitarist in Nashville, was put in charge.

Among the songwriters who now gravitated to Nashville was Mel Tillis, who had grown up in rural Florida and discovered that music—and a sense of humor—helped him cope with a speech disorder. "My daddy stuttered a bit, and my brother stuttered a little bit, too, and I thought that's the way we talk," Tillis said:

And I started to go to school in the first grade at Woodrow Elementary, in Plant City, Florida. And I came home, the first day, and I said, "Mama, do I stutter?" And she said, "Yes, you do, son." I said, "Mama, they laughed at me." And she said, "Well, if they're going to laugh at you, give them something to laugh about." And that was my first day, I think, in show business.

Miss Short, my teacher, found out that I could sing without stuttering. And she'd take me around to the other classes, up to the sixth grade, and let me sing. And I'd sing an old song, a Gene Autry song, "I'm Going

to Drink My Coffee From an Old Tin Can."

During a stint in the Air Force, Tillis started playing in a country group, but found it difficult to make a living as a musician after his discharge. He took a job as a railroad fireman for a while, until they fired him because of his stutter. But in Nashville, his songs started being recorded by established artists, particularly Webb Pierce, who, like Elvis Presley and some other stars, often insisted on sharing the writing credit—and therefore a share of the royal-

ABOVE *Young Mel Tillis (left) was made fun of because he stuttered when he talked. But he didn't when he sang, and a teacher encouraged him by having Mel perform for other students.*

BELOW *Mel Tillis and a backup band perform in a shoe store.*

ties—on tunes he recorded: "He told me, 'Your songs aren't hits unless I do them.' Okay, so I'd give him half of this one and half of that one. And it ended up quite a few."

One of them, called "I Ain't Never," was inspired by something a waitress said to Tillis at a local diner before he went to a barber shop where Pierce was getting a haircut. Pierce heard him working on the song and offered him $50 for half of the writing credit. When Tillis refused, he upped the offer to $150. Tillis finally agreed—if Pierce would throw in his fancy cowboy boots as well. The song was recorded by Pierce and ultimately fifty-six other artists, Tillis said, bringing in half a million dollars in royalties over the years. Pierce got half of that. "I learned a lesson on that," Tillis said. "Just don't do that. I'd have had a half a million instead of $250,000. That's a lesson."

A year after Tillis came to Nashville, another aspiring singer-songwriter arrived in town. Roger Miller was born in Fort Worth, Texas, but after his father died, when Miller was a year old, his destitute mother sent him away to be raised by an uncle near Erick, Oklahoma. It was a town so small, he later remembered, "we didn't have a town drunk [so] we had to take turns."

Precocious and mischievous, he wrote poems and silly songs as a boy, dreamed of leaving farm life far behind, and was expelled from two different high schools for his constant pranks. "He didn't fit," one classmate remembered, "because his brain operated different than the rest of us."

Miller took up the fiddle—he could play "Bonaparte's Retreat" standing on his head—and joined a country band. But after being caught for a petty theft in Amarillo, he was given the choice of jail or the Army and ended up in Korea, where he spent most of his time performing at military bases. Back in the States, he moved to Nashville in 1957 and took a job as a bellhop at the Andrew Jackson Hotel, not far from WSM and the Ryman Auditorium, where he hung out, trying to interest artists in his songs.

When Tillis got him a chance to be the fiddler in a band Minnie Pearl was forming for an upcoming tour, he jumped at it. Tillis was the opening act, and during the first shows, still too self-conscious to speak in public, he asked Miller for help:

Roger would introduce my song for me. And I'd finish the song and he'd come back and he'd say, "Melvin said thank you."

And Miss Minnie Pearl, she watched me for a little while, and then one day she called me over and she said,

LEFT *A young Roger Miller, outside his school in tiny Erick, Oklahoma*

ABOVE *Miller performing with Ray Price on KWKH's* Louisiana Hayride

"Melvin, if you're going to be in our business, you're going to have to learn to introduce your own songs and you've got to thank them. And you've got to sign autographs."

I said, "Miss Minnie, I can't do it. They'll laugh at me." And she said, "No, they won't, Melvin, they'll laugh *with* you."

She told me to talk. Go out there and talk. And the more I talked, the less I stuttered. And she taught me the timing. "Melvin," she said, "don't step on your laughter." And I said, "Why?" And she said, "It's too hard to get."

On the road, Tillis and Miller became close friends: "I told him, I said, 'You ain't never going to make it, writing them old stupid songs you're writing.' He said, 'You ain't going to make it with that damn stutter, either.'"

After the tour, Miller had trouble finding more work and moved to Amarillo, where he got a job in the fire department and played clubs as "the Singing Fireman." There, he met Ray Price, who asked him to join his new band, the Cherokee Cowboys, and liked Miller's song "Invitation to the Blues" well enough to record it, with Miller singing harmony. With its success, he moved back to Nashville and signed a recording contract with Owen Bradley and Decca. Though his own records did not sell, other artists had success with his songs: Ernest Tubb, Faron Young, and Jim Reeves, who had a hit with "Home," a tune Miller had written in the space of fifteen minutes because he needed $300 to buy a riding lawn mower, which he then drove eight miles down busy streets to his house.

Miller encouraged another songwriter, Bill Anderson, to come to Nashville. Anderson was a nineteen-year-old journalism student at the University of Georgia, working nights at a country radio station, when he first met Miller at a Wanda Jackson concert. Sitting on the roof of his apartment building in tiny Commerce one night, he was inspired to write a song about the view. "City Lights" got recorded by Ray Price at the same session Price recorded Miller's "Invitation to the

Blues," and after it spent thirteen weeks as the number one country song, Anderson headed to Music Row.

Like others in the growing music industry, he quickly learned that Nashville's elite still wanted their city to be known as "the Athens of the South" and looked down on the songwriters and performers as second-class citizens:

And Roger told me, when I got to Nashville, he said, "When you go to get credit anywhere, like to get a telephone, or whatever, don't tell them you're in the music business. Whatever you do, don't admit to being in the music business."

I went to get my first telephone and the lady says, "It's a $15 deposit," and she said, "By the way, what do you do?" Well, I was kind of proud of it—I had just written a couple of hit songs—and I said, "I'm in the music business." And she said, "That will be a hundred dollars."

RIGHT *Like Roger Miller, Bill Anderson, seen here performing on the* Louisiana Hayride, *got his big songwriting break when Ray Price recorded one of his songs.*

WALKIN' AFTER MIDNIGHT

When she moved to Nashville in 1959, Patsy Cline seemed more like a throwback to country music's past than a bridge to its future. She wore a cowgirl outfit, complete with a hat and boots; many of her songs featured steel guitars and fiddles and had honky tonk themes, like cheating; when she sang Hank Williams's old hit "Lovesick Blues," she could yodel as well as Hank did—and she intended to be as big a star as he had been.

Virginia Patterson Hensley had been born on September 8, 1932, in the small town of Winchester, in Virginia's Shenandoah Valley, and dropped out of high school at age fifteen after her abusive father deserted the family. "Ginny," as she

Virginia Patterson Hensley (top) at age sixteen in Winchester, Virginia, and singing with the Melody Boys at the armory in her hometown (right). From the start, she had a powerful voice and an equally powerful personality.

was called, began working in a drugstore during the day and singing in bars and supper clubs at night to help support her mother and two younger siblings.

Her rich voice had a remarkable range and power that impressed anyone who heard it. By 1954 she had won first place at a national country music contest in Virginia and began appearing regularly on a country television show in Washington, D.C., hosted by Jimmy Dean.

She married a businessman named Gerald Cline, changed her first name to Patsy, and signed a recording contract with a small independent label, 4 Star, which she learned later was notorious among insiders for cheating its artists—a royalty rate half of what other companies paid, and an insistence that she sing only songs published by the label's owner.

But the studio it used was in Nashville, where Owen Bradley instantly recognized her talent and struggled to make the most of the mediocre songs she was required to sing. "We tried rock and roll on the country songs; we tried Western swing," according to Harold Bradley. "They tried everything. But the songs weren't there."

After a string of singles that failed to sell, 4 Star insisted that she record a song originally written for the popular artist Kay Starr. Cline resisted at first: "It's nothing but a little ol' pop song," she said, "I hate it." But under Bradley's guidance—and with steel guitar solos by Don Helms, a former member of Hank Williams's Drifting Cowboys—she turned "Walkin' After Midnight" into something special. Singing it on CBS television's *Arthur Godfrey's Talent Scouts*, she won the night's competition, and the exposure pushed

the song to number two on the country charts and number twelve on the pop charts.

Billboard magazine named her the Most Promising Country & Western Female Artist of 1957, though for the next several years none of her other 4 Star recordings sold well. The label released her, saying she owed them nearly $5,000 in unrecovered royalty advances.

Divorced from Gerald Cline, she married Charlie Dick, had a daughter, and moved to Nashville, where the *Grand Ole Opry* offered her a spot in its cast. There, and on tour with *Opry* package shows, she quickly became known not just for her power-

ful voice, but also for her equally powerful personality. She argued with everyone; swore like a sailor; walked out of concerts if promoters didn't pay her and her band on time. She called people "Hoss," and referred to herself as "the Cline."

Among those traveling with her was a singing prodigy named Brenda Lee. "Well, let me tell ya, you didn't mess with Patsy," said Lee. "She'd tell you in a New York minute what she thought and what she was gonna do and how it was gonna be done."

Lee was born in 1944 in a charity hospital in Georgia to a family of sharecroppers. Even as a toddler, her talent was unmistakable. By the time she was three years old, she would stand on the wooden counter of the local grocery store and sing, while people dropped pennies and nickels at her feet, which helped her destitute family buy food. When she was seven, her father died, and she started singing professionally. "And I became the primary

ABOVE *As Patsy Cline, Hensley began her recording career with 4 Star, an independent label known by insiders for cheating its artists.*

CENTER, RIGHT *Patsy Cline and her second husband, Charlie Dick, with their daughter Julie, moved to Nashville in 1959.*

breadwinner for the family," Lee said. "My mom was working odd jobs and doing all that she could working in a cotton mill, sixteen hours a day. My goal was to help my mom and my siblings get out of the situation that we were in."

She belted out Hank Williams songs in a voice that belied her age and tiny stature, working so many late nights her third-grade teacher sometimes let her put her head on her desk and nap during class. In 1956, her television appearances on ABC's *Ozark Jubilee*, billed as "the little girl with the big voice," landed her a contract with Decca, and her family moved to Nashville, where Owen Bradley became her producer. "We started recording her when she was eleven or twelve years old," Harold Bradley said. "She was just amazing—the energy and the things that she was doing vocally, just none of us had heard of. We were cutting one day and we started and hardly played just eight bars and she stopped. And my brother said, 'Hey, what's wrong?' She said, 'Bass player missed a note.'"

Lee's first single was "Jambalaya," and with her mother along to chaperone, she soon began touring on package shows that included everyone from Kitty Wells to Chuck Berry and Patsy Cline. On one tour, the promoter didn't pay the performers, Lee remembered, "and Patsy put us in her car, she paid us out of her own pocket, took us back to Nashville, fed us on the way. And that's what kind of gal she was. She was so bighearted and so kind." Despite the age difference, the two became friends:

> Patsy, I think, was thirteen years older than I was. So, she was kinda like a big ole sister to me. And I'd go to her house and she'd let me clomp around in her cowboy boots and try her spangledy-dangledy outfits on. And boy I was in heaven. We just were the greatest of friends.
>
> And she, as I like to say in the kindest sense of the word, she was a great broad.

Nashville has always been proud and pleased and eager to go on any ride that a hit engenders. That's what a music capital is about—and there is no music capital like Nashville. So it could mount a running horse faster than any city I've ever seen. Country music has always been happy to take a ride on a fast horse.

DEL BRYANT

In 1959, at the inaugural ceremony of the Grammy Awards, the winner for Best Country and Western Performance went to a group totally unlike anything associated with Nashville. The Kingston Trio—three clean-cut college graduates from the San Francisco Bay Area—had released an old murder ballad from North Carolina, based on the story of a Confederate Civil War veteran who stabbed his sweetheart to death and was hanged for the crime. "Tom Dooley" had first been recorded in the 1920s, during the country music industry's early years. Now, it was sweeping the nation.

"The Kingston Trio's version of 'Tom Dooley' had an impact that no previous song had had," according to Bill C. Malone. "It was just a huge, huge hit. And it set off a hunger, an enthusiasm, for old songs, both real and newly made. It was mainly a Northern urban phenomenon in its beginnings, but it had a great impact on country music because country musicians eventually began trying to capitalize on what had been unleashed."

In their search for anything that would sell, suddenly, it seemed, every country artist was releasing a folk or story song, returning to one of the deepest roots of the music.

The Louvin Brothers came out with an even older murder ballad, "The Knoxville Girl," that traced its origins all the way back to the 1700s in the British Isles. Riley Puckett had released a version in 1924, and the Louvins said it was the first song they themselves had ever sung. They had recorded

THE DAY THE MUSIC DIED

In early 1959, a concert tour aimed at teenagers called the "Winter Dance Party" was winding its way through the Midwest, headlined by Buddy Holly. He had come a long way since opening for Elvis Presley and Johnny Cash in his native Lubbock, Texas, back in 1955.

Frustrated about creative control during some recording sessions in 1956 in Nashville, Holly and his band, the Crickets, had gone into a studio in New Mexico and developed their own sound—two electric guitars, an electric bass, and drums—that produced a series of hits: "That'll Be the Day," "Maybe Baby," and "Peggy Sue."

Holly had appeared twice on *The Ed Sullivan Show*; made triumphant appearances in England, where his raw, rocking sound was especially popular; and now was in the middle of a tour to twenty-four Midwestern cities in as many days, made all the more grueling by constant troubles with the bus. It had broken down a few times, and its heat often didn't work well enough to fend off the bitter winter weather.

Other acts included Dion and the Belmonts; a seventeen-year-old rising Hispanic star named Ritchie Valens; and J. P. Richardson, a Houston deejay better known as "the Big Bopper." Because of a dispute with his regular band, Holly had asked a close friend of his from Lubbock to come along to play bass: Waylon Jennings.

On February 2, they rolled into Clear Lake, Iowa, to play in front of 1,100 adoring teenage fans at the Surf Ballroom. When the show ended, around midnight, Holly arranged for himself and two musicians to fly ahead to the next gig. Valens won a coin toss for one of the seats. Jennings gave up his seat to the Big Bopper, who was suffering from the flu.

A few minutes after its takeoff from Clear Lake, some time before 1 a.m., the single-

ABOVE *Photo booth shot of good friends Waylon Jennings and Buddy Holly in Grand Central Station, January 1959*

LEFT *With Jennings playing bass (back, left), Holly performs at the Surf Ballroom in Clear Lake, Iowa, February 2, 1959.*

RIGHT *Poster for the Winter Dance Party tour headlined by Buddy Holly and the Crickets, along with the Big Bopper, Ritchie Valens, and Dion and the Belmonts. The day of the plane crash in Iowa that killed Holly, Valens, and the Big Bopper would come to be known as "the day the music died."*

engine plane flew into a blizzard and plummeted into a corn-field. The pilot and all three passengers were killed instantly in the crash—but its impact would reverberate for years within the world of music.

The tragedy transformed Holly from a rock-and-roll star into a legend. His record sales skyrocketed. Two British bands, heavily influenced by his music, named themselves in his and the Crickets' honor: one band was the Hollies; the other was a quartet from Liverpool, who decided to call themselves the Beatles.

In Nashville, a rising *Opry* singer named George Jones, a lifelong friend of the Big Bopper from his days in Houston, recorded "White Lightnin'," which Richardson had written. It would be Jones's first number one country hit.

Waylon Jennings was so devastated by Holly's death, he gave up performing for a time and took a series of jobs as a disc jockey. "All the sparkle had gone out of me," he remembered. "I had lost my center of gravity." But he would never forget his friend's advice to stay true to his own instincts and make music the way he wanted to.

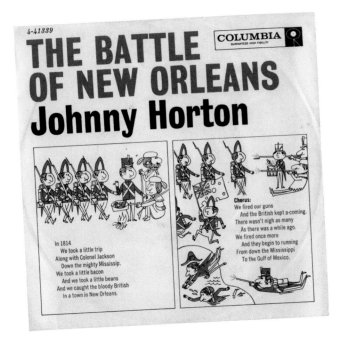

it in 1956, but until the success of "Tom Dooley," their label had considered it too morbid to release as a single. Country singer Stonewall Jackson had success with "Waterloo," which related the story of three men who each had to "meet his Waterloo"—Adam eating the apple, Napoleon at the famous battle, and . . . Tom Dooley.

Johnny Cash released two songs he had written: a Western saga called "Don't Take Your Guns to Town" and a remembrance of his family's experience evacuating their home in Dyess, Arkansas, during the great Mississippi River flood of 1937, "Five Feet High and Rising." Eddy Arnold got caught up in the folk craze, too, releasing two albums, including one that featured "Tennessee Stud," his biggest hit in four years.

The Browns, three siblings from Arkansas who had toured with Elvis Presley for the *Louisiana Hayride*, were getting out of the music business and had come to Nashville for their final recording session, when Chet Atkins asked them what they'd like to sing as a swan song for RCA. They decided on a plaintive tune by Jean Villard, made popular in France by Edith Piaf. "Les Trois Cloches" (The Three Bells) told the story of a man's life—his birth, his marriage, and his death—through the chiming of his village's chapel bells. The Browns' version of "The Three Bells" hit number one on both the pop and country charts, and sold more than a million copies. Johnny Horton's "The Battle of New Orleans" recounted Andrew Jackson's victory against the British

ABOVE *With the success of his single "The Battle of New Orleans," Johnny Horton's performance fees ballooned from $350 to $6,000 a night.*

Johnny Cash was so enamored of it, he included it on a list of one hundred essential American songs for his daughter Rosanne to learn. "'Long Black Veil,' I thought, was a perfect country song," she said. "It had everything. It was a ghost story; there was a death; the central character had integrity. The scene was laid out—the scaffold, the judge, her veil, the graveyard—I mean, it was chilling in every way. And the fact that Marijohn had co-written that, that was hugely inspiring to me. That song is timeless. It's like Stephen Foster's 'Hard Times'; it's bedrock, it's rooted somewhere in the mist of time. You can't imagine the fabric of music without these songs."

"If Shakespeare were sitting there, he would have to go, 'That's a good song.' I don't care, Irving Berlin would have to go, 'That's a great song,'" Marty Stuart added. "I loved rock and roll. But that was the kind of song that captivated my heart. It made me want to play country music. It was like a beam that said, 'Come here, Marty. Come here, Marty.' I had to get there. It knew more about me than I knew about it."

during the War of 1812. It had been written by Jimmie Driftwood (also the writer of "Tennessee Stud"), a former Arkansas elementary school teacher who composed songs to help his students learn American history. "The Battle of New Orleans" reached number one on the country and pop charts and won a Grammy Award, and Horton's performance fees went from $350 a show to $6,000. He bought a new house for himself and his wife, Billie Jean, the widow of Hank Williams.

But it was another murder ballad that would rescue another country singer's fortunes. Lefty Frizzell had once challenged Hank Williams for supremacy in the world of honky tonk. Then, from 1955 to 1958, as rock and roll took off, he had failed to chart a hit. His new hit song seemed to spring from another century, but in fact had just been written by Danny Dill and Marijohn Wilkin. It, too, was a murder ballad: "The Long Black Veil."

ABOVE *Lefty Frizzell hadn't had a hit for nearly four years; he finally got one in 1959 with "Long Black Veil," a song that seemed timeless but had recently been written by Marijohn Wilkin and Danny Dill.*

RIGHT *Marty Robbins gave up his white sport coat to record* Gunfighter Ballads and Trail Songs, *which included his favorite song, "El Paso." He had written it on a car ride from Nashville to his native Arizona. He named the cantina dancer in the song Faleena, in honor of a girl from his fifth grade.*

Marty Robbins wasn't trying to tap into the folk boom when he cajoled his label into letting him record the album *Gunfighter Ballads and Trail Songs*. He just wanted to sing something that harkened back to growing up in the West, watching Gene Autry's singing cowboy movies, hearing the harmonies of the Sons of the Pioneers, and listening to stories his maternal grandfather had told him about the frontier. "This album won't sell five hundred records," he told his producer, "but it's something I've always wanted to do and I think Columbia owes it to me."

The inspiration for one of the album's songs had come to him while driving his family from Nashville to Arizona one Christmas, seeing a road sign for El Paso and thinking it would be a good setting for a tune. "The song came out like a motion picture," he said later. "I really didn't have too much to do with that song. It just came out." He had it finished by the time he got to Phoenix.

A combination love story, murder ballad, and West-ern outlaw saga with a surprise twist at the end, "El Paso" begins in a place called Rosa's Cantina, where a young cowboy shoots another man vying for the affections of a pretty dancer named Faleena, named in honor of a Mexican girl Robbins had known in fifth grade. In the studio, Grady Martin added a distinctive Spanish guitar that is as unforgettable as Robbins's voice as he recounts his tale. Robbins overrode his label's objections that at four and a half minutes, the song was much too long to ever be played on the radio. "We didn't play records that long," deejay Ralph Emery said, "but it was a story. You had to play it all. And, the fact is, Columbia reissued it, edited some of the story out. But nobody played that. To get the story, you had to play the whole record."

Of all the songs he would record, Robbins would consider "El Paso" his favorite, and later he would use the same characters to write two more—one called "Faleena" and the other "El Paso City"—that essentially were sequels to the original song. The Grateful Dead would add "El Paso" to their repertoire in the late 1960s and keep it on their set list for more than twenty-five years, calling it their most-requested song.

As 1959 ended, Robbins's version was headed to number one on the pop and country charts. Six of the ten top country songs that year had been story songs.

ABOVE *In the recording studio for "El Paso," no one wore cowboy clothes. The three Glaser brothers (left) sang the tight harmonies that were as distinctive as Grady Martin's guitar licks.*

My father knew thousands of songs—and not just "kind of" knew them—he could *sing* you thousands of songs. He had the instincts of a musicologist. And he had a deep and wide knowledge of roots music, folk music, country music, Appalachian music, blues, and then the sub-genres of death songs, songs about Mother, songs about trains—he loved them all.

He also was a natural poet. You combine those two things, and it's powerful.

ROSANNE CASH

By 1959, Johnny Cash had moved Vivian and his growing family—they now had three girls—from Memphis to an expensive house in Southern California. Only five years earlier, he had been making $50 a week as an appliance salesman and would-be performer; now he was on track to bring in $250,000 a year.

Cash had left Sun Records to sign with Columbia, a bigger label that promised him not only a $50,000 bonus and a better royalty rate, but also greater creative freedom in choosing what songs to record. He finally was able to release an album of gospel songs, just as he'd promised his mother after his brother Jack's death. He soon followed it with his first concept album, *Songs of Our Soil*, featuring a collection of folk-type tunes filled with stories of hardship and death.

"Jack's death was central to everything," Rosanne Cash said. "Even in the end of my grandmother's life, my dad went up, every year, on the day of Jack's death, and sat with his mother all day. And they just sat together. And Dad always said that he dreamed of Jack his whole life, and Jack would age as he did; Jack was always two years older than he was."

Like every other singing star, Cash spent most of his time traveling from one personal appearance to another, promoting his records—an existence that required ceaseless miles, punctuated only momentarily with performances before fans who thought it must be both easy and glamorous to make a living giving a two-hour concert and creating three-minute songs.

Now headlining his own package tours, Cash added a

ABOVE *Johnny Cash with his mother. Every year, he made sure to visit her on the anniversary of his brother Jack's death.*

LEFT *Vivian and Johnny Cash at their new home in California with their girls, from left, Kathy, Rosanne, and Cindy. He had left Sun Records and signed a lucrative contract with Columbia.*

drummer—W. S. "Fluke" Holland, formerly with Carl Perkins—and the Tennessee Two became the Tennessee Three as they barnstormed from Texas to Toronto, New York to California.

Out on the road, Cash and his band developed a reputation for pulling outrageous pranks wherever they went. At one hotel, they spray-painted their rooms black; at another, they strung a rope to every door handle on their floor late one night so no one could get out of the rooms. In Omaha, Cash bought five hundred baby chicks and turned some of them loose at every stop on the elevator. Other artists complained that Johnny Cash and his Tennessee Three were making it hard for *any* country act to book rooms at some hotels.

Cash knew that spending so much time on tour posed many dangers to the musicians who logged all those miles. Buddy Holly and three others had perished in a plane wreck trying to get to the next concert. On his way to a television appearance, Carl Perkins had been nearly killed in a car accident that took the life of two men, including Perkins's brother. And Cash's close friend Johnny Horton died on a country road in Texas when his car was hit by a drunken driver.

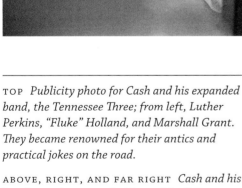

TOP *Publicity photo for Cash and his expanded band, the Tennessee Three; from left, Luther Perkins, "Fluke" Holland, and Marshall Grant. They became renowned for their antics and practical jokes on the road.*

ABOVE, RIGHT, AND FAR RIGHT *Cash and his band toured constantly. He would call Vivian each night to say how much he missed her and their girls, but he also loved the road, he said, because it meant adventure and freedom. Like many touring artists, to cope with the grueling schedule he became addicted to amphetamines.*

Life on the road held other perils, too. Every night, Cash would call Vivian to say how much he missed her and the girls, to reassure her that he would soon be back with them—and that he was being faithful. In truth, Marshall Grant had found it necessary to constantly remind his friend that he was a married man. But the road, Cash said, meant "adventure . . . creativity, freedom. . . . I love being a gypsy."

"He was addicted to it," Rosanne Cash said:

If he was home more than ten days, he started to get very restless and had to get back out there again. They would get in a car and put the big bass guitar on the roof and drive two hundred miles and do a show. Sometimes drive and do two, three, four shows a day. Then drive all night, get someplace, do it again, afternoon show, evening show, drive all night, over and over.

Well, somebody finally said to Dad, when he was at the point of utter exhaustion, "Here's how you get through it. You take this pill." That was it. That's how he got through it. But then you had to have something to come down off the pills, so he had to take something else. And then he was locked in a terrible, terrible cycle.

When my dad took that first pill, he didn't take it to get high. He did it because he hadn't slept in days and he had three shows to do the next day. "Here's how you get from here to here. Here's how you can keep this up and build your career. Take this pill, it'll help you." And that was a very slippery slope. And he went down it.

As his addiction to amphetamines increased, Cash did his best to hide it from his family—and from his fans, though part of his appeal was his image as a rebel, fueled in part by one of their favorite songs, "Folsom Prison Blues," which he had written and recorded during his time with Sam Phillips.

It was inspired by a movie he had seen in the Air Force, *Inside the Walls of Folsom Prison*, and borrowed heavily from a song by Gordon Jenkins, "Crescent City Blues." In his reworking of it, Cash reconfigured a line from his hero, Jimmie Rodgers's first blue yodel: "I'm gonna shoot poor Thelma, just to see her jump and fall." In Cash's song it becomes, "I shot a man in Reno, just to watch him die."

Since its release in 1956, "Folsom Prison Blues" had been one of Cash's signature songs. And though he'd never served time in prison himself, many fans assumed the song had been drawn from personal experience.

During an appearance at the Texas state prison

LEFT *Handwritten lyrics to Cash's "Folsom Prison Blues." The line in the song "I shot a man in Reno, just to watch him die" was inspired by his hero Jimmie Rodgers's line "I'm gonna shoot poor Thelma, just to see her jump and fall."*

My parents probably could not have made it in the creative industry that they chose to operate in if they hadn't loved each other so dearly. My father brought the complete experience of music, the tremendous knowledge of how music works. My mother brought a tremendous desire to make it in popular music. I think that her biggest contribution was pushing my father as hard as he would allow anyone to push. This incredible love allowed her to push and push until he wrote.

She gave him incredible ideas. She had a tremendous amount of talent; he could polish, he could finish. And she made him finish and kept him excited. But my mother wanted it more than my father. My father wanted my mother more than anything.

DEL BRYANT

rodeo in Huntsville, he was profoundly moved by the reception it received: the inmates begged him to sing it again, even when a rainstorm soaked everyone in the crowd and caused a power failure that required him to continue without electrical amplification. After the show, Cash asked to be booked for the New Year's Day show at California's maximum-security facility at San Quentin.

Sitting in the San Quentin audience that day was a young inmate named Merle Haggard, who had just turned twenty-one in prison. "He had blown his voice the night before at a New Year's Eve party in San Francisco, and he had nothing but a whisper," Haggard remembered. "But with that only, he was able to totally subdue the crowd—and in competition with strippers and all kinds of things, an eight-hour show. I was really worried for him because men are cruel in San Quentin. They don't applaud unless they like you. But they were crazy about him. He identified with us. And he was the kind of guy that might have been in there with us had things gone the wrong way for him."

Merle Haggard decided that if he ever got out of prison, he would try to follow in Johnny Cash's footsteps.

Boudleaux and Felice Bryant's success writing hit songs for the Everly Brothers had allowed them to move from a tiny trailer on the outskirts of Nashville into a real house, and more artists were now interested in what they could offer.

Boudleaux had once written song ideas on scraps of paper he stuffed in his pockets, until one day, fourteen new songs were lost when his raincoat disappeared. His friend Chet Atkins bought him a leather-bound ledger—similar to the kind Stephen Foster had used, he said—and the Bryants became more systematic about their writing, filling ledger after ledger with songs they pitched to producers and artists in a setting that always worked for them: over a steaming plate of Felice's spaghetti.

ABOVE *In the audience at Johnny Cash's first San Quentin concert was convict A 45200, young Merle Haggard.*

RIGHT *At Chet Atkins's suggestion, Boudleaux and Felice Bryant started writing their lyrics and music in leather-bound ledgers.*

And, quite often, he would find something they liked. They really sold hard and fed well."

If an artist performed one of their songs at the *Grand Ole Opry*, Felice had other tricks to improve its chances, Del Bryant said: "My mother would run out around the back and start screaming at the end of the song—because she could scream louder than anyone—and start an encore. And if you had an encore, they'd play it again. And you had a better chance of firmly setting something in the public's mind."

To promote their songs, she also courted radio disc jockeys—by writing them letters or sometimes going on the road to visit stations in person—and got their two sons involved in the family business. For "Georgia Piney Woods," the Bryant boys got a thousand pine seedlings from a government agency and sent them to every country deejay in the nation.

"There weren't many Sicilians in Nashville, and she was an incredible cook," Del Bryant explained. "So the fixings were there. The folks would arrive. The wine would be poured. The people were just waiting for the meal because you could smell it throughout the house and no one had had food like this, this good of that type. And you'd eat. You would drink. And then they would bring out their books, the ledgers that they wrote in. And then they would pitch songs.

Over time, more than nine hundred of the Bryants' songs would be recorded, selling more than half a billion records worldwide.

The Bryants may have been the first to prove that songwriters could make a good living in Nashville without being recording stars in their own right, but by 1960 more songwriters were following their trail. The city now was home to more than a hundred music publishers, as well as a thousand members of the musicians' union—and so many booking agents, one magazine wrote, "they have to wear badges to keep from booking each other."

The publishing companies hired salesmen called "song pluggers" to make regular visits to record producers and play them demo tapes of their writers' newest material. But many of the songwriters did some of the plugging themselves at a hangout on Lower Broadway called Tootsies Orchid Lounge. Its back door opened onto the alleyway near the artists'

The success of the songs they wrote for the Everly Brothers allowed Felice and Boudleaux Bryant and their growing boys to move out of their trailer and into a lake house near Nashville (top, left). There, Felice's famed spaghetti dinners (center) were part of the attraction for recording stars to come and hear some of the Bryants' new songs (left).

entrance to the Ryman Auditorium, making it a convenient place for performers to drop in for a beer between shows—and a good place for a writer to pitch a new song to an established star.

Its proprietress, Hattie Louise "Tootsie" Bess, had a big heart for songwriters, but little patience for troublemakers. "She wore her hair in kind of a bun, as I remember, and kept a big hatpin in there," said songwriter Tom T. Hall, "and if somebody got out of hand, she'd take it and she'd just walk up and hit him on the butt with it. She got the attention of some pretty rowdy songwriters in those days. . . . I never got stuck."

Among the new arrivals who began frequenting Tootsies were Hank Cochran and Harlan Howard, who signed with Pamper Music, a publishing company co-owned by Ray Price.

Not far from the Ryman's stage door, Tootsies Orchid Lounge on Broadway (top) became a hangout for songwriters to introduce their tunes to recording stars. Hattie Louise "Tootsie" Bess (right) kept unruly patrons in line by prodding them with the sharp end of her hatpin.

The essence of a good country song, Harlan Howard said, was "three chords and the truth." He had been working as a forklift operator at a printing company in California when Price made a hit out of his song "Heartaches by the Number" and encouraged him to come to Nashville, along with his wife, Jan, who often sang on Howard's demos and would soon have a recording contract of her own.

Another aspiring songwriter who showed up was a twenty-seven-year-old from Abbott, Texas, who arrived in his 1946 Buick and rented a trailer for $25 a week for his wife and three children—the same trailer Roger Miller and Hank Cochran had once used. His name was Willie Nelson.

Born on April 29, 1933, Nelson was raised by his paternal grandmother after his mother abandoned him and his older sister. He grew up in central Texas during the Great Depression, surrounded by music. He would sit on a piano stool as

his grandmother taught his sister to play the family pump organ; at night the radio brought him the songs of his first musical heroes, Gene Autry, Bob Wills, and Ernest Tubb.

"I think I knew what I wanted to do from the beginning," Nelson said, "because I grew up with my sister Bobbie playing the piano and me sitting on a piano stool, trying to learn 'Stardust.' I just kind of felt like that's what I wanted to do, and I seemed to have a talent. I had written poems earlier, before I could play the guitar."

TOP, LEFT *Young Willie Nelson with the grandmother who raised him in Abbott, Texas. His older sister, Bobbie (right), would go on to play piano in his bands.*

ABOVE AND RIGHT *Twelve-year-old Willie Nelson's handmade songbook, with a cardboard cover and the lyrics to one of his first songs, "I Guess I Was Born to Be Blue"*

CENTER, RIGHT *Willie (left) and his band in 1948; sister Bobbie at the piano*

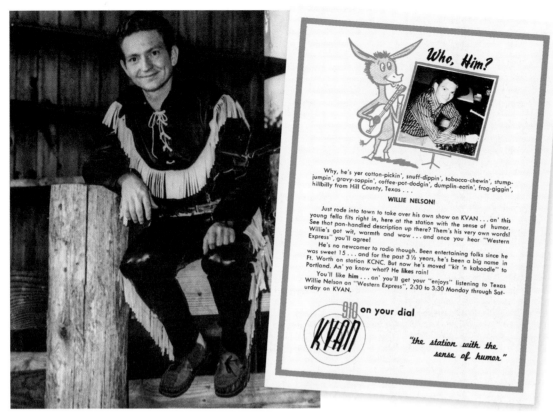

spent most of his time writing lyrics, he moved to Houston, where he recorded a few songs that didn't sell. He was always short on money. "I hocked my guitar so many times," he said later, "the pawnbroker played it better than I did."

Strapped for cash, he sold his writing credit on two songs for only $200, giving up all future royalties. One of them, "Family Bible," became an immediate hit on country radio when someone else recorded it. The other, "Night Life," would later go on to sell thirty million records.

Encouraged by the success of his two songs—even if he didn't profit from them—Nelson decided to try Nashville. When he arrived in early 1960, Hank Cochran befriended him, persuading Pamper Music to take Nelson on for $50 a week. (Cochran gave up a raise for the same amount to seal the deal.)

By age ten, he was good enough to accompany himself when he sang at the town's barbershop, and to strum in a band that performed polkas and waltzes at local gatherings, earning more in a night than he had made picking cotton and baling hay. By twelve, he had written enough lyrics to fill a makeshift songbook he constructed with a cardboard cover and string holding the sheets of paper together.

After graduating from Abbott High School in 1950, he began a restless existence: marrying his first wife when they were both teenagers; moving from one Texas city to another and spending a short time in the Pacific Northwest before returning home; working as a radio disc jockey; performing on weekends with a series of country bands; and sometimes selling encyclopedias, Bibles, sewing machines, and vacuum cleaners door to door to support his growing family.

Along the way, he became fascinated with the jazz stylings of the guitarist Django Reinhardt. And during his time as a disc jockey, he became convinced, he said, that he could "write better songs than the ones I'm playing on the radio."

After being fired from a job as a carpet installer because he

---

TOP, LEFT AND RIGHT *Willie Nelson, the disc jockey with "wit, warmth and wow" at KVAN in Portland, Oregon*

RIGHT *For a time, Nelson played in fellow Texan Ray Price's Cherokee Cowboys.*

'Hello picture frame.' Just anything in the room, 'Hello doorknob.' And they were making fun of the song. Well, Faron Young thought it was a hit. He said, 'I think I can do something.' And so he recorded it."

Before the record's release, Nelson offered to sell Young the writing credit for just $500. Instead, Young gave him a loan of $500—if he promised not to sell it to anyone else. "Hello Walls" topped the country charts, became a top twenty pop hit, and was soon covered by Perry Como, Lawrence Welk, and Willie's hero Ernest Tubb.

When his first royalty check arrived—for $14,000—Nelson rushed to Tootsies and in front of everyone else gave Faron Young a big kiss, square on the lips. "I ain't never had nobody," Young said, "kiss me that good in my life."

THE NASHVILLE SOUND

There's a fine line between art and business. Sometimes we make business decisions that affect the art. But we have to keep in mind, it is the music *business*. I mean, if you just want to be a troubadour, go play for fun; but if you want to do this for real and get it out to all the people, then you have to approach it from a business standpoint.

We don't have a lot of geniuses like Owen Bradley and Chet Atkins who are capable of both sides of the art and the business.

CHARLIE MCCOY

Sitting in a converted garage, which served as his writing space, Nelson looked around one day and on a piece of cardboard jotted down some lyrics to a song he entitled "Hello Walls." Then he went to Tootsies Orchid Lounge to play it for the other songwriters and singers gathered there. Ralph Emery remembered the moment: "People were making fun of the song. And they would say, 'Hello glass,' 'Hello beer,'

In a garage-turned-office, Nelson wrote "Hello Walls" before taking it to Tootsies to try it out in front of singers and songwriters. Only Faron Young (top, right) liked it––and made it a hit.

It was a great relationship, because Owen and Chet had the big picture. The big picture is that whatever is good for Nashville is good for everybody. And they were great friends.

They never viewed themselves as competitors. They rejoiced if one of them got a hit, because that meant four, five other artists were going to come to town and record. It was going to be good for the business. Which it was.

HAROLD BRADLEY

Back in 1958, a group of industry executives, concerned about the declining number of radio stations playing country and western records, had formed the Country Music Association (CMA) to actively promote their business with station managers and advertising executives, trying to counteract age-old stereotypes about the music's fans. Jo Walker-Meador, a young college-educated Nashville woman who had never been to the *Grand Ole Opry*, became its executive director.

"We felt they had an image that people who liked country music were a bunch of unwashed hillbillies, to put it bluntly, people who didn't have money to spend," she said. "But that was not true. We were trying to tell them that country music sells. Country listeners *do* have money to spend, and you can make money with this music."

By the early 1960s, the CMA had persuaded *Billboard* to refer to the music as "country" instead of "country and western," and started a Hall of Fame—modeled after the one for baseball in Cooperstown, New York—to recognize important figures in the music's history. The first three to be inducted were Jimmie Rodgers, Hank Williams, and the influential song publisher Fred Rose.

But by now, most of the music being recorded in Nashville no longer sounded anything like that of Rodgers or Williams.

In their recording studios on Music Row, Chet Atkins and Owen Bradley had been experimenting with ways to reach a wider audience: adding a few sweet violins instead of a hard-driving fiddle; a soft piano; and the subdued background vocals of either the Anita Kerr Singers or the Jordanaires, a gospel quartet—all allowing the lead singer to be front and center.

"Chet Atkins, Owen Bradley were doing everything they could to make it more elegant, and more 'listenable,' more

palatable," Marty Stuart said. "They 'de-twangified' it, if you will. If that's a word."

What they created came to be called "the Nashville Sound."

"I wasn't trying to change the business," Chet Atkins said, "just sell records." He helped Jim Reeves make the transition from a hillbilly singer doing novelty songs like "Mexican Joe" to a crooner of aching heartbreak with "Four Walls." And over at his Quonset hut studio, Owen Bradley was moving Brenda Lee away from rockabilly with a song called "I'm Sorry."

"I think rockabilly was more that raw, rhythmic sound," Lee said. "'I'm Sorry' was more of your uptown, big ballad, classy kind of a sound. And it changed my sound because then I became a ballad singer."

By 1961, despite her brief success with "Walkin' After Midnight," Patsy Cline hadn't had a hit in four years and her family was barely getting by. They didn't even have a telephone;

ABOVE *As executive director of the Country Music Association, Jo Walker-Meador worked to improve the music's image and led the drive to build a Hall of Fame to highlight its history.*

people were told they could reach her by leaving a message at WSM. But once she was freed from her contract with 4 Star records, she signed with Decca, and for her first session Owen Bradley was looking for a song that could easily straddle the country and pop markets. He came across one written by Hank Cochran and Harlan Howard: "I Fall to Pieces."

The song was set to a familiar 4/4 shuffle beat, but Cline at first resisted Bradley's insistence on a hushed accompaniment and the addition of the

TOP, LEFT AND RIGHT *Chet Atkins, behind the glass in the control room, steered Jim Reeves toward the smoother Nashville Sound, while Owen Bradley moved Brenda Lee away from rockabilly to big ballads like "I'm Sorry."*

LEFT *Don Gibson (at the microphone) wrote and performed some of the early Nashville Sound songs, like "Sweet Dreams." He said that on an afternoon in 1957, when his vacuum cleaner and television set were both repossessed from his trailer near Knoxville, he sat down and wrote "Oh Lonesome Me" and "I Can't Stop Loving You."*

Jordanaires, whose male voices, she feared, might overwhelm her own. She finally relented—and with "I Fall to Pieces" scored her first number-one country hit, and reached number twelve on the pop charts.

Ray Walker remembered Cline's response to her change in fortune: "We're on a session. She's upstairs with Owen in the control room and she came down those steps, sassy, sassy. She put her hand on her hip, cocked her hip, threw her head back, and said, 'Boys, they say I got a hit. Ain't nobody taking my Frigidaire and my car now.' And from then on she just loved us."

As more and more artists turned to the Nashville Sound, "country music," *Time* magazine

---

ABOVE *Patsy Cline, seen here with daughter Julie and baby son Randy, was struggling financially when "I Fall to Pieces" hit number one. "Ain't nobody taking my Frigidaire and my car now," she told the Jordanaires.*

RIGHT *Producer Fred Foster (far right) helped former rockabilly star Roy Orbison (standing in center with white shirt) come out with a string of hits, like "Crying." Harold Bradley, sitting center, and Hank Garland, left, played guitar, and the Anita Kerr Singers provided smooth background vocals.*

proclaimed, "is now wearing city clothes." The studios on Music Row were busier than ever.

Working with producer Don Law of Columbia Records, Ray Price put the shuffle beat momentarily aside to lay down a slow and bluesy version of Willie Nelson's "Night Life." Even though the steel guitar accompaniment was brief and so subtle that it was almost overwhelmed by the orchestral strings on Skeeter Davis's melancholy ballad "The End of the World," some pop stations initially considered it "too country" to play—until one deejay in New York put it on the air, and it became a million-seller.

Fred Foster, who had documented the stunning drop of country music sales when rockabilly burst on the scene in the mid-1950s, now decided the time was right to go to Nashville and start a record label and publishing company. He developed his first star, the former rockabilly singer at Sun Records, Roy Orbison, by encouraging him to branch out in a new direction with songs like "Running Scared," "Only the Lonely," and "Crying."

Many purists complained that the drive to become more mainstream—and profitable—meant forsaking the raw, homespun roots that had always distinguished country music. But there was no disputing how well it sold.

"What is the Nashville Sound?" Chet Atkins was asked. He reached into his pocket and jingled his change. "That," he said, "is the Nashville Sound."

HONKY TONK GIRL

Country music, if you ain't got a steel guitar or a fiddle, then you ain't got no country band. That's it.

JEAN SHEPARD

Some country artists preferred to stick with tradition. One of them was a sharecropper's daughter from Oklahoma named Jean Shepard. Born in the depths of the Depression, one of ten children, she had grown up listening to Bob Wills's broadcasts on the radio at noon, when her mother called the children in from the fields. She learned to yodel from the Jimmie Rodgers records her father would save for months to buy.

After her family migrated to California's Central Valley, her parents pawned their furniture to buy Jean an upright bass so she could perform with a band called the Melody Ranch Girls at a nearby dance hall. One night in 1952, honky-tonk star Hank Thompson heard her singing and persuaded Ken Nelson of Capitol Records to sign her when she was still a teenager.

By 1955, Shepard had joined Kitty Wells as one of the few female lead singers in country music, releasing a string of honky tonk tunes that often pushed the boundaries of what a woman could say in a song. In "Beautiful Lies," a woman wants to hear her lover tell her what she wants to hear, true or not; in "I Thought of You," she tells a previous lover she still thinks of him while she's with someone else. "Girls in

Disgrace" is from the perspective of a woman still waiting for her lover to keep his promise to marry her.

After becoming a star on the *Ozark Jubilee* television show, broadcast from Springfield, Missouri, Shepard joined the cast of the *Grand Ole Opry* in Nashville. She soon fell in love with a charismatic cast member, Hawkshaw Hawkins, a six-foot-five West Virginian who had fought in the Battle of the Bulge and earned four medals in World War Two.

As a rising star on Wheeling's WWVA, Hawkins had been booked for the Hank Williams concert in Canton, Ohio, on January 1, 1953, when the news arrived that Williams, his musical hero, had died en route. The show went on nonetheless, and Hawkins was said to have given one of the best performances of his career.

In 1960, when Hawkins proposed to Shepard, he told her he wanted to do what Williams had done in his second marriage: have the ceremony onstage, in front of several thousand people. After their wedding at a concert in Wichita, Kansas, Hawkins and Shepard moved to a home near Nashville, and set about starting a family.

LEFT *When Jean Shepard and Hawkshaw Hawkins (far right) fell in love and got engaged, he insisted they have the ceremony onstage, just like his hero Hank Williams had done.*

ABOVE *Shepard and Hawkins named their baby boy Don Robin Hawkins after their close friends Don Gibson and Marty Robbins.*

That same year, another female singer arrived in town. Like Jean Shepard and Patsy Cline, Loretta Lynn had survived a childhood of abject poverty to emerge as a strong-minded, outspoken woman determined to make her mark on country music.

She was born on April 14, 1932, in a one-room cabin in Butcher Hollow, Kentucky, an impoverished coal-mining region in the foothills of the Appalachians. The oldest girl in a family of eight children, she grew up wearing dresses made from flour sacks and tending to her younger siblings, singing them to sleep in a rocking chair. For entertainment, Lynn remembered, they listened to the *Grand Ole Opry*:

Well, there was one person in that hollow who had one of these little tiny radios. And, on Saturday night, everybody would end up at that one house. And we listened to the *Grand Ole Opry*. And I remember Ernest Tubb, Little Jimmy Dickens, Roy Acuff, and "the Wabash Cannonball."

Daddy, when he got his job in the coal mines, we got a Philco radio. And that was the greatest thing that ever happened to us, was that radio. When Bill Monroe would start to singing the bluegrass, Mommy would hit the floor and start dancing. She'd do that little, I don't know what you call it, "Hillbilly Hoedown." And when Mommy would hit the floor and start dancing, you'd see Daddy, with his head down, and he'd look up and he would grin, you know, and put his head back down.

I'd go to sleep every night with that radio, with a

blanket over the top of me. Sometimes I'd be froze to death, but I listened to the radio.

At age fifteen, she met Oliver "Doolittle" Lynn, a twenty-one-year-old war veteran, who outbid everyone else for her pie at a schoolhouse social. He was the first boy she ever kissed—and they married within a month, beginning a turbulent relationship that included arguments and fistfights

TOP, LEFT *Loretta Webb, age nine, from Butcher Hollow, Kentucky*

TOP, RIGHT *"Doolittle" Lynn and his young bride Loretta, 1948*

but never drove them apart. She and Doolittle moved to Washington State, near the Canadian border, where he had found work on a ranch. She had four children in quick succession while the couple scraped to get by.

Hearing his young wife sing to their kids, Doolittle bought Loretta a $17 guitar from Sears. She taught herself to play it, composing songs of her own and playing them to her children. "I'd line these kids up and I'd sing and sing," she remembered, "and I'd say, 'Now, which one, which one of these songs do you like?' And, 'Do you think Mommy can sing?' And every one of them would say, 'Yeah, Mommy, you can sing.'"

Soon she was performing with a small country band for five dollars a show at a local tavern and won a talent contest on a Tacoma television show hosted by Buck Owens. A wealthy lumberman offered to finance a recording of a song she had written, "I'm a Honky Tonk Girl."

"I like the very first record she did," Merle Haggard said. "I think that's the best she ever sounded. I love that record. She had authenticity in it, and

she was hungry and she wanted out of that life she was in. And kind of sung her way out of prison."

To promote the record, the Lynns started sending it, along with a photograph of Loretta dressed in a cowgirl outfit, to disc jockeys around the nation. In a trade magazine, they read about Felice and Boudleaux Bryant publicizing songs by going from station to station, and in early 1960 decided to do the same thing—sleeping in their car, living on baloney and cheese sandwiches, washing their clothes in a basin in the back seat and drying them by holding them out an open window. Loretta said she fell into a routine on the trip:

ABOVE *Loretta Lynn performs on Buck Owens's television show,* The Bar-K Jamboree, *in Tacoma, Washington.*

LEFT *To promote Loretta's first record, "I'm a Honky Tonk Girl," she and Doolittle sent a photograph of her along with the record to disc jockeys around the nation and then went on the road to personally encourage them to play it.*

I had one little dress. It was a little black and white dress. Doo got it for me for my seventeenth birthday. I had kept it all this time, you know, and I kept that one dress so I could go someplace. And I'd get in the back seat and change into my little black and white dress and pull my jeans off and go in the radio station.

Sometimes, I'd sit there for three or four hours before they'd play my record. It wasn't easy, either. I walked in one station and there was my record down in the garbage can. He said, "I don't know. I've never heard you sing. I don't know if this record's any good, or not." And I told him, "Well, like you probably won't ever find out, 'cause it's laying in the garbage can."

Then, when I'd come back [to the car], I'd pull my dress off, hang it back up, and we'd go on down the road to the next radio station. That's how we did it.

In Tucson, they stopped at a station where young Waylon Jennings was the deejay; he liked her music and played it on air. By the time they reached Dallas, "I'm a Honky Tonk Girl" had reached number fourteen on the country charts. They decided it was time to head for Nashville. "I sat up in WSM till four o'clock in the morning before Ralph Emery played my record," she said. "And he got off at four. So just before four, he played my record."

She pestered officials at the *Grand Ole Opry* until they granted her a guest appearance, and the reception to "Honky Tonk Girl" was enthusiastic enough to win her a spot on the show.

ABOVE *Loretta and Doolittle celebrated when Ralph Emery played her song on WSM in Nashville.*

LEFT *She celebrated again when Ott Devine told her the Opry had made her an official member.*

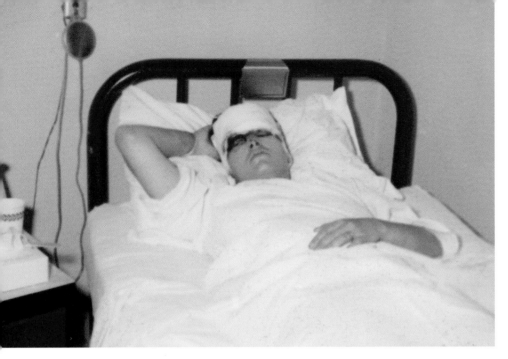

tiled bathroom. "I guess she saw in Loretta what she had seen in her own career," Ralph Emery said: "having a hard time making it."

Looking for a contract with a major label, Loretta got to know Brenda Lee through Owen Bradley, who, Lee said, had an offer to make: "He brought me in and he said, 'There's this new girl. Her name is Loretta Lynn. She brought me a song yesterday. It's called "Fool Number One." I don't think it's a good song for her, but I think it's a great song for you. So here's what I'm gonna do, and tell me what you think. I'm gonna offer her a contract with Decca if she'll give me "Fool Number One" for you.' She took the deal. I got the song. I had a number-two record with it, and look what Decca got: They got Loretta."

Meanwhile, one of Loretta's idols, Patsy Cline, was involved in a horrible automobile accident that killed two people. Patsy was catapulted through her car's windshield and hospitalized in critical condition, with broken bones, a dislocated hip, and a deep gash that sliced across her forehead.

After an appearance on the *Opry*, Loretta was scheduled to be on Ernest Tubb's *Midnite Jamboree*. She sang "I Fall to Pieces" and dedicated it to Patsy in the hospital. "So she sent her husband out to town to get me, to bring me to the hospital," Lynn said. "And that's where I met her, was in the hospital."

Loretta and Patsy soon became close friends. As Cline slowly recovered—appearing once at the *Opry* in a wheelchair to show her fans she was mending—she started giving Lynn advice on her career, offering any help she could: money for rent, nicer clothes, and styling tips in Patsy's gold-

ABOVE *Patsy Cline was in the hospital after a terrible car accident when she heard Loretta Lynn sing Cline's song "I Fall to Pieces" on the* Midnite Jamboree. *The two soon became friends.*

RIGHT *Loretta credited Patsy for giving her career advice and nice clothes and styling tips.*

CRAZY
By WILLIE NELSON.

Recorded by
PATSY KLINE
on BRUNSWICK Records

Acuff-Rose Publications Ltd.
50, NEW BOND STREET, LONDON. W.1
PAMPER MUSIC INC. TENNESSEE

12091

Made in England

2/-
NET

CRAZY

God, you know, that's another voice that just transcends any genre of music. Someone might hear Patsy Cline sing "Crazy" and think, "What the heck is that?"

That performance and that record—all of a sudden, there's this window that they're looking through into a genre of music that they would never think about otherwise. That's the beautiful thing about those transcendent voices.

KATHY MATTEA

Patsy Cline's near-fatal car accident had generated a wave of publicity—and sympathy—for her, and fueled even more sales of her song "I Fall to Pieces." As soon as she felt up to

it, Owen Bradley brought her back to his studio to record an album featuring more of the Nashville Sound.

She performed an eclectic assortment of songs: "Foolin' Around" by Harlan Howard and Buck Owens, and a Mel Tillis tune called "Strange"; Cole Porter's "True Love" and the pop standard "The Wayward Wind"; and covers of Bob Wills's "San Antonio Rose" and Gene Autry's "South of the Border." But the song that produced the album's biggest hit was the one she had the most trouble recording: a slow, soft lament Willie Nelson had written during his time in Houston. He had originally entitled the song "Stupid," but changed his mind and called it "Crazy." Once again, as Nelson recalled, the

ABOVE *The sheet music for Willie Nelson's "Crazy," which Patsy Cline was the first to record. It was, Nelson said, "a perfect rendition."*

story of getting one of his songs recorded started at Tootsies Orchid Lounge:

Charlie Dick, Patsy's husband, was there. He and I were having a beer. I had a demo on "Crazy," and I got it on Tootsies jukebox. And he heard it and said, "That would be a great song for Patsy. Let's go play it for her." And I said, "It's a little late," you know, it was about midnight. And he said, "That's okay."

So we went over to her house. It was about twelve thirty, one o'clock when we got there, and I wouldn't get out of the car. So he went in, and Patsy came out and made me get out of the car and come in, and listened to the song.

I thought it was a good song. You know, when you write one, you know whether it's good or whether it's not great. But I always thought it was a really good song. And I played it for Patsy Cline, and she thought it was a great song.

"I'm glad you woke me up," Cline said. "I'm recording it." But in the studio, as Owen Bradley and his musicians struggled at first to compile an arrangement, Patsy was having trouble herself. Her bruised ribs from the accident made it hard to sustain some notes, and she couldn't get Nelson's unique phrasing on his demo version out of her head.

A Nashville recording session usually laid down three or four songs in three hours. This time, even after adding an extra hour in the studio, Bradley still didn't have a completed take. "It was just a constant back-and-forth," said Harold Bradley, a guitarist on the session. "Owen was refining [the arrangement] while she was having that problem. He finally told her, 'There's no use beatin' yourself up. Why don't we just make a track?'"

Bradley sent Cline home while he and the musicians finished the background track. Two weeks later, she returned to lay down her vocals over it—an unusual procedure at the time—and in her first take delivered the kind of performance they had been searching for: turning her powerful voice into an intimate, quavering instrument that matched the anguish and vulnerability of the lyrics.

"I think the thing was that Patsy finally figured out how to style it herself, where she felt it," Harold Bradley said. "And I think she just took it and made it her own."

"When you hear her sing, it sounds to me like she is in the room, right here. And you feel the emotion in every lyric," according to country star Trisha Yearwood. "For me, she was the example of when you sing, you want to make people feel what you're feeling. And she did it so well. If you can find that perfect song and then you marry it with that, with the voice it's supposed to go with, it's timeless."

"Of all the versions of my songs covered by other artists," Nelson would say, "it's my favorite . . . a perfect rendition" sung with "delicacy, soul, and perfect diction." He added: "She understood the lyrics on the deepest possible level." Released as a single, "Crazy" quickly crossed over to the Top Ten on the pop charts, just as Owen Bradley had wanted.

That fall, at the annual country deejay convention in Nashville, still needing crutches to get around, Cline walked up to accept the award as *Billboard* magazine's Female Artist of the Year, ending Kitty Wells's unbroken string dating back to 1952. Then she embarked on an arduous tour to promote her new sound—and a new look. Instead of a fringed cowgirl outfit, she now appeared in elegant dresses, with a new hairdo and heavy makeup meant to mask some of her facial scars.

She joined an *Opry* entourage that played New York City's Carnegie Hall. It included Jim Reeves, Faron Young, Marty Robbins, Minnie Pearl, and Bill Monroe, and won a review from *The New York Times*, which praised her "convincing way with 'heart songs,' the country cousin of the torch song." But she paid more attention to a biting column in the *New York Journal-American* by Dorothy Kilgallen, who disdained all country music and referred to the visiting musicians as

"hicks from the sticks" and the "Carnegie *Hall*billies." Outspoken as ever, Cline fired back at her next concert. Kilgallen, she said, was "the Wicked Witch of the East."

Just as she had befriended young Brenda Lee on the road years earlier, Cline now took a thirteen-year-old steel guitar prodigy named Barbara Mandrell under her protective wing. "She was loving and caring, and soft and feminine, and motherly," Mandrell said. "She wanted me to room with her. So, of course, gladly, I would do that." Patsy let young Barbara comb her hair every night before performances, and the future star would stand in the wings and watch Cline interact with the audiences:

And I remember Patsy said, "I just had this song that you all made a hit, called 'I Fall to Pieces,' and I was in this horrible car accident." And I remembered in combing her hair, that she had a scar here, here, and here. And I was told that, in the wreck, the first thing she saw was just a big flap of [skin], you know, it was horrible. So, anyway, she said, "'I Fall to Pieces,' and then I had this horrible wreck." She says, "I'm going to premiere a new song for you tonight that's brand new, coming out, and I'm a little worried about it for me because it's called 'Crazy.'"

OPPOSITE *As Patsy Cline recovered from her car accident, she started performing again, and Owen Bradley brought her into his studio to record more songs.*

ABOVE *Cline, now in furs, promotes a new Decca record with a deejay, while Charlie Dick, her husband, listens in the background.*

MODERN SOUNDS

What's interesting about "I Can't Stop Loving You" and Ray Charles and country music is that country music claims triumphs of the heart and traumas of the heart as the most elemental space. Well, I think that he was able to bring jazz and a kind of refinement, a different kind of black refinement of cool to country. He refined country music while keeping it still rooted.

ALICE RANDALL

Country music was crossing over as never before. Owen Bradley's reworking of Brenda Lee—using her big voice to turn out records that mixed pop, country, and rhythm and blues—made her a sensation in Europe as well as the United States. England's *Melody Maker* magazine ranked her as the top female artist in the world.

Touring in Hamburg, Germany, her opening act at the Star Club was the Beatles, who were still struggling to break through. Brenda, a teenager at the time, was captivated by their music, their look, and their irreverent personalities. She brought home a photograph and a demo recording—and tried without luck to interest Decca into signing them. Skeeter Davis's "The End of the World" became an international number one song, and she toured briefly with the Rolling Stones.

The boundaries between musical genres had always been porous. But in 1962, no one proved it more than a blind rhythm and blues singer and piano player named Ray Charles. Given creative control of an album for the first time in his career, he surprised everyone—and had to overcome initial reluctance by his label—by recording a collection of country songs.

"He's listening to the radio, is he not going to hear country music?" said the jazz musician and composer Wynton Marsalis. "We tend to think of it one way, like these white musicians heard these black musicians play. The black musicians were listening to the white musicians, too."

For his album *Modern Sounds in Country and Western Music*, Charles chose songs like Hank Williams's "Hey Good Lookin'" and "You Win Again," the Everly Brothers' "Bye Bye Love," Eddy Arnold's hit "You Don't Know Me," and country singer Don Gibson's song "I Can't Stop Loving You."

LEFT *Ray Charles performs at New York's Carnegie Hall.*

"Ray didn't have to go out and make that record; he could have kept making the records he was making," Darius Rucker said. "He was a huge star. But he loved country music so much, he wanted to go make a country record. And he did, and it's one of the all-time classic records in American history."

"When you hear Ray Charles singing some great Hank Williams song or a great Don Gibson song, and in a way that was soulful and more from an R&B place," said Vince Gill, "to me, it showed how great these songs were."

"You take country music, you take black music," Ray Charles said, and "you got the same goddamn thing exactly." "And he was absolutely right," said Ronnie Milsap, also a blind singer and piano player with hits that crossed over between country and pop. "'I Can't Stop Loving You' hit the radio, and that whole summer of 1962, it just played all summer long. He took the song into a brand-new place."

Within just three months of its release, *Modern Sounds of Country and Western Music* was already certified gold—with 500,000 copies sold—and replaced the soundtrack of *West Side Story* as the nation's best-selling album. As a single, "I Can't Stop Loving You" topped the charts in the United States and Britain, won a Grammy for best R&B release, and sold so briskly, one Atlanta record store owner reported, "people who don't even own record players are buying it."

"That was a huge record for us, maybe even more so than for Ray," according to Gill, "for us to be able to hang our hat on how soulful this music could be." Ralph Emery agreed: "Ray Charles was a step. That was another step in popularizing what many considered to be a 'second-class music.' He made country music more popular. And I think he caused people to take a second listen, who might have said, 'I don't like country music.' He gave them a second choice, and people here [in Nashville] really appreciated it. We'd been looking for legitimacy for years. And this was just another step."

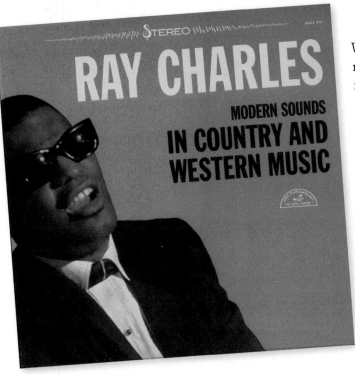

ABOVE *With* Modern Sounds in Country and Western Music, *Ray Charles "did more for country music than any one artist has ever done," said Willie Nelson.*

We all thought, like what Kennedy said, 'When the tide comes in, all the boats rise.' We thought that would help all the boats rise here in Nashville."

Ray Charles, Willie Nelson said, "did more for country music than any one artist has ever done."

"Music is always striving to the best thing. And the best thing is the mix, you know? It always is," said the singer Rhiannon Giddens. "You have these two things, which are pretty cool on their own. Then you put them together and all the strengths multiply and become this beautiful thing. And I think that's one of the reasons why American music has taken over the world—because everybody can feel that it comes from one plus one equals a hundred."

LOVE IS A BURNING THING

Being the daughter of a really famous guy was fraught with so much anxiety, partly because of my mother. She was so afraid of fame, and she was afraid we'd be kidnapped.

She didn't want anything in the papers and she wanted a quiet life, a contained life. And my dad did not have a quiet and contained life. So there was always this conflict and struggle about that.

ROSANNE CASH

By the early 1960s, Johnny Cash was on the road more than ever, consuming twenty amphetamine pills a day to feed his addiction and keep him going, then using alcohol and barbiturates to get to sleep.

He had appeared in a low-budget film, *Five Minutes to Live*, which bombed at the box office. Another concept album, *Ride This Train*, failed to sell many records. Arrested in Nashville for public drunkenness, he spent a night in jail; later, he was stopped for driving more than ninety miles an hour on a California freeway.

Rodgers's clothes and was "as skinny as rain," one band member said.) The audience sat in confused silence for a few minutes—and then started calling out for "Folsom Prison Blues." Cash handed the lantern to someone onstage and, in an almost inaudible voice, launched into his regular set of songs. "It was just a nightmare," he later recalled, "awful, start to finish."

Cash and Vivian now had four daughters, and he moved them to a big house in Casitas Springs, an hour from Los Angeles, though he was seldom at home—and when he was, the tensions with Vivian were palpable. "I wasn't going to give up the life that went with my music," Cash said later, "and Vivian wasn't going to accept that. So, there we were, very unhappy. There was always a battle at home."

After one road trip, Cash brought his whole band to the house, along with Patsy Cline, who was part of his tour. Vivian became friends with Patsy, but not with another woman now appearing regularly with her husband: June Carter.

Carter had divorced her first husband, Carl Smith, and married her second, Edwin Nix, who operated a body shop in Nashville while June pursued her career. When Rose Maddox departed from Cash's package show—partly because of all the cancellations and postponements caused by his drug use—Carter had been hired to replace her.

Cash's interest in Jimmie Rodgers had grown into an obsession: he collected Rodgers memorabilia; recorded two of his songs, "In the Jailhouse Now" and "Waiting for a Train"; and even considered producing a movie about Rodgers's life in which he would play the lead role.

"Jimmie Rodgers was a profound influence," said Rosanne Cash. "I think it was his own restlessness and Jimmie Rodgers's restlessness. There's so many songs about travel in country music, about longing for home, being away from home, never going to get back home, never going to see Mother again, hoboing, waiting for a train. Those themes are central. And Dad really responded to that restlessness."

Booked for a concert at Carnegie Hall, Cash showed up onstage wearing his hero's railroad outfit and carrying his lantern, intending to open with a set of Rodgers's songs. (He had been taking Dexedrine diet pills to lose enough weight to fit into

ABOVE AND RIGHT *Johnny Cash was on the road more than ever, leaving Vivian and their four girls at home. From left, standing, Cindy, Kathy, and Rosanne; in back, Cash holding Tara, alongside Vivian's mother, Irene Liberto, and Vivian.*

Cash soon added June's mother, Maybelle, and her sisters to the act, and they appeared with him at a big show at the Hollywood Bowl, where eighteen thousand fans came to hear him, Patsy Cline, Roger Miller, Marty Robbins, Don Gibson, and Flatt and Scruggs perform. Vivian took the girls to the concert. When it was over, they watched as Johnny jumped into a waiting Cadillac to drive off with June. "The look on Vivian's face," one band member remembered, "was pure anguish." Patsy Cline was upset enough to upbraid June Carter about it the next time they saw each other.

By the end of 1962, Johnny Cash and June Carter's affair had deepened. "A lot of people were in the dark about it," said Carlene Carter, June's daughter. "But it was pretty evident to even me, a small child, that there was something there between them, a special bond." But Johnny and June were conflicted about it: they were both still married to other people and had children of their own to consider.

June poured her feelings into a new song, co-written with Merle Kilgore, that her sister Anita recorded. "When she wrote 'Ring of Fire,' I believe that she wrote that about John," Carlene Carter said. "It was about something real. It was about true passion and true love—and the scary factor of that. You know, 'I fell into a burning ring of fire'—that is scary."

Anita Carter's "Ring of Fire" had not resulted in a hit record, so in March 1963 Cash decided to record it himself. To help him, he turned to "Cowboy" Jack Clement, a friend from his Sun Record days, who enjoyed pushing musical boundaries. In Memphis, Clement had persuaded Sam Phillips to record Roy Orbison and Jerry Lee Lewis, and had written and produced two hits for Cash, "I Guess Things Happen That Way" and "Ballad of a Teenage Queen." Now he was working as a producer in Beaumont, Texas.

Cash wanted something fresh for "Ring of Fire"—maybe even Mexican mariachi horns—to give his "boom chicka boom" sound a new twist, and he thought Clement was just

---

ABOVE *Cash's extravaganza at the Hollywood Bowl included many of the top country stars of the day. Patsy Cline would upbraid June Carter for leaving the event with Johnny while Vivian looked on.*

BELOW *June Carter was now a permanent part of Cash's touring show.*

remember I went back to Beaumont and a few days later, I'm hearing it on the radio, all over the place," Clement said. "It was good."

"Ring of Fire" spent seven weeks at number one on the country charts, and an album featuring it lasted more than a year on the pop charts, earning Cash his first gold record when it sold more than 500,000 copies. Afraid he might leave for another label, Columbia signed him to a new five-year contract guaranteeing Cash half a million dollars.

Vivian hated "Ring of Fire"—and did her best to avoid the radio stations that seemed to play it constantly. She associated it with June Carter, whose voice could be heard on the record, singing backup with her sisters. "The mere mention of her name annoyed me," Vivian would remember. "I longed for the days when Johnny told me he'd always walk the line for me."

the man he needed. "The phone rang and Johnny Cash said he's going to cut a record in Nashville with trumpets on it," Clement remembered. "And he wanted me to come up and help him figure it out. So I flew up and got in there and he had these two, two or three trumpets and they didn't know what they were going to do. They had music, but it was blank." Clements suggested the notes the trumpets should play— and they became the signature sound of "Ring of Fire." "I

TOP *Johnny Cash and June Carter were both married with children, but falling in love. June described her feelings about the affair by co-writing "Ring of Fire."*

ABOVE, LEFT *Cash's album* Ring of Fire *would sell more than 500,000 copies to become his first gold record.*

SWEET DREAMS

I think there were people in Nashville, in the early days, when I came here, in the late '50s, early '60s, I think they wished we'd go away. I think there were people here that actually wished that there was no such thing as the *Grand Ole Opry*.

I think there was a certain amount of people that were ashamed of it—who were these hillbillies coming down here, wiping the mud off of their boots on our sidewalks?

And when tragedy struck, some people in Belle Meade, or the fancy places in Nashville, couldn't have really cared less, I think it just brought us together that much more because it hurt us all. It was like one person got cut and we all bled.

BILL ANDERSON

Nashville's music industry was thriving, even if the city's leaders still viewed the singers, songwriters, and session players with barely concealed disdain. The recording studios on Music Row were pushing out hits, and every Saturday night, thousands of people from hundreds of miles away converged on the Ryman Auditorium to see their favorite stars on the *Opry*—a place many Nashville residents studiously avoided.

"They didn't come to the *Opry*," according to Ralph Emery. "The *Opry* was a tourist business. I was onstage at the *Opry* one night and I looked down and saw this guy, part of the Belle Meade group, and I said, 'What are you doing down here?' Because I knew he wouldn't come on his own. He said, 'Oh, I got these people from out of town; they insisted I bring 'em to the *Grand Ole Opry*.'"

When they were home from the road, the artists tended to stick together. Everyone knew everyone else—personally as well as professionally. Jan Howard and her songwriting husband, Harlan, often hosted friends like Patsy Cline at their house on Music Row. Roger Miller and Hank Cochran attended "pickin' parties" at their home, where songwriters sang their latest creations; June Carter came by whenever she was in Nashville. The Howards were especially close friends with Jean Shepard and Hawkshaw Hawkins.

Hawkins and Shepard now had a son, named Don Robin in honor of two other friends in the close-knit musical com-

TOP *Bill Anderson and Patsy Cline*

ABOVE *Anderson (right) talks with Marty Robbins, Hawkshaw Hawkins, and Jean Shepard.*

CLOCKWISE FROM TOP, LEFT *Patsy Cline with her close friends Harlan and Jan Howard; Tompall Glaser and Mother Maybelle Carter at a "pickin' party" at the Howards' home; Jan and Harlan join in; Patsy with, from left, Owen Bradley, her manager and guitarist Randy Hughes, Justin Tubb, and songwriter Hank Cochran. Within Nashville, the country music artists were like a close-knit family, Bill Anderson said.*

munity, Don Gibson and Marty Robbins. The day the boy was born, Hawkins was so proud that he rushed to Ralph Emery's all-night show on WSM to announce his arrival and his name.

Patsy Cline was now a mother of two. Following the success of "Crazy," she was in demand for appearances everywhere, and to cut down on her time away from home, she now often flew to and from concerts in a four-seat Piper Comanche flown by her guitar player and manager, Randy Hughes.

Her latest single, "Leavin' on Your Mind," was climbing the charts when she and Owen Bradley started work on a new album in February 1963. Over four days, Cline and Bradley recorded enough material for it: songs that ranged across all musical genres, from Bill Monroe's "Blue Moon of Kentucky" and the old standard "Bill Bailey, Won't You Please Come Home" to Irving Berlin's "Always" and Ray Price's "Crazy Arms"—and a dreamy version of Don Gibson's "Sweet Dreams."

Cline called Jan Howard one day to invite her to the recording session in Bradley's Quonset hut studio. One of the tracks they laid down that night was an old Bob Wills fiddle tune, "Faded Love," which Bradley planned on being the album's title song. He had reworked it

to incorporate the Nashville Sound—with the Jordanaires again singing background vocals, Floyd Cramer on the piano, Harold Bradley on guitar, and a smooth string section.

"I went to the session," Howard recalled. "I had always heard 'Faded Love,' the Bob Wills version, which was great. But when she sang 'Faded Love' it was just unbelievable. When she changed keys and hit the high note and then went to the low note, that did it. It gives me cold chills."

With the album completed, Patsy made an appearance on the *Opry*, hosted by Cowboy Copas, a former member of Pee Wee King's band and now a solo artist known as "the Country Gentleman of Song." Then she flew off to a string of concerts—Lima and Toledo, Ohio; New Orleans; Birmingham—before a few weeks' break at home in early March.

That February, Hawkshaw Hawkins was excited about a new single of his that had just been released, a swinging heartbreak song written by Ernest Tubb's son, Justin, entitled "Lonesome 7-7203." He was even more excited that Jean was pregnant with their second child.

Hawkins was just starting to promote his new record when word reached Nashville that a popular disc jockey in Kansas City, "Cactus" Jack Call, had been killed in an automobile accident. Call had no insurance, and a local promoter was putting together a benefit concert to help his family. A troupe of *Opry*

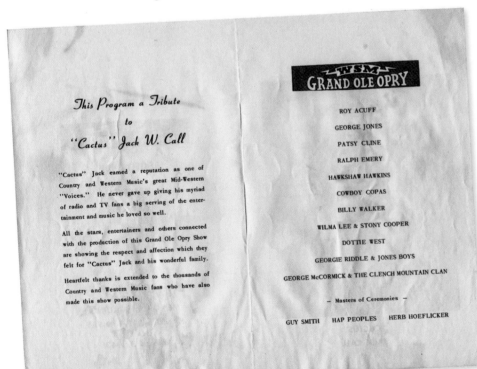

ABOVE *Patsy Cline and Owen Bradley working on a new album*

LEFT *The benefit concert in Kansas City for the family of disc jockey "Cactus" Jack Call featured a number of Opry stars.*

stars agreed to come to Kansas City for the show, including Hawkins. "He was one of the first ones to volunteer because, back then, you did stuff like this," Jean Shepard said. "If you had a friend in need, you went and helped fill that need."

Before he left for Kansas City, Hawkins told his pregnant wife, "I hope this one's a boy, too," and stopped by the WSM studio to hand-deliver a copy of his new single. "Play the hell out of it," he urged Emery, and headed to the concert.

Besides Hawkins, the benefit show in Kansas City's Memorial Building on Sunday, March 3, included Dottie West, Billy Walker, George Jones, Cowboy Copas—and, as a last-minute addition to the roster, Patsy Cline, who had flown in from her recent tour. She was tired and had come down with a bad cold, but she closed the concert with a set of her hits, along with a few she had just recorded, including "Faded Love" and "Sweet Dreams."

The audience response to Cline was so overwhelming, Dottie West remembered, that "she was moved to tears and thanked them. Patsy said how much they meant to her and that she'd be nowhere without them."

The concert raised $3,000, and the next morning the musicians prepared to make their separate ways home. Billy Walker had learned in the night that his father had suffered a heart attack; Hawkins gave him his commercial airline ticket and said he'd fly back later with Patsy Cline and Cowboy Copas on Randy Hughes's small plane.

CLOCKWISE FROM TOP, LEFT *Patsy Cline, Hawkshaw Hawkins, and Cowboy Copas perform at the benefit concert in Kansas City, March 3, 1963.*

After a day's delay because of bad weather, the four-seater finally departed Kansas City early on the afternoon of March 5. West of Nashville, they flew into dense rain clouds as darkness fell. Hughes was not trained to fly by instruments.

Word began to spread on country radio stations that the plane and its four famous passengers were missing. Jean Shepard had put her son to bed and dozed off when her phone rang. "It was about ten o'clock, ten thirty, and Hawk had a fan club president out of Minneapolis who took care of his fan club," she remembered. "And she said, 'What are you doing?' I said, 'Well, I'm trying to go to sleep.' And she said, 'Oh, my God, you don't know.' I knew then." Friends started showing up at the house, including Jan Howard and Minnie Pearl, who helped her through the long night as they waited for more news.

Early in the morning, Bill Anderson also got a phone call, from the wife of a friend: "She said, 'Go turn on WSM right now.' So I turned on the radio and they were talking and they were crying. You could actually hear the tears in their voice as they were telling their audience, and the world, for the first time, that this plane had gone down."

Meanwhile, a frantic search was under way near Camden, Tennessee. Roger Miller, who had been visiting Patsy Cline's husband, joined the team combing the forest, calling out his friends' names in the darkness. As the sun came up, he climbed a fire tower, saw some torn treetops, and led the group to the crash site, which was littered with debris: a hairbrush, gold slipper, and cigarette lighter of Patsy's; Hawkshaw Hawkins's leather belt, one of his cowboy boots, the broken neck of his guitar.

CLOCKWISE FROM TOP, LEFT *The broken neck of Hawkshaw Hawkins's guitar, on the site where he, Patsy Cline, Cowboy Copas, and Randy Hughes died in an airplane crash; Roger Miller surveying the site where four of his friends were killed; the body of one of the victims is carried from the scene.*

OPPOSITE *June Carter cries backstage before the Opry's tribute. A fifth star, Jack Anglin, had died in a car accident on his way to one of the funerals.*

No one had survived. "It was like a cloud fell over country music and Nashville and the *Grand Ole Opry*," Jan Howard said. "It was devastating to everybody. It was just a horrible, horrible time. Four good friends." The four became five on the day of the funeral. Jack Anglin, of the singing duo Johnny and Jack, was killed in a car accident going to Patsy Cline's memorial service. Jan Howard, on her way to the funeral home with Anita Carter, heard the ambulance sirens. "And we got to the funeral home and it was like chaos," she said. "When Ernest Tubb heard that Jack Anglin had been killed, he just fell apart." Bill Anderson was there and got the news at the same time. "My goodness," he thought, "when is this going to stop?"

A short time after the funerals for Hawkshaw Hawkins, Patsy Cline, Cowboy Copas, Randy Hughes, and Jack Anglin, the *Grand Ole Opry* paid tribute to them all at the start of its Saturday-night program. The country music family was grieving and in shock, but wanted to give their lost friends a proper good-bye.

With everyone gathered onstage, they bowed their heads and asked the audience to stand to join them in a silent

LEFT AND ABOVE *The* Opry *members bow their heads to remember their fallen friends and offer comfort to their families. Minnie Pearl (far left corner) had to return to the stage and perform so the regular show could go on.*

prayer. "Everybody was there who was a member," Ralph Emery recalled. "And they decided they would have that service and then move on, move back to regular programming. Minnie Pearl went out and she did her 'Minnie Pearl.' She was just as 'Minnie' as she could be. But she came offstage crying. I've never forgotten that picture. And I thought, 'Minnie just really did the hardest show she's ever done in her life.'"

In the weeks that followed, Hawkshaw Hawkins's "Lonesome 7-7203" would rise to the top of the country charts—the only number-one hit of his career. Jean Shepard had their baby a month later—a boy she named Harold Franklin Hawkins, after the father he would never know. Marty Robbins, for whom their older son had been named, wrote a song, "Two Little Boys," and he listed the Hawkins children as the songwriters, which gave them any royalties it would receive. "And that meant a lot," Shepard said. "I was just kind of lost. I just took it one day at a time."

Like those of Jimmie Rodgers and Hank Williams, Patsy Cline's life and career had ended far too soon. She was just thirty years old. "Faded Love" and "Sweet Dreams" were released and would reach the Top Ten on the country charts. Her loss would resonate in country music for decades. And her signature song, "Crazy," would go on to become the number-one jukebox tune of all time.

I was a *Grand Ole Opry* announcer in those days. And honest to God, I don't think anybody realized the impact she was going to have on history. We had no idea that she was going to be a "goddess" and that she was going to be immortal.

RALPH EMERY

She was funny; she was energetic; she was sweet and thoughtful. But she was also tough and powerful—and strong, too. She was what a woman should be. All of it. She was very special. I think I learned from Patsy Cline that it's not just a man's world. Women can do things, too.

BARBARA MANDRELL

ABOVE *Jean Shepard with her two boys, Harold Franklin and Don Robin Hawkins, Christmas 1965*

ABOVE, RIGHT *The album cover for* Sentimentally Yours, *the last album Patsy Cline released before her death*

OPPOSITE *Patsy Cline at the* Opry. *"We had no idea," Ralph Emery said, "that she was going to be immortal."*

THE SONS
AND DAUGHTERS
OF AMERICA

*In the 1960s, Johnny Cash would come to embody
everything the nation was going through.*

DURING THE MID-1960s, as the generation known as baby boomers came of age and began asserting itself against older ways of doing things, the United States found itself torn in different directions—between impatient demands for change and stubborn resistance to it; between peaceful protests and senseless violence, hopeful idealism and angry despair.

All of it would be reflected in country music. Its songs and its stars would respond, in their own way, to the same swirls of change sweeping across the nation.

And a dark-eyed, deep-voiced troubadour from Dyess, Arkansas, would somehow embody nearly everything the '60s came to stand for: heedless self-destruction and selfless concern for social justice, an eagerness to experiment with new ideas, and a yearning for old-fashioned, personal redemption.

> My dad was the physical embodiment of folk music, gospel, Delta blues, Appalachian, searing folk poetry. Dad was the embodiment of that. There is everything in him. And, yet, totally original.
>
> ROSANNE CASH

By 1964, Johnny Cash's erratic career seemed back on track. The phenomenal success of his album *Ring of Fire* prompted his label to re-sign him to a half-million-dollar contract. He was headlining package tours that played to packed auditoriums in major cities with a regular show that featured a gospel quartet from Virginia called the Statler Brothers; Cash's old friend from his rockabilly years, Carl Perkins; and Maybelle Carter and her three daughters, Helen, Anita, and June.

"People were hypnotized by him," said Don Reid of the Statler Brothers. "He didn't even have to try. He just walked out and there was charisma all around him. His presence was electric." At each show, after the opening acts had performed, Reid would be the one to introduce the star of the evening: "And he would always say, just before I went onstage, practically every night, 'Donny, be sure to tell them where I got that scar.' He had this deep scar on the side of his face, and there was about a dozen stories about where he got that scar. I don't think I ever did tell them the truth. [Some people] thought it was a knife fight and then somebody thought it was [from] when he was in prison—which, he never was in prison. I think the final one was something about a barbed wire fence, as best I remember, something when he was a kid. But he saw the humor in all of those colorful stories."

Cash was billed as a country singer, but he was fascinated by *all* forms of American music. "I've never known a guy that knew as many songs as he did," Reid remembered. "He knew every old gospel song. He knew every old pop song. He taught us a song we put on an album one time, an old Ink Spots song that we'd never heard, and he taught us the lyrics to it, wrote them down on a piece of paper, and showed us the melody. He would carry a record player and stacks of records with him on tour, and we'd sit in hotel rooms at night and he'd play all these old folk songs. He was into every field and knew every song that had ever been written."

Cash's newest interest centered on the folk music revival emanating from New York City's Greenwich Village and focusing not only on old, traditional tunes but also on newly written, highly personal lyrics and songs of social protest. At its forefront was a prolific young songwriter from Hibbing, Minnesota, named Bob Dylan, whose work was being turned into hit after hit by artists like Joan Baez and Peter, Paul, and Mary. When *The Freewheelin' Bob Dylan* was released, Cash added it to the albums he took on the road. "He played the album in his dressing room

before he went onstage," Rosanne Cash said, "and when he came off, he played it again."

Cash sent Dylan a fan letter, and got one back in return. Cash soon wrote and recorded a new song of his own, "Understand Your Man," with a melody that echoed Dylan's "Don't Think Twice, It's All Right." It spent six weeks at number one on the country charts. His cover version of Dylan's "It Ain't Me, Babe" reached number five.

At Dylan's invitation, the country celebrity appeared at the 1964 Newport Folk Festival, where Cash performed songs ranging from his best-known hits, like "Folsom Prison Blues" and "I Walk the Line," to the Carter Family's "Keep on the Sunny Side." "With a masterly set of story-telling songs," *The New York Times* reported, "the Nashville star closed the gap between commercial country and folk music." After the

concert, Cash presented Dylan with his guitar as a token of appreciation.

At the same time, another folk singer in Greenwich Village caught Cash's attention. Peter La Farge's "The Ballad of Ira Hayes" told the story of the Pima Indian who had been one of the Marines who hoisted the American flag at Iwo Jima during World War Two. After being hailed as a hero upon his return to the States, Hayes had descended into alcoholism and died along a lonely road on his Arizona reservation.

La Farge's song—which linked Hayes's fate with the mistreatment of his people—struck a powerful chord with Cash. He took La Farge with him on tour, but was angered when audiences didn't seem to respond. Undeterred, Cash decided to record an entire album, *Bitter Tears*, dedicated to the nation's troubled history with Native Americans. When "The Ballad of Ira Hayes" was released as a single, Cash became outraged that radio stations wouldn't play it and *Billboard* magazine didn't even mention it.

He took out a full-page ad in *Billboard* with an open letter

OPPOSITE AND ABOVE *On December 7, 1963, Cash sent a fan letter to folk star Bob Dylan, and Dylan sent him one back. The two soon became good friends.*

to deejays and station managers. "Where are your guts?" it asked. Referring to recent race riots, the burgeoning civil rights movement, and the growing American war in Asia, he added, "'The Ballad of Ira Hayes' is strong medicine. So is Rochester—Harlem—Birmingham—and Vietnam."

In response, some stations considered boycotting all of Cash's records. But enough began playing the song that it gradually reached number three on the country charts. Cash added some benefit concerts on Indian reservations to his schedule, including Pine Ridge in South Dakota, where he visited the site of the Wounded Knee massacre of 1890. Moved by the experience, Cash wrote a song that recounted the tragedy. In the suburbs of Washington, D.C., a young folk singer named Emmylou Harris came across *Bitter Tears* and thought, "Oh, he's one of us; he's a 'folkie' too," and became a lifelong fan.

Meanwhile, Cash's personal life was in shambles. His constant touring had strained his ten-year marriage to his wife, Vivian, the mother of their four

TOP *Cash's album* Bitter Tears *contained three songs written or co-written by Cash and five written by Peter La Farge, including "The Ballad of Ira Hayes."*

RIGHT *His growing addiction to amphetamines made Cash unreliable as a performer and strained his marriage with Vivian.*

daughters. She now suspected—correctly—that he was having an affair with June Carter, who traveled with Cash as part of his package shows.

But his close friend and bass player in the Tennessee Three, Marshall Grant, who already worried about Cash's deepening relationship with June Carter, was even more concerned about his drug use, which had mushroomed into a dangerous dependence. "He felt tremendously protective of Dad," Rosanne Cash said. "And he took it upon himself, he and June—they would go in his room, find his pills, flush them, do everything they could to get him from Point A to Point B and show up for the shows and not be high." "Sometimes, you wouldn't see anything 'cause he didn't show up," Don Reid said. "Sometimes, when he did show up, he was a different person. You wouldn't have any idea what his next thought and action was going to be, and he didn't either."

The addiction caused Cash to lose weight, hollowed out his cheeks, and made him fidgety and jumpy. Appearing on Pete Seeger's television show with June Carter, he squirmed and rocked in his chair, uncomfortably fussed with his hair and scratched his neck, nervously lit and relit a series of cigarettes, even ended the show with his shoes off.

In 1965, the Federal Drug Administration tightened its

else could do seemed able to keep Cash away from his drugs. "I just went on and on," he later remembered. "I was taking amphetamines by the handful . . . and barbiturates by the handful too, not to sleep but just to stop the shaking from the amphetamines."

On the road, shows were canceled when he was unfit to perform. Promoters sued him. He was sued again—by the federal government—when his carelessness was blamed for starting a fire in a national forest near Los Angeles; he made a settlement for $82,000.

At the *Grand Ole Opry* one night, he ended his set by smashing all the footlights with his microphone stand. The managers told him he was no longer welcome at the Ryman Auditorium.

By now, Cash rarely went home to Vivian and their four girls in California. He had "become almost a stranger in the house," she recalled. And during his rare visits, he would disappear for days without any explanation. "I couldn't just stand by," she added, "and continue to simply hope that things would get better." In 1966, she filed for divorce.

That same year, June Carter divorced her second husband, and though she loved Johnny Cash, she turned down his repeated requests that they now get married. He seemed too intent on destroying himself.

ABOVE *Johnny and Vivian leaving the federal courthouse in El Paso, after his sentencing on drug charges. The National States Rights Party in Alabama used the photo in its publication* The Thunderbolt *to claim that Cash was married to a black woman and to call for a boycott of his concerts.*

regulations on prescriptions for amphetamines. Undeterred, Cash found them easy to get in Mexico, hiding them in his guitar case when he crossed back into the States. In 1965, he got caught in El Paso, was arrested for possession of more than a thousand amphetamines, and spent the night in jail before being released on bail. When his case came up for trial, the judge gave him a thirty-day suspended sentence and a $1,000 fine, but a picture of him leaving the courthouse, with Vivian by his side, made national news.

"She was so humiliated," Rosanne Cash said. "She was such a private person. All of her friends knew. It was just terrible. My mother is very exotic looking, and her people were Italian. And the Ku Klux Klan jumped on this picture and said that my dad was married to a black woman, and started a firestorm." The National States Rights Party in Birmingham, Alabama, reprinted the photo in its newsletter, saying "Money from the sale of records goes to scum like Johnny Cash to keep them supplied with dope and negro women." It referred to his children as "mongrelized" and called for a boycott of his shows and records.

Cash's manager mounted a publicity campaign that earned his artist sympathy in the press. But nothing he or anyone

KING OF THE ROAD

The road, as we like to say, is a bitch. We travel all the time, and it's the hardest part. The guys in the band make a joke, they say, "We don't get paid for playing. We get paid for riding." It was a Gypsy world. It was like joining the Foreign Legion.

RAY BENSON

Most country artists were not major stars like Johnny Cash, with a lucrative record contract and albums that sold well, so for them the road was even more important if they wanted to make a living as a musician. "The artist had to get in the car or the station wagon and hightail it out of Nashville and get up the road to [people in] the hinterlands," said Bill Anderson. "We would take their music to them."

For these artists, instead of large auditoriums, the venues were more likely to be firemen's festivals, county fairs, and the multitude of outdoor music parks that featured Sunday festivals—like Ponderosa Park in Goshen Township, Ohio, three hundred miles from Nashville, or Sunset Park in West Grove, Pennsylvania, more than twice the distance from Music City. The musicians would drive all Saturday night to get there and perform three consecutive shows on Sunday, then drive all night for another performance somewhere else on Monday.

At the festivals, stars were expected to share meals with their fans, who brought plates of ham and potato salad, pies and iced tea. And regardless of the venue, the musicians were also expected to linger after their performances, to mingle with the people and sign autographs. "The industry

was truly built one handshake at a time, one autograph at a time," said Marty Stuart. "And somewhere along the way, the relationship between country performers and country fans became unlike any other genre of music. Ernest Tubb was one of those legendary examples. He would sit on the edge of a stage in a folding chair and sign popcorn boxes till the very last soul was gone. The word was, 'Those people put us up here.'"

"Once they accept you as part of their family, they're there for life," added Roy Clark. "You may not have another hit record, but you already made enough that they know who you are and they like you. I can't imagine anybody going up to Frank Sinatra and patting him on the back and saying, 'How you doing, Frank?' I mean you wouldn't do that. But you can do that to Red Foley or Ernest Tubb, or me, and I appreciate your loyalty."

• • •

TOP AND LEFT *Donna Stoneman at the wheel of the touring bus the Stoneman Family used to get from concert to concert—often at outdoor music parks, where the fans usually insisted on feeding their favorite country stars homemade food.*

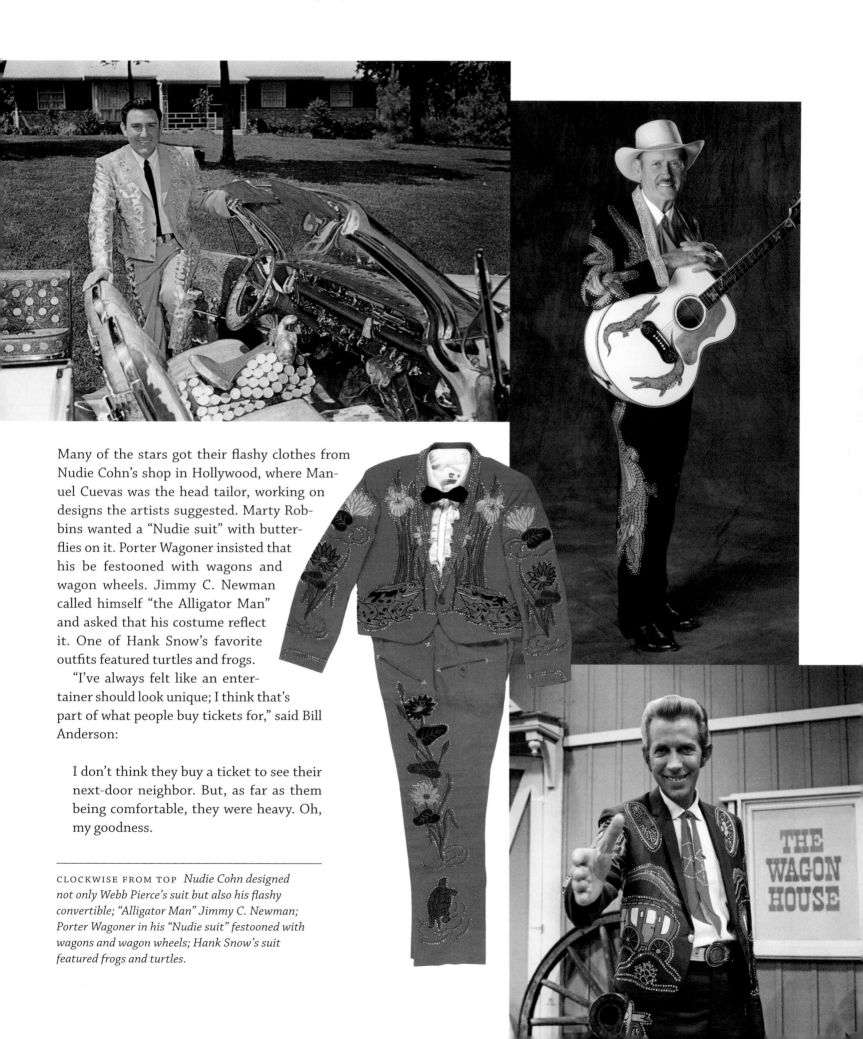

Many of the stars got their flashy clothes from Nudie Cohn's shop in Hollywood, where Manuel Cuevas was the head tailor, working on designs the artists suggested. Marty Robbins wanted a "Nudie suit" with butterflies on it. Porter Wagoner insisted that his be festooned with wagons and wagon wheels. Jimmy C. Newman called himself "the Alligator Man" and asked that his costume reflect it. One of Hank Snow's favorite outfits featured turtles and frogs.

"I've always felt like an entertainer should look unique; I think that's part of what people buy tickets for," said Bill Anderson:

> I don't think they buy a ticket to see their next-door neighbor. But, as far as them being comfortable, they were heavy. Oh, my goodness.

CLOCKWISE FROM TOP *Nudie Cohn designed not only Webb Pierce's suit but also his flashy convertible; "Alligator Man" Jimmy C. Newman; Porter Wagoner in his "Nudie suit" festooned with wagons and wagon wheels; Hank Snow's suit featured frogs and turtles.*

You get on a summer stage at a fair-grounds in the middle of August, in the day-time, and you're wearing one of those things, you're going to lose ten pounds while you're out there trying to sing.

The necessity to travel so much came with a cost. On tour, Skeeter Davis lost her singing partner in a car accident; *Opry* member Ira Louvin was killed in another one. A year after Patsy Cline, Hawkshaw Hawkins, and Cowboy Copas perished in a small-plane crash, Jim Reeves's single-engine plane went down, ending his life just as his singing career was reaching its peak.

Like Johnny Cash, many artists turned to pills that kept them awake and energized during the ceaseless travel. Before new regulations were enacted, amphetamines were readily available from physicians, who prescribed them as diet pills. They had various nicknames: Old Yellers, White Crosses, Black Mollies, L.A. Turnarounds, Speckled Birds.

"I could finish playing a show, pack up, and now I've got five hundred miles to drive," Ray Benson, of the band Asleep at the Wheel, said. "'Asleep at the Wheel' was a good name because it reminded you, don't do that. It was 'medicine.' Somebody would say, 'Here, take a pill,' and I was alert as hell. What they didn't tell you was that it will kill you if you keep using it." Disc jockey Ralph Emery got hooked on Old Yellers after someone told him they would help him get through his all-night show on WSM.

Despite his heavy use of amphetamines, Roger Miller—

CLOCKWISE FROM TOP LEFT *Bill Anderson with Loretta Lynn at a country music park; performing onstage, while a chicken watches the show; with fellow star Ray Price, the Cherokee Cowboy.*

unlike Johnny Cash—never let it keep him from showing up to perform. "How long can he stay up?" one concert promoter asked Miller's tour manager. "I don't know," the man answered, "I've only been with him a year and a half; I don't know how long he was up before then." He was "the King of the Pill Takers," according to Ralph Emery: "Roger said, 'You've got to be careful where you keep your change and where you keep your pills. The other night I got confused and before I knew it, I'd taken thirty-five cents.'"

After coming to Nashville in 1957 and working for a while as a bellhop at the Andrew Jackson Hotel to scrape by, Miller was now an established songwriter in Music City, with hits recorded by Jim Reeves and Ray Price. But his dream of becoming a major singing star in his own right had never materialized. Four different labels had dropped him in six years because of weak record sales, and he spent most of his time on the road playing small solo gigs or as an extra act for one of his many friends, who enjoyed having him around because of his lightning wit and offbeat sense of humor. "Hanging out with Roger Miller was like hanging out with

TOP *June Carter at New River Ranch country music park in Maryland, where young fans sat on the stage.*

LEFT *Ernest Tubb signs autographs at New River Ranch. "Those people put us up here," he said of country fans.*

than a thousand dollars for the move. As a favor, Jerry Kennedy, his producer at Mercury Records, arranged to pay him $100 a song if he'd come in for two days of recording. With nothing to lose, Miller showed up with more than a dozen of the sillier songs he had written. One of them was from the point of view of a married man who spends all his money buying drinks for his friends: "Dang Me."

Of the songs they recorded in the two days, Kennedy thought another one, not "Dang Me," should be released as the album's single, and the company began pressing five thousand copies to send to radio stations. Meanwhile, Kennedy took a tape of all the tracks home, so he could listen to them in his basement office and map out the album. When he got to "Dang Me," his two boys came bounding down the steps, asking him to play it again.

a sparkler," said Marty Stuart. "It went in all directions at the same time. You never knew what was going to be said or done. He didn't know what was going to come out of his mouth."

"He came up to me one night at a concert," Larry Gatlin remembered, "and he said, 'Lorenzo'—that's what he called me—he said, 'Did you ever notice how much weight a chicken can gain and never show it in the face?'"

"He had that brilliant, quick sense of humor," added his good friend Bill Anderson:

We used to say, "We follow Roger around and pick up his droppings." He used to say that his family was so poor, "If the wolf had ever come to our door, he'd have had to have brought a picnic lunch."

Well, I thought that was the funniest line I ever heard. And when I started writing a song called "Po' Folks," early in my career, I put that line in there. And I went to Roger and I said, "Roger, I've borrowed your line." And he said, "Oh, did I say that?"

In early 1964, Miller decided to give up on Nashville and leave for Los Angeles, where he hoped he could find work as a comic on television. But he was broke and needed more

Based on his sons' enthusiasm, Kennedy made a nervous call to the company president and urged him to grind up copies of the other song and press "Dang Me" instead. Miller was already in California when it was released—cutting radio ads for $50 each to make spending money and playing at a small club for $75. Four people were in the audience, and the club's check bounced when he tried to cash it. Driving home on the freeway, he heard "Dang Me" on the radio for the first time. It was taking off across the nation.

Fueled by Miller's appearances on several national television shows, "Dang Me" was soon the top hit on country charts, and the number-seven pop song in the nation, just ahead of "I Get Around" by the Beach Boys. Another song from the session, "Chug-a-Lug," did nearly as well, and the

ABOVE *Roger Miller's manic sense of humor endeared him to other artists, who also respected his songwriting skills.*

RIGHT *Believing his album of silly songs had little chance of success, Miller named it* Roger and Out *and left Nashville.*

album Miller had recorded for moving expenses was headed for gold. (As an inside joke about his expectations for the album, he had named it *Roger and Out*.) He came back to Nashville to record a follow-up album. From it came an even bigger hit, "King of the Road," which rose to number three on *Billboard*'s pop charts. In England, it knocked the Beatles' "Ticket to Ride" from its perch at number one. Its album also went gold.

Roger Miller, the poor boy from Oklahoma, was on top of the world. Supper clubs in Las Vegas and Reno now paid him $25,000 a week to perform. A royalty check for a quarter of a million dollars arrived in his mailbox. For 1964, he won five Grammy Awards; for 1965, he won six. When he visited Nashville, he liked to stay at the most expensive suite at the Andrew Jackson Hotel, where he had once worked as a bellhop.

Miller would go on to have his own network television show; open a "King of the Road" motor inn; travel to performances in a private jet; write and sing songs for Walt Disney's animated film *Robin Hood*; and then provide the score for *Big River*, a Broadway musical based on Mark Twain's *Huckleberry Finn*, which won seven Tony Awards. "Old songwriters never die," he said. "They just decompose."

CENTER *Miller wrote the opening lines for his hit song "King of the Road" on a credit card application.*

BELOW *Miller in front of five Grammy Awards. His international stardom permitted him to stay in the most expensive suite of Nashville's Andrew Jackson Hotel, where he once worked as a bellhop.*

THE A-TEAM

The noise used to be called mountain music, and it was a twangy, nasal thing that went with corn liquor, family feuding, and barefoot courting. A few years back, though, Nashville image builders rechristened their musical lingo, added new songs and lyrics, and came up with the style that's called Country.

Since then, the Nashville Sound has come rolling down the mountains, spread to the far corners of the continent, and now is beating on distant shores.

Despite all this burgeoning acceptance, no one has yet defined just what country music is. It has roots in the songs and laments the earliest colonists brought over from 17th-century England, but it has since had infusions of new vitality from almost every mode of popular music from high society jazz to lowdown blues to gospel songs.

Today, it is as cosmopolitan as Rome.

MEMPHIS *COMMERCIAL APPEAL*

By the mid-1960s, Nashville was home to more than 250 music publishers. Two dozen record companies had offices in town. Country music had become a $100 million business, employing five thousand people. Among the busiest were the musicians who backed up the singing stars during recording sessions in the studios on Music Row.

They were all virtuosos on the instruments they played, though only a few could read sheet music and relied instead on a chart with numbers that indicated what chords accompanied a song's lyrics. Each three-hour session was expected to produce a usable take on three or four songs, whose arrangements were usually improvised collaboratively on the spot.

"The way a typical Nashville session works, when you're called for a session, there's no preparation," said Charlie McCoy, a veteran session musician. "When you hit the door, you hear the song for the first time. And you have a session leader. He'll say, 'Okay, let's have harmonica behind the second verse and let's have steel guitar behind the chorus.' They tell you *where* to play. They never usually told you *what* to play. That was up to you—and the people who had the right instinct were the ones who get to work."

Over time, producers like Owen Bradley and Chet Atkins tended to draw from a core group of session musi-

CLOCKWISE FROM TOP LEFT *The Jordanaires; A-Team guitarist and session leader Grady Martin; the Anita Kerr Singers*

CLOCKWISE FROM TOP LEFT *A-Team guitarists, from left, Grady Martin, Ray Edenton, and Harold Bradley, in the studio with bass player Bob Moore; singer George Hamilton IV runs through a song with his session musicians before recording begins in RCA's Studio A; harmonica player Charlie McCoy, who could play a variety of instruments; producer Billy Sherrill goes over a song with piano player Hargus "Pig" Robbins; Lloyd Green on the pedal steel guitar; Floyd Cramer at the piano; and a chart with the chord numbers and notes to musicians for Anita Carter's recording of "God Is."*

albums and on Jeannie Seely's 'Don't Touch Me,' and on Charlie Rich, 'Mohair Sam.' I played organ on 'Easy Loving,' Freddie Hart. I played vibes and bells on 'Blue Velvet,' Bobby Vinton. But more harmonica than anything else."

The Anita Kerr Singers or the Jordanaires provided harmony in the background. In one year alone, the Jordanaires sang on hits that sold more than thirty-three million copies.

A typical week for a member of the A-Team was fifteen to twenty sessions, each lasting three hours: 10 a.m. to 1 p.m., 2 to 5, 6 to 9, and 10 p.m. to 1 a.m. They all followed a simple rule, passed on from one veteran session musician to another. "Check your ego at the door," said McCoy. "The song and the artist are the picture, we're the frame. What we need to do is anything we can do to make this song better. Most of the time, less is better." Pig Robbins put it another way: "Listen to the lyric, and let your licks and feel determine what you play. You learn to play in between the lines, the singer. The singer is the main thing." McCoy said he learned the lesson from legendary guitarist Grady Martin, who was acting as a session leader at one of Owen Bradley's sessions:

cians, knowing they were both efficient and creative in the studio. Insiders called them the "A-Team."

It included piano players Floyd Cramer, who popularized a distinctive "slip note" style, and Hargus "Pig" Robbins, who had been blind since the age of four and learned classical music at the Tennessee School for the Blind.

Buddy Harman played the drums. On bass, Bob Moore would take part in eighteen thousand sessions and more than fifty thousand songs. Pete Drake mastered the intricacies of the pedal steel. So did Lloyd Green.

Among the top guitarists were Grady Martin, Hank Garland, Jerry Kennedy, Ray Edenton, Velma Smith—and Harold Bradley, who would become the most-recorded guitarist in music history, working with thirty artists who entered the Rock and Roll Hall of Fame, and eighty-three in the Country Music Hall of Fame.

Charlie McCoy was best known for his harmonica, but he could play almost any instrument. "I was a guitar player; pretty comfortable with keyboard; I learned to play vibraphones," he said. "I play a little sax, a little trumpet. Trumpet on 'Rainy Day Women #12 and 35' by Bob Dylan; baritone sax on 'Pretty Woman,' Roy Orbison; the tuning guitar on 'Detroit City,' Bobby Bare. I played bass on three Dylan

I'm twenty-one years old, I'm living my dream. I'm playing with the Nashville musicians. I'm playing with big country music stars. And I was feeling my oats. And one day, we're on a session, and [Martin] said, "You're playing too much."

He said, "You listen to the lyrics. If you can't hear and understand every word, you're playing too much." And the light went off in my head. That was the best piece of advice I ever had.

"In the sense that there was a certain formula involved, that we had to get one song every forty-five minutes, it was an assembly line process," Lloyd Green said. "But during that forty-five minutes a lot of things were happening, musically and creatively. We cut a lot of brilliant stuff. We cut a lot of junk stuff, too, to be honest. You can't cut four songs every three hours and do three and four sessions a day, year in and year out, and not have a lot of disasters. But when the magical moments happened, they really were magical."

ABOVE *A recording session in progress in Owen Bradley's Quonset hut studio on Music Row*

THE MOTHER CHURCH

It was the personification of America—the bayous, the valleys, the wheat fields, the mountains, the West. All of its children had come to "the Mother Church of Country Music" to sing country music at the *Grand Ole Opry*.

It was almost like a badge of honor, that you had to bring your culture with you to the table. Bob Wills and his guys brought us Western music; Bill Monroe brought bluegrass music out of Kentucky. Hank Williams brought the South with him, from honky tonks. Johnny Cash brought the black land dirt of Arkansas. Patsy Cline brought her heartache from Virginia. Willie Nelson brought his poetry from Texas.

It was the most wonderful parade of sons and daughters of America that brought their hearts and their souls and their experiences with them to the microphone. And it gave us a great era in country music.

MARTY STUART

Nashville's Music Row was now the center of the country music industry. But in the minds of most fans, the music's home was firmly located on Fifth Avenue in downtown Nashville, where every Saturday night, radio station WSM beamed out the *Grand Ole Opry*, broadcast live from the stage of Ryman Auditorium.

Between six thirty and midnight, more than forty different acts were ushered on and off the stage for brief appearances— from square dancers and old-time string bands like the Fruit Jar Drinkers to comedy routines by Minnie Pearl and younger singing stars with the latest hit record. Over the airwaves, it all sounded orderly. In person, it was organized mayhem.

"It looked like the chariot race in *Ben-Hur*," said Larry Gatlin of the Gatlin Brothers. "Different musicians coming on, then someone would sing and they'd clap. And then another bunch of people would come out there. And they were milling around. It's chaos back there."

At the center of the frenetic activity—onstage and backstage—stood the man who had joined the *Opry* back in 1938 and helped transform the show from an old-fashioned barn dance into a vehicle for personal stardom: Roy Acuff.

Acuff was now in his mid-sixties. His days of recording big hits were behind him, and after nearly being killed in a car accident, he had given up touring. But his hugely successful Acuff-Rose publishing company had paved the way for other publishers in the city; and many of the industry's current stars had grown up listening to him on the radio. Within the walls of Ryman Auditorium, Roy Acuff was king.

"It was 'the Mother Church of Country Music' and we were kind of a congregation," said singer-songwriter Tom T. Hall. "We had our own religion, which was country music. Roy Acuff was the pastor of the church. He's the 'king' of country music. And we were all his children and God's children. We'd go backstage and then we'd sing and then we'd fan out in all directions and go play shows and then come back on Saturday night. It was a family, a very spiritual thing." Vince Gill recalled the story of an *Opry* fan asking Acuff for an autograph: "And he's writing his name. The guy said, 'I bet you wish you had a dollar for every one of those you signed,' and he goes, 'Oh, I do,' and handed him back his piece of paper."

RIGHT *Fans line up for* Grand Ole Opry *tickets at Ryman Auditorium.*

The National Life and Accident Insurance Company, which had started WSM in the 1920s as a sales vehicle for its policies, was as interested in who came to the *Opry* shows as who listened to it at home. Company surveys showed that the fans drove an average of more than six hundred miles to Nashville for the chance to see their radio heroes in person.

Thousands of them made the pilgrimage each week, lining Fifth Avenue and the corner of Broadway for their ticket into the Ryman, filling the wooden pews on the ground floor and the balcony called the Confederate Gallery to its capacity—more than three thousand people per show. Bud Wendell, who had once sold National Life policies door to door in Ohio, was now the head of WSM and the *Opry*. Sometimes, he said, the show was oversold, so they raised the backdrop and let several hundred people stand behind the artists onstage: "They're looking at the backs of the artists, but the artists have all got to walk around and through them. They were like in 'hog heaven,' you might say, to be onstage at the *Opry*."

OVERLEAF, LEFT PAGE *While one act performs on the* Opry *stage, others wait nearby for their turn.*

OVERLEAF, RIGHT PAGE *Within the walls of the Ryman, Roy Acuff (top) was king. As Hank Snow finishes his performance and waves (bottom right), the dancers have moved onstage, and other musicians prepare for their turn at the microphone. If the night was oversold (bottom left), the extra guests were crowded onto the back of the stage and watched the show from behind.*

ABOVE *Outside the Ryman, fans prepare to tour Music City on a bus that will take them past the homes of their favorite stars.*

Tour buses now roamed some of Nashville's finer neighborhoods, jammed with outsiders eager to see the homes of their favorite rhinestone-clad stars—like Webb Pierce, who had a giant, guitar-shaped swimming pool in his yard, and sold Mason jars of his pool water for a dollar each.

Many of Nashville's upper-class citizens feared that "the Athens of the South" was being ruined forever. Jean Shepard remembered Acuff being asked to speak at a Nashville Chamber of Commerce dinner: "And he said, 'You people might as well get used to the idea. We're here to stay in Nashville.' And we were, because us rednecks didn't care; we had things going our way."

Another *Opry* star took a different approach and tried to repair relations between the two cultures in town. Sarah Ophelia Cannon, better known as Minnie Pearl, was as much a fixture on the Ryman stage as Roy Acuff—and even more beloved. She was so popular that, in 1966, at its annual country music awards, *Billboard* magazine named her "*Man* of the Year."

But she had grown up in a prosperous Tennessee family, attended the fashionable Ward-Belmont finishing school, and now lived in one of Nashville's most exclusive neighbor-

Webb Pierce

Webb has been voted #1 Male Vocalist in Country Music eight times. He has starred in movies and TV shows, and is an accomplished songwriter. He's from West Monroe, Louisiana, and is a former member of the Opry, Louisiana Hayride, and Ozark Jubilee. His hit singles include "Wondering," "I Ain't Never," "More and More," "There Stands the Glass," and "Slowly." Webb's house is one of the showplaces of Nashville—and those rumors about him having a guitar-shaped swimming pool are true.

hoods, next door to the governor's mansion, with her husband, who ran a successful air charter service. "She was really a very sophisticated lady," said Bud Wendell. "She belonged to a bridge club. She played tennis over at Belle Meade with four or five other ladies. She could just put that hat on and she could be Cousin Minnie Pearl, or she could take it off and be Ophelia Cannon."

Margaret Ann Robinson, whose family owned National Life, often enlisted Cannon to raise money from the music industry for highbrow causes, like the symphony or the celebration of the town's founding:

I went out to Minnie's one morning, to talk to her about her part in this citywide celebration. In the middle of our conversation, she said, "Oops, we've got to go. Follow me to the mailbox." And I thought, "Well, for heaven's sakes, Sarah, can't you wait?"

We walked down the driveway, and coming around the hill I could see one of the sightseeing buses in Nashville. They stopped at her mailbox like they always did and opened the door, and she climbed on the bus. And she'd say, "How-DEE, I'm

ABOVE Homes of the Stars, *a guidebook for visiting fans, included two pages about Webb Pierce's lavish estate, which had a swimming pool shaped like a guitar. Pierce sold Mason jars filled with his pool water for a dollar.*

LEFT *Sarah Ophelia Cannon, also known as Minnie Pearl, lived near the governor's mansion and helped bridge the gap between Nashville's upper crust and country music's "hillbillies."*

so glad to see you." Then those people in the bus would go home and they'd say, "We met Minnie Pearl."

Then she was Sarah Cannon again, and we talked about what we would eat for lunch or what she wanted to do in this Nashville celebration. You see, she bridged the gap between the two.

Eventually, the city surrendered, putting up signs reading "Welcome to Nashville, Home of the Grand Ole Opry, Music City USA"—though the old signs, welcoming visitors to "the Athens of the South," remained in place too. "We finally reconciled that," said Tom T. Hall. "And you know how we did it? You follow the money. Once they find out that these hillbillies are making, you know, a half a million dollars a night singing through their nose and playing the guitar, we'll have them out to lunch to help out with their charity."

MAKE THE WORLD GO AWAY

Funny thing about Nashville. It stands at the crossroad of several great music traditions that have roots deep in America's memory: Negro blues, Southern mountain balladry, bluegrass string bands, and work songs.

And yet the city has become to many music fanciers the international symbol for a musicality of such numbing mindlessness and banality that some either won't or can't listen to it.

TV GUIDE

Country music's image problem in the mid-1960s was even bigger nationally than it was within Nashville. Americans were awash in wave after wave of fads and trends that emphasized the new and the hip; country music and its fans seemed just the opposite. "There was a line of demarcation," Ralph Emery said. "We were those 'hillbillies.' People who love country music are 'ignorant.' 'They don't have any money. They are the poor working class. And if this music is their representative, we don't want any.'"

"BLUE-COLLAR" BUYING POWER

The INDUSTRIAL WORKER'S INCOME has rocketed OVER 500% in TWO DECADES, from $18.50 per week to $102.00 per week, this plus a working wife and/or son or daughter creates a multi-salaried income of over $7,500 a year.
Dr. Roslow — PULSE

58% of the nation's spendable income is in the hands of the "BLUE COLLAR" industrial worker, 42% in the white collar professional market!

The truck driver earns more than a bank clerk, a bricklayer more than an office manager; he earns twice as much as a bookkeeper or an accounting clerk! The "BLUE-COLLAR" Market accounts for more expensive Hi-Fi sets, more air conditioners, and for more than half of big ticket items than the white collar worker.

OVER 50% OF THESE BLUE-COLLAR WORKERS HAVE A COUNTRY-WESTERN HERITAGE!

They support OVER 50 COUNTRY-WESTERN NIGHT CLUBS in LOS ANGELES ALONE!

91.9%
OF THE BLUE COLLAR WORKERS
LISTEN TO
RADIO EVERY WEEK

Source: IBM Supermarket; RSA-Pulse "Blue Collar Market"   15

The number of radio stations playing country music full time had dropped to fewer than one hundred at the start of the decade. Even Chicago's WLS, once the home of the *National Barn Dance*, had switched to an all rock-and-roll format.

To combat the decline, the Country Music Association embarked on an aggressive campaign to persuade station owners and major advertisers that they were ignoring a lucrative market, and that the common stereotypes about the music and its fans were wrong. The group hosted elaborate events in New York, Detroit, and Chicago, with Tex Ritter as the host. "The fans of our music elect the presidents, run the factories, grow the food, trans-

ABOVE AND LEFT *Jo Walker-Meador, head of the CMA, seen here with Gene Autry, led the efforts to persuade radio stations and advertisers that country music fans had "blue-collar buying power." Another brochure proclaimed "The 'C' in country music means cash."*

port our goods, and in general manipulate the gears of this country every day," Ritter told the businessmen.

Jo Walker-Meador, who was CMA's executive director, described the points she would then make: "It's no longer just a hillbilly and rural music. It's city music. It's widely known and liked. You're just missing out if you don't get in on using it to sell your company's products. The selling point is the loyalty of the country music fans; if they buy your product, they will stick with you." "The 'C' in country music," a brochure added, "means cash."

The sales pitch convinced some stations to give country music a try. In Chicago, WJJD made the switch and saw its ratings skyrocket: an estimated 500,000 households tuned in, representing a quarter of the radio audience at certain times. Others followed suit around the nation. By the end of the decade, more than six hundred stations were programming country music full-time, and two thousand played it during part of the broadcast day.

Take everything you've heard about Nashville, Tennessee—about the jug-eared hillbillies who subsist on corn "likker"; about the barefoot mountaineers who play squalky fiddles—take all that, and throw it into a cocked hat.

Because Nashville is "Music City, U.S.A." . . . home of the hottest sound on the national airwaves today. It's the home of the "Nashville Sound."

BOSTON RECORD AMERICAN

For anyone worried about country music's image or the limits of its acceptance, Eddy Arnold—and the way he sang his songs—seemed like something of a savior. "The word 'hillbilly' did not apply to Eddy Arnold," Marty Stuart said. "He was one of the breakout guys that could take country music beyond its own borders, beyond its own culture, to where people from other parts of the world, and other parts of the culture, could go, 'Those guys ain't so bad after all. I can listen to that.' And, at the same time, they might not have known it, but they were getting snookered by a country guy saying, 'Come on in.'"

By 1965, Arnold had already had two different careers—first as the popular "Tennessee Plowboy" on the *Grand Ole Opry* and then as a crooner of love songs whose records outsold those of Hank Williams. But the rise of rockabilly left

him behind in the 1950s, making him wonder if his days at the top had ended. Now, with the lush arrangements associated with the Nashville Sound, he proved that a mellow voice surrounded by soothing strings and background vocals could cross over to large audiences.

In concerts, he appeared in a tuxedo, not a rhinestone-encrusted Nudie suit, with entire orchestras behind him. His label of twenty years, RCA Victor, invested a million dollars to build a second, larger studio in Nashville to accommodate his recordings—and he repaid them with hit after hit, like Hank Cochran's "Make the World Go Away" and "The Tip of My Fingers" by Bill Anderson, which consistently scored on both the country and pop charts.

"Eddy Arnold has often been referred to as 'the man who took country music uptown,'" said WSM announcer Eddie Stubbs. "One of the complaints about him was that he was too smooth," added Ralph Emery. "He never understood that; how could you be too smooth?"

Arnold wasn't the only country singer reinventing himself. Ray Price had been a friend and honky tonk imitator of Hank Williams; then he switched gears in the late 1950s with his 4/4 shuffle sound, featuring a prominent fiddle and steel guitar. Now Price changed styles again, with "Danny Boy,"

ABOVE *Eddy Arnold (left) with fellow crooners Dean Martin and Frank Sinatra. Arnold had repeated crossover successes, taking the Nashville Sound and country music "uptown."*

Country music belongs first to the laboring and rural people of this country. They have no musical training and often can't read music, but when the day's work is done they can take down the old guitar, banjo, or fiddle and play the simple songs that tell about their way of life.

They don't want your horns or drums—they don't want your chorus singing in the background or even the Jordanaires making little noises behind them.

All that stuff is for the city people who jumped on the country music bandwagon when there turned out to be so much money in it.

JAMES KENNISON, *MUSIC CITY NEWS*

Two thousand miles west of Nashville, in California's San Joaquin Valley, a different kind of country music—unafraid of its rough edges—was coming out of the rowdy and smoky dance halls in Bakersfield. Many of the working-class patrons had been displaced from their homes in Texas and Oklahoma during the Dust Bowl, or were lured to California during World War Two by the prospect of better jobs.

The music *they* preferred came to be called the Bakersfield Sound. "It was more hardnosed, unapologetic, had a honky tonk bass to it, and a snap to it, and there's a defiance to that music," Marty Stuart said. "The worries and the heartaches and the struggles of the common man are understood, and

a song many country deejays had urged him to record after hearing him sing it at one of their conventions. But when it first came out, complete with an orchestral background, many of the same disc jockeys turned on him, according to Eddie Stubbs: "The disc jockeys wouldn't play the record. Some broke the record on the air, literally. You could hear them throwing the record in the trash can. He had people that came up to him at concerts and said, 'Why don't you sing like you did back in 1956?'—that was the year 'Crazy Arms' came out. He said, 'I don't want to sing like I did in 1956.' He alienated a lot of his longtime fans. The worst of all was some people came up and literally spit on him."

But the album was a big seller, and thanks to the Nashville Sound that Price, Arnold, and many others had adopted, 30 percent of the nation's hit singles were being recorded in Nashville. "The fiddle and the steel seemed to disappear more into the background," said Marty Stuart. "The hard-hitting, hard-nosed honky-tonk sounds of the 1950s and early 1960s seemed to give way to more of a velvet glove touch. A lot of people thought it was forward thinking; a lot of people thought it was the beginning of the end."

ABOVE *Ray Price put away his Nudie suit for a coat and tie—and sang songs like "Danny Boy" that broadened his audience.*

RIGHT *Even as a boy, Dust Bowl refugee Buck Owens had what Dwight Yoakam called a "Tom Joad glare."*

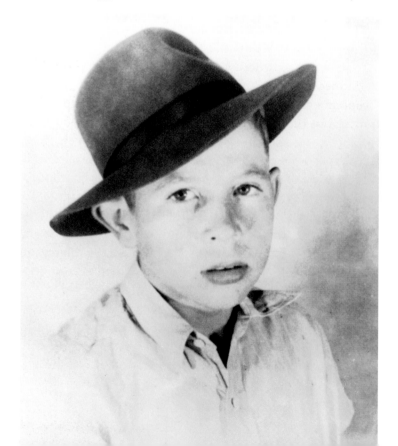

it's set to a twanging Telecaster and a driving steel guitar and some mighty good vocals and some mighty powerful songs." The personification of the Bakersfield Sound was Buck Owens and His Buckaroos. "Buck took the shuffle beat and he took the lyrics and the style of honky tonk, and he added the spunk, the vitality of rock and roll to his sound," said Bill C. Malone. "He had a sort of a fusion of a honky tonk sound and rock-and-roll energy."

Alvis Edgar Owens Jr. was born to a family of sharecroppers on August 12, 1929, in north Texas, just across the Red River from Oklahoma. Before he was four, he adopted the nickname "Buck" after a mule he admired.

Ruined by the Dust Bowl, in 1937 his desperate family struck out for California, but they only made it as far as

Mesa, Arizona, where they took whatever farm jobs they could find. "When I get big," Owens remembered thinking, "I'm not going to go to bed hungry [and] I'm not going to wear hand-me-down clothes."

He quit school in ninth grade in order to work: washing cars, driving a truck, picking oranges—and playing guitar in local honky tonks with a group called Mac's Skillet Lickers. By 1951, Owens had moved to Bakersfield, performing at one of its dance halls, the Black Board, with the Orange Blossom Playboys and sitting in as a session guitarist in Los Angeles at Capitol Records. Six years later he was in Washington State, hosting a Tacoma television show, *The Bar-K Jamboree*, where young Loretta Lynn got her first break as a country singer in his local talent contest.

But Owens's ambition was to be a recording star, and he was soon back in California, chasing his dream and developing a sound of his own. He fashioned it for AM radios—even did playbacks in the studio on car speakers—with less bass; higher, cleaner-sounding Fender Telecaster electric guitars; pedal steel; and a danceable beat. The melodies and lyrics, often written with Harlan Howard, were simple, so that any bar band could play them easily.

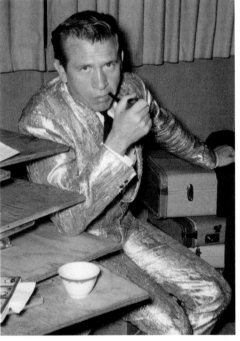

TOP *Owens (second from right) with Mac's Skillet Lickers in Bakersfield. Bonnie Campbell (third from right) would become his wife.*

CENTER *Like many stars, Buck got his clothes made by Manuel Cuevas at Nudie Cohn's tailor shop in Hollywood.*

RIGHT *Buck Owens, holding microphone, plays a gig at a school gymnasium with his Buckaroos. Don Rich (second from left) added harmony and a hard-driving Telecaster guitar that was part of the Bakersfield Sound.*

places at number one on the country charts.

So that no one could mistake where he stood, Owens published a pledge to country music in Nashville's *Music City News*. "I Shall Sing No Song That Is Not a Country Song," he wrote. "I Shall Make No Record That Is Not a Country Record. I Refuse to Be Known as Anything But a Country Singer. I Am Proud to Be Associated With Country Music. Country Music and Country Music Fans Have Made Me What I Am Today. And I Shall Not Forget It."

"Buck had a chip on his shoulder," according to Dwight Yoakam, "and I didn't realize it was there until I got to know him some years into our relationship, how suspect he was of being thought 'less than.' And it's ironic, because he didn't really write about that in his music. Buck was very effervescent in his music. It's a way for him to cope, I think, with what he had to deal with growing up. So Buck carried that with him in his music and it's always there in the tension, underneath the exposed part of his songs and songwriting."

"I was an AM radio kid, and I used to flip through the stations and I would stop when I heard a song I liked," said Darius Rucker. "I remember hearing a Buck Owens song and just being blown away by it because he came out of the radio so different. Buck came out with all this brightness and no bass, just all treble guitar. He had a way of just making me want to turn the radio up."

"It was a distinct sound," Ralph Emery said. "It had a biting rock sound to it; he had an edgy sound." Dwight Yoakam, who later became a friend and collaborator of Owens, added, "Buck came in with a raw, work camp, Tom Joad glare. You see it. You see it through the smile. Buck, sonically, did things that were as bold, or bolder, than anybody ever in the history of country music. It was not a singer's approach; it was an instrumentalist's. And he also sang with that kind of staccato."

With unabashed twang—and with Don Rich playing guitar and adding harmony—Buck Owens's Bakersfield Sound was defiantly the opposite of the Nashville Sound, which Owens called "soft, easy, sweet recordings, and then they pour a gallon of maple syrup over it." "I always wanted to sound like a locomotive comin' right through the front room," he said. Fans responded to his hardcore approach. On one record, both the A *and* B sides traded

When the Beatles began dominating the American airwaves, launching the so-called British Invasion, most people in the country music industry viewed them as mop-haired interlopers. John Lennon's much-publicized comment "We're more popular than Jesus" resulted in a burning of Beatles records in Nashville. Buck Owens, however, became an outspoken supporter. "I liked their music and their attitude . . . refusing to let anybody push them around," he said, though "I was still old-fashioned enough not to like their hair."

As it turned out, the Beatles were country music fans themselves. George Harrison's initial interest in guitars was prompted by listening to his father's Jimmie Rodgers records,

After the Beatles (above) released Buck's song "Act Naturally" on the flip side of "Yesterday," the Buckaroos (top) added a comic impersonation of the Fab Four to their act.

and he was so enamored of Chet Atkins, he insisted on playing the same kind of guitar he had seen on Atkins's album covers. As a teenager, John Lennon sang Hank Williams's "Honky Tonk Blues" around his home in Liverpool. Young Paul McCartney liked Marty Robbins. Of the four, drummer Ringo Starr was the most avid about country music. He cited Gene Autry, the singing cowboy he had seen in the movies at age eight, as "the most significant musical force in my life."

In 1965, when the Beatles were recording a new album and wanted a song for Ringo to sing, he suggested either Roger Miller's "Husbands and Wives" or "Act Naturally," which had been Buck Owens's first number-one hit two years earlier. They settled on Buck's tune, and released it on the flip side of "Yesterday."

Owens loved it. On tour, he and the Buckaroos incorporated a comedy routine into their act, donning Beatles wigs and playing their songs. His own records benefited from the exposure. "I started developing a whole new audience of young people," he later recalled. "I guess they figured if the Beatles recorded one of my hits, then I must be all right."

In 1965, he spent 302 days on the road—and earned more than half a million dollars in royalties, third highest for Capitol Records, behind the Beatles and the Beach Boys. He used his money to buy sole interest in a publishing company, bought radio stations in Bakersfield and Arizona—and, just as he had dreamed, never went to bed hungry again.

"I am who I am, I am what I do, and I ain't never gonna do it any different," Owens said. "I don't care who likes it and who don't."

BELOW *Owens's success—in music and business—took him a long way from his impoverished roots. Here, he and the Buckaroos prepare to perform at New York's Carnegie Hall.*

WOMAN ENOUGH

If you write the truth and you're writing about your life, it's going to be country. It will be country because you're writing what's happening. And that's all a good song is.

LORETTA LYNN

Loretta Lynn had now been in Nashville for five years, cutting records for the Decca label, billed as "the Decca Doll from Kentucky," touring constantly and hoping for a breakthrough. Her producer, Owen Bradley, realized that something different was needed—and it wouldn't be found in the Nashville Sound he and Chet Atkins had been pushing other artists to adopt. There was, he believed, nothing smooth and polished about Loretta Lynn.

Bradley encouraged her to return to the way she had first

started, writing her own material, just as she had done as a teenage wife, making up songs to entertain her four children. "He said, 'You write your next record. No matter what it is, it's going to be a hit because the times are changing,'" Lynn remembered. "And he said, 'You're out there working and you see the changes. You write about it.' So, we did that."

She turned to themes drawn from the experiences of women like herself—including her own turbulent marriage to Doolittle. In 1966, she came out with "You Ain't Woman Enough to Take My Man," in which a wife bluntly confronts another woman who has designs on her husband. It rose to number two on the country charts. It was quickly followed by another song from a wife's perspective—only this time aimed at a husband who stumbles home drunk, expecting to have sex: "Don't Come Home a'Drinkin' With Lovin' On Your Mind."

"I was writing about life, what was going on that day," Lynn explained. "You don't write about fantasies; you write about life and true life. That's the way I did it. Just life. I mean, the songs are just life. I've seen it, or I've lived it—and I never would tell my husband which one it was." The same year that

ABOVE *Loretta Lynn works on a new song, as her husband Doolittle writes down her words.*

the National Organization for Women was founded, and the year the phrase "women's liberation" was first used, "Don't Come Home a-Drinkin' with Lovin' on Your Mind" became her first number-one hit.

"It's an acknowledgment of the right of women, even a married woman, to define when she will and will not have sex with her husband," said songwriter Alice Randall. "That is absolutely a feminist statement and that song needs to be played on campuses today. I mean, Loretta was calling it out back then. You can put Loretta on the jukebox, put Loretta on the radio, put Loretta on the stereo, and have your say. You can hide behind her strength."

Lynn didn't consider herself part of any movement—nor did her growing legions of female country music fans. But they believed that at last, someone was speaking for them. "I would get mail, that they were going through the same thing," she said. "They would know that I'm going through the same thing. They went out and bought the record, and then they'd see their husband coming, they'd put it on and turn it up. That's what they did."

"These were some songs that people weren't writing, and certainly no woman was writing songs like that," said Elvis Costello. "She wrote all these amazing commentary songs—you know, sexual politics when nobody was singing that. Nobody in rock and roll was singing those ideas." Jack White agreed: "You're talking about things like spousal abuse and alcoholism, and a woman's right to her own body and her own rights. There's nothing more feminist than that."

"They were happening to everybody, but nobody would write about it. They thought they'd insult people," Lynn said. "Well, I never thought about that, because people were living that kind of life."

She had more to say—in her own feisty, unfiltered way. In "Two Mules Pull This Wagon," a harried housewife scolds her husband that he's not the only one working hard. In "Fist City"—based, she later said, on a real event in her life—she's ready to punch out and pull the hair of a woman trying to steal her husband's affections.

Her most controversial song focused on a wife who feels like a hen in a brooder house, confined to an existence of having one child after another—until she learns of a new form of birth control that had

ABOVE *Loretta and Doolittle show off her gold record for "Don't Come Home a-Drinkin' with Lovin' on Your Mind." Like many of her hits, she said, "the songs are just life. I've seen it or I've lived it."*

LEFT *Loretta holding her twins, Peggy and Patsy, who brought the number of her children to six*

I was borned a coal miners Daughter in a cobom on a Hill in Butche Holler. [handwritten original lyrics]

It wasn't dirty. In fact, if they'd have had the pill out when I was having kids, I'd have ate 'em like popcorn. I don't know where I'd have got the money to buy them, but I might have had to steal them."

When "The Pill" *did* come out, a number of country stations refused to play it, until the publicity about the boycott—and demands from her female fans—made it a top-five country hit and crossed it over to the pop charts.

But her biggest success came from a song that simply recounted her humble beginnings in Butcher Hollow, Kentucky, and how she was proud to be a coal miner's daughter. It would become her signature song—and lead to her being the first woman ever named the Country Music Association's Entertainer of the Year.

"Loretta opened the door for the subject matter in country music, for women to sing about anything they wanted to, anything that was on their mind, anything they felt like singing about," according to Marty Stuart. "I think she shattered a glass wall for all the females that followed her." Singer Kathy Mattea said she "studied 'Coal Miner's Daughter' like it was a textbook. It's a Rosetta Stone. It goes back to bluegrass and mountain music, and [it's also] the edge of the beginning of modern country."

"I've watched her, studied her," said Reba McEntire. "Loretta Lynn is honesty, bluntness. She'll say anything; there's no filter. She reminds me of Mama a lot: she's strong-willed and a survivor." Rosanne Cash remembered seeing a picture of Loretta: "She had a white Telecaster and she had on her short fringe skirt, and her cowboy boots, you know, singing 'The Pill,' and I thought, 'Oh, man.' She was radical. She was a badass."

come on the market. "All these years I've stayed at home, while you had all your fun," she sang. "And every year that's gone by, another baby's come. There's gonna be some changes made right here on nursery hill; you've set this chicken your last time, 'cause now I've got the pill."

Decca was worried enough about the song's topic, sung by a mother of six, that it held back release of "The Pill" for two years. Lynn recalled the mind-set behind the label's reluctance: "Everybody would look at me like, 'Another dirty song.'

ABOVE *The original handwritten lyrics to "Coal Miner's Daughter," which told Loretta's life story*

OPPOSITE *With her plain-spoken honesty, Loretta Lynn became the first woman to be named the CMA's Entertainer of the Year.*

PRIDE

My dad used to say, now, "Pride. Just think about the name itself." He said, "Whatever you want to do, you want to try to do it good and do it quick."

CHARLEY PRIDE

He's a pioneer. He broke down tons of barriers. The reason he was able to make it in country music was because of his voice. Eventually, it didn't matter what the color of his skin was 'cause his music was way too good.

DARIUS RUCKER

By the mid-1960s, the long struggle by African Americans to end the South's "Jim Crow" laws, which had legalized discrimination against them for nearly a hundred years, was finally producing victories. Schools could no longer be segregated. The hard-won Civil Rights Act of 1964 banned employers and public places from denying them jobs or providing them equal access to everything from drinking fountains to seats in cafeterias or on a bus. And in 1965, after peaceful marchers in Selma, Alabama, were viciously attacked by the police, shocking a nation that watched it all on television, President Lyndon Johnson signed a bill passed by Congress, overriding state laws meant to keep black people from exercising their right to vote.

That fall, in Nashville, a thirty-one-year-old from Sledge, Mississippi, with a deep, resonant voice entered a studio to record some country songs there for the first time. He was a black man. His name was Charley Pride.

He was born on March 18, 1934, the fourth of eleven children in a sharecropper's family that lived in a three-room shotgun shack in the Mississippi Delta. He remembered walking four miles to school each day, while white children passed him in their bus on their way to their whites-only school and encouraged the driver to splash him if he was near a mud puddle: "The kids would say, 'Hey, nigger,' you know, taunting me and that sort of thing." But he had big dreams:

I always wanted to be somewhere and do something different than picking cotton beside my dad. I used to sit on the porch and I'd look up at the clouds. And I said,

"Boy, to float on them clouds." And I'd think of that, you know, when I was little.

I didn't realize what it would be. When I saw Jackie Robinson go to the major leagues, I said, "There's my way out of the cotton field." I believe every kid grows up and has a dream. When I saw Jackie Robinson, that was my dream.

Pride's ability as a pitcher landed him a spot on the Memphis Red Sox in the Negro League when he was still a teenager. After some injuries and a stint in the Army delayed his career, he moved to Helena, Montana, where he played on a minor league team and worked in the smelting plant.

But he had also grown up listening to the *Grand Ole Opry*, admiring Hank Williams, and in Montana he began performing in a local bar. Passing through town, *Opry* stars Red Foley and Red Sovine heard him sing Williams's "Lovesick Blues," and were impressed enough to encourage him to try

---

ABOVE, LEFT *As a youngster in the Mississippi Delta, Charley Pride dreamed of someday doing bigger things than picking cotton as a sharecropper.*

ABOVE *Inspired by Jackie Robinson's breaking of baseball's color barrier, Pride started out as a pitcher for the Memphis Red Sox in the Negro League.*

OPPOSITE *At early concerts, many fans who had heard him on the radio didn't know Pride was a black man until he stepped out onto the stage.*

Clement had Charley Pride record two songs by Mel Tillis and one Clement had written, "Just Between You and Me," and began shopping them around to different labels. Meanwhile, Pride's manager started making introductions to other people in the business—people who could make Pride's life easy, or very difficult. One of the latter was Faron Young, one of the most outspoken stars in town. "People listened to Faron," Emery said. "People respected Faron. People were afraid of Faron."

According to Pride, his manager warned him that Young might "walk up to you and say, 'You're that N-word that's trying to sing music.' And I said, 'Let's go find him. We might as well get it over with right now.'"

They tracked Young down at one of his favorite clubs. Pride walked up and introduced himself, and soon enough they were trading songs: "Now I don't know where the guitar came from. But he would sing one, and I would sing one. He would sing one, and I would sing one. And, finally, he said, 'Well, I'll be. Who would have ever thought I'm sitting here singing with a "jig" and don't mind it.'" According to session musician Lloyd Green, "From that moment on, they were friends. The word spread immediately all over Music Row that Faron was a fan of Charley's and so it was okay to like Charley Pride."

But most of the labels in Nashville weren't interested in signing him. Then, Chet Atkins took the tapes to his bosses at RCA—waiting until they liked what they heard before showing them a photograph of Pride. They decided to release his early singles without making any mention of Pride's race. Many of the radio disc jockeys—and the people listening—

Nashville, if his dream of becoming a big-league baseball player didn't work out. When the Los Angeles Angels and New York Mets turned him down, Pride showed up in Music City, where he caught the attention of Cowboy Jack Clement, the maverick producer and songwriter. Clement had helped Sam Phillips revolutionize music at Sun Records in Memphis in the 1950s, and later helped Johnny Cash make "Ring of Fire" into a huge hit.

"Charley had the good fortune to meet Cowboy Jack Clement," said Ralph Emery. "He always marched to the beat of a different drum, and it was a marriage made in heaven. If any producer should have taken on a black kid, it was Jack. Because Jack liked to be different, and Jack wasn't afraid of anything."

"I thought country music was getting a little stale at that time," Clement recalled. "I thought it needed some . . . a kick in the butt. And a friend of mine was telling me about this 'Negro' that was a great country singer. Well, I heard him sing, and he was great. And I said, 'Let's get him in here. I'd like to record him.'"

ABOVE *Pride and the Nite Hawks, the band he performed with in Helena, Montana. From left, Pride, Monty Cowles, George Owens, and Jimmy Owens.*

RIGHT *Cowboy Jack Clement, the maverick producer in Nashville who produced Pride's first records*

assumed he was just another white, Southern country singer, but with an especially good voice.

One of his early live performances was as the third act in a big country show in Detroit, where Ralph Emery was the emcee. After asking the crowd how many of them were originally from the South,

and most of the hands went up, Emery said the next singer was from Mississippi and encouraged them to "give him a big Detroit welcome: Country Charley Pride." They started clapping enthusiastically, Emery remembered, until Pride walked out on the stage.

It was "like turning down the volume," Pride said. "You could hear a pin drop. I said, 'Ladies and gentlemen, I realize it's kind of unique, me coming out here on a country music show wearing this permanent tan.' The minute I said that, big applause. I guess they said, 'Well, let's sit back and see what he's got to offer.' But once they saw me sing and heard me sing, [it was like] 'I don't care if he's green; I like his singing.'"

TOP LEFT AND RIGHT *Charley and some of his growing legions of fans*

CENTER *For this concert in Minneapolis, Pride was the headliner, over Slim Whitman, Jimmy Dickens, and Grandpa Jones.*

LEFT *Though his label at first avoided mentioning Pride's race, once his music proved popular on country radio, publicists highlighted it.*

who he's singing to. There ain't many 'hair of golds' that's his color.'"

But his talent was so undeniable, Pride kept releasing hits, including six consecutive number ones. His biggest, "Kiss an Angel Good Morning," spent five weeks at the top of the country charts and crossed over to pop markets. He would become the first black member of the *Grand Ole Opry* since DeFord Bailey decades earlier, the first black artist to have a number-one country record—and the first artist of *any* color to win the Country Music Association's Male Vocalist award two years in a row. (At one award ceremony, Loretta Lynn was the presenter, and was told that if Pride was the winner, she should step back when he reached the podium. Instead, she recalled, "I hugged him. You can't let people tell you where to stand and what to say—or I never could.")

Charley Pride would go on to be named the CMA's Entertainer of the Year; have twenty-nine number-one hits and twelve gold albums; be inducted into the Country Music Hall of Fame—and remain a lifelong friend of Faron Young. "We went into the Country Music Hall of Fame together," Pride said. "Faron Young, one of my best, best friends there ever was."

But there were still more barriers to overcome. At a convention in Nashville, a visiting disc jockey told Faron Young that when they learned Charley Pride was black, the station decided to stop playing his records. Young set the man straight, according to Emery: "You son of a bitch, you go back there and tell that son of a bitch that manages your station if he takes Charley Pride off, take all my records off."

When his single "Just Between You and Me" reached number ten on the country charts, Charley Pride's career was launched, though for a while his label was still skittish about which songs he recorded—especially love songs. They turned down his request to sing Curly Putman's "Green, Green Grass of Home." The lyrics talk of Mary, with "hair of gold," Pride said. "That one line, 'Look

ABOVE *Charley Pride and his best friend Faron Young chat with Buck Owens (left).*

RIGHT *Pride became the first African American to have a number-one country record and the first artist of any color to win the CMA's Male Vocalist award two years in a row.*

MAMA TRIED

The human being has a history of being awful cruel to something different. "Okie" was not a good word, you know? They were talked down to and looked down on. It might have been something comparable to the way that they treated the blacks.

MERLE HAGGARD

When Merle Ronald Haggard was born on April 6, 1937, his family had already been living near Bakersfield, California, for three years. But they were still looked down upon as "Okies." Haggard's parents and his two older siblings had migrated from eastern Oklahoma, not far from Muskogee, in 1934, after a fire destroyed their barn, farm equipment, and livestock and ruined them financially. In California, his father found work on the railroad and made the family a new home out of an abandoned boxcar a few hundred yards from the tracks in the town of Oildale.

"There was a lady named Miss Bona who owned a lot with

a boxcar sitting on it," Haggard said. "And she said, 'If you have a mind to be a hard enough worker, you could probably make this into a pretty nice home.' She said, 'But I never heard of an Okie that would work.' And my dad took a little offense to that, and he said, 'Well, ma'am, I never heard of one that *wouldn't* work.'"

Haggard was only nine years old when his father died from a stroke. "Something," he said later, "went out of the world that I was never able to replace." To support the family, his mother got a job as a bookkeeper, and to fill the gap in her young boy's life, she encouraged Merle's budding interest in music, hoping it would keep him out of trouble. It didn't.

"He began to rebel more and more," his older sister remembered, "against all forms of authority." He ran away for a while at the age of ten by hopping a freight train, then ran away again at fourteen, hitchhiking all the way to Texas and back. His freshman year in high school, he showed up for classes a total of ten days.

TOP, LEFT *James Haggard and his infant son Merle, 1937*

TOP, RIGHT *When Haggard's father died, "something went out of the world that I was never able to replace," he said.*

Merle Haggard became Prisoner Number A-45200, confined with several thousand of California's most hardened criminals, some of them on death row. He was twenty years old—and intent as ever on breaking out.

An older inmate everyone called Rabbit invited Haggard to join in an escape he was plotting (they would hide inside a desk he was building in the prison's furniture factory), but at the last minute advised the young man not to take part in the dangerous plan. "You can sing and write songs," he told Haggard. "You can be somebody someday."

Haggard took the advice. "It was a big decision to not go," he remembered, "but it was kind of neat to know that I could get out of there if I wanted to." Rabbit's escape was successful, but only for a time. During his recapture, he killed a policeman, was brought back to San Quentin—and later executed.

Haggard would spend more than two and a half years in San Quentin, at first getting into enough trouble to be kept

But he steeped himself in country music: listening endlessly to the Jimmie Rodgers records his mother bought him; sneaking off to see Bob Wills perform at Bakersfield's Beardsley Ballroom; taking in local concerts by the Maddox Brothers and Rose and his personal hero, Lefty Frizzell, who let him come onstage at age sixteen and do an uncanny imitation of the honky tonk star. "Lefty," he said, "gave me the courage to dream."

Haggard spent most of his teenage years running from the law. He was constantly arrested for truancy (then for stealing cars for joy rides) and just as constantly escaping from juvenile detention centers. Married at age seventeen, he started selling stolen scrap iron, got caught and jailed—only to escape again. "Somebody was always after me, it seemed like," he said. "I escaped seventeen times from different places in California. For several years, I was Bonnie and Clyde all rolled into one, just running from the law and then doing time when they'd catch me."

In 1957, the police brought him in for a minor burglary. This time, based on his long rap sheet of escapes, more than the severity of any of his crimes, he was sentenced to fifteen years in San Quentin, a maximum-security prison; no one had escaped from it in eight years.

ABOVE *A young Merle Haggard, outside the family home—a converted boxcar—near Bakersfield. He started running away from home and from school, getting arrested for truancy and then escaping from the detention centers.*

RIGHT *Music was Haggard's other escape. When his idol Lefty Frizzell let him sing at a concert, Merle said, he "gave me the courage to dream."*

the textile mill, and played in the prison band. One New Year's Day, he attended Johnny Cash's concert for the inmates and became inspired that someday he, too, might do the same. "I would have been a career criminal . . . and died young," he remembered, "if music hadn't saved me."

His wife had stopped visiting, even writing. But his mother never gave up on him, he said:

We've all got a Mama, and, you know, the majority of them tried. My mother was a Christian lady, raised me in a church. And she lived what she believed in. But she was never too good to come and see me in San Quentin; rode a Greyhound bus up there, every time she could afford to come.

I was the only one, am the only one, in our whole family to have ever been to jail. So she had a lot of guff from the rest of the family, I'm sure. And it was good when I started getting popular, because she kind of got back at them.

in solitary confinement for a week and being turned down for parole, before deciding that his only way out was to become a model prisoner. "Something happened to me there," he said. "I came to the fork in the road and took it, you might say. And I kind of started back in the other direction, trying to make something out of myself rather than to dig myself in a deeper hole."

He volunteered for the toughest job, in

TOP *During his two and a half years in prison, Haggard's wife stopped visiting, but his mother would regularly take a Greyhound bus to San Quentin to see her son.*

ABOVE, LEFT *At first, Haggard was a problem inmate, as this prison sheet notes; he spent time in solitary confinement and was turned down for parole until he decided to work at being a model prisoner.*

ABOVE, RIGHT *Released from prison, Merle joined Buck Owens and the Buckaroos. He later married Bonnie Owens, Buck's ex-wife, and recorded duets with her.*

Finally paroled, he returned to Bakersfield and took a day job digging ditches. Seven nights a week, he played music in the city's honky tonks: the High Pockets, Rainbow Gardens, the Lucky Spot. He toured briefly with Buck Owens, playing bass with the Buckaroos. In 1965, he married the singer Bonnie Owens, Buck's former wife, and recorded duets with her.

Then Haggard's solo career started picking up steam on its own. Some of the songs he wrote—"Swinging Doors" and "The Bottle Let Me Down"— were classic honky tonk tunes with a Bakersfield sound. But increasingly he turned to themes reflecting his own experiences: "Hungry Eyes," about growing up poor; "Sing Me Back Home," drawn from his time in prison; and "Mama Tried," about his reckless younger years.

People started calling him "the Poet of the Common Man." Haggard's song "Hungry Eyes" epitomizes his point of view, according to Dwight Yoakam: "It starts with him singing, 'A canvas-covered cabin in a crowded labor camp, stand out in this old memory I revive. 'Cause my daddy raised a family there with two hard-working hands and tried to feed my mama's hungry eyes.' In the second verse of that song, he sings, 'Another class of people kept us somewhere far below. One more reason for my mama's hungry eyes.' He sang that for Buck and Buck's family, the Maddox Brothers, and all those unnamed 'Okies' and 'Arkies' and Texans. Merle Haggard is one of the greatest poets ever in American music, independent of genre."

"He's Woody Guthrie's seed," added Marty Stuart. "He's the guy that hauls the timber of Jimmie Rodgers's ghost on a blue train headed to anywhere he wants to take it. He looks to the left and the right of the human condition and reports the struggles, the affairs, the injustices."

"Poetry for the common man," said Dierks Bentley. "Words and songs and stories that could take these complex subjects of life and love and whittle them down to a three- or four-minute song that really helps someone have a better understanding of the life they're living."

During a three-year stretch in the late 1960s, Haggard put out a number-one hit every four months. (He even had a role in a B movie, *Killers Three*, playing a sheriff killed by an outlaw, who was played by his good friend and future television music host Dick Clark.) "The first thing we noticed about him, well, he was Hollywood handsome," said Ralph Emery. "I had girls stop me on the street asking me how to meet Merle Haggard. Stewardesses on airplanes said, 'You know Merle Haggard?' He was handsome. He could sing. And he could write. He was the total package."

BELOW *Haggard recording at Capitol Studios in Hollywood*

ily together. He sings, 'Today was Angie's birthday. It must have slipped your mind. I tried twice to call you, with no answer either time. But the postman brought a package, I mailed some days ago. I signed it 'Love from Mama,' so Angie wouldn't know.' You don't have to say anything more about Merle Haggard."

Future country star Ronnie Milsap remembered being a Motown fan in the 1960s and uninterested in country music, until he heard Haggard on the radio. "He was playing 'The Bottle Let Me Down,' or 'Swinging Doors'—and all those great songs that he's written. Single-handedly, he saved country music for me, for sure."

"Well, what is country music?" added Emmylou Harris. "I would say, just get any Merle Haggard record, it doesn't matter which one, and just drop the needle on any track. And this will give you an idea, and you can take it from there."

Loretta Lynn said her all-time favorite song is "Today I Started Loving You Again," which Haggard wrote for his wife at the time, Bonnie Owens: "And 'crying time again has just begun, because today I started loving you again.' That covers my whole life, right there, in that one little song."

"Bonnie and I had been on tour for ninety-three straight days, without a break," Haggard remembered. "We were in the L.A. International Airport, and I told her, 'Today I started loving you again. I had the time to tell you about it.' And that's where it came from. It's a circle—a circle of words that surround a subject, best way to describe it. It's been recorded almost five hundred times by some of the greater artists in the business. So I'm awfully proud of that copyright."

"My favorite song of Merle's is 'Holding Things Together,'" said Dwight Yoakam. "It's chronicling a family who's broken apart. And in this case, it's not the father who's left, it's the mother who left, and the father's left there to hold the fam-

"I felt like I was on a roll," Haggard recalled. But "I couldn't help but wonder what would happen to my little growing public if they found out I was a San Quentin graduate. Mama even suggested I change my name." He decided to stick with Haggard. "It was my daddy's," he said, "and it's mine."

TOP *At the end of a long concert tour with his wife Bonnie, Haggard wrote "Today I Started Loving You Again," which Loretta Lynn cited as her favorite country song of all time. "That covers my whole life, right there," she said, "in that one little song."*

ABOVE *The cover of Haggard's album* Mama Tried. *People started calling him "the Poet of the Common Man."*

DUMB BLONDE

Those days, men were the headliners. Men were selling the records. And women were the opening acts. Women were kind of like "the girl singer" in the band.

REBA MCENTIRE

The "token" girl singer, that was a truth. But some women changed some things. And that's good.

BARBARA MANDRELL

As Loretta Lynn expanded the boundaries of what topics women songwriters and singers could confront in their music, other female artists began making strides of their own.

Connie Smith had grown up in Ohio, painfully shy but possessing an extraordinarily powerful voice. Bill Anderson heard it for the first time in 1963 at the Frontier Ranch music park outside Columbus, when she took part in a talent contest that he was asked to judge:

I remember I had a legal pad and a pen they gave me to sit down and make notes. I saw two or three people come out onstage and they were good; there weren't any bad performers on the stage.

ABOVE AND RIGHT *Connie Smith's powerful voice impressed Bill Anderson so much, he wrote a song for her to record in Nashville. When she arrived, Loretta Lynn befriended her, just as Patsy Cline had once done for Loretta.*

But, all of a sudden, I looked up and here came this little bitty girl with a guitar as big, or bigger than she was; beautiful, long blond hair and a little white cowgirl dress with a musical treble clef kind of embroidered onto the skirt. And I thought, "That's a beautiful little girl."

And she started singing. I actually thought she was pantomiming a record. I had never heard a voice that big come out of somebody that small. I thought, "Goodness, gracious." The talent contest was over when she opened her mouth.

Anderson persuaded Smith to come to Nashville in 1964, where she recorded a song he had written, "Once a Day," and appeared on Ernest Tubb's *Midnite Jamboree* radio broadcast. Loretta Lynn was there and asked to meet her, Smith recalled: "And she told me, she said, 'Now Patsy did this for me and I'm going to do it for you.' And she told me what to expect out of Nashville, who to watch out for and

who to watch for, and all that. We became friends, the very first day we met."

Smith's single "Once a Day" became the first debut single by a female country artist ever to reach number one. Her debut album did the same. She was soon touring, not as a "girl singer" in a band, but as a headliner. One show was at the Choctaw Indian Fair in Philadelphia, Mississippi, where Hilda Stuart brought her eleven-year-old son, Marty, along to see her favorite female singer. "When she stepped out onstage," Stuart remembered, "she was breathtakingly beautiful, wearing a blue sparkle dress. And I got my picture made with her that night, me and my sister did. I got her autograph—and she didn't really notice me. So, on the way out of the grandstand, I saw her go sit down in a station wagon, and I said, 'Mama, can I borrow your camera?' And Mama loaned me her camera, so I went over and said, 'Miss Smith, can I take your picture?' And I stuck it right up in her face and took her picture. She still didn't notice me. But, on the way home that night, I declared that I was going to marry Connie Smith one day."

"In the 1960s is when there were a few of us who were coming into it totally on our own," said Jeannie Seely. "I think Connie Smith is one who came in on her own. I certainly was one who came in trying to fight my own battles. We were just starting to stand up a little bit for ourselves."

Growing up in Titusville, Pennsylvania, Seely had considered getting Jean Shepard's autograph at the local country music park as one of the biggest thrills of her childhood. After spending four years in California trying to make it as a songwriter, she moved to Nashville in 1965 at the suggestion of Hank Cochran, one of Music City's top songsmiths. Her first job was as a "girl Friday" for a publishing company—typing up song contracts, setting up demo sessions, and sending the tapes to artists and labels for consideration.

But Seely also continued writing songs of her own that artists like Connie Smith, Dottie West, Faron Young, and Ray Price recorded. She sang, too—in a soulful voice that landed her a contract with Monument Records. In 1966, she came out with a song Cochran wrote for her, "Don't Touch Me," that rose to number two on the charts and won Seely a Grammy Award.

Invited to appear on the *Grand Ole Opry*, she shocked the management when she walked onstage wearing a miniskirt. "I really didn't give that much thought about it," she said. "I wanted to wear whatever was in style at the time. Mov-

---

ABOVE *When Connie Smith performed at the Choctaw Indian Fair in Philadelphia, Mississippi, Marty Stuart's mother took him to see her. He got his picture taken with her and then snapped another photo himself—and vowed that he would marry her someday.*

RIGHT *When Jeannie Seely made her first appearance at the* Opry, *wearing this dress, the management told her it was too short.*

girl, who's got on a pretty little outfit. Come on and put your hands together and make her feel welcome.' The connotation being, 'She isn't welcome, just make her feel that way.' And yet night after night, we would see the men being introduced, talking about their fine bands or the songs they had written; the awards they had won; the records they had in the charts. We weren't introduced that way."

Nowhere was that practice more evident than on *The Porter Wagoner Show*, the most popular of the many syndicated country music television shows coming out of Nashville in the 1960s, carried by nearly a hundred stations and watched by more than three million fans. For seven years, viewers could count on seeing one of the show's favorite stars, Norma Jean Beasler, introduced by Wagoner every week simply as "Pretty Miss Norma Jean."

In 1967, Beasler left the show, and for her replacement, Wagoner turned to a younger woman from East Tennessee who had been knocking around Nashville for three years, trying to make it as a songwriter and performer. Dolly Rebecca Parton was twenty-one years old, but she had been preparing all her life for her big chance.

ing from Southern California, where everyone was wearing miniskirts, it just didn't enter my mind. It wasn't even a real mini-mini. It was kind of a 'sort-of' mini, but it was shorter than what they were used to." The show's manager called her into his office to say she couldn't wear such a short skirt again onstage, but when she asked to see the rule prohibiting it, he couldn't show her one. "And finally, I said, 'Okay, this is what America is wearing, and I'll make you a deal. I won't wear a miniskirt in the back door if you don't let anybody wear one in the front door,'" she recalled. The matter was settled: she wore what she wanted.

Seely became known for her strong opinions. She openly criticized the condescending way male country announcers introduced women artists: "They'd say, 'Here's a cute little

ABOVE *Jeannie Seely's first single for Monument Records, "Don't Touch Me," which won her a Grammy, was written by Hank Cochran (in a studio with Seely), who later became her husband. Other artists had hits with songs Seely had written.*

RIGHT *Young Dolly Parton, center, and her family in the foothills of the Great Smoky Mountains*

The fourth of twelve children, she was born on January 19, 1946, in the foothills of the Great Smoky Mountains, in a one-room cabin without electricity, running water, or indoor plumbing. The doctor who delivered her was paid with a sack of cornmeal for his services.

"My mother's people were very musical," Parton said. "They all played musical instruments—the guitar and banjo, autoharp, dulcimer—and we were the family that always would sing at funerals, or weddings, and all the shindigs. There was a lot of gospel music. There was a lot of bluegrass music, and a lot of just pure old country music."

From the time she was a little girl, Parton was vivacious, precocious, and ambitious. She started writing songs at age five—her first one, "Little Tiny Tasseltop," was inspired by the doll her father had made for her out of a corncob. Grade school teachers recognized her remarkable ability at memorizing almost anything.

By the time she was ten, she was making $20 a week appearing on Cas Walker's Knoxville television show, though none of her family could watch it since they didn't have a TV set at home (her earnings on the show eventually paid for a family television). As a teenager, she recorded a few songs in the mold of rockabilly star Brenda Lee, and set her sights on Nashville.

In 1964, the day after becoming the first in her family to graduate from high school, Parton packed a cardboard suitcase, boarded a bus, and headed for Music City. There, she worked part-time as a waitress and receptionist, and auditioned for Ralph Emery's early-morning local television show. "I had a dream," she said, "and I had a talent, I thought, and I really believed it was going to happen."

TOP, LEFT *At age ten, Dolly was appearing on a Knoxville television show; the money she made allowed her family to buy a TV so they could watch her.*

TOP, RIGHT *Parton, during the time she was appearing on Ralph Emery's early-morning television show in Nashville*

LEFT *Dolly Parton performs on* The Porter Wagoner Show, *a nationally syndicated program.*

which she sang on Wagoner's television show, after he introduced her as "Pretty Miss Dolly Parton."

Parton's career was picking up speed. Wagoner took her with him on tour more than two hundred nights a year; recorded a series of duets with her; and helped guide her to a bigger label, RCA. But Wagoner could also be controlling and domineering, insisting on overseeing every aspect of her career.

Parton bristled at the double standard, as her self-written hit, "Just Because I'm a Woman," made perfectly clear. "Porter thought he was just finding another girl to fit that spot," she said. "I went in with a whole barrel of stuff, you know, I was a whole ball of wax. And Porter wasn't used to that. So I had a mind of my own, too. And I wasn't just going to be told what to do, or just be that and nothing else."

Emery remembered her first appearance: "She sang a George Jones song called 'You've Got to Be My Baby' and just killed us. I mean, from day one, she wasn't nervous. It was like she'd been doing it a hundred years." He asked her to come back once a week, and when she admitted she didn't have a car, he offered to drive her. "One morning, she had her laundry with her," he recalled, "and she said, 'When we get back, would you drop me off at the Wishy-Washy up the street? I need to do my laundry.' So, when it was over, I took her by the Wishy-Washy, said good-bye to her, and she went in there to do her laundry and met Carl Dean, that she's still with today. She met her husband in the Wishy-Washy."

Meanwhile, she kept trying to interest publishing companies in her songs and record labels in her singing. Fred Foster at Monument Records finally took her on, he said, after Chet Atkins turned her down, saying she sounded like a screech owl. By 1967, other artists were having success with some of the songs Parton had written; but her own first single to attract any attention was not one of her own compositions. It was written by Curly Putman; its title was "Dumb Blonde,"

• • •

In 1967, the same year Dolly Parton debuted on *The Porter Wagoner Show*, a song about a mysterious suicide on the Tallahatchie Bridge in the Mississippi Delta swept the airwaves, doing even better on the pop and rhythm and blues charts than on country charts.

"Ode to Billie Joe" was written and performed by Bobbie Gentry, who had been born in Chickasaw County, Mississippi, before going on to study philosophy at UCLA and music at the Los Angeles Conservatory. She was working in Las Vegas—as a secretary and nighttime showgirl—when she recorded her song. It won three Grammy Awards and sold three million copies. Rosanne Cash considers it a classic:

That song, the plaintive quality of her voice, it's like a Walker Evans photograph, it's so stark. You see every scene: The mother saying, "You wipe your feet when you come in the door." The father saying, "Oh, that boy never had any sense, pass the black-eyed peas." The brother saying, "Didn't I just see him up at the saw

ABOVE *Parton and Porter Wagoner in the studio. "I wasn't just going to be told what to do," she said.*

mill?" And, "We went to the picture show with him." And then the mama saying, "Why aren't you eating? What's wrong?"

And then the last verse, where she says, "I spend a lot of time picking flowers up on the ridge and throwing them into the water." And you think, "That was her up there with him. They were throwing something off the bridge. What did they throw off the bridge?" So that scene, laid out like a movie, [has] cinematic quality, although you feel it's in black and white, somehow. And the family and the food, and the mystery at the heart of it. What did they throw off the bridge? And forty years later, forty years after the song was a hit, people are still saying, "I wonder what they threw off the bridge."

I performed it at this big benefit at Carnegie Hall, and President Clinton was in the audience. I sang the song and at intermission, the Secret Service comes back and says, "President Clinton wants to speak to you." Clinton waxed poetic on "Ode to Billie Joe" for fifteen minutes. He had all of these theories about the shame of the South and what the song really meant, and teenage pregnancy, and what that meant in the South in the 1960s. The song is so powerful that the leader of the free world had formulated fifteen minutes' worth of thought about this song.

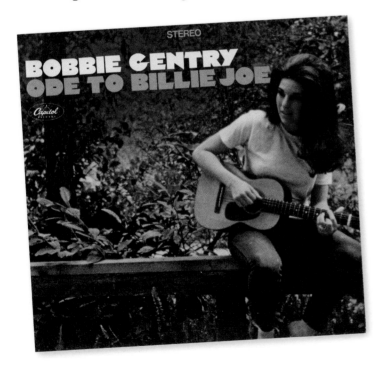

The next year, a singer named Jeannie C. Riley had even more phenomenal success with a song that took direct aim at small-town hypocrisy and a woman's image. "Harper Valley PTA" told the story of a spirited young widow confronting

the city's establishment after receiving a note that accused her of setting a bad example for her daughter.

Songwriter Tom T. Hall, who had arrived in Nashville in 1964, originally had ambitions, he said, to "write the great American novel. I read Mark Twain, Hemingway, but I loved Sinclair Lewis. I was fascinated by *Main Street*, and I lived in one of those towns, and I was always fascinated by the social structure, you know, the hypocrisy."

"Harper Valley PTA" was based on something he remembered from his hometown of Olive Hill, Kentucky: "I recalled an incident where this lady had gotten a note from the PTA and she wasn't buying into the aristocracy of this community. And when she got this note that said she shouldn't be bringing up her daughter this way, or wearing makeup and everything, and having little parties on Saturday night at her house, she just marched into the meeting and told them off."

Riley, who had grown up in a deeply religious family in a tiny town in Texas, had been in Nashville for two years—exposed to executives who tried to seduce her and deejays who groped her at conventions, as she struggled to make her way in the music business.

ABOVE *Tom T. Hall wrote "Harper Valley PTA" based on an incident he remembered from his hometown in Kentucky, when a mother stood up against the local PTA after it criticized the way she was raising her daughter. Jeannie C. Riley's recording sold seven million copies.*

LEFT *Bobbie Gentry's song "Ode to Billie Joe," about a mysterious suicide on a bridge in the Mississippi Delta, won three Grammys.*

She recorded the song after getting off work as a secretary. "I was mad at the whole world," she remembered. "I stood close to the mike and let it all pour out, sassing everything I hated."

In its blunt critique of shallow mainstream mores, the song seemed to strike a chord with the nation's mood, rising to number one on both the country and pop charts, and selling seven million copies. When it won Single of the Year at the 1968 CMA awards, held at Ryman Auditorium, Riley showed up planning to wear a floor-length dress to the ceremonies. But her record producer had ordered someone to cut off the bottom of the dress, so she appeared instead in a makeshift miniskirt and go-go boots.

ABOVE *When Riley's performance won CMA's Single of the Year, she planned on wearing a floor-length gown. Before she got to the ceremony, label executives had ordered it cut into a miniskirt.*

IF THEY FREED ME FROM THIS PRISON

My dad had a deep connection to that sorrowful, mournful Celtic music, the ballads about death and murder and war, all of those images and stories that were full of so much sadness because he had that mournful quality at the center of his music.

The most compelling weaving together for me, personally, is when Appalachia and Delta blues somehow marry, which actually happened in my family—my dad marrying June, in case you missed the point.

ROSANNE CASH

By 1968, June Carter was not yet forty years old, but, as a member of "the First Family of Country Music," she had already spent three decades in the business. As a young girl in the 1930s, she had performed with her mother, Maybelle, and aunt and uncle, Sara and A.P.—the original Carter family—on radio broadcasts that spread their music from coast to coast. In the 1940s, June and her sisters, Helen and Anita, along with Maybelle, had continued the family tradition, ultimately bringing it to the stage of the *Grand Ole Opry*. In the 1950s, they had appeared with nearly every major country star, including Hank Williams and the young Elvis Presley. Now, they toured regularly with Johnny Cash.

June was deeply in love with Cash, but his addiction to amphetamines was threatening his career. He hadn't recorded a number-one record in four years, and he failed to show up for half of his concerts on the road. She feared worse was in store.

"Even as children, we knew that they had something special," her daughter Carlene Carter said. "Mom was saying, 'If he didn't have me out here, he'd be dead.' She really felt like that if she wasn't out on the road with him, kind of watching what was going on, to a certain degree, that he would get too messed up, and might be gone like Hank. That's what Mama would say, 'I don't want to lose him like I lost Hank.'"

No one seemed to be able to get Cash to quit. Arrested for public drunkenness in Georgia, he spent a night in jail, but was released the next day because the judge's wife was a big fan. "You want to kill yourself," the judge told him, "I'm going to give you your God-given right to go ahead and do that; so, take your pills and go."

Maybelle Carter tried kindness, always welcoming Cash to her home late at night when he needed someone to talk to, just as she had done with Hank Williams. "Grandma would get that little cup of coffee, and she'd sit there and she'd play cards and smoke cigarettes and drink coffee and

talk and laugh and giggle and tell jokes all night long," Carlene said. "Well, that was fine with John. And so, he always had a soft place to land. Mom would get a call, and Mom would say, 'I've got to go over to Grandma's house. John's there and he's in bad shape. And I need to go.'"

Finally, June gave him an ultimatum: if he wanted her to marry him, he had to get professional help to fight his drug habit. "This was the condition," according to

TOP *Johnny Cash at the microphone; June, Anita, a barely visible Maybelle, and Helen Carter provide the background harmonies. The Carter women feared that Cash was headed toward self-destruction, just like their late friend Hank Williams.*

BELOW, LEFT *Cash presents Maybelle with the* Music City News *award for Mother of the Year, 1966. She had been a source of comfort to Hank Williams in some of his darkest hours in the early 1950s; now she was doing the same for Cash.*

BELOW, CENTER *June Carter with her daughters, Carlene (left) and Rosie*

BELOW, RIGHT *Johnny Cash and his daughters, visiting him in Tennessee. From left, Rosanne, Tara, Cindy, and Kathy.*

Carlene. "'If we're getting married, if we're going to ever be together, and you're going to be around my daughters and we're all going to be a family with your daughters, all of us together, you have got to get cleaned up.'"

A doctor was brought in, and for weeks he and June and her parents kept constant watch over Cash at his house near Nashville—taking away any pills he had managed to hide and blocking anyone else from showing up with fresh supplies.

It worked well enough that in early 1968, Cash was ready to attempt making a new album. Cash's idea was to record a live performance at a prison, something he had wanted to do ever since his first prison concert, when he realized how inmates responded to his music. But Columbia Records had continually turned him down. With a new producer, Bob Johnston, in Nashville, Cash tried again.

They settled on the place that had inspired one of his biggest hits—and now the place he hoped would revive his career: Folsom Prison in California. "Redemption themes played out in my dad's life and his career, over and over and over," said Rosanne Cash. "Every day of his life, there was this struggle and a search for redemption. The same guy who sang, 'I shot a man in Reno just to watch him die,' sang, 'Were

you there when they crucified my Lord' in the same show."

On Saturday, January 13, 1968, Cash arrived at Folsom. With him were the Tennessee Three, Carl Perkins, the Statler Brothers, and June Carter. Inside, three thousand inmates gathered in the huge prison cafeteria, seated at tables bolted to the floor, while guards with shotguns watched from a safe perch above it all.

Carl Perkins warmed them up with his early rockabilly hit "Blue Suede Shoes"; then the Statler Brothers performed "Flowers on the Wall," while Cash waited just offstage for his turn. "I knew this was it," he later remembered, "my chance to make up for all the times I had messed up."

TOP *June rebuffed Johnny's repeated requests that they get married— unless he got professional help for his drug addiction.*

OPPOSITE, CLOCKWISE FROM TOP LEFT *At Folsom Prison, Cash sang the prisoners songs about bad luck and bad choices, about rebellion and the hope for redemption; armed guards watched over the concert; as a final song, Cash chose "Greystone Chapel," written by inmate Glen Sherley, who was sitting in the front row; Cash's album from Folsom Prison won praise from every corner of the nation's cultural divide and redeemed his career.*

When his time came, at Bob Johnston's suggestion, Cash tried a new way of opening his act. Instead of having Don Reid doing the usual introduction, he simply introduced himself. "Hello," he said, "I'm Johnny Cash," and launched into "Folsom Prison Blues."

The convicts loved it. "Their response," Marshall Grant said, "inspired us to perform every song better than we had ever done it before." "My father had never been convicted of a felony, but you couldn't hardly tell a convict that," John

Carter Cash said. "They took him in as one of their own because he accepted them; he appreciated them. He had that magic onstage that connected with the people in the audience."

During his two concerts that day, Cash seemed to be singing directly to each prisoner, choosing songs that touched on loneliness and confinement, bad luck and bad choices, as well as irrepressible rebellion—sometimes mixing in a little profane banter with the audience and taunts at the warden. When June Carter joined him onstage, the men went wild.

But the biggest response came at the end, when Cash sang "Greystone Chapel," which had been written by one of the Folsom inmates, Glen Sherley, who was sitting in the front row. Cash and his musicians had only learned the song a day earlier, but he had insisted on using it as the show's finale because it dealt with the possibility of redemption for even the most hardened sinner.

That spring, Columbia released the Folsom Prison album to rave reviews from all corners of the nation's deepening cultural divide. Commentators from every style of music saw in Cash something they all could agree on. "Talk about magical mystery tours," said *The Village Voice.* "Cash's voice is as thick and gritty as ever, but filled with the kind of emotionalism you seldom find in rock." *The New York Times* called his performance "soul music of a rare kind—country soul from the concerned and sensitive white South that Northerners tend to forget." Jazz critic Nat Hentoff, writing in *Cosmopolitan* magazine, proclaimed, "There's no hemming Johnny Cash into any one category."

In *Rolling Stone,* the Bible of the emerging counterculture, Jann Wenner pointed out Cash's friendship with Bob Dylan, calling them both "master singers, master story-tellers, and master bluesmen." After noting Cash's early connection with Elvis Presley to young readers who might be unaware of it, Wenner told them, "Johnny Cash is meaningful in a rock-and-roll context."

In its promotion of Cash as an anti-establishment rebel, Columbia Records was happy to leave the impression that he was a former inmate himself, and that the scar on the right side of his face—which was the result of a botched dental procedure—might have come from a knife fight.

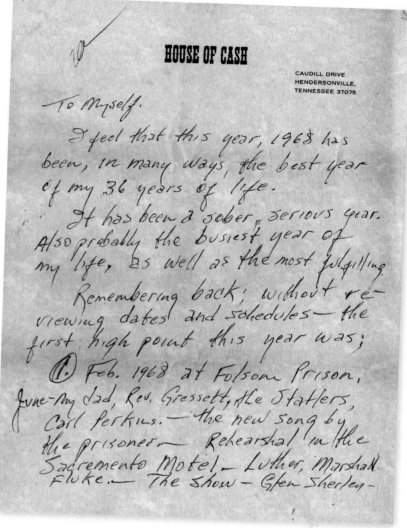

OPPOSITE *A month after the Folsom Prison concert, Johnny proposed to June again. This time, she accepted.*

ABOVE *In a letter to himself, Cash called 1968 "the best year of my 36 years of life."*

Twelve years earlier, country fans had pushed Cash's initial recording of "Folsom Prison Blues" to the top five; now, the live version spent four weeks at number one. The album's sales would soon reach 500,000, achieving gold status. It would remain on the pop charts for more than two years and sell more than three million copies in the United States alone.

Johnny Cash had become a superstar.

One month after the Folsom Prison concert, in February 1968, he proposed to June Carter during a concert in Canada. This time, she accepted. The day before they got married, they were awarded a Grammy for their song "Jackson," a spirited back-and-forth duet about a couple who get "married in a fever, hotter than a pepper sprout." It would become their signature song.

Cash would later write out a six-page note to himself. The year 1968, it began, was "the best year of my 36 years of life." But 1968—one of the most divisive and turbulent years in American history—had only just begun.

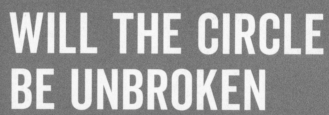

WILL THE CIRCLE BE UNBROKEN

"Will the Circle Be Unbroken" is a song that really encompasses what country music is about, because of how timeless it is. It changes, but in a way, it doesn't change at all. And it is a song about sadness, hope, redemption, love.

It's a song that starts off with someone who is dead and being buried and carried away—how sad this moment is. But there's a better home awaiting, you know, "in the sky, Lord, in the sky." And it's about how we're all going to be together.

TRISHA YEARWOOD

With Mother Maybelle Carter at the center, the Nitty Gritty Dirt Band and other country stars record Will the Circle Be Unbroken.

BY 1968, with the war in Vietnam intensifying, America was more divided than it had ever been since the Civil War. The wounds that the nation seemed to be suffering—and inflicting on itself— sometimes appeared too deep to heal. Americans were being forced to take sides on everything: from the rights of women and minorities to the justification for a war in Asia; from the kind of clothes people wore or the length of their hair to the kind of music they listened to. The gulf between one generation and the next seemed too wide to be bridged. More and more people, from all walks of life, felt that their voices were not being heard.

Country music was not immune to the divisions.

A young poet and troubadour would reject the path his parents had chosen for him, and in Nashville find salvation in his art, bringing to country music an honesty and lyricism rarely heard before; while another gifted songwriter from Texas would reluctantly decide that his music simply didn't fit in Music City.

A restless rebel who had been expelled from the Mother Church of Country Music would triumphantly return to its stage—then welcome others from *every* style of music to join him.

Two remarkable singers, pursued and beset by their own inner demons, would turn their troubles into songs—and find for a time some peace with each other.

And just when one of the most traditional forms of country music seemed to have been left behind by the rush of change, it would resurface and find a way to bring the generations together, answering in its own way the question posed in the old Carter Family song, "Will the Circle Be Unbroken?"

• • •

ABOVE *While his comrades listen, a soldier with "Oklahoma Kid" on his helmet plays a song from home.*

OPPOSITE, TOP *When string band music had disappeared from country radio, the New Lost City Ramblers brought Mother Maybelle Carter back on the road and introduced her to a new generation of listeners.*

OPPOSITE, BOTTOM *A small crowd in Ashland, Kentucky, turns out for Bill Monroe and the Blue Grass Boys playing on a stage set up on the top of a concession stand.*

By the late 1960s, acoustic bluegrass and string band music had all but disappeared from country music radio stations, where the electrified Bakersfield Sound and smoother Nashville Sound still held sway. "I don't know who the alien brainchild was that come up with the idea that, 'Hey, we need to separate bluegrass and country on radio,'" said Ricky Skaggs, "but there was definitely a time that bluegrass got marginalized."

Eddie Stubbs, a WSM announcer and expert on country music history, explained the phenomenon that occurred in stations around the nation: "The music was changing in a big-time way. And if you had an acoustic band like the Stanley Brothers, being played back to back with a record by Skeeter Davis, say 'The End of the World,' with the voices and the strings, it was a head-on collision. And a program director would come in and say, 'What in the world was that?' 'Well, that was the latest bluegrass record.' 'Well, no more bluegrass. We don't want any of that.'"

A number of groups lost their contracts with major labels, and found themselves performing at smaller and smaller venues. There was a total of eleven thousand bluegrass fans in the entire nation, Sonny Osborne joked to an interviewer; he knew, he said, because he and the Osborne Brothers had been making bluegrass records for years, and each one sold only eleven thousand copies.

APRIL 2 - 21
ASH GROVE
8162 MELROSE AVE. OL 3-2070

MAYBELLE CARTER
&
THE NEW LOST CITY RAMBLERS

"I think, to many music executives, bluegrass was just too old-fashioned," said music historian Bill C. Malone. "They were singing about the old cabin home and about the old ways of life, and about the mountains. I think it just created an image that mainstream country wasn't too comfortable with. And so bluegrass had to begin looking for its own way of survival."

But old-time music began to find new fans among one of the nation's youngest audiences—middle-class college students caught up in the folk revival, who disdained the more commercial versions of country music and were often unfamiliar with its deep roots, until groups like the New Lost City Ramblers exposed those roots to them. "They gave it the term 'folk,' but they were actually embracing hillbilly music and race music, and gospel music, and Cajun music," Malone said. "It was exciting. It was so old that it was new. And once that happened, then the next step is for people to go back and start finding records by the people from whom the New Lost City Ramblers had borrowed. 'Let's go see if we can find a Carter Family record. Let's see if we can find some Uncle Dave Macon records,' and so on."

Maybelle Carter, of the original Carter Family, had been moonlighting as a practical nurse in a Nashville hospital, when the New Lost City Ramblers took her with them to play in some big-city folk music clubs; then to the Newport Folk Festival, where she held workshops on her guitar and autoharp techniques.

Soon, festivals dedicated exclusively to bluegrass and old-time music began sprouting up in places as diverse as tiny Luray, Virginia, and metropolitan Chicago. Combined with concerts on college campuses, they became the principal lifeline to keep many string bands afloat. "Bluegrass began to create its own world," Malone said. "Bluegrass continued to be, in my opinion, the most authentic form of country music, the most reflective of its roots, but, nevertheless, it still had to come up with something different in order to survive."

The exception was Lester Flatt and Earl Scruggs, who had eclipsed every other bluegrass act in the nation, including Bill Monroe's. Under the energetic and inventive management of Earl's wife, Louise, they had a syndicated television show, played at Carnegie Hall, and recorded a live album at Vanderbilt University.

When the producers of a new television show, *The Beverly Hillbillies*, approached them about helping with the theme

---

LEFT *Bluegrass festivals and college audiences, like these students at Berkeley in California, seen here with the New Lost City Ramblers, kept traditional music alive.*

ABOVE *Lester Flatt and Earl Scruggs and the Foggy Mountain Boys, seen here at Carnegie Hall, became the most popular string band in the nation.*

year, "Well, bluegrass will be big this year!" And not much would happen. "Oh, 'Counting Flowers on the Wall' has got a banjo in it. It's a hit. Bluegrass is going to be big this year." Nothing for another year. "Oh, *Bonnie and Clyde*, 'Foggy Mountain Breakdown' is on pop radio. It's going to be big this year." And nothing for a couple of years. "Dueling Banjos" comes out: "Bluegrass will be big this year."

And the thing about bluegrass is it's always been big. But it's a relation of big. If you look at all these careers, they all kind of went up very slowly. They didn't have pop success and then disappear. But it's just been kind of moving along and they're doing fine, thank you. And bluegrass has always been big to the people that play it.

song, Flatt and Scruggs were hesitant. "We'd worked so hard to get away from . . . the hillbilly image," Earl said. But Louise screened an early episode, decided that the main characters were portrayed more favorably than the city slickers, and okayed the deal. "The Ballad of Jed Clampett" hit number one on the country charts—unheard of at the time for a bluegrass band—and even crossed over to the pop charts. "The song wasn't our favorite," Flatt conceded, but "after it sold a hundred thousand copies we just learned to love it."

A few years later, Warren Beatty used their recording of "Foggy Mountain Breakdown" in the hit movie *Bonnie and Clyde*. The exposure from the film transformed the song into the nation's best-known bluegrass tune. "*Bonnie and Clyde* completely took Flatt and Scruggs to another level," said Randy Scruggs, one of Earl and Louise's sons. "They did some concerts in Japan and it was like the Beatles coming to the United States. I mean, literally, they had to go through tunnels to get to their cars to take them away from the venues and all that sort of thing."

But for the most part, acoustic string band music remained a relatively small and separate world from commercial country music—though it had some of the most fervent advocates, as concerned about the music's roots as its future, and always looking for signs of a resurgence in popularity. John McEuen of the Nitty Gritty Dirt Band remembered the cycles:

A funny thing about bluegrass is when I started playing it, in the mid-1960s, the first thing you heard was, "Bluegrass is going to be big this year!" And the next

POSSUM

George Jones. I'm not sure whether he didn't know he was important or fought being important. But the minute we heard him, we'd never heard a voice like that.

RAY WALKER, THE JORDANAIRES

Well, I think the trials and tribulations that George went through had everything to do with his music. I think when he was hurting you could hear it in a song. I always say George didn't sing country songs, George *was* a country song.

BRENDA LEE

"If I could have made a living doing some other things, I know I would have been a lot happier," George Jones confided to a reporter in 1966. "I would have had more peace of mind," he said, but "you don't get that in this business." Singing had helped raise him from the poverty of his childhood, but never let him escape its most painful memories.

ABOVE *This publicity shot for Flatt and Scruggs's appearance on* The Beverly Hillbillies *did double duty, when they dressed like characters from* Bonnie and Clyde, *which also featured one of their songs.*

OPPOSITE *As a boy, George Jones sang on the streets of Beaumont, Texas, for spare change; his alcoholic father took the money to buy booze for himself.*

Born on September 12, 1931, in a log shack in south-east Texas, the youngest of eight children, Jones inherited a gift for music from his mother's family. "The little feller could carry a tune before he could even talk good," a cousin remembered. But his father had a weakness for hard liquor, which turned him mean and uncontrollably violent. Returning home drunk many nights, he would roust young George from bed and demand some songs, belt-whipping the boy if he hesitated. George would perform with tears streaming down his face.

When the family moved to a government housing project in Beaumont, the father took his eleven-year-old son to a bus stop and forced him to sing for strangers passing by—and then confiscated the coins they tossed into George's tin cup to go on a bender. Jones soon learned to do street performance on his own—and quickly spent all the money on candy and soda pop.

By the time he was in his mid-teens, after two years in seventh grade without passing, Jones had quit school and was singing in local bars for tips and free beer. His favorite songs were Roy Acuff's, because of the way Acuff put so

TOP LEFT AND RIGHT *As a teenager, Jones quit school, joined a band that played in local honky tonks, and developed his own weakness for liquor.*

ABOVE *George's drinking led to bar fights and times when his band searched for him in lonely corners of nearby establishments to get him back onstage.*

much emotion and conviction into his music. In 1949, he was playing on radio station KRIC when Hank Williams stopped by, promoting his first big hit, "Lovesick Blues." Williams became Jones's next hero.

By the late 1950s, working as a deejay at station KTRM while trying to get his recording career launched, Jones became friends with J. P. Richardson, "the Big Bopper," and acquired a nickname of his own: "Possum," because of his close-set eyes, turned-up nose, and tight-lipped grin. His first number-one hit, "White Lightning," was written by Richardson and released in 1959, after the Big Bopper's death in the plane crash that also killed Ritchie Valens and Buddy Holly.

Jones was well into a second unhappy marriage by then. On the road, he had developed his own taste for whiskey—Jack Daniels and 7Up—and was having the same troubles with it as his father. Though only five feet seven and weighing 145 pounds, he'd regularly pick fights with bigger men in the audience. At one concert, he was so drunk he fell off the stage. Sometimes he would simply disappear, until his bandmates finally found him, sitting alone, drinking in a dark corner of a bar.

Still, there was no denying the brilliance of his singing, especially once he stopped imitating his musical heroes and developed his own style. Jones began singing in a lower register, sometimes through nearly clenched teeth, holding back the power of his voice until the drama of the song required it, bending and embroidering notes. "He had this quality of a musical instrument," said session musician Lloyd Green. "He had range from as high as you want to go to as low as you want to go. And he always hit the notes precisely

accurately. And wherever he wanted to go, he had complete control of his voice, much like an operatic singer, except it was country."

Jones said he approached each recording "until you're just like the people in the song, and you're living it and their problems become your problems, until you're lost in the song and it just takes everything out of you." When he recorded in Nashville, other musicians started coming to his sessions, just to listen to Jones sing. In the early 1960s he released a string of hits, including "She Thinks I Still Care," "A Girl I Used to Know," "The Race Is On," and "Walk Through This World with Me."

In 1968, his second wife—who didn't drink and didn't really like country music—divorced him, and he moved from Texas to Nashville. He opened a nightclub on Lower Broadway, called Possum Holler, and marketed a line of souvenirs, including women's lingerie called Possum Panties. Jones was thirty-seven years old and a major star now. He told his friends, "You can just say ole Possum ain't gettin' married again until he's sixty-nine."

ABOVE *Jones's first number one hit, "White Lightning," had been written by his friend "the Big Bopper," who died in a plane crash with Buddy Holly.*

RIGHT *Jones at the New River Ranch country music park in Maryland. Other artists, who nicknamed him "Possum" because of his close-set eyes, were amazed by the virtuosity of his voice.*

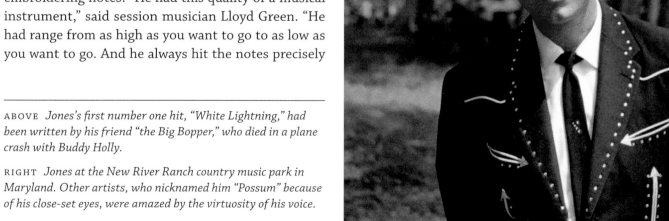

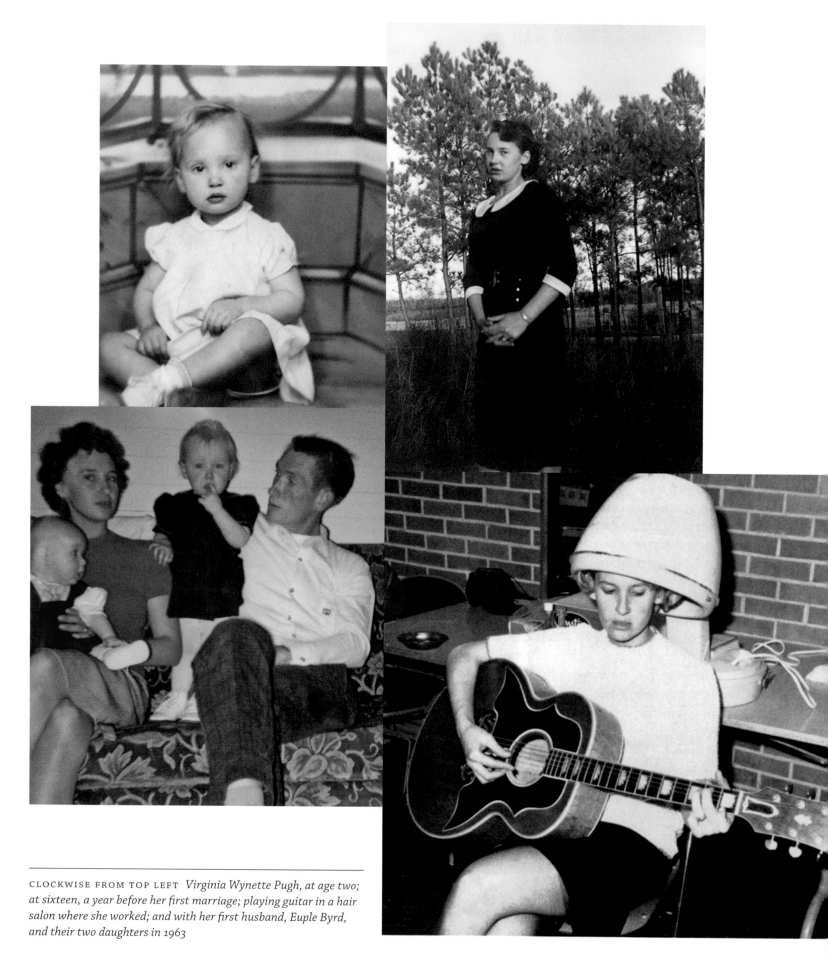

CLOCKWISE FROM TOP LEFT *Virginia Wynette Pugh, at age two; at sixteen, a year before her first marriage; playing guitar in a hair salon where she worked; and with her first husband, Euple Byrd, and their two daughters in 1963*

STAND BY YOUR MAN

Tammy's snatches at happiness were few and far between. That is what I observed. And you always wanted her to be happier because you felt like she wasn't. And you didn't know how to fix it.

Tammy was one of those people that you always just wanted to hug and envelop her and say, "It's gonna be alright. It's gonna be fine."

BRENDA LEE

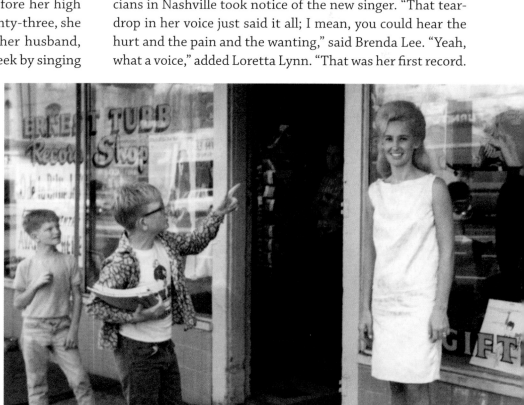

George Jones's vow to stay single for the next thirty years lasted less than one. By the fall of 1968 he was proudly telling people he was married once again. Jones and his new wife, Tammy Wynette, shared a number of things in common. Both had already been married twice before. Both had extraordinary voices. And Wynette's personal life seemed just as fragile and tormented as her new husband's.

Born Virginia Wynette Pugh on May 5, 1942, in Itawamba County, Mississippi, close to the Alabama border, she had been raised on a cotton farm by her grandparents. Her father died before she was one and her mother moved to Memphis to work in a defense factory during World War Two.

She married at age seventeen, a month before her high school graduation. By the time she turned twenty-three, she was the mother of three girls, had divorced her husband, and was living in Birmingham, making $45 a week by singing on a local television show early each morning, before going to work all day at a beauty salon.

In 1966, she packed her children and a few belongings into her car and moved to Nashville, where she started making the rounds along Music Row, hoping someone would sign her to a contract. When an executive offered her that possibility—in exchange for sexual favors—she ran out of his office.

Eventually she began showing up at the office of Billy Sherrill, a young producer at Epic Records. "She would come to my office

and sit out in the lobby and wait around, and finally, she'd give up and leave," Sherrill recalled. "One day, a friend of mine—another record producer, and she had seen him—made some kind of derogatory remarks about their relationship, and it made me really, really mad at him. So the next time she came in, I said, 'Send her in.' She came in and I said, 'I've got this song. Learn this and tomorrow we'll record this.' And she said, 'You wouldn't be kidding me, would you?' I said, 'Do I look like I'm kidding? You learn the song and tomorrow we'll make a little history.'"

The song, "Apartment #9," did not make history, but musicians in Nashville took notice of the new singer. "That teardrop in her voice just said it all; I mean, you could hear the hurt and the pain and the wanting," said Brenda Lee. "Yeah, what a voice," added Loretta Lynn. "That was her first record.

TOP *Billy Sherrill changed her name to Tammy Wynette and took her into a recording studio. After hearing Tammy's powerfully expressive voice, Loretta Lynn said, "I've got competition."*

RIGHT *Tammy outside Ernest Tubb's Record Shop after the release of her first two albums.*

And I heard it on the radio, and I said, 'I've got competition.'"

The record was released under her new name, given to her by Sherrill, who had just seen a movie called *Tammy and the Bachelor:* "I said, 'Pugh's the ugliest name I've ever heard. Let's call you Tammy and forget Pugh, and use your middle name, Wynette. From now on, you'll be Tammy Wynette.'"

Sherrill was fascinated by the rich arrangements that rock producer Phil Spector was creating in Los Angeles, known as "the Wall of Sound." When Sherrill wrapped his own version of it around Tammy Wynette's dynamic voice, the result was a steady string of number-one country hits.

One of them was "D-I-V-O-R-C-E," written by Bobby Braddock and Curly Putman, in which a mother tries to shield her little son from the agony of the breakup of her marriage by spelling out words like "divorce" and "custody." (Some stations refused to play it, Braddock said, because another word that was spelled

out was "h-e-l-l.") The song, Wynette would say, "fit my life completely." As it hit the top of the country charts, her second marriage—to songwriter Don Chapel—was already disintegrating.

By this time, George Jones's second divorce had just been finalized. Jones, eleven years older, was Wynette's idol as a country singer—she had arrived in Nashville with all of his song lyrics handwritten in a loose-leaf notebook—and the two had gotten to know each other performing at concerts on the road.

One night, Jones stopped at Wynette and Chapel's house. She was playing Jones's latest hit, written by her husband, over and over. Chapel began ranting and cussing, calling her a "bitch." Jones, who had been drinking, exploded. Turning over a dining table and tossing a chair through the plate glass window, he shouted at Chapel, "You don't talk to her like that."

"She's *my* wife," Chapel answered. "What the hell business is it of yours?"

"Because I'm in love with her," Jones said, "and she's in love with me, aren't you, Tammy?" It was the first time he'd expressed his feelings toward her, and now she revealed her own. "Yes," she said, "I am."

Jones ushered Wynette and her girls from the home and put them up in a hotel. A few days later, he flew her to Mexico City so she could get a quick divorce. Upon their return, they found themselves each being sued by Chapel—Wynette for desertion and adultery; Jones for alienation of affection—and Tennessee law did not recognize Mexican divorces.

In the midst of all the turmoil, Billy Sherrill brought Tammy back into the studio to record a song they had co-written that borrowed its melody from a Johann Strauss waltz. It was called "Stand By Your Man." "She didn't want to cut it," according to Ralph Emery. "It was a strange time for her. But Billy insisted that she cut it."

"Stand By Your Man" quickly became the top country song in the nation and would be Tammy

TOP *Wynette began touring with her idol, George Jones. She had all of his song lyrics written out in a loose-leaf notebook.*

RIGHT *As her album* D-I-V-O-R-C-E *hit the charts, Tammy's marriage to her second husband was falling apart; when she was recording* Stand By Your Man, *he was suing her for desertion.*

Wynette's biggest record ever, selling five million copies, earning her a Grammy Award, and making her the Country Music Association's Female Vocalist of the Year, beating out the previous recipient, Loretta Lynn.

"One amusing thing to me about Tammy and Loretta," said Jeannie Seely, "Tammy's songs were always about standing by your man and treating your man right, and being there for him, and yet she divorced several times. Loretta was always threatening, 'Don't come home drinking, don't do this, or I'll do that,' and she always stayed with her man. So I always kind of thought they wrote each other's songs."

Wynette's lawyers eventually settled Don Chapel's lawsuits by finding a technicality that established that her marriage to him hadn't been legal in the first place. Having told people for six months that they had been married in Mexico, George Jones and Tammy Wynette were finally legally united on February 16, 1969, and began touring together in a bus emblazoned "Mr. and Mrs. Country Music."

Jones had his own hit song rising in the charts at the time, "I'll Share My World With You." It reached number two— blocked from the top by "Stand By Your Man."

TOP AND LEFT *After their marriage, Tammy and George toured together as "Mr. and Mrs. Country Music" and performed regularly on the* Grand Ole Opry.

YOU AIN'T GOIN' NOWHERE

It was the 1960s and you had this unrest in society, Haight-Ashbury in San Francisco, and the spokesperson for this generation was *Rolling Stone* magazine. For some reason, *Rolling Stone* magazine didn't take a liking to Nashville very much. They called it "a recording factory," because we would do three songs a session. They'd think, "Oh, these people are selling out to commercialism."

But what they didn't realize is that we were not only being commercial, we were being creative, too, and efficient.

CHARLIE MCCOY

Back in 1965, during a visit to New York City, Charlie McCoy, one of Nashville's "A-Team" session musicians, stopped by the Columbia Records studio where his friend Bob Johnston was producing a new album with Bob Dylan, *Highway 61 Revisited*. When McCoy was introduced to the star, he was surprised when Dylan said, "I'm getting ready to do a song, why don't you grab that guitar and play along." It was "Desolation Row"—eleven minutes long, with just Dylan, a bass player, and McCoy, suddenly expected to provide the guitar accompaniment. The session time was nearly over.

"So we had time to record the song once; listen to it once; and record it one more time," McCoy remembered. "And that was it. Done. After I left, Bob Johnston started selling Nashville to Bob Dylan. I guess he was saying, 'Now did you see how easy that went, with this guy? That's the way they do it in Nashville.'"

The next year, when Dylan became dissatisfied with the slow and uneven progress on a new album, Johnston ignored the objections of the label's New York executives and moved everything to Nashville, where McCoy, pianist Harold "Pig" Robbins, and other A-Team musicians sat in.

The sessions were incredibly productive—turning out a double album, *Blonde on Blonde*, that was both a critical and commercial success. Dylan "was the quintessential New York hipster; what was *he* doing in Nashville?" his friend and organ-

ABOVE *Impressed by the skills of Nashville's session musicians, especially multi-instrumentalist Charlie McCoy, Bob Dylan recorded a number of albums on Music Row.*

LEFT *Charlie Daniels (far right) also played several instruments during the recordings. More artists from other genres soon followed Dylan to Nashville.*

ist Al Kooper said. "But you take those two elements, pour them into a test tube, and it just exploded." In 1967, Dylan came back to Music Row to record his next album, *John Wesley Harding*.

The nation was becoming more politically and culturally polarized, and musical tastes increasingly accentuated that divide. But in the recording studios of Nashville, at least, there seemed to be room for everyone. "It was almost like all of these folk-rock artists said, 'Now, wait a minute, there's something going on there,'" said McCoy. "It was like the floodgate opened. Here they came: Joan Baez; Buffy Sainte-Marie; Peter, Paul, and Mary; the Manhattan Transfer; Leonard Cohen; Gordon Lightfoot; Dan Fogelberg; the Byrds. It's just like the gates opened and here they came."

"The old world of rhinestone-encrusted, fiddle- and steel-driven country music had left a lot of people from the Woodstock generation cold," added Marty Stuart. "That was Grandpa's music. That was Mom and Dad's music. And, all of a sudden, here are these hipsters and these rock stars coming to Nashville and making music that's playing on FM radio and getting talked about in *Rolling Stone*. It telegraphed to a lot of bands in New York and L.A., 'There's a lot going on

here. You need to come see about it.' And a lot of bands did. It further expanded the term 'Music City,' because they blew the walls down around here and changed the rules. And that's just what you have to do from time to time to keep things moving forward."

Among those who followed Dylan to Nashville was an eclectic rock band from Los Angeles called the Byrds. They had pioneered what came to be called folk-rock by turning Dylan's song "Mr. Tambourine Man" and Pete Seeger's "Turn, Turn, Turn" into national hits. Then they helped popularize psychedelic-rock with a song called "Eight Miles High."

In 1968, led by founding members Roger McGuinn and Chris Hillman, they showed up on Music Row with the intention of creating an album of country music. With them came their newest member, Gram Parsons.

Parsons himself seemed an unlikely prospect to become a country music advocate. Born Ingram Cecil Connor III, the

---

ABOVE *The Byrds, seen here performing on the* Grand Ole Opry, *arrived to record a country album. At the microphones, from left, Gram Parsons, Roger McGuinn, and Chris Hillman; at the drum, Kevin Kelley. The crowd didn't like their look and booed them.*

structure. I'm thinking, 'Okay, we're going to do this in a structured fashion like that.' And I said, 'Where do you want me to fill?' In unison, they said, 'Everywhere. Everywhere.' And I said, 'Hey, my kind of guys. Turn it on.' So, if you listen to the *Sweetheart of the Rodeo* album and 'You Ain't Goin' Nowhere,' you'll hear steel guitar from the first note to the end of the song, the last note. They let me play everywhere."

But when the Byrds' record label used its influence to get them an invitation to perform at the Ryman Auditorium—the first rock band ever to play the *Grand Ole Opry*—no one was prepared for the reaction. "People saw them coming out and started booing," according to Green, who was onstage. "They saw this young group of hippie-looking guys and with longer hair than what they were used to, they literally booed. Welcome to Nashville."

The songs the Byrds recorded for *Sweetheart of the Rodeo* included ones written by Bob Dylan, Merle Haggard, the Louvin Brothers, Woody Guthrie—and two by Gram Parsons, including the plaintive ballad "Hickory Wind," which he sang at the *Opry* and dedicated to his grandmother. The album would not be a big commercial success: country stations avoided it, and many rock stations weren't sure what to make of it. But some reviewers saw in it the beginnings of something new.

"In doing country as country," one critic wrote in *Rolling Stone*, the Byrds "show just how powerful and relevant unadorned country music is. And they leave just enough rock in the drums to let you know that they can still play rock and roll. That's what I call bringing it all back home."

heir to a family fortune based on a Florida citrus empire, he was sent to a prestigious private school as a teenager and attended Harvard University. Originally drawn to folk music—and surrounded by people who looked at country music with contempt—Parsons switched allegiances after a friend played him some Buck Owens and Merle Haggard records. He soon immersed himself in the work of other country artists: George Jones, Loretta Lynn, the Louvin Brothers, and Ray Charles's soulful interpretations of country tunes.

When the Byrds got to Nashville, Lloyd Green was called in to provide a pedal steel guitar: "And the first song was 'You Ain't Goin' Nowhere,' a Bob Dylan song. So they're standing over my steel and I'm sitting there and I say, 'Well, where do you guys want me to fill?' because I was used to more of a formulated recording environment where the steel might play the intro, then a guitar may fill for eight bars, and then piano may fill the chorus, that kind of

Parsons would later refer to it as "Cosmic American Music"—a hybrid of various roots music forms, from American folk and soul and blues to country's honky tonk. Most people would come to call it "country-rock."

ABOVE *Before his conversion to country music and joining the Byrds, Gram Parsons, seen here playing in his Harvard dorm room, preferred folk music.*

LEFT *Sweetheart of the Rodeo was not an immediate commercial success, but it was a breakthrough in what came to be called "country-rock."*

heard across the river, in Matamoros, I think that probably put the heart in it for me."

His father, a general in the Air Force, and his mother had their own ideas for his future. After moving to California, they were proud that their son entered the prestigious Pomona College, where he played rugby and football, joined the Reserve Officers'

FREEDOM'S JUST ANOTHER WORD

I remember I used to do demo sessions at Columbia Studio, and there was this guy there who was the janitor. He would always lay aside his push broom, and he'd start asking me questions about songwriting. And, as I got to know him, I realized this guy was not just a janitor.

I think he was like three or four years older than I was. And I found out that he had been to Oxford and that he had been an officer in the military and a helicopter pilot. I got to know him pretty well. I thought he was an amazing songwriter, and his name was Kris Kristofferson.

BOBBY BRADDOCK

Born in Brownsville, Texas, on June 22, 1936, Kristoffer Kristofferson had shown an early interest in poetry and music. He especially enjoyed listening to Hank Williams on the radio and to the Mexican music that seemed to permeate the streets of his border town. "The *rancheras* influenced me as much as country music, maybe more," Kristofferson said. "The music I

TOP, LEFT *Growing up in Brownsville, Texas, Kris Kristofferson, seen here with his sister Karen, loved listening to the Mexican music he heard in the border town.*

TOP, RIGHT *A Christmas card from the Kristoffersons, who were immensely proud of their oldest son's academic and athletic accomplishments.*

ABOVE AND LEFT *At college, Kristofferson played rugby and football and joined ROTC, before graduating Phi Beta Kappa and going to Oxford as a Rhodes scholar.*

father's. He was a captain and helicopter pilot in the Army's Airborne Rangers and had volunteered for duty in Vietnam, but instead was assigned to be an instructor at West Point.

Before he started that job, he had come to Nashville for a few days in 1965, still harboring his childhood dream. The songwriter Marijohn Wilkin, a cousin of Kristofferson's platoon leader, agreed to show him around. She introduced him to Cowboy Jack Clement, who in turn took him behind the scenes at the *Grand Ole Opry*. Backstage, he was introduced to Johnny Cash. "He was skinny as a snake," Kristofferson said, "like he was going to end up like Hank Williams. But he was still exciting to watch perform, even when he was messed up. And I got to shake his

Training Corps, and graduated Phi Beta Kappa in English literature, before going on to Oxford, England, as a Rhodes scholar to continue studying the Romantic poets. He was especially captivated by William Blake, and more than fifty years later could still quote from memory a piece of advice from the poet-philosopher: "If you, who are organized by the Divine Providence for spiritual communion, refuse, and bury your talent in the earth, even though you should want natural bread, sorrow and desperation pursue you through life, and after death shame and confusion of face to eternity."

"He's telling you that you'll be miserable if you don't do what you're supposed to do," Kristofferson said. "And I felt, from a time as early as I can remember, that that's what I was supposed to do, is to write songs."

When Kristofferson turned twenty-nine, his life was at a crossroads. He had a wife and a small child and was well on his way toward a distinguished military career, like his

ABOVE *Kristofferson was working as a janitor in Columbia's recording studio when Bob Beckham of Combine Music (right) took him to Fred Foster to try out for a songwriting job that provided a modest weekly salary.*

RIGHT *Kristofferson at work in the Combine Music offices*

For four years, Kristofferson struggled to make it. He and his wife divorced. He got a part-time job helicoptering workers and supplies to oil rigs in the Gulf of Mexico, but always returned to Nashville and his songwriting. His parents lost patience with the direction his life had taken. "Well, my mother just disowned me," Kristofferson said. "She sent me a letter saying, 'We thought it was cute when you were little and you liked country music, but nobody over the age of fifteen listens to that trash—and if they did, it wouldn't be anybody we'd want to know.' And, 'Please don't write or come home because you're an embarrassment to us.'"

He showed the letter to Cowboy Jack Clement, who borrowed it and showed it to Cash, who had

hand. That's probably why I left the Army. It just electrified me."

He resigned his West Point position, moved his small family to Nashville, and set about trying to interest people in his songs. To earn money—and hoping to meet some artists who might record something he wrote—Kristofferson took a job as the janitor at Columbia Records' studio: sweeping floors, cleaning ashtrays, and sometimes slipping demo tapes and lyric sheets to the stars who passed through. Johnny Cash was one of them, but he tended to throw demo tapes away without listening to them.

ABOVE *Kristofferson in a studio with Fred Foster, who thought the songwriter also had a distinctive voice and encouraged him to record his own songs*

RIGHT *Embarrassed that he had given up a promising military career in favor of being a songwriter, Kristofferson's parents disowned him.*

had his own strained relations with his father. The next time the superstar saw the janitor at Columbia's studio, Cash came up to Kristofferson and made a joke about it: "He said, 'It's always good to get a letter from home, isn't it, Kris?' And from then on, he insisted—all of his sessions were closed to everybody there, and nobody but the producer and the band could be in there—but he always let me in."

In 1969, Bob Beckham of Combine Music decided to take a chance on Kristofferson and brought him to his boss, the record producer and publisher Fred Foster, to audition. Kristofferson was hoping to be hired as a songwriter with a weekly salary, called a "draw." Foster had a formula for deciding if he thought a songwriter had talent: "If you were going to play me songs that you've written, I want to hear four. Anybody might luck up and write one. A miracle could happen and you might do two. You're not going to write four great songs unless you're a writer. So he sang me four songs. And I thought, honestly, before he finished those four songs, that I was hallucinating. They were just sophisticated, and yet 'rootsy' and country. Not a wasted word. I said, 'Okay, I'll sign you. I'll agree to the draw you want, but on one condition.'"

Foster insisted that Kristofferson also record an album, singing some of his own songs. Kristofferson was flummoxed, according to Foster: "'Man,' he said, 'you're crazy. I can't sing. I sound like an effing frog.' I said, 'Possibly, but one that can communicate, because you've sold me.' He said, 'Okay, if you're crazy enough, I guess I am too.'"

As he predicted, Kristofferson's debut album did not sell well; but one day, Foster came to him with an idea for a new song. It wasn't much, just a phrase that came to Foster when he met Boudleaux Bryant's new secretary, Barbara McKee. Everyone called her Bobbie. "Fred said he had a song title for me," Kristofferson remembered. "He says, 'Me and . . . ,' I thought he said, 'McGee.' But he said, 'Bobbie McKee. How does that grab ya? Me and Bobbie McKee?' I didn't know how I was going to write that."

Kristofferson had one more trip to the Gulf of Mexico, taking oil workers to their rigs, and while he was there, he mulled over Foster's suggestion. At the same time, he started thinking about the film *La Strada*, by the Italian director Fed-erico Fellini, in which the hero, played by Anthony Quinn, abandons the woman he loves after a long and tempestuous journey. "And then it started coming together for me," he said. "At the end of the film, Anthony Quinn is getting drunk in a bar and he goes out by the beach and he's looking up, on his knees, looking up at the stars and just weeping. And that's what I was trying to get, because I was trying to get the same feeling in 'Me and Bobby McGee.' So, I owe it to Fellini."

"And he got caught in a bad rainstorm in Baton Rouge," Foster said. "And he wrote the first verse in his car: 'Busted flat in Baton Rouge, heading for the train, feeling nearly as faded as my jeans, Bobby thumbed a diesel down just before it rained, and took it all the way to New Orleans'; then to 'I pulled my harpoon out of my dirty red bandana and was blowin' sad while Bobby sang the blues. With them windshield wipers slapping time and Bobby clapping hands, we finally sang up every song that driver knew. Freedom's just another word for nothing left to lose.'"

"I was just trying to write as good a song as a Hank Williams song," Kristofferson added. "I was trying to move the emotions in. It was a statement of loss at the end, by the end of the song. Most of the song, talking about how good it was. And then it's over."

Roger Miller would be the first to record the song, taking it to number twelve on the country charts in 1969. Others soon came out with their own versions. Then, just before her death from a drug overdose in 1970, the blues and rock singer Janis Joplin recorded it. Her single, released posthumously, became the number one record in the country.

Out of gratitude for providing him with the title of his first big hit, Kristofferson insisted that Fred Foster share half of the writing credit.

ABOVE *Barbara McKee, whom everyone called Bobbie, was a secretary in the office of Boudleaux Bryant. After meeting her, Fred Foster suggested a song title, "Me and Bobbie McKee," to Kristofferson, who misheard him and thought he had said "Bobbie McGee."*

A BOY NAMED SUE

In 1968, Johnny Cash had redeemed his career by recording an album at Folsom Prison. A year later, he had even greater success with one recorded live at San Quentin.

The biggest hit on the album was a novelty tune called "A Boy Named Sue," about a man who searches all his life to find the father who named him Sue, finally confronts him in a bar and beats him in a fistfight, only to be told that it was the name that had made him a tough enough man to defeat his father.

It was written by a friend of Cash's with an unlikely background for a country songwriter. Shel Silverstein was a cartoonist for *Playboy* magazine and a celebrated author of children's books. "His love for country music was not fake; it was the real deal," said singer Bobby Bare. "His favorite singer as a kid was Ernest Tubb, and it's very difficult to imagine a small, Jewish boy growing up around Chicago loving Ernest Tubb. I mean it's strange—of course, Shel *was* strange. But he was the most creative person I ever met in my life."

"A Boy Named Sue" would be Cash's biggest single ever. It was part of a long tradition; country music fans had always enjoyed silly—and sometimes suggestive—songs called "hokum."

"Me and Shel, one day, were sitting around whining about, 'We ain't got no record deal, what are we going to do?'" Bare remembered. "And I said, 'Well, hell, why don't we just do an album about people our age?' And so Shel wrote twenty-some songs about the realities of getting older in Music City. And [with Mel Tillis, Waylon Jennings, and Jerry Reed] we did songs like, 'I'm an Old Dog, but I Can Still Bury a Bone.' Waylon did one called 'Lord Ain't It Hard When It Ain't.' I did one called 'She'd Rather Be Homeless Than Here at Home With Me.' Mel did one called 'I'm Not Too Old to Cut the Mustard, Just Too Tired to Spread it Around.' Jerry said it was the most fun he ever had with his clothes on."

Silverstein wasn't the only master of silly songs. Other artists and songwriters also had success with titles like "She Got the Gold Mine, I Got the Shaft," "My Wife Ran Off with My Best Friend, and I Sure Do Miss Him," "(I've Been) Flushed from the Bathroom of Your Heart," and "If I Said You Had a Beautiful Body, Would You Hold It Against Me."

The only number-one song Little Jimmy Dickens ever had was "May the Bird of Paradise Fly Up Your Nose."

Roy Clark had a hit with "Thank God and Greyhound (You're Gone)."

Bill Anderson wrote "Walk Out Backwards and I'll Think You're Walking In," "We Ran Out of Anything to Call It, So We Called It Quits," and "Peel Me a Nanner, Toss Me a Peanut, 'Cause You Sure Made a Monkey Out of Me."

One of Conway Twitty and Loretta Lynn's most popular duets was titled "You're the Reason Our Kids Are Ugly."

"My favorite, and it came from my father," Vince Gill said, "is 'It's Hard to Kiss the Lips at Night That Chew Your Ass Out All Day Long.' It's pretty hard to beat."

TOP *Shel Silverstein was a* Playboy *cartoonist, author of children's books, and writer of novelty songs like Johnny Cash's "A Boy Named Sue," which became Cash's biggest single.*

ABOVE *Little Jimmy Dickens's only number-one hit was also a novelty song, "May the Bird of Paradise Fly Up Your Nose."*

By the summer of 1969, Johnny Cash had reached a level of national stardom virtually unequaled by any previous country music artist. His San Quentin album spent twenty weeks at number one on the country charts, and four weeks on top of the pop charts.

His live performances were commanding higher fees and were played before huge audiences: twenty thousand people at New York's Madison Square Garden; fifteen thousand in San Antonio; two sold-out shows at the eighteen-thousand-seat Hollywood Bowl; and an appearance in Detroit that grossed $93,000, nearly twice the previous record for a single country concert.

Other country artists, like Porter Wagoner, Marty Robbins, the Stonemans, Flatt and Scruggs, and Ernest Tubb had television shows that were distributed to stations in many states; but Cash had his own weekly network television show that aired on every ABC affiliate in the nation. Cash insisted that his show be taped at the Ryman Auditorium. Only a few years earlier, high on drugs, he had knocked out all of the footlights on the stage and the Ryman had told him never to come back. Now he provided the Mother Church of Country Music with an unprecedented spotlight.

"I think the TV show was more than a gig; it was almost a mission," said Rosanne Cash. "He wanted to expose and bring to national television some of the people he most admired—this diversity and ecumenical attitude he had toward all music."

His guests ranged across the musical and cultural divide: from country legends like Eddy Arnold to Motown's Stevie Wonder; from rock stars Eric Clapton and the Who to a long list of rising folk artists Cash thought more people should hear—including James Taylor, Ian and Sylvia, Odetta, Gordon Lightfoot, and Joni Mitchell. When he suggested having the folk singer Pete Seeger on the show, network executives balked because of Seeger's left-wing politics. Cash brought him on anyway.

Johnny Cash sings of trains, prisons and hard times

LIFE

JOHNNY CASH
The Rough-cut King of Country Music

NOVEMBER 21 · 1969 · 40¢

Roger Miller came on and had some fun with one of Cash's signature songs. "I keep my pants up with a piece of twine," Miller sang. "Please say you're mine, and pull the twine." One night, Louis Armstrong played "Blue Yodel No. 9," the same tune that Armstrong and Cash's idol, Jimmie Rodgers, had recorded back in 1930.

Merle Haggard was invited to appear, and during rehearsals, Cash learned that Haggard had been one of the inmates at Cash's first San Quentin concert nearly a decade earlier. Merle confessed that he had been keeping his prison record secret from his fans and the press. "Well, it was just not anything that you want to brag about," Haggard explained. "So I didn't want anybody to know it. And he said, 'Well, why don't you let me tell the people where you've been?' And I said, 'Why would you want to do that, Cash?' And he said, 'Listen, Merle, you let me tell the people where you've been. Them goddamn dirty magazines will never be able to touch you.' I thought about it. I thought, well, there's nothing like honesty. So he told the folks that night on network television; he said, 'When this guy and I first met, he was in the audience.' And he told them where he was talking about. And you know, I've never been sorry."

Cash also instituted a regular segment on his program in which he explored what he considered forgotten segments of society—including prisoners and Native Americans—and, over the objections of the network, he included a gospel song in every show, just as he had promised his mother.

LEFT *With his weekly network television show, Johnny Cash had reached a new level of stardom. He used it to draw attention to issues he considered important and to highlight all styles of American music.*

OPPOSITE, CLOCKWISE FROM TOP LEFT *Among the eclectic array of music stars Cash featured on his show were Louis Armstrong, who played "Blue Yodel No. 9," which he had recorded with Johnny's hero, Jimmie Rodgers, in 1930; folk singer-songwriter Joni Mitchell; the fun-loving Roger Miller; Cash's mother, who accompanied him on a gospel song; Merle Haggard, who let Cash reveal Merle's prison record so the tabloids wouldn't; and Pete Seeger, whom Cash insisted on inviting despite the network's objections.*

Meanwhile, Bob Dylan had returned to town to record yet another album, *Nashville Skyline*, to be filled with songs that had even more of a country flavor. Dylan invited Cash to stop by the recording studio, and the two friends spent time in the studio laying down some songs and having fun together. Cash then persuaded Dylan to make a rare television appearance by coming on his show at the Ryman. "And that seared itself into the consciousness of everyone who cared about music," Rosanne Cash said:

> Those two young men, sitting side by side, playing "Girl From the North Country." Dad said later, "I didn't realize how important that was. All I did was sit there and strum some G chords." Yeah, from G chords mighty revolutions come, because those of us of my generation who saw that, [we were] utterly changed.
>
> My own husband saw that on TV, and he said it opened the door to his love of country music. It opened to everything, it opened to Merle Haggard, opened

to the Louvin Brothers. He started seeking this out. He already knew Dylan, but this—Dylan and Dad together—it was an explosion.

I remember going to school the next day and feeling like I was the coolest thirteen-year-old in the world. My dad and Bob Dylan had just sung together the night before, on national television, and nobody could touch me.

ABOVE, RIGHT *When Bob Dylan returned to Music Row to record* Nashville Skyline, *he invited Cash to join him. Bob Johnston (right) was a producer for both stars.*

TOP *Cash got Dylan to make a rare television appearance on his show, where they sang "Girl From the North Country."*

player. He's not the greatest banjo player. He's not the greatest fiddle player. He's not the greatest singer. And he's not the greatest comedian. But he does it *all* better than anybody else."

When Clark and his manager, Jim Halsey, arrived for the first taping, they were appalled at what they saw. It was not going to be anything like Cash's and Campbell's shows—or any other country music show. And its name, they learned, was *Hee Haw*.

"Here are all these bales of hay, and overalls, and straw hats, and corncob pipes," Halsey said. "Frankly, I was a little upset about it and I told Roy, I said, 'We've been fighting this all of our life,' to get away from the hay bales and the barn doors and the pigs, and all this stuff, and here we are right in the middle of it." "They tried to paint a picture that everybody in country music, they were barefooted and they wore bib overalls," Clark said, "and the most of us raised up and said, 'Look, I have two custom-made tuxedos. But I'm not ashamed to say that I did grow up in bib overalls, and probably you did too.' It should have a little more class. But being third class is better than being no class."

What the producers intended was, at heart, a comedy show, based loosely on Rowan and Martin's hugely popu-

· · ·

At the same time *The Johnny Cash Show* was being taped at the Ryman Auditorium, two other country music programs were appearing on network television.

One originated in Los Angeles, hosted by guitarist and singer Glen Campbell. Born near Delight, Arkansas, Campbell had become one of the most sought-after session musicians on the West Coast—he had played with the Beach Boys—before he broke out on his own, with hits like "Gentle on My Mind," "By the Time I Get to Phoenix," and "Wichita Lineman."

The other show was being taped at Nashville's CBS affiliate. Its hosts were Buck Owens, from Bakersfield, California, and a musical virtuoso from Virginia named Roy Clark. "I heard someone describe Roy Clark once," said Charlie McCoy, who became the show's musical director. "He's not the greatest guitar

---

ABOVE *Glen Campbell's* Goodtime Hour *was broadcast from Los Angeles.*

RIGHT *From Nashville, CBS broadcast* Hee Haw, *a comedy show that also featured country music, with hosts Buck Owens (left) and Roy Clark.*

lar *Laugh-In* program. But instead of hip humor, *Hee Haw* would be full of cornpone jokes, delivered by people acting like stereotypes of hillbillies. The country music would be secondary.

As word about the show spread across Nashville, industry insiders started to worry. "There was a lot of talk about, 'Oh, Lord, I hope not,'" Bud Wendell of WSM and the *Opry* said. "'I hope it's not what we hear. I hope it isn't hay bales and 'hee haw,' and all that. That's an image that we try to live down and they're going to play it up.'" Clark remembered country music executives saying, "You've put country music back twenty years."

But the show was an immediate hit with audiences across the nation. And besides making Owens and Clark into even bigger stars, it revived the careers of some fading country music legends like David "Stringbean" Akeman and Grandpa Jones. "What made it work was, 'Okay, we can laugh at ourselves,'" said Charlie McCoy, "and that's what we were doing. We were laughing at ourselves. But when they did the music, it was serious. We had the stars of the day with hit records. We had nice sets. We had great sound. So, okay, we had this cornball over here, but with it, we had this legitimate look at country music." Bud Wendell conceded, "After that show had been on a few weeks, then I think everybody began to see that it was not damaging to the image of country music. And it was wonderful exposure for the artists." Jim Halsey added, "They forgot about it on the way to the bank."

Hee Haw would be broadcast for twenty-five years—three years with CBS and the rest as one of the most successful syndicated shows in television history.

CLOCKWISE FROM LEFT *Following in the wake of Charley Pride's success, other African Americans were making their mark on country music. Stoney Edwards was discovered at a benefit show for Bob Wills in 1970 and signed with Capitol Records; he had fifteen charted hits, including "Hank and Lefty Raised My Country Soul" and "Blackbird," which told the story of a young black boy who meets resistance from the "scarecrows" in the music industry. In 1969, Linda Martell, shown below with Roy Acuff, became the first black woman to sing on the Grand Ole Opry; her single "Color Him Father" was the first by a black woman to reach the country charts. O. B. McClinton charted fifteen hits, including some that addressed racial issues with biting humor, including "Obie From Senatobie," which borrowed its melody from Merle Haggard's "Okie From Muskogee" and lampooned stereotypes of southern blacks.*

SUNDAY MORNING COMING DOWN

Kris Kristofferson is probably the best songwriter. You can just go right down the road and you can compare Kris with anybody—Gershwin, or anybody else.

WILLIE NELSON

I think he's the greatest lyricist in the English language. And people say, "Well, Johnny Mercer," and Johnny Mercer was great. But, let me tell you, "See him wasted on the sidewalk in his jacket and his jeans, wearing yesterday's misfortune like a smile. Once he had a future full of money, love, and dreams, which he spent like they were going out of style. But he keeps right on believing, for the better or the worse, searching for the shrine he's never found, never knowing if believing was a blessing or a curse, if the going up was worth the coming down." That is William Blake. That is Robert Louis Stevenson. That is Lord Byron.

LARRY GATLIN

Nashville was now a songwriting capital, and Kris Kristofferson was one of the city's hottest songwriters, having elevated what was possible to say in a country song. Other artists were eager to record what he had written, though he was still unsure about his own singing voice.

In 1970, Sammi Smith released Kristofferson's "Help Me Make It Through the Night." It was one of several of his songs that dealt more directly, though poetically, with sexual relations between a man and a woman—more directly than some people in the country music industry were accustomed to. Smith's label let her record it for an album, but feared the lyrics were much too suggestive for radio, and released a different song as the single.

Then a disc jockey in Los Angeles called to say that when he played Smith singing Kristofferson's song off the album, he was so jammed with calls requesting it again, he had to announce that he would play it every hour, just to keep his phone lines open. Both the album—and the single the company quickly released—hit the top of the country charts.

ABOVE *Though his own recordings were not hits, many artists were having great success with songs that Kris Kristofferson was writing.*

"Until Kris, it was like, 'Hold my hand, darling.' Or, 'May I kiss you on your cheek?'" said Hazel Smith, a Nashville industry insider. "But Kristofferson just went right to the core of it. 'Put your warm and tender body close to mine,' he sang. And he knew what he was singing about, and America knew what he was singing about." "I never thought of it as being that radical," Kristofferson said. "I am a little surprised now that I wasn't worried about offending people, because it's talking about sex. But I'm glad I didn't censor myself."

He had more hits, with songs like "For the Good Times," about a man and a woman making love one last time as they break up; and "Loving Her Was Easier (Than Anything I'll Ever Do Again)," about the sweet memory of a lost love. When Ray Price heard the demo of "For the Good Times," Eddie Stubbs said, "he told his bandmates, 'This is going to be the biggest song of my career.' And it ultimately became just that." Charley Pride considered the lyrics of "Loving Her Was Easier" some of the most beautiful of any song he ever recorded.

The Kristofferson song that caught Johnny Cash's attention had nothing to do with love. Instead, it painted a despairing picture of a lonely man waking up on a Sunday morning, hungover from Saturday night, and his feelings of isolation as he walks the streets of a peaceful town on the Sabbath. "It was just autobiography," Kristofferson said. "It was just describing a day in my life, at the time, on a Sunday morning, because all the bars were closed on Sunday morning. I can remember walking down the street there. I was describing what I was going through at the time. I think more people like that song than anything I've written."

A number of songwriters are among its admirers. Rodney Crowell called it "the perfectly sustained narrative for those sixteen lines that make the song. You step into this emotionally charged scene of sorrow and woe, and a strange kind of hopefulness, at the same time." Larry Gatlin pointed to the vivid storytelling, matched by an unusual rhyme scheme that "only an English major and professor would know how to do, and some of the greatest alliteration in the English language: 'The beer I had for breakfast

wasn't bad, so I had one more for dessert. I fumbled through my closet for my clothes and found my cleanest dirty shirt. I washed my face, and combed my hair, and stumbled down the stairs to meet the day.' You can see that old boy stumbling through there and he's hungover and he's smoked a bunch of dope, and he stayed up too late. And he's depressed, or he's lost his job, or his woman's left, or something, and he stumbles through that. 'And far away I heard a lonely bell a-ringing, and it echoed through the canyon like the disappearing dreams of yesterday.' Hey, all those words are in the dictionary, but nobody else before Kris knew what damn order they came in."

When Johnny Cash heard "Sunday Morning Coming Down," he said later, it felt as if he'd written it himself. "The lines of the song started running through my head," he remembered, "and I realized I could identify with every one of them. I was so caught up in the song I didn't even want to

RIGHT *When Kristofferson wrote "Sunday Morning Coming Down," he said, "it was just describing a day in my life."*

wait to go into the studio." Cash decided to record the song live, during a performance on his television show.

The network objected to a line in the chorus—"wishing, Lord, that I was stoned"—and insisted that Cash change it to "wishing, Lord, that I was home," according to Rosanne Cash: "Well, Kris was in the audience that night. And Dad just couldn't, in good conscience, change that word with the songwriter sitting in the audience. So when he was performing it, he sang, 'Wishing, Lord, that I was stoned,' a little emphasis on 'stoned.' And Kris was very happy. The network was not."

For Johnny Cash, "Sunday Morning Coming Down" became another number-one record. For Kris Kristofferson, it meant his decision to follow his heart to be a songwriter, despite his family's objections, had been the right one. Later, Cash invited the shy janitor who thought he had a froggy voice to come on his show and sing for himself.

"John was always encouraging me; even when he didn't record my songs, he was always on my side," Kristofferson said. "And he put me on his show. That was the first time I was ever in front of people doing that. I was a performer all of a sudden. And I never had to work for a living after that."

ABOVE AND RIGHT *Johnny Cash "was always on my side," Kristofferson said, and after Cash got Kris to perform on his television show, "I never had to work for a living after that."*

THE MAN IN BLACK

Historically, country music has been apolitical. The writers tend to write about love and the everyday problems of the average man. But when they did venture into politics, I think the best description would be "populism"—music that was suspicious of banks and corporations and railroads, or of so-called experts and intellectuals.

But the real upsurge of a political conservatism came in the 1960s, not so much as a defense of the Vietnam War, but as a protest against the protesters—to criticize those "long-haired hippies" who were attacking the war and the other values that some had seen to underlay it.

BILL C. MALONE

Of all the issues that divided the nation during the 1960s, none proved to be more polarizing than the United States' steady escalation of the war in Vietnam. At the outset of the conflict, most country songs—like a majority of Americans—voiced support for the military buildup, just as they had for the nation's involvement in World War Two and Korea.

Johnny Wright had a number-one hit in 1965 with "Hello Vietnam," written by Tom T. Hall, in which a departing soldier tells his sweetheart, "America has heard the bugle call, and you know it involves us, one and all." In 1966, Dave Dudley released "Vietnam Blues," an early song of Kris Kristofferson's, written in response to an antiwar demonstration he encountered while he was still in the Army.

The soldiers serving in Vietnam disproportionately came from country music's core audience: working-class families. Sixty-five percent of all records sold at military bases were country music. And most of the songs dealt less with the politics of the war than with its human cost—to the soldiers as well as those who loved them.

Loretta Lynn's "Dear Uncle Sam" was told by a wife, saying that she needed her husband just as much as the nation did. In "Little Boy Soldier," Wanda Jackson sang about a boy at a train station with his mother, holding a toy gun and a tiny flag, waiting for his father—who returns home in a pine box. Although they didn't deal directly with the war, two of Bobby Bare's songs—"Detroit City" and "500 Miles Away

from Home"—were particularly popular with the troops, Bare said, because "homesickness and nostalgia are one of the strongest emotions there is. On the evening news, I'd see a bunch of soldiers sitting around and singing one of those songs, because they were homesick."

Two of country singer Jan Howard's three sons enlisted. Jimmy, her oldest, was the first to ship off to Vietnam, ahead of his younger brother Corky, and Howard wrote him a long letter, recounting some of her fondest memories of his childhood, and her motherly concern for his safety. Corky

ABOVE *A soldier in Vietnam heads out with his guitar and rifle slung over his shoulder.*

persuaded her to put it to music, and, with Owen Bradley's help in the studio, she managed to make it through one take before saying she couldn't do any more. She sent a tape of it to Jimmy, but never heard back from him; he was killed when his armored personnel carrier hit a land mine south of Da Nang. (Later, she received a letter from a comrade of Jimmy's saying that he had received the tape, listened to it, "and he was so proud that he cried.")

Her middle son, Corky, survived his tour of duty, but her youngest, David, still not old enough to enlist, was so traumatized by his big brother's death that he had a mental breakdown and committed suicide. "So, the Vietnam War took two," Howard said.

When Mel Tillis wrote one of the biggest country songs of the Vietnam era, it was not meant as a political comment. It focused on the emotional turmoil of a veteran, paralyzed from the waist down and confined to his bed at home, watching while his young wife prepares to go out for the night; and though the

narrator refers to "that old crazy Asian war," Tillis's inspiration came from remembering a disabled World War Two veteran he had known twenty years earlier in Florida.

"Ruby (Don't Take Your Love to Town)" was recorded by more than half a dozen artists, before Kenny Rogers and the First Edition's version exploded on the charts in 1969. It was one of those songs, Rogers said, "that really touched your soul. I mean you can just feel the pain from this guy, after he's done everything he could do for his country and come back the way he is, and then to deal with that." One night on the NBC network, after reporting the latest news from Vietnam and the sacrifices made by so many veterans and their families, *The Huntley-Brinkley Report* concluded its broadcast by playing the song in its entirety while showing an empty room.

"Country music is known for patriotic songs and sometimes belligerently patriotic songs," songwriter Alice Randall said. "But what I think is far more significant is some of the greatest anti-war songs ever are country music songs." She pointed to "Ruby" and to "Galveston," a hit song for Glen Campbell. "These are two songs appearing in the Vietnam era. One of them talking about a man in a wheelchair and impotent; the other talking about

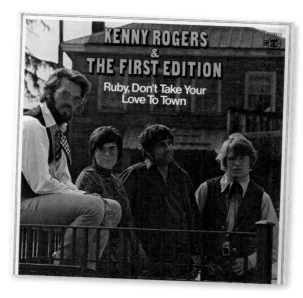

a young man, separated from his lover, and he is so afraid of dying: 'I clean my gun and dream of Galveston.' These are antiwar songs, but they are pro-American songs."

By late 1969, the nation seemed more divided than ever—not just over the war in Vietnam, but also over the many cultural upheavals that had been going on for a decade. America was split between those pushing for faster, more transformative change, and those President Richard Nixon now called "the great silent majority." No one was unaffected.

Kris Kristofferson and Tom T. Hall eventually opposed the war. Willie Nelson wrote one of the few overtly antiwar songs, "Jimmy's Road," after a bandmate got drafted. Lester Flatt abruptly broke with Earl Scruggs over musical disagreements that reflected some of the larger tensions within American society: Scruggs, influenced by his young sons, added Bob Dylan songs and other contemporary material to their repertoire; Flatt had insisted on sticking with traditional bluegrass music.

On November 15, 1969, Scruggs and his sons, along with Charlie Daniels, agreed to help entertain the hundreds of thousands of protesters converging on Washington, D.C., to call for a moratorium on the Vietnam War. "There wasn't any other artist from Nashville," Randy Scruggs remembered. "Dad did it with no reservations at all, of whether he feared a backlash from going there. He felt it was the right thing to do."

At the same time as the march on Washington, a song by Merle Haggard became the number-one country song in the nation, and crossed over to the pop charts, just behind a song by Bob Dylan and just ahead of one by the Byrds. Accounts of how "Okie From Muskogee" came to be written have varied over the years, but most begin with Haggard and his band on

a bus traveling through Oklahoma, while some of them were enjoying a joint. Someone saw a sign for Muskogee and joked, "I bet they don't smoke marijuana in Muskogee." Haggard quickly turned the comment into a song. Although it started as "sort of a joke," historian Bill C. Malone said, it became "a tribute to small-town American life and to those people who paid their taxes and defended their government and fought in the wars. And to Merle's great surprise, the song was a huge hit."

Haggard himself later said that the song was prompted in part by his memories of the discrimination his father had experienced as an "Okie" in California: "The main message, I think, is I'm proud to be something: I'm proud to be black; I'm proud to be white; I'm proud to be an Okie. And there's a lot of people that identify with that." But, he added, "I don't think we realized the impact of the many different messages that it had." They performed it first at an Army base in North Carolina, and the crowd demanded an encore. The next night, in front of an audience of civilians, the same thing happened. "Well," Haggard remembered thinking, "I think we've got something here."

RIGHT *Influenced by his sons Gary (left) and Randy (right), Earl Scruggs broadened his repertoire to include more contemporary songs—and went with them to perform at a massive antiwar demonstration in Washington, D.C.*

ABOVE *Merle Haggard's "Okie From Muskogee" may have been written partly as a joke, but it became a crossover sensation, especially among the so-called Silent Majority who supported the war and despised the protesters.*

Writing about the response to the song during a concert in Ohio, one magazine noted, "Suddenly they are on their feet, berserk, waving flags and stomping and whistling and cheering . . . and for those brief moments the majority isn't silent anymore." Jukebox operators reported extremely heavy play of the record, and speculated that it was from older patrons trying to irritate younger people in bars.

Emmylou Harris, at the time a self-described "quasi-hippie folksinger in New York City," heard Haggard singing it on the radio and thought, she said, "He's gone over to the dark side." Ray Benson, still in his late teens, noted, "We loved Merle Haggard because what a great songwriter and a great singer he is. All of a sudden, he comes out with 'Okie From Muskogee,' and we're going, 'Wait a minute. Wait, what?' Here it is: rednecks, hippies; anti-Vietnam, pro-Vietnam; America, love it or leave it, or America, we think you need to change. Here was Merle Haggard, who we loved, and how could you do this to us? Not only that, everybody in country music knew that Merle smoked marijuana. But the audience didn't."

"Okie From Muskogee" would be Haggard's biggest hit, the rallying cry of the so-called Silent Majority who supported the war in Vietnam. Whether he intended to or not, he found himself in the middle of a storm that was tearing his country apart.

• • •

[Johnny Cash] is at once an underground hero and a favorite of the great mass of adult record buyers. His song material and style of performance cut across practically all key categories and appeal to all markets. . . .

He is the epitome of the music man who embraces realism and draws for his inspiration upon the inexhaustible accounts of his own and his fellow man's experience.

The nation and its history are his reference books.

The people are his audience.

PAUL ACKERMAN,
BILLBOARD MAGAZINE

With one foot planted firmly—and unapologetically—on each side of America's cultural divide, Johnny Cash was at the peak of his popularity as the 1970s began. His popular television show came from the Mother Church of Country Music, and his records played constantly on country radio. But he was also a hero to many members of the counterculture, because of his image as an anti-establishment rebel, his advocacy for prison reform and Native American rights, and his open association with artists from rock and roll, and especially folk music.

He could have a hit with a novelty song, "The One on the Right Is on the Left," poking fun at the fierce political disputes of the time; and then come out with a somber, serious song like "The Man in Black," in which he explained the color

ABOVE AND OPPOSITE *Johnny Cash sang for the troops but opposed the war, and when President Nixon invited him to sing at the White House, he performed "What Is Truth," a defense of young people challenging the status quo, instead of the song Nixon had requested, "Welfare Cadillac," which Cash considered demeaning to poor people.*

of his wardrobe by saying it was a reminder of all the Americans left behind and forgotten by mainstream society.

He and June made a tour of American military bases in Vietnam, performing and visiting hospitals, and he wrote a song about the experience, "Singing in Vietnam Talkin' Blues." "We did our best to let 'em know that we care," it said, "for every last one of 'em that's over there—whether we belong over there or not. They're our boys, and they belong over here somewhere."

He told his brother that American soldiers "may be dying for a cause that isn't just," and he would sometimes flash a peace sign during a concert. But he consistently refused to publicly criticize President Nixon for continuing the war. A reporter asked Cash if that didn't make him a hawk. "No," he answered, "but when you watch the helicopters bringing in the wounded, that might make you a dove with claws."

"That was him in a nutshell," said Rosanne Cash. "He could hold two opposing thoughts at the same time and believe in both of them with the same degree of passion and power. As Kris says, he's a 'walking contradiction.' And he was."

President Nixon invited him to perform at the White House, and, though many of his younger fans objected, Cash said he was honored to accept. Then he learned that the president wanted him to sing Guy Drake's song "Welfare Cadillac," which was popular on country radio at the time, but disparaged poor people who relied on public assistance to survive.

Cash was in a bind between his respect for the office of president and his disgust with the song. "He felt he couldn't betray himself by singing 'Welfare Cadillac,'" according to Rosanne. "It would be the antithesis of who he was—a proponent, a strong supporter of the downtrodden, the poor, the prisoner, the Native American. This was part of who he was. Even though it was the president, he couldn't say yes to that. He did it very respectfully. But then, instead, he sang one of his own songs. He stayed true to himself."

The song Cash performed was "What Is Truth," a full-throated defense of young people who challenged the status quo—from the music they danced to and the length of their hair to questions about war and the need to speak out against injustice. "Yeah, 'What is Truth,'" Rosanne said. "'The lonely voice of youth cries, what is truth?' He loved young people. He said, 'I can learn more from a nineteen-year-old than I can from someone my own age.'"

WHAT CAN YOU DO TO ME NOW?

Johnny Gimble once said that there's only two songs ever written, "The Star-Spangled Banner" and the "blues." Bands that I liked a lot, country music players play jazz.

Bob Wills and the Texas Playboys, a whole lot of jazz musicians there. Johnny Gimble was a great jazz player, but he was also a great country music player. A lot of the great country music players could also play great jazz.

WILLIE NELSON

For Willie Nelson, the late 1960s proved to be a frustrating time, both personally and professionally. Two marriages ended in divorce, fueled in part by troubles with alcohol. And though other artists, from Patsy Cline to Ray Price, had enormous hits with songs he had written, his own career as a singer seemed hopelessly stuck.

Nashville didn't know quite what to make of him. At his debut as a member of the *Grand Ole Opry*, the announcer introduced him as "*Woody* Nelson," and he quit the show after a year. Like the man himself, Nelson's music was impossible to pigeonhole—influenced as much by the jazz stylist Django Reinhardt as it was by his other hero, Ernest Tubb. His vocal phrasing was unlike anybody else's. His guitar was different, too—a gut-string Martin he had electrified and lovingly named "Trigger," as a reminder of Roy Rogers's trusted horse.

"This didn't sound anything like Nashville—and Willie didn't want it to," said Tom T. Hall. "If you listen to him sing, he sort of has a jazz approach to his singing and his playing," said songwriter Bob McDill. "He's obviously influenced by a lot more people than what he might have heard on the *Grand Ole Opry* growing up." Fred Foster had this advice for him: "People hadn't caught up to him. I said, 'Willie, they're going to catch up someday. Sooner or later, they'll dig you, they'll know what you're doing. Right now, they don't know what you're doing.'"

"I didn't think it was that bad," Nelson joked. "I was having fun being rejected. You know, they liked my songs, but they didn't care for my singing and phrasing, a little crazy, so to speak. I was probably stubborn, and not really wanting to do anything anybody wanted me to do. But they weren't all wrong."

Chet Atkins, his producer at RCA, struggled to come up with album ideas that would sell. Nothing seemed to work. He had recorded fourteen albums, without any breakthrough hits. Atkins, Nelson would say, was "the ultimate Nashville insider [who] saw me as an outsider writing outsider songs and singing in an outsider style." But "even though his vision and mine were different," Nelson said, "I couldn't get mad at a man who believed so deeply in my talent."

But if he couldn't get mad, he did get discouraged. Late one night at Tootsies Orchid Lounge, he walked out onto Broadway Avenue and lay down in the middle of the street. "Well, I had a little bit to drink and I decided I'd go out and lay down on the highway," he remembered. "It was right there on Broadway in Nashville at like two in the morning. I don't know what happened up until then. I just woke up a-laying on the highway. I'm surprised I'm still here."

With his songwriting royalties, Nelson bought a farm east of Nashville, and started raising hogs and cattle, trying for a while to concentrate solely on his writing. But his true love was performing his music in front of people, so he and his band were soon back out on the road. One tour took them fifteen thousand miles in just eighteen days; on another, they drove from a concert in Connecticut to their next one in California. During the long trips, he began switching from alcohol to marijuana.

His favorite performances were always in his native Texas. "We were stars in Texas," he said. "In Nashville I was looked upon as a loser singer." In the Texas beer joints, he said, "I wouldn't have to change a thing. And they all liked what I did. So I knew that what I was doing, I could do it forever, whether I pleased everybody in Nashville, or not."

Back in Music City, he and his friend Hank Cochran wrote seven songs together one winter night. One of them, "What Can You Do to

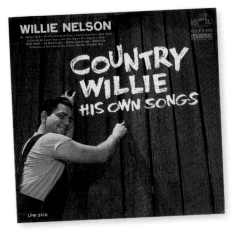

OPPOSITE *At his debut on the* Opry, *Willie Nelson was introduced as "Woody Nelson."*

RIGHT FROM TOP TO BOTTOM *While other artists had top hits with Nelson's songs, his label struggled unsuccessfully to come up with a sound and image for him as a solo artist.*

Me Now," described a man at the end of his rope, filled with both existential sadness and a determination to overcome it.

Not long after the song was finished his farmhouse caught fire. Nelson told his nephew to drive the family car into the garage—so he could collect insurance on it after it went up in flames, too. Then Nelson rushed into the burning house and came out with two guitar cases containing his most prized possessions. One was his gut-string guitar called Trigger. The other contained two pounds of Colombian marijuana.

He rebuilt his farmhouse, but his singing career was still seemingly going nowhere. "Everybody [in Nashville] was doing whatever they were told to do," Tom T. Hall said. "Willie went back to Texas and said, 'To hell with it, I'm just going to be Willie Nelson.' So he taught everybody a lesson." Back in his native Texas, Nelson would start over—and revive his career.

ABOVE *Frustrated by the trajectory of his singing career, Nelson bought a farm and raised livestock, while living off his songwriting royalties.*

BELOW *Nelson in a Nashville recording studio; with his singing career stalled, he decided to move back to Texas and start over.*

WHY ME, LORD?

I wouldn't want to go to a church that didn't let sinners in. I don't belong there.

LARRY GATLIN

From the time he was a little boy growing up in west Texas, Larry Gatlin sang gospel music. Every weekend, he and his two younger brothers—and later their sister—were driven by their mother in a Rambler station wagon to perform at multiple churches, captivating the congregations with their close harmonies.

At the age of twenty-three, Gatlin moved to Nashville, where he and Kris Kristofferson soon became friends, while each one held janitor jobs to make ends meet as they tried to sell their songs and get recording contracts. Gatlin struggled with drug addictions and alcoholism, but never lost his faith. He regularly attended the Evangel Temple just outside of Nashville, where the pastor was the colorful Jimmie Rodgers Snow, son of country star Hank Snow and namesake of his father's idol, Jimmie Rodgers. Snow also hosted the *Grand Ole Gospel Time,* broadcast each week from the Ryman Auditorium.

One Sunday at the church, June Carter Cash heard Gatlin sing a song he had written, "Help Me," and told her husband about it. Cash came the next week to hear it himself, and introduced himself to Gatlin after the service. "And he said, 'I like that song, boy,'" Gatlin remembered. "He said, 'We're

making a movie about the life of Jesus, and we're writing some songs over there at Columbia Studio tomorrow. Could you come help us?'"

It was part of Cash's lifelong commitment to the religion his mother had instilled in him as a young boy. "My dad always kept a gospel song in his stage show, for his whole life," Rosanne Cash said. "I always sense that he felt an obligation to his mother. Not to say his faith wasn't powerful. It was. But that was something that was for his mom."

When Cash got his national television show, he had told the network he wanted to include a gospel segment in each episode. The executives were against it, but Cash persisted, even when some local stations began complaining that the program featured too much religion and seemed out of step with the times. In response to the network's concerns, Cash doubled down. Over the producers' objections, he made an on-camera profession of his faith and described how the forces of good and evil, God and the Devil, battled over the

LEFT AND BELOW *Larry Gatlin was brought up as a gospel singer in west Texas before coming to Nashville. Singing his song "Help Me" at the Evangel Temple near Nashville, where a number of country stars worshipped, caught the attention of Johnny Cash. The church's pastor was Jimmie Rodgers Snow, who was named in honor of Jimmie Rodgers, the hero of his father, Hank Snow.*

lives of people like himself. Then he dedicated an entire program to gospel music and invited the evangelist Reverend Billy Graham to preach on it.

Cash's feature film project sprang from the same religious impulse. The ninety-minute film, *The Gospel Road: A Story of Jesus*, was shot on location in Israel. Cash appeared as the narrator, occasionally singing some songs; June Carter Cash played the role of Mary Magdalene. Neither it, nor the double-album soundtrack that Larry Gatlin helped with, was commercially successful. The record stalled on the charts, the worst showing of any Cash album up to that point; and Cash never recouped his half-million-dollar personal investment in the film. He didn't care. It was, he later said, his "proudest work."

Meanwhile, one Sunday morning, Kris Kristofferson ended up at Evangel Temple, too, after driving through the night back to Nashville from a concert with Connie Smith. "We talked all night, because my goal was to get him to go to church with me," Smith remembered. "He hadn't been in church in twenty years. And I wanted him to go to church with me."

Kristofferson had not been raised in the evangelical tradition, and felt a little out of his element. He listened intently as Larry Gatlin sang "Help Me." Then, he recalled, Reverend Snow began to preach:

I can't remember how he phrased it, but something like, if you felt like you needed to be saved, to come down to the front of the church. I remember thinking, "That will be the day." And the next thing I knew, I found myself getting up and walking down with a few other people to, it turned out, kneel down.

And he asked me, when I was there, he said, "Are you ready to accept this?" And I said, "I don't know." And he says, "Get down." And he pushed me down to the kneeling position. And I can't even remember the things he was saying. I was weeping. It was an experience unlike anything I'd gone through before. And then the words to the song came to me shortly after. It was straight from the heart.

The song Kristofferson wrote that day, "Why Me"—melodically simple, lyrically straightforward—is a sinner's admission of his failings and his surprise that he might be forgiven. "Why me, Lord," it begins, "what have I ever done to deserve even one of the pleasures I've known." He played it for Connie Smith and Larry Gatlin soon after completing it, and the three of them sang it on Jimmie Rodgers Snow's *Grand Ole Gospel Time* before the week was out. Kristofferson's recording of it, with Gatlin singing harmony, would become his biggest hit as a solo artist. "It's still kind of a mystery to me," Kristofferson said. "I sing it every night I sing. I close the show with it now."

ABOVE *Larry Gatlin helped Johnny Cash with the music for* The Gospel Road, *a feature film shot in Israel. Neither the film nor the soundtrack recouped Cash's half-million-dollar investment, but he considered it his "proudest work."*

LEFT *During Reverend Snow's (left)* Grand Ole Gospel Time *at the Ryman, Kris Kristofferson (right) and Gatlin sing "Why Me," the song Kristofferson had written after hearing Snow preach.*

A BETTER WORLD AWAITING

In the summer of 1971, American combat troops were being withdrawn from Vietnam, but the divides at home were as great as ever. That summer, a group of long-haired musicians from Southern California began setting up in the Woodland Studios in East Nashville, across the Cumberland River from Music Row. It was the Nitty Gritty Dirt Band. Their version of Jerry Jeff Walker's song "Mr. Bojangles" had been a Top Ten pop hit, but they were still trying to find their own sound.

"We were not a country band," said John McEuen, a member of the band. "I was the banjo player. We played a bluegrass-sounding kind of music, but it wasn't bluegrass. We played jug band music; we played some folk-rock music." Now they were in Music City to cut a record with McEuen's banjo-playing hero, Earl Scruggs. With his help, they started recruiting other legends in country and bluegrass music to join them.

Merle Travis, from Kentucky, had been in the business since the 1930s. Songs he had written included classics like "Sixteen Tons" and "Dark as a Dungeon," but he was best known for popularizing a syncopated guitar style, called "Travis picking," that had inspired a generation of guitarists. Doc Watson was a blind guitar player and folk singer from North Carolina. He had named his own son Merle, in Travis's honor—even though the two had never met until they showed up for the sessions. Jimmy Martin, from East Tennessee, who had been a member of Bill Monroe's band in the late 1940s and now called himself "the King of Bluegrass," joined in, as did Vassar Clements, a fiddle prodigy from South Carolina.

Maybelle Carter also agreed to take part. Her roots reached back to the earliest recordings of country music in the 1920s, but recently she had been touring with some of her grandchildren and had no prejudices against young people's musical tastes. (Carlene Carter, one of her grandchildren, remembered them practicing for a show, and Maybelle suggested "One Toke Over the Line, Sweet Jesus"; she thought it was a gospel song.)

ABOVE *Maybelle Carter, Randy Scruggs, and Doc Watson in the recording studio for* Will the Circle Be Unbroken

But Roy Acuff proved harder to get. "We sat in Acuff's office for about an hour and a half, hearing his history of country music," McEuen said. "Roy Acuff was 'the King of Country Music,' and he thought everybody had a right to his opinion. And he'd let you know what it was, just so you didn't miss it. And a staunch Republican—ran for governor—and he's meeting with a bunch of hippies." Acuff told a reporter doing an article about the newcomers to Nashville, "I don't know if they're young boys or old men. If I ever saw them again without their hair, I'd never know them."

Acuff wasn't the only one in Nashville initially distrustful about the Dirt Band and their intentions. Bill Monroe

turned them down. And many industry insiders were perplexed about the project, because they considered the artists now being gathered at the studio as more or less washed up, far beyond their prime.

Once the sessions began, with William McEuen producing, it became clear that the West Coast hippies weren't interested in having country and bluegrass artists accompany *them*; the Nitty Gritty Dirt Band wanted to back up the legends. Together, they started recording some classic songs that hadn't been widely popular in a generation.

"For us, it was like going back to 1928 and making early records; we wanted to make an 'old' record," John McEuen said. "We set up in a big studio in a circle, facing each other," added Jeff Hanna, another band member. "All of us on chairs with the great microphones and a two-track tape. So there were no baffles between us. And it was so warm and so immediate. I think the idea was to try to recreate a living room or a back porch."

They kept at it for six days, performing one song after another, usually in one or two takes: half a dozen Carter Family standards, like "Keep on the Sunny Side" and "Wildwood Flower"; a few of Merle

CLOCKWISE FROM TOP LEFT *Vassar Clements, the fiddle prodigy; Merle Travis, who had a style of guitar picking named after him. Guitarist and folk singer Doc Watson (right) met Travis for the first time at the session and said he had named his own son Merle, in Travis's honor.*

Travis's hits; banjo tunes written by Earl Scruggs, and other instrumentals that allowed the collection of talented musicians to shine; even some classics of Hank Williams.

Everyone involved felt a special magic in the studio. "It was more [like] being at your home and just having a 'picking party,'" said Randy Scruggs, who was there with his father. "It just felt like a big family." "The Vietnam War was raging, and marches were going on, and churches were being burned, and the president was lying," said John McEuen. But with that turmoil going on around them, he said, "it came together in the studio. The music transcended everything."

made famous from the stage of the Ryman Auditorium back in the 1940s: "The Precious Jewel" and "Wreck on the Highway." For the album's climax, they chose another Carter Family song, "Will the Circle Be Unbroken," which would become the name of the album. Everyone joined in.

"I think the song 'Will the Circle Be Unbroken' shows hope," McEuen said. "It shows a better future may be ahead. Things may be bad, but they'll get better. 'Undertaker, please drive slow.' That's my mama going. But she'll be okay."

"America was in the midst of a great upheaval, especially the youth of America in the early seventies," Jeff Hanna said:

I think because country music looked a certain way and represented a conservative view, sort of the antithesis of what most kids in America were, you were choosing up sides.

To get in this recording studio and make a record with folks that kind of bridged that cultural gap and

On the last day, Roy Acuff himself showed up—and asked to hear a little of what they had already recorded. "He said something like 'How would you boys describe this music?'" Hanna recalled. "And we're going, 'Well, uh, it's mountain music,' or 'It's kind of bluegrass,' or 'It's got kind of an Appalachian vibe.' And he said, 'It ain't nothing but country.'"

Then Acuff led them through some of the songs he had

The sessions—and the album it produced—brought two generations together at a fractious time for the nation. Jimmy Ibbotson (top, at left) and Jeff Hanna sing with Roy Acuff. Maybelle Carter (above, at left) and Merle Travis play, while Hanna listens.

that generation gap, that was significant. We heard stories later where a good friend of mine said that he and his dad were kind of estranged. And they sat down and bonded on that *Circle* album.

Released as a triple-disc set, *Will the Circle Be Unbroken* got little play on country radio. But *Rolling Stone* magazine praised it; some progressive FM stations started featuring it; and, especially on college campuses around the nation, it caught on, spread by word of mouth. Eventually it would be selected for the Grammy Hall of Fame and the Library of Congress's prestigious National Recording Registry and ultimately be recognized as one of the most iconic albums in country music history. When it sold half a million copies to reach the status of a gold record, John McEuen went to see Maybelle Carter to personally give her the good news: "She said, 'Well, I never thought that many people even heard my old songs.'"

ABOVE *Jimmy Martin (on guitar) and Vassar Clements*

BELOW *John McEuen and Earl Scruggs relax as they listen to the playback of* Will the Circle Be Unbroken, *which would eventually be recognized as one of the landmark albums in American music history.*

7

ARE YOU SURE HANK DONE IT THIS WAY?

I don't like fences built around music, because fences, sure they keep things out, but they also don't let things in.

BILL ANDERSON

I think the lines are only imaginary and that you have to put them there, because they're not there in the beginning. It's music, you know? You can't say it's this, that, or the other. It's not a Democrat or Republican.

WILLIE NELSON

OPPOSITE, CLOCKWISE FROM TOP LEFT *Townes Van Zandt, Emmylou Harris, Waylon Jennings, Dolly Parton*

THOUGH ITS ROOTS were older than the nation itself, by the 1970s, country music was just fifty years old as a commercial enterprise. Throughout that half century, it had struggled with the tensions pitting its working-class origins and hillbilly image against its yearning to be accepted by the mainstream of American culture; between hewing to the music's traditions versus branching out in new directions.

Now those tensions would come to a boil. In Nashville, industry leaders would redouble their push for both respectability and bigger sales by further smoothing out the music's sound, even if it meant offending some hard-core purists. "I think there's a paradox that's always existed in country music," said historian Bill C. Malone. "How much change do you embrace? And how much change can you make without completely obliterating what you were and where you came from?"

From its beginnings, country music had never been one style. Like all art forms, it had always resisted being confined within arbitrary borders. And like all artists, its greatest stars had always pushed the boundaries to their limits. "As fans, we may want them to do the old stuff; we're unhappy when they branch out into something new," Malone added. "But

musicians, they're innovative. They're experimental. They want to do something fresh, something new. Of course, the question is, where does it end? When does it cease to be country when they've made all these changes?"

During the 1970s and early 1980s, defining country music would be debated as never before. But the argument would spark one of its most vibrant eras, making room for different voices and new attitudes—and out on the edges, where different types of music meet and mingle, and art is always created, somehow find a dramatically larger audience.

Meanwhile, a musical prodigy from Mississippi would somehow find himself in the middle of it all.

• • •

When I was growing up on Route 8, Kosciusko Road, in Philadelphia, Mississippi, the Gulf, Mobile & Ohio ran right behind our house. It sounded like the train was coming through my bedroom at night, and I loved it.

I used to dream about getting on that train and riding and just going to . . . I didn't want to go to New York, I didn't want to go to Hollywood, I wanted to go to Nashville and play that kind of music that touched my heart.

MARTY STUART

From the time he was a little boy, growing up in Mississippi in the 1960s, music was a central part of Marty Stuart's life. His mother had named him after her favorite country singer, Marty Robbins, and gave him a cowboy guitar when he was only three. By the age of nine he had mastered the instrument and performed wherever he could.

The first record he ever owned was by his musical hero, Johnny Cash. "He was my Beatles," Stuart said. "His songs took me to places. They took me on mind trips away from my bedroom on Kosciusko Road."

The highlight of his eleventh year was meeting country star Connie Smith, after hearing her perform at the local fairgrounds. He got her autograph and his picture taken with Smith—and vowed to his mother that he would marry her when he got old enough.

At a different concert, Bill Monroe ignited a passion for the mandolin. Stuart got Monroe's autograph and told the

OPPOSITE *Marty Stuart, still in diapers, tries out the piano with his grandmother Velma Moore in Philadelphia, Mississippi.*

LEFT *Marty Stuart shows an album of his hero Johnny Cash to his sister Jennifer, 1968.*

Father of Bluegrass that he wanted to play the instrument "just like you." Monroe gave the boy his mandolin pick and said, "This right here will help you out," Stuart remembered. "And I carried that pick to school with me every day like it was Kryptonite in my pocket. I felt special because I had something in my pocket that nobody else had and nobody else knew about."

Stuart was soon good enough on the mandolin to impress a member of Lester Flatt's bluegrass band, who happened to hear him play and suggested that someday the boy might travel with the band. The chance came in 1972, when he was thirteen. He got permission from his parents to travel to Nashville and try out for the group. The only disappointment was that he had to take a bus, not the train. It dropped him off in the decaying downtown of Nashville, not far from the Ryman Auditorium, at two in the morning.

"Downtown Nashville was really seedy at that time. Two o'clock in the morning, on any night, around the Ryman, was not the place to be," Stuart recalled. "You had a lot of peep shows and honky tonks, late-night restaurants with a real edgy atmosphere. It was not a place to be found after dark, unless you had evil and sin and sorriness on your mind. I walked around the corner of the Greyhound station and there was the Ryman Auditorium, the building that I knew so much about. And it was tired and it was weary, and the paint was cracked on [the doors] and some of the windows were out. But it looked beautiful to me."

Stuart's skill on the mandolin impressed Lester Flatt, and within a week he brought the boy along to perform on the *Grand Ole Opry*. "Walking into the *Grand Ole Opry* with Lester Flatt, toting his guitar, was like walking into the Vatican with the pope," Stuart said. "It was like that old scene in *The Wizard of Oz*, where the world went from black-and-white to color. That's what it was like for me. Everything I'd ever

dreamed of came true when I was thirteen years old:

And I was so little, I had to hold the mandolin way up in the air like I was shooting birds, or something. At the end of the song, the crowd just kept applauding and applauding and applauding. And I thought I had done something wrong, and I looked at Lester and I said, "What do I do?"

He said, "Do it again."

And my life changed at the end of that song. I knew I had found a home. And I knew I was where I belonged and that was where I wanted to be.

CENTER *When young Marty Stuart (second from left) and the Musical Rangers performed at the Neshoba County Fair in 1970, they had to lower the microphone for him to reach it.*

ABOVE *Marty with his instrument of choice, the mandolin*

GOODBYE, DEAR OLE RYMAN

By the time young Marty Stuart debuted on the *Grand Ole Opry*, the decision had already been made that, because of its condition and location, the Ryman Auditorium was no longer suited for an attraction drawing 400,000 tourists a year. The former tabernacle was more than three-quarters of a century old and surrounded by Nashville's downtown, which, like the centers of so many other American cities, was suffering from neglect.

National Life and Accident Insurance Company, owner of radio station WSM and the *Opry*, was thrilled that thousands of fans poured into town each week. But executives worried that the aging building, with its wooden pews and sawdust on the floor, might be a fire trap, and that the increasingly shabby neighborhood around the Ryman would reflect badly on the image that the company—and everyone else in the country music industry—was trying to project. "The insur-

ance company got very sensitive as time went on," said Bud Wendell, the *Opry* manager at the time. "It was really a PR problem."

Wendell had also been fielding complaints from the performers about their cramped working conditions: one tiny changing room for female artists; a men's bathroom squeezed under a stairway, so artists had to hunch over when using it. "No other musicians would put up with this place," said Roy Acuff, the unofficial King of Country Music, who had been an *Opry* star since the 1930s. "Most of my memories of the Ryman," he added, "are of misery, sweating out there on [the] stage, the audience suffering too."

Summers were the worst for artists and audiences alike, when temperatures inside the un-air-conditioned brick building rose to 100 degrees or higher. (The *Opry* did a brisk business selling small fans for a quarter, all emblazoned

---

ABOVE *Stuart performs with Lester Flatt and the Nashville Grass onstage at the Ryman.*

with National Life's name and logo.) Marty Stuart remembered Lester Flatt suggesting a solution to Wendell: "He said, 'Bud, we've talked about it amongst ourselves, and why don't some of us older artists pitch in and maybe come up with an air-conditioning system?' And Bud said something to the effect, 'Well, we've checked into that, Lester, and it's a little over $2 million.' And Lester said, 'Ain't as hot as I thought.'"

Wendell's bosses decided that the only solution was to build a new home for the *Opry*. On more than three hundred acres of land, six miles up the Cumberland River from the downtown, they spent more than $65 million to build an elaborate theme park, Opryland USA; a sprawling, 615-room hotel; and the spacious Grand Ole Opry House—fully air-conditioned, with comfortable seating for 4,400 people, twelve dressing rooms for the artists, and a separate, state-of-the-art television studio.

By March 1974, everything was ready. "There were some artists who thought this was the grandest thing that's ever happened," according to Wendell. "'We're going to have a

parking place. We're going to have dressing rooms. We're going to have toilets. We're going to have lockers—all of this is going to be wonderful.' Then you had some artists who said, 'This is going to be the end of the *Grand Ole Opry*. It's in this house [the Ryman]. It's in this floor. It's in these boards. It's in this stage. We can't leave all of this and go to a new house out there. It won't be the *Grand Ole Opry*.' So you had two sides to it."

On March 15, the Ryman hosted its final *Grand Ole Opry*. The evening was still vivid in Bill Anderson's memory forty

---

ABOVE *By the early 1970s, the area around the Ryman had decayed. An adult cinema was operating across the street. The owners wanted to move to the suburbs.*

OPPOSITE, TOP *Roy Acuff comforts a crying Minnie Pearl as they say goodbye to the Ryman.*

OPPOSITE, BOTTOM *Bill Anderson performing "Po' Folks" on the last night of the* Grand Ole Opry *at the Ryman.*

years later: "It was on a Friday night, and we were going to open at the Opry House the next night, on Saturday. There was a feeling there I've never felt at the *Opry* before. It was a little bit of sadness, a lot of sadness. It was a little bit of joy. There was anticipation. There was a fear of the unknown. There was like, 'Well, where do we go from here? Are we cutting off our nose to spite our face here? Is this really what we ought to be doing?'"

Anderson sang his hit song "Po' Folks" to the sellout crowd. Hank Locklin performed a song he had written for the occasion, "Goodbye, Dear Ole Ryman." Roy Acuff did "Wabash Cannonball," before introducing his old friend Minnie Pearl.

After eight half-hour segments of the *Opry*, the Reverend Jimmie Rodgers Snow took over for the final *Grand Ole Gospel Time*. His father, the legendary Hank Snow, was a featured guest, as were Mother Maybelle Carter and her daughters—along with the man who had once been banned from the Ryman for knocking out its footlights and who then brought it greater fame by hosting his national television show from its stage: Johnny Cash.

The last song performed late that evening was the old Carter Family classic, "Will the Circle Be Unbroken."

Listening to it all was a young reporter named Garrison Keillor, who had come to the Ryman to cover the

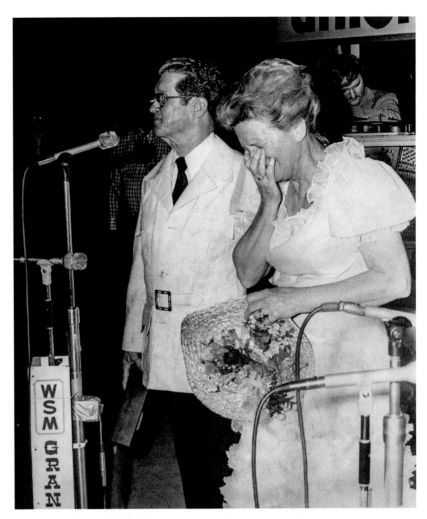

event for *The New Yorker*. He had grown up in Minnesota, 860 miles away, glued to his family radio every Saturday night to hear the *Grand Ole Opry*—to listen to its music and especially to Minnie Pearl's stories from the make-believe village of Grinder's Switch. On this night, Keillor worked his way into the broadcast engineers' booth, leaned against the back wall, and closed his eyes. "It was good," he wrote, "to let the *Opry* go out the same way it had first come to me, through the air in the dark."

Then it was over. As the music faded, and the crowd quickly dispersed, workmen wasted no time stripping the Ryman of some of its memories before sentimental fans would have a chance to. The sign directing guests to the balcony called the Confederate Gallery came down; then the one over the front door that had welcomed so many people for so many years. In the Mother Church of Country Music, the pews were now empty.

The next night, the *Opry* debuted from its brand-new home in the suburbs. To make the connection clear between the past and the present, at the center of the new stage was a wooden circle, cut from the Ryman's floorboards. For the opening, a movie from the 1940s with Roy Acuff singing "Wabash Cannonball" was projected on the curtain; then the curtain lifted, Bill Anderson remembered, and "here's Roy Acuff, now in the '70s, still singing 'Wabash Cannonball.' It

never missed a beat. I stood there and cried. I can almost sit here and cry just thinking about it."

Many of the artists that night were the same ones who had performed twenty-four hours earlier at the Ryman. Anderson sang "Po' Folks" once more. But this audience reflected country music's rising prominence in America's mainstream culture and was filled with VIPs: thirteen congressmen, two senators, and four governors, including Alabama's George Wallace, who had been a presidential candidate two years earlier.

The guest of honor, however, was the man who had won the election: President Richard Nixon. In Washington, he was embroiled in the Watergate scandal and impeachment proceedings; in Nashville, he seemed happy to find a

---

ABOVE *Johnny Cash and June Carter Cash performed on* Grand Ole Gospel Time, *the last show at the Ryman before it closed. With them were Johnny's daughter Rosanne (center holding microphone) and June's daughters Carlene Carter (right) and Rosie Nix (left).*

OPPOSITE, TOP *Workers pack away the* Opry's *welcome sign as they close the Ryman.*

OPPOSITE, BOTTOM *As a connection to the* Opry's *past, a circle of wood from the Ryman stage was set into the floor of the brand-new* Grand Ole Opry House.

friendly audience to help him celebrate his wife Pat's birthday. Onstage, Nixon played the piano—serenading the First Lady with "Happy Birthday" and "My Wild Irish Rose," then leading the audience in a verse of "God Bless America." Roy Acuff tried to teach the president how to use the yo-yo . . . without success.

Minnie Pearl was introduced by country stalwart Ernest Tubb. "I've waited so long to come on," she told the high-toned crowd, "my dress has done went out of style." She said she was delayed by a handsome Secret Service agent who "frisked me all up and down—so I turned around and went out and came back in again."

The show—and the move to the suburbs—proved to be a huge success. Three-quarters of a million people would come to the *Opry* in the next year, and 1.4 million would attend Opryland. Four months after the opening, Garrison Keillor would launch his own radio program, *A Prairie Home Companion*, on Minnesota Public Radio, and captivate audiences with tales from his own make-believe town of Lake Wobegon.

LEFT *Minnie Pearl and Roy Acuff welcome the crowd to the expanded and modern new home of the* Opry, *March 16, 1974.*

ABOVE *President Richard Nixon, the guest of honor, played the piano on opening night.*

I WILL ALWAYS LOVE YOU

Dolly got smart; I guess she came smart. I think Dolly learned that she was not going to go any further with her career as long as she was in Porter's shadow.

RALPH EMERY

Her voice was spellbinding. What I think people are drawn to the most is it sounds exactly like where she's from, you know? That's exactly what you'd think East Tennessee is supposed to sound like. And then, on top of that voice, you have one of the greatest songwriters in history.

VINCE GILL

By 1974, Dolly Parton had been performing on Porter Wagoner's syndicated television show for seven years, and during all seven of them, Wagoner had exerted tight control over her career. Wagoner's own star as a country singer was fading—his duet albums with Parton outsold his own solo records—but on the road and in the studio, he insisted on being in charge. "I signed the checks," he said, "so we did things my way."

With Wagoner producing, Parton recorded the old Jimmie Rodgers tune from 1930, "Mule Skinner Blues," which became her first Top Ten single. (Wagoner cracked the bullwhip used as a sound effect in the background.) "There are songs like the 'Mule Skinner Blues' that are just classics," Parton said. "From Jimmie Rodgers and his version of it to Bill Monroe's, to Rose Maddox's, there are songs that go all the way back. Somebody hears that and Daddy loved that and Grandpa loved that, and they pass that song down. It's a little like an heirloom. It's something that they can hold in the family. They're like keepsakes."

But Wagoner also encouraged Parton to record more and more of the songs she had written herself, starting with "Joshua," which became her first number-one country hit, and then "Coat of Many Colors" and "Jolene." In the early 1970s, Parton had five number-one country solo hits, all of them self-written; Wagoner had none. He was competitive and possessive, and industry insiders could see tensions building.

"I think Porter had a real hard time after other people started recording my songs, and I was getting to be pretty popular," Parton said. "It was his show. I wasn't trying to hog it, but I just kind of carved out a little place for myself. But it was a love-hate relationship. We fought like cats and dogs; we were just both very passionate people. There was no way that I wasn't going to do what I was going to do. And no way I was going to not do what he thought I was going to do."

But every time she broached the topic of striking out on her own, Wagoner wouldn't hear of it. "Porter dreamed of me staying with his show forever, and I dreamed of having my own show," Parton said. "I wrote more and more songs, and dreamed bigger and bigger dreams," she added, and "nothing and nobody has ever been able to stand in the way of me and my dreams."

Finally, she decided, "He's not going to listen to me, because I've said it over and over. And so, I thought, 'Do what you do best. Just write a song.' So I wrote the song, took it back in the next day, and I said, 'Porter, sit down. I've got something I have to sing to you.' So I sang it, and he was sitting at his desk and he was crying. He said, 'That's the best thing you ever wrote. Okay, you can go, but only if I can produce that record.'"

The song was "I Will Always Love You." Released a few months after she and Wagoner announced in early 1974 that Parton

LEFT AND OPPOSITE *Dolly Parton stayed with Porter Wagoner's show for seven years before finally going off on her own. As a way to honor what he had done for her—and to soften the blow of her leaving—she wrote "I Will Always Love You."*

was going off on her own, it would go on to become her best-selling song. "It was an anthem to Porter Wagoner," Ralph Emery said. "She wrote it, I think, because she felt guilty for leaving him, because he had done so much for her. But she felt if she didn't leave him, she would just remain 'Porter's Girl Singer.'"

Holly Williams, the granddaughter of Hank Williams and a songwriter herself, considers it a classic: "Writing a beautiful song from the most simple words—'I will always love you, I will always love you, I will always love you,' when she sings it over and over, it's just something that any of us can relate to. She was able, like Hank Williams, to take the most basic one-liners, 'I will always love you,' and turn it into a masterpiece."

WE'RE GONNA HOLD ON

Porter Wagoner and Dolly Parton had broken up, but other famous duet teams were staying together. There was Bill Anderson and Jan Howard, who sometimes wrote each other's songs. Dottie West, who had been in Nashville for more than a decade, joined with Kenny Rogers, who had recently arrived. Loretta Lynn teamed up with Conway Twitty, the

former rockabilly star who had returned to country music; together, they released nearly a dozen duet albums, had five number-one singles, and were named Duo of the Year ten times by the *Music City News*.

But no couple captivated audiences—and headlines—more than George Jones and Tammy Wynette. "I think people really felt like they were getting a lot of the true story and getting the story of their own lives when this incredibly talented male singer was singing with this beautiful and incredibly talented female singer, and they're singing songs like 'We're Gonna Hold On,'" said Bill Anderson. "Okay, if they can hold on, me and old Fred can hold on, too, or me and old Ethel, you know? And I think people saw their own lives in these George and Tammy songs."

When they got married back in 1969, both Tammy Wynette and George Jones were already well-known artists. Billed as "Mr. and Mrs. Country Music," they drew large, adoring crowds on tour—and their producer, Billy Sherrill, made sure they fed their fans a steady string of duet albums. "They brought the greatest country talent that I'd ever dreamed of working with," Sherrill said. "Tammy was one of these people, you'd sing a new song to her one time and she knows it. 'The Possum' would have to think about it a while. I see Tammy looking at George's lips, trying to figure out if he's ever going to do it twice the same way and doing her damnedest to phrase with him. And him with that little beady-eyed possum look about him, loving every second of it."

"When we were onstage," Jones said, "we were in our own little heaven." Offstage, he lavished her with gifts—expensive jewelry and clothes, automobiles, a houseboat named *The First Lady*, and three different houses in as many years. She encouraged him to grow his hair longer, in keeping with the times, and, as a former hairdresser, insisted on taking care of it each day herself.

But this was a third marriage for both of them, and it was never tranquil. His binge drinking made him unpredictable and uncontrollable; she could be equally volatile. "He nipped," she said, "and I nagged." One night, hoping to keep him from sneaking out to the bar, Wynette hid the keys to their large collection of cars, as well as to his riding lawnmower. After she was asleep, Jones hot-wired the lawnmower and drove it six miles to the nearest tavern.

Jeannie Seely was friends with both of them: "I have to say, I thought, 'Oh, my. I don't know whether this can work or not.' I truly think that George and Tammy had a great love affair. I think that was very obvious, how much in love

LEFT *Tammy Wynette and George Jones in the studio with their producer Billy Sherrill (at the piano)*

They weren't just making things up. They were telling their life story to music. And that's hard to beat."

Two years later, Wynette filed for divorce again. This time, there was no turning back. "George is one of those people who can't tolerate happiness," she told a reporter. "If everything is right, there is something in him that makes him destroy it . . . and destroy me with it."

They each released popular albums; but as solo acts on the road, their bookings suffered. At Wynette's concerts, disappointed fans often shouted out, "Where's George?" Jones's drinking increased, and he started developing a reputation for missing his own performances. "All my life I hid when I hurt," he remembered. "At that time, I hid in a bottle."

He moved to Alabama, but would sometimes be seen, in one of the twenty-seven cars he bought and sold that year, aimlessly circling the driveway of the home the couple had once shared in Nashville. She embarked on a series of highly publicized—and short-lived—romances: with a movie star, a professional football player, a country singer, a politician, and others.

At a recording session in late 1975, she sang a song she had co-written with Billy Sherrill and George Richey, which she later called the favorite of all her singles: "Til I Can Make It on My Own." As the session musicians gathered to hear the playback of the song, no one in the studio spoke a word for a long time. "They knew," Wynette recalled, "the song was about Jones."

Four months later, Sherrill was able to get the two of them together for one more duet album.

they were. But there are certainly problems that arise from two strong careers, a strong duet career thrown in there, family added, and George's drinking was just always a problem, too. So all of those elements add to either living out a country song or writing a damn good one, I don't know which."

In 1973, Wynette filed for divorce, but after a fragile reconciliation, withdrew her petition. Billy Sherrill, meanwhile, brought them in to record "We're Gonna Hold On," which rose to number one. "If you lived the life that George lived and the life that Tammy lived, you almost have to say they lived all their songs, whether happy or whether they're unhappy songs," Sherrill said. "I think it came out in those songs because they lived them.

CENTER *Jones and Wynette recorded "We're Gonna Hold On" after she withdrew her divorce petition in 1973, but the reconciliation didn't last.*

TOP *Tammy recorded the solo song "Til I Can Make It on My Own" after their breakup.*

RIGHT *Out on the road on his own, George said, "I hid in a bottle."*

Its title track, "Golden Ring," written by Bobby Braddock and Rafe Van Hoy, tells the story of a young couple's engagement, wedding, and eventual breakup, by following a golden ring from its purchase in a Chicago pawn shop to its return when the marriage is dissolved. "When Bobby Braddock brought in 'Golden Ring,' I said, 'Whoa! That's a good one. That's a keeper,'" Sherrill said. "And so I brought them in on that one and they loved it too. And that was an easy record to make—their abiding love for the music; their abiding love for each other. And I've never really seen anything quite like that before or since in two musicians."

"Golden Ring" would top the country charts. It was playing on Wynette's car radio on the day she was on her way to marry her fourth husband in 1976. It was still on the charts when she divorced him forty-four days later.

COUNTRYPOLITAN

I grew up in Astoria, in Queens, right outside of the 59th Street Bridge in New York City. And my exposure to country music was zero. My exposure strictly was what was on pop radio. I was a British Invasion baby. I was a Motown baby. I was a Doors baby.

Everything that was going on, on college campuses in the late 1960s and early 1970s, I was part of. Whether it would be anything from Cream to the Doors, to the Beatles, to the Stones, that's what I grew up on. And that's what I loved.

JOE GALANTE

Joe Galante had graduated from Fordham University in 1971 with a degree in finance and marketing, and was working for RCA Records in New York as a budget analyst when they told him he was being transferred to their Nashville operation, which focused on country music. "I started immersing myself in things like Porter Wagoner and Hank Snow," Galante recalled, "and just went, 'Oh, my God, I can't do this.' But I moved."

Some people in Music City viewed Galante as an interloper, but at RCA, Chet Atkins welcomed him to town and explained the differences between how things worked in Nashville versus the home office in the Big Apple. Despite its growing popularity, country music's sales were still dwarfed by the pop market, so expectations were lower. "It wasn't a big risk for them if we

screwed up," Galante said. "We were making some money"—maybe $20,000 to $30,000 on a typical album that cost perhaps $6,000 to make—"but New York was 'Mom and Dad.' They supplied all your room and board and we got to go to school down here and play in our little sandbox. Everything we had to do, we had to go to them."

Within the close-knit country music community, the feeling of being looked down upon extended beyond record sales. "Country music has always longed for acceptance," said Marty Stuart. "I think country music, from day one, was always treated, within the realms of popular culture, as a second-class citizen."

In 1975, acclaimed Hollywood director Robert Altman released a sprawling feature film, *Nashville*, which followed the lives of two dozen fictional characters, with Music City—from the new Opryland to the famed replica of the Parthenon—as its backdrop. Country music insiders had initially been thrilled that their city and their industry would be

tion was overwhelmingly negative. Many country stars felt that they—and their fans—had been unfairly parodied and once more looked down upon by the nation's elites. Music Row felt slighted, because Altman had let his actors write their own songs.

But there was no denying that country music had now penetrated mainstream American culture as never before. Thirty-five million people listened to it regularly, buying $350 million worth of records a year. Nashville—where 90 percent of the recordings took place—was the industry's undisputed capital city.

And while the name "country" wasn't abandoned, a new term came into use, describing the type of music that more and more producers were turning out

the focus of a major film, seeing in it the opportunity to burnish the image they had been working so hard to project: that theirs was no longer the music of rustic hayseeds, but the soundtrack of middle America. (Having previously shed the label of "hillbilly music" and "country-western music," some now favored dropping the term "country music" entirely, in favor of calling it "American music" and broadening its appeal even further.)

When *Nashville* premiered—with its vision of the swirling interaction between celebrity culture and commercialism, politics and religion, and, ultimately, violence—critics hailed the movie as a satirical metaphor for what American society had become in the early 1970s, and it earned five Oscar nominations. Within Nashville, however, the reac-

OPPOSITE *At first, Music City insiders thought Robert Altman's film* Nashville *would be a major boost to country music's image; when it was released, they felt betrayed.*

ABOVE, RIGHT AND CENTER *By adding even more strings to their arrangements, often played by symphony musicians, producers like Billy Sherrill (seen with Charlie Rich) edged their artists into something even smoother than the Nashville Sound. It was called Countrypolitan.*

country music. Now, as a brash, upstart producer in Music City, he antagonized many traditionalists by pushing artists like Jones beyond the Nashville Sound toward the even smoother Countrypolitan.

"Oh, I'm killing him," Sherrill said of the reaction. "'Sherrillizing' him. That was a new word that came out. 'Oh, he's fallen a victim of Sherrillization. Putting those violins with George Jones is criminal.' I said, 'Well, sue me. I'm doing it anyway.' So I did."

Sherrill also helped Charlie Rich, a journeyman rhythm and blues singer, reinvent himself as an easy-listening, country-pop star with a string of number-one songs. Tanya Tucker was a precocious thirteen-year-old with a big voice when Sherrill discovered her. The songs he gave her—like "Delta Dawn," about an aging Southern belle waiting for the return of the lover who had betrayed her years earlier; and the more overtly sexual "Would You Lay With Me (In a Field of Stone)"—had adult themes that raised eyebrows among country music's more conservative fans, but earned Tucker two Grammy nominations before she turned seventeen.

Up and down Music Row, other producers—including

to cross over into the lucrative pop market. They called it "Countrypolitan."

Billy Sherrill was Nashville's most reliable Countrypolitan hit maker. As a boy, Sherrill had been steeped in gospel music, playing piano for his evangelist father at church services, funerals, and baptisms in Alabama, before he became enamored with jazz and the blues. Hearing a George Jones song on the radio as a young man had fired his interest in

ABOVE *As a teenager, Tanya Tucker had hits with songs with adult themes.*

In 1974, the Country Music Association named Newton-John as its Female Vocalist of the Year, beating out Dolly Parton and Loretta Lynn. Country traditionalists were both surprised and angry. When Roy Acuff announced the winner as "Oliver Newton," many people suspected he was making a statement, not a slip of the tongue. "It shocked me—that the music was getting away from 'us,'" Jean Shepard recalled. "We were losing our identity, so to speak."

The furor was even greater at the next year's awards show, when CMA's top honor—Entertainer of the Year—went to the folk-pop singer John Denver. Charlie Rich, who opened the envelope to announce the winner, lit the card on fire with his cigarette lighter as he read Denver's name.

Chet Atkins and Owen Bradley, who had popularized the Nashville Sound in the 1960s—steered their artists even farther away from country twang and toward the middle of the musical road.

"People criticized Chet when he started doing the Countrypolitan stuff, and at that time he kind of apologized," said Harold Bradley. "And then, later on, he said, 'I must have been having a bad day, because it wasn't all that bad.' It's a natural progression, where the music is going to change and the artists are going to change. They just kind of moved it forward. Think of it this way: What would have happened if they hadn't done it? We would have just been in kind of a stalemate there. They moved the town forward, Owen and Chet, by kind of gussying it up, you might say."

The bridge to crossover success went both ways. Anne Murray was a former folk singer from Canada; Lynn Anderson had been a regular on *The Lawrence Welk Show*. Australia's Olivia Newton-John got her career launched when her early pop-sounding songs—"Let Me Be There" and "If You Love Me (Let Me Know)"—were promoted to country radio stations.

OPPOSITE, BOTTOM, AND THIS PAGE, ABOVE *When Olivia Newton-John won CMA's Female Vocalist of the Year in 1974, country traditionalists were outraged. A year later, the furor was even greater when John Denver was named Entertainer of the Year. Charlie Rich burned the card announcing Denver's victory.*

For some established artists, the CMA seemed to be pushing the fusion of country and pop music too far. They formed the Association of Country Entertainers to publicize their grievances, announcing that their intention was to "preserve the identity of country music" and claiming that the Top Forty format adopted by most radio stations meant that songs by older, more traditional stars weren't getting any airtime. "Crossover music, pop music, or middle-of-the-road or whatever you want to call it," Hank Snow said, "has come in and drowned the basic country artist."

Justin Tubb, the son of Ernest Tubb, expressed the same feeling in a song he wrote and recorded, "What's Wrong With the Way That We're Doin' It Now." "What's wrong with fiddles and steel," it asked, "what's wrong with telling the world that you're country, if that's how you really do feel?" Like several other songs of its kind, it was ignored by Top Forty country stations.

"Things were changing, and not everybody agreed with it," Marty Stuart said. "I think a lot of people saw it as the boundaries were being broadened and expanded upon. And other people saw it as that country music is losing its soul. And, to this day, that's still an argument that exists out there."

The Association of Country Entertainers soon faded out of existence, unable to stem the Countrypolitan tide. Some of its own members were already crossing over toward the mainstream—and finding more success there.

The thing about Nashville, it's not that they're squashing your creativity; they will to make a buck, but the point is they're in business. You know, they're here to make money, not to support your artistic bent.

GUY CLARK

While older, traditional artists engaged in a tug of war with the Countrypolitans, Nashville was also attracting a new wave of young singer-songwriters who had their own ideas about the direction of country music. For them, creating a well-crafted song was more important than writing a hit—though they all dreamed that they might have both, like the hugely successful Kris Kristofferson, with his vividly poetic lyrics. And like Kristofferson, many of the new arrivals were from Texas.

"People ask me and say, 'What, what is it about these Texas songwriters?'" said Rodney Crowell, from Houston. "And I say, 'We're the best liars in the world.' Truly. You know, Texas's fight for independence was based on a lie." "I guess Texans have always had this independent streak of doing shit the way they want it, the way they hear it, and the way they

want to do it," added Guy Clark. "They don't follow rules, and it's pretty much been like that with everything since about 1836."

When Guy Clark was a little boy in the small west Texas town of Monahans, his family didn't own a record player and instead spent their evenings reading poetry aloud to each other. Clark got his first guitar when they moved to south Texas, and the first songs he learned were in Spanish.

By his early twenties, he was performing in folk clubs around Houston. After a year in Los Angeles, with his wife, Susanna, a painter and songwriter, he relocated to Nashville, where Kristofferson and fellow Texan Mickey Newbury had achieved success with their compositions. Two of Clark's songs, "L.A. Freeway" and "Desperados Waiting for a Train," received attention on FM radio stations when Jerry Jeff Walker recorded them, but Clark's own albums sold poorly. He toured at coffee houses and campuses to make ends meet—and kept writing.

At the newly opened Exit/In, a small live-music venue on Elliston Place near Vanderbilt University, Clark and others found a place to try out their latest songs in front of younger, more progressive audiences. "It was kind of like what Paris in the 1920s must have been," Marty Stuart said, "because it was all bohemians and new-thinking, forward-thinking country music people."

"When I arrived in Nashville, in August 1972, the Exit/In was the primo showcase folk club in Nashville," said Rodney Crowell. "The whole idea out on the street was that, 'Man, I've got to work hard enough and have the dedication to lift

my art up to a level where I can get on the Exit/In stage,' where you would see Kris Kristofferson perform and Guy Clark perform."

Rodney Crowell had grown up being steeped in country music. His parents met at a Roy Acuff concert, and Crowell was only two years old when his father insisted on taking him to see Hank Williams perform. By age eleven, he was playing in his father's honky tonk band; at fifteen, Crowell had his own group that toured small towns promising to perform everything from the Beach Boys and the Beatles to rhythm and blues and, their business card said, "country, if you want it."

He had just turned twenty-two when he came to Nashville, at first spending his days at Centennial Park, near the city's replica of the Parthenon, and sometimes spending his nights sleeping in his car. Soon enough, Crowell began showing up at the home of Guy and Susanna Clark, the unofficial gathering place for like-minded musicians.

"We never called," Crowell recalled. "We just showed up, banging on the door. Sometimes Guy just said, 'Go home. Not tonight.' Then, other times, he and Susanna would crawl out of bed and get dressed, and stay up with us till daylight,

OPPOSITE, TOP *Young Guy Clark and his sisters, with their grandmother Rossie Clark in Monahans, Texas*

OPPOSITE, BOTTOM *Guy Clark in the photo session for his first album,* Old No. 1. *The painting of the denim shirt was by his wife, Susanna.*

LEFT *Guy and Susanna Clark after their arrival in Nashville. Their home became a gathering place for young singer-songwriters.*

ABOVE *Young Rodney Crowell with his parents J.W. and Cauzette in Houston. They had met at a Roy Acuff concert.*

just trading songs and talking about how to get it done." "It was very casual and very open," Clark added. "Anybody was welcome that played good music and wasn't too much of an asshole."

Crowell came to look on Clark as a mentor: "I remember Guy Clark telling me, the second time we ever sat in conversation, he said, 'You're a talented guy. You can be a star, you probably have the talent to do it. Or you can be an artist. Pick one. They're both worthwhile pursuits. Pick one.'"

Clark's advice to any aspiring songwriter was always the same: "Write with a pencil that has a big eraser." Rosanne Cash also grew to respect him: "He had a very precise hand in his songwriting and a discipline that I really admired. He said, 'You have to throw out the best line of your song if it doesn't serve the rest of the song.' He was ruthless; ruthless, as a songwriter."

The most frequent visitor to the Clarks' house was their best friend, another troubadour from Texas: the brilliant and equally eccentric Townes Van Zandt. He was born in Fort Worth to a prominent family—Van Zandt County was named for one of his ancestors, a signer of the Republic of Texas's constitution—but Townes had turned away from his father's and grandfather's profession as lawyers to pursue a vagabond's life as a singer-songwriter.

The Houston blues guitarist Lightnin' Hopkins had the biggest influence on his music, but another hero was Hank Williams, whose turbulent and tragically short life Van Zandt seemed determined to follow. He drank heavily and constantly; became addicted to heroin for a while; was hospitalized for manic depression; and spent his twenty-ninth birthday convinced he was going to die, just as Hank had at that age.

ABOVE *Rodney Crowell practicing with a bandmate as a teenager.*

BELOW *Crowell (with guitar) at a late-night pickin' party at the home of Susanna and Guy Clark (in center). Clark became Crowell's songwriting mentor.*

"He didn't want to be a star as such," Clark said. "He wanted to be a poet. I was always inspired by him. But to be inspired by Townes was different than being like him. If you wanted to be like Townes, you had to be dead."

Van Zandt spent most of his time on the road—sometimes hitchhiking from one performance to another; living in run-down motels or rented shacks; writing all the time, including "If I Needed You," which he said he composed in his sleep.

But it was another song of his that would attract a startling array of musicians who would feel compelled to perform it. It tells the tale of a Mexican bandit named Pancho and his friend Lefty, who may have betrayed him. Pancho dies young and is buried in Mexico; Lefty lives to an old age, singing in a bar far north of the border, in Ohio.

" 'Pancho and Lefty' was one of those songs that you really can't pick it apart, you know, and have it make sense," according to Clark. "You have to just let it be. He came in and played it, and I was just stunned by it. The images were just mind-boggling." "It's perfectly written," Crowell added. " 'He wore his gun outside his pants for all the honest world to feel.' I mean, who wouldn't want to write that line? 'Pancho was a bandit, boy, his horse was fast as polished steel.' Beautiful writing. I mean, elevated poetry and melodically perfect. The lyrics and the melody are so perfectly joined. It's right there with 'Sunday Morning Coming Down' and 'Like a Rolling Stone.' " "First of all, it's like a Wallace Beery movie, in my mind," said Emmylou Harris:

I visualize these characters. And what is the worse tragedy? That Pancho, who is betrayed and killed—it's almost a Christ-like kind of story, not to put too much into it—but you can't help but have this compassion for Lefty, who has to grow old, living with what he's done.

I love the sad part. "The poets tell how Pancho fell, Lefty's livin' in a cheap hotel. The desert's quiet and Cleveland's cold. So the story ends, we're told." I mean, that's it. It's so poignant; it's heartbreaking. "Pancho needs your prayers, it's true. But save a few for Lefty,

TOP, LEFT *Townes Van Zandt performs for his younger cousins in Texas.*

TOP, RIGHT *Townes Van Zandt with Susanna and Guy Clark and Daniel Antopolsky on the Clarks' porch in Nashville*

LEFT *Van Zandt recording an early album with producer Cowboy Jack Clement*

too. He only did what he had to do, and now he's growing old." The older I get, the more that song resonates for me, because the weight of our lives, it gets heavier and lighter at the same time.

By 1975, Townes Van Zandt had recorded six studio albums, filled with self-composed tunes revered by other songwriters. None of the albums was commercially successful—the sixth was titled *The Late, Great Townes Van Zandt*, more or less as an inside joke—but he was developing a small, cult-like following.

Like his good friend Guy Clark, he performed mostly at smaller venues across the nation. "Nashville," he told a reporter, "is just not geared for minor keys." "His songs were dark," Clark said. "Somebody at a show asked him, he said, 'Man, why don't you do a funny song?' He said, 'Those *were* the funny songs.'"

A review of one of his concerts, however, compared him favorably with his hero, Hank Williams. "Both men live in their music," it said, "as if singing and writing and being human were the same thing, and all as natural as breathing . . . the direct, untrammeled expression of a man's soul." "For men like these," it continued, "the highway is heritage and home."

ABOVE *Townes "didn't want to be a star," his friend Guy Clark said. "He wanted to be a poet."*

THE SAME THING, JUST IN DIFFERENT LANGUAGES

I was drawn to country music because I could relate more about what they were singing about. It was just like the music of our people. In Mexican music, you have stories. Mexican music and country music said almost the same thing, just in different languages.

JOHNNY RODRIGUEZ

Growing up in the south Texas town of Sabinal, ninety miles north of the Mexican border, young Johnny Rodriguez loved mariachi music, but also the songs of Jimmie Rodgers, Hank Williams, and Merle Haggard.

In the early 1970s, Rodriguez was nineteen and working

at a Texas tourist attraction called Alamo Village when the country stars Tom T. Hall and Bobby Bare happened to hear him performing. Hall offered to buy him a beer if he would translate Hall's favorite country song, "I Can't Stop Loving You," into Spanish: "And he started singing that song—the hair just stood up on my arms and I said, 'Holy cow, somebody else has got to hear this; I've got to share this with somebody.'"

Rodriguez was performing as "Johnny Rogers," and Hall

asked him, "How did a Mexican guy get a name like 'Johnny Rogers'?" Rodriguez explained that his manager idolized Roy Rogers and said that "Johnny Rogers" sounded more like a country music name. Hall replied, "Well, if you come to Nashville and pick with me, we're going to call you Johnny Rodriguez. That's a much prettier name, and it's who you are."

True to his word, Hall helped Rodriguez come to Nashville, hired him to join Hall's touring band, and arranged an audition with a record label: "I said, 'I'm not a talent scout, but listen to this kid sing this song.' So he started off singing 'I Can't Stop Loving You,' half in English and half in Spanish. And they said, 'We'll sign him up.'"

Rodriguez became an overnight sensation. He would have fifteen consecutive Top Ten hits, including six number ones—and become the first Mexican American to be a major country music star.

In 1975, two years after Rodriguez was nominated for the Country Music Association's Male Vocalist of the Year award, another Hispanic singer broke through. Baldemar Huerta,

the son of migrant farmworkers in south Texas, had dabbled in rockabilly under the stage name of Freddy Fender. His song "Before the Next Teardrop Falls" topped both the pop and country charts and won the CMA's top honor for Single of the Year.

Later, he and accordion player Flaco Jiménez would help form the Texas Tornados, a Grammy-winning band featuring the distinctive working-class *conjunto tejano* music that had grown up along the border.

CLOCKWISE FROM OPPOSITE PAGE *Young Johnny Rodriguez in Sabinal, Texas; as a young singer calling himself "Johnny Rogers"; signing a contract using his real name with Frances Preston of BMI and country star Tom T. Hall, who encouraged him to come to Nashville; Johnny with fellow country star Freddy Fender.*

Waylon Jennings's voice—let's not even talk about his songwriting—is one of the greatest voices in country music, or music, period. That voice, you couldn't ignore it. If it was on the radio, you had to stop. If you were in a store and he came on, you had to just stop and take it in. He was undeniable.

ROSANNE CASH

He sang as good as Hank Williams, and he was really a good songwriter. His voice was what tore me up, though. It's just like the way Hank Williams tore me up. He could sing songs that I can't.

KRIS KRISTOFFERSON

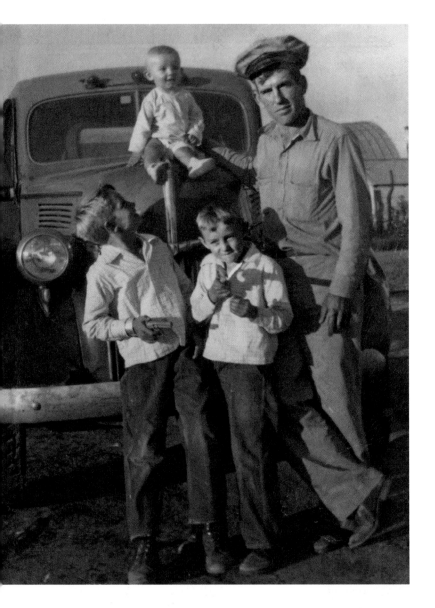

By 1975, Waylon Jennings had spent a frustrating decade in Nashville, occasionally trying to fit in with the country music establishment and just as often rebelling against it. "I never did feel at home," he remembered. "I was being told, over and over, 'You just don't do this,' or 'You can't do that.' 'There's a certain way we do things in Nashville.' 'We know what's best for you.'" Jennings was now thirty-eight years old, and his career had already followed many of the same twists and turns country music itself had taken in his lifetime.

Born during the Dust Bowl in Littlefield, Texas, on June 15, 1937, Jennings's earliest childhood memory was of his father connecting the family's radio to the pickup truck's battery, so they could listen to the Carter Family out of Del Rio's "border blaster" station, and to the *Grand Ole Opry* out of Nashville. "In my house," he recalled, "it was the Bible on the table, the flag on the walls, and Bill Monroe's picture beside it." His mother cried every time Roy Acuff sang "Wreck on the Highway."

As a teenager, Jennings was especially drawn to Hank Williams and honky tonk music, and started performing it in local bars. Working as a disc jockey at a small radio station, he also soaked up other types of music: rhythm and blues,

LEFT *Young Waylon Jennings, left, with his father, Albert, and two brothers. His dad hooked the family radio to the truck's battery so they could listen to country music.*

ABOVE *Jennings put his name on his guitar as a teenager.*

and then rockabilly and rock and roll. In 1959, he had gone on tour with his good friend Buddy Holly, from nearby Lubbock, and it was only by chance that Jennings wasn't in the small airplane that killed Holly and two other musicians when it crashed in an Iowa cornfield.

By the early 1960s, Jennings was in Arizona, where he formed his own band and became a local celebrity, packing in huge crowds and clearing $1,500 a week at a night spot called JD's in Scottsdale. Country star Bobby Bare heard him there and was so impressed he immediately called Chet Atkins at RCA in Nashville to arrange for a recording contract.

Before he agreed to leave his well-paying steady gig in Arizona for Nashville, Jennings asked fellow Texan Willie Nelson for his advice. "Stay away from Nashville," Nelson told him. "They'll just break your heart."

He went to Nashville anyway, deciding that the chance to work with Atkins at a major label was impossible to resist. But just as he had with Willie Nelson, Atkins had trouble trying to mold Jennings into

a country star. Their first album together was *Folk-Country*; their second was filled with the lush Nashville Sound of the time; a third included a ballad by the Beatles; and on another, Jennings crooned the pop hit "MacArthur Park."

None of it sounded like Waylon's performances back in Arizona. "They were good, smooth records," he said, "and there I was, rougher than a goddamn cob. All the damn sand I swallowed [in Texas] is in my singing."

TOP, RIGHT AND LEFT *Waylon, with his brother Tommy on bass, was making good money at JD's in Scottsdale when he was invited to come to Nashville.*

RIGHT *Producer Chet Atkins struggled to find the right combination of songs and sound to make Jennings a star.*

Like many people in the industry, Atkins believed that Jennings had the makings of a big star, but nothing seemed to be working on getting him there: an album's worth of songs by Nashville's most reliable songwriter, Harlan Howard; even a leading role in a movie, *Nashville Rebel*, in which he played a naive young singer being manipulated by managers and promoters.

In 1969, he married Jessi Colter, a Los Angeles–based singer who was used to the way pop and rock music was being recorded, with artists having greater creative control in the studio. "You could take your musicians; you could take your songs; you could have a hand in choosing your own producer, and basically be more independent in putting it together, so it's truly a result of who you are," Colter said. In Nashville, she added, "there was an 'old guard.' It was kind of like a large conglomerate making refrigerators, like RCA making TVs. I didn't quite understand what they were doing. I knew what Waylon was and the greatness of his talent. I kind of put it in very simple terms: they took a thoroughbred and treated him like a mule."

ABOVE *Jennings with his wife, the singer Jessi Colter, who urged him to demand greater creative control over his career*

RIGHT *When he brought his band to "Hillbilly Central" on Music Row, Jennings could record with greater freedom. People wondered what was going on inside, office manager Hazel Smith remembered, because the windows were always closed.*

"All Waylon wanted was for his music that he was doing live, on the stage, and driving the people crazy, to sound exactly like it did on the record," explained Hazel Smith, who was working on Music Row. "And it didn't. It didn't." His friend Willie Nelson knew the problem firsthand: "Waylon was a real artist. He knew what he wanted and he was running into the same things that a lot of us were running into there. And he decided he wanted to do it his own way, which was basically take his band in the studio, which was not that easy to do back in those days."

In 1972, Jennings changed managers and negotiated a new contract with RCA that broke all the prevailing Nashville rules: he would have his own production company to oversee his recordings; choose his own songs; use his own band in the studio. (He named his new company WGJ—Waylon Goddamn Jennings—Productions.) Then he quickly broke another rule, which required RCA albums to be recorded with RCA engineers, in RCA studios. Instead, he began using the studio owned by his friend Tompall Glaser, where he could have sessions as long as he wanted, at any time of day or night.

In seeming defiance of the image Nashville and the country music industry had worked so hard to push aside, Jennings and his friends called their new hangout "Hillbilly Central." Hazel Smith was the young office manager: "I would go to work and go into my office and there would be people

William had that rare gift and so does Waylon Jennings."

"If I had an outlaw hero," Jennings admitted, "it was Hank Williams. I wanted to be like him. We all did." One of his prized possessions was a pair of Williams's cowboy boots someone had given him, though after he wore them to a recording session and lightning toppled a tree onto his Cadillac and overloaded the studio's circuits, he became superstitious about putting them on.

In 1974, he invited Nashville's most free-spirited producer to work on his newest album. Cowboy Jack Clement had helped Sam Phillips break new ground in American music at Sun Records in Memphis in the early days of rock and roll. His creative touches had boosted Johnny Cash's career at critical moments. And it was Clement who had stepped forward in the mid-1960s to produce Charley Pride, country music's first African-American superstar. Musicians recording for him knew that Cowboy Jack liked what they were doing when they saw him dancing behind the control board.

"Jack Clement was the antithesis of phony; he had a nose for what was phony, and spurned it," said Allen Reynolds,

asleep in my office, had been asleep in there all night long, just stoned out of their mind, one of them asleep with his head on my typewriter and the other one asleep over there in the chair. And I chased them out. I told them they better not come up there no more when I wasn't there. But they came back, of course they did."

Jennings let his hair grow longer and shaggier, added a beard and moustache, and gave up shiny suits completely, in favor of blue jeans and leather vests. He started making the music *he* wanted to make—and started having some hits. "He had conviction, and it was the honesty in his voice," Joe Galante recalled. One review compared him favorably to his personal hero, Hank Williams, another artist who had bucked the Nashville status quo, a generation earlier. "There's nothing faddish or contrived or artificial about [Jennings]," it said. "If he sings it, you can believe it. Hank

TOP *Waylon's friend Tompall Glaser (right) with an engineer at Hillbilly Central*

ABOVE *Cowboy Jack Clement, the maverick producer who had recorded Charley Pride's first records, went into the studio with Jennings for* Dreaming My Dreams. *When he liked what he was hearing, Cowboy couldn't help but start dancing.*

LEFT *Jennings let his hair and beard grow as he started breaking many of the industry's rules on Music Row.*

who worked with Clement. "He was always looking for quality and looking for a performance. In the studio, he was looking for magic." Jessi Colter said he was an "intuitive sensor—and when you'd get it to the right place, Jack would dance. He felt it from the inside out. It wasn't about marketing, he was looking for great songs and he was looking to sense it. And that's what he did."

Jennings brought his band into the studio at Hillbilly Central, where he and Clement began recording an album called *Dreaming My Dreams*. An eclectic collection of melodies—from sweet ballads to a cowboy song, a blues number to a driving honky tonk tune—it also paid homage to some country artists who, by following their own instincts instead of the current musical fashion of their time, became legends: Jimmie Rodgers, Bob Wills, Roger Miller—and especially Hank Williams.

Jennings included a Williams song on the album, but chose to open it with one he had written himself on the back of an envelope on the way to the studio. With a driving guitar beat, it summarized his personal experience in the business, as well as his opinion on the way Nashville operated, by posing a simple question: "Are you sure Hank done it this way?"

"This is a commentary on country music and brilliant; it was a call to arms," said Ray Benson. "'It's the same old tune, fiddle and guitar, where do we take it from here? Rhinestone suits and big shiny cars, it's been the same way for years.' It

says it all right there. This has got to change." According to Jessi Colter, "It was Waylon's way to say, 'Just a minute. Is this all there is to this? It's not moving in the right direction.' It was like using Hank as a barometer, 'Are you sure Hank would have done it this way?'"

Dreaming My Dreams, Jennings later said, was "my favorite album I've ever done"—and his first to be certified as a gold record by selling half a million copies. Soon, other country artists were demanding contracts like Waylon's. And, according to Hazel Smith, more people were showing up at Hillbilly Central:

> First of all, the building didn't have windows. And everybody up and down Music Row wanted to come in that building to see what is going on there because Willie would come to town and he would be there. Kinky Friedman and the Texas Jewboys practically lived there; they'd be walking up and down the hall. Shel Silverstein hung out there. And the great Cowboy Jack Clement.
>
> The hip people of Nashville, Tennessee, hung out at that building. People thought, "They've got something going on and they ain't got no windows."

ABOVE *Waylon's song "Are You Sure Hank Done It This Way?" was a "call to arms" against the industry's status quo, Ray Benson said.* Dreaming My Dreams *was Jennings's first gold album.*

ANCIENT TONES

I think every generation comes up with their own sound. Music starts out raw, you know what I mean, funky, raw. And it gets more polished, more polished, more polished, and the next generation comes along and goes, "We don't like that slick stuff." And it becomes funky and raw again.

RAY BENSON

By the 1970s, with Countrypolitan ruling the airwaves, acoustic string band music—one of the principal wellsprings of country music—had virtually disappeared from country radio. But there were still plenty of people playing it. "Bluegrass festivals were doing great," said Marty Stuart. "The roots of it were great. Everybody that mattered was still making plenty of good music, they just weren't getting recognized as much."

Stuart, still a teenager, was now officially part of Lester Flatt's band, the Nashville Grass. On occasion, he also traveled with Bill Monroe, the patriarch of bluegrass, and as the bus drove through the night, the old man would play a lick on his mandolin and expect Marty to replicate it:

He kept one mandolin that was tuned with strange tunings that were very ancient sounding. He called them the "ancient tones." He was never one of those guys to say, "Listen to this tune."

He would [just play] and look off; and I was supposed to [repeat it]. And when I would get it, he'd move on. And when I'd miss it, he'd just kind of shake his head and run off and do something else. And it would kill me if I couldn't keep up.

Other bluegrass musicians were also coming of age. Ricky Skaggs was from the mountains of eastern Kentucky. When he

was little, his parents listened to bluegrass records; his older sister liked rock and roll. "I'd stand in the middle of the house, and I'd hear Mom and Dad listening to Flatt and Scruggs or Ralph Stanley, and then I'd hear my sister listening to the Beatles. And I would stand in the middle, and it's like I would hear two worlds going off and on. But the harmonies that John [Lennon] and Paul [McCartney] were doing were not different than what Ralph and Carter [Stanley] were doing; I could hear it."

Like Marty Stuart, Skaggs had taken up the mandolin at an early age—and he was good at it, too. At the age of six, he was in the crowd when Bill Monroe came to town, and

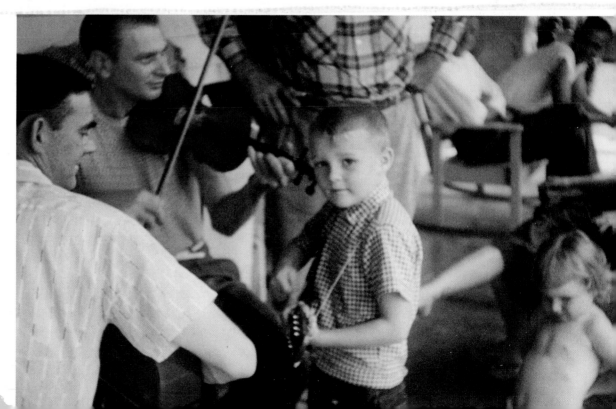

TOP *Bill Monroe, the patriarch of bluegrass music, performs with Marty Stuart at a festival in 1975.*

RIGHT *Little Ricky Skaggs plays mandolin on the family porch in Kentucky; his father, Hobert (left), is on guitar.*

there and watched us for at least ten or fifteen minutes.

And I'm seeing Ralph Stanley listening to me out of my peripheral vision, and I'm just like, "Would you please leave? I don't want to sing in front of you." I was shy that I was singing his songs, singing his tenor licks, and everything.

But it set us in good stead with Ralph. Ralph hired us to go work the summer with him. We were still in high school. So we worked the summer and went to our first bluegrass festivals. It truly was a life-changing moment.

In Norman, Oklahoma, young Vince Gill became proficient on banjo and guitar, and in high school dabbled in rock and roll. "When you're a kid, you're soaking so much in," Gill remembered. "I didn't care if it was a jazz guitar player, a rock god, a country guitar player, a bluegrass player, I loved it all. I never differ-

Skaggs's neighbors chanted for Monroe to let the little boy play a tune. Monroe relented, handed Skaggs his mandolin, and asked him to play "Ruby, Are You Mad at Your Man." The prodigy did it, even though, Skaggs remembered, "I never knew what she was mad about." Skaggs's skills soon caught the attention of Earl Scruggs, who invited him, at age seven, onto the Martha White Flour television show that he and Lester Flatt hosted. With Scruggs accompanying him on banjo, Skaggs played "Ruby" once again.

By the time he was in high school, Skaggs and a close friend, Keith Whitley, developed a show in which they performed the Stanley Brothers' repertoire, note for note. In 1970, they went to see Ralph Stanley at a small club near their home, and when the star's bus was delayed, Skaggs recalled, the club owner put the two boys onstage while everyone waited for the main act:

Well, the only songs that me and Keith knew were Stanley Brothers songs from the 1940s and early 1950s. That's all we knew. So we're standing up there singing songs that's thirty-five, forty years old already. And then Ralph walks in. He pulled up a barstool and sat

ABOVE *As a teenager, Skaggs (center) and his friend Keith Whitley performed with one of their heroes, Ralph Stanley.*

RIGHT *Vince Gill grew up in Oklahoma playing guitar and banjo.*

entiated any style or anything; I was just moved by people that could play the instrument. I've always been drawn to the instrument."

Then he joined a bluegrass band, Mountain Smoke. They thought they had caught their big break when they were asked to fill in at the last minute as the opening act at a concert in Oklahoma City. It turned out to be a KISS concert. The hard-rock fans, he said, did not appreciate having to listen to bluegrass music while they waited for KISS and their fireworks:

These people flipped completely out, they hated us so bad. They started booing from the first note and

ABOVE *When Vince Gill (sitting, far right) and the bluegrass band Mountain Smoke were a last-minute opening act for a KISS concert, it did not go well.*

screaming, and I must say, it was kind of a neat feeling, having that many people pissed off at you, and screaming at you.

But we only lasted about three songs, and then the beer bottles started flying. And we said, "Well, we better get out of here." So I turned around and flipped them off, and told them to kiss my ass.

The next day, there was a review in the paper. And it said, "Group member Vince Gill, on his departure, showed the crowd which part of his anatomy the crowd could KISS."

Marty Stuart found himself in a similar situation when Lester Flatt and the Nashville Grass, hoping to get signed for some campus appearances, auditioned at a college showcase. Competing with them were the jazz pianist Chick Corea and the funk band Kool & the Gang. "I remember putting my head down on the bunk in the bus, going, 'They're going to laugh us off of the stage,'" Stuart said:

But we went out there, in that traditional dress, all these old guys, and me, as a youngster. The movie *Deliverance* was pretty hot at the time. And, unknowingly, Lester had always done "Dueling Banjos" as a part of his show, for years. And it was on the new record. So it was just simply one of the instrumentals that we played that night.

Well, that unlocked, and we encored, and we kept getting encores throughout the night. At the end of the night, we had encored nine times throughout the set. And the next day, Lester's manager booked seventy-two college shows and rock shows off of that one thirty-minute performance.

And the next thing I know, we go from being a tired old *Opry* band that's playing "Mom and Pop" shows and bluegrass festivals to we were rock stars.

One of their first new bookings was a big concert at Michigan State University. Besides Lester Flatt's bluegrass band, the show that night featured an up-and-coming rock group, the Eagles. The other act was Gram Parsons, who had brought along a new harmony singer named Emmylou Harris.

Back in 1968, Parsons had come to Nashville with the Byrds to record *Sweetheart of the Rodeo*, one of the first albums to popularize what came to be called country-rock. "He was passionate about real country music, the real washed-in-the-blood stuff," according to Harris. "But he was also a child of the '60s; rock and roll was also a passion of his. He kind of had one foot in both worlds. He really believed that you could bring the two together."

Country-rock had gained a foothold on the West Coast, where Parsons and Chris Hillman, another former member of the Byrds, formed the Flying Burrito

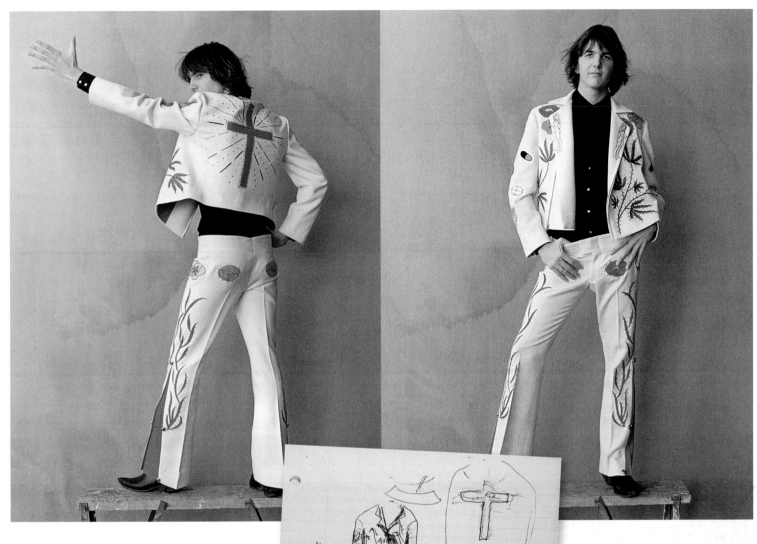

Brothers. "The music that was going on in Southern California was the Byrds and the Flying Burrito Brothers," Ray Benson said. "In Northern California, the Grateful Dead had a spinoff band, the New Riders of the Purple Sage, and there was Commander Cody. There was this incredible crossing of people very interested in the roots of country music and folk music

and rock and roll, and how it all fit together. It was the burgeoning of this baby boom generation, reinterpreting country music."

Parsons's passion for country music also extended to the flamboyant outfits many of its stars got at Nudie Cohn's tailor shop in North Hollywood. Parsons wanted some for himself and his band—but decorated much differently than Porter Wagoner's iconic outfit with its wagon wheels motif. Parsons told Nudie's top designer, Manuel Cuevas, that his suit should feature tall, green marijuana plants; red-petaled poppy flowers, the source of morphine, opium, and heroin; and hypodermic needles.

As the self-appointed apostle of the fusion he called "Cos-

OPPOSITE *After Marty Stuart (second from right) performed "Dueling Banjos" at a college showcase with Lester Flatt and the Nashville Grass, the band enjoyed a big boost in its bookings. One of their first gigs was at Michigan State University, where they opened for the Eagles and Gram Parsons.*

ABOVE AND CENTER *Gram Parsons took the typical country star's "Nudie suit" in a new direction. He asked Manuel Cuevas to design one that included marijuana plants and poppies.*

record he could find. The sessions helped influence the creation of the Stones' song "Wild Horses," which they tested out on Parsons—and then allowed the Flying Burrito Brothers to record a year before their own version was released.

Parsons's next prospect for conversion to country music was Emmylou Harris. "Except for Johnny Cash, I couldn't be fooled with country music," she said. "Folk music was what really spoke to me. I had been in New York trying to make it as a folk singer, still trying to be Joan Baez."

Born in Birmingham, Alabama, and raised in Virginia,

mic American Music," Parsons became friends with the Rolling Stones, especially Keith Richards, and spent days playing them every George Jones, Merle Haggard, and Ernest Tubb Emmylou Harris dropped out of college, got married and had a baby, got divorced, and had bounced around the East Coast folk scene for several years, when Chris Hillman of the Burrito Brothers heard her performing at a small club in suburban Washington, D.C. Impressed, he told Parsons about her remarkable voice.

A year later, as Parsons prepared to record his first solo album, he sent Harris a plane ticket for Los Angeles and they began rehearsals, which included his tutorials on the country music he loved—like melodies written by Felice and Boudleaux Bryant or the tight harmonies of the Louvin Brothers. "I had no idea who the Louvin Brothers were," Harris said. "I thought

TOP, LEFT *Four-year-old Emmylou Harris near her home in Birmingham, Alabama*

TOP, RIGHT *Harris at the University of North Carolina with her folk group, the Emerald City*

LEFT *Emmylou learns a new country song from Gram Parsons, who converted her from folk music. "I had finally discovered who I was as a singer," she said.*

Ira Louvin was a girl—the high tenor sound. They have these wonderful harmonies; there's such a tension in the voice that you feel like you're starting to vibrate. I became a big fan of the Louvin Brothers and started trying to track down their records."

Harris's own exquisitely tender harmonies added the special element Parsons had been searching for, and they went on tour to promote the result. "I had finally discovered who I was as a singer from singing with him and becoming this huge country music convert," she remembered. "I finally felt I had found where I was supposed to be as a singer. I felt like I truly was no longer a Joan Baez wannabe. I was a country singer, a singer who was coming through the country music door."

Walking through that door had brought her to the concert at Michigan State, where Marty Stuart had a revelation:

That night at Michigan State was the first time I ever saw rock and roll and bluegrass and honky tonk and folk music and gospel music collide. And she was dead center of every bit of it, like sparks were flying off of her as much as they were anybody. She absolutely brought something new and fresh to the table.

And I remember thinking: It can all exist under the umbrella of country music.

ABOVE *Parsons and Harris, on tour to promote his new album, perform at Max's Kansas City nightclub in New York City.*

I tell people, "Willie's not from around here." I mean Earth.

LARRY GATLIN

Obviously, his voice is different. When I first moved to Texas, people would say, "That Willie Nelson sings through his nose." Yeah, it's a hell of a nose.

We really didn't think that Willie could ever break through to the mainstream because he was too different. He was too good and too different. And the stuff that made it in the mainstream was not different. Then the mainstream found out—and then it got really nuts.

RAY BENSON

Willie Nelson had experienced the same difficulties as Waylon Jennings fitting into the Nashville system. In 1972, after ten discouraging years in Music City—where the songs he wrote provided huge hits for other artists, but his own records didn't do well—he had returned to his home state of Texas.

In Austin, he discovered an emerging music scene that seemed much more freewheeling than the Nashville he knew, less concerned about labeling music for commercial reasons and more welcoming to offbeat artists like himself. Its focal point was an old National Guard armory, just across the Colorado River from downtown Austin, a place called Armadillo World Headquarters, where live music ranged from B. B. King, Jerry Jeff Walker, and Taj Mahal to Frank Zappa, the Flying Burrito Brothers, Commander Cody and His Lost Planet Airmen—and Ray Benson and *his* band, Asleep at the Wheel.

As a Jewish kid growing up near Philadelphia, Benson had drifted into a hippie lifestyle, before he somehow came across the Western swing music of Bob Wills. He fell in love with it, and formed Asleep at the Wheel to keep that sound alive. They played rough-and-tumble honky tonks in West Virginia; moved to California's Bay Area for two years, where country-rock was popular; then showed up to perform in Austin.

The Armadillo sold more Lone Star beer than any other place in Texas except Houston's Astrodome. And after the county sheriff announced that he wasn't interested in busting people for personal use of marijuana, the smoke inside the concert hall had an unmistakable aroma. The crowds were free-spirited, raucous—and overwhelmingly young. "It

TOP *The Armadillo World Headquarters was the hub of Austin's progressive music scene.*

CENTER *Inside the Armadillo, the crowds were young and rowdy. Lone Star beer sold more product there than anywhere in Texas, except in the Astrodome, and pot was available and cheap.*

LEFT *When they arrived in Austin, Ray Benson (in black cowboy hat) and Asleep at the Wheel thought they had found "heaven on earth."*

was like, 'This is it. We found heaven on earth.'" Benson said:

> There's people our age who love our music. They have beer. There were college girls to chase. Rent was a hundred dollars a month. And pot was cheap and plentiful from Mexico.
>
> We needed money, but we were not motivated just by making money. Yeah, we wanted to make money, but it was more important that we had the freedom. And the great thing about Austin, it was cheap. So you didn't need a lot of money to be free.

Willie Nelson was nearly a generation older than most of the patrons—and the other musicians—at the Armadillo, but from his first appearance on its stage, they fell in love with him. "He was on a personal journey to play the music and create the music, and become the person that he was going to become," according to Benson. "This was a town that allowed him to do that."

Nelson let his hair grow longer; exchanged the turtlenecks and suits he had worn in Nashville for blue jeans and a straw cowboy hat or bandana. He could sense from the strange mixture of people showing up—long-haired college students and

redneck truck drivers—that something new was happening. He called his friend Waylon Jennings in Nashville and urged him to come down to check it out.

"Willie said, 'Waylon, I've got preachers and pilgrims and poets, poor people, hillbillies, college graduates, they're all sitting side by side watching me play my songs and sing my music,'" Hazel Smith recalled. "You need to come down here and see what's going on." When Jennings arrived for the first time, he looked out into the crowd and said, "Someone get that redheaded son of a bitch who brought me here."

"It was unusual to see Waylon really caught off guard," said Jessi Colter. "In those days, the country music audiences were very reserved. But here were these young people

---

ABOVE AND TOP *The poster for Willie Nelson's appearance at the Armadillo notes his early hit song from his time in Nashville, "Hello Walls," a decade earlier. Though he was a generation older than his fans, they clamored for his music—and his bandana.*

blown away. They were young and vibrant—and responded. And Waylon was blown away. He said, 'This is something.'" Jennings agreed to return for an even bigger outdoor concert, when the same diverse crowds showed up in even larger numbers for what became Willie's annual Fourth of July picnics.

The picnics, Benson said, were "the most disorganized gathering of the tribes. I don't know how to describe them except chaos. Nobody was in charge. Nobody knew what was going on. I don't know, twenty or thirty thousand people, but who paid? It was like Woodstock: nobody paid. Willie would lose money every time. We didn't care. Lone Star Beer would sponsor everything." Willie didn't seem to care, either. He simply enjoyed making music with his friends, and watching the throngs in the audience having a good time. "They're out there drinking beer, smoking pot," Nelson said, "and finding out that they really didn't hate each other." He invited his

hero Ernest Tubb to perform before the young crowd, and even put a recliner on the stage for the aging star so he could watch the whole show. When it was over, Tubb said, "Well,

---

ABOVE *At Willie Nelson's Fourth of July picnics, his eclectic musical interests were evident in the artists he invited. Here, Leon Russell dances while Willie looks on.*

OPPOSITE, TOP LEFT AND BOTTOM LEFT *Willie's picnics, Ray Benson said, were "the most disorganized gathering of the tribes. . . . It was like Woodstock." Willie liked the notion that rednecks and hippies were "finding out that they really didn't hate each other."*

OPPOSITE, TOP RIGHT *Waylon Jennings was amazed at the young people in the audiences.*

OPPOSITE, BOTTOM RIGHT *Willie also invited one of his heroes, Ernest Tubb, to perform. After singing, Tubb tipped his hat and—just like his hero Jimmie Rodgers—flipped his guitar that said "THANKS" on its back.*

it might be a little loud, but I believe you boys are doing just fine."

Going back to Texas has sure been good for Willie Nelson. You get the impression that when he was living in Nashville he was sending out his songs like a stranded man sends out messages in bottles, and that when he moved to Austin, he suddenly discovered that all those bottles had floated to shore among friends.

DAVE HICKEY, *COUNTRY MUSIC* MAGAZINE

When Nelson signed a new contract with Columbia Records, he negotiated the same terms Waylon Jennings got—the right to use his own musicians in the studio and more freedom in producing his music. Then he put his new artistic

TOP *With his favorite guitar, Trigger, Nelson recorded* Red Headed Stranger *at Autumn Sound Studio in Garland, Texas. He wanted a simpler sound than Nashville studios were producing. Executives there predicted it would flop.*

RIGHT *After the album's breakthrough success—critically and commercially— "everybody left Willie alone, including me," Billy Sherrill said.*

control immediately to work on his next album: *Red Headed Stranger*, a collection of haunting songs that together tell the story of a man who kills his unfaithful wife and her lover, then rides off across the West, grieving and seeking redemption.

Many of the songs were his own, but Nelson also included "Blue Eyes Crying in the Rain," written by Fred Rose, which had been recorded by Roy Acuff in the 1940s, Hank Williams in the early 1950s, and many other country artists over the years, though none of their versions had become big hits.

To make the album, Nelson chose a small studio near Dallas, because he thought his previous records had been overproduced, with too many musical elements added on top of the basics. He spent only $4,000 recording *Red Headed Stranger* and got the simple, unvarnished sound he was looking for: his singular voice untouched by any engineering tricks, and the sparest backup instrumentation, including his idiosyncratic guitar playing.

Columbia Records didn't know what to make of it when he turned it in. "We were in agreement that it was a poor, lousy-sounding record," said Billy Sherrill. "And they said, 'We can't put this out.' I said, 'Well, I agree. It sounds like a bad demo.'"

As it happened, Waylon Jennings was there when the head of the label suggested adding string arrangements and other overdubs to sweeten the album's sound. Jennings's reaction was swift—and characteristic. "I called him a tone-deaf, tin-eared sonofabitch who didn't know nothin'," Jennings recalled. "You ain't got a goddamn clue what Willie Nelson's music is about. . . . That album is what he is."

Billy Sherrill advised the executives to try a different approach: "I said, 'Let's do this. Let's appease Willie by releasing the record. It will die a quick death, anyway, and that way he'll be more receptive to what everybody wants him to do.' So we put it out. And we were wrong as hell. [It was] a big, big record, and, after that, everybody left Willie alone, including me."

Thirty years after it was first written, "Blue Eyes Crying in the Rain" rocketed to the top of the country charts and crossed over onto the pop charts. The album attracted critical acclaim: one reviewer called it a masterpiece; another compared Nelson's unsentimental style to Ernest Hemingway's—and it sold steadily, staying on the charts for an unprecedented 120 weeks.

In Texas, Willie and his band (with his sister, Bobbie, on piano) seemed to be everywhere: performing at a fundraiser for a Houston radio station after it was firebombed by the KKK; drawing

ten thousand people to a concert in his tiny hometown of Abbott; and doing the pilot show for his adopted city's public television station, experimenting on the idea of an hour-long program devoted exclusively to one artist's live performances. *Austin City Limits* would go on to become the longest-running music program in television history.

Only a few years earlier, drunk and despairing over his career, Nelson had sprawled out in the middle of Broadway Avenue in Nashville, not caring if he got run over. Now *Newsweek* called him "the King of Country Music," and *Rolling Stone* put him on its cover.

RIGHT Newsweek *crowns Nelson as country music's new king.*

BELOW *During the sessions for his album, Willie takes a break to stretch out while standing on his head.*

IF I COULD ONLY WIN YOUR LOVE

The simplicity of country music is one of the most important things about it. It's about the story and the melody, and the sound, and the voice, and the sincerity of it.

EMMYLOU HARRIS

When they hear her voice, they feel like they've been touched by an angel, whether you believe in angels or not. That's the beauty and the transcendental quality of Emmy's voice. It just somehow gets past everything and winds up somewhere in your heart. And it feels good in there.

RODNEY CROWELL

Emmylou Harris's collaboration with Gram Parsons ended tragically and suddenly when he died at the age of twenty-six of an alcohol and drug overdose, a few months before the release of his second solo album. His death, she said, "was like falling off a mountain."

In 1975—the same year as Willie Nelson's *Red Headed Stranger* and Waylon Jennings's *Dreaming My Dreams*—Harris came out with two albums of her own. "I didn't really know what I was doing, but I had some songs that I wanted to do," she said. "And I knew that I wanted to make a country record, almost like in memory of Gram."

She filled *Pieces of the Sky* and *Elite Hotel* with songs drawn from the lessons in country music that Parsons had provided: Merle Haggard's "The Bottle Let Me Down," Dolly Parton's "Coat of Many Colors," George Jones's "One of These Days," Hank Williams's "Jambalaya," and others. "When I became a convert to country music," she said, "there's no other word for it, I became obnoxious, trying to get people to listen to everything."

Released as a single, her version of an old Louvin Brothers song, "If I Could Only Win Your Love," went to number four on the country charts; then her renditions of Buck Owens's "Together Again" and Patsy Cline's "Sweet Dreams" both reached number one. One reviewer, noting her background in folk music, and that she was based in Los Angeles, nonetheless declared that her music was "more country than Nashville."

She surrounded herself with some of the leading rock instrumentalists on the West Coast—including several from Elvis Presley's act in Las Vegas. They called themselves the

---

ABOVE *Devastated by the death of Gram Parsons, Emmylou Harris embarked on her own solo career featuring country songs he had taught her.*

OPPOSITE, TOP *With Rodney Crowell, Harris said, their different musical backgrounds combined to make country music "outside the lines, but with total respect for tradition."*

OPPOSITE, BOTTOM *Emmylou Harris and the Hot Band. Top row, from left: Rodney Crowell, Hank DeVito, Emmylou, Albert Lee; front row: John Ware, Emory Gordy, Glen D. Hardin*

"Rodney was kind of like my kid brother," Harris said. "We were the same kind of sort of quasi-hippie kids, but we had totally different upbringings. He grew up with country music. He was kind of my partner in this wonderful 'crime' of making country music—outside the lines, but with total respect for the tradition of country music." Crowell agreed: "We just took traditional country music, and Southern rock and roll, and rockabilly, and just played it. Just let it have its voice. And it was good fun."

With the Hot Band, Harris played in every type of venue: from the Palomino Club in North Hollywood to Armadillo World Headquarters in Austin. They were the opening act for folk and pop star James Taylor, as well as Merle Haggard—and for the sixty thousand fans who came to hear Elton John at Dodger Stadium.

Hot Band. The one she became closest to was Rodney Crowell, fresh from the all-night gatherings at Guy and Susanna Clark's home in Nashville. After hearing some of his songs, Harris had invited Crowell to California to work on her albums.

Reporters were intrigued by her musical journey and the way she had seemingly bridged so many styles. FM stations picked up certain songs to broadcast for their progressive audiences, while AM stations played different ones for their hard-core country listeners.

Bob Dylan invited her to sing harmony with him on a new record; so did Linda Ronstadt and John Sebastian. During a whirlwind visit to Nashville, Crowell introduced her to his circle of friends, and she was asked to judge a talent contest at the Exit/In, then performed at the fiftieth anniversary show of the *Grand Ole Opry*.

She provided vocal backup on a Guy Clark album; chose a painting of Susanna's for the cover of her own next record, in which she sang one of Susanna's songs; and recorded Townes Van Zandt's song "Pancho and Lefty." *Rolling Stone* hailed her

music as "Country without Corn." Everyone seemed to love Emmylou Harris.

Tony Brown, a member of the Hot Band, said, "To me, she was like a rock star. She wore little hippie dresses and the tight jeans, and she was just so cool, against-the-grain kind of an artist for a female, because most country females had the coiffed hair and they were dressed in the rhinestones and stuff, and Emmy was not that. She was the hippie chick. But her music was so traditional. She drew from bluegrass and she drew from country-rock. But she always had that focus on the tradition of country music."

"She didn't care which banner anyone flew," said Rosanne Cash. "She could do a Carter Family song next to a full-on rock-and-roll song and it all sounded of a piece. And it came from her own authenticity. This wasn't contrived. The authenticity was so palpable that it gave a lot of people permission, myself included, to open our minds."

When Rodney Crowell left the Hot Band to pursue his own career, Harris replaced him with Ricky Skaggs,

---

With the release of her first two albums, Emmylou seemed to be everywhere—and everyone responded to the way she gave country music a new sound and a new look.

CLOCKWISE FROM TOP *Emmylou Harris at the Palomino Club in Hollywood; talking with Guy Clark—she sang on one of his albums and chose a Susanna Clark painting for a new album cover; hugging Merle Haggard at Giants Stadium; and opening with the Hot Band for Elton John at Dodger Stadium.*

who brought with him a deeper connection to bluegrass, which she wanted to learn more about. "I think it was a cross-pollination with Emmylou and me," Skaggs said. "I think I influenced her and brought that element of bluegrass and old-time mountain music, a lot of gospel songs we were doing. But, in the process, I was getting Albert Lee's guitar playing style; I was getting Emery Gordy's bass style. I was getting John Ware's shuffle on the drums back there. So I was learning all of this stuff. I'd never worked with any band other than just a bluegrass band. I was going to school for those two years that I was with Emmy."

Harris's label wanted her to capitalize on her success by crossing over to mainstream music. Instead, she came out with two albums tinged with bluegrass, *Blue Kentucky Girl* and *Roses in the Snow*. "I was actually told that it would be a disaster," she said. "And [one of them] turned out to be my most successful record in the sense that it went gold earlier than any of the other records did, because there was this huge audience for bluegrass music that the regular music industry didn't know about. I mean, bluegrass music people sold their records from the back of the station wagon. All of a sudden, this was a bluegrass record that was able to be put into the music business machinery. And I think that Ricky's presence on that record had a lot to do with it. There were people who bought that record because of Ricky, not because of me."

With seven gold albums in a row, three Grammy Awards, and recognition by the Country Music Association as Female Vocalist of the Year, Emmylou Harris had accomplished much more than selling millions of records and winning some prestigious awards. The recent convert to country music had transferred her enthusiasm for its unadorned roots to a wider audience—and pointed some people in the industry toward a future that could appreciate the music's past.

"Emmylou is the glue, for me, that bridged the gap between '70s folk, rock and roll, and traditional country, with bluegrass thrown in," said Trisha Yearwood. "She's the bridge, to me, that brings that music and makes that music live side by side on country radio with George Jones and the Louvin Brothers. She's able to somehow encompass it all and make it work—and with class and grace."

Dwight Yoakam was another future country star caught in her spell: "Emmylou didn't explode onto the scene. She bloomed into the musical consciousness and scene. And she'll forever be that rose that bloomed into our collective consciousness, and our musical consciousness. She was a navigational beacon for all of us."

ABOVE *When he joined the Hot Band, Ricky Skaggs helped add a tinge of bluegrass to Emmylou's music.*

LEFT *Harris would bring a new generation of fans—and new artists—to country music. "She's the bridge," Trisha Yearwood said.*

OUTLAWS

On the strength of his song "Are You Sure Hank Done It This Way?" Waylon Jennings was named the Country Music Association's Male Vocalist of the Year in 1975. But his battles for creative control of his records made many people in the industry distrustful. "I was the black sheep of Nashville," he recalled. "They thought I was a troublemaker."

Jennings's chronic drug use had been a source of friction with Chet Atkins, and now he had switched from amphetamines to cocaine, which fueled long periods of time when he simply didn't sleep. With his friend Tompall Glaser, he would spend hours on end—and hundreds of dollars—playing pinball all night at the Burger Boy.

Hazel Smith was the office manager at Hillbilly Central, where Jennings and his friends were now turning out hit after hit. Reporters started asking her how to describe the music he and Willie Nelson and others were creating, and Smith came up with a name for it:

In my mind, I thought everything needed a title for it to happen. So I always did, and still do, have a dictionary under my desk. Well, one day, I reached under there and I pulled it out and just went through it and came to the word "outlaw."

And it was about that much information there that meant very little, but the last sentence said it all. And here's what it said: "Living on the outside of the written law." And I leaned back in my chair and I went, "That's

ABOVE *Despite his commercial success, Waylon Jennings had become "the black sheep of Nashville," due to his battles with his label and his increasing use of drugs.*

LEFT *Texan Billy Joe Shaver (left) wrote or co-wrote all but one of the songs on Waylon's album* Honky Tonk Heroes.

term "outlaw music" caught on, the younger Bradley sensed an opportunity. Willie Nelson and Waylon's wife, Jessi Colter, were now with different labels, but RCA still had some unreleased recordings of them in the company vaults, which RCA still had the rights to release. In his office, Bradley had some copies of the *Time-Life* book series on the Old West, which gave him another idea—about what the album cover should look like.

Bradley put together the previously recorded material of Colter, Nelson, and Jennings—and, at Waylon's insistence, some Tompall Glaser—and in 1976 released a compilation album, *Wanted! The Outlaws*, with the images of the four artists added to a facsimile of an old Western poster. "It was a marketing tool, when Jerry came up with that idea for the cover," said Joe Galante. "And it was brilliant. It was a campaign we put together."

The album rose to the top of the country charts, crossed over to the Top Ten on the pop charts, and, after selling a million copies, became the first certified platinum album in country music history. Then it sold a million more. The Jennings-Nelson duet on "Good Hearted Woman," which they had written years earlier during a poker game, became a number-one single—and

it." They are not going along with the Nashville establishment; they're doing their own thing, and they're doing it the way they want to. That was what outlaw music was, right there.

Chet Atkins had recently retired from producing, and RCA had chosen Jerry Bradley, the son of Owen Bradley, to take his place. As the

TOP AND CENTER *At Hillbilly Central, Hazel Smith gave the Outlaw sound its name; RCA made it even bigger with an album that looked like a wanted poster from the Old West. It was the first country album to sell a million copies.*

LEFT The Outlaws *album was a "turning point for country music," said Joe Galante (far right), seen here celebrating another successful Waylon Jennings/Willie Nelson collaboration. Producer Jerry Bradley is at far left.*

of course, what did everybody want to do? They wanted to capitalize on that," said Del Bryant, who was working for BMI. "So, immediately, the town turned 'outlaw' happy. Everybody that had been walking through the alleys, looking like an outcast, wearing a hat, was immediately signed as an artist. And everybody who loved that record, who thought that they were an 'outlaw,' who were somewhere else other than Nashville, came to Nashville. It did change music. Fads change music. What causes a fad? A big hit." (Some of the artists had actually been real outlaws. Singer-songwriter David Allan Coe had done time in the Ohio State Penitentiary; Johnny Paycheck had spent two years in military prison, and years after his hit "Take This Job and Shove It" came out in 1977, he was imprisoned again for two years after a barroom gunfight.)

Willie Nelson, as usual, was more philosophical about it: "Oh, we thrived on it. We thought it was the best thing that happened to us, 'Hey, they're calling us outlaws.' Everybody who's in the creative business has to have a little outlaw in him. I think there's a lot of people out in the audience who have a little outlaw in them, too. So they were willing to forgive us, as long as the music was good."

Trying to make the most of the surge in popularity, Way-

permanently enshrined the two as outlaws, albeit lovable ones.

"My God, that was a song worth singing, wasn't it?" said Hazel Smith. "I mean, you ain't got no songs like that coming out of this hillbilly town now. It was truth. If there was ever a truer song than that one, I don't know what it is. 'A long time forgotten are dreams that just fell by the way. And the good life he promised ain't what she's living today.' Ain't that great?"

"*Outlaws* was a turning point for both country music and for Waylon, because we weren't, on a regular basis, having gold and platinum records, and then this one shot up," according to Joe Galante. "We had New York's attention. Absolutely."

"Suddenly, we didn't need Nashville," Jennings recalled. "They needed us." In 1976, the CMA honored the two "outlaws" with four awards: Vocal Group of the Year, Vocal Duo of the Year, Album of the Year, and Single of the Year. "And,

TOP *With their records selling so briskly, "we didn't need Nashville, they needed us," said Jennings (seen here with Nelson in the background). More artists and labels climbed onto the Outlaw music bus.*

RIGHT *Jessi Colter helped Jennings fight his way out of bankruptcy and an addiction to cocaine.*

Bit's Done Got Out of Hand"—but in a few years, he was advised that his only financial option was to declare bankruptcy. Contrarian as always, Jennings refused and instead trimmed his costs and worked even harder to repay all his debts. Jessi Colter stuck with him through it all. She was with him when he rented a house in the Arizona desert and finally kicked his addiction.

Willie Nelson was now bigger than ever, and even more steadfast in refusing to bow to any musical orthodoxy. He slipped some old pop standards—like "Stardust" and "Georgia on My Mind"—into his live performances in Austin, and discovered an enthusiastic response. "The kids in the crowd thought 'Stardust' was a new song I had written," he explained. "The older folks remembered the song well and loved it as much as I did."

Against his label's objections, he recorded *Stardust*, an entire album of similar songs, produced by Booker T. Jones and with a cover painting by Susanna Clark. Radio deejays initially resisted it, on the grounds that it wasn't country music, but listener demand drove two of the singles to number one. The album also reached the top—and stayed on the charts for 551 weeks.

President Jimmy Carter was a fan, and brought Nelson to the White House for a special performance, then invited him back to spend the night in the Lincoln Bedroom. That evening, Willie went up on the White House roof with one of Carter's sons, and they smoked a joint.

lon Jennings bought a fleet of buses, hired a big road crew, and set out on elaborate tours. Everywhere they went, they played to packed houses, but he was spending more than he was taking in. Jennings's cocaine habit was costing him $1,500 a day, and he barely escaped prosecution when federal drug agents tracked a shipment to the Hillbilly Central studio where he was recording.

None of it hurt his image. His records kept selling—including one song he wrote, "Don't You Think This Outlaw

---

ABOVE AND CENTER *Willie Nelson surprised many people with* Stardust, *an album of old standards that sold phenomenally well. The cover was a painting by Susanna Clark.*

FAMILY TRADITION

By the mid-1970s, Hank Williams had been dead for nearly a quarter century, but the shadow of his superstardom still loomed over any country musician dreaming of success. No one felt it more keenly than his only son, Hank Williams Jr.

Only three and a half years old when his dad died, Hank Junior had few actual memories of his famous father, beyond listening on the radio to hear him say goodnight to "Bocephus," Hank Senior's affectionate nickname for his little boy. But Audrey Williams was determined that he would be the vehicle to keep her former husband's memory alive—and

provide her a chance to be in the spotlight in ways she hadn't been during Hank Senior's short career.

"When I was eight years old, I went out and did the very first show," Hank Junior remembered. "I thought, 'Oh, my gosh.' You know, this is an eight-year-old boy that's the son of a God-like figure. So, an eight-year-old boy's out there and you've got people that are crying and people that are laughing. What's going on here? Does it sound that bad? It has quite an effect on a little guy."

Williams made his *Grand Ole Opry* debut at age eleven,

TOP *Hank Williams Sr. lovingly called his son "Bocephus."*

an appearance on *The Ed Sullivan Show*, and then began a tour that opened in Canton, Ohio, on New Year's Day, 1964—the same place his father was headed exactly eleven years earlier when he died in the backseat of his car. At a promotion in Nashville, Audrey brought the car itself.

"My dad was dealing with his dad's shadow from day one, not only from fans and friends, but from his own mom," according to Holly Williams, his daughter. "She was right there with other people going, 'You need to sing your daddy's songs. You need to write like your daddy did.' It was very hard for him."

When a Hollywood movie was made about Hank Senior—*Your Cheatin' Heart*, starring George Hamilton— Audrey insisted that Hank Junior sing the songs on the soundtrack. As his manager, she pushed him to record more albums, and sent him on the road with a band called the Cheatin' Hearts in a bus called "The Cheatin' Heart Special." She had Nudie Cohn outfit him in shiny suits, even a customized convertible, festooned with 547 silver dollars, fancy guns in leather holsters, and a horse saddle between the driver and passenger seat.

DIRECT FROM NASHVILLE - TENN.
IN PERSON
AUDREY
"MRS. HANK"
WILLIAMS
— FEATURING —
HANK WILLIAMS JR.
STARRING
RCA VICTOR
RECORDING STAR
JOHNNY RIVERS

singing the same song his father had at his own debut, "Lovesick Blues." By the time he was fourteen, his mother had negotiated a contract for him to record an album of Hank Senior's songs. One of them, "Long Gone Lonesome Blues," reached number five on the country charts.

To promote the album, Audrey arranged

"Loosen up a bit," Johnny Cash urged Audrey. "Let him be Hank Williams *Junior* a while." She didn't pay any attention. In 1966, the year he turned seventeen, he released one of his first self-written hits, "Standing in the Shadows," which summarized his life so far. He was starting to rebel: "I remember laying up in the back of a car, touring, and they'd want to put it onto the *Grand Ole Opry* and I said, 'I am not listening to country at all. I'm listening to 'Soul Twist' and Fats Domino, and Jerry Lee Lewis. And I ain't listening to country. I ain't. Bye-bye to the cloning.'"

ABOVE AND CENTER *Audrey Williams pushed her son, Hank Williams Jr., to follow in his father's footsteps, but she always wanted to be in the spotlight in ways she never was when Hank Senior was alive.*

LEFT *Young Hank Junior debuts on the* Opry.

As soon as he reached eighteen and became entitled to his inheritance and legally able to make his own decisions, Williams dropped his mother as his manager and set out to make his own way in the music world: "I said, 'I'm done with this,' because there's one simple reason: Daddy don't need me to promote him. How dumb can you be? He does not need me to promote him. What a joke. I said, 'I think I better start writing my own and doing my own style of stuff.'"

But he wasn't prepared for the reaction from his father's fans, according to Holly Williams: "He told me his first few shows of his own music, he's getting boos from the crowd. He said 50 percent of them, sometimes 80 percent would be gone. There'd be a few people left sitting there. They'd throw stuff at him. He'd say, 'If you all don't mind, I'm going to sing a song of mine for you tonight'—and just gone. Which, just on a basic, human, being-nice-to-people level is so shocking to me, that people would just turn away and walk out. But they didn't want to hear it; they wanted to hear 'Cold, Cold Heart' and 'I Saw the Light.' So he really struggled for years."

By 1974, Williams had entered what he called "an endless nightmare of bars and shows . . . of Jim Beam and . . . multicolored pills." He recalled, "I'd never realized how deeply

ingrained my daddy's myth really was. At twenty-five years old, I was more like him than I ever figured I'd be—drunk, on dope, divorced."

Convinced that he was on the same trajectory as his father, he attempted suicide by swallowing a bottle of painkillers. A doctor advised him to leave Nashville and rethink his life, or he would certainly not even make it to twenty-nine. He moved to Alabama and lived in a small cabin.

"From my point of view," said his friend Charlie Daniels, "Hank reached a point where he said, 'I am me. My name is Hank Williams, but I am me. And I've got things that I want to do and I want to say. So I am going to pursue that,' and he just did a complete turn. He's got his own talent. He's got Hank's blood in his veins; he's got Hank's talent flowing in his veins. But it's manifesting itself in a different way, and he's

ABOVE, LEFT *"Let him be Hank Williams Junior a while,"* Johnny Cash (left) advised Audrey (center). She ignored his advice.

ABOVE, RIGHT *When he turned eighteen, Hank Junior decided "Daddy don't need me to promote him," and tried to strike off on his own. But many fans still wanted to hear his father's music.*

going to let it out that way. He could have ridden on that name for his whole career. He could
have gone around singing 'Your Cheatin' Heart'
for the rest of his life and made a great living at
it. But he didn't do that. He took quite a chance
when he did that."

In 1975, Williams went into a studio in Muscle
Shoals, Alabama, to record a new album, *Hank
Williams, Jr. and Friends*. He was attracted to
what was called "Southern rock," music by
groups like the Allman Brothers, Lynyrd Skyn-
yrd, the Marshall Tucker Band—and Charlie
Daniels, who had just released an album of his
own, *Fire on the Mountain*, and like Williams
was totally uninterested in musical categories.
"We were country, but not what was accepted by
the country music establishment at the time,"
Daniels said. "Every other music was changing
and moving, and cooking. It was time for country to do that,
too."

When the sessions ended, Williams took off for Montana,
to relax before releasing his new album and going on tour.
He was happy with his new record, which included "Living
Proof," a song that mentioned the early deaths of his father,
Jimmie Rodgers, and Johnny Horton, and lamented, "I don't
want to be a legend, I just want to be a man."

Hiking along a ridge on Ajax Mountain, near the Idaho

border, he slipped on the snow and tumbled nearly five hundred feet down the rocky slope. By some miracle, he survived,
though every bone in his face had been broken, one eye was
permanently damaged, his nose was torn off, and parts of
his brain were exposed through a deep gash in his forehead.
Three surgeons worked seven and a half hours trying to put
him back together.

The news quickly reached Nashville and his godparents,
Johnny Cash and June Carter, who raced to be with him.
"I'm in the hospital and they're
basically saying, 'He's probably not
going to make it,'" Williams said,
"and Johnny and June came there,
and John sat down on the side of
the bed. It was something I really
needed at that time. There wasn't
any better medicine than having
him there with me."

TOP *Williams wanted to record a new
album, influenced by what was called
"Southern rock," and make his own
musical statement.*

LEFT *His new album,* Hank Williams,
Jr. and Friends, *included Charlie Daniels
(with guitar, with Daniels's band).*

OPPOSITE, TOP *After recovering from
his near-fatal accident, Hank Junior was
invited by Waylon Jennings to go on tour.
"He believed in me," Williams said.*

Over the next sixteen months, and after nine surgeries, Williams's face was reconstructed. When his album was finally released, another member of his country music family interceded to help him promote it. "Waylon Jennings and my dad were very, very close friends," according to Holly Williams. "Waylon was huge and selling out arenas and my dad's going, 'I'm going to open for Waylon Jennings.' It was a risk; my dad wasn't huge at the time. But Waylon believed in him, and believed in his songs, not him covering his daddy's songs, and gave him his first break on the road."

"There was nobody—nobody—in this business that was more special to me than Waylon Jennings," Hank Junior added. "He believed in me. Here's a guy that looks in the camera and says, 'Well, you might be put off by this, but I'm going to tell you right now, this kid here, he's way more talented than his father was.'"

Three years later, when he made it to age twenty-nine, Williams released *Family Tradition*. "I am very proud of my daddy's name," he sang in the title song, "although his kinda music and mine ain't exactly the same." The album began an uninterrupted string—through the 1980s and early 1990s—of twenty-one gold records. He would win five country

Entertainer of the Year awards, two from the Country Music Association and three from the Academy of Country Music.

"The Williams family tradition is to follow our own passion," said Holly Williams. "Find your own way. Write what you know and what inspires you. My dad came along and plugged in the guitar and shot guns offstage and ran around to every instrument. Just the most amazing shows where you're just entertained. I'll never forget a security guard saying, 'Your dad's shows were wilder than our Guns N' Roses, and Metallica, in the '80s. More fights and drinking and whiskey.' But then Dad would do his acoustic set, and that's when you go, 'He does have Hank's blood in him.' He can rip your heart out with songs like 'Old Habits' and 'Blues Man.' So he's known for his party songs, but he still had that gene to just make you stop and listen, and really relate to his music."

And like his father, Hank Williams Jr. would leave his mark on the young artists who followed him. "There are key characters in country music that are a bridge between generations and between genres," said Dierks Bentley. "That's the reason why I got into country music. I heard a song [of Hank Junior's] called 'Man to Man' and right away, it's like a coin going down a slot machine and just every-

thing lining up. I just knew I wanted to move to Nashville and be a country singer because of one song that Hank Junior sang. And I heard that and, all of a sudden, the guitars come in and it was just so rocking. This is country music? Wow. If this is country music, I want to be part of this music. For my contemporaries, he is such a bridge. This would sound sacrilegious to some people, but I don't know who had a bigger influence in country music, Hank Williams or Hank Junior."

CLOCKWISE FROM LEFT *Family tradition: Hank Williams Jr. finally emerged from his famous father's shadow to become a major star in his own right; his daughter, singer-songwriter Holly Williams; his son, singer-songwriter Hank Williams III; and his half sister, singer-songwriter Jett Williams, daughter of Hank Senior and Bobbie Jett.*

SEVEN YEAR ACHE

There was this Countrypolitan era that was happening in Nashville at the time, and Johnny Cash did not fit within the mold. You could not make a Countrypolitan record and add Johnny Cash on top of it and it would work. And so, a lot of people, I think, figured that my father was passé.

JOHN CARTER CASH

Johnny Cash was now in his early forties, still putting out a steady stream of records, though few of them sold well; some didn't even make the country charts. Cash still drew large crowds on tour. His regular appearances in Las Vegas brought in good money. And his public stature was such that when the nation celebrated its bicentennial in 1976, he was chosen to be the grand marshal of the Fourth of July parade in Washington, D.C.

At home, Cash's personal life seemed better than it had ever been. His long battles with drug addiction appeared to be behind him. His marriage to June Carter was a happy one, especially with the addition of their son, John Carter Cash. Trying to make up for his shortcomings as a father during his first marriage, Cash did everything he could to spend time

TOP, LEFT *On July 4, 1976, Johnny Cash served as grand marshal of the national parade celebrating the country's bicentennial.*

TOP, RIGHT *Cash with his children: from left, Tara, Kathy, Rosanne, Cindy, and John Carter Cash*

RIGHT *The two Cash men head out together.*

with all the children in his and June's family, whether it was at their home outside of Nashville or out on tour.

His oldest child, Rosanne, had been twelve when he divorced her mother. She and her little sisters spent summers with Cash, but grew up mostly in Southern California, surrounded by music much different than her father's. "I loved country music when I was a little kid," Rosanne said. "But then, as a preteen and teen, that was my parents' music. I didn't care; I didn't want to know. I'm going to go with Buffalo Springfield for the moment."

The day after her high school graduation, she left California with her father and went on the road with him, joining his package show that included Maybelle Carter and the Carter Sisters and Carl Perkins. During the shows, she would hang out in the dressing room, learning Carter Family songs from Anita, Helen, and June; getting some guitar instructions from Maybelle and Perkins; and then joining the entire cast for the finale of the night, a singing of "Will the Circle Be Unbroken."

When she first started on the road with her father, she thought it would be an extended vacation—"travel the world,

ABOVE *After her graduation from high school in 1973 in California, Rosanne Cash went on tour with her father.*

RIGHT *On the road, Cash gave Rosanne a list of one hundred essential country songs.*

stay in nice hotels, and see Dad play [and] I'll go to college later," she said—but it turned into much more than that:

We were on the bus one day and talking about songs. It had started to dawn on me that I wanted to be a songwriter. I had been writing poetry, and I wanted to start putting them to music.

I was talking to Dad about wanting to be a songwriter. And he said, "Well, do you know this song?" And I said, "No." And he played it for me. And he said, "Do you know *this* song?" I said, "Never heard that one either."

And he got really alarmed. And he sat on the bus and made this list, and he wrote across the top, "One Hundred Essential Country Songs." And he said, "This is your education." And I took that very seriously.

Still, like Hank Williams Jr., Rosanne was uncertain about following in her father's footsteps. She carried painful childhood memories about what his career had done to her family, and though she aspired to being a songwriter, "I was just torn with how to do that and not be completely eclipsed by my dad's shadow. So I did a lot of things. I lived in Europe for

a while. I made my first album in Europe. I thought, 'Maybe I'll try to do this quietly and no one will notice that he's my dad.'"

After releasing her first album in Germany, she returned to the United States, where Rodney Crowell began work on producing her second album in California. "She was shy," he remembered, "and a little reticent to put her own sensibilities out there. She was keenly aware of the finer points of her father's creative mastery [and] why he was a global icon—a very articulate, intelligent young woman right on the cusp of becoming a fully realized artist when I met her." They married in 1979.

TOP *In Germany, Rosanne recorded her first album.*

LEFT *Rosanne Cash in the studio with her husband and producer Rodney Crowell in Los Angeles*

ABOVE *Cash performing at the Bottom Line, 1981*

One of her father's greatest hits—"I Walk the Line"—had been drawn from tensions in his relations with his first wife. Rosanne now turned a dispute with Crowell into her first number-one song. The couple had an argument outside a restaurant on Ventura Boulevard, she remembered: "I started writing what was a long poem, like three, four pages, and I distilled it down to 'Seven Year Ache.' And I didn't know if it was a country song; I didn't know if I had achieved what I was trying to do. I took it before the 'tribunal,' Guy [Clark] and Rodney, and I was so afraid of what Guy would say. So I kind of played it to myself, off in a corner, and his head whipped around and he said, 'Who wrote that?' I said, 'I did.' I just got this nod, like, 'Okay, you can join the party.'"

Crowell recognized that "she wrote it because I was being an idiot," but also thought it was "a fine piece of music, beautifully written. It stands as one of those songs, like her dad's 'I Walk the Line,' which is, I can't find its prototype."

The song would top the country charts and reach number twenty-two among pop records. The album would also hit number one, become a gold record, be nominated for a Grammy Award—and spin off two additional top singles.

Rosanne Cash was twenty-five years old. With her liberated attitude and her songwriting so attuned to the times, she was, the *Village Voice* proclaimed, "country music's first modern woman." Vince Gill, who now has a daughter of his own trying to make it in the music business, said, "I probably have some good knowledge of how hard it was for Rosanne to be taken seriously. But the cool thing was that she was nothing like her dad. The music was nothing like her father's.

Using some of his friends from Emmylou Harris's Hot Band—renamed the Cherry Bombs—as session players, Crowell took Rosanne into the studio. Her songs and her sound reflected her own life and experiences as distinctively as her father's life had marked his music. "Very quickly she had her own voice," Crowell said, "the same way her father had his own particular voice—obviously two different generations." "Her look, everything about her, was very 'Cash,'" said Tony Brown, one of the Cherry Bombs. "And I think Rosanne brought attitude to country music, not contrived, just natural cool. She had to live up to that 'Cash' iconic thing that he established, and she pulled it off. She was relevant, musically, and she was cool."

At one point, Vince Gill, who had left bluegrass to join the country-pop group Pure Prairie League, was brought in to play lead guitar and sing backup on the Cherry Bombs. It was a big decision on his part, since his new group was so successful. "When I left Pure Prairie League, it wasn't a move about money," Gill said. "It's got to be about the music. The group of musicians that Rodney had put together to play music was as good as it got, and [Rosanne's] a world-class songwriter."

TOP *Rodney Crowell and Rosanne Cash perform with Rodney's mentor Guy Clark. Clark's approval of her song "Seven Year Ache," she said, meant "Okay, you can join the party" as a songwriter.*

RIGHT *With Columbia executive Rick Blackburn, Rodney and Rosanne celebrate her album becoming a gold record.*

She came from a totally different place, and she was her own artist from day one."

By this time, Johnny Cash had made an addition to his musical family. Lester Flatt had died, and his young mandolin player, Marty Stuart, needed a job. He got one—as part of Cash's traveling band. "It's interesting," Stuart said. "The first two records I ever owned in my life was a Johnny Cash record and a Lester Flatt and Earl Scruggs record. And the only two jobs I've ever had was with Lester Flatt and Johnny Cash." Stuart's connection became even closer when he married one of Cash's daughters, Cindy.

Meanwhile, at age forty-eight, Johnny Cash had recently been inducted into the Country Music Hall of Fame, the youngest person to achieve that status. When communist China sent its first ambassador to the United States, one of the places he wanted to visit was Nashville. Johnny Cash was among the country music dignitaries who shared a private brunch with him at the home of Tom T. Hall one Sunday morning. As the crowd prepared to eat, there was an awkward pause in the moment when a prayer would normally be said. Johnny and June saved the day: they began singing "Will the Circle Be Broken," and everyone joined hands and sang along.

TOP *Marty Stuart joined Cash's band and married into his family.*

ABOVE *Carlene Carter (top, left) also went into the family business, touring with her mother June (front, left) and aunts Anita (top, right) and Helen.*

RIGHT *When communist China sent its first ambassador to the United States and he wanted to visit Music City, Cash and his wife June were among those to welcome him.*

She's crossed all boundaries. Dolly's not country; Dolly's not rock; Dolly's not pop. Dolly's everything. And everybody from every genre loves her. And she loves them back.

She didn't want to be just Nashville. Nashville was great to her and she reveres it. But Dolly wanted to be everywhere. And that's what she did. And she brought fans to country music probably that maybe we would have never had.

BRENDA LEE

Dolly Parton's ambition to be a major star in her own right had prompted her to leave Porter Wagoner in 1974. Three years later, frustrated with the trajectory of her solo career, she hired a new management team in Los Angeles—and traveled there to record a new album.

"I'm not leaving country music," she told reporters, "I'm taking it with me to new places." She added: "Abraham Lincoln was great not because he was born in a cabin, but because he got out of it."

"Her choice was absolutely correct," said Joe Galante. "It propelled her career to another level. But you couldn't change that voice. I mean, Dolly is not a disco singer. She's not a rock-and-roll singer. She's a country singer." "Everybody was saying I was betraying country," Parton recalled. "How could I not be country? I'm a country girl at heart, in my voice, in my feelings, in my attitude."

Previously, Parton's number-one country singles had sold about sixty thousand copies. "Here You Come Again," her first crossover success, sold a million. Then the album it came from did the same and went platinum. In 1978, the Country Music Association named her Entertainer of the Year—the second woman, after Loretta Lynn, to win the top honor.

Asked if she considered her music country or pop, she had a ready answer. "I prefer," she said, "to call it Dolly Parton music." More and more people wanted to hear it—and learn about the petite and shapely blonde with the big hair who performed it. With her refreshing sense of humor, especially about herself, Dolly never disappointed them. "It costs a lot of money," she said, "to look this cheap."

Playboy put her on its cover. *Cosmopolitan* did a lengthy profile of what they called "country music's mega-star." She posed with body builder turned actor Arnold Schwarzeneg-

OPPOSITE *Dolly Parton mixed glamour with down-home country songs.*

BELOW *Dolly, at a press conference in Tokyo, also became an international star.*

ger for *Rolling Stone*. In New York, she gave a free concert at City Hall Plaza, and Mayor Ed Koch presented her with the keys to the city. Later she was the guest of honor at a party at the famous Studio 54.

"Although I look like a drag queen's Christmas tree on the outside, I am at heart a simple country girl," Parton said. "I look a certain way because I choose to. This is a country girl's idea of glamour. I wanted to have beautiful clothes; I wanted to wear makeup. I'd pattern my look after the town trollop in our hometown because I thought she was beautiful."

Joe Galante accompanied her on some promotional trips: "She walks into a room and she lights everything up. Her smile, her laugh, just the way she looks at you, you feel like you've known her forever. She gets everybody excited. We'd rent a ballroom in a hotel and bring in all the radio [executives] and the retailers. We'd have to

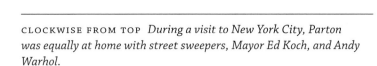

CLOCKWISE FROM TOP *During a visit to New York City, Parton was equally at home with street sweepers, Mayor Ed Koch, and Andy Warhol.*

go through the kitchen, because she was a celebrity. And she would be slapping the butts of the waiters walking through there, just playing. And these guys would turn around and go, 'What, what just happened to me?' It's like pouring gasoline on a fire."

But beneath the flashy exterior, and despite her poor Appalachian upbringing, Parton was one of the savviest artists in the business. She had her own publishing company; marketed a successful line of Dolly dolls; and negotiated a three-year deal with a Las Vegas hotel, said to be worth from six to nine million dollars. "I've never had a problem being a woman; that's worked for me more than it's worked against me," Parton said. "I just always believed that I was strong in myself and strong in my work. I do know, and I have seen that it can be a hindrance, but I would always just go in saying, 'I think I've got something to offer, and I think we can both make a lot of money from it.' And, usually, by the time the deal was done, I'd have the money and be gone."

In 1980, she achieved an entirely new level of national stardom when she joined Jane Fonda and Lily Tomlin in the Hollywood movie *9 to 5*, about three women working for an insufferable, chauvinistic boss in a big insurance com-

pany. The film's title song, written and performed by Parton, won her two Grammy Awards and an Oscar nomination, became *Billboard*'s most performed country song of the year—and, as an anthem for working women across the nation, was the first performance by a woman in more than a dozen years to reach number one on both the country and pop charts.

Back in 1964, fresh out of high school, Dolly Parton had arrived in Nashville with a cheap cardboard suitcase containing all her possessions. It had taken three years of hard work to finally have a song—"Dumb Blonde"—reach the charts. Now, thanks to her songwriting talent, her unmistakable voice, her bigger-than-life persona, and her tireless drive, she had become the most famous woman in country music.

"I'm not offended by all the dumb-blonde jokes, because I know I'm not dumb," she said. "And I'm not blonde, either."

TOP, LEFT *Record executive Joe Galante (left) credited Dolly Parton as one of the three artists whose work persuaded him to stay in Nashville. The other two were Waylon Jennings and Ronnie Milsap.*

TOP, RIGHT *In the Hollywood movie 9 to 5, Dolly starred with Jane Fonda (left) and Lily Tomlin. She also wrote the title song, which was nominated for an Oscar.*

CENTER *Dolly the businesswoman shows off a Dolly doll.*

I WAS COUNTRY
WHEN COUNTRY WASN'T COOL

We say "country," but mean something else when we buy a recording by Anne Murray, Linda Ronstadt, John Denver . . . and now Dolly Parton, Barbara Mandrell, Larry Gatlin, or perhaps even Conway Twitty, among others.

What about Kenny Rogers, the current darling of the pop-rock set? Willie Nelson? He's turned his back on country. Charley Pride has a string section.

[They] have strayed from traditional country music. Can we, in all good conscience, support and extol those who have broken with the old traditions and allowed country music to slide into gradual oblivion?

EVERETT J. CORBIN, *STORM OVER NASHVILLE*

In the late 1970s and early 1980s, the debate over defining country music was growing increasingly shrill—yet also less relevant. Country music's embrace was bigger than ever. Artists were exploding the old definitions and exploring every possible combination of styles, and many of them didn't care what it was called. Record labels were more intent on reaching as many listeners as possible than on dealing with complaints about how they did it.

Whether it was the outlaw music of Willie Nelson, Waylon Jennings, and Hank Williams Jr.; Emmylou Harris and

Rosanne Cash's infusion of West Coast sensibilities; or Dolly Parton's phenomenal breakthroughs to pop audiences, old boundaries were being stretched more than ever. So were record sales, which had more than tripled during the 1970s. Gold albums, once a rarity, were now being announced nearly twice a month. The money spent on producing an album had also ballooned. Between 1973 and 1983, the number of full-time country radio stations would nearly triple, rising from 764 to 2,266.

Joe Galante, at RCA, had been in the middle of it all: "I was going to stay in Nashville for two years. One of the main reasons why I didn't leave was I met Waylon. And when I met Waylon, my entire view of this format changed. There were three acts in my life that changed what I felt about this town. One was Waylon. The second was Dolly. And the third was Ronnie Milsap. When I met those three, I was hooked for life."

Ronnie Milsap was born in Robbinsville, North Carolina, with congenital glaucoma. When faith healers couldn't cure it, his mother considered his blindness as divine punishment and sent him away to a state school, where he was subjected to harsh treatment, including a beating so severe that his one eye that *could* detect a little light had to be removed. But nothing could dampen his musical talent—or his ambition: "I learned Braille at six, violin at seven, piano at eight—twelve years of classical training. And I went to my counselors and I said, 'I want to become a professional musician.' And they said, 'We won't let you do that because you'll end up out on the street. You won't have a job.'"

Milsap managed to meet his hero, Ray Charles, who encouraged him to follow his heart, and he ended up in Memphis, playing piano on an Elvis Presley record. His own tastes leaned toward Motown and rhythm and blues, but hearing some of Merle Haggard's songs got him interested in country music, as well. Then, in the early 1970s, Charley Pride happened into one of Milsap's performances at the Whisky a Go Go nightclub in Los Angeles. After hearing Milsap sing Haggard's song "Today I Started Loving You Again," Pride told him, "You need to play more songs

LEFT *Young Ronnie Milsap would not let his blindness keep him from following his love of music.*

like that." He moved to Nashville, Milsap said, "and I've been here ever since."

With dozens of number-one hits, an Entertainer of the Year award, and six Grammys, Milsap became one of Nashville's top Countrypolitan artists. His music mixed country and rock, blues and soul. His biggest hit, which topped the country charts and hit number five among pop records, would be "There's No Getting Over Me."

At RCA, Joe Galante and Jerry Bradley also signed a band called Alabama, formed by three cousins from the Fort Payne area. Randy Owen, the lead singer and songwriter, had performed in his family's gospel group as a boy; as a teenager, he considered Merle Haggard and the Beatles equal influences on his music. He and his group had supported themselves playing at a rowdy dance hall and beer joint on Myrtle Beach in South Carolina, which also featured "Bouncin' Betty, the Largest Go-Go Dancer in the United States."

The experience of being in a bar band in the 1970s, Owen said, meant "you're there playing what they want to hear as

RIGHT *Milsap turned to country music at the suggestion of Charley Pride—and went on to become a CMA Entertainer of the Year.*

BELOW *The band Alabama began its career playing in a bar on Myrtle Beach; soon, their rock-style production values thrilled audiences at huge venues, as well as here at the* Opry.

opposed to what you may want to play: rhythm and blues, beach music, rock music, dance music. We had to play KC and the Sunshine Band. We had to do all those songs because we had to work for tips."

Their first single for RCA, "Tennessee River," was a song they had already tried out on crowds of young people. "It had all the ingredients of Southern rock, gospel, country," Owen said, but at the end included a bluegrass fiddle breakdown. "I wanted to see how the audience reacts," he said. "Well, the audience went crazy." The single went straight to number one.

An unprecedented twenty consecutive number-one hits followed. Every one of Alabama's albums in the 1980s sold at least a million copies. Their live concerts became legendary for incorporating rock-style production values. "It was about a change in terms of generations," Galante said. "When they came through, you had people that were of the prior generation really pissed off: 'This is not country music.' We go through that every ten years or so, somebody always telling us what we're not supposed to be doing, but at the end of the day, it's up to the people." In Oklahoma, young Garth Brooks was paying attention: "Well, as a teenager, you grew up on '70s rock, which was filled with bands. Alabama was

known as a band. They traveled that way. And that was cool, especially in country music. I played more Alabama than Alabama has."

At the other end of the spectrum from Alabama was Don Williams, a former folk singer from Texas, who was having hits with ballads that featured his warm baritone voice and kept the accompaniment at a minimum. Many of his hits came from the pen of fellow Texan Bob McDill, a prolific songwriter with a literary bent. In 1980, McDill came up with "Good Ole Boys Like Me," which he said was inspired by a novel by Robert Penn Warren: "I was so impressed with that and wanted to create a song about the real South, the one I'd grown up in—not *The Dukes of Hazzard* or whatever—and put all those themes in there. They're in Faulkner, and they're in Warren: a reverence for the land, the father-son battles, race. All those things."

Alice Randall, a novelist and songwriter, considers "Good Ole Boys Like Me" one of her favorite songs of all time: "That song opens, 'When I was a boy, Uncle Remus would put me to bed.' But a picture of Stonewall Jackson is hanging over the bed—the Confederate general, but the tale being told is an Uncle Remus story. The father is, 'Daddy would come in with gin on his breath and his Bible in his hand.'"

ABOVE *Joe Galante (far left) celebrates another platinum album with Alabama.*

RIGHT *Balladeer Don Williams recorded many songs written by Bob McDill, including "Good Ole Boys Like Me," inspired by a novel by Robert Penn Warren.*

"It's almost like a really good Southern novel," said songwriter Bobby Braddock. "He mentions 'Thomas Wolfe whispering in my ear.' And I daresay a lot of country music fans probably didn't know who Thomas Wolfe was. And when he said, 'Those Williams boys still mean a lot to me, Hank and Tennessee,' I think probably a lot of people who would listen to it on the radio and liked it probably didn't know who Tennessee Williams was. But it didn't matter."

"But when you get all those images, near the end, it says, 'We're all going to be what we're going to be, so what do you do with good old boys like me?'" said McDill. "Meaning, I don't care if you go to LA and change your accent, this is still who you are. You can't get rid of it."

With that and other songs, including a duet with Emmylou Harris of Townes Van Zandt's "If I Needed You," Don Williams became one of the most successful country artists in the world, extending the music's popularity to Europe, Australia, and Africa.

There were other stars who moved across the musical boundaries and found success. The Oak Ridge Boys had been trying for years to expand their fan base from the tiny gospel market; with songs like "Elvira," they became one of the top-selling groups in country music. Crystal Gayle was Loretta Lynn's youngest sister. Her songs, her sound, and her look—sophisticated, smooth, and glamorous—could not have been more different from Lynn's hard-country style, and she easily crossed over to the pop charts in ways her big sister couldn't.

> I think country music should decide if they're an art form or if they're a business. If they're an art form, get rid of everybody that doesn't sound like Hank Williams. If they're a business, take the money wherever it comes from.
>
> KENNY ROGERS

Kenny Rogers grew up in the public housing projects of Houston, where at age twelve he won a quart of ice cream singing Hank Williams's "Lovesick Blues" in a music contest. But as a teenager he played in a rockabilly band, then switched to jazz for

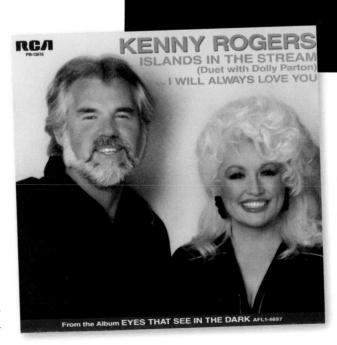

ABOVE *Kenny Rogers spanned genres, but had his greatest success in country music. One song, "The Gambler," was turned into four television movies.*

LEFT *Rogers and Dolly Parton had a huge crossover hit, "Islands in the Stream," written by Barry Gibb of the Bee Gees.*

a while, and later joined a folk group, the New Christy Minstrels. In the late 1960s, as the lead singer for the First Edition, he had success with a psychedelic song, "Just Dropped In (To See What Condition My Condition Was In)" and an even bigger hit with "Ruby (Don't Take Your Love to Town)," Mel Tillis's song about a disabled war veteran.

By the late 1970s, Rogers was on his own, releasing crossover singles like "Lucille" and "The Gambler," a song so popular, four made-for-television movies were based on it. Then, with songs like "Lady," written by R&B star Lionel Ritchie, he edged even further away from straight country music. "Islands in the Stream," a duet with Dolly Parton, was written and produced by Barry Gibb of the Bee Gees—and spent two weeks at the top of the country and pop charts.

"When you have a career, you want success wherever you can find it," Rogers said. "I think there's always been a certain resentment from country music for my going to the pop side. I've always felt that, rightfully or not. My goal was to introduce country music to people who wouldn't normally listen to it because I know this: Once you come into country, you don't leave, because that's where the truth is. And people come up and they say, 'You know what? I didn't realize that was country.' I thought I was doing a good thing. I don't know whether it was or not, but that's really something that I was very proud of, that I was bringing people from New Jersey who had never listened to country music."

Barbara Mandrell

Wright~Custom

· · ·

They would call us artists. Well, artists are creative people. And how does one create, if you keep doing the same thing over and over again? I just think that's wonderful when it can stretch out.

And if you are a purist of country music, I don't even know that I would know what that is. But if you are, and you're happy with that, enjoy it and let everybody else enjoy every other place that country music goes. It's wide open. It has no boundaries.

BARBARA MANDRELL

ABOVE *Barbara Mandrell's first publicity as "Sweetheart of the Steel Guitar"*

LEFT *Mandrell with Loretta Lynn. Both of them had been befriended by Patsy Cline years earlier.*

If some people complained that Barbara Mandrell had become too Countrypolitan, no one could argue that her country music credentials weren't impeccable. A musical prodigy, she had mastered the steel guitar by the time she was eleven years old and began appearing on a country television show in California. "When I'd go back to school, on Mondays, after the show on Saturday night," she said, "I would hear things like, 'Hee-haw—that country music,' kids poking fun."

Billed as "the Sweetheart of the Steel Guitar," at the age of thirteen she was part of Johnny Cash's package tour, along with George Jones and Patsy Cline. Jones asked her to back him up during his songs; Cline gave her motherly advice and watched out for her.

In 1973, working with Countrypolitan producer Billy Sherrill, Mandrell had a breakthrough hit with "The Midnight Oil," a cheating song originally written for George Jones. It broke new ground when she changed the lyrics to the perspective of a woman planning to betray her husband.

Mandrell released records that R&B stations played and did remakes of soul music by Aretha Franklin. She also starred in her own network variety show on NBC, along with her two sisters, that aimed squarely at the broadest mainstream audience with its mixture of comedy sketches, celebrity appearances, and music, including her displays of

versatility on a range of instruments and the black gospel songs she loved.

In 1980 and 1981, Mandrell became the first artist to be named the Country Music Association's Entertainer of the Year two years in a row. At one of the awards ceremonies, she sang her latest hit song, which two friends had written for her after listening to her stories about being made fun of back in junior high school. Its title was "I Was Country When Country Wasn't Cool," and it included a line about listening on the radio to George Jones. He had once asked her to accompany him on steel guitar; now, he sang a cameo verse on her song. "It is the story of my life," she said. "It's my signature song, because that's what I lived."

ABOVE *Mandrell performs "I Was Country When Country Wasn't Cool" with George Jones at the CMA Awards.*

LEFT *Barbara accepts some flowers from the next generation of country fans.*

who were required to remain at the top-secret nuclear research plant near Oak Ridge, Tennessee, during World War Two.

By the 1970s, after a number of changes in personnel, they had won a dozen of gospel music's Dove Awards, but were struggling to make ends meet, when Johnny Cash asked them to join his package tour to replace the Statler Brothers, who had gone off on their own.

"He called us up and said, 'Fellas, there's something special about you guys. You have to find a way to stick it out. You have to find a way to stay with it,'" said Richard Sterban, one of the group's members. "'If you don't, you'll never realize your dreams, and people will never realize how special you guys are.' We said, between ourselves, 'If Johnny Cash thinks we can make it, we are going to make it.'" According to fellow member Joe Bonsall, they began wearing big belt buckles that said, "Johnny Cash is a friend of mine."

Part of Cash's tour included an extended stay at a Las Vegas casino, which put the Oak Ridge Boys in bad standing with the gospel community; whenever they appeared at gospel singing conventions, the purists would walk out while they performed.

HE BELIEVES IN ME

Gospel and country will always be connected because they're cousins of each other. Just like R&B and black gospel. R&B and country always have embraced some form of gospel music because it's the soul part of their music.

I think that the relationship of country music and gospel music is because I think country folks feel like if they are bad on Saturday night, all they've got to do to make it right is go to church on Sunday.

TONY BROWN

The Oak Ridge Boys traced their lineage back to the 1940s, when the gospel quartet formed to sing for workers and their families

Things got worse when they found themselves in debt, behind on their taxes, and in desperate need of $25,000. They went to Cash and offered to sell him their publishing company for that amount. Cash told them to hold on to the publishing company, because its value would increase over time, and instead wrote them a check for $25,000 and tried to hand it to them, remembered lead singer Duane Allen.

He said, "Here, now go pay off your bills and you guys stay together and just know that Johnny Cash believes in you."

Instead of taking the check, I went past the check he was holding out and hugged his neck. And I said, "Johnny, I think you've taught us a big lesson." And I said, "You believe in the Oak Ridge Boys more than we do. And I want you to keep that check. We just need to go get our heads together and tell each other that Johnny Cash believes in us that much."

Johnny Cash was dressed in black, but he could have dressed in any color and he would have been an angel to me.

Soon after, in 1977, their career started to take off when the Oak Ridge Boys finally had a hit. "The Y'all Come Back Saloon" tells the story of a woman who sings in the church choir on Sunday, but on Saturday nights makes her living singing at the saloon. They had even greater success with "Elvira," which reached number one on the country charts and crossed over to number five among pop songs.

When they were named the Vocal Group of the Year by the CMA, Johnny Cash was hosting the show. "When we were announced," Sterban said, "instead of running to accept our awards, we went over and all hugged Johnny Cash's neck. He told us, 'See, fellas? I told you so.'"

OPPOSITE, TOP *Caught between the gospel and country music markets, the Oak Ridge Boys were struggling when Johnny Cash gave them the confidence to keep going.*

OPPOSITE, BOTTOM *With Cash's encouragement—and songs like "Elvira"—they went on to win every possible award (like this Grammy) and became one of the top-selling groups in country music.*

NO-SHOW JONES

I am convinced George Jones might be the most soulful singer the planet has ever known.

GARTH BROOKS

I think I was sweeping the floor, or something, and I had a George Jones record on. All of a sudden, I heard him. I don't know how to explain it, but it was like a veil lifted from my ears, attached to my soul and my heart. And the way I listened to music, I heard him, truly heard him, for the first time, the soulfulness in his voice. And it was just this incredible "aha" moment where I thought, "There's just no one like him." He could have sung the phone book, probably, and moved me after that.

EMMYLOU HARRIS

It was always a heartfelt song, and he could tear it up and he could make you cry while he was singing. That's what made George Jones, because he could take a song and you could feel it. You could go through the pain while he was singing it. I'm telling you. He's the greatest singer in the world when it comes to country music.

LORETTA LYNN

I don't think you can understand George Jones. I don't think there's a way on God's green earth to understand George Jones. I quit trying a long time ago.

BILLY SHERRILL

In the years following his divorce with Tammy Wynette, George Jones's life spiraled out of control. Some people thought it was because he still loved Tammy, while she had moved on. Already prone to violent bouts of heavy drinking, he now became addicted to cocaine. He continued to record, and no one disputed the singular power of his voice, but Jones seemed intent on self-destruction. As a song he released explained, "I Just Don't Give a Damn."

"George's behavior could become quite volatile out on the road," said WSM announcer Eddie Stubbs. "There were times that he'd get paid a thousand dollars for a show date and he'd go and flush a thousand dollars right down the commode and think nothing of it. He'd light a cigarette with hundred-dollar bills."

On the whole, however, his fans forgave him, according to Charlie Daniels: "He touched such a nerve in people that very rarely an artist can reach that point. Hank Williams did it. George Jones did it. Very few people reach the point that you're willing to accept them like they are. So he didn't show up: 'Well, I'll keep my ticket. I'll come see him next time. I'm not going to be mad at him.' It just identified him as being more like them. We're all human. We all make mistakes. That's just 'Old George. He's our hero. We love him.'"

Jones's mixture of whiskey and cocaine made him chronically sleepless and paranoid. He lost weight, dropping to under a hundred pounds. Friends grew alarmed when he started having conversations with two imaginary friends—Deedoodle Duck, who sounded like the cartoon character Donald Duck, except for his cussing; and the Old Man, who sounded like the actor Walter Brennan and dispensed homespun advice. Sometimes Jones would argue with people in the Duck voice—and later apologize in his own.

In one drug-crazed rage, Jones fired his pistol at his best friend. He had repeated run-ins with the police for speeding around in one of his Cadillacs while drunk. Doctors at a psychiatric hospital told him he'd be dead in two months if he didn't change his habits. He ignored them all. Entangled in lawsuits for bad debts and canceled shows, he filed for bankruptcy, lost his house, and lived in his car for a while.

He began missing concerts—so many that promoters and fans alike gave him a new nickname. It had been "Possum." Now it was "No-Show Jones." "I worked on a couple of shows with him during that time," Marty Stuart said. "He didn't make it, and the crowd got hostile. I mean, it was riot time. They were throwing and yelling and screaming and wanting money back. But you know what? Just the sight of his bus and his band was better than most people showing up and giving it their best shot."

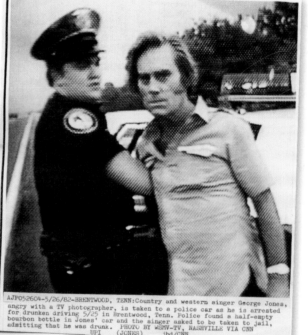

AJP052604-5/26/82-BRENTWOOD, TENN:Country and western singer George Jones, angry with a TV photographer, is taken to a police car as he is arrested for drunken driving 5/25 in Brentwood, Tenn. Police found a half-empty bourbon bottle in Jones' car and the singer asked to be taken to jail, admitting that he was drunk. PHOTO BY WSMV-TV, NASHVILLE VIA CNN UPI (JONES) jbd/CNN

Tammy Wynette's life was in shambles, too. Now married to her fifth husband and plagued with health problems, she had become hooked on prescription painkillers, and then was involved in a string of bizarre incidents that kept her constantly in the tabloid news: reports of mysterious break-ins and fires at her house, and a sensational claim that she had been kidnapped and beaten up before being released.

CLOCKWISE FROM TOP *As his life seemed to spiral out of control and he added cocaine to his alcohol addiction, George Jones was besieged by reporters; arrested for drunk driving; and in the news as "No Show" Jones while he filed for bankruptcy.*

Wynette hadn't had a number-one hit for four years—and neither had George Jones—when Billy Sherrill brought the two of them back into the studio in January 1980 for another album of duets, *Together Again*. "It was kind of like two wounded animals," Sherrill said, "not too wounded to keep doing what they wanted to do and what they loved doing."

"[George] is still the greatest voice in country music," Wynette told a reporter. "Even though we couldn't live together, he'll always be my favorite singer." A single from the album, "Two Story House," which she had co-written especially for the occasion, would rise to number two on the country charts

in the spring of 1980. But its success paled compared to a song Jones recorded by himself less than a month later.

"He Stopped Loving Her Today" was written by Bobby Braddock and Curly Putman, two veteran Nashville songsmiths who had already collaborated on Tammy Wynette's breakthrough hit, "D-I-V-O-R-C-E," about a mother's worries for her child as her marriage breaks apart. Their new song had even more pathos. It describes a man who waits all his life, pining away for the woman who's left him. Midway through the song, it's revealed that the only reason he stopped loving her is because he has died.

ABOVE *Tammy Wynette's life was also falling apart.*

TOP, RIGHT *Bobby Braddock (left) and Curly Putman wrote "He Stopped Loving Her Today," which Billy Sherrill believed could provide George Jones with a much-needed hit.*

ABOVE, RIGHT *But Jones thought the song was too morbid and at first resisted recording it.*

Billy Sherrill believed the song was a perfect fit for George Jones. The only problem was that Jones thought the song was too depressing—and once he got into the studio, he had trouble getting the melody straight. He kept confusing it with Kris Kristofferson's "Help Me Make It Through the Night," until Sherrill finally got him straightened out.

With some of Nashville's best session musicians, Sherrill created an arrangement that had a classic Countrypolitan sound: a faint, weeping steel guitar without a hint of twang;

sweet background vocals; and an ensemble of strings that built steadily toward the song's climax.

"A lot of the critics of that day found great fault with Billy Sherrill's production," Braddock remembered. "They said it was 'slick,' too orchestrated. This may sound strange coming from the songwriter, but I think that roomful of cellos and violas and violins, ascending on that record, sounding like the man's soul going up to heaven—I thought that was the most powerful thing on the record."

When the session ended, Sherrill was happy with the result; Jones was not. "Word for word, after I played him the finished product, so help me God, Jones said, 'You've got your record, but listen, son, nobody will ever buy that morbid son of a bitch,'" Sherrill recalled. "And I said, 'They may not, but they're going to get it in two weeks and we'll find out then.'"

Three months after its release, "He Stopped Loving Her Today" reached the top of the country charts—George Jones's first solo number-one hit in six years. It would go on to sell a million records and win every possible award for the songwriters and the artist.

"There's not one beat, not one bar, that's not perfect," said Barbara Mandrell. "It's supreme; it's superb, everything about it. It just yanks your heart out—and it was George's voice." Eddie Stubbs called it "one of those songs that was meant to be, and it was one of those songs that George Jones was meant to record. And when he got done with it, it had been *done*. Anybody who was around when that record came out can tell you where they were, the first time they heard it on the radio. They could take you to the spot they were, if they were driving, or a room in the house they were in when they heard 'He Stopped Loving Her Today' for the first time. It had that much of an impact."

Hazel Smith is one of those people: "The first time I heard it, I was driving out Interstate 65 where it turns there and goes into 265. I had to pull off the road. I couldn't see, I was crying so hard. That song just really touched me—and I honestly think it may have happened."

"I was back on top," Jones recalled. "A four-decade career had been salvaged by a three-minute song." With the help of a new wife, he would eventually beat his addictions to drugs and alcohol, release dozens more albums—many of them gold and platinum—and live another thirty-three years.

For Tammy Wynette, "Two Story House" would be her last song to reach the top five. With her husband, instead of Billy Sherrill, producing her, her career drifted. But she would still be called "the First Lady of Country Music" when she died in 1998, at the age of fifty-five.

George Jones attended the private and public memorials. "Life is too short," he said. "In the end, we were very close friends. And now I have lost that friend. I couldn't be sadder."

ABOVE *With the success of "He Stopped Loving Her Today," George Jones was back on top. "A four-decade career," he said, "had been salvaged by a three-minute song."*

TURN ME LOOSE, SET ME FREE

I think sometimes songs, they're like dreams. They're hanging around, and different songwriters reach up and get them. And if they just bring me up in the same sentence with some of the great writers, that would be my ultimate, to have that.

MERLE HAGGARD

I asked Merle, one time, who his favorite country singer was. He said, "George Jones." I asked George who his favorite country singer was. He said, "Merle Haggard."

RALPH EMERY

By the early 1980s, Merle Haggard was one of country music's major stars. *Time* magazine had put him on its cover; California governor Ronald Reagan had issued a pardon that expunged his prison record; he had recorded more than forty albums and more than thirty number-one singles. He was already considered one of the greatest singer-songwriters, "the Poet of the Common Man." Many people—especially those in the business—also considered him country's greatest singer, ranked alongside George Jones.

"I got him in the studio one day, and it came right off the top of my head, I hadn't even planned to say it. I said, 'Merle, you're my favorite country music singer,'" said Bill Anderson. "And I meant it. I just feel like there is a depth of quality to his voice, the songs that he sings, the way that he sings them, what he chooses. Whether he's singing a gospel song or a low-down honky tonk song or a love song, Merle Haggard's voice resonates inside of me. And when I told him that he was my favorite singer, I noticed he grew very quiet. And I thought, 'Oh, goodness, I hope I haven't offended him in any way.' And I looked over there, and there was a tear running out of the corner of his eye."

If much of country music seemed to have moved to the

white-collar suburbs, Haggard's songs were firmly attached to his working-class roots. In 1981, Haggard's album *Big City* became his first gold record. Its title song was inspired by a remark his tour bus driver made—"I'm tired of this dirty old city"—and when Haggard asked him where he'd rather be, the man said, "Somewhere in the middle of Montana." In thanks for the inspiration, Haggard decided to share the writing credit with the bus driver, Dean Holloway, which earned Holloway half a million dollars in royalties.

The next year, Haggard and George Jones collaborated on an album of duets, *A Taste of Yesterday's Wine*. And in 1983, he had even greater success with an album recorded with another country icon, Willie Nelson.

They had been recording for five days at Willie's studio in Texas, but still hadn't found the right song to anchor the album. Haggard had gone to sleep on his bus. Meanwhile, Nelson's daughter played her father a tune he had never heard before. It was on an Emmylou Harris album, a bittersweet ballad written by Townes Van Zandt. Thirty years later, Haggard still remembered the moment:

And Willie came and knocked on my bus, late one night, about four in the morning, actually, and I had just laid down. And he said, "I think I've found a title [song] for

ABOVE *Merle Haggard (left) said George Jones was his favorite singer; Jones said Haggard was his.*

our album." And he had a paper sack rolled out and these words [on it].

"Willie," I said, "I can't even see those lyrics." I said, "You guys go ahead and put it down and I'll put my voice on in the morning."

"No," he said. "Get up and come in there with me. Let's do it all at once."

So I went in there. I was real sleepy, and we recorded that thing. And I was thinking, while I was doing it, "Well, I'll do this over in the morning." So I got up the next morning and went in the studio and I said, "Can I do that vocal track over?" And they said, "Hell, that's on the way to New York." I don't even remember singing it. I was asleep.

The song was "Pancho and Lefty." The album of the same name would shoot to number one on the country charts,

cross over to pop, and sell more than a million records.

To get there, the song had traveled a long, meandering road. Two of country music's legendary songwriters—the musical "outlaw" from Texas and "the Poet of the Common Man" from the hardscrabble streets of Bakersfield—had listened to an album recorded by a former hippie folksinger, who had been converted to country by a cosmic cowboy, and in doing so stumbled upon a song written by an eccentric vagabond, who spent his days trying to write the perfect song, and some of his nights crashing with friends, at a home where the focus was on art, not commercial success.

TOP AND ABOVE *Merle Haggard fiddles while Willie Nelson stands by with his guitar, Trigger, at one of Willie's picnics. Their duet album,* Pancho and Lefty, *catapulted Townes Van Zandt's song to the top of the charts.*

On his sixtieth birthday, Willie Nelson would sing "Pancho and Lefty" again, this time with someone who also defied musical categories, Bob Dylan. Backing them up on the mandolin was the kid from Philadelphia, Mississippi, who had played in Lester Flatt's and Johnny Cash's bands: Marty Stuart.

"Music cuts through all the boundaries, and a lot of us know that," Nelson said. "So we're not afraid to play anything for anybody, because music will get through."

BELOW *Willie Nelson performs "Pancho and Lefty" with Bob Dylan at Willie's sixtieth-birthday concert. Marty Stuart (center background) accompanies them on the mandolin.*

URBAN COWBOYS

In the early 1980s, Hollywood ignited a boom in country music. It began with *Urban Cowboy*, set in an actual Texas dance hall called Gilley's and starring John Travolta, who only a few years earlier had popularized the disco music scene in *Saturday Night Fever*. Now he was dressed—and dancing—in jeans, boots, and a cowboy hat.

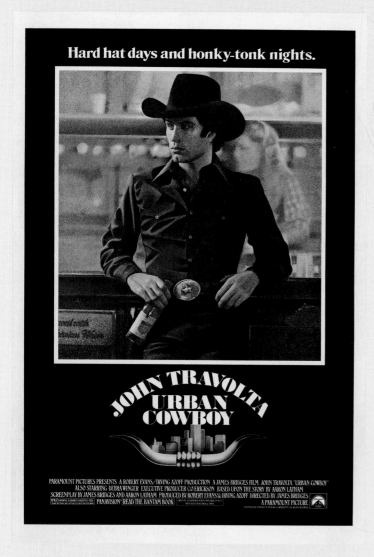

The movie's huge success turned Gilley's into a major tourist destination, boosted sales of Western wear among suburbanites, got them learning the Texas two-step—and sold lots of records.

"I remember when the movie *Urban Cowboy* first came out," said Del Bryant. "My brother, who is in publishing, had gotten the song 'Could I Have This Dance?' cut, which was the Anne Murray hit. Well, everybody who was on that album, as it turns out, was on the ride of their life, because the album sold about five or six million units. Country music became, once again, not only hot in country, but hot in pop. And it became hot in the movies. All of a sudden, every movie thought, 'Well, the recipe might be to have a country song in your movie, or might be to have a country movie.'"

A string of other country music films followed in quick succession.

Coal Miner's Daughter told the life story of Loretta Lynn—and won Sissy Spacek an Academy Award for her portrayal. Jessica Lange was nominated for an Oscar playing Patsy Cline in *Sweet Dreams*, which revived interest in Cline's music. In *Tender Mercies*, Robert Duvall won an Academy Award as a washed-up, alcoholic singer-songwriter whose wife is still a star performer.

A number of actual country stars, including Marty Robbins, appeared in *Honkytonk Man*, a story very loosely based on the career of Jimmie Rodgers, in which Clint Eastwood is a country singer dying of tuberculosis.

Willie Nelson appeared with Robert Redford in *The Electric Horseman* and with Kris Kristofferson in *Songwriter*. Then, in *Honeysuckle Rose*, Nelson portrayed a performer who spends all his time on the road. "There was no acting there," he said. His movie band was his real band. Emmylou Harris had been slated to appear opposite Nelson in a major role, but her pregnancy reduced it to a cameo.

Though much of the music in *Honeysuckle Rose* comprised songs Nelson had written and recorded earlier, the film's executives wanted something new for a theme song. "They asked me if I could write a song about the road," Nelson remembered. "I said, 'You mean, like "On the road again. I can't wait to get on the road again?" And they said, 'Well,

does it have a melody?' And I said, 'It will have by the time we get to the studio.'"

"On the Road Again" was nominated for an Oscar, topped the country charts, and reached the top twenty in pop. It became one of Nelson's signature songs, neatly summarizing his life—"like a band of gypsies" going down the highway—and his preference for playing before live audiences night after night. "The life I love," it said, "is making music with my friends."

LEFT TO RIGHT *The movie* Urban Cowboy, *starring John Travolta, set off a boom in country music and touched off a string of similar films; Sissy Spacek played Loretta Lynn in* Coal Miner's Daughter; *Jessica Lange became Patsy Cline in* Sweet Dreams; *and Willie Nelson portrayed a character very much like himself in* Honeysuckle Rose.

8

DON'T GET ABOVE YOUR RAISIN'

If you look at it over the last ninety years now, that it's been recorded, it wouldn't be one thing. It wouldn't be anywhere close to one thing. It's been a million different things in a million different ways. And that, to me, is the way it should be. I don't think I would enjoy country music if it stayed the same. It's not supposed to.

VINCE GILL

LEFT *Garth Brooks shakes hands with the next generation of country fans.*

BY 1984, despite the mainstream popularity of the smooth Countrypolitan sound, and the *Urban Cowboy* boom that seemed to broaden its appeal, actual sales of country music records had decreased by more than 27 percent. "Urban Cowboy Goes to Boot Hill," *Variety* magazine proclaimed. "Those good times are gone," *The New York Times* declared, "and they won't be coming back." "It's not just the Nashville Sound that seems to be dying," the reporter added, "it's the Nashville dream."

But no sooner had the dip in commercial success been noticed and mourned than it began reversing itself. Two new cable networks dedicated exclusively to country music—CMT and TNN—brought interviews and stories about a new generation of stars to fans across the nation, using music videos to promote their new songs. In the last half of the 1980s, sales would double—and never look back.

Within the broad embrace of its extended family, the age-old question of what is—and what isn't—country music would only intensify. Could a music of everyday people, described as "three chords and the truth," survive the changes of the late twentieth century with its soul and its simplicity intact? Would its stars and the music itself lose their way, or would they heed the old saying, "Don't get above your raisin'?"

"*Don't get above your raisin'* is a term I associate with the South," the music historian Bill C. Malone said. "It's the kind of advice that parents would give their children: 'As you go into the world, don't forget where you came from. Don't get so uppity that you forget us and you forget the values that you were taught back home.' And I think for country music, it's just a reminder to the music in general: Don't forget where you came from."

We are all related when it comes to country music and to country songs. We're like "blood kin." Anybody that loves country music, they're related to you. You've got that in common.

DOLLY PARTON

By the mid-1980s, Johnny Cash was about to start his fourth decade in country music. To many people, he *was* country music—a living legend within the industry, already in the Hall of Fame, though he had just turned fifty-two. He no longer had a weekly network television show, but he and June Carter Cash hosted an annual Christmas program on CBS.

ABOVE *From left, Carl Perkins, Jerry Lee Lewis, Roy Orbison, and Johnny Cash remembered their days at Sun Records in Memphis by recording* Class of '55.

LEFT *From left, Willie Nelson, Waylon Jennings, Cash, and Kris Kristofferson performed as the country music super-group the Highwaymen.*

With his friends Willie Nelson, Waylon Jennings, and Kris Kristofferson, Cash formed a country super-group called the Highwaymen, who toured the world and appeared in a made-for-television version of the classic film *Stagecoach*. Then Cash reunited with Carl Perkins, Jerry Lee Lewis, and Roy Orbison—fellow artists who got their start at Sun Records in Memphis—for an album called *Class of '55*.

Appearing on David Letterman's late-night show, he felt secure enough about his image to talk openly about the drug addictions that were part of his past. *Saturday Night Live* asked him to New York City to host an episode.

But despite his status as an icon, Cash's solo records were no longer selling. Only two singles had reached the Top Ten in more than a decade; many of his recent albums failed to chart at all.

His last number-one hit, "One Piece at a Time," back in 1976, was a novelty song—a talking blues about an auto-worker who builds his own Cadillac out of parts he sneaks out of the assembly line in his lunch box. Now, Cash's label hoped something similar might get him back on top. The song they chose told a silly story, made even sillier in the music video they also released: Cash undergoes a brain trans-plant, but the brain he gets is a bank robber's, which trans-forms the singer into an outlaw. Cash's brain gets placed inside a chicken—who begins performing across the nation as "The Chicken in Black."

"Columbia Records was trying anything and everything, and John was trying anything and everything to find something that worked, that had any kind of fresh appeal to it,"

said Marty Stuart. "'The Chicken in Black' is probably one of the low points." Rosanne Cash agreed: "I was embarrassed about that. I just thought, 'Why is Dad listening to these people?'" Cash would later say "The Chicken in Black" was the only thing he ever recorded that he hated—so much so that he begged Columbia Records to reclaim copies of it from stores and the music videos from television stations, and he canceled plans to promote it on tour.

Meanwhile, Cash's eldest daughter, Rosanne, was carving out her own career in country music. She carried painful memories of her father's neglect of her mother and sisters in the 1960s, when he was strung out on drugs and never at home. But she also shared his deep love of music and his fierce individualism as an artist:

> I didn't want people to think that I was using my dad in any way or trading on his fame, or trying to get doors open because of him. It was so important to me that I do it on my own. Even thought of changing my name.
>
> And my dad didn't say anything about that. He knew I was considering that; and then, when I didn't, he said, "I'm so happy that you kept your name. I'm so proud of our name. I'm so happy you didn't give it up." And I realized that would have hurt him terribly.

ABOVE *Rosanne Cash in the studio. When she moved to Nashville from Los Angeles, she had trouble fitting in. But her records were topping the charts.*

LEFT *Rosanne and her father, backstage at the* Opry

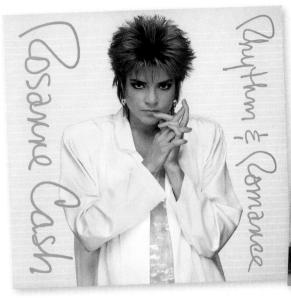

chute pink, big-shouldered jacket on. I walked out, just kind of proud of myself, and people in the audience actually laughed."

But her 1985 song, "I Don't Know Why You Don't Want Me" went to number one and won a Grammy; the album it came from produced three other singles in the top five. "She was selling records and the people were getting her music," Crowell said, "and that will endear you to the establishment pretty quick, because

After making some successful albums in Los Angeles, Rosanne and her husband, Rodney Crowell, who was also her producer, had moved to Nashville, where she had trouble fitting in. "I had purple hair," she said. "I was a little bit streetwise, urban girl, straight from Los Angeles, and brazen. And I really put people off. I remember walking onstage once, at this multi-artist show, and I had this Japanese para-

TOP *Rosanne Cash was winning awards and charting hits with each album.* King's Record Shop *went gold and produced four consecutive number-one singles.*

BELOW *But Johnny Cash was unceremoniously dropped from his label after twenty-eight years as one of Columbia's major stars. The news, one insider remembered, hit Nashville like "an atom bomb," and Cash felt adrift.*

'Man In Black' without a label

ROBERT K. OERMANN
Staff Writer

Johnny Cash is without a country music record label.

The Country Music Hall of Fame member who is arguably the most legendary star in Music City has been with Columbia Records since 1958, but sources at the company say that his contract will not be renewed.

Columbia/Epic/CBS Nashville head Rick Blackburn would say only that, "This is the hardest decision that I've ever had to make in my life."

Others on Music Row say that Cash's contract was allowed to expire at the end of March because Cash has not had a solo Top-10 hit since 1981's *The Baron*.

"We don't know where we'll be going," said Cash's manager Lou Robin yesterday during a telephone conversation. "Other people are talking to us. There's a lot of places where they're interested in somebody like Johnny Cash.

"And not just in Nashville. We're negotiating all over the world."

Although Cash has had recent duet hits with Waylon Jennings (1978's *There Ain't No Good Chain Gang*, 1986's *Even Cowgirls Get the Blues*) and has enjoyed success in 1985 as a quartet (with Jennings, Willie Nelson and Kris Kristofferson), his solo record sales are not nearly what they were during his 1960s heyday.

"Johnny has a lot going on besides records," Robin commented, "TV, movies, concerts, overseas.

"And his book was published today." Harper & Row has just issued *Man In White*, Cash's first religious novel.

Cash could not be reached for comment on his recording situation.

The country superstar is currently represented on LP by a compilation on PolyGram's Smash/America label. It is the *Class of '55* Memphis reunion album that pairs him with Jerry Lee Lewis, Roy Orbison, and Carl Perkins.

Robin did not discount the possibility that PolyGram might be among the negotiators for Cash's country recording services.

For his gospel records, Cash is affiliated with the Word/Nashville Records label. That firm has just released Cash's *Believe In Him* religious effort.

Because of the lapsed Columbia deal, this is the first time in over 30 years that Cash has not had a country recording contract. He began his career at Memphis' Sun Records la-it adds to the bottom line. You'd be surprised at how much respect you get when your records are selling. And you probably wouldn't be surprised how little you get when they're not."

In 1986, Columbia Records abruptly dropped Johnny Cash from its roster. He had been with the label since 1958. No one—including Cash—saw it coming; he was on tour in Canada when the news broke. "It was like somebody had dropped an atom bomb in Nashville," said record producer Tony Brown. "The guy that ran Columbia at the time, Rick Blackburn, everybody thought that he was the devil. Because Johnny Cash was more than an artist; he was a way of life for America. He was like John Wayne, and he was just bigger than music."

Dwight Yoakam considered it "regrettable and reprehensible that he was just kind of summarily, disrespectfully dismissed and cast aside by a label that had made millions and millions of dollars with Johnny Cash's music. The fact that Columbia Records would drop Johnny Cash was an insult to anybody who had ever listened to music." Marty Stuart—part of Cash's touring band and the husband of one of his daughters, Cindy—had recently released his own first solo album for Columbia. When he protested Cash's dismissal, he said, executives retaliated by cutting back on the album's promotion. His next one would be with a different label.

Johnny Cash signed with Mercury Records, where his first album sold poorly. Country deejays didn't play it, and *USA Today* named it one of the ten worst albums of the year. "In the '80s, if you weren't selling records, you couldn't get a record deal," said Kenny Rogers. "It is a business, after all. You can have the most talent in the world, but if you can't sell records, who's going to throw away their money? I remember Johnny Cash said something that just broke my heart when he said, 'I feel like a stranger in my own hometown.'"

Rosanne Cash, however, was still on a roll. Her newest album, *King's Record Shop*, was certified as a gold record, and produced four consecutive number-one singles, including "Tennessee Flat Top Box," a song her father had first recorded in 1961. "I felt kind of guilty that I was having a lot of number-one records and getting a lot of attention at the same time my dad was dropped from Columbia and he was really floundering," she said. "I felt bad for him, because he put a lot of stock in being Johnny Cash and everything that that meant, including the fame and the hit records. And to not have that, he was a little disconcerted and at sea, and depressed."

In all things country music, we see a response. How far are they going to take country music? Well, it will come back around again. It's always reminding itself who it is. And the old ghosts are always rising up and refusing to be cast aside.

KETCH SECOR

There is a tension, always. It's how big can you make your audience, and how pure you can keep your heart. I think the way country music was puffed up and so hung up on itself and its sound and image, and all that—I think maybe it was a little prideful, and we needed to have a heart check.

RICKY SKAGGS

No one had more impeccable bluegrass credentials than Ricky Skaggs from eastern Kentucky. A prodigy on the mandolin, he had played for Bill Monroe at age six; appeared on the Flatt and Scruggs television show when he was seven; and as a teenager joined Ralph Stanley and the Clinch Mountain Boys.

But in the late 1970s, Skaggs had moved to Los Angeles to be part of Emmylou Harris's Hot Band—infusing her music with a tinge of bluegrass, and at the same time learning a greater appreciation for electric guitars and drums. Now he was on his own, experimenting with a sound that combined the acoustic instruments of a string band with something more electric, more honky tonk. It was traditional. And it was brand new.

"The bluegrass purists, they didn't like the electric part," Skaggs said. "The real pure bluegrass people really saw me almost as a traitor." At the same time, Skaggs's music didn't conform to the sound radio stations were playing on their Top Forty format. "It was so country, I mean, it was barnyard," he said. "You could smell it, it was so country. The radio stations would say, 'You're just *too* country. We're not going to play this stuff.' But, you know, most people, they just loved it."

Skaggs's music caught on, and during the mid-1980s he released a steady stream of hits. He enjoyed nothing better than taking a song one of his bluegrass heroes had written and recorded a generation earlier, and injecting it with something fresh. He transformed "Don't Get Above Your Raisin'," an old Lester Flatt and Earl Scruggs song, into something he called "a slamming kind of country song; it's almost like rock and roll."

Then he did it again with a remake of a song his mentor, Bill Monroe, had written back in 1950 about Monroe's mentor, "Uncle Pen." Monroe's version had never charted; Skaggs's jumped to number one. "I was at the *Opry* one night," Skaggs recalled, "and Mr. Monroe come up to me and he said, 'Ricky, I just got a powerful check on that song you put out. I'm telling you, it was a *powerful* check. I paid all my land taxes.' And he said, 'You can record all my songs if you want to.'"

Monroe even agreed to appear in a music video for Skaggs's song "Country Boy," pretending to be Uncle Pen from the sticks, paying a visit to his nephew in New York City. The video included a cameo by Mayor Ed Koch, mouthing the words "I'm just a country boy at heart," showed kids break-dancing with Monroe on the subway to the music—and helped the album become Skaggs's third number one in a row.

Ricky Skaggs, Chet Atkins said, "saved country music." But there were other young artists who were also reconnecting the music with its roots—and having great success.

George Strait was raised on a ranch near his birthplace of Poteet, Texas, and studied agriculture at Southwest Texas State University. His music—influenced by Hank Williams, Lefty Frizzell, Ernest Tubb—had an old-fashioned dance hall feel to it, anchored by his smooth, easy voice and his no-frills approach. He took the song "Right or Wrong," which had been recorded by Emmett Miller in the 1920s and Bob Wills in the 1930s, and in 1984 made it a number-one hit. Though it wasn't fashionable among most country

singers at the time, Strait insisted on dressing the way he had growing up: blue jeans, a big belt buckle, a pressed button-down shirt, and a clean Stetson cowboy hat.

His first album, *Strait Country*, sold a million copies. So did every other album he released for the rest of the century. He would ultimately record sixty number-one singles—more than any other artist in any musical category.

Strait's sound—and his clean-cut cowboy look—would affect a whole new crop of country stars. "I was going to the store with my dad and I remember coming out of Turtle Creek, up there where I was going to take a left by the blue church, heading north to Snyder's IGA," said Garth Brooks. "And Dad had the radio on and this lady said, 'Here's a new kid from Texas and I think you're going to like his sound.' And it was George Strait. And it was 'Unwound.' There's something about the beat; something about that fiddle lick; and then that whole first opening line, when George opens his mouth, you just, there you are. And that's what happened to me. And it was that day, I looked and said, 'That's what I want to be.'"

OPPOSITE, TOP *Ricky Skaggs and bluegrass patriarch Bill Monroe recording together*

OPPOSITE, BOTTOM *When Skaggs added electric instruments and drums to the traditional bluegrass sound, some purists were outraged, but Monroe loved how it brought new fans to the music.*

CENTER *The title of George Strait's first album says it all about his sound.*

TOP *Strait would go on to record sixty number-one singles—more than any other artist in any musical genre.*

Meanwhile, in Charlotte, North Carolina, Randy Travis had barely survived a troubled youth—drugs, alcohol, scrapes with the police—when "Lib" Hatcher, the manager of a local club where he was singing, intervened and promised authorities she would take responsibility for keeping him out of trouble.

Hatcher brought him to Nashville, where Travis worked as a short-order cook while she took demo tapes to producers up and down Music Row. They admired his deep baritone

voice, but thought it had too much twang in it and uniformly turned him down. Finally, after rejecting him twice, one label relented. To everyone's surprise, his debut album in 1986, *Storms of Life*, ended up selling three million copies. Travis would sell thirteen million records by the end of the 1980s—and marry Hatcher in 1990. "Randy helped get the rudder back under country music," said record producer Allen Reynolds, "because he was so pure country and the audience embraced him, a big audience. And that was evidence enough for me that the audience out there was bigger than people thought."

ABOVE *Record executives thought Randy Travis had too much twang in his voice—until his albums started selling in the millions.*

RIGHT, TOP *Reba McEntire, with her brother Pake, on the family ranch in Oklahoma*

RIGHT *The Singing McEntires, with Reba at the microphone*

Because of the way I talk and the way I sing, I can't cross over that much. It's a big old bar that comes up; the barriers do come up. My accent has been with me forever. And I'm very proud of my Oklahoma twang. Why would I get rid of it? God gave it to me.

REBA MCENTIRE

Reba McEntire grew up on an eight-thousand-acre cattle ranch near Kiowa, Oklahoma. Her father, a three-time world-champion calf roper, taught his four children to work hard and love horses. Her mother, who had an excellent voice, taught them to harmonize and love music.

By high school, Reba was performing with a brother and sister as the Singing McEntires—and competing in rodeos

as a barrel racer. When she sang the national anthem at the National Finals Rodeo in 1974, her powerful voice prompted an invitation to Nashville, where she signed a recording contract and released several albums.

But as the years went by, she grew dissatisfied with the way her label tried to mold her into a Countrypolitan-style artist. "Of course, me, being a strong-willed third child out of four kids, and a redhead, I had my own opinion of how things would be done," McEntire said. "And then when they'd say, 'Well, you can't do it that way,' I'd just kind of sit back and bide my time. Later on, I got to do it my way."

In 1984, a new label finally listened to her. "I said I would really like things more country," she remembered. "I don't want orchestra and violins. I want a steel guitar and a fiddle.

ABOVE, LEFT *Reba competing in a rodeo*

BELOW *McEntire's songs touched on themes that women across America were facing, and she attracted legions of fans.*

I wanted to help to bring country music back to more traditional. That was really something that I loved: George Strait, Ricky Skaggs, Randy Travis, all in that era. That started me having more control of the songs that I recorded."

McEntire's instincts proved to be right. Just as Loretta Lynn had done in the 1960s, many of her hits touched on issues women all over America were facing: dealing with a troubled marriage in "Somebody Should Leave" and "Whoever's in New England," or deciding to finish their education after starting a family in "Is There Life Out There." "I would be doing that song onstage and women would stand up in the audience, hold up their diploma," she said. "They'd write me letters saying, 'I didn't get to go to college' or 'I didn't get my high school diploma.' 'And so when the kids got out of the house, I went back and got my GED,' or 'I went back to college and got my degree there.' And they said, 'That song inspired me to do that.'"

By 1988, McEntire took even firmer control over her career. She formed an entertainment company that handled song publishing, concert booking, publicity, and recording facilities. But after a concert one night in San Diego in 1991, eight members of McEntire's band perished in an airplane accident. For the tight-knit country music community in Nashville, it was the biggest tragedy since Patsy Cline and three others were killed in a plane crash in 1963, after a concert in which Cline had performed "Sweet Dreams," a song she had recently recorded but not yet released. "Sweet Dreams" was the last song McEntire had sung that night in San Diego.

In the 1980s and '90s, Reba McEntire would have twenty-two number-one singles and sell 33.5 million albums; be the first artist to be chosen the Country Music Association's Female Vocalist of the Year four years in row; appear in movies, television shows, and on Broadway—and become the most successful female country artist of her era.

"I did find my own way," she said. "But I went back to my teachers—Dolly, Loretta, Tammy. I saw what they did to pave the way for the women in country music. It's women standing up for themselves in all walks of life. Any job you have, women have to work twice as hard, sometimes three times as hard. That's just the way it is in life. And you do it. You do it with a smile. But you win."

TOP, LEFT *When she finally took control of what songs she would record, McEntire's career took off.*

LEFT *Reba with Kenny Rodgers in the made-for-television movie* The Gambler Returns

George Strait, Reba, Randy Travis—there was a little community of us. And we all sort of burst down the doors of the pop stuff that was coming out of the *Urban Cowboy* genre. We were so gutsy and so real. Reba was discovered singing "The Star-Spangled Banner" at rodeos, okay? George was a real cowboy down in San Marcos, Texas.

We were real. We didn't need a focus group or a marketing meeting and any of that kind of stuff. And people were hungry for that.

NAOMI JUDD

Back in 1976, Naomi Judd was a divorced mother of two strong-willed daughters, Wynonna and Ashley, living in Los Angeles, when she decided to move back to her native Kentucky. "Wynonna was twelve, Ashley was eight," she said, "and I had taken them back home to a mountaintop in Kentucky to expose them to their ancestry. I wanted to plug the kids into their incredibly rich, eighth-generation Kentucky heritage. We lived on a mountaintop, Morrill, Kentucky, very isolated. No TV or telephone. It was in that splendid solitude that I handed the twelve-year-old nemesis, I handed Wynonna a plastic string guitar. And, voila!"

Wynonna had a different perspective: "The truth is, I wasn't into music. I was not into even being a singer. I just was bored out of my mind, living on a mountaintop with a single parent and a sister who wouldn't leave me the heck alone. And I think the guitar became my friend because I was just so lonesome."

While Wynonna practiced the guitar, Naomi studied nursing, and the two of them managed to ease some of their mother-daughter tensions by learning to harmonize

TOP, LEFT *Naomi Judd, holding Ashley and hugging Wynonna in Morrill, Kentucky*

RIGHT *Ashley (left) and big sister Wynonna, with cousin Erin at a store in Morrill where the proprietor played the banjo*

an appointment with Joe Galante, the head of RCA Records in Nashville, and two of his producers.

"Wynonna and I had had a huge fight, of course, and we weren't speaking," according to Naomi. "It felt very much like going to the principal's office," Wynonna said, "and, yet, I knew that these were men who had a business that could help us, musically. I was used to singing. I just wasn't used to being in a boardroom full of men."

"So we go into this room," Naomi continued, "and she was so scared and I felt very, I guess the word is *guilty*. I felt guilty that I had put her in that situation—I mean she was only like seventeen and a half years old, and she was terrified, just frozen. And I looked at her and I said, 'Okay. Here you go, kiddo. We're back on that mountaintop, and there's a storm rolling in, and we're sitting on the porch. Let's just sing.'"

together. "We were studying the Delmore Brothers, and they had the most tempestuous relationship," Naomi said, "and it occurred to me, if you look at the word 'kindred,' it's 'dread of kin.' Hmm . . . And Lord knows, there are many times Wynonna and I couldn't talk to each other. But we could sing together."

They moved to Nashville, where they appeared on Ralph Emery's local television show at five thirty each morning, before Naomi went to work at a hospital and Wynonna went to high school. Naomi spent her days off knocking on every door on Music Row, trying to get an audition with a record label. Finally, through the help of the family of a patient Naomi had nursed back to health, the Judds managed to get

The moment was just as vivid in Joe Galante's memory: "They came in, and Wy had braces, and Naomi was stunning, as always. And they opened up their mouths and it was . . . we all just kind of went, 'Oh, my God.'"

Their first album, *Why Not Me*, released in 1984, hit the top of the charts. The Judds would be the dominant country music duo for the rest of the 1980s, until Naomi was diagnosed with hepatitis C and, after a 124-show farewell tour,

TOP, LEFT *After Wynonna started playing the guitar, she and Naomi often worked out their mother-daughter tensions through music.*

RIGHT *Joe Galante (right) and fellow RCA executive Robert Summer celebrate the label's contract with the Judds over milkshakes.*

retired. Wynonna went on to a successful solo career (and her little sister, Ashley, went into the movies).

"That song became our anthem, 'Why Not Me,'" according to Wynonna. "My mom would say, 'We wake up every day and we just look up and say, "Why not me?"' I'll never forget her saying that, because we were America's sweethearts, in a sense, because everyone wanted us to make it. We were a mother-daughter; they knew our story. And they knew that we had nothing, and they wanted to see us make it. We were the underdog. And 'Why Not Me' became our anthem."

Naomi and Wynonna Judd, Reba McEntire, Randy Travis, George Strait, and Ricky Skaggs were all part of a group that came to be called the neo-traditionalists. "I think there was just a general feeling among many people, that something needed to

be done to revitalize country music and move it away from what seemed to be just an all-out, unending fusion with pop music," said Bill C. Malone. "The new traditionalists were there because country had now gone so far into pop music and was so consumed with making a buck that we had forgotten what it was like to cry in our beer," added Ketch Secor. "I mean, we had forgotten what it was like to go honky tonking."

"Well," said Ricky Skaggs, "they were calling me 'neo-traditionalist'; and I didn't even know what 'neo' meant. I had no idea."

ABOVE AND LEFT *The Judds became the dominant country duo of the 1980s. In their farewell concert in 1991, before Wynonna went on to a successful solo career, they performed with the Jordanaires.*

of country music records—Hank Williams, Johnny Cash, Buck Owens, Johnny Horton—and the hymns his family sang each week at the Church of Christ, a denomination that encouraged a capella gospel singing, readings from the Bible—and total abstinence from alcohol.

He started playing guitar at the age of six. The Yoakams moved to Ohio when Dwight was one, but returned constantly to his grandparents' home in Floyd County, Kentucky. One day, at age ten, sitting on their porch, he began singing the Hank Williams song "My Bucket's Got a Hole in It," which includes the line, "I can't get no beer" in its chorus. "I didn't really know what it was about, 'I can't buy no beer,'" he said. "My mother came out on that porch, and she looked at me and she said, 'I don't believe you need to be singing that'— because it was a guy drinking beer. And about that time, we

GUITARS, CADILLACS, AND HILLBILLY MUSIC

My earliest memory, probably at three, four years old, was [being] wedged in that great womb-like squish that you'll get between your mother and your aunt. And we were singing at the record player—not with it, but directionally at it. It was in this little den that my aunt had at her house, and it was on a Saturday evening, and I was squished between them.

They were singing one of the popular crossover hits of the day, "Send Me the Pillow That You Dream On." And we, literally, it was just with abandon that I sang with them. We were hollering. It was, "Send me the pillow that you dream on, so darling I can dream on it too." That's my first memory.

DWIGHT YOAKAM

Dwight Yoakam was born in Pikeville, Kentucky, in 1956. His earliest musical influences were his mother's collection

TOP, LEFT *For Dwight Yoakam (seen with his grandmother in Kentucky), music was part of his life from the beginning. His earliest memory was singing "Send Me the Pillow That You Dream On" with his mother and his aunt.*

ABOVE, RIGHT *Yoakam (seated at left, with guitar) with some young friends. When he sang a Hank Williams song about drinking, his mother scolded him—but a neighbor asked for more.*

The band changed its name to Dwight Yoakam and the Babylonian Cowboys—and found work instead within LA's post-punk rock scene, opening for groups like the Blasters, Gun Club, and Los Lobos. Young, hip audiences went wild for Yoakam and his music—songs he'd written himself, as well as one that Johnny Horton had released back in 1956, the year Dwight was born, "Honky Tonk Man." "I started doing it with the band, and the audience responded very immediately to it," he said. "In December of 1985, we went and recorded it, and it launched what I was about to do for the next thirty years of my life."

According to Marty Stuart, "He brought a spark and a sass, and an interesting sensibility to country music that country music so needed at that time. He brought style back; he brought absolute swagger, a rock-and-roll swagger with absolute hard-hitting country music. He single-handedly kind of kicked it and restarted it."

Yoakam's first album, released in 1986, also included a song of his own, which included the line "guitars, Cadillacs, and hillbilly music." His label told him to drop the hillbilly reference. "Warner Music, Nashville, was not prepared to have us release a song with the term 'hillbilly music' in it," he said. "They were ashamed of the term 'hillbilly.' They thought it was derogatory. And I said, 'Oh, no. That's something I'm proud of.' I'm proud of it because I watched my own family

heard across the holler—about two acres down, there was an older couple, the Hunleys—I heard her voice come across as my mother had scolded me, she said, 'That was good. Do it again.' She had been listening across the holler."

In high school, Yoakam was active in theater and formed a rockabilly band called Dwight and the Greasers. Then, after dropping out of college, he headed to Nashville to see if he could make it as a singer. He auditioned for the Opryland amusement park, which had live performances throughout the summer, but failed the audition and headed back home.

Inspired by the early records that Emmylou Harris was recording in Los Angeles, his next stop was the West Coast. "The beacon that I navigated toward was Emmylou Harris," he said. "I would not have become the artist I became without her first two albums, because they are the direct tissue connection, if you will, musically, to Buck Owens and Merle Haggard for my generation. I've often said, 'I was born in Kentucky. I was raised in Ohio. But I grew up in California.'"

He worked as a short-order cook, drove delivery trucks, and formed Dwight Yoakam and Kentucky Bourbon, a bar band that played regularly at the Palomino nightclub in North Hollywood.

Yoakam preferred the hard-core honky tonk tunes he had heard in his mother's record collection, or the Bakersfield Sound that Buck Owens and Merle Haggard had popularized in the 1960s. But it was the early 1980s, and they were constantly told to perform popular songs from the *Urban Cowboy* craze. They refused and got fired.

TOP, LEFT *Yoakam, in gold lamé, with his high school rockabilly band, Dwight and the Greasers*

ABOVE *With a later band, Dwight performs at the Palomino Club in North Hollywood.*

jacket, similar to what his hero Buck Owens had worn. The album's popularity prompted thousands of requests from all over the world for a jacket just like Dwight's.

But Yoakam's outspokenness put him at odds with some industry insiders in Nashville. He had used a string of profanities when reporters asked him about Johnny Cash being dropped by his label, and his opinions about Music Row's Countrypolitan sound were equally harsh. "The rawness," he complained, "has left country music."

"Dwight Yoakam was a big influence on me," said Darius Rucker. "He ain't afraid to be old school, dirt country, all the time. He ain't afraid to sing about any subject he wants to sing about. I said, to myself, 'I'm going to make a country record someday. I want to do this.'"

Yoakam found a good friend in Buck Owens, who had always chafed at what he considered Nashville's slights toward country artists from California—a tension that had prompted the creation of the Academy of Country Music on the West Coast, a rival of the Nashville-based Country Music Association. "Buck was keenly aware of being the outsider and relished in it," Yoakam said, "although he resented that he didn't get the respect he was due."

Like Johnny Cash, by 1988, Owens had faded from the limelight. He was surprised to be asked to perform at the CMA awards—and reached out to his young friend, knowing that Yoakam, too, had made some enemies in Nash-

submitted to ridicule and being called hillbillies. But, generationally, I didn't have the same open wound. So I was able to be proud of what that musical legacy was about."

Yoakam stuck to his guns about the song's lyrics, though the label titled the album *Guitars, Cadillacs, Etc., Etc.* When the album sold more than two million records, his label had no problem at all with the title of his next album: *Hillbilly Deluxe.* For its cover, Yoakam asked Manuel Cuevas, who had once been the head tailor at Nudie Cohn's shop in Hollywood, to design him a jacket—just as Cuevas had done for country stars ranging from Little Jimmy Dickens to Johnny Cash, Porter Wagoner to Gram Parsons. Yoakam wanted a bolero-style

TOP AND RIGHT *Yoakam "brought a spark and a sass" back to country music, Marty Stuart said. And as his second album's title proclaimed, he was proud to call himself a hillbilly.*

ville. The song Owens suggested they sing together was one he had recorded back in 1972, with little success, "The Streets of Bakersfield." Its chorus makes a blunt statement: "You don't know me but you don't like me. You say you care less how I feel. But how many of you that sit and judge me, ever walked the streets of Bakersfield."

"He sent a cassette down to me, and I started playing it in the car," Yoakam recalled, "and I thought, 'They're going to tar and feather us. They're going to run us out of town on a rail.' I said, 'Buck, honestly, I don't think this is a good idea, I just don't think it's smart.' And he said, 'Now, Dwight, you just, you leave it to old Buck. They're going to like that we came and sang':

So, we went down there, against my better judgment, but Buck was right. The larger theme, which addresses the displaced from anywhere, which belies time and place, but has to do with the universal that we all feel, going back to those that came on the *Mayflower* to now, of being "less than"—that's what "The Streets of Bakersfield" was about.

TOP *Yoakam, Buck Owens said, "should have been one of my sons." Their duet of "The Streets of Bakersfield," which Owens had first recorded back in 1972, provided Buck with his first number-one hit in sixteen years.*

And I realized at that moment it will be cheered by people who are the outcasts, the outsiders in every culture. And when Pete Anderson and I decided to record our version of it, that Buck came and sang on, we added Flaco Jiménez playing the Tex-Mex California border culture accordion, because I thought, "That's also part of displaced groups of disparate people, from the white Okies from the Dust Bowl to the migrant workers of those same fields around Bakersfield by the 1960s, 1970s, and 1980s." It was a marriage of that that Buck just had a sense of, because of his own outsider credentials.

When it was released, the Dwight Yoakam–Buck Owens duet of "Streets of Bakersfield" gave Owens his first number-one single in sixteen years and briefly revived his career. He went back on tour for a while and started releasing his own albums again. Dwight Yoakam, he said, "should have been one of my sons."

Darius Rucker was in the rock band Hootie & the Blowfish at the time, and a fan of Yoakam's music, which prompted him to buy a Buck Owens record: "So I go home and I put on this Buck Owens record and I was like, 'Man, I see exactly what Dwight was listening to as a kid.' There's a chain you can see from *here* to *here* to *here*—Jimmie Rodgers to Buck Owens to Dwight Yoakam. You see that chain, and I love it."

The rise of the new traditionalists helped resuscitate the sales of country music records, which in 1984 had dipped to $393 million, its low point for the decade, before starting to climb back up. But country artists of all ages—and all styles—were also contributing to the rebound.

Willie Nelson was still on the road and still hosting his annual Fourth of July picnics. Now he added another outdoor extravaganza: Farm Aid, an outdoor concert, organized with Neil Young and John Mellencamp, to raise money to help the nation's embattled family farmers. Nelson's guests were as eclectic as his musical tastes—from young rockers to some of his older friends in country music. Eighty thousand people attended the first Farm Aid concert in 1985, which raised $9 million. They would still be holding the annual event more than thirty years later.

That chain of connection runs throughout American music, jazz musician and composer Wynton Marsalis said:

Everybody has an ethnic heritage of some sort. It's more integrated than we think. But we have a human heritage that's much more fundamental and greater. There are things that are a part of the landscape of human life that we all deal with: the joy of birth, the sorrow of death, a broken heart, jealousy, greed, envy, anger. Music, because it is the art of the invisible, it gets inside of that and it does not get inside of it less for you than it does for me.

I think a lot of our music is the same. If you just deal with the church music, "I let God down. I need to go do this to find redemption." What else are they talking about? "Man, look what I did to my old lady." Or, "Oh, boy, look at my old lady, what she did to me. Damn."

Now, it's coming out in different forms, but the root of it is that. And if you can tell those stories that way, then you are Patsy Cline. Hank Williams, he had that thing. You hear that cry and that yearning in it.

There's a truth in the music. And it's too bad that we, as a culture, have not been able to address that truth. That's the shame of it. And not letting that truth be our truth.

In 1987, Merle Haggard had his thirty-fourth number-one single with a song he had written, "Twinkle, Twinkle Lucky Star." That same year, Dolly Parton released an album with Emmylou Harris and Linda Ronstadt, which included a Jimmie Rodgers song, as well as ones Parton had written. It won two Grammy Awards and sold more than four million copies. For the album cover, Manuel Cuevas designed special embroidered cowgirl outfits for each of them.

After Rosanne Cash's album *King's Record Shop* went gold, her husband and producer, Rodney Crowell, came out with his own album that did the same—and included an unprecedented five number-one singles.

With his rocking party song "All My Rowdy Friends Are Coming Over Tonight," Hank Williams Jr. was bigger than

---

ABOVE, LEFT *When he recorded "The Streets of Bakersfield," Yoakam invited Flaco Jiménez to add a Mexican-American sound with his accordion.*

CENTER, RIGHT *Dolly Parton, Linda Ronstadt, and Emmylou Harris released* Trio—*and asked Manuel Cuevas to design Nudie suits for them to wear on the album's cover.*

ever—the hell-raising host who welcomed millions of television viewers to Monday-night football every week and the artist with an unbroken stream of gold or platinum albums over the course of thirteen years. In 1989, he came across a previously unissued recording of his famous father singing "There's a Tear in My Beer." Williams overdubbed himself singing along—and, thirty-six years after Hank Senior's death, created a music video that made it appear as if they were performing together at last. The Grammys gave the father-and-son duet its award for best vocal collaboration.

Regardless of whether it was new traditionalists or old traditionalists, country-rock or Countrypolitan, all of it was good for Music City, according to Joe Galante:

> We were making music at that point, reaching lots of different audiences and beginning to go around the world. So we were getting more notoriety from the companies, because we were delivering more money to them.
>
> With that, I had the ability to take on even more from New York and take them out of the loop. We were a self-sustaining company. We made our decisions on our own; we made the calls. And that was a big defining moment. I don't want to say we were declaring independence, but the Nashville labels were starting to be no longer satellites; we were really full-fledged offices at that point and we were profit centers.

TOP *With his song "All My Rowdy Friends Are Coming Over Tonight," Hank Williams Jr. welcomed football fans across the nation on television every Monday night.*

The financial resurgence made room for other artists who were harder to categorize. Lyle Lovett, a singer-songwriter from Texas with an edgy voice and a quirky perspective, came out with albums tinged with everything from folk to honky tonk, gospel to rhythm and blues. He even released his own version of Tammy Wynette's "Stand by Your Man."

Nanci Griffith had been a kindergarten teacher before making a name for herself with plaintive ballads and songs she described as "folkabilly."

In Alberta, Canada, k. d. lang adopted a persona as a punk reincarnation of Patsy Cline and began touring in fringed cowgirl dresses and singing with a voice as powerfully expressive as Cline's. She came to Nashville, recorded an album produced by Owen Bradley, and won a Grammy singing a duet with Roy Orbison, before moving on in new musical directions.

As a rebellious teenager, Steve Earle had dropped out of high school and claimed Townes Van Zandt as his songwriting mentor and role model. He struggled for ten years to get known, until 1986, when he emerged with a sound somewhere between country and early rock. His album *Guitar Town* went to number one.

CLOCKWISE FROM TOP, LEFT *Nanci Griffith, Lyle Lovett, Steve Earle, and k.d. lang each brought unique sensibilities to country's sound and look.*

We kind of all think of it as a Golden Age in country music, where everybody was welcome. You heard Nanci Griffith on the radio. You heard Steve Earle's voice on the radio. You heard Lyle Lovett. It was like all of the fringes were welcome.

My picture of it in my mind is these big doors opening up, instead of being like the gatekeepers who were just letting a few people in. Suddenly everybody was welcome. I mean, we were country music. We didn't know it was going to last for such a short amount of time.

KATHY MATTEA

Growing up in West Virginia, Kathy Mattea originally sang folk music and bluegrass. Her tastes broadened when she took a job as a tour guide at the Country Music Hall of Fame—and broadened again when she started earning extra money singing on demo tapes for songwriters pitching their tunes on Music Row.

Along the way, Mattea got a recording contract and ended up with Allen Reynolds, an independent producer who had learned to trust his own instincts working for many years with the iconoclastic Cowboy Jack Clement. "I always

have felt that we're all so many snowflakes," Reynolds said, "so what you try to do as a producer is help the artist find their own uniqueness and lift that forward."

He had decided to leave the business and sell his recording studio when he met Mattea. "I liked her mind and I liked her talent," he said, "and I got to working with her and it ended up being very nourishing for me. Her roots were more folk music, but she wanted to be a country singer. She was very clear about that. She didn't want to straddle the fence and be country-pop or that kind of thing. She wanted to present herself as a country singer, but brought something fresh to country music."

Mattea remembered the first advice Reynolds gave her: "He would look at me and say, 'It's the song, pal. It's the song. It's not all the bells and whistles. It's a good song, sung honestly, and well framed. Don't ever forget it. When they start telling you it's about all this other stuff, you just come back to that and you will always be okay.' And he got that from Cowboy Jack."

TOP *Kathy Mattea started out with folk music, before leaving West Virginia for Nashville, where she worked as a tour guide at the Country Music Hall of Fame.*

LEFT *Mattea with her producer, Allen Reynolds. His early advice to her was, "It's the song. It's not all the bells and whistles."*

"and it wasn't until I had been running it for a few months that I realized what I had gotten myself into. Once the Bluebird was up and running, at that point, I just followed where it took me."

Soon, the music became more important than the menu. (Kurland focused on finger food to keep the noise of the diners down, and to encourage them to look at the performers instead of their plates.) She held auditions for aspiring songwriters and opened a weekly writers' night for the winners to perform; then she added a special "writers in the round" format, in which four of them could sit in the middle of the audience, rather than on a stage, and exchange stories and new songs.

In 1988, a songwriter from Minnesota named Jon Vezner took the stage at the Bluebird. He and his friend Don Henry had written a song based on an event in Vezner's life, and he decided to sing it that night in front of an audience.

Kathy Mattea was there; she was now Vezner's wife and knew the story behind the song. His grandmother had been hospitalized and was suffering from dementia, unable to recognize visitors and not talking with anyone. Then Jon brought his grandfather into her room in a wheelchair. "She just kept looking at him and looking at him," according to Mattea. "And she said, 'Where've you been?' And that was the last thing she said; she died days after that."

Under Reynolds's guidance, Mattea had a string of hits, including Nanci Griffith's "Love at the Five and Dime"; a truck driver's love song called "Eighteen Wheels and a Dozen Roses"; and a tune written by Susanna Clark and Richard Leigh, "Come from the Heart," whose chorus declares, "You've got to sing like you don't need the money."

Early in her career, Mattea began performing regularly at a newly opened dinner-and-music venue five miles from downtown Nashville—an intimate space that welcomed young singers and songwriters, called the Bluebird Café. Its founder was Amy Kurland, the daughter of a classical violinist who had become one of the lead session musicians in Nashville's recording studios.

Her original interest, Kurland said, was to be in the restaurant business, but she was dating a guitar player who suggested that she put a stage in the dining room, so he and his friends could perform. "I was just trying to keep my boyfriend happy," she admitted,

TOP, LEFT *Among Mattea's hits were songs written by Nanci Griffith and Susanna Clark.*

RIGHT *Amy Kurland (far left) and friends at the opening of the Bluebird Café, 1982. It soon became a favorite venue for aspiring songwriters to be heard.*

The song, "Where've You Been," describes the couple's lifelong love, from their courtship to their marriage to her dementia and that final moment together. Recording labels and artists throughout Nashville told Vezner what a powerful song it was, but everyone had turned it down—including his wife. "I loved it," Mattea said, "but I was so scared because it was so personal for Jon. And it was so sad."

"Around Nashville," Amy Kurland explained, "sometimes a songwriter will write a great song, take it out to their publisher, or record label, and be told, 'Yeah, a great song, but that's a Bluebird song.' In other words, it's too long; it's too serious; it's too meaningful; it's not going to fly, so to speak, on the radio. But that night, in the Bluebird, the people were weeping. And suddenly it became obvious, this is a song that can make a real impact, and it's okay that it's slow and it's a little long. And it's about death. This song can be a hit."

"And I was sitting in the audience, I feel so lucky to have gotten to have this experience," Mattea remembered. "You could hear audible sobs all over the room. People were like dumbstruck. They didn't even clap at the end of it. They just stopped for like a couple of beats before they clapped. That night, at the Bluebird, when he played it, I got to see, collectively, the universal poignancy of that song. And I just

became obsessed with recording it, because I felt that it needed to be heard."

"And she knew how she wanted to record it," Allen Reynolds said. "She wanted two bass players and a guitar player, an acoustic piano. It was that simple. Kathy just gave this great performance of the song, and all we did was try to be true to the song. We weren't thinking about it as a single—and it certainly was not jumping to the front in the eyes of the record label as a single. And, of all things, radio [stations] began to call for that as a single, and it was a strong enough call that the record label said let's try it. And people loved it."

"Where've You Been" was declared Song of the Year by the Academy of Country Music, which named Mattea as that year's top female vocalist; was chosen as Single of the Year

ABOVE, RIGHT AND LEFT *Minnesota songwriter Jon Vezner performs a new song at the Bluebird. The crowd's emotional reaction to "Where've You Been," about his grandparents' love and final moment together, persuaded his wife, Kathy Mattea, to record it.*

RIGHT *"Where've You Been" was a commercial and critical success for Mattea and Vezner (seen here with one of the awards it won) and his cowriter Don Henry.*

by the Country Music Association; and it won two Grammy Awards—one for Jon Vezner and Don Henry for writing it; one for Kathy Mattea's performance of it. But it would not be the only surprise hit to come out of the Bluebird that night and prove that record executives' initial instincts could be wrong.

GO REST HIGH ON THAT MOUNTAIN

I don't know whether you write the song, or the song writes you. The language has been around for longer than any of us, you know, and it's just our job to pick pieces of language up that move us and tie them together.

VINCE GILL

By 1989, Vince Gill had been in Nashville for seven years, struggling to make it in country music. He had started out in bluegrass, where his high tenor voice and supreme skill on stringed instruments had made him a local star in his home state of Oklahoma, then Kentucky and California.

In Los Angeles, he switched gears to become lead singer in the country-pop group Pure Prairie League, before Rodney Crowell persuaded him to join the Cherry Bombs and back up Rosanne Cash.

Gill soon moved to Nashville to record his own albums, but they didn't sell well enough to support himself and his family. He sat in on other artists' sessions as a guitarist and harmony vocalist, kept writing songs and playing them at the Bluebird Café—and, because of his talent and easygoing nature, became well liked within Music City's country family. George Jones affectionately called him "Sweet Pea."

Impressed by Gill's guitar playing, Mark Knopfler of the rock band Dire Straits asked him to leave Nashville and join the group on a world tour. "I was struggling to pay the house note at the time," Gill said. "This would have cured everything for me, financially, and it would have been a great experience. You know, the musician in me wanted to do that so badly, because I love the way he plays and sings. But I told myself, 'If you're not going to believe in you, who else is? And I'm going to have to say no. I don't want to say no, but I have to try. I think I have something to offer for this world of country music.'"

Working with Tony Brown, a former member of Emmylou Harris's Hot Band and now a producer at RCA, Gill came out with an album that included a Western swing duet with fellow Oklahoman Reba McEntire and songs he had co-written with Rosanne Cash and Guy Clark. The album's title song,

TOP, RIGHT *Like many young artists in Nashville, Vince Gill often appeared at the Bluebird.*

LEFT *On Music Row, Gill found work as a session musician and harmony vocalist while he tried to launch his solo career as a singer-songwriter.*

"When I Call Your Name," was one Gill had co-written with Tim DuBois.

"At the end of the day, all I've ever wanted out of music was to be moved," Gill said. "All I wanted someone to do was play something that just makes me go, 'Oh!' I love the emotion of music. There's something that it does to my DNA that I can't explain. I just think that's all it ever is, is you want to hear somebody do something that moves you."

The album went to number one and sold two million copies. The song was named Single of the Year by the CMA and won the special praise of Roy Acuff, the aging King of Country Music.

That same year, Gill began work on another song that was even more emotional—and more personal. In his

early bluegrass days, Gill had played in a band with Ricky Skaggs and Keith Whitley. Whitley was now a rising country star, married to singer Lorrie Morgan, and many people believed that the young couple would be the next George Jones and Tammy Wynette.

But Whitley was an alcoholic. Sometimes his wife tied their legs together at night so he couldn't sneak off to drink some more. On May 9, 1989, while she was performing on the road, he was discovered at home, dead from alcohol poisoning at the age of thirty-three.

CLOCKWISE FROM TOP, RIGHT *Vince Gill (center) backed up Rosanne Cash in California before coming to Nashville; he and George Jones became friends, and the Possum gave Gill an affectionate nickname: Sweet Pea; Roy Acuff particularly liked Gill's song "When I Call Your Name."*

Like many others in Nashville, Vince Gill was devastated by the news. In his grief, he began writing a song, "Go Rest High on That Mountain." The first verse was "centered around Keith," Gill said, "with the words, 'I know your life on earth was troubled and only you can know the pain. You weren't afraid to face the devil. You were no stranger to the rain.' That was his song. Then I just put it down. I didn't fin-

ish it. I felt a little uneasy about it for some reason; I don't know why. And I never kept going."

Four years later, Gill's brother died: "All of a sudden, I remembered that verse, and I said, my brother had that story. You know, my brother really struggled in his life. And I pulled that out and finished that song. So, in the real sense, it really is about my brother. But those first few lines were because of a friendship with Keith and admiration for him. I had written it and had no intention of recording it. Tony Brown heard it and said, 'You've got to record that.'"

With Ricky Skaggs and country star Patty Loveless singing harmony, Gill released the song, and won another CMA award and two more Grammys. In time, "Go Rest High on That Mountain" would become a classic, joining "Amazing Grace" and "Will the Circle Be Unbroken" as a song grieving people request to hear when they've lost a loved one.

Nearly twenty-five years after he first started writing it, Vince Gill would be asked to sing it at George Jones's memorial service at the Grand Ole Opry House. That day, overcome by emotion, he had trouble finishing it again.

TOP, LEFT *When Keith Whitley, a rising country star and friend of Vince Gill's, died of alcohol poisoning, Gill began work on a new song, but put it aside.*

TOP, RIGHT *After the death of his older brother Bob (seen here holding Vince in 1958), Gill finished the song "Go Rest High on That Mountain" in his honor.*

LEFT *Patty Loveless tries to comfort Gill as he struggles to perform "Go Rest High on That Mountain" at the memorial service for George Jones.*

FRIENDS IN LOW PLACES

The same night that Jon Vezner sang "Where've You Been" in public for the first time at the Bluebird Café, another singer-songwriter also performed there. His name was Garth Brooks.

Growing up in Yukon, Oklahoma, in the 1960s and '70s, the youngest of six children, Brooks was exposed to every kind of music—the country stars like George Jones and Merle Haggard his parents liked, and the younger artists his older siblings listened to, "bands like the Eagles, guys like James Taylor," Brooks said, "everything from Townes Van Zandt to Tom Rush, everything from Janis Joplin to Rita Coolidge and Emmylou Harris."

He attended Oklahoma State University on a track scholarship; worked as a bouncer at a local night spot called the Tumbleweed Ballroom; and formed his own band, Santa Fe,

that became a favorite at Willie's Saloon near the campus, where he learned to play whatever the audience wanted.

In 1987, Brooks moved to Nashville and began making the rounds at publishers and record labels. He worked as the manager at a store selling cowboy boots, got paid to sing on demo tapes for other songwriters, and, like many unknown musicians at the time, played at the Bluebird whenever they would let him. Amy Kurland remembered his first audition:

> He blew me and everybody else in the room away. I don't remember the name of the song right offhand, but I do remember that it was about loving a woman,

BELOW *Garth Brooks performing at the Bluebird Café*

which I'm sure Tony thought, "Well, I'm not going to go spend that money right now."

By the spring of 1988, Brooks had been rejected by every record label in Music City. On May 11, he was back at the Bluebird, on the same bill with Jon Vezner. At the last minute, when one of the other singers didn't show, Brooks was moved up to an earlier slot on the program. He began singing a song he had co-written, "If Tomorrow Never Comes."

Sitting in the audience was Lynn Shults, an executive for Capitol Records, who had come to hear the singer who hadn't shown up. Only a few days earlier, Shults had turned down the chance to sign Garth Brooks, but something about the performance at the Bluebird that night changed his mind.

With a modest advance of $10,000, Brooks was assigned to a producer to create his first album. It was Allen Reynolds. Their initial session got off to a rocky start, according to Reynolds: "He was doing, I don't remember what song, but it sounded like someone else. It didn't sound like Garth to me, and I was questioning him about it, and he said, 'Well, I'm trying to put a little of that George Strait thing in there.' I just stopped everything right then, and I said, 'Look, we've already got a George Strait. We don't need another one. And what I'm trying to do is get the best Garth Brooks to step forward.'"

Brooks recalled the moment, too: "And he says, 'Look, man, just be yourself. That way, if you're yourself, there's never been anybody else like you. And anybody that comes after you is going to be called a copycat. So just be yourself and if it doesn't work, then you go down being true to yourself, because that's who you have to live with the rest of your life.'"

For his debut album, in addition to songs he had co-written—like "If Tomorrow Never Comes" and "Much Too Young (To Feel This Damn Old)"—Brooks asked Reynolds about including "The Dance," the song he had heard Tony Arata sing at the Bluebird writers' night: "I said, 'Allen, I'm worried it's not country enough. I really am.' And he said, 'Look, don't worry about what's country and what's not.' He says, 'You're country. That's all that matters. And I'm going to tell you this: If you don't cut 'The Dance,' it will be the biggest hit you never had.'"

putting her up on a pedestal, and I'm thinking, "I want to be that woman."

And then he came back and played the writers' night, maybe a month or so later. And again, the audience was just blown away. I think it's the first time I ever saw a standing ovation in the middle of a song—you know, end of the first chorus, and people were like going crazy.

Another time, Garth Brooks and Tony Arata and two other friends were playing In the Round one night. Nobody had a record deal; nobody had a publishing deal. They were just hanging out. And Tony played a song he had written by himself called "The Dance." Garth always says he was the only one listening. And he said, "If I ever get a record deal, I'm going to record that song." To

---

ABOVE AND RIGHT *The sheet from Brooks's audition for songwriters' night at the Bluebird Café. A record executive who had previously turned Garth down heard him at the Bluebird and decided to sign him for his first album.*

Released in 1989, the album sold well at first, but not spectacularly—until "The Dance" came out as a single, and the sales doubled in a single month.

Garth Brooks now joined another generation of young artists who were beginning to make their mark.

Vince Gill's *When I Call Your Name* was topping the charts. Alan Jackson, a lanky singer-songwriter from Georgia, who had been working in the mailroom at TNN for four years, finally got to record his own album, *Here in the Real World*. And a former construction worker and part-time bar singer from Houston, Clint Black, broke out on the charts with *Killin' Time*.

"We were all betting on Clint Black," said Ralph Emery, who now was a host on TNN's popular talk show. "We thought he was more handsome and we thought his songs were just as good. And he could sing better. Garth came on and he surprised all of us, I think, with his showmanship. I began to hear about his stage shows and how different they were, how big the crowds were, and how the crowds were reacting to him."

Garth Brooks would surpass them all. Out on the road, he could hold an audience spellbound with his sensitive and soulful ballads. But he absolutely tore them up with his rocking songs. He applied what he had learned while playing in college bars, and in watching the bands he admired growing up—Alabama, Queen, and KISS—to his stage performances.

"The first time I ever saw Garth Brooks, he was opening the show for me, I think in Davenport, Iowa, 1990," said Reba McEntire, "and I thought he was the wildest guy on a stage I'd ever seen." "He had a very country sound," added Trisha Yearwood. "But what made Garth different was his show wasn't country. He didn't walk out there and stand in one spot. There's nothing pop about Garth Brooks; his show is pop, but his music is 'countrier' than I'll ever be."

ABOVE *Brooks in the studio with his producer, Allen Reynolds (center), who advised him to "just be yourself"*

His biggest crowd pleaser was "Friends in Low Places," written by Dewayne Blackwell and Earl Bud Lee, who had asked Brooks to sing it as a demo back when he was selling cowboy boots. Now, Brooks added it to his second album, *No Fences*. "That's what kind of song you want to write," said Darius Rucker, who remembered the first time he heard it on a jukebox. "You want to write a big drinking song like that, where everybody's in the bar singing it at the same time. Even people that don't know it, by the second chorus, they know it."

Propelled by the astonishing popularity of "Friends in Low Places," Brooks's second album sold 700,000 copies in its first ten days and reached number four on the pop charts. It would soon become the first country album to hit five million in sales.

His third album would *debut* at number one on the pop charts—another first for a country artist—and sell more than eight million copies. Magazines put him on their covers. *Forbes* called the Brooks phenomenon "Led Zeppelin meets Roy Rogers . . . country conquers rock." NBC devoted a prime-time television special to him and his music.

"And he did this without ever once allowing his record label to promote his records across into other markets, like the pop market," said Allen Reynolds. "His loyalty was to country

Wall Street fashion report: from junk bonds to junk equity

Here come the real estate tax shelters again

March 2, 1992 Four Dollars

Forbes

Led Zeppelin meets Roy Rogers... country conquers rock

Country music's Garth Brooks

radio and his attitude was, 'Let them come to us. Let's be so good at what we do that they come to us, and leave pop radio or whatever kind of radio and come listen to country.'" "And when they do," Brooks added, "they're going to get to hear Vince Gill, Alan Jackson. They're going to hear the great ones, Strait, McEntire, Keith Whitley—I don't know if there's ever been a greater voice to sing country music than Keith Whitley. So that was our job, to anybody that said, 'Hey, I didn't know anything about country music.' Well, come over, and while you're here, take a look around because you're going to be impressed."

"It wasn't about being hip," Kathy Mattea said. "I think country music had kind of been self-conscious for a long time about, 'Are we cool? Do the big people in New York accept us? Are we kind of the unwanted stepchild? Are we kind of the afterthought?' And, all of a sudden, this guy is selling out the stadiums and doing specials, and blowing the tops off record sales across the board. And he's one of us."

TOP, LEFT AND RIGHT *Clint Black and Alan Jackson were also breaking out with big hits.*

CENTER AND OPPOSITE *His wild energy onstage, particularly with songs like "Friends in Low Places," helped propel Brooks to a new level of country stardom—and onto the cover of magazines like* Forbes.

In 1993, Brooks announced that he would be doing a concert at Texas Stadium. All 65,675 seats were sold out within ninety-two minutes, beating a previous record held by Paul McCartney. A second show was added—and sold out in the same time. So did a third. Angered when he heard about the extravagant prices being charged by scalpers, Brooks announced a fourth concert—with free tickets.

The four concerts were like nothing any country star had ever delivered. In front of the massive crowd, preparing for the biggest stunt he had ever attempted—being lifted by a wire and ascending over the audience, all the way to the high seats at the back of the stadium—he remembered the first Queen concert he attended, when he was seventeen:

I'm standing in the thirteenth row, on my chair. And all I want that whole night is for Freddie Mercury to look at me for three seconds so I can go, "Thank you, dude. Thank you. It's what I listen to before I play football; it's what I listen to when I'm down. Thank you. Thank you."

And it was funny, you start to get to do this for a living, you're the guy that gets to do it for a living, and now all I do is scan the audience, every night, for that three seconds, to go, "Thank you. Thank you." Coolest gig ever.

I've got to tell you, flying over a crowd at Texas Stadium, singing, I'd love to tell you, "Oh, it was nothing." It scared me to death. But it was such a rush, so much fun. You could see every face as they passed underneath

your boots. And then you saw all the people out there. And then the last night, I told the guy that was operating, the Foy flyer guys, I said, "How close you want to get?" And it was that night, I felt someone clap the boot on the very top row. I said, "A little too close for me." But that's great.

• • •

Starting in 1991, *Billboard* had instituted a new way of gauging a record's success. Instead of taking a telephone poll of record store clerks, it now relied on SoundScan, which used bar codes to keep track of actual sales. What the new system proved was that Garth Brooks and his contemporaries were doing even better than anyone had imagined. "If you were making country music records in the '90s, you were selling records," said Trisha Yearwood. "And it was largely due to Garth."

OPPOSITE *At Texas Stadium, Brooks broke sales records with four concerts—and then astonished the crowds by being launched toward the upper tiers.*

ABOVE *Garth refused to have his records promoted on anything but country stations, where, he said, listeners would also hear "the great ones," like George Strait. At Fan Fair he posed with a cardboard cutout of his hero.*

twenty million, every record. It just changed the whole landscape of what the expectations were of Nashville."

Marty Stuart, now working with Tony Brown at his new label, had a string of gold records, proudly embracing a flamboyant hillbilly image and honky tonk sound. So did his good friend Travis Tritt. Neither of them conformed to the clean-cut cowboy look projected by George Strait, Alan Jackson, Clint Black, and Garth Brooks—the so-called "hat acts." Stuart and Tritt announced a "No Hats" tour of the United States. It was a huge success. "Tradition was still alive, but the sky was the limit," Stuart said. "Everybody was buying tractors and trailers and big sound systems, and we were putting on stadium

Between 1989 and 1991, sales of country music had doubled, from $460 million to nearly $1 billion; then, between 1991 and 1994, they doubled again. In 1995 alone, twenty-seven country albums sold more than a million copies and went platinum. The number of radio stations playing country music had jumped from 1,800 to 2,600—and with seventy million listeners, it had become the biggest format on the airwaves.

"It was just unbelievable," producer Tony Brown said. "Every record label was selling millions of records. My first George Strait record I produced, *Pure Country* [1992], sold six million records. Up to that point, he had only sold a million. Then my first record on Wynonna Judd sold six million records. And then Garth Brooks was selling ten, fifteen,

shows. And it was about how big can you get it; how loud can you get it; and how many people can you get to come see you."

From Canada, Shania Twain burst onto the scene with a sassy persona and performance style that filled big arenas and sold records in the tens of millions, as she edged her version of country music further toward pop and rock.

Mary Chapin Carpenter, from Princeton, New Jersey, was more folk oriented, but still had five platinum albums.

CLOCKWISE FROM TOP, LEFT *Marty Stuart (right) and Travis Tritt on their hugely successful "No Hats" tour; Mary Chapin Carpenter, whose songs were more folk oriented but had five platinum albums; Shania Twain, who sold more records than any previous woman country star*

I was a teenager, just graduated from high school, when Reba really hit it big. She was the first kind of, I would say, contemporary artist for me. I had grown up on the classic women of country. I listened to Patsy; I listened to Loretta; I listened to Tammy Wynette.

When I heard Reba, it was kind of, okay, this is the next step for me. If Loretta and Tammy opened the door for Reba, Reba opened the door for me.

TRISHA YEARWOOD

When Trisha Yearwood arrived in Nashville in 1985 and entered Belmont College, it was the farthest she had ever been from home: the small town of Mon-

ticello, Georgia, only three hundred miles away.

She took a part-time job as a receptionist at a record label; led tours of the old RCA Studio B, which was now considered a part of Music Row history; and started singing in a student bar band. (A Merle Haggard song, "I Think I'll Just Stay Here and Drink," became one of her favorite numbers.) After graduation from Belmont, she got work singing on demo tapes for ten to twenty dollars a song. For duet demos, she had been put together with a young Garth Brooks, before his career took off.

When Yearwood got her own record deal, Brooks invited her to be the opening act on one of his early tours as she promoted her first album. Its signature song, "She's in Love With the Boy," hit number one on the country charts, and she became the first female country singer to have a debut album sell more than a million copies. (Fourteen years later, Yearwood and Brooks would marry.)

For the record labels, the expectations that defined success in country music had ballooned. But the expectations of country fans were unchanged: Don't get above your raisin'.

TOP *Trisha Yearwood treasured the autograph she got from Reba McEntire, who "opened the door for me."*

ABOVE *As a college student at Nashville's Belmont College, Yearwood played in a bar band. Merle Haggard's "I Think I'll Just Stay Here and Drink" was a favorite number.*

RIGHT *Before either one became a star, Trisha and Garth Brooks sang duets on demo tapes for ten to twenty dollars a song. He then helped launch her career by inviting her to be an opening act on his tours. More than a decade later, the two got married.*

"Minnie Pearl said, 'Love them, and they'll love you back.' That was always her advice about country music fans," said Dierks Bentley. "These fans are not just investing in a song. They're investing in you as a person. It all goes back to the songs. They get woven into the fabric of people's lives, and they associate you with that song. You really feel like you know them, even if you've never met them before."

"Part of the journey of being a country music star, you go talk to your fans," said Kathy Mattea:

You sign autographs. You look them in the eye, and when you look those people in the eye, they are you and you are them. There is no being above.

People come through and they're like, "This song changed my life." "I had this song sung in my wedding." "My grandmother died the same way."

ABOVE AND RIGHT *Minnie Pearl and Kathy Mattea carry on a country music tradition connecting with the fans.*

OPPOSITE, CLOCKWISE FROM TOP, LEFT *Hawkshaw Hawkins, Johnny Cash, Eddy Arnold, Charley Pride, Brenda Lee, Little Jimmy Dickens sign autographs.*

There was a moment, where I was signing autographs, and this woman just walked up to me on the line and she just looked at me. And I looked at her and she didn't say a word and she just started crying, tears just came down her face. And I just looked at her and she looked at me, and we just hugged.

And her husband just leaned down and he grabbed her arm, [and] when they were walking away, he said, "She buried her mom this morning, but she really wanted to come and see you tonight." And, I mean, that's it, you know? That's it. That's country music.

For decades, the Country Music Association had hosted Fan Fair, a chance for people to hear some live music, but most of all meet their favorite stars and get their autograph. Five thousand fans showed up for the first one, in 1972, held in Nashville's Municipal Auditorium; by the mid-1990s, it was an outdoor event with a crowd of 24,000.

At the peak of his unprecedented popularity, Garth Brooks showed up—not to play, but to sign. "He went there unannounced," Yearwood remembered. "He drove in his truck. He got out of his truck and he went and stood under a tent somewhere, not a Garth Brooks booth, and just stood there. And I think somebody said, 'Oh, my gosh, there's Garth Brooks.' And it started. And people lined up."

Kathy Mattea remembered that day, too: "Usually you have a window and everyone knows when it is. And so that people don't get disappointed, you have someone stand at the end of the line and say, 'Look, this is the last person, we're not going to take any more.' But Garth just didn't stop. He just decided he was going to sign until everybody was done."

He stayed at it for more than twenty hours.

OPPOSITE, FROM TOP LEFT *Merle Haggard, Waylon Jennings, Dolly Parton (with Porter Wagoner), June Carter, Emmylou Harris, Loretta Lynn with their fans*

ABOVE AND LEFT *Garth Brooks carries on the tradition—for more than twenty hours at Fan Fair.*

BLUE MOON OF KENTUCKY

Record labels have a terrible tendency to chase whatever is the current hit. I have always said that marketing men would clone today's number one forever, without a sense of guilt, if they could get away with it, just because it would eliminate risk.

ALLEN REYNOLDS

Country music may have been bigger than ever, but by the mid-1990s, record sales were concentrated on a smaller and smaller number of new releases. Executives at the labels in Nashville were under increasing pressure to only produce albums that sold in the millions, at the expense of experimenting with new artists and new sounds and giving them the opportunity to find an audience over time.

"Expectations became part of the creative decision making," according to Rodney Crowell. "That means that the record companies' bottom line had risen to such great heights with the likes of Garth Brooks and Shania Twain that their shareholders were never going to be happy if they were out trying to develop a new act who sold one-fifth, or one-one-hundredth of what those artists sold. It just wasn't going to happen."

Then, a change in federal law allowed large corporations to consolidate their ownership of radio stations across the nation. Decisions on which songs would be broadcast were being made by fewer people. Playlists got shorter. It became even harder for new, unconventional artists to break in, and harder for many established artists to hold on.

"The days of an artist dropping in to see a disc jockey, like was the case with Loretta Lynn, those days are virtually gone," said Eddie Stubbs of WSM. "And now," Allen Reynolds added, "instead of having a lot of possibilities to get to try your record out and see if the public will respond, you're going through the eye of the needle, one person who is pro-

ABOVE *By the 1990s, sales were soaring, but the Mother Church of Country Music was shuttered and decaying. Many older, established artists felt that they were being neglected and forgotten.*

gramming for thirteen, fourteen hundred stations and his say-so is *the* say-so. And if he says no, that's it."

Many artists found themselves in a musical no-man's land, seemingly shut out from being heard. Emmylou Harris recalled being at a radio station to talk about a new album, when the news was announced that Loretta Lynn was to be inducted into the Country Music Hall of Fame: "And I said, 'Oh, this is so fantastic. Let's play something by Loretta Lynn.' And he said, 'Oh, we can't do that, because she's not on our playlist.'"

But some independent stations still existed and continued featuring alternative country artists, as well as the classics. To prove that it and other roots music still had an audience, a new term had to be invented, with its own chart—and later, its own awards. It was called Americana.

No one was more supportive of the movement than Emmylou Harris. Twenty years earlier, when she became a convert to country music, her best-selling albums, featuring songs by older stars, had shone a spotlight on what was being overlooked. "Every so often," Johnny Cash told a reporter, "country has to get back to Emmylou Harris."

"She made people remember Buck Owens," Vince Gill said. "She made people remember Merle Haggard, and made people remember Kitty Wells and the Louvin Brothers. Every now and then, there's someone that's going to be the great conduit to connect you back to where we come from."

By the 1990s, Harris decided to do an all-acoustic album. To record it, she chose the Ryman Auditorium, which had been closed since the early 1970s. "It was just an old building where the *Grand Ole Opry* used to be, and with an old history that was tired," Marty Stuart said. "The windows were bro-

ken out, and pigeons were flying around, and they conducted two-dollar tours."

When Harris and her band recorded their live album at the decaying Ryman, the crowd that was permitted to witness it was restricted—for safety reasons—to only two hundred people, all gathered near the stage to make it appear that the audience was much larger.

The only guest she invited to perform with her was Bill Monroe, the aging patriarch of bluegrass, who had first appeared at the Ryman back in 1939 and now danced with Emmylou when he came onstage. "For country music, perhaps it's a reminder of where we all came from, and not to

forget that," Harris said. "Not to just constantly be recycling that and trying to go back, because you can't go back. Every generation is different. But we mustn't forget where we came from, because it's going to make the music that we make in the future better."

LEFT *When Emmylou Harris and the Nash Ramblers recorded an all-acoustic live album at the Ryman, it boosted a campaign to renovate the historic structure to its old glory.*

ABOVE *Emmylou and Bill Monroe sing and dance at the* Opry.

The event—and the album that it produced, *At the Ryman*—reminded people of the building's incomparable acoustics, as well as its place in music history. Harris and others joined a campaign to save the Ryman from destruction, and the owners of WSM and the *Grand Ole Opry* invested more than $8 million to completely restore it. The Mother Church of Country Music reopened as a performance venue on June 3, 1994, with Little Jimmy Dickens, Porter Wagoner, and Marty Stuart cutting the ribbon.

The next year, when the *Grand Ole Opry* celebrated its seventieth birthday, two of the

ABOVE, LEFT AND OPPOSITE *During Bill Monroe's final days, Marty Stuart brought his camera to Monroe's farm, where they talked and played music together.*

show's favorite stars were no longer there. Roy Acuff, who had joined the cast in 1938, had died. Minnie Pearl had delivered the news from Grinder's Switch every Saturday night since 1940, but she was now incapacitated by a stroke and would pass on a few months later.

But Bill Monroe, at age eighty-four, showed up. In tribute to him, more than fifty fiddlers performed his song "Uncle Pen," and Vince Gill sang Monroe's signature tune, "Blue Moon of Kentucky." Monroe and Emmylou Harris danced again for the crowd. Then a seven-foot statue of the Father of Bluegrass was unveiled.

By now, Monroe had put aside the bitter feuds that had splintered bluegrass music for so long. He and Lester Flatt had made amends with each other. And when Carter Stanley had died, Monroe attended the funeral and sang "Swing Low, Sweet Chariot" in his honor.

But Monroe's health began failing, and he spent most of his time alone at his farm. Marty Stuart paid a visit to take photographs of his mentor: "I loved that old man. And toward the end of his life, I thought, 'I want to go hang out

with him one more time and just spend the afternoon with him.' And at the end of it all, we were standing by his barn, just me and him, playing mandolins. We played a couple of tunes together, and he put his hand on my shoulder and he said, 'You learned pretty good, boy. You learned pretty good.'"

As Monroe faded even more, Ricky Skaggs made pilgrimages to his bedside: "I could tell, in his last few days, that he was really concerned about where bluegrass was going, what was going to happen to it, where's it going to end up. And I just said, 'Bill, listen, this music is bigger than you. You got to hear it first. You got to play it first. And you got to sow great seeds with this music. I'm part of your seed. Marty's part of your seed. Vince is part of your seed. All of us that love bluegrass are part of your seed. It's never going to die. So you can go home and rest in peace. Don't worry about where the music's going. We're going to take care of it. Just be free.' I made a promise to him that I would play this music all the days of my life. And I would always tell people where it came from."

After Monroe died on September 9, 1996, Ricky Skaggs, Marty Stuart, and Vince Gill were among the performers at his funeral, held at the newly restored Mother Church of Country Music. Ralph Stanley was there, too, and sang "Swing Low, Sweet Chariot" over Monroe's casket, just as Monroe had done for Stanley's brother.

In the wake of Monroe's death, both Ricky Skaggs and Marty Stuart would refocus their careers. "I just kept hearing this deep calling-unto, deep thing in me," Skaggs said. "And it was like, 'simple life, simple life, simple life.' I can take these acoustic instruments, I don't have to have microphones. I don't have to have amps. If we wanted to pull off the road and go to a little schoolhouse, we could go play and entertain the kids. Back into the kitchen, that's just where I wanted to take it. I wanted to take it back to the front porch. And so that's what I did."

Stuart had been touring constantly, playing big venues and chasing record sales; his marriage to Johnny Cash's daughter had ended in divorce. "I had become a success machine," Stuart said. "I simply wanted success. I wanted

to be accepted, and my heart got left behind. And one day I was riding through the woods and I was noticing barns and cows and tractors, and clothes blowing on the line, and the smell of the country, and I listened to the kind of music I was making, and it did not line up with what I was looking at. And then I went back and started listening to the Carter Family, and I listened to Bill Monroe, and Tammy Wynette, and George Jones, and Hank Williams. And I started to cry. My heart came back to life, and I went, 'I think I know what I need to do: Go back to myself and start again, and take it up again.' I left charts behind. I left demographics behind. And I simply followed my heart."

A year later, Stuart married country star Connie Smith—just as he had predicted he would do when he was eleven years old and got her autograph at the Choctaw Indian Fair in Mississippi.

ABOVE *Patty Loveless, Vince Gill, Ricky Skaggs, and Marty Stuart perform at Bill Monroe's funeral, held at the renovated Ryman Auditorium. Both Stuart and Skaggs would refocus their careers in his memory. "I left charts behind," Stuart said, "and I simply followed my heart."*

RIGHT *Stuart and his wife Connie Smith. He had taken her picture and gotten her autograph when he was eleven.*

I STILL MISS SOMEONE

Take every piece of American music, every piece of that stream, all those tributaries that go into that pool of whatever we call it, country music, American music—from blues, gospel, bluegrass, rock and roll—that was all in John. I mean it was all in him.

EMMYLOU HARRIS

I was always so averse to using my dad or appearing to use my dad, or trading on my dad in any way. I so wanted to be my own agent, as he always was.

ROSANNE CASH

As the 1990s began, Rosanne Cash was coming off a string of number-one singles and successful albums. But her relationship with Nashville was as complicated as the one she had with her famous father, who had been absent for much of her and her sisters' childhood. "I was kind of famous, when I was in Nashville, for not touring," she said. "I grew up think-

---

ABOVE AND CENTER *Rosanne Cash was proud of her album* Interiors, *but label executives said they couldn't promote it. "Stay true to yourself," her father said. She left Nashville for New York City.*

ing that becoming famous was about the worst thing that could happen to you, because then you had to go on the road. And if you went on the road, you got divorced and you didn't see your kids and you got on drugs. And everything fell apart. My mother thought that, too, so it was something kind of ingrained in us, 'This is not a good way to live.'"

As he aged, Cash had taken to writing poignant letters to his daughters, asking them to forgive him for his many absences. But he and Rosanne shared the same stubborn willingness to take artistic risks. He had recorded a prison album over his label's reluctance and, in keeping a promise he had made to his mother after his brother's death, continually released gospel albums—ten of them by now—even if they didn't sell. Now it was Rosanne's turn.

Following the phenomenal success of *King's Record Shop*, she told her label she wanted to produce a different kind of album—all of the songs to be written by her, "very acoustic, really rooted, really pristine." She was proud of the finished product, *Interiors*, but, she said, the executives at Columbia told her "there's nothing here we can work with; there's nothing we can send to the radio on this record." When she saw that they weren't pushing it, "I was just devastated," she said, "and I called my dad and I said, 'What do I do?' He said, 'Screw 'em, do what you want. Stay true to yourself.' Eventually I moved to New York. I didn't have any more hits. But I was happy. I was writing my own songs."

Rosanne was in New York City when her father came to town for a concert. He asked her if she'd join him onstage for a song—one he had co-written and recorded back in 1958: "I Still Miss Someone." She refused at first:

I was mad at him about something. Some childhood transgression he had committed, or something I was going through, something he hadn't done. I don't even remember what it was. And I very petulantly said, "No, I don't think I will." Can you imagine? And he said, "Okay."

And he turned and he walked out of the room. And, as he walked out, I looked at his back and I thought of the thousands of times I had seen his back from sitting in the wings offstage, and seen his back with the light coming down on him and his guitar. And there's something about his back—I mean, that image of his back is as powerful to me, about my dad, as anything.

So, I said, "Dad, I'll do it." That night, he called me out and we sang "I Still Miss Someone" together. It's one of his most beautiful ballads. And everything got dissolved; everything got fixed, just looking at him.

He worked out all of his problems onstage. That's where he took his best self; that's where he took all of his anguish and fears and griefs, and he worked them out with an audience. That's just who he was. And got purified by the end of the night. So that happened with me that night with him. That just all got fixed.

Johnny Cash's own career seemed to have bottomed out. He was inducted into the Rock and Roll Hall of Fame in 1992, at age fifty-nine, but his albums on his new label still sold poorly. Like many fading country stars, he and June Carter found themselves encamped in the tourist town of Branson, Missouri, where a group of theaters had sprouted up and turned the old business model of live performances on its head: it was the *audience* who showed up in big buses; the musicians stayed in one place and gave two or three shows a day.

"It's not what I wanted to do with my life," Cash said. "I wanted to . . . do something new." Some days, he looked out at the 2,500-seat theater and fewer than two hundred people were in the seats.

Then, in 1993, a young producer named Rick Rubin—who had helped popularize hip-hop music, and recorded successful rap, punk, and heavy metal artists—approached Cash about doing an album for his label, American Recordings. Many of Cash's friends and family—with memories of "The Chicken in Black" fiasco in mind—were against it, afraid the collaboration would be damaging to his already faltering career. He went ahead anyway.

Cash and Rubin began their collaboration, according to John Carter Cash, with Rubin saying, "Let's just think about the song. Let's think about where your heart is." "And so, they began to focus on material," John said. "And they put together this collection of songs that was very diverse, but everything was honestly connected with my father and who he was as a person: songs of faith; songs of my dad's love for my mother; songs of his humor; songs of the elemental darkness within him."

Released in the spring of 1994, *American Recordings* won rave reviews for its sparse arrangements, Cash's still-commanding voice, and his song choices—from a traditional cowboy tune to compositions by Tom Waits, Leonard Cohen, and Kris Kristofferson, and the nearly century-old

LEFT *His career fading, Johnny Cash still toured, though his crowds were getting smaller.*

OPPOSITE, TOP AND CENTER *With producer Rick Rubin, Cash went back to the studio with just his guitar and remarkable voice to record a selection of songs Cash personally selected. "Let's think about where your heart is," Rubin told him. The album won a Grammy in the folk category.*

OPPOSITE, BOTTOM *From left, Tom Petty, Cash, Rick Rubin, and Marty Stuart working on* Unchained, *the second in a series of* American Recordings. *It won a Grammy as Best Country Album.*

roots, but of the roots of country music, and proved that you could have this simple sound, this pure sound of a voice and a guitar," said John Carter Cash. "He was casting back and looking upon the sound of the Carter Family. He was remembering what it sounded like to stand in front of a Victrola and hear Jimmie Rodgers. It was all from him going back to his roots. It was all from him just stepping up there with a guitar and saying, 'This is me. This is what I do.'"

Rosanne Cash noted a change in her father: "Everything was new again. He was back. It was like the light shined on him again. And he was so grateful and relieved that somebody saw his essence and who he was, and just wanted to bring that out, just wanted him to be Johnny Cash again."

Most country radio

murder ballad "Delia's Gone." The *Los Angeles Times* called it a "milestone work" that "peer[s] into the dark corners of the American soul." *Rolling Stone* said it was "at once monumental and viscerally intimate, fiercely true to the legend of Johnny Cash and entirely contemporary."

"He came back to the simplicity not only of his

stations ignored the album, claiming it didn't fit their play-list. But it sold 150,000 copies—more than any album of his since 1971—and won Cash a Grammy Award for Best Contemporary Folk Album. Young audiences began turning out to hear him at rock clubs and auditoriums. At an outdoor concert in England, where he shared billing with rock star Peter Gabriel, an interviewer asked him, "How does it feel to be cool again?" "It feels," he answered, "like no time has passed."

Two years later, in 1996, Cash and Rubin came out with the equally successful *Unchained*, with Marty Stuart and Tom Petty and the Heartbreakers as backup musicians. When it won a Grammy for Best Country Album, Rubin took out a full-page ad in *Billboard*, using a photograph that had been taken backstage in 1969 at Cash's San Quentin concert of him defiantly giving the middle finger to the camera. "American Recordings and Johnny Cash," the ad said, "would like to acknowledge the Nashville music establishment and coun-

try radio for your support." Willie Nelson put it on the wall of his tour bus. "John," he told a reporter, "speaks for all of us."

Over the next several years, even as his health deteriorated and he could no longer make live appearances, Cash would record three more albums with Rick Rubin, with an equally wide range of songs: from ones Cash had written to those by Bono, Sting, and Lennon and McCartney, as well as Marty Robbins, Hank Williams, and the Carter Family.

One of the albums, *The Man Comes Around*, opened with a song that Cash had recently written, based on passages from the Bible's Book of Revelation. But the track that got the most attention was "Hurt," written by Trent Reznor of Nine Inch Nails. The album would eventually sell nearly two million copies, earn Cash yet another Grammy—and, as a sign

ABOVE AND OPPOSITE, TOP *After June died, Cash went back to perform at the Carter Fold in Virginia, where she had been born and raised. Their son, John Carter Cash, helps his father tune his guitar.*

that the country music industry wanted him back as one of their own, won the CMA's award for Album of the Year.

Shortly after the album's release, on May 15, 2003, June Carter Cash died. Johnny hung on for four months without her. "In the last few months of his life, it seems like I sang a lot of Carter Family songs to him," Rosanne Cash remembered. "It comforted him. I read the Psalms to him, and I read some poetry to him. The last song he heard was 'The Winding Stream.' That's what I sang to him when he was dying. It was June's favorite Carter Family song, and I just liked to sing it, and he liked to hear me sing it. The Carter Family songs on the radio when he was a kid, that pulled him forward; and Carter Family songs sent him out, sent him away." He died on September 12, 2003.

At his funeral, people sang "Will the Circle Be Unbroken"—and then Johnny Cash was buried next to June Carter Cash in the Memory Gardens cemetery near their home in Hendersonville, Tennessee. Later, a memorial tribute concert was staged at the Ryman Auditorium, with performances by a grand array of stars. It began, as his mother would have liked, with the Fisk Jubilee Singers doing a gospel song. Then Rosanne stepped to the microphone and sang "I Still Miss Someone"—this time, on her own.

LEFT *In his last days, Rosanne Cash read the Bible and sang songs to her dying father—and sometimes simply held his hand. The last song he heard was a Carter Family tune, "The Winding Stream."*

It was now 2003, and a new century was under way. As a commercial enterprise, country music was still less than a hundred years old. But as a uniquely American art form, it was ageless—a complicated chorus of American voices, joining together to tell a complicated American story, one song at a time. It has been handed down from generation to generation, moving from farm fields and churches and family porches into every corner of the country, changing and growing at every turn, tethered to its past but always reaching toward its future.

PREVIOUS SPREAD *"Take every piece of American music,"* Emmylou Harris said of Johnny Cash. *"It was all in him."*

ABOVE *Ketch Secor, center, and Old Crow Medicine Show perform on The Grand Ole Opry, 2014.*

RIGHT *A boy plays his homemade banjo under his father's guidance on their front porch in Perry County, Kentucky.*

It rose up out of nothing—uneducated, from the soul—and came into what it is, which is probably never been anything like it and there will never be anything like it again.

MERLE HAGGARD

It's always going to be connected to the past, but we don't want to stay there. We've got to move ahead, but we carry it forth with us. Who was it that said, "You never step into the same river twice"? Music has to change, too.

The river has to constantly be changing. And all those tributaries that move into that river of country music—it's the same and yet it's different.

EMMYLOU HARRIS

It's so rich and so vast, and nobody has to stake a claim or make a line or draw a definition. It's not a religion that you have to stick to this doctrine. There are multitudes. We contain multitudes.

ROSANNE CASH

There will be songs that should have been hits that never were. There will be songs that are hits that shouldn't have been. There will be people that you'll fall in love with and they'll be gone in three weeks, or after the next record. Then there will be stars that come and get inside of your heart and stay with you for the rest of your life.

Somewhere along the way you'll discover an old country song that will speak to that divorce you're going through or that tax problem you're going through, or you losing your best friend. Country music has something for everybody, and it's inside the songs. It's inside the lives of the characters. It's really colorful in here. I invite you in.

MARTY STUART

ABOVE *Elizabeth "Libba" Cotten picks her guitar in Rhode Island.*

OPPOSITE *Dellie Norton strums her banjo while her laundry dries in North Carolina.*

AFTERWORD

WAYLON, EMMYLOU, AND JOE: THE GOOD STUFF AND COUNTRY MUSIC

My own journey with country music began in an unlikely place: the basement of the Friends Church in tiny Ackworth, Iowa, a few miles from the farm where my mother had grown up. I was eight years old, in late 1957, and I was singing solo in public for the first time. A group of mostly elderly women, including my Quaker grandmother, sat listening politely. Mom was at the piano, accompanying me as I sang "A White Sport Coat and a Pink Carnation," Marty Robbins's big hit that year.

Robbins was known as the singer with a teardrop in his voice. I have no idea how someone would have described mine, except to note that at that young age I was a soprano. I also don't remember the small crowd's response. At best, I imagine they thought it was "cute" to hear a small boy with a high voice (dressed, of course, in a white sport coat with a pink carnation on its lapel) singing the lament of a jilted beau attending a prom and feeling "all alone in romance." If they'd wanted an encore, I knew Elvis's "Heartbreak Hotel," but I think my mother must have wisely decided this was not the place, or the audience, for that.

What strikes me now, sixty years later, is that at age eight the two songs I was drawn to were about heartache. If, as I've learned since then, the two sides of the country music coin are Saturday night and Sunday morning, my life at the

OPPOSITE *A miner in Kentucky totes his guitar over a creek, on his way to relax with some music after a hard day's work.*

ABOVE *Sheet music for "A White Sport Coat and a Pink Carnation" by Marty Robbins*

time was all Sunday morning (perfect attendance at Sunday school and singing in church choirs, mainly); but clearly, Saturday night was already tugging at my subconscious.

Neither song qualifies as classic or "pure" country, though both Presley and Robbins had roots there. While Elvis would move on to become the King of Rock and Roll, Marty would return from his foray in the world of crossover, trade in his white sport coat for a cowboy outfit, create *Gunfighter Ballads and Trail Songs*, and ride it into the Country Music Hall of Fame. But at the time I was debuting in a Quaker church basement with a song about a broken heart, genre classifications didn't mean a thing to me. It was just music I liked.

I liked a lot of music. In our home in nearby Indianola, a town of about six thousand people (and therefore a "city" compared to Ackworth), the LPs in my parents' collection in their mammoth wooden console centered on Glenn Miller, Louis Armstrong, Ella Fitzgerald, Spike Jones, and every Rodgers and Hammerstein musical soundtrack available. I listened to them all. My older sister had a small machine for 45 rpm singles in her room, and I remember sneaking in, whenever she was out of the house, to play Gogi Grant's "The Wayward Wind" and Pat Boone's "Love Letters in the Sand"—two more songs about broken promises and broken hearts.

By the time I started high school, still singing in church choirs and now school choruses, my voice (now a tenor) and tastes were changing. On the AM radio in our kitchen, I listened to station WHO in Des Moines early every morning as I did my homework. A typical rotation might include Johnny

Cash's "Ring of Fire" followed by Perry Como, then the Beach Boys, Bobby Darin, and Peter, Paul, and Mary. I enjoyed them all, but turned up the volume whenever Roger Miller sang "Dang Me" or "King of the Road." My family watched the Beatles on *The Ed Sullivan Show*, which launched the British Invasion of American music; and I learned to like Flatt and Scruggs by hearing (and memorizing) the theme song of *The Beverly Hillbillies*.

Every Saturday night, my best friend, Joe Blake, and I would watch a little of *The Lawrence Welk Show* with his parents, before getting in a car to drive endlessly around the town square in the vain hope two girls in some other car would hear the music on our radio (we always had the windows down, just in case) and decide we were so cool they'd ask if they could ride with us. Some of our favorites were the Righteous Brothers doing "You've Lost That Lovin' Feelin'" and

---

ABOVE *High school buddies Joe Blake, number 42, and Dayton Duncan, number 20, 1967*

LEFT *The New Frontier Four, Indianola, Iowa, 1966. Clockwise, from seated left: Dayton Duncan, guitar; Rob Bower, banjo; Wayne Peterson, bass fiddle; Gary Brown, guitar.*

Sonny and Cher's "I Got You, Babe" (we thought it showed our sensitive side) and the Rolling Stones' "I Can't Get No Satisfaction" (which more accurately expressed our situation). As the fruitless cruising wore on, we gravitated to the Animals' "We Gotta Get Out of This Place." When I drove him back to his house, and we had the windows up, Joe often did his dead-on impersonation of Eddy Arnold singing "Make the World Go Away."

At home, I tuned in to *American Bandstand* to check out the latest dance moves, but became particularly fascinated with *Hootenanny*, a folk music show staged at college campuses, and I came to the conclusion that sitting around and singing folk songs was what college students did, so I'd better start getting ready.

I ended six years of piano lessons (all classical), bought a guitar, and with three classmates formed the New Frontier Four, a folk quartet that ultimately earned us all

a little money for college, performing at Rotary meetings, church suppers, and in front of any other group that would pay us $50. We did well enough on a televised talent scout show to compete (unsuccessfully) for a bigger payout at the Iowa State Fair two years in a row. Our repertoire included "Long Black Veil," "Tom Dooley," "Wagoner's Lad," and "Blowin' in the Wind," though our big number was the gospel song "This Little Light of Mine."

When I arrived at college in the East in the late 1960s, the days of *Hootenanny* had ended. We occupied the college president's office and had teach-ins about the Vietnam War instead. I danced to Motown, became obsessed with *Tommy* by the Who (it told a story), adored Marvin Gaye and Tammi Terrell's duets, but still was drawn mostly to folk music. In my dorm room, I had Tom Rush and Joni Mitchell (*lots and lots* of Joni Mitchell) on my stereo and learned their songs on my guitar.

The only TV show I watched regularly was *The Johnny Cash Show*, where I got to know the Man in Black and his ecumenical embrace of American music. He was unabashedly country, but he seemed to be saying that our national songbook has many styles, wonderfully intermixed; let's enjoy it all. Tun-

ing in to his show also meant I could see Joni Mitchell (a big moment), Bob Dylan, James Taylor, and Pete Seeger perform. Sometimes I caught an episode of *Hee Haw* and *The Glen Campbell Goodtime Hour*. Back in Iowa in the summers, I came across *The Porter Wagoner Show*, syndicated on a local station, and Dolly Parton joined Joni Mitchell in my pantheon of woman singer-songwriters. In quick succession, the Byrds' *Sweetheart of the Rodeo*, Dylan's *Nashville Skyline*, and the three-disc *Will the Circle Be Unbroken* by the Nitty Gritty Dirt Band got me leaning toward country music in ways I never had before.

• • •

My real "come to country" moments came in 1975, four years out of college, living in my adopted state of New Hampshire. Emmylou Harris, a fellow "folkie," came out with *Pieces of the Sky* and *Elite Hotel*, filled with country songs I hadn't heard: from the Louvin Brothers' "If I Could Only Win Your Love" to Felice and Boudleaux Bryant's "Sleepless Nights," from Buck Owens's "Together Again" to Don Gibson's "Sweet Dreams" and many more. Her voice called me to country.

Then Joe, my friend from my hometown, called me up and insisted that I buy Waylon Jennings's *Dreaming My Dreams*. It seemed important to him, so I did—and it clinched the deal.

I wore that album out. Every song spoke to me. I would begin some days singing to myself, "I'm sick and tired of waking up sick and tired," the opening lines of "High Time (You Quit Your Lowdown Ways)." Some acquaintances at work would look at me askance when I quoted the words of wisdom from "Waymore's Blues": "If you want to get to heaven, got to D-I-E; got to put on your coat and T-I-E. If you want to get the rabbit out of the L-O-G, got to make a commotion like a D-O-G." I could feel the anguish

ABOVE, TOP AND BOTTOM *Emmylou Harris's albums* Pieces of the Sky *and* Elite Hotel

in Waylon's renditions of "I Recall a Gypsy Woman," "She's Looking Good," and "The Door Is Always Open"—and especially in the tender "Dreaming My Dreams." ("Someday I'll get over you; I'll live to see it all through. But I'll always miss dreaming my dreams with you.") I delighted at the word-play in "I've Been a Long Time Leaving (but I'll Be a Long Time Gone)," not even knowing that Roger Miller had written it. And, as I grew restless with the direction my life was taking, I appreciated the rebellious drive of "Are You Sure Hank Done It This Way," without really understanding its context to Waylon's career (or even to Hank Williams's standing in country music history).

It's no coincidence, I believe, that I became a country fan as an adult. "You have to have lived a little bit to really understand good country music," country star Dierks Bentley told us when I interviewed him for our film series. "It's one thing to listen to country music. Anyone can listen to it, but to really hear it, is two totally different things. You can listen to it and enjoy it, but to really hear the words, the lyrics, to hear the heartache, to hear the steel guitar and to understand what the steel guitar is speaking to you, you have to have been through some hardships in your own life to really understand. The good stuff—it takes a little bit of life's living to really get it." Emmylou Harris and Waylon Jennings were definitely part of the good stuff.

By the early 1980s, I was a serious fan. WOKQ, a country station in New Hampshire, was the station I listened to. Something about "You're the Reason God Make Oklahoma," sung by Shelly West and David Frizzell, captivated me (I think it was the simple yearning of two lovers who lived in different parts of the country)—and it led me to learn more about her mother, Dottie West, and his father, Lefty Frizzell. I adored Willie Nelson and Merle Haggard's "Pancho and Lefty" (as I had Emmylou Harris's version)—which led me to its songwriter, Townes Van Zandt. More good stuff.

By then, my own life had caught up with country music's core themes. I had gone through a divorce, some other per-

sonal and professional failures, and the untimely death of a man who was a father-like figure to me. The heartbreaks I had intuited in the songs I sang as an eight-year-old were now lived experiences.

Haggard's sad drinking songs resonated inside me, especially "No Reason to Quit" ("There's a circle of people where I'm no longer welcome, and I'm ashamed to say that I no longer fit"). I listened again—really listened—to Kris Kristofferson's "Sunday Morning Coming Down," which I remembered first hearing on *The Johnny Cash Show.* I identified with the song's protagonist, hungover from Saturday night and now unable to find any comfort or redemption, only deeper isolation and despair, in the tranquil Sunday-morning scenes that he encounters yet can no longer be part of—from the scent of chicken frying in a family kitchen to the sound of hymns being sung in a nearby church: "And it took me back to something that I'd lost somehow, somewhere along the way." He seemed to be telling my story. (Johnny Cash had felt the same thing.) I, too, woke up on many mornings, not just Sundays, with no way to hold my head, figuratively and literally, that didn't hurt.

I went, alone, to see Emmylou Harris perform, and when she sang the mournful "Boulder to Birmingham," written in response to the death of her mentor, Gram Parsons, I thought she was singing to me. I spent the darkest holiday season of my life listening over and over to Dolly Parton singing "Hard Candy Christmas," focusing on the lines, "Maybe I'll move somewhere, maybe I'll get a car, maybe I'll drive so far they'll all lose track," and "I'm barely getting through tomorrow, but still I won't let sorrow bring me way down."

ABOVE, TOP *Waylon Jennings's album* Dreaming My Dreams

ABOVE, BOTTOM *Merle Haggard's album* Big City

OPPOSITE *Kathy Mattea's* Willow in the Wind *included the song* "Where've You Been."

I embarked on a vagabond's life for a while, as much to be on the move as to pursue the life of a writer chasing stories about the way the vast American landscape has shaped our history and our character. I retraced the Lewis and Clark trail; visited the nation's most sparsely settled counties (all in the West); traveled the rodeo circuit; crisscrossed the continent on a Greyhound bus; rode with a long-haul trucker as he brought a load of Boston lettuce from Yuma, Arizona, where it was picked, to Boston, where it was eaten.

Country music became the soundtrack of my travels. Every time I crossed the border into Montana, which was often, I played Merle Haggard's "Big City," with its line of "turn me loose, set me free, somewhere in the middle of Montana." Ian Tyson's cowboy ballads and Chris LeDoux's rodeo songs (as well as George Strait's "Amarillo by Morning") accompanied me across great stretches of two-lane highways. I blasted the Sons of the Pioneers' "Cool Water" out my car windows as I crossed endless deserts. Emmylou and Waylon, of course, were constant companions on lonely nights when it was just me, the big, dark sky, and my headlights on the road. On the first Memorial Day after his death, I found a station playing only Marty Robbins songs; I knew the words to every song.

I had started writing some of my own songs by then. They were predominantly about heartache (no surprise there), with a few cowboy tunes thrown in, and were never intended for recording or public performance. Writing them and singing them to myself simply helped me get through. When my future wife, Dianne, and I began an off-and-on courtship, I sang them to her—and wrote some more, at first inspired by the "off" times (more heartbreak), but eventually turning, at least occasionally, to love songs.

She had not been a country music fan, and I introduced her to it. She says now it was a "test." When she mentioned how much she liked Ed Bruce's "My First Taste of Texas," about a road-hardened older man meeting a younger woman in an airport, if it was in fact a test, she had passed it. Don Williams's "Yellow Moon" (a man on the road wonders if his lover is looking at the same moon) became our theme song, along with Ian Tyson's "What Does She See" ("What does she see in that old cowboy; he's no longer young, the battles that he's won, they're all in his past").

We married, started our family, and moved temporarily from New Hampshire to Kansas, while I worked on a book that required me to be on the road once more. When I was home, I took Dianne and our two-year-old daughter, Emme, to the rodeo in Kansas City. We went because I wanted to share a rodeo experience with them, but as it turned out, the music performance just before the finale of all rodeos, the bull riding, was by a young artist, not yet a phenomenon, named Garth Brooks. Aside from us, the crowd was all Future Farmers of America teenagers attending a national conference. Dianne and I were captivated by a song Brooks sang, "If Tomorrow Never Comes." The FFA kids were blown away by another song, "Friends in Low Places." By the second chorus, they and Emme were singing along at full throat.

Not long after that, my buddy Joe Blake called again. He said it was imperative that I listen to an artist named Kathy Mattea. He listed off a string of her hits—"Love at the Five and Dime," "Goin' Gone," "Eighteen Wheels and a Dozen Roses," and "Come From the Heart"—as songs I simply had to hear. I had learned a long time ago to follow Joe's advice. When I discovered that Mattea was coming to Kansas City, I invited Joe and his wife, Chris, to drive down from Iowa. Kathy performed all her hits that night, and then added a song that had not yet been released: "Where've You Been."

We were all transfixed. The story steadily unfolds about Claire and Edwin—in the first verse, she has almost given up on finding a lover; in the second, now married to him, she worries about him being on the road as a salesman; in the third, they are both elderly, in separate hospital rooms, and her dementia has robbed her memory and she has stopped speaking, until he is wheeled into her room—and between each verse, the intervening chorus takes on added meaning each time it's sung: "Where've you been? I've looked for you forever and a day. Where've you been? I'm just not myself when you're away."

We didn't know the story behind the song: that it was co-written by Mattea's husband, Jon Vezner (with Don Henry), and was based on his grandparents' courtship, marriage, and final moment together; or that its first public performance was at the Bluebird Café the same night Garth Brooks sang "If Tomorrow Never Comes" and got his first recording contract. But as with any truly great song, or any great work of art, that background information was unnecessary for us to be profoundly moved by it.

"Where've You Been" became another theme song for our life together. We would whisper it to each other every time I returned, often late at night after a long drive, from a road trip. When we moved back to New Hampshire and I played it in the car, our two children (Will had been born in Kansas) always noticed my eyes getting teary, the same way I responded to "If Tomorrow Never Comes." They started calling me "the waterworks." And as time went on, and Dianne's mother descended into Alzheimer's, the song took on even deeper personal meaning, offering solace in the notion that whatever life throws at you, you are not alone. That, too, is what a great country song does.

· · ·

My journey with country music took another turn in 2010, when Ken Burns suggested that for our next film project together we tell the music's history, just as he had done with jazz. It took me about forty-five seconds to agree.

For most of a decade, my "job" has been delving into the stories and characters that created this uniquely American art form, learning as much as I could to construct a narrative, however imperfectly, that attempts to explain its tangled roots and its many branches as it grew and changed (and sometimes returned to its roots) in the twentieth century. What I learned is that country music isn't—and never was—one music. It's always been a mixture of styles. Its boundaries— both in terms of incorporating other styles and influencing other styles—have always been porous. And its power—at least the good stuff's—has always been its honesty, its ability to connect to people's real lives. It's always personal. There are many doors that can lead someone to country music, and as Waylon's song says, "The door is always open, and the light's on in the hall."

Along the way, in ways no other book or film project ever has, I've been privileged to meet some of the people whose works had touched my own life. Kris Kristofferson told me the story of writing "Sunday Morning Coming Down," pausing for a long time when he finished to add, "It was a bless-

ing." Yes, it was. Talking to Emmylou Harris, to say the least, was also a blessing—and a personal thrill.

Rosanne Cash deepened my understanding and appreciation of her remarkable father, who perhaps more than any other figure somehow embodied all the swirling crosscurrents of country music, just as he embodied the cultural crosscurrents of American culture in the last half of the twentieth century. When she said *The Johnny Cash Show* attracted a new generation to at least consider country music, I knew she was right—I was one of them.

In what was probably his last extended filmed interview, Merle Haggard talked to me about the mysterious art of songwriting: "It's about those things that we believe in but we can't see, like dreams and souls. They're hanging around here and different songwriters reach up and get them." His passion for some of the artists who preceded him—Jimmie Rodgers, Bob Wills, Lefty Frizzell, the Maddox Brothers and Rose—was infectious. I told him that his moody ballad "Kern River," what one reviewer called "heartbreak by geography," had become Dianne's favorite song of his, and he smiled appreciatively. Then he added it to his playlist that night at his concert, with her smiling back in the audience.

I met Guy Clark and Rodney Crowell, whose stories about Townes Van Zandt and the group of country bohemians who used to gather at Guy and Susanna's home for nightlong picking parties made me wish I could have taken part. I later took our son, Will, an aspiring poet and singer-songwriter, to meet Guy, who had become one of Will's heroes. He invited Will to sing him one of his own compositions on a guitar Guy had made. That's a moment a proud father will never forget. During the interview with Crowell, Rodney mentioned he was going next to a doctor's appointment, where they would "take a picture of my heart." Will overheard it, and turned it into one of his songs.

In the interview with Cowboy Jack Clement, a month

ABOVE *Dayton Duncan with Emmylou Harris*

OPPOSITE *Dayton Duncan with Merle Haggard*

before he died, he sang me "Let's All Help the Cowboy Sing the Blues," which he had written and which Jennings performed on *Dreaming My Dreams*, an album Clement produced. I sang along. Allen Reynolds, who wrote that album's title song, told me it sprang from "the confluence of some sadnesses in my life," some marriage troubles and professional setbacks. I could relate to that. Reynolds also described his work producing Garth Brooks and Kathy Mattea, who in their interviews both credited him with helping them stay true to themselves in their music.

I had the pleasure of meeting Kathy Mattea and Jon Vezner early in the project, told them about my friend Joe's role in bringing us to her concert and hearing "Where've You Been" for the first time, and from them learned the backstory of the song and Jon's first performance of it at the Bluebird. I'm happy to report that, over time, they've become friends of our family. When Kathy sang it again at the Bluebird in early 2018, on the thirty-fifth anniversary of her first appearance there, I was honored to be in the small audience.

How I wish that Joe could have been there. I had kept him

informed about my progress on the project—he was, after all, more responsible than anyone in my life for connecting me to country music. To make him a little jealous, I had sent him photos of me and Jessi Colter, Waylon Jennings's widow, after my interview with her; and I had kidded him that Kathy Mattea seemed to remember seeing me in the audience at Kansas City but couldn't remember seeing him. My plan was to bring him to Nashville and introduce him to her in person. But, as I've learned, life is a country song, and there's usually hardship or heartbreak around the corner. Joe died, too soon, in a car accident near our hometown in 2015.

Maybe someday I'll write a song about him. It will be a country song, of course, but it can't be a sad song. Joe wasn't that way; I was the one with melancholy baked into his soul, while Joe was an artesian well of bubbling enthusiasm, fun, and laughter. Instead, I'll concentrate on the advice Wanda Jackson gave me about country music, interrupting my questions in the middle of one of the first interviews I conducted for our film. "Don't overthink it," she said. "Just enjoy it. That's your lesson for the day."

ACKNOWLEDGMENTS

The first thing we need to acknowledge is that this book—and the film it accompanies—is not an encyclopedia of country music. It is meant as a narrative story, describing a uniquely American art form and how it grew, through the advent of radio, records, and television in the twentieth century, from something that had once been transmitted person to person into a major cultural force in the nation.

As storytellers, we are drawn to the biographies of the people, famous and unknown, who make history, but from the outset we recognized that not everyone's story could be told within our limits of time and space. Each artist whose story we chose to include, each moment we described, each song we decided to highlight required choices about people, moments, and songs that had to be left out. Those were hard choices. We realize that others might have made different ones. This represents our collective best effort in telling the sprawling, complicated story of what many people consider a simple art form.

In each agonizing choice we made, we found some comfort in what two legendary songwriters had told us. Loretta Lynn's original version of "Coal Miner's Daughter" had nearly twice as many verses as the final version, she said, because she wanted to tell a fuller story of her life. Owen Bradley, her producer, told her it was simply too long to fit on a record. We're sure that her longer song was terrific; we're equally sure that the released version is an enduring classic. Guy Clark's advice to aspiring songwriters was also instructive: "You have to be willing to throw out the best line of a song if it doesn't serve the rest of the song. Use a pencil with a good eraser."

Because of the myriad hard choices we needed to make, we also decided to end our principal narrative in the mid-1990s, following the phenomenal rise of Garth Brooks, which took country music's popularity to an entirely new level; the death of bluegrass patriarch Bill Monroe; and the redemptive story of Johnny Cash's recordings with Rick Rubin, which revived his career and further cemented his place as one of the major artists in the music's long history. We are historians, not journalists. That means, as in other series we've done, like *Jazz* or *The National Parks*, that we need a historical arm's-length from our topic, the space in time that provides a perspective between what may have seemed popular or important at the moment and what was historically significant—about a generation's distance.

Over the course of more than six years we conducted 101 on-camera interviews, collected more than 100,000 still images and six hundred hours of footage, listened to more than fifteen thousand songs from our accumulating CD library, and spent nearly two years in the editing studio winnowing and refining it all into our final film. Like any song recorded on Music Row, it was a collaborative endeavor from the start, and we were fortunate to have our own "A team" of supremely talented and dedicated coworkers to create it.

Our fellow producer, Julie Dunfey, was our equivalent of a session leader, making sure everything got done, creating harmony out of cacophony, art out of noise. Coproducer Pam Tubridy Baucom took on an array of tasks—everything from being our principal contact with families of artists whose story we were telling and professional photographers whose works were essential to bringing those stories to life, to overseeing the logistics of our regular screenings. Associate producers Susanna Steisel, Susan Shumaker, and Katy Haas relentlessly pursued photographs and footage (some never publicly seen before) across the country; research / production associates Emily Mosher and Sam Frickleton helped organize the wealth of images that came in. Peter Miller, a consulting producer, managed the complex task of clearing all the music rights, and Craig Mellish served as a field producer for many of the interviews. Buddy Squires, Florentine Films' principal cinematographer from the moment of its founding, shot most of the interviews; Allen Moore filled in when Buddy was unavailable.

Our editors, Erik Ewers, Craig Mellish, Ryan Gifford, and Margaret Shepardson-Legere, were masterful at turning a script on paper into a compelling visual story that somehow also kept the music—the beating heart of the story—front and center. They were ably assisted by Evan W. Barlow, J. Alex Cucchi, Richard Rubin, and Brian T. Lee, with Caleb Garcia and Rebecca Branson Jones as apprentice editors. Technical director Dave Mast kept the array of equipment in the editing house running smoothly. Postproduction supervisor Daniel J. White made sure the final six months of "finishing" the film created what we had hoped it would be. The Florentine Films family in Walpole, New Hampshire, also includes Elle Carrière, Jennifer Fabis, Patty Lawlor, Brenda Heath, Chris Darling, Cauley Powell, Jillian Hempstead, Stephanie Greene, Bree Camber, Chris Sink, and Karen Domina; without their hard work behind the scenes, nothing gets accomplished.

We feel fortunate that Peter Coyote (a country music fan

OPPOSITE *Bluegrass legend Ralph Stanley*

of long standing) agreed to narrate our film, that Jim Free gave us crucial guidance as our senior adviser, and that our panel of knowledgeable experts read an early draft of the script and then attended an early screening of the film in progress, offering constructive criticism and valuable suggestions in both instances. At the beginning of the project, a number of country music artists kindly took the time to listen to our tentative plans for the narrative and provided us with helpful ideas on how to improve it: Marty Stuart, Rosanne Cash, Ketch Secor, Kathy Mattea, Vince Gill, Emmylou Harris, Ricky Skaggs, and Dwight Yoakam. Del Bryant graciously connected us to other people in the industry.

We were overwhelmed by the generosity of people, too many to be named here, who consistently opened their doors and invited us in to help us tell the story of the music they love: families who shared precious photographs, museum archivists and record executives, and especially the 101 people who sat down to be interviewed and added immeasurably to our understanding of country music, whether or not they ended up in the final film. We thank them all—and we mourn the passing of the twenty interviewees who have died as of this writing.

More than a decade ago, Cappy McGarr first suggested country music as a topic to explore; this is our chance to publicly thank him, with hopes that we've lived up to his high expectations. And we wish to remember our dear friend Anne Harrington, who for many years assisted our efforts from her post at WETA with equal amounts of calm grace and fierce determination; we're grateful she saw our film in its early stages, but deeply regret she will not see the finished project. We will miss her.

Our film could not have been made without the financial support of our funders: Bank of America, members of the Better Angels Society, the Annenberg Foundation, the Arthur Vining Davis Foundations, Belmont University, the Tennessee Department of Tourist Development, the Metropolitan Government of Nashville and Davidson County, Rosalind P. Walter, the Corporation for Public Broadcasting, and the Public Broadcasting Service. For forty years, PBS has provided a home for Florentine Films documentaries, and we urge anyone who believes in the mission of quality, educational television to donate to their local PBS station. Among the people at PBS we thank are Paula Kerger, Jonathan Barzilay, Ira Rubenstein, Perry Simon, and Beth Hoppe. We also wish to thank our long-standing producing partner, WETA-TV in Washington, D.C., including Sharon Percy Rockefeller, Dalton Delan, Jim Corbley and Karen Fritz. Joe DePlasco and his team at DKC Public Relations help us reach millions of Americans with the news that a new project is coming, and we greatly appreciate all they do.

For this book, we thank our agents, Jennifer Rudolph Walsh and Jay Mandel of William Morris Endeavor Entertainment; Sonny Mehta of Knopf; our editor Andrew Miller; and designer Maggie Hinders.

Finally, we wish to acknowledge our families for the support they provide that sustains us: Sarah, Lilly, Olivia, and Willa Burns, and Dianne, Emme, and Will Duncan. They are the sweet melody in the song of our lives, whose title is "I Can't Stop Loving You."

KEN BURNS
DAYTON DUNCAN
Walpole, New Hampshire

BIBLIOGRAPHY

What follows is a selected bibliography of the principal written sources used in this book and the film series it accompanies. Many other sources—newspaper accounts, magazine articles, liner notes, and the extended interviews we conducted with more than a hundred people—are not included.

We are grateful to all the authors listed below, upon whose scholarship and hard work we have built our narrative. Special thanks goes to Bill C. Malone, whose comprehensive *Country Music, U.S.A.* has recently celebrated its fiftieth anniversary in print with an updated fourth edition. Begun as his doctoral dissertation at the University of Texas in the mid-1960s, when the topic was deemed beneath the worthiness of serious academic study, Malone's book is widely considered the headwaters of scholarly research into the history of country music. We're all lucky that Bill got things moving.

———— (no author). *The Bakersfield Sound: Buck Owens, Merle Haggard, and California Country*. Nashville: Country Music Foundation Press, 2012.

———— (no author). *Dylan, Cash and the Nashville Cats*. Nashville: Country Music Foundation, 2015.

———— (no author). *Johnny Cash: An Illustrated Biography*. New York: LIFE Books, 2013.

———— (no author). *Patsy Cline: Crazy for Loving You*. Nashville: Country Music Foundation Press, 2012.

———— (no author). *Reba: All the Women I Am*. Nashville: Country Music Foundation Press, 2013.

Allen, Bob. *George Jones: The Life and Times of a Honky Tonk Legend*. Milwaukee, WI: Backbeat Books, 2014.

Anderson, Bill. *I Hope You're Living as High on the Hog as the Pig You Turned Out to Be*. Hermitage, TN: TWI, Inc., 1994.

————. *Whisperin' Bill: An Autobiography*. Atlanta: Longstreet Press, 1989.

Arnold, Eddy. *It's a Long Way from Chester County*. Old Tappan, NJ: Hewitt House, 1969.

Atkins, Chet, with Bill Neely. *Country Gentleman*. Chicago: Henry Regnery Company, 1974.

Atkinson, Brian T. *I'll Be Here in the Morning: The Songwriting Legacy of Townes Van Zandt*. College Station: Texas A & M University Press, 2012.

Bane, Michael. *The Outlaws: Revolution in Country Music*. N.p.: Country Music Magazine Press, 1978.

Berry, Chad, ed. *The Hayloft Gang: The Story of the National Barn Dance*. Urbana: University of Illinois Press, 2008.

Bogdanov, Vladimir, Chris Woostra, and Stephen Thomas Erlewine. *All Music Guide to Country: The Definitive Guide to Country Music*. San Francisco: Backbeat Books, 2003.

Bonsall, Joseph S. *An American Journey: The Oak Ridge Boys*. Green Forest, AR: New Leaf Press, 2004.

Bowen, Jimmy, and Jim Jerome. *Rough Mix: An Unapologetic Look at the Music Business and How It Got that Way—a Lifetime in the World of Rock, Pop, and Country as Told by One of the Industry's Most Powerful Players*. New York: Simon and Schuster, 1997.

Braddock, Bobby. *A Life on Nashville's Music Row*. Nashville: Vanderbilt University Press and Country Music Foundation Press, 2015.

Bragg, Rick. *Jerry Lee Lewis: His Own Story*. New York: Harper Collins Publishers, 2014.

Brock, Pope. *Charlatan: America's Most Dangerous Huckster, the Man Who Pursued Him, and the Age of Flimflam*. New York: Three Rivers Press, 2008.

Brown, Jim. *Emmylou Harris: Angel in Disguise*. Kingston, Ont.: Fox Music Books, 2004.

Brown, Maxine. *Looking Back to See: A Country Music Memoir*. Fayetteville: University of Arkansas Press, 2005.

Bufwack, Mary A. and Robert K. Oermann. *Finding Her Voice: Women in Country Music, 1800–2000*. Nashville: Country Music Foundation Press and Vanderbilt University Press, 2003.

Burke, Kathryn. *The Dust Bowl, the Bakersfield Sound, and Buck*. North Charleston, SC: BookSurge Publishers, 2007.

Burke, Ken. *Country Music Changed My Life: Tales of Tough Times and Triumph from Country's Legends*. Chicago: A Cappella Books, 2004.

Byworth, Tony, ed. *The Billboard Illustrated Encyclopedia of Country Music*. New York: Watson Guptill Publications, 2007.

Canfield, Jack, Mark Victor Hansen, and Randy Rudder. *Chicken Soup for the Soul: Country Music, the Inspirational Stories Behind 101 of Your Favorite Country Songs*. Cos Cob, CT: Chicken Soup for the Soul Publishing, 2001.

Cantwell, David. *Merle Haggard: The Running Kind*. Austin: University of Texas Press, 2013.

Cantwell, David, and Bill Friskics-Warren. *Heartaches by the Number: Country Music's 500 Greatest Singles*. Nashville: Vanderbilt University Press and Country Music Foundation, 2003.

Carlin, Richard. *American Popular Music: Country*. New York: Checkmark Books, 2006.

————. *The Big Book of Country Music*. New York: Penguin Books, 1995.

————. *Country Music: The People, Places, and Moments That Shaped the Country Sound*. New York: Black Dog and Leventhal Publishers, 2006.

Carlisle, Dolly. *Ragged but Right: The Life and Times of George Jones*. Chicago: Contemporary Books, Inc., 1984.

Carr, Patrick, ed. *The Illustrated History of Country Music*. New York: Random House, 1995.

Cash, John Carter. *Anchored in Love: An Intimate Portrait of June Carter Cash*. Nashville: Thomas Nelson, 2007.

————. *House of Cash: The Legacies of My Father, Johnny Cash*. San Raphael, CA: Insight Editions, 2011.

Cash, John R., with Patrick Carr. *Cash: The Autobiography*. New York: Harper Collins, 1997.

Cash, Rosanne. *Composed: A Memoir*. New York: Penguin Books, 2010.

————. *Songs Without Rhyme: Prose by Celebrated Songwriters*. New York: Hyperion, 2000.

Cash, Vivian, with Ann Sharpsteen. *I Walked the Line: My Life with Johnny*. New York: Scribner, 2007.

Clark, Roy, with Marc Eliot. *My Life—In Spite of Myself*. New York: Pocket Books, 1994.

Colter, Jessi, with David Ritz. *An Outlaw and a Lady: A Memoir of Music, Life with Waylon, and the Faith That Brought Me Home*. Nashville: Nelson Books, 2017.

Cooper, Peter. *Johnny's Cash and Charley's Pride: Lasting Legends and Untold Adventures in Country Music*. Nashville: Spring House Press, 2017.

Corbin, Everett J. *Storm Over Nashville: A Case Against "Modern" Country Music*. Nashville: Ashlar Press, 1980.

Cosby, James A. *Devil's Music, Holy Rollers and Hillbillies: How America Gave Birth to Rock and Roll*. Jefferson, NC: McFarland and Company, Inc., 2016.

Cox, Patsi Bale. *The Garth Factor: The Career Behind Country's Big Boom*. New York: Center Street, 2009.

Crowell, Rodney. *Chinaberry Sidewalks: A Memoir*. New York: Vintage Books, 2011.

Cusic, Don. *Baseball and Country Music*. Madison: University of Wisconsin Press, 2003.

————. *The Beatles and Country Music*. Nashville: Brackish Publishing, 2015.

————. *The Cowboy in Country Music: An Historical Survey with Artist Profiles*. Jefferson, NC: McFarland and Company, Inc., 2011.

————. *Discovering Country Music*. Westport, CT: Praeger, 2008.

————. *Eddy Arnold: I'll Hold You in My Heart*. Nashville: Rutledge Hill Press, 1997.

————. *Elvis and Nashville*. Nashville: Brackish Publishing, 2012.

————. *Gene Autry: His Life and Career*. Jefferson, NC: McFarland and Company, Inc., 2007.

————. *Roger Miller: Dang Him!* Nashville: Brackish Publishing, 2012.

————. *Saved by Song: A History of Gospel and Christian Music*. Jackson: University Press of Mississippi, 2002.

Daley, Dan. *Nashville's Unwritten Rules: Inside the Business of Country Music*. Woodstock and New York: Overlook Press, 1998.

Daniel, Wayne W. *Pickin' on Peachtree: A History of Country Music in Atlanta, Georgia*. Urbana: University of Illinois Press, 2001.

Daniels, Charlie. *The Devil Went Down to Georgia.* N.p.: Zenda, Inc., 1990.

Davis, John T. *Austin City Limits: 25 Years of American Music.* New York: Billboard Books, 2000.

Dawidoff, Nicholas. *In the Country of Country: A Journey to the Roots of American Music.* New York: Vintage Books, 1997.

Dean, Eddie. *Pure Country: The Leon Kagarise Archives, 1961–1971.* Port Townsend, WA: Process Media, 2008.

Delmore, Alton. Edited by Charles K. Wolfe. *Truth Is Stranger Than Publicity: The Delmore Brothers.* Nashville: Country Music Foundation Press, 1999.

Diekman, Diane. *Live Fast, Love Hard: The Faron Young Story.* Urbana and Chicago: University of Illinois Press, 2007.

———. *Twentieth Century Drifter: The Life of Marty Robbins.* Urbana and Chicago: University of Illinois Press, 2012.

Emery, Ralph, with Tom Carter. *Memories: The Autobiography of Ralph Emery.* New York: Macmillan Publishing Company, 1991.

———. *More Memories.* New York: G. P. Putnam's Sons, 1993.

Emery, Ralph, with Patsi Bale Cox. *50 Years Down a Country Road.* New York: William Morrow, 2000.

———. *The View from Nashville.* New York: William Morrow and Company, Inc., 1998.

Eng, Steve. *A Satisfied Mind: The Country Music of Porter Wagoner.* Nashville: Rutledge Hill Press, 1992.

Erlewin, Michael, with Vladimir Bogdanov, Chris Woostra, and Stephen Thomas Erlewine. *All Music Guide to Country: The Experts' Guide to the Best Recordings in Country Music.* San Francisco: Miller Freeman Books, 1997.

Escott, Colin. *The Grand Ole Opry: The Making of an American Icon.* New York: Center Street, 2006.

———. *Lost Highway: The True Story of Country Music.* Washington, D.C.: Smithsonian Books, 2003.

Escott, Colin, and Kira Florita. *Hank Williams: Snapshots from the Lost Highway.* New York: Da Capo Press, 2001.

Escott, Colin, with George Merritt and William MacEwen. *Hank Williams: The Biography.* New York and Boston: Little, Brown and Company, 2004.

Flippo, Chet. *Everybody Was Kung-Fu Dancing: Chronicles of the Lionized and the Notorious.* New York: St. Martin's Press, 1991.

———. *Your Cheatin' Heart: A Biography of Hank Williams.* London: Plexus, 1981.

Foster, Pamela E. *My Country: The African Diaspora's Country Music Heritage.* N.p., 1998.

Fowler, Lana Nelson. *Willie Nelson Family Album.* Amarillo, TX: H. M. Poirot and Company, 1980.

Fox, Aaron A. *Real Country: Music and Language in Working-Class Culture.* Durham, NC: Duke University Press, 2004.

Frizzell, David. *I Love You a Thousand Ways: The Lefty Frizzell Story.* Solana Beach, CA: Santa Monica Press, 2011.

Gatlin, Larry, with Jeff Lenburg. *All the Gold in California: The Man, His Music, and the Faith That Saved His Life.* Nashville: Thomas Nelson Publishers, 1998.

George-Warren, Holly. *Public Cowboy No. 1: The Life and Times of Gene Autry.* London and New York: Oxford University Press, 2007.

George-Warren, Holly, and Michelle Freedman. *How the West Was Worn.* New York: Harry N. Abrams, Inc., 2000.

Goldsmith, Thomas, ed. *The Bluegrass Reader.* Urbana and Chicago: University of Chicago Press, 2004.

Grant, Marshall, with Chris Zar. *I Was There When It Happened: My Life With Johnny Cash.* Nashville: Cumberland House, 2006.

Gregory, James N. *American Exodus: The Dust Bowl Migration and Okie Culture in California.* New York and Oxford: Oxford University Press, 1989.

Green, Douglas B. *Singing in the Saddle: The History of the Singing Cowboy.* Nashville: Country Music Foundation and Vanderbilt University Press, 2002.

Grissim, John. *Country Music: White Man's Blues.* New York: Paperback Library, 1970.

Gubernick, Lisa Rebecca. *Get Hot or Go Home: Trisha Yearwood; The Making of a Nashville Star.* New York: William Morrow and Company, 1993.

Guralnick, Peter. *Last Train to Memphis: The Rise of Elvis Presley.* New York: Little, Brown and Company, 1994.

———. *Sam Phillips: The Man Who Invented Rock 'n' Roll.* New York: Little, Brown and Company, 2015.

Haggard, Merle, with Tom Carter. *My House of Memories: An Autobiography.* New York: Cliff Street Books, 1999.

Haggard, Merle, with Peggy Russell. *Sing Me Back Home: My Story.* New York: Pocket Books, 1981.

Hall, Tom T. *The Songwriter's Handbook.* Nashville: Rutledge Hill Press, 1976.

———. *The Storyteller's Nashville.* New York: Doubleday and Company, Inc., 1979.

Hall, Wade. *Hell-Bent for Music: The Life of Pee Wee King.* Lexington: University Press of Kentucky, 1996.

Halsey, Jim, with John Wooley. *Starmaker: How to Make It in the Music Business.* Mustang, OK: Tate Publishing, 2011.

Hardy, Robert Earl. *A Deeper Blue: The Life and Music of Townes Van Zandt.* Denton, TX: University of North Texas Press, 2008.

Harkins, Anthony. *Hillbilly: A Cultural History of an American Icon.* Oxford: Oxford University Press, 2004.

Havinghurst, Craig. *Air Castle of the South: WSM and the Making of Music City.* Urbana: University of Illinois Press, 2007.

Hay, George D. *The Story of the Grand Ole Opry.* (Missing publication pages.)

Hazen, Cindy, and Mike Freeman. *Love Always, Patsy: Patsy Cline's Letters to a Friend.* New York: Berkley Books, 1999.

Hemphill, Paul. *Lovesick Blues: The Life of Hank Williams.* New York: Penguin Books, 2005.

———. *The Nashville Sound.* Atlanta: Everthemore Books, 1970, 2005.

Hentoff, Nat. *Listen to the Stories: Nat Hentoff on Jazz and Country Music.* New York: Da Capo Press, 1995.

Hicks, Darryl E. *Marijohn: Lord, Let Me Leave a Song; the Unforgettable Life Story of Nashville's Famous Songwriter.* Waco, TX: Word Books, 1978.

Hilburn, Robert. *Johnny Cash: A Life.* New York: Little, Brown and Company, 2013.

Hitchcock, Stan. *At the Corner of Music Row and Memory Lane.* Hendersonville, TN: Hitchcock Enterprises, 2009.

Horstman, Dorothy. *Sing Your Heart Out, Country Boy.* Third edition. Nashville: Country Music Foundation Press, 1996.

Howard, Jan. *Sunshine and Shadow: My Story.* New York: Richardson and Steirman, 1987.

Huber, Patrick. *Linthead Stomp: The Creation of Country Music in the Piedmont South.* Chapel Hill: University of North Carolina Press, 2008.

Hume, Martha. *You're So Cold I'm Turnin' Blue: Martha Hume's Guide to the Greatest in Country Music.* New York: Penguin Books, 1982.

Hurd, Mary G. *Kris Kristofferson: Country Highwayman.* Lanham, MD: Rowman and Littlefield, 2015.

Hurst, Jack. *Nashville's Grand Ole Opry: The First Fifty Years, 1925–1975.* New York, Abradale Press, 1989.

Isenhour, Jack. *He Stopped Loving Her Today: George Jones, Billy Sherrill, and the Pretty-Much Totally True Store of the Making of the Greatest Country Record of All Time.* Jackson: University Press of Mississippi, 2011.

Jarrett, Michael. *Producing Country: The Inside Story of the Great Recordings.* Middletown, CT: Wesleyan University Press, 2014.

Jennings, Waylon, with Lenny Kaye. *Waylon: An Autobiography.* New York: Warner Books, 1996.

Jennings, Dana. *Sing Me Back Home: Love, Death, and Country Music.* New York: Faber and Faber, Inc., 2008.

Jones, George, with Tom Carter. *I Lived to Tell It All.* New York: Dell Publishing, 1996.

Jones, Margaret. *Patsy: The Life and Times of Patsy Cline.* New York: Da Capo Press, 1994.

Judd, Naomi, with Bud Schaetzle. *Love Can Build a Bridge.* New York: Villard Books, 1993.

Kealing, Bob. *Calling Me Home: Gram Parsons and the Roots of Country Rock.* Gainesville: University Press of Florida, 2012.

Kennedy, Dan S., and Chip Kessler. *Making Them Believe: The 21 Principles and Lost Secrets of Dr. J. R. Brinkley-Style Marketing.* Garden City, NY: Glazer-Kennedy Publishing, 2010.

Kienzle, Rich. *Southwest Shuffle: Pioneers of Honky-Tonk, Western Swing, and Country Jazz.* New York: Routledge, 2003.

Kingsbury, Paul. *The Explosion of American Music: 1940–1990.* Nashville: Country Music Foundation, 1990.

———. *The Grand Ole Opry History of Country Music: 70 Years of the Songs, the Stars, and the Stories.* Foreword by Dolly Parton. New York: Villard Books, 1995.

Kingsbury, Paul, ed. *Country: The Music and the*

Musicians, from the Beginnings to the '90s. Revised second edition. New York: Abbeville Press, 1994.

———. *The Country Reader: 25 Years of the Journal of Country Music.* Nashville: Country Music Foundation Press and Vanderbilt University Press, 1996.

Kingsbury, Paul, and Alanna Nash. *Will the Circle Be Unbroken: Country Music in America.* London: DK and Country Music Foundation, Inc., 2006.

Kingsbury, Paul, Michael McCall, and John W. Rumble, eds. *The Encyclopedia of Country Music.* Second edition. Oxford and New York: Oxford University Press, 2012.

Kosser, Michael. *Acuff-Rose Publishing.* Nashville: SONY/ATV Tree, 2005. (Booklet.)

———. *How Nashville Became Music City, U.S.A.: 50 Years of Music Row.* Milwaukee, WI: Hal Leonard Corporation, 2006. (Multiple copies.)

———. *SONY/ATV Tree: Fifty Years of Inspiration.* Nashville: SONY/ATV Tree, 2002. (Booklet on fiftieth anniversary.)

Laird, Tracey E. W. *Louisiana Hayride: Radio and Roots Music Along the Red River.* Oxford: Oxford University Press, 2005.

Lee, Brenda, with Robert K. Oermann and Julie Clay. *Little Miss Dynamite: The Life and Times of Brenda Lee.* New York: Hyperion, 2002.

Lee, R. Alton. *The Bizarre Careers of John R. Brinkley.* Lexington: University Press of Kentucky, 2002.

Leverett, Les. *Blue Moon of Kentucky: A Journey into the World of Bluegrass and Country Music as Seen Through the Camera Lens of Photo-Journalist Les Leverett.* Madison, NC: Empire Publishing, 1996.

Leverett-Crew, Libby. *Saturday Nights with Daddy at the Opry.* Nashville: Rutledge Hill Press, 2003.

Logan, Horace, with Bill Sloan. *Elvis, Hank, and Me: Making Musical History on the Louisiana Hayride.* New York: St. Martin's Press, 1998.

Lomax, John III. *Nashville: Music City USA.* New York: Harry N. Abrams, Inc., 1985.

Louvin, Charlie, with Benjamin Whitmer. *Satan Is Real: The Ballad of the Louvin Brothers.* New York: Harper Collins, 2012.

Lynn, Loretta. *Coal Miner's Daughter.* New York: Vintage Books, 1976, 2010.

———. *Honky Tonk Girl: My Life in Lyrics.* New York: Alfred A. Knopf, 2012.

Lynn, Loretta, with Patsi Bale Cox. *Still Woman Enough: A Memoir.* New York: Hyperion, 2002.

Mack, Bill. *Bill Mack's Memories from the Trenches of Broadcasting.* Fort Worth, TX: Branch-Smith, 2004.

Malone, Bill C. *Classic Country Music.* Washington, D.C.: Smithsonian Institution Press, 1990.

———. *Don't Get Above Your Raisin': Country Music and the Southern Working Class.* Urbana: University of Illinois Press, 2002.

———. *Singing Cowboys and Musical Mountaineers: Southern Culture and the Roots of Country Music.* Athens: University of Georgia Press, 1993.

Malone, Bill C., and Judith McCulloh. *Stars of Country Music.* New York: Da Capo Press, 1975.

Malone, Bill C., and Jocelyn R. Neal. *Country Music, U.S.A.* Third revised edition. Austin: University of Texas Press, 2010.

Mandrell, Barbara, with George Vecsey. *Get to the Heart: My Story.* New York: Bantam, 1990.

Masino, Susan. *Family Tradition: Three Generations of Hank Williams.* San Francisco: Backbeat Books, 2011.

Mazor, Barry. *Meeting Jimmie Rodgers: How America's Original Roots Music Hero Changed the Pop Sounds of a Century.* Oxford and New York: Oxford University Press, 2009.

———. *Ralph Peer and the Making of Popular Roots Music.* Chicago: Chicago Review Press, 2015.

Marshall, Jim. *Pocket Cash.* San Francisco: Chronicle Books, 2010.

McCloud, Barry, et al. *Definitive Country: The Ultimate Encyclopedia of Country Music and Its Performers.* New York: Perigree Books, 1995.

McDonough, Jimmy. *Tammy Wynette: Tragic Country Queen.* New York: Viking, 2010.

McGee, David. *Steve Earle: Fearless Heart, Outlaw Poet.* San Francisco: Backbeat Books, 2005.

McLeese, Don. *Dwight Yoakam: A Thousand Miles from Nowhere.* Austin: University of Texas Press, 2012.

Meyer, David N. *Twenty Thousand Roads: The Ballad of Gram Parsons and His Cosmic American Music.* New York: Villard, 2008.

Millard, Bob. *Country Music: 75 Years of America's Favorite Music.* New York: Da Capo Press, 1998.

Miller, Karl Hagstrom. *Segregating Sound: Inventing Folk and Pop Music in the Age of Jim Crow.* Durham, NC: Duke University Press, 2010.

Miller, Stephen. *Smart Blonde: Dolly Parton.* London: Omnibus Press, 2008.

Milsap, Ronnie, with Tom Carter. *Almost Like a Song.* New York: McGraw-Hill Publishing Company, 1990.

Montgomery, Charlene, with Earl Peanutt Montgomery. *The Legend of George Jones: His Life and Death.* Monterey, CA: Heritage Builders Publishers, 2014.

Morgan, Lorrie, with George Vecsey. *Forever Yours, Faithfully: My Love Story.* New York: Ballantine Books, 1997.

Morris, Edward. *At Carter Stanley's Grave: Musings on Country Music and Musicians.* Nashville: Storm Coast Press, 2010.

———. *Garth Brooks: Platinum Cowboy.* New York: St. Martin's Press, 1993.

Morton, David C., with Charles K. Wolfe. *DeFord Bailey: A Black Star in Early Country Music.* Knoxville: University of Tennessee Press, 1991.

Nash, Alanna. *Behind Closed Doors: Talking with the Legends of Country Music.* New York: Cooper Square Press, 1983.

Nassour, Ellis. *Honky Tonk Angel: The Intimate Story of Patsy Cline.* Chicago: Chicago Review Press, 1993, 2008.

Neal, Jocelyn R. *Country Music: A Cultural and Stylistic History.* New York and Oxford: Oxford University Press, 2013.

———. *The Songs of Jimmie Rodgers.* Bloomington and Indianapolis: Indiana University Press, 2009.

Nelson, Shirley Caddell Collie. *Scrapbooks in My Mind.* N.p.: Booklocker.com, Inc., 2009.

Nelson, Willie. *Roll Me Up and Smoke Me When I Die: Musings from the Road.* New York: William Morrow, 2012.

Nelson, Willie, with Bud Shrake. *Willie: An Autobiography.* New York: Cooper Square Press, 1988.

Oak Ridge Boys, with Ellis Widner and Walter Carter. *The Oak Ridge Boys: Our Story.* Chicago: Contemporary Books, Inc. 1987.

Oermann, Robert K. *America's Music: The Roots of Country.* Atlanta: Turner Publishing, Inc., 1996.

———. *Behind the Grand Ole Opry Curtain: Tales of Romance and Tragedy.* New York: Center Street, 2008.

Oermann, Robert K. *A Century of Country Music: An Illustrated History of Country Music.* New York: TV Books, 1999.

Owen, Randy, with Allen Rucker. *Born Country: How Faith, Family, and Music Brought Me Home.* New York: Harper One, 2008.

Owens, Buck, with Randy Poe. *Buck 'Em!: The Autobiography of Buck Owens.* Milwaukee: Backbeat Books, 2013.

Parton, Dolly. *Dolly: My Life and Other Unfinished Business.* New York: Harper Collins, 1994.

Patoski, Joe Nick. *Willie Nelson: An Epic Life.* New York and Boston: Little, Brown and Company, 2008.

Pearl, Minnie, with Joan Dew. *Minnie Pearl: An Autobiography.* New York: Simon and Schuster, 1980.

Pecknold, Diane. *The Selling Sound: The Rise of the Country Music Industry.* Durham, NC: Duke University Press, 2007.

Peterson, Richard A. *Creating Country Music: Fabricating Authenticity.* Chicago: University of Chicago Press, 1997.

Plantenga, Bart. *Yodel-Ay-Ee-Oooo: The Secret History of Yodeling Around the World.* New York: Routledge, 2004.

Porterfield, Nolan. *Jimmie Rodgers: The Life and Times of America's Blue Yodeler.* Jackson: University Press of Mississippi, 2007.

Pride, Charley, with Jim Henderson. *Pride: The Charley Pride Story.* New York: William Morrow, 1994.

Pruett, Barbara J. *Marty Robbins: Fast Cars and Country Music.* Lanham, MD: Scarecrow Press, Inc., 2007.

Pugh, Ronnie. *Ernest Tubb: The Texas Troubadour.* Durham, NC: Duke University Press, 1996.

Reid, Jan. *The Improbable Rise of Redneck Rock.* Austin: University of Texas Press, 2004.

Ribowsky, Mark. *Hank: The Short Life and Long Country Road of Hank Williams.* New York: W. W. Norton and Company, 2017.

Riley, Jeannie C. Riley, with Jamie Buckingham. *Jeannie C. Riley: From Harper Valley to the Mountain Top.* Lincoln, VA: Chosen Books, 1981.

Rodgers, Carrie. *My Husband Jimmie Rodgers.* Nashville: Country Music Foundation Press, 1975, 1995.

Rorrer, Kinney. *Rambling Blues: The Life and Songs of Charlie Poole.* Danville, VA: McCain Printing Company, Inc., 1982.

Rosenberg, Neil V. *Bluegrass: A History.* Urbana and Chicago: University of Illinois Press, 2005.

Russell, Tony. *Country Music Originals: The Legends and the Lost.* Oxford and New York: Oxford University Press, 2010.

St. John, Lauren. *Hardcore Troubadour: The Life and Near Death of Steve Earle.* New York: Fourth Estate, 2003.

Schlappi, Elizabeth. *Roy Acuff: The Smoky Mountain Boy.* Gretna, LA: Pelican Publishing Company, 1978.

Self, Philip. *Guitar Pull: Conversations with Country Music's Legendary Songwriters.* Nashville: Cypress Moon, 2002.

Sgammato, Jo. *For the Music: The Vince Gill Story.* New York: Ballantine, 1999.

Sheldon, Ruth. *Bob Wills: Hubbin' It.* Nashville: Country Music Foundation Press, 1995.

Silverman, Jonathan. *Nine Choices: Johnny Cash and American Culture.* Amherst and Boston: University of Massachusetts Press, 2010.

Sisk, Eileen. *Buck Owens: The Biography.* Chicago: Chicago Review Press, 2010.

Smith, Richard. *Can't You Hear Me Callin': The Life of Bill Monroe, Father of Bluegrass.* New York: Da Capo Press, 2000.

Snow, Hank, with Jack Ownbey and Bob Burris. *The Hank Snow Story.* Urbana: University of Illinois Press, 1994.

Stanley, Dr. Ralph, with Eddie Dean. *Man of Constant Sorrow: My Life and Times.* New York: Gotham Books, 2009.

Stevens, Ray, with C. W. "Buddy" Kalb. *Ray Stevens' Nashville.* Nashville: Clyde Publishing, 2014.

Stimeling, Travis D. *Cosmic Cowboys and New Hicks: The Countercultural Sounds of Austin's Progressive Music Scene.* Oxford: Oxford University Press, 2011.

Streissguth, Michael. *Always Been There: Rosanne Cash, the List, and the Spirit of Southern Music.* New York: Da Capo Press, 2009.

———. *Eddy Arnold: Pioneer of the Nashville Sound.* Jackson: University Press of Mississippi, 1997.

———. *Johnny Cash: The Biography.* Philadelphia: DaCapo Press, 2006.

———. *Johnny Cash at Folsom Prison: The Making of a Masterpiece.* New York: Da Capo Press, 2004.

———. *Like a Moth to a Flame: The Jim Reeves Story.* Nashville: Rutledge Hill Press, 1998.

———. *Outlaw: Waylon, Willie, Kris, and the Renegades of Nashville.* New York: It Books, 2013.

Streissguth, Michael, ed. *Ring of Fire: The Johnny Cash Reader.* New York: Da Capo Press, 2002.

Stuart, Hilda. *Chocktaw Gardens.* Taylor, MS: Nautilus Publishing Company, 2012. (Pictures of the Stuart family.)

Stuart, Marty. *Country Music: The Masters.* Naperville, IL: Sourcebooks Inc., 2008.

———. *Pilgrims: Sinners, Saints, and Prophets.* Nashville: Rutledge Hill Press, 1999.

Thomson, Graeme. *The Resurrection of Johnny Cash: Hurt, Redemption, and American Recordings.* London: Jawbone Press, 2011.

———. *Willie Nelson: The Outlaw.* London: Virgin Books, 2006.

Tillis, Mel, with Walter Wager. *Stutterin' Boy: The Autobiography of Mel Tillis.* New York: Rawson Associates, 1984.

Tosches, Nick. *Country: The Twisted Roots of Rock 'n' Roll.* New York: Da Capo Press, 1985.

Townsend, Charles R. *San Antonio Rose: The Life and Music of Bob Wills.* Urbana and Chicago: University of Illinois Press, 1976.

Tribe, Ivan. *Country: A Regional Exploration.* Westport, CT: Greenwood Press, 2006.

———. *The Stonemans: An Appalachian Family and the Music That Shaped Their Lives.* Urbana: University of Illinois Press, 1993.

Urbanski, Dave. *The Man Comes Around: The Spiritual Journey of Johnny Cash.* Lake Mary, FL: Relevant Books, 2003.

Ward, Michael K. *Ghost Riders in the Sky: The Life of Stan Jones, the Singing Ranger.* Tucson, AZ: Rio Nuevo Publishers, 2014.

Whitburn, Joel. *Hot Country Songs, 1944 to 2008.* Menomonee Falls, WI: Record Research, 2008.

———. *Joel Whitburn's Top Country Singles, 1944–1988.* Menomonee Falls, WI: Record Research, 1989.

Whiteside, Jonny. *Ramblin' Rose: The Life and Career of Rose Maddox.* Nashville: Country Music Foundation Press and Vanderbilt University Press, 1997.

Williams, Hank Jr., with Michael Bane. *Living Proof: An Autobiography.* New York: Dell, 1979.

Williams, Lycrecia, and Dale Vinicur. *Still in Love With You: The Story of Hank and Audrey Williams.* Nashville: Rutledge Hill Press, 1989.

Wills, Rosetta. *The King of Western Swing: Bob Wills Remembered.* New York: Billboard Books, 2000.

Wilson, Lee. *All I Have to Do Is Dream: The Boudleaux and Felice Bryant Story.* N.p.: House of Bryant Publications, 2001.

Wolfe, Charles. *In Close Harmony: The Story of the Louvin Brothers.* Jackson: University Press of Mississippi, 1996.

———. *A Good-Natured Riot: The Birth of the Grand Ole Opry.* Nashville: Country Music Foundation Press and Vanderbilt University Press, 1999.

———. *Tennessee Strings: The Story of Country Music in Tennessee.* Knoxville: University of Tennessee Press, 1977.

Wolfe, Charles K., and James E. Akenson, eds. *Country Music Goes to War.* Lexington: University of Kentucky Press, 2005.

Wooley, John. *The Colors of Oklahoma Music: From the Blue Devils to Red Dirt.* Tulsa, OK: Hawk Publishing, 2006.

Wynette, Tammy, with Joan Dew. *Stand by Your Man: An Autobiography.* New York: Simon and Schuster, 1979.

Zwonitzer, Mark, with Charles Hirshberg. *Will You Miss Me When I'm Gone: The Carter Family and Their Legacy in American Music.* New York: Simon and Schuster Paperbacks, 2002.

INDEX

Page numbers in *italics* refer to photo captions.

FILM PRODUCTION CREDITS

Directed by
KEN BURNS

Written by
DAYTON DUNCAN

Produced by
DAYTON DUNCAN
JULIE DUNFEY
KEN BURNS

Edited by
ERIK EWERS, ACE
CRAIG MELLISH, ACE
RYAN GIFFORD
MARGARET SHEPARDSON-LEGERE

Coproducer
PAM TUBRIDY BAUCOM

Associate Producers
SUSANNA STEISEL
SUSAN SHUMAKER
KATY HAAS

Narrated by
PETER COYOTE

Cinematography
BUDDY SQUIRES, ASC

Voices
TRINA CARMODY
TIM CLARK
KEVIN CONWAY
MURPHY GUYER
GENE JONES
CAROLYN MCCORMICK
MICHAEL POTTS

Assistant Editors
EVAN W. BARLOW
J. ALEX CUCCHI
RICHARD RUBIN
BRIAN T. LEE

Postproduction Supervisor
DANIEL J. WHITE

Technical Director
DAVE MAST

Apprentice Editors
REBECCA BRANSON JONES
CALEB GARCIA

Senior Advisor
JIM FREE

Program Advisors
MARY BUFWACK
BRENDA COLLADAY
DON CUSIC
COLIN ESCOTT
ERIN MORRIS HUTTLINGER
BILL IVEY
JEFF JONES
PAUL KINGSBURY
WILLIAM E. LEUCHTENBURG

BILL C. MALONE
BARRY MAZOR
LYNN NOVICK
ROBERT K. OERMANN
ALICE RANDALL
TAMARA SAVIANO
DAVID SCHMIDT
MICHAEL STREISSGUTH
GEOFFREY C. WARD

Field Producer
CRAIG MELLISH

Consulting Producer
PETER MILLER

Archival Producer
SUSAN SHUMAKER

Research/Production Associates
SAM FRICKLETON
EMILY MOSHER

Additional Cinematography
ALLEN MOORE

Sound Recording
FRANK COAKLEY
MATT HAMILTON
JAMESON HERNDON
DAVID HOCS
JOHN OSBORNE
JAMIE PFEFFER
MARK ROY

Assistant Camera
JARED AMES
JT SUMMER
JILL TUFTS

Chief Financial Officers
JENNIFER FABIS
BREE CAMBER
BRENDA HEATH

Accountants
CHRISTOPHER SINK
STEPHANIE GREENE

Associate Financial Officer for Ken Burns
PATTY LAWLOR

Coordinating Producer for Ken Burns
ELLE CARRIÈRE

Assistants to the Director
CHRISTOPHER DARLING
CAULEY POWELL

Administrative Assistant
JILLIAN L. HEMPSTEAD

The Better Angels Society
AMY MARGERUM BERG, President
COURTNEY CHAPIN, Executive Director

Sound Effects Editors
ERIK EWERS
RYAN GIFFORD
DAVE MAST

MARGARET SHEPARDSON-LEGERE
IRA SPIEGEL

Music Editor
CRAIG MELLISH

Dialogue Editors
MARLENA GRZASLEWICZ
MATT RIGBY

Assistant Sound Editors
J. ALEX CUCCHI
MATT RIGBY

Voiceover Recording
LOU VERRICO
CITYVOX, New York, NY

Stills Animation
RICHARD RUBIN

Motion Graphics and Visual Effects
BRIAN T. LEE

Digital Image Restoration
EVAN W. BARLOW
LYNNE CARRION
REBECCA BRANSON JONES
BRIAN T. LEE
KRISTEN WOODS

Transcription Services
MARY L. BAILEY

Legal Services
DREW PATRICK
MICHAEL McCORMACK

Instrumental Arrangements and Performances
BOBBY HORTON

Production Assistants
RACHEL ABESHOUSE
BILL BADI
TESS BARRY
JON BLISTEIN
NICK BONEY
SAM BOYETTE
MARIAH A. DORAN
WILL DUNCAN
MATT FOLLETT
HILLARY JO GOOD
PHILIP HAAS
SARAH HAAS
SCOTT HEAD
ZACH HERZER
STEPHANIE JENKINS
LOGAN LANIER
DAWN MAJORS
CAITLIN MEYER
SALAR RAJABNIK
TEJAS REDDY

OPPOSITE *A young girl enjoys the* Opry *show at Ryman Auditorium in Nashville.*

SEBASTIAN LASAOSA ROGERS
AILEEN SILVERSTONE
TYLER STEIN
KYLE TURGEON
MOLLY WEINBERG

Interns
CLAIRE M. ANDREAE
NICOLE BEVANS
LEAH BODIN
PHILIP BRAND
MILES BRAUTIGAM
KEELAN BROWN
MARLEY R. BROWN IV
R. TYLER BUCKINGHAM
REBECCA BURTEN
CARLOS STEINKAMP CALANDRIA
LYNNE CARRION
REBECCA M. CONNOLLY
J. ALEX CUCCHI
MIRANDA R. DEAN

CHARLES DEWEY
ANDREW FLESHER
FRANK ADAM FORTINO
SAM FRICKLETON
CALEB GARCIA
HANNAH GREEN
CAROLINE HALL
COOPER HARDEE
MICAH C. HEANEY
LUKAS IRIZARRY
CHRISTOPHER JACOB JONES
REBECCA BRANSON JONES
QUINN KELLEY
BRIAN T. LEE
FERNANDO MALDONADO
DANIEL DECLAN MCAULIFFE
EMILY MOSHER
JASON NELKEN
MAX P. NEMHAUSER
MACKEY O'KEEFE

SAMANTHA PROVENCHER
NATALIE REES
HALLIE REICHEL
MATT RICE
ELENA RIDKER
MEGAN RUFFE
ALI SCATTERGOOD
EMILY SEARLES
NICHOLAS MAZZOCCA SENNOTT
AUGUSTA SMITH
YINAN SONG
SAMANTHA SPIELBERG
QUINN THOMASHOW
DANIEL UPDEGRAFF
SAM VAIL
MARGARET VANCE
T. CAMILLE WANG
GRETCHEN WELLS
KRISTEN WOODS

Original Production Funding Provided By
Bank of America
Corporation for Public Broadcasting
Public Broadcasting Service
Annenberg Foundation
The Arthur Vining Davis Foundations
Belmont University
Tennessee Department of Tourist Development
Metropolitan Government of Nashville and
Davidson County
Rosalind P. Walter

and members of
THE BETTER ANGELS SOCIETY
The Blavatnik Family Foundation
Schwartz/Reisman Foundation
The Pfeil Foundation
Diane and Hal Brierley
John and Catherine Debs
Fullerton Family Charitable Fund
Perry and Donna Golkin Family Foundation
Jay Alix and Una Jackman
Mercedes T. Bass
Fred and Donna Seigel
Gilchrist and Amy Berg
James R. Berdell Foundation
David Bonderman
Deborah P. and Jonathan T. Dawson
Senator Bill and Tracy Frist
Susan and David Kreisman
Rocco and Debby Landesman
Lillian Lovelace
John and Leslie McQuown
Mindy's Hope Foundation
The Segal Family Foundation
Michelle Smith

ILLUSTRATION CREDITS

When there is more than one credit for a page, the images will be listed clockwise from top left.

ABBREVIATIONS

Cash and Carter Family Photos — Cash and Carter Family Photos courtesy of John Carter Cash, Cash Cabin Enterprises, LLC

Cash Family Photos — Cash Family Photos courtesy of Rosanne Cash, Kathy Cash Tittle, Cindy Cash, Tara Cash Schwoebel

CMHoF — Country Music Hall of Fame® and Museum

GAE — Gene Autry Entertainment

GI — Getty Images

GOO — Grand Ole Opry Archives

JRP — Jimmie Rodgers Properties I.L.P.

Leverett Coll. / GOO — Les Leverett Collection courtesy Grand Ole Opry Archives

Leverett / GOO — Photograph by Les Leverett courtesy Grand Ole Opry Archives

McGuire / GOO — Jim McGuire Collection courtesy Grand Ole Opry Archives

MSA — Marty Stuart Archives / Congress of Country Music, Philadelphia, Mississippi

NPLSC — Nashville Public Library, Special Collections

SMA — Sony Music Archives

UNC — Wilson Special Collections Library, Southern Folklife Collection, University of North Carolina at Chapel Hill

ENDPAPERS
Front: GI 635930943 Corbis Historical/David Turnley
Back: GOO

FRONTMATTER
ii: Library of Congress LC-DIG-ppmsc-00252
vi: Leverett/GOO
viii: Danielle Osfalg
x: John Doubler Collection
xi: courtesy Ricky Skaggs
xii: Kern County Museum/used by permission
xiii: ©The Dorothea Lange Collection, Oakland Museum of California
xiv: GOO
xv: MSA
xvi–xvii: Charles Wolfe Collection

CHAPTER 1
xviii–1: CMHoF
2: (l t-b) Greg French Early Photography; Beinecke Library, Yale University 2002047; (r both) Jim Bollman Collection
3: UNC 20001_pf0371_01_0001
4: UNC 20001_pf0849_01_0001; CMHoF
5: JRP; Marshall Wyatt, Old Hat Records
6: (all) CMHoF
7: Princeton Theological Seminary Library
8: Danny and Bobby Ricketts; *Bluefield Daily Telegraph* Feb 17 1925
9: kansasmemory.org/Kansas State Historical Society 451054
10: Doris Ulmann Foundation, Berea College courtesy International Center of Photography

11: West Virginia and Regional History Center, WVU Libraries 037659; Pitts Theology Library, Candler School of Theology, Emory University
12: Library of Congress LC-DIG-pga-03164
13: Colonial Williamsburg Foundation 1935.301.3/T1995-1; Kinney Rorrer
14: Library of Congress LC-USZ62-46758; Robert K. Oermann Photo Archive; California Historical Society Coll. at USC CHS-915
15: Foster Hall Coll., Center for American Music, U. of Pittsburgh
16: Jim Bollman Collection; African-American Sheet Music Collection, John Hay Library, Brown University; BenCar Archives
17: Library of Congress LC-USZC4-10004; Jim Bollman Collection; Library of Congress LC-USZ62-107659
18: UNC 20001_PF2013_01_0001
19: Jim Bollman Collection; kansasmemory.org/Kansas State Historical Society 208349
20: Scott Childers, WLSHistory.com
21: Library of Congress LC-USZ62-35069; GOO
22: GOO
23: Leverett Coll./GOO
24: Macon-Doubler Family Collection; Leverett Coll./GOO
25: courtesy Craig Havighurst; GI 529490126 Corbis Historical
26: GOO
27: Leroy Troy
28: Georgia State University Library, Special Collections, WSB Radio Records M004_0034
29: *Variety* Dec 29 1926 p1; Hooks Bros–Memphis ©Delta Haze Corp/All rights reserved/Used by permission; Library of Congress Okeh Race Records Form 2566
30: Archives of Appalachia, East TN State U., Stoneman Family Papers; Bristol Historical Association
31: UNC Archie Green Papers; Birthplace of Country Music, gift of Denise Smith
32: Carter Family Museum, Rita Forrester
33–34: Leverett Coll./GOO
35: SMA; Tony Russell Collection
36: Jimmie Rodgers Foundation, Inc.; JRP
37–38: JRP
39: Jimmie Rodgers Foundation, Inc.
40: SMA; Jimmie Rodgers Foundation, Inc.
41: JRP; (next two) C.F. Martin & Co. Archives
42–43: (all) JRP
44: (t-b) JRP; *Variety* Jan 8 1930; Louis Armstrong House Museum 1987.14.53
45: (all) JRP
46: (all) Jimmie Rodgers Foundation, Inc.
47: Carter Family Museum, Rita Forrester
48: Smith Family
49: Cash and Carter Family Photos; Carter Family Museum, Rita Forrester
50: JRP
51: Nolan Porterfield Collection; "The Carter Family Visits Jimmie Rodgers" by A.P. Carter ©1931 Peer International Corp., copyright renewed/used by permission/all rights reserved, courtesy Crossroads of Music Archive and Southwest Coll., Texas Tech University
52: Nolan Porterfield Collection
53–55: (all) JRP
56: "T.B. Blues" by Jimmie Rodgers and Raymond E. Hall © 1931 Peer International Corp., copyright renewed/used by permission/all rights reserved, courtesy Crossroads of Music Archive and Southwest Coll., Texas Tech University; JRP
57–59: (all) JRP

CHAPTER 2
60–61: Library of Congress LC-DIG-fsa-8a36111
62: Library of Congress LC-DIG-fsa-8b21509
63: Library of Congress LC-DIG-fsa-8b38113
64: San Francisco History Center, San Francisco Public Library AAK-0435; *Oakland Tribune* Apr 11 1933 p3

65: Arhoolie Foundation; Woody Guthrie Archive/Woody Guthrie Center, Tulsa, OK
66: Library of Congress LC-DIG-ds-00832; Marshall Wyatt, Old Hat Records; scan from original
67: Berea College Southern Appalachian Archives/Southern Music & Radio Collection
68: Berea College Southern Appalachian Archives/John Lair Papers; UNC 20001_pf2454_0001
69: GOO; Scott Childers, WLSHistory.com; Berea College Southern Appalachian Archives/John Lair Papers
70: GAE
71: GAE; GAE courtesy Autry Museum, Los Angeles T87-36-35
72: Robert K. Oermann Photo Archive; GAE courtesy Autry Museum, Los Angeles T94-11-111-2
73: GI 104714944 Archive Photos; Douglas B. Green Collection; Old State House Museum, Little Rock, Arkansas 1996.017.48
74–75: (all) GAE
76: Douglas B. Green Collection; Alamy Everett E5NNYT, E5NHHK
77: Douglas B. Green Collection
78: GI 74253056 Michael Ochs Archives
79: GAE Research Binder; GI 128008506 Archive Photos
80: Cash and Carter Family Photos
81: Cash and Carter Family Photos; BenCar Archives
82: scan from original; "Can the Circle Be Unbroken" by A.P. Carter ©1935 Peer International Corp., copyright renewed/used by permission/all rights reserved, courtesy University of South Carolina, Music Library, Claude Casey Coll., Box 7 Folder 2
83: N. M. "Billy" Bays, Jr.; Carter Family Museum, Rita Forrester
84: Carter Collection, Flo Wolfe
85: Carter Family Museum, Rita Forrester
86: (all) Estate of Bob Wills courtesy Charles Townsend
87: Crossroads of Music Archive and Southwest Coll., Texas Tech U.
88: Hank DeVito; Estate of Bob Wills courtesy Oklahoma Historical Society
89: Oklahoma Historical Society P2011-025-087
90: Oklahoma Historical Society P2011-025-010
91: scan from original
92: Margaret Ann Craig Robinson
93: Peggy Motley Collection courtesy Ruth and Roy Cunningham; GOO
94: Peggy Motley Collection courtesy Ruth and Roy Cunningham; Leroy Troy
95: Leroy Troy
96: David Morton; Crossroads of Music Archive and Southwest Collection, Texas Tech University
97: GOO; CMHoF
98: The Estate of Roy Neill Acuff; GOO
99: CMHoF
100: James Monroe/Monroe-Vandiver Family Collection; CMHoF; courtesy Roger Givens
101: CMHoF
102: Ken Spain Photograph Collection
103: (all) GOO
104: Mary Beth Pruett; GOO; Belmont University 1932 Milestones
105: GOO; NPLSC; GOO
106: GAE courtesy Autry Museum, Los Angeles T87-36-6018-2-2; GAE BIO_273; GAE Champion Binder 1
107: Oklahoma Historical Society 21412.B36.69
108: CMHoF; Kent Archives
109: Dennis Wile; David Morton courtesy NPLSC
111–112: The LIFE Collection, Eric Schaal/GI 3054844, 50947780, 50472029
113: Thomas Sims Archives; Hawkshaw Hawkins Family Collection; GAE courtesy Autry Museum, Los Angeles T87-36-3920
114: GOO; courtesy Stephen Parry
115: GOO
116: Estate of Bob Wills courtesy Charles Townsend
117: Life Magazine Jun 28 1948 courtesy GAE; GAE; GI 3207403 Hulton Archive

118: Oklahoma Historical Society P2011-025-062; Estate of Bob Wills courtesy Oklahoma Historical Society
119: Lorrie Carter Bennett Collection; Vicki Langdon Collection
120: Ed Clark Collection
121: CMHoF; GOO

CHAPTER 3
122–123: Leverett Coll./GOO
124: Library of Congress LC-DIG-fsac-1a34090
125: Ray Sczepanik/Texas Top Hands Band, San Antonio, TX
126: Ken Spain Photograph Collection
127: JRP; Ronnie Pugh
128: Ronnie Pugh; Library of Congress LC-GLB23-0873
129: Bob Grannis/grannisphotography.com; GOO
130: MSA black binder 4; MSA lyrics/corr. lg gray box Ephemera 1 2017.021
131: MSA black binder 4
132: (all) MSA black binder 3
133: Bear Family box set/Tubb Walking the Floor Over You; Mitch Diamond/kardboardkid.com
134: (all) Leroy Troy
135: GOO
136: The Estate of Eddy Arnold notebook 1; Richard Weize/and more bears
137: GOO; The Estate of Eddy Arnold
138: CMHoF
139: GOO
140: Mitch Diamond/kardboardkid.com; CMHoF
141: Joshua Rinkel; Leverett Coll./GOO
142: Leverett Coll./GOO
144: Arhoolie Foundation
145: (t-b) Glenn E. Mueller; Scotty Broyles photo/©Deke Dickerson Photo Archive; Glenn E. Mueller; Thomas Sims Archives
146: Bear Family box set/Dickens Country Boy
147: Leverett Coll./GOO
148: (all) courtesy Dane and Del Bryant
149: Leverett Coll./GOO; courtesy Jimmy Key
150: MSA black binder 1
151: MSA lyrics/corr. lg gray ephemera box 3 2017.153, box 3 2017.0156, box 1, box 3 2017.153
152: Ken Campanile; MSA lg gray box ephemera 4 2017.0109 (B), used by permission from Sony/ATV Music Publishing; MSA
153: Kent Archives courtesy MSA Williams black binder 1
154: Ken Spain Photograph Collection
155: CMHoF; Robert F. Menasco
156: The LIFE Collection, Eric Schaal/GI 72384760
157: Jimmie Rodgers Snow; Bear Family box set/Snow The Yodelling Ranger
158: Bob Grannis/grannisphotography.com
159: Cash and Carter Family Photos
160: (first two) Chet Atkins Family; Vicki Langdon Collection; Bob Grannis/grannisphotography.com
161: Leverett Coll./GOO
162: scan from original, used by permission from Sony/ATV Music Publishing; MSA black binder 5
163: Dana Blevins Russ; (r both) Lomax Photo Archives
164: MSA; MSA black binder 1
165: CMHoF; MSA black binder 3; MSA black binder 4
166: MSA; scan from original, used by permission from Sony/ATV Music Publishing
167: scan from original, used by permission from Sony/ATV Music Publishing; scan from original
168: GOO; Bob Grannis/grannisphotography.com
169: (all) Thomas Sims Archives
170: Leverett Coll./GOO; CMHoF
171: (all) MSA black binder 4
172: CMHoF; Dr. Dennis Hickey, Missouri State University
173: MSA black binder 3; photo by John E. Kuhlman courtesy Sue Morris
174: (all) Colin Escott

175: Mitch Diamond/kardboardkid.com; *Akron Beacon Journal* Jan 29 1953 p37
176–179: MSA red binder funeral

CHAPTER 4
180–181: Leverett/GOO
182: CMHoF; Ken Spain Photograph Collection
183: Bill Anderson; GI 535084507 Teenie Harris Archive/Carnegie Museum of Art
184: Cash Family Photos; courtesy Museum of Pop Culture, Seattle, WA 2001.306.2
185: (all) Cash and Carter Family Photos
186: Cash Family Photos; MSA lg gray box MS 1A 2014.0415
187–188: Cash Family Photos
189: (t all) Sam Phillips Family; (b l-r) GI Michael Ochs Archives 73908040, 74259045
190: Sam Phillips Family
191: Sam Phillips Family; Kent Archives courtesy Colin Escott
192: Opal Walker; Cash and Carter Family Photos
193–194: Cash Family Photos
195: scanned reproduction; GI 74254323 Michael Ochs Archives
196: Oklahoma Historical Society; UNC 20484_36-01_0001
197: Sam Phillips Family
198: Wanda Jackson; Oklahoma Historical Society P2011-025-067
199: (t) GI Michael Ochs Archives 74290665, 74290666, 74290667, 74290671; (m) MSA black binder 2; (b) Kent Archives
200: Cash Family Photos; Leverett Coll./GOO
201: CMHoF; SMA
202–203: Leverett Coll./GOO
204: Thomas Sims Archives
205: GOO
206: Marty Robbins Family; Leverett Coll./GOO; Sony/ATV Music Publishing courtesy Vanderbilt University Special Collections, Grand Ole Opry Coll.; MSA/photo by Hilda Stuart
207: (all) Leverett Coll./GOO
208: GI 521923659 CMHoF/Elmer Williams; (other three) Dane and Del Bryant/courtesy CMHoF
209: NPLSC Banner Archives BP Bradley 3-10-1955; GOO
210: Owen Bradley Family Collection; GOO
211: (all) Mel Tillis Family courtesy Doris Y. Tillis
212: Kent Archives; Alamy CE5J20 Pictorial Press
213: Kent Archives courtesy Bill Anderson
214: Celebrating Patsy Cline, Inc.; Patricia Patterson Brannon
215: (all) Patsy Cline Enterprises
216: CMHoF; Elmer Williams photo/source unknown; Brenda Lee and Ronnie Shacklett; GI 74291272 Michael Ochs Archives; (next two) Brenda Lee and Ronnie Shacklett; Kent Westberry; (center) Brenda Lee and Ronnie Shacklett
217: *Billboard* Jul 20 1959
218: Personal Collection of Waylon Jennings; James McCool and Sevan Garabedian
219: SMA; James McCool and Sevan Garabedian
220: SMA; Marty Robbins Family
221: GI 521920817 CMHoF/Elmer Williams
222: Cash Family Photos; SMA
223: Cash Family Photos; Guy Gillette; GI 524865670 Corbis Historical/Marvin Koner; SMA
224: MSA
225: California State Archives; Dane and Del Bryant/ledgers courtesy CMHoF
226: (all) courtesy Dane and Del Bryant
227: CMHoF; Al Clayton Photography LLC/U. of North Carolina, Southern Historical Coll. 04859_0381_29A
228: CMHoF; Lana Nelson Collection; (next two) Willie Nelson courtesy Wittliff Collections, Texas State University
229: (t both) Lana Nelson Collection; (b) Thomas Sims Archives
230: (l both) Willie Nelson and Friends Museum, Nashville; (r) scan from original

231: *The Tennessean*/Part of the USA TODAY Network
232: Colin Escott; GOO; Leverett Coll./GOO
233: Celebrating Patsy Cline, Inc.; Fred Foster Collection
234: Family of Jean Shepard and Hawkshaw Hawkins; Leverett Coll./GOO
235: (all) Loretta Lynn Foundation dba Coal Miner's Daughter Museum
236: Buck Owens Private Foundation; Loretta Lynn Foundation dba Coal Miner's Daughter Museum
237: Loretta Lynn Foundation dba Coal Miner's Daughter Museum; Leverett/GOO
238: Patsy Cline Enterprises; Leverett/GOO
239: Mario Munoz, used by permission from Sony/ATV Music Publishing
240: Donald Harvey
241: Leverett/GOO
242–243: The LIFE Collection, Bill Ray/GI 92925434
244: scan from original
245: (all) Cash Family Photos
246: Thomas Sims Archives; Cash and Carter Family Photos
247: photo by Judy Mock/courtesy Cash and Carter Family Photos; SMA
248: Thomas Sims Archives; GOO
249: Harlan Howard and Melanie Howard Collection; (next two) Jan Howard; Patsy Cline Enterprises
250: GI 521919849 CMHoF/Elmer Williams; Dottie West Photographs courtesy Ron Harman
251: UNC 20484_pf1038_003; UNC 20484_pf1038_001; UNC 20484_pf1038_002
252: (l both) Gerald Holly Photographs courtesy GOO; (r) *The Tennessean*/Part of the USA TODAY Network
253–254: AP Images/Brian Calvert 6303091125, 6303091117
255-256: Leverett/GOO
257: scan from original; Family of Jean Shepard and Hawkshaw Hawkins

CHAPTER 5
258–259: GI 135992281 Premium Archive/David Gahr
260: unnamed source
261: ©Daniel Kramer
262: SMA; Dan Poush
263: *El Paso Times*/Part of the USA Today Network; *The Thunderbolt* Jan 1966 p2
264: (all) Joe Lee/photo by Leon Kagarise
265: (first two) GOO; Leverett/GOO; photo by Richard Connors
266: (all) Bill Anderson
267: (all) Joe Lee/photo by Leon Kagarise
268: Colin Escott; scan from original
269: MSA; The LIFE Collection, Ralph Crane/GI 50329094
270: Jimmy Moore JMO182 neg 18A; (other two) GOO
271: Harold Bradley Collection; Jimmy Moore JMO261 neg 23; GOO; Billy and Charlene Sherrill, Cathy and George Lale; Jimmy Moore Vern Oxford neg 9; GOO; (center) Vicki Langdon Collection
272–274: Leverett/GOO
275: Leverett/GOO; Leverett Coll./GOO; GOO
276: Leverett/GOO
277: *Homes of the Stars* 1975; GOO
278: CMHoF; Thomas Sims Archives
279: The Estate of Eddy Arnold notebook 3
280: CMHoF; Buck Owens Private Foundation
281: (t and b) Buck Owens Private Foundation; (m) Judy Mock
282: Buck Owens Private Foundation courtesy Capitol Records; scan from original
283: Buck Owens Private Foundation
284: Leverett/GOO
285: NPLSC Banner Archives BP 1967 Jack Gunter; Leverett/GOO
286: Loretta Lynn Foundation dba Coal Miner's Daughter Museum
287: Leverett/GOO
288: Jimmy Moore JMO131 neg 12A
289: ©Dr. Ernest C. Withers, Sr. courtesy Withers Family Trust BB95; Charley Pride Photo Archives
290: Monty Cowles Collection; Cowboy Jack Clement courtesy Niles and Alison Clement

291: GOO; Hope Powell Collection by Singleton/Curb; Mitch Diamond/ kardboardkid.com; CMHoF

292: NPLSC Goodman Negs Owens Party 002; Jimmy Moore JMO160 neg 35A

293–294: (all) Lillian Haggard Rea courtesy Gandulf Hennig

295: California State Archives; Lillian Haggard Rea courtesy Gandulf Hennig; Colin Escott

296: Capitol Records

297: NPLSC Banner Archives BP Haggard 1970 Bill Goodman; scan from original

298: Jimmy Moore JMO181 neg 34A; *The Tennessean* (Oct 1966)/Part of the USA TODAY Network

299: MSA–photo by Marty Stuart; MSA/photo by Hilda Stuart; Jeannie Seely Photographs courtesy Ron Harman

300: CMHoF; Dolly Parton

301: UNC 20245_pf0616_0001; Center for Popular Music, Middle Tennessee State U./Everett Corbin; Leverett/GOO

302: SMA

303: (all) scan from original

304: NPLSC Banner Archives BN 1968-2853-f1-27 Bill Goodman

305: Leverett/GOO; Cash Family Photos; Judy Mock; Leverett/GOO

306: SMA

307: (all) ©Jim Marshall Photography LLC

308: GI 592162516 Mirrorpix/Charlie Ley

309: Cash and Carter Family Photos

CHAPTER 6

310–311: William E. McEuen

312: National Archives 530617/111-C-CC45804

313: John Cohen; photo by Carl Fleischhauer

314: John Cohen

315: MSA

316: Leverett Coll./GOO

317: Nancy Jones

318: (t both) Nancy Jones; (b) Thomas Sims Archives

319: Colin Escott/*Billboard* May 18 1959; Joe Lee/photo by Leon Kagarise

320: CMHoF; Red Bay Museum/Scotty Kennedy; Donna Chapel; Red Bay Museum/Scotty Kennedy

321: Donna Chapel; Red Bay Museum/Scotty Kennedy

322: CMHoF; (other two) SMA

323: SMA; Leverett/GOO

324: (all) SMA

325: Bill Grimes courtesy SMA

326: Ted Polumbaum/Newseum Collection; SMA

327: (first two) David A. Hilliard Family; (other two) Pomona College Archives

328: Al Clayton Photography LLC/U. of North Carolina, Southern Historical Coll. 04859_0331_18, 04859_0366_22

329: Al Clayton Photography LLC 04859_10452_14; Al Clayton Photography LLC/U. of North Carolina, Southern Historical Coll. 04859_0339_14

330: Bobbie McKee Eden

331: ©Jim Marshall Photography LLC; SMA

332: The LIFE Collection, Michael Rougier/GI 50950250

333: (l all) Leverett/GOO; (r t-b) ©Jim Marshall Photography LLC; Roger Miller Music; Jimmy Moore JMO122 neg 18

334: ©Jim Marshall Photography LLC; Al Clayton photo, Bob Johnston Coll. di_11636/Dolph Briscoe Center, UT Austin

335: GI 170133856 CBS; GOO

336: GOO

337: (t-b) Stoney Edwards Collection; GOO; GI 887739680 Michael Ochs Archives; *Ebony* March 1970 pg 68

338: ©Jim Marshall Photography LLC

339: Al Clayton Photography LLC 04859_10086_19

340: ©Jim Marshall Photography LLC; GI 117069239 Disney ABC Television Group

341: GI 517322508 Bettmann

342: (t both) Jan Howard; scan from original

343: scan from original; photo by Carl Fleischhauer

344: MSA black binder 3

345: U. of North Carolina, N. Carolina Coll./Hugh Morton

346: Leverett/GOO

347: (all) SMA

348: Lomax Photo Archives; CMHoF

349: John Reggero; Les Leverett

350: Alamy E5NC3X Everett; Jimmie Rodgers Snow

351: CMHoF

352-355: (all) William E. McEuen

CHAPTER 7

356–357: Wood Newton; GI 111563534 WireImage/Paul Natkin; ©Jim Marshall Photography LLC; McGuire/GOO

358–359: MSA/photo by Hilda Stuart

360: MSA/photo by Hilda Stuart; MSA

361–362: (all) Leverett/GOO

363: *The Tennessean*/Part of the USA TODAY Network; McGuire/GOO

364: NPLSC Banner Archives BN 1974-841-28 Bob Ray

365: McGuire/GOO; GOO

366-368: (all) McGuire/GOO

369: Leverett/GOO

370: Clark Thomas

371: Slick Lawson; (other two) SMA

372: Alamy PNN04H Prod DB ©ABC-Paramount

373: (t-b) SMA; *Orlando Sentinel* Apr 15 1969 p20; Billy and Charlene Sherrill, Cathy and George Lale

374: Leverett/GOO; John Reggero

375: Leverett/GOO

376: Guy Clark Family Collection; Jim McGuire courtesy Guy Clark Family Collection

377: Rodney Crowell; Guy Clark Family Collection

378: Rodney Crowell; Graham Leader, producer *Heartworn Highways*

379: Rice Family, cousins of Townes Van Zandt; Al Clayton Photography LLC 04859_10118_28A, 04859_10120_18

380: Marshall Fallwell Jr. courtesy Tom and Susan Fallwell; Ricardo Rodriguez and Melanie Clark

381: Ricardo Rodriguez and Melanie Clark; Estate of Alan L. Mayor and Theresa Mayor-Smith; NPLSC Banner Archives BN 1975-2087-f3-6 Don Foster

382: (all) James Jennings Collection

383: Richard Weize/and more bears; Personal Collection of Waylon Jennings; SMA

384: Leverett/GOO; CMHoF

385: CMHoF; *The Tennessean* (Loftin Dec 1976)/Part of the USA TODAY Network; ©Jim Marshall Photography LLC

386: Scott Newton Archive

387: Sue & John Averill courtesy Bluegrass Music Hall of Fame & Museum; courtesy Ricky Skaggs

388: Tom Henderson courtesy Bluegrass Unlimited; Patrick J. Wood

389: Patrick J. Wood

390: *Michigan State News* May 3 1973 p9; Leverett/GOO

391: GI Redferns/Jim McCrary 85237442, 85351057; Autry Museum, Los Angeles T94-293-2

392: (first two) Emmylou Harris; ©Kim Gottlieb-Walker/www.lenswoman.com

393: Lily Hou

394: Alan Pogue; Steve Northup Photo Archive e_spn_0065/Dolph Briscoe Center, UT Austin; Scott Newton Archive

395: Personal Collection of Waylon Jennings; Dr. Dennis Hickey, Missouri State University/Micael Priest artist

396: ©Jim Marshall Photography LLC

397: (first two) Burton Wilson Photography; Scott Newton Archive; Clark Thomas

398: Shelly Katz; SMA

399: scan from original; Shelly Katz

400: Dan Reeder

401: Rodney Crowell; Dan Reeder

402: (all) Dan Reeder
403: Dan Reeder; Guy Clark Family Collection; John Reggero; Dan Reeder
404: Leverett/GOO; McGuire/GOO
405: ©Jim Marshall Photography LLC; Burton Wilson Photography
406: CMHoF; SMA; Personal Collection of Waylon Jennings
407: Estate of Alan L. Mayor and Theresa Mayor-Smith; Personal Collection of Waylon Jennings
408: GI 1143765078 Corbis Historical/Wally McNamee; SMA
409: CMHoF
410: Thomas Sims Archives; Mitch Diamond/kardboardkid.com; UNC 20484_37-26_0001
411: GI 521920479 CMHoF/Elmer Williams; Thomas Sims Archives
412: UNC 20484_pf0037_0024_0001; John Reggero
413: C. V. Gouveia
414: (t) Leverett/GOO; (m l-r) Jett Williams and Kelly Zumwalt; GI 453934638 Getty Entertainment/David A. Smith; (b) Lawson Little
415: GI 2578269 Archive Photos/Picture Parade; (other two) Cash and Carter Family Photos
416: (all) Cash Family Photos
417: Cash Family Photos; SMA; Alan Messer | www.alanmesser.com
418: Guy Clark Family Collection; Don Putnam courtesy Danny Fields
419: (t-b) Bill Thorup courtesy MSA; Cash and Carter Family Photos; photo by Don Putnam courtesy Jim Free
420: Nancy Barr-Brandon
421: AP Images 7907231216/Tsugufumi Matsumoto
422: GI 139345506 Premium Archive/David Gahr; John Reggero; SMA
423: NPLSC Banner Archives BP Parton 1984 Oct 9 McCormick; courtesy NPLSC Banner Archives BP Parton 1980 Nov_02; NPLSC Banner Archives BP 1977 Apr
424: CMHoF
425: McGuire/GOO; Leverett/GOO
426: Lomax Photo Archives; McGuire/GOO
427: Leverett/GOO; SMA
428: Barbara Mandrell; Loretta Lynn Foundation dba Coal Miner's Daughter Museum
429: John Reggero; CMHoF
430: Lomax Photo Archives; GI 174285540 Ron Galella Coll.
432: John Lomax III; WSMV-TV; *Philadelphia Inquirer* Dec 16 1978 p21
433: (t) John Lomax III; (other two) Clark Thomas
434: CMHoF
435: Alan Messer | www.alanmesser.com
436: Scott Newton Archive; SMA
437: Scott Newton Archive
438–439: (l-r) Alamy Paramount Pictures PY9W3P, Everett E5N0AY, E5MTMP, E5MFP4

CHAPTER 8:
440–441: Estate of Alan L. Mayor and Theresa Mayor-Smith
442: Lomax Photo Archives; Beth Gwinn
443: Cash Family Photos; Leverett/GOO
444: SMA; Hank DeVito; Alan Messer | www.alanmesser.com; From *The Tennessean.* ©1986 Gannett-Community Publishing. All rights reserved. Used under license.
446: photo by Larry G. Dixon courtesy Ricky Skaggs; Leverett/GOO
447: T. Hale; scan from original
448: Metro Nashville Archives/Jim Hagans Collection; (other two) courtesy Reba's Business, Inc.
449: photo by Kenneth Springer courtesy Reba's Business, Inc.; Estate of Alan L. Mayor and Theresa Mayor-Smith
450: Beth Gwinn; courtesy Reba's Business, Inc.
451: (all) The Judds Photographs courtesy Naomi Judd
452: The Judds Photographs courtesy Naomi Judd; CMHoF
453: Scott Newton photo courtesy Lomax Photo Archives; The Judds Photographs courtesy Naomi Judd

454: courtesy Dwight Yoakam; UNC 20484_38_09_0001
455: courtesy Dwight Yoakam; GI 74301727 Michael Ochs Archives
456: GI 486147837 Michael Ochs Archives; CMHoF; scan from original
457: Buck Owens Private Foundation
458: GI 477736942 Getty Entertainment/Gary Miller; scan from original
459: CMHoF
460: McGuire/GOO; GI 502487341 Toronto Star/Erin Combs; Alan Messer | www.alanmesser.com; GI 74280570 Michael Ochs Archives
461: Kathy Mattea; Estate of Alan L. Mayor and Theresa Mayor-Smith
462: CMHoF; Amy Kurland
463: Jon Vezner; Amy Kurland; photo by Ellen McDonald courtesy Kathy Mattea
464: Amy Kurland; McGuire/GOO
465: SMA; Vince Gill Archive; GOO
466: McGuire/GOO; Vince Gill Archive; AP Images 13050203782/Mark Humphrey
467: Amy Kurland
468: Amy Kurland; scan from original
469: Allen Reynolds
470: (t both) McGuire/GOO; (b) scan from original
471–473: (all) Estate of Alan L. Mayor and Theresa Mayor-Smith
474: photo by Bill Thorup courtesy GOO; Beth Gwinn; Estate of Alan L. Mayor and Theresa Mayor-Smith
475: (t and m) Trisha Yearwood; (b) Estate of Alan L. Mayor and Theresa Mayor-Smith
476: GOO; Estate of Alan L. Mayor and Theresa Mayor-Smith
477: GOO; Cash Family Photos; CMHoF; SMA; UNC 20484_pf0057_0001; Ken Spain Photograph Collection
478: John Reggero; SMA; Thomas Sims Archives; GOO; Dan Reeder; Loretta Lynn Foundation dba Coal Miner's Daughter Museum
479: (all) Estate of Alan L. Mayor and Theresa Mayor-Smith
480: McGuire/GOO
481: Leverett/GOO; NPLSC Banner Archives BT 1991-1675-10 Steve Lowry
482-483: (all) MSA/photo by Marty Stuart
484: GOO; MSA 59905 23A
485: Larry Busacca; SMA
486: Personal Collection of Waylon Jennings
487: MSA/photo by Marty Stuart; scan from original; Kevin Estrada Photography
488: Alan Messer | www.alanmesser.com
489: Daniel Coston/danielcoston.com; MSA black binder 2
490-491: Leverett/GOO
492: GI 458669384 Getty Entertainment/Terry Wyatt
493: John Cohen
494: GI 149380102 Premium/David Gahr
495: David Holt

AFTERWORD
496–497: The LIFE Collection, Eliot Elisofon/GI 897060114
497: scan from original, used by permission from Sony/ATV Music Publishing
498: Indianola High School 1967 yearbook courtesy Dayton Duncan; Dayton Duncan
499: (all) scan from original
500: (all) SMA
501: scan from original
502–503: (all) Florentine Films photo by Jared Ames

BACKMATTER
504: Jean Laughton
526: GOO
534–535: Jon Evan Glaser/Images by Jon Evan
536: The LIFE Collection, Eliot Elisofon/GI 92935849

A NOTE ABOUT THE AUTHORS

Dayton Duncan, writer and producer of *Country Music*, is the author of twelve other books, including *Out West: A Journey Through Lewis & Clark's America*, in which he retraced the historic route of the expedition, and *Miles from Nowhere*, about the most sparsely settled counties in the United States. He has worked with Ken Burns on documentary films for nearly thirty years and won prizes ranging from Spur Awards from the Western Writers of America to two Emmy Awards. He lives in Walpole, New Hampshire.

Ken Burns, the producer and director of numerous film series, including *The Vietnam War, The Roosevelts: An Intimate History,* and *The War,* founded his own documentary film company, Florentine Films, in 1976. His landmark film, *The Civil War,* was the highest-rated series in the history of American public television, and his work has won numerous prizes, including Emmy and Peabody Awards, and two Academy Award nominations. He lives in Walpole, New Hampshire.

OPPOSITE *A father serenades his children with a country song.*

PREVIOUS SPREAD *A country road in Cades Cove in East Tennessee*

A NOTE ON THE TYPE

This book was set in Chaparral, an Adobe original typeface designed by Carol Twombly and released in 1997. The inspiration for Chaparral was a page of lettering from a sixteenth-century manuscript, adapted by Twombly into a readable slab serif design. Unlike geometric slab serif fonts, Chaparral has varying letter proportions that give it an accessible and friendly appearance. Chaparral was the last typeface Twombly designed before she left Adobe and perhaps retired from type design in 1999.

Composed by North Market Street Graphics,
Lancaster, Pennsylvania

Printed and bound by LSC Communications,
Kendallville, Indiana